RELIGION AND THE SPECTER OF THE WEST

INSURRECTIONS

CRITICAL STUDIES IN RELIGION, POLITICS, AND CULTURE

INSURRECTIONS
CRITICAL STUDIES IN RELIGION, POLITICS, AND CULTURE

Slavoj Žižek, Clayton Crockett, Creston Davis, Jeffrey W. Robbins, editors

The intersection of religion, politics, and culture is one of the most discussed areas in theory today. It also has the deepest and most wide-ranging impact on the world. Insurrections: Critical Studies in Religion, Politics, and Culture will bring the tools of philosophy and critical theory to the political implications of the religious turn. The series will address a range of religious traditions and political viewpoints in the United States, Europe, and other parts of the world. Without advocating any specific religious or theological stance, the series aims nonetheless to be faithful to the radical emancipatory potential of religion.

After the Death of God, John D. Caputo and Gianni Vattimo, edited by Jeffrey W. Robbins
The Politics of Postsecular Religion: Mourning Secular Futures, Ananda Abeysekara
Nietzsche and Levinas: "After the Death of a Certain God," edited by Jill Stauffer and Bettina Bergo
Strange Wonder: The Closure of Metaphysics and the Opening of Awe, Mary-Jane Rubenstein

RELIGION AND THE
SPECTER OF THE WEST

Sikhism, India, Postcoloniality, and the
Politics of Translation

Arvind-Pal S. Mandair

Columbia University Press   New York

Columbia University Press
Publishers Since 1893
New York   Chichester, West Sussex
cup.columbia.edu

Copyright © 2009 Columbia University Press
Paperback edition, 2016

Library of Congress Cataloging-in-Publication Data
Mandair, Arvind-pal Singh.
   Religion and the specter of the West : Sikhism, India, postcoloniality, and the politics
of translation / Arvind Mandair.
      p.   cm. — (Insurrections : critical studies in religion, politics, and culture)
   Includes bibliographical references and index.
   ISBN 978-0-231-14724-8 (cloth : alk. paper)—ISBN 978-0-231-14725-5 (pbk. : alk. paper)—
   ISBN 978-0-231-51980-9 (ebook)

   1. Sikhism and politics—India—History. 2. Translating and interpreting—Political
aspects—India—History. 3. Religion—Philosophy. I. Title. II. Series.

BL2018.5.P64M36 2009
294.6'172—dc22   2009020690

Printed in the United States of America
c 10 9 8 7
p 10 9 8 7 6 5 4 3 2 1

Cover image: "Nineteen Eighty-Four," © The Singh Twins (www.singhtwins.co.uk)
Cover design: Milenda Nan Ok Lee

For Preet, Aman, and Sukhmani

Contents

Preface

This book has had a long and unusual development. The central issues with which it grapples—religion, translation, subjectivity, and the politics of knowledge construction—first became an issue for me in the mid- to late 1980s, when significant sections of the Sikh community, within and outside India, were embroiled in an often violent conflict with the Indian state. With the global media thoroughly fixated on issues such as fundamentalism, sectarianism, and the unwelcome return of religion into the public domain, Sikhs and Sikhism were often in the media spotlight. By the time this conflict had peaked in 1992, not only was it routinely driving local Sikh politics in the UK and North America, as organizations fought for control of newly established political parties and institutions, but it had also spawned vigorous intellectual debate as many Sikhs, myself included, tried to come to terms with the events that had transformed them into a rogue community vilified by the state, media, and academic apparatus.

At the time I had just left the chemicals industry to take up an academic position researching superconductors. Despite constantly bemoaning this decision—as it would continue to deprive me of the intellectual tools and the time necessary to comprehend the complex relationship between state, media, and academia, particularly as it impinged on the representation of Sikhism on the one hand, and the production of Sikh subjectivity on the other—I was eventually able to embark on a program of retraining in the humanities while continuing my scientific research.

The discipline that initially attracted my attention was the history of religions, with an area focus on South Asian studies. I was interested specifically in the philosophical hermeneutics of Sikh scripture. Somewhat naively, I had hoped to find a way to reinterpret "Sikh theology" from a postcolonial perspective, thereby avoiding the growing impasse between traditionalist Sikhs and the strictly academic (phenomenological) perspective. While I never relinquished this task, I quickly discovered that any hermeneutic project had to acknowledge the encounter between Sikhism and the West in the nineteenth century, and particularly the politico-philosophical consequences of translating Sikh scripture into European languages. In other words, there was an important historical dimension to the emergence of "Sikh theology" and its enunciation as a part of modern Sikh identity. This realization dovetailed neatly with the work of some scholars of South Asian religions who at the time were producing ground-breaking social histories that suggested that the turn to religion in Sikh (and more broadly South Asian) politics could be traced back to the encounters between Sikhism (or India) and the West in the nineteenth century. This historical work provided support for the broader thesis emerging in the study of religions that the category of religion, defined as a set of beliefs and practices supposedly found in all cultures, dates from the modern period, during which Europe expanded its trade and established colonial networks throughout the world. The idea that the category of religion was, at least in some sense, fabricated in the nineteenth century found a convenient and useful ally in postcolonial theory, which helped to highlight issues of domination and power.

But while a combination of history of religions and postcolonial theory provided a useful critique of religion, it proved to be less useful than—and in some ways it firmly resisted—a similar critique of the category of secularism. Indeed, both history of religions and postcolonial theory have maintained a doctrinaire adherence to the concept of secularism in the sense that the latter constitutes the very ground from which critique itself arises. This is best seen in the prevalence of historicism as the central methodology for these disciplines and in the general inertia involving any questioning of history. The root of this problem is that these disciplines view the distinction between religion and secularism in terms of a conventional narrative that states that modernity, humanism, and its offspring, secularism, constitute a radical break with prior traditions of thought, especially theology. What this story misses, however, is the essential—i.e., ontotheological or metaphysical—*continuity* between different moments in the Western tradition: specifically, the Greek (*onto-*), the medieval-scholastic (*theo-*), and the modern humanist (*logos* or *logic*). The active forgetting of the ontotheological continuity between religion and secularism—the religious nature of the formation called the secular, or the secular nature of the formation called religion—has, however, been thoroughly probed by the discipline that has come to be called "continental philosophy of religion." With its parallel critiques of secularism and religion, continental philosophy of religion proved to be a somewhat unlikely though useful ally in my attempts to understand the various turns toward, or the returns of, religion in India.

Despite the obvious cultural and intellectual tensions between these three divergent disciplines—the material of continental philosophy of religion is drawn almost exclusively from the European philosophical and religious traditions, while history of religions and postcolonial theory apply themselves to non-Western cultures also—it was possible to harness these differences by focusing on the intellectual encounter between India and the West made possible by European imperialism. This intellectual encounter must be considered a form of contact, that is, a social relation capable of transforming both parties in the encounter. As such this imperial encounter cannot be examined unless some attention is given to the problematic of translation. By doing so I was able to formulate a doctoral thesis, entitled "Thinking Between Cultures: Metaphysics and Cultural Translation," which laid the basis for the present book. This was by no means a straightforward task, for it required forging an idiom that tested the limits of normal multidisciplinary practice. As I soon discovered when presenting or publishing earlier versions of my work at conferences and in journals related to these respective disciplines, continental philosophers (and philosophers of religion) showed little or no interest in reading materials that they considered to be too "specialist" (i.e., non-Western) and that belonged, properly speaking, to ethnic or area studies. Likewise, scholars in South Asian, and especially Sikh, studies tended more often than not to regard my engagements with continental philosophy, theology, and critical theory as either superfluous to the "real" labor of producing and interpreting archival data, or simply irksome insofar as my investigations were also attuned to the

politics of knowledge production. And postcolonial theory, as I mentioned above, simply avoided any attempt to blur the lines between religion and secularism.

Although these disciplines have different outlooks, I remained con-
vinced that there were ways of productively mediating the tensions between them. This could be done by emphasizing a long-standing lacuna
in all three that thus links them together. This is the theoretical relationship between the concept of translation and the concept of religion, what
Jacques Derrida has called the "theology of translation," or, more specifically, "a problematics of ontotheology that is located at the founding
of a certain concept of translation."[1] This theoretical relationship can be
usefully applied to the colonial (and postcolonial) context, where, for example, the concept of religion may not have existed in the lexicon of a
particular culture prior to its encounter with European colonialism, but
"suddenly" enters into their idiom as if it were their own. In such a case,
"religion," inasmuch as it emerges or takes shape in the language of the
colonized, is better considered a response to the imposition of a certain
concept of translation, which surreptitiously obliterates the gap between
there *not being* a lexical term "religion" and *there being* "religion." Apart
from signaling the birth of a new subjectivity, this gap reveals the active
forgetting that replaces the real work of translation with a *representation
of* translation (and contact) construed as a one-way process of transmitting ideas, doctrines, or values.

It is this latter concept of translation that comes to be deployed by
the three seemingly different disciplines—continental philosophy (of
religion), history of religions, and secular postcolonial theory—in any
relation to the other, even when the other is a particular knowledge formation. If these disciplines can be brought together in a mutual confrontation, this gap (inasmuch as it signifies a repression of translation) can
help to shed light on the essential cartography of knowledge production
in the humanities. Consequently, the humanities shows itself to be not
so much the bastion of disinterestedness and impartiality, but a location
that institutes a division of knowledge that parallels the division of humanity into native versus ethnic, host versus guest, etc. In a sense, therefore, it could be said that the humanities grants *belonging* to some forms
of knowledge (those that are expected to take an active attitude toward

---

[1] Jacques Derrida, "Theology of Translation," in *Eyes of the University: The Right to Philosophy II* (Stanford: Stanford University Press), 65.

studying and knowing, which in turn enables them to engage in a historical self-overcoming of knowledge, to change and recreate the means of knowing in the manner of "theory") and *nonbelonging* to others (those who participate in knowledge production primarily as passive suppliers of raw data and factual information). As such it is a location that must be ceaselessly contested by these other forms of knowledge. What the "theology of translation" reveals is an immigration policy toward different kinds of knowledge formation that is intrinsic to the architecture of the humanities, and that reflects the immigration policy ingrained in the fabric of the nation-state.

By reworking the particulars of the Sikh and South Asian archive via the self-consciously generalized idiom of continental philosophy, I have sought to revive the disavowed memory of contact and contamination between Indian and Western thought and culture that has existed since the early colonial encounters. To revive the memory of this mutual imbrication, the being-with, of West and non-West, is best seen as a response to the demand for a truly comparative cultural theory, a form of thinking that remains attentive to the global connectedness of cultures and knowledge formations. This project therefore explores how the effects of theory can be altered when performed in sites of (de)colonization, one of which is religion. The idea of theory as a thinking that always occurs between cultures, such that this "between" is always already a "being-with" another culture, will inevitably be organized around the work of translation. It is the act of translation that not only brings differential phenomena and modes of thought onto a plane of comparison, but also prefigures the very possibility of comparison. Such an enterprise will inevitably be political in nature insofar as it seeks to challenge the essentialized opposition between native and foreign, self and other that underpins cultural identity and knowledge formation.

Acknowledgments

During the course of this work I have incurred many debts, intellectual and otherwise. My primary intellectual debt is to Jacques Derrida, whose writings have inspired me and have allowed me to locate new spaces for engagement within the humanities.

Many individuals have helped me to begin this project and eventually bring it to completion. In particular I want to thank Christopher Shackle for his support, generosity, and encouragement and, not least, for all the wonderful conversations we have had over the years. I also want to thank my former philosophy advisors at Warwick (Martin Warner, David Wood, Andrew Benjamin, Christine Battersby, and Keith Ansell Pearson) for their receptiveness to my ideas and for helping me to make the intellectual transition from the natural sciences to continental philosophy. I want especially to thank Martin Warner for helping me to initiate the project that eventually became this book. I owe much to my close friends and colleagues Gurharpal Singh and Pal Ahluwalia, who have both gone out of their way to support me during some very testing times.

Many people have read or engaged with different parts of this book, either as the audience for journal articles, book chapters, conference presentations, or graduate seminars or as conversation partners. In particular, my thanks go to Richard King, Cosimo Zene, John Hinnells,

Warren Frisina, Terry Godlove Jr., Anne Murphy, Balbinder Bhogal, Ann O'Byrne, Michael Nijhawan, Virinder Kalra, Markus Dressler, Brian Axel, Navdeep Mandair, Paulo Gonçlaves, Purushottama Bilimoria, the late Grace Jantzen, Darshan Singh (Punjabi University Patiala), Srilata Raman, Giorgio Shani, James Robson, Dermot Killingley, Inderpal Grewal, Nikky Singh, Sunit Singh, Jasdev Rai, Davinder Panesar, Gurbinder Kalsi, Daljit Singh, Prabhsharandeep Singh, Nirinjan Khalsa, Harjeet Grewal, and Punnu Jaitla. I also want to thank former colleagues Darshan Tatla, Shinder Thandi, and Ian Talbot from the Punjab Research Group, which provided an early forum for my work.

Parts of these chapters were presented and honed at various venues, including the University of London (SOAS), the University of Warwick, the University of Birmingham, Oxford University, Lancaster University, U.C. Berkeley and U.C. Irvine, Hofstra University, Stony Brook University, Imperial College, the University of Wisconsin–Madison, and the University of Michigan, and at annual meetings of the American Academy of Religion (Toronto, Philadelphia, Atlanta, and San Diego) and the Association of Asian Studies (Boston). Portions of chapters 2 and 3 appeared in the following publications: *Journal of the American Academy of Religion* 74.3 (2006): 646–673; *History of Religions* 44.4 (2005): 277–299; and *Bulletin of the School of Oriental and African Studies* 68.2 (2005): 253–275.

This book could not have been completed without a period of leave generously provided by the University of Michigan. I want to thank Don Lopez and Nancy Florida for supporting this and for helping to make my transition to Ann Arbor as smooth as possible.

Jeff Robins kindly suggested that I consider publishing this volume in the exciting new series "Insurrections: Critical Studies in Religion, Politics, and Culture." I want to thank the series editors, and particularly Clayton Crockett, for providing such speedy and positive feedback. At Columbia University Press, Wendy Lochner provided enthusiastic backing for this book, and Kerri Sullivan has been a wonderfully efficient and helpful editor.

Without doubt, I owe the greatest debt to my family for their unstinting love and support. In particular I want to mention my parents, Karnail Singh Mandair and Parkash Kaur Mandair. My wife, Preet, and children, Aman-vir and Sukhmani, have been fellow travelers and sufferers during the course of this project. It is to them that I dedicate this book, in love and gratitude.

RELIGION AND THE SPECTER OF THE WEST

It is impossible to undo the consequences of the history of imperialisms no matter how desperately one wishes that imperialisms had never been effectuated. We live in the effects of the imperialist maneuvers of the past and the progressive present, in their pervasive effects in which everyone in today's world is inevitably implicated. From those effects some may be able to extract almost inexhaustible privileges; because of the same effects, others may be condemned to what appears to be unending adversities.

—Naoki Sakai, Translation and Subjectivity

Introduction

    A certain repetition of the colonial event seems to haunt the very manner in which different portions of humanity have attempted, or indeed have been permitted, to engage with what has come to be called "the political." This repetition can be visualized in terms of the revived function and reassigned place of the phenomenon called "religion"—more specifically, its recent return as "political religion," or its seeming incompatibility with the demands of secular liberal democracy and multiculturalism. For South Asians the relationship between religion and repetition continues to be a vexed issue in their attempts to rethink the questions of identity and difference beyond a neocolonial imaginary. This move "beyond" has routinely followed a deconstruction of the "religious effects"[1] of Orientalism, whose conceptual matrix can be located in the political history of European ideas.

    Taking its theoretical cue from an enigmatic remark by Jacques Derrida—"What if *religio* remained untranslatable?"[2]—this book explores the possibility of connecting past imperialist structures with their repetition in the lives and thought of postcolonials today. In doing so it reveals the workings of an ontotheological matrix[3] that underpins not only the recent resurgences of religious nationalism and political religion in South Asia and the South Asian diaspora, but also, paradoxically, the secular frameworks of contemporary multiculturalism and anti-imperialist critique. The ontotheological matrix effectively took on the role of a blueprint for domination encoded in the structures of thought, practice, and order necessary for the maintenance of Empire in the nineteenth century. Contrary to what is often thought, this very matrix continues to be replicated and repeated in the postmodern incarnations of Empire, such as global capitalism. Specifically my aim is to trace the circuit of this repetition to the nexus of ideas feeding one particular site where the subjectivity of South Asians is formed, namely the site where religious tradition is retrieved and reproduced, projected and introjected. To do this the book pursues an oblique and often impossible engagement between several discourses not usually thought to be connected: (i) the theorization of religion and "world religions" in relation to the specialist discipline of Indology; (ii) the secular form of postcolonial theory inspired by Edward Said, particularly as it impinges on modern South Asian formations; (iii) a study of the relationship between the religious reform movements and the enunciation of the colonial subject in nineteenth-century South Asia; (iv) the role of translation as a site of colonial hegemony and as a site of anti-colonial resistance; and (v) underpinning all of the above, the continuing influence of European philosophy, especially the writings of G. W. F. Hegel, whose spectral presence was thought to have been safely exorcised by postcolonial theory.

Far from being accidental, the juxtaposition of these seemingly disparate themes points to their mutual imbrication in colonial and contemporary South Asian experience. More importantly, however, it focuses attention on the central role played by religion as a driving force behind the circuit of repetition. Despite the predictions of secular modernity, recent years have witnessed a global and "machinelike" return of religion from the periphery to the center of debates on the future of democracy, multiculturalism, and globalization.[4] The obvious example is 9/11, an event that highlighted the importance of faith in motivating contemporary religious interventions in the political. Less visible, but in consonance with this, would be the redefining of politics in South Asia in terms of pancontinental religious traditions; or perhaps the effort expended by South Asian immigrants and settlers in Britain to reproduce their heritage traditions in a manner that does not necessarily conform to the ideological demands of contemporary multiculturalism. The latter scenario is highlighted by Talal Asad in his perceptive article "Multiculturalism and British Identity in the Wake of the Rushdie Affair."[5] Responding to the hysteria of

British liberal intellectual elites over the political mobilization by British Muslims to have *The Satanic Verses* banned, Asad identifies the insidious tactics of institutionalized and interventionist power respectively at work in the liberal/conservative and radical left notions of multiculturalism. For Asad the real dilemma for British-Asian immigrants in Britain was how to defend, develop, and elaborate the collective historical difference exemplified by their religious traditions, but under the proviso that the politicization of religious traditions has no place within the cultural hegemony that has defined British identity over the last century.

Although Asad is perfectly correct in emphasizing the reproduction of religious tradition as a site of postcolonial contestation, the impression could be given, however unintentionally, that "religion" is conceptualized as something that both is universally translatable and has strictly defined boundaries. While evidence would appear to suggest that this is indeed the case (in addition to the seemingly straightforward case of Islam and British Muslims, one only has to cite the revival or return of religious nationalisms—Hindu, Sikh, Muslim—in India and the diaspora, or the seeming transparency of the relationship between religion and identity in the enunciations "I am Hindu," "I am Muslim," "I am Sikh," to show how empirically unassailable this position is), there is, however, a problem in simply assuming the same understanding in the case of South Asian traditions. Recent thinking about the *question* of religion, as opposed to assuming ready-made definitions of it (for example that religion is necessarily opposed to the political, meaning thereby that the political is necessarily based on the overcoming of the religious) suggests that there is a much stronger and often invisible connection between religion, enunciation, and the political than is normally given credit.

Questioning this invisible link between religion, enunciation, and the political exposes the effects of imperialism well beyond the target areas on which it was originally designed to take effect. Indeed the connection between religion, enunciation, and the political brings into view not only its historical root, but its repetition *today* in and as the place of its origination. To see how this works consider for example those—mainly Europeans and Americans—who identify themselves, intellectually, psychologically, existentially, with the formation called "the West," as opposed to those who, because they might be identified, or identify themselves, as South Asian, belong by default to "the Rest." In both cases the repetition of the colonial event is rather well illustrated by the different ways in which European-Americans and South Asians narrate, or are expected to narrate, their respective movements through modernity to the present moment, and in so narrating situate themselves or their cultures within the "ontological script of liberation,"[6] that is, the ability to overcome a particular stage of culture and to move beyond it, the efficacy of the so-called *post-*.

For most European-Americans, modernity was born with the Enlightenment project that broke with a world centered around Christianity. It comprises a variety of different movements: the Enlightenment project, the separation of Church and State, the crisis of European identity through its encounter with non-Christian cultures, followed by the rise of nationalist identity politics and the development of modern nation-states, the colonization of non-European territories—all of which lead in the twentieth century to modernity's seemingly divergent political projects (communism versus the secular liberal democratic model based on an all-powerful state) that eventually did away with the "political" and settled into routine politics.[7] With the end of the Cold War and the onset of globalization, and the global "return of religion" in the form of violent identity politics, the secular narrative of modernity undergoes a crisis and mutates into a *post*-secular form. Post-secularism does not imply any worldwide increase in religiosity but rather a changed attitude by the secular state in regard to the existence of religion(s) and religious communities.[8] Although it is part of the "death of God" phenomenon and not simply a reemergence of Christianity, the era now being identified as postsecularism implies a more overt relinking of the political to religious (especially Christian) conceptuality, and therefore a need to understand politics and the political in terms of the "theologico-political."

More important, though, and what remains a hidden or silent aspect of this narrative, is that this return of religion to the heart of the political, or alternatively, the return of the political to its religious sources, is a self-legitimating or self-referencing phenomenon. The movement of this narrative from Christianity through secularism to postsecularism is legitimate because it is self-referential. The narrative returns the West to itself despite its various transformations. This ability to return to itself despite its continual alteration is the singular privilege that is drawn by the West even, or especially, when the West is not named in this narrative.

One of the reasons this narrative can be considered legitimate is that it purports to be universal. It describes a set of events that supposedly encompass other cultures as well. However, similar phenomena, such as the entry into secular modernity, the crisis of secularism, and the "return of religion," also appear to have taken place within South Asian society and culture. But unlike Europe's passage to modernity, which entailed a certain death or privatization of religion, India's passage to modernity happened through its being reawakened to the notion that it once had religion, that it had forgotten its original religion(s), but that this religion could be recovered through the colonizer's benign intervention, in order to progress toward a form of modern national self-governance. As a result India's passage to globalization is limited to a stand-off between secularism and/or global religions such as Hinduism, Islam, and Sikhism. Indian society remains at the level of identity politics, at the stage of politics rather than the political, properly speaking, since the latter is not yet achieved. Because the god(s) of Hinduism or the "God" of Sikhism was being reborn at the time when Christianity was suffering the death of its own God, consequently, the narrative goes, India cannot manifest a *post*-secularism. Hence the equation of global Hinduism or global Sikhism with the postsecular phase is illegitimate.

Consequently, even when it is not the West, but the non-West, that is being evoked, the West is being automatically constituted. This self-constitution, which takes place through a process of exclusion, the creation of a boundary between "the West" and "the Rest," is what Rey Chow and others have termed the "self-referentiality" of the West.[9] And it is this innate ability to self-reference, even when the discourse is about the West's other, that I refer to as the repetition of the colonial event.

This book interrogates the self-referential aspect of the West from the standpoint of a postcoloniality that not only is fully aware of being immersed and inflected by the history of modernity, but also acknowledges the need to disrupt the limits now signified by the modern. Its aim is to find critical spaces for engaging with the reality called "the West" and hence to find a meaning for the "post-," whose disruptive potential has come to be monopolized by the West's self-referential narrative, a tendency that might simply be termed "Occidentalism."[10] From the critical space of the postcolonial this kind of Occidentalism consists of the historical and conceptual space in which the subject has been constituted, initially through the discourses of the Enlightenment, modernity, and postmodernity and more recently through the various "returns" of religion and the political that comprise the intellectual space that has come to be termed postsecularism. It is a narrative that has become hegemonic through the universalizing tendencies inherent in modernity, through the spread of European colonization, and, today, through the ineluctable movement of global capital. Today the postcolonial world may be present everywhere but it is filtered and relocated for the West through representational devices inherent within consumer culture and within the university, more specifically the humanities and its division of knowledge into theory and empiricism.[11] By being filtered in this way, the postcolonial world appears as a silent witness whose presence can never coincide with events that make up the *post-*. Invariably the postcolonial appears to coincide only with the backward, the underdeveloped, or the catastrophic outside.[12] I want to let the postcolonial appear, to demonstrate its effects at the heart of the modern, the secular, the postmodern, and now the postsecular.

However, I do not think I am alone in suspecting that there is something that manages to remain constant in the narrative of the *post-*, especially when this narrative not only claims to speak for the West but tries to encompass the encounter between Europe and India. One of the central arguments of the book is that this "constant something" is an idea that is mostly taken for granted, an idea that seems fairly innocuous because of its apparent ubiquity. This constant something happens to be the concept of religion-in-general, which is comprised of two interconnected themes: (i) the idea that religion is something that exists in all cultures, and (ii) the idea that it does so because religion as a concept is generally translatable. There is, in other words, an indissociable link between religion and translatability that will be explored more fully here.

There is now a growing consensus among scholars that questions the prevalent notion of religion as a cultural universal. "Religion" is now understood to be a relatively recent invention that emerged during the course of the nineteenth century at the intersection of a variety of different discourses.[13] It is increasingly accepted that the construction of religion as a concept cannot be separated from the formation of the comparative imaginary of the West. Indeed, Daniel Dubuisson has argued that "religion . . . must be considered the locus in which the identity or figure of the West has in principle been constituted and defined."[14] This is why, he suggests, that "instead of speaking about the religious consciousness of the West, it would surely be more judicious to say that the West is religious only in the very exact and strict sense that religion, as a notion intended to isolate a set of phenomena thenceforth considered homogenous, is the exclusive creation of the West, and is thus what may constitute its innermost nature."[15]

In her recent book, *The Invention of World Religions*, Tomoko Masuzawa echoes these sentiments, arguing that since the discourse of religion and religions was "from the very beginning a discourse of secularism, . . . these two wings of the religion discourse did the work of churning Europe's epistemic domain" and "forged from that domain an enormous apparition: the essential identity of the West."[16] This essential identity not only crystallized into a self-sustaining belief in the West's unique and sovereign nature, it also helped to preserve and promote its universalizing tendency, paradoxically, through a language of pluralism as found in the discourse of "world religions." For Dubuisson, it is through the language of pluralism embedded in the discourse of "world religions" that the West has in a sense drawn around itself a magic—and narcissistic—circle. This charmed circle "both limits its reflections and flatters its epistemological talents. And with the inevitable reassuring effect that such a mechanism produces, the West believes all the more willingly in the relevance of this concept, since other civilizations merely faithfully reflect its own chimeras. And this will be the state of things as long as the debate is conducted exclusively on the conceptual field chosen and defined by the West alone."[17]

In this book I explore the mechanisms by which this apparition—what I call the "specter of the West"—has been, and continues to be, produced every time Indians retrieve for themselves a mode of identification through which they see themselves, and are seen by others, as members of a particular "world religion" (Hinduism or Sikhism) or as members of a nation (Indian or Sikh), for in doing so they must rely on a comparative imaginary and inadvertently help to solidify the specter that calls itself the West. It needs to be stated, however, that this exploration is very far from reducing religion to scientific categories or simply dismissing it as an obsolete phenomenon. My approach, rather, is to conceptualize the identification that Indians make with "religion" or "world religion" as an *aporia*, an experience that is simultaneously possible and impossible. Perhaps the clearest indication of this *aporia* is that way in which Indians have attempted to engage the political through a mode of identification that once upon a time did not exist, yet which today is repeatedly brought to life through their responses to the word "religion." The *aporia* can be visualized in terms of the relationship between "religion" and "response," in the sense that religion not only informs the Indian response to the political, but is also the response that gives rise to the Indian experience of political modernity. This aporetic response would be one that on the one hand accepts *without resistance* the translatability of the term "religion," and at the same time *must resist* what is encompassed by the term "religion."

The term *aporia* reflects the deeply ambivalent nature of Indian decolonization and is indicative of a combination of knowledge and experience that manifests in two very different ways. On the one hand there is the experience of there being, prior to the encounter with European thought, no exact equivalent for the term "religion," no referent that signifies what "religion" signifies in European languages, and therefore, no history of a response to this term.[18] After European conceptuality becomes hegemonic, however, and once Indians were coerced into responding to its call by appropriating and internalizing this term as if it had been part and parcel of their traditions of *longue durée*, it has become a matter of historical fact that "Indian religions" have existed.

What seems to be so peculiar about Indian decolonization was not just the unavoidability of responding to the term "religion," but that even today Indians continue to respond to the call of "religion" even, or especially, when they consider themselves to be absolutely secular. Consider, for example, the continued rejection of the term "religion" in favor of its secular other by those who identify themselves as Indian Marxists or as Indian left liberal secularists, the argument being that "religion" cannot be disassociated from the phenomenon of colonial violence. Consider too the fact that those who belong to India's religious right, such as the various Hindu nationalist parties (BJP, VHP, RSS, Shiv Sena, etc.)[19] or Sikh political parties such as the Akali Dal, have all accepted what the term "religion" signifies in the name of a particular religious tradition: Hinduism, Sikhism, etc.

In both cases the response has still taken place. Nowhere is the ineluctability of the response more evident than in some of the violent events that define India's difficult passage to political modernity. Examples that immediately spring to mind include the partitioning of India in 1947 along religious lines, Muslim versus Hindu; the Indian army's invasion of the Golden Temple complex in Amritsar in June 1984 to oust Sikh militants; Indira Gandhi's assassination in October 1984, followed by the state-orchestrated anti-Sikh pogroms in the capital, New Delhi; the symbolic destruction of the Muslim Babri Masjid in Ayodhya in 1992 by mobs of Hindu militants, once again indirectly assisted by the secular state but directly orchestrated by Hindu nationalist parties; and the anti-Muslim pogroms in Gujerat in 2002.

With these examples in mind, let me turn to what seems at first sight an unlikely source for insights into the operation of this colonial event and therefore for the nature of Indian decolonization, namely, Jacques

Derrida's oblique meditations on religion, violence, and law. From seemingly different angles, Derrida argues that religion and violence are intrinsically connected to the question of law and the (im)possibility of experiencing justice.[20] In this view, every time an Indian responds to the word "religion" s/he is obliged to speak (whether in English or Hindi) in another's language, breaking with her own and in so doing give herself up to the other. In this obligation "the violence of an injustice has begun when all members of a community do not share the same idiom throughout. For all injustice supposes that the other, the victim of the languages' injustice, is capable of a 'language in general,' that the other is a subject capable of responding and insofar, a responsible subject."[21] Furthermore, Derrida argues, to address oneself to the other in the language of the other is the impossible condition of all justice since I can speak the language of the other only to the extent that I am able to appropriate it according to the law of an implicit third, an appeal to a third party who suspends the unilaterality or singularity of all idioms, implying thereby the element of universality and, specifically here, the implied translatability/universality of the term "religion."[22] Accordingly, every time an Indian responds, quite responsibly, as "I am Hindu / Hinduism is my religion," or even if one rejects this response in favor of a purely secular enunciation, what is never questioned, because it is always assumed, is the concept of religion operating in this case, indeed, the relation between religion and conceptuality. In responding at all one will always have conformed to a certain law—which is first and foremost a law of thinking, or an assumption about *what thinking is* that itself constitutes a law—according to which the meaning and concept of religion is accepted universally and without resistance.

A strange scenario: Indian's have no exact word for religion yet they cannot avoid answering to its call. As Derrida notes, "there is no common Indo-European term for what we call religion, no omnipresent reality that is religion. There has not always been nor will there always and everywhere be *something*, a thing that is *one and identifiable*, identical with itself, which whether religious or irreligious, all agree to call 'religion.'"[23] Why then do Indians continue to respond? And to respond precisely in terms of something that is identifiable and one? More to the point, why do they feel obliged to respond in conformity with a law? To feel obliged is already to have interiorized that law, to have imposed the law on oneself, to have *intro*jected it as a self-censorship, the *pro*jection of which would be the response or enunciation: "I am Hindu" or "Hinduism is my religion" or "I am a secular Indian." The law itself is never seen. It is simply assumed as a law of thinking, and the work of thinking is in turn assumed to incorporate a "fundamental translatability."[24] Indeed to make visible the law that obliges one to respond to religion would entail a trespass, a violation of a meaning that all are supposed to know, whence its universality. Clearly, though, a universal that needs to be shown in evidence is no longer a universal since not everybody will have assented to its meaning.

Prior to even questioning religion, therefore, what needs to be interrogated is the invisible link, the law as a law of thinking that connects, on the one hand, religion as the response that conforms to the enunciation of an identity ("I am Hindu/Sikh," etc.) and, on the other, the violence that results not from simply *not*-responding, but from a response that resists conforming to the law that demands identity and identification. Elsewhere Derrida refers to this law as an interdict.[25] The interdict works by preventing a certain kind of speech or thought from being articulated, instead specifying access to certain identifications, while in that very moment actively repressing other identifications. Moreover, the interdict doesn't simply work at the level of language. It is the language of law: language as Law.

Derrida's notion of the interdict is indebted to Jacques Lacan's psychoanalytic account of the subject.[26] For Lacan the subject is formed around a lack and in the face of a trauma. In order to become who we are we have to find our place in a social order that is produced through language into which we are born. We are therefore born as subjects of language. Language forms our subjectivity. Each language has its own way of dividing up the world in certain ways to produce for every social group what it calls "reality." But this process is never complete and therefore no language can ever completely produce a "reality." There is always something lacking, something that fails or refuses to be symbolized into "reality." This lacking something that refuses or resists symbolization is what Lacan calls "the Real." So when the subject is born into a language or a social order, it is formed by covering up what cannot be symbolized, or what is prohibited from being symbolized: the traumatic real. This real has to be forgotten, hidden, because it threatens the subject's imaginary completeness. The subject exists only insofar as the person manages to find a place in the social order or language. But this place always leaves out something that could not be symbolized in that language or social order.

The relation between language and response can therefore be recast in a Lacanian frame as follows. By responding to the word "religion" in the form of a religious identity ("I am a Hindu / Hinduism is my religion"; "I am not a Muslim"; "I am a Sikh"/ "Sikhism is my religion"; "I am not a Hindu," etc.), the Indian (i) already believes that religion is a universal, and (ii) assumes in advance that s/he has mastered the meaning of the word "religion" through normal acquisition of English. But according to Lacan, one cannot *acquire* language, all one can do is accede to it, which means that one willingly agrees to submit to it as Law, such that one is first mastered by language. Thus the enunciation "religion" is the locus of an identification that represses the traumatic real: namely, that which does not conform to what "religion" signifies, or which resists the very concept of religion. In other words, the possibility that arises here is that the constitution of the Indian subject through the enunciation of "religion" during the colonial encounter does not reflect the operation of a culturally universal meaning, but the site of a trauma that marks the nature of Indian engagement with European conceptuality. This traumatic entry into the enunciation of religion, the response as religion, religion as the response, is concomitant with a depoliticization of India and everything associated with it. Consequently "religion" does not constitute the same "reality" for South Asians as it does for those who identify themselves with the formation called the West. Rather, the enunciation "religion" enjoins South Asians to hide the traumatic real and to instead identify with the fantasy of social reality created by nationalism.

Here then is the central issue that is interrogated in this book. If the notion of religion as a cultural universal is deconstructed, if we accept that religion as a concept cannot be unproblematically translated across cultures, that is, without leaving some residue, is it possible to dissipate the mechanism by which such identifications occur? What might be the political and psychological implications of this dissipation, particularly at a time when the specter of the West appears to be achieving its final incarnation in the form of capitalist globalization? What can the deconstruction of religion as a cultural universal teach us about the history of colonialism in India, about India's decolonization, and about the task of postcoloniality in an era of globalization?

As recent scholarship has shown, the undertaking of such a task can no longer be isolated either from a knowledge of the events that transformed the indigenous cultures of India during its encounter with European imperialism, or from the construction of autonomous disciplines such as the study of religion(s) in the Western academy. Events such as these profoundly affected the self-understanding of South Asians. Having been forced to articulate what they stood for to the Raj, it appears that their articulation was framed in terms of questions and concepts drawn largely from the Western experience. However, any attempt to bring the experience of the South Asian diaspora in Europe today into a relationship with contemporary critical thought also calls for the need to excavate the history of encounter between India and Europe. This encounter was deeply colored by the articulation and development of the concept of religion. Moreover, such excavation prompts the question as to whether this encounter, and specifically the *work of translation as the site of encounter*, was as innocent or transparent as is still presumed. Indeed, the traditional view of translation underwritten by Western philosophy and classical Western theism enabled by the operation of "resemblance"—which makes possible the translation of one thing into another given that both are based on the identity of the general and the particular[27]—has helped colonialism to construct an exotic "other" as unchanging and ahistorical, thereby rendering it easier to appropriate and control. Any attempt to examine the mechanisms of colonial installation, and the possibility of a postcolonial project, must therefore take into account the interrelated roles of theology and the political in relation to subject formation.

"Indian Religions" and Western Thought

This book is divided into three parts, each consisting of two chapters. Part I, entitled " 'Indian Religions' and Western Thought," reexamines the encounter between India and Europe through: (i) the closely connected roles of religion and language in the formation of the colonial subject, (ii) the transformation of indigenous traditions and the projects of social reform as Indian elites acceded to a newly formed public sphere, and (iii) the politico-religious debates in European philosophy that formed the intellectual backdrop to this activity. A key theme that emerges from this study is the interplay between mimesis and power, which helped to establish the ruse of a communicational economy that on the one hand facilitated the transparent movement of Indic cultural logics initially under the project of "religion" and eventually their installation within the secular humanist framework of the modern university, a movement that is often represented as India's transition (or "conversion") to modernity, but which in fact involves a displacement of Indian forms of thinking into the domain of European conceptuality. On the other hand, the ruse of transparent communication helped the West to flesh out its own sense of identity and difference from India, Indic thinking, and culture. Although this will be disavowed by both parties, Indian and Western thought are mutually transformed in this encounter. The first two chapters will track this act of mutual disavowal whose form is threefold: (i) the disavowal of the work of translation in encounters between India and the West, (ii) as a consequence of the disavowal of translation, the reconceptualization of religion-as-universal; and (iii) the removal of India and everything associated with it from the realms of theory and the political.

In chapter 1 I explore the possibility of connecting the operations of an imperialist technology in a past historical moment (specifically during the encounter between Britain and India) with its legacies in the present, namely, the crisis of secularism and/or the "return of religion" into the heart of the Indian nation-state and the projects of the South Asian diaspora. The ability to crystallize this link between past and present centers around a reassessment of the role of religion and language, which are normally analyzed as separate but crucial components in the formation of nationalisms. Recent theorizing of the nexus religion-language-subjectivity has shown that language and religion, far from being separate, are inextricably linked. Indeed, it could be claimed that the work of monotheism and monolingualism that is central to the formation of nationalist ideologies can be considered part of a single process that might be termed *mono-theo-lingualism*.

In order to examine this claim, this chapter begins by reassessing recent scholarship that has identified religion as the primary site of encounter between Britain and India during the colonial period.[28] During this period Britons and Indian elites mutually affected each others' self-understanding in such a way that religion and the process of thinking about religion were transformed. If religion is considered to be the privileged site of this encounter between India and Europe, this is because it has been assumed to be totally transparent, that is to say, universally translatable in the process of encounter. By reconsidering the emergence of public spheres in Britain and across a set of geographically and culturally specific sites across North India (Bengal [1820s–1830s], Banaras [1850s–1870s], Punjab [1880s-1920s]), I attempt to shed a rather different light on the role of religion and the "religious reform movements" during the late nineteenth century. My aim is to materialize the operations of representation that constitute the transparency of religion, and this will be accomplished in two ways.

I will first trace a genealogy of religion within the colonial discourse of Indology and the neocolonial discourses of the religious reform movements. This genealogy shows that the concept of religion being used by Indologists and by native elites was always affected by ongoing intellectual debates within the domains of Western philosophy, theology, and politics. Second, I will demonstrate the dependency of religion on a mode of homolingual address that was established between colonizer and colonized in the Anglo-Vernacular schools of nineteenth-century North India. The multiple effects of this mode of address include: (i) the production of an economic (fluent) exchange between English as the First Idiom of the Raj and the regional vernaculars represented by the imaginary figure of the mother tongue, that is to say, the invention of the mother tongue (Punjabi, Hindi) as the monolingual other of English; (ii) closely related to this, the colonizer's paternalistic demand for "true religion," fostered through a belief in the unhindered translatability of *religio*, and the reciprocation of this demand by neocolonial elites who produced monotheistic versions of Sikhism and Hinduism in order to inscribe themselves within the political and ideological space of Christianity.

By reading the Indian experience of colonization through writings by Jacques Derrida, Naoki Sakai, and Jacques Lacan that address the connections between language and religion, it is possible to work out an alternative model for conceiving the interaction between colonizer and colonized, and thus a different way of thinking about the formation of colonial subjectivity. As a result of this model one can no longer take for granted that religion exists as naturally within Indian cultural formations as it does within European cultural formations. Rather, if, as Derrida maintains, "religion is the response,"[29] it is more accurate to suggest that religion comes to be enunciated by native elites as the result of their emergence into the dominant symbolic order, the language of the colonizer. Moreover, even within the colonial idiom, the concept of religion is not a stable one. The discourse of religion, and hence its concept, is subject to fundamental shifts within European philosophy. The nature of these shifts and their effect on the discourse of Indology — specifically a reversal in the nature of Indological discourse during the mid-nineteenth century — and hence on the modern conceptual formations known as Hinduism and Sikhism, is taken up in chapter 2. More importantly, this model enables us to see how the politics of language-making and the politics of religion-making are intrinsically linked in a process that might be termed *mono-theo-lingualism,* which continues to haunt not only the access that Indians have to their past, but the possibilities for engaging the political present.

Chapter 2 considers in greater detail what was identified above as a reversal in the nature of Indology during the first half of the nineteenth century. I argue that these shifts and reversals can be traced to the work of redefining the nature of religion (the question, "what is religion?"), a task that proceeds in relation to debates in aesthetics, the philosophy of history, and the problem of classifying non-Western cultures (the "other") in relation to Western identity. The mechanism of the reversal is illustrated most powerfully in the work of G. W. F. Hegel (though not limited to Hegel alone). What follows is a close reading of some of Hegel's key moves in the often overlooked *Lectures on the Philosophy of Religion.* Hegel's main concern in these texts was to bring the chaotic diversity of (newly discovered) Oriental religions into some kind of manageable order, and in so doing to counter the growing influence of the early Orientalists and the Jena Romantics, in whose work the prevailing definition of the nature of Oriental religion coincided with the origin of history, of reason, and consequently of civilization itself. Given that a situation such as this threatened to displace or undermine the dominant vantage point of European identity based on its exclusionary claims to history/reason/civilization, Hegel's key move was to establish a firm theoretical standpoint for religion-in-general, and as a result of this, a way of classifying Oriental cultures according to a new framework based on ontotheology. The work of framing this ontotheological schema is performed by the Hegelian narrative itself. It serves as a classic example of the way in which ontotheology is harnessed on the one hand for disciplining knowledge of other cultures by *hermeneutically* structuring discourse about them, and on the other hand for *practically* structuring nondiscursive practices.

The ontotheological schema is a means for rendering the encounter with non-Western cultures politically harmless by installing them on a standardized graph of history/religion/reason. Mediated via new disciplines as seemingly different as the philosophy of religion and Indology, the results of the ontotheological schema are far reaching. Deploying for the first time the terms "pantheism"/"monotheism"/"polytheism" as "world historical" categories, the schema provides an intuitive comprehension of the "meaning-value" of each culture that happens to be plotted on the graph.[30] In effect the schema provides a principle of "generalized translation"—to use Derrida's term—a mechanism for bringing different cultures into a system of equivalence in which the relative meaning-values can be assigned to each culture, in order for them then to be exchanged/compared. By bringing the meaning-value of different cultures into a system of exchange/comparison Hegel effectively replaces the very real problem of translation with the work of representation proper to the political economy of the sign. As cultural exchange/comparison begins to parallel commodity exchange in the political economy of Empire, Hegel's schema can be seen as a precursor of Marx's analysis of global monetary exchange. In practice, the principle of "generalized translation" or exchange/comparison begins to empower the task of future missionaries and Indologists as translators and interpreters of indigenous texts and cultural practices. The task of the Indologist-cum-translator will be to enact a simultaneous passage to, and installation of, Indic cultures. Stated differently, the Indologist can at the same time be a theologian and an anthropologist without there being any contradiction between the two positions. Lack of contradiction implies perfect translatability (infinite and at will) between the Indologist's identities as theologian and as anthropologist, since the law by which one position translates into the other is the law of thinking itself.

More precisely than any other thinker, Hegel's work both fleshes out the contours of "the West" and "the Rest," and provides the conceptual tools for future disciplines within an emerging humanities to theoretically exclude non-Western cultures, to "ban them from entering signification (the realm of human contact and interaction)" and yet at the same time to "retain, rename and elevate them in a benevolent second-order gesture as signification's spectral other."[31] Central to this double act of exclusion-through-inclusion is the gesture of denying coevalness in time, or the assertion of temporal disjunction, the classification of non-Western others as noncoincident and essentially discontinuous with the West. This gesture becomes ingrained in the various theoretical and empirical projects of the humanities: Indology (chapters 1, 2, and 3), history of religions (chapters 4 and 5), theory of religion (chapter 2 and 6), area studies (chapter 2 and 4), and political theory (chapter 6).

I am well aware that Hegel's role should not be overestimated. Indeed, there may be a tendency for some to misread my interpretation of the Hegelian influence too literally—believing that I see him as a master architect whose agency is omnipresent throughout the chain of intellectual exchanges being explored particularly in later chapters. However, I want to stress that Hegel's role is better perceived as a spectral presence rather than a literal agent. Hegel's ideological influence functions like a cipher. It is more like a post-hoc justifier rather than an actual initiator of what are in fact complex large-scale cultural and political processes. In this sense one could simply replace the name "Hegel" with the metonym "ontotheology." Nevertheless Hegel continues to be named in these explorations partly because he is directly responsible for reformulating the matrix of knowledge-power in relation to Asian cultures, and partly because this very matrix, if not the name "Hegel," continues to influence not only the production of theory in the humanities but the way this theorization continues to be put into practice. One way or another, Hegel continues to haunt the very movements that have tried to overcome modernity: postcolonialism, postmodernism, and postsecularism. Perhaps the key cipher of this haunting is the presence of a "fundamental translatability" between religion and secularism that continues to structure unholy alliances between academic theory, media, and the state.

Disorders of Identity and the Memory of Politics

Part II of this book, entitled "Theology as Cultural Translation," investigates the spectral passage of ontotheology into the various projects—cultural, theoretical, and political—of the native elites, giving rise over a period of about fifty years (1870s to 1920s) to what could be termed the politics of religion-making, responsible for the specifically religious underpinning of the Indian passage into modernity.[32] The term "religion-making" here refers to the nature of the space in which are mutually fleshed out the specters of India as a nation and the West. No site reveals the political consequences and limits of this religion-making better than the marginal space inhabited by Sikhs and Sikhism.

I have chosen to focus on Sikhism for several reasons. First, in the history of the encounter between India and the West, Sikhs occupy a somewhat ambivalent position. As early as the 1780s, Sikhism was construed by the British as the indigenous other of Hinduism. Their apparent difference from the "Hindoo multitude" was hailed by the British as a reason for their rise to power and attainment of a sovereign kingdom under the Sikh ruler Maharaja Ranjit Singh. Implicit references to Sikh sovereignty continued in the British reports until the onset of hostilities between Sikhs and the British in the 1840s, which resulted in the Anglo-Sikh wars of 1848. However, after March 24, 1849, the imperial narrative introduced a new component, which Brian Axel has aptly termed the "colonial scene of surrender." For Axel this surrender was "perhaps the most spectacular the British had witnessed in India. Governor-General Dalhousie, the director of this spectacle, wrote to Queen Victoria, describing the event in order to include the absent monarch in the "experience" of taking possession:

> Your Majesty may well imagine the pride with which the British Officers looked on such a scene, and witnessed this *absolute subjection and humiliation* of so powerful an enemy[33]

In this scene of surrender, Axel tells us, "Sikhs are at once transformed into prisoners and liberated as new colonial subjects."[34] Due to the sheer ambivalence of these representations—sovereignty/surrender, imprisonment/liberation—in the colonial narrative, Sikhs were able to find a device that conveniently allowed them to retain at least a memory of their former sovereignty and at the same time to resist complete assimilation into the evolving nationalist imaginary of India and Hinduism.

On the other hand, though, because Sikh literature and tradition remained culturally and conceptually continuous with the broad themes of North Indic cosmography—indeed, because it had to be *constructed* as a religion—neither could it ever be totally assimilated into a colonial or Western frame. This is best seen through the moment in which Sikh scripture enters into the economy of colonial translation and thus into the dominant symbolic order of English through the work of Indologists. This site of translation into English is potentially the scene of a second surrender—a surrender not only to English this time but to a newly resurgent Hindu consciousness—which had to be resisted. Sikhs and Sikhism today continue to occupy this ambivalent subaltern space that is simultaneously inside and outside the figures of the Indian nation and the West.

There is, however, another, and somewhat more personal, reason for me to focus on Sikhs and Sikhism in this book. For this is a space in relation to which I have also chosen to work out and reveal my own theoretico-political position. This position, as I shall clarify below, is influenced partly by the increasingly prevalent recognition within the discipline of religious studies that the safe and privileged standpoint of liberal humanist scholarship, with its belief in a proper disinterested method of inquiry, is little more than a "secularized version of theology's dream of an unconditional principle of principles,"[35] and partly by the realization that it is not necessary to try to transcend one's own "passionate attachments"[36] to cultural and social identity even as one writes from an academic perspective. Clearly though, one cannot claim to derive a theoretico-political position simply from the fact that one belongs to a particular society. Such a position, as Antonio Gramsci reminds us, has to be struggled for and constituted through different kinds of intellectual struggle.[37] The excerpt from Naoki Sakai at the beginning of this chapter reminds us that part of this struggle involves a realization that it is not possible to simply undo the consequences of past imperialisms. This is especially the case for South Asians, for whom the task of undoing the colonial event came to be inscribed with a double prohibition. On the one hand was the effort to forget that identification with a mother tongue and a determinate religion—two events that characterize India's birth to modernity—entailed a transformation and jettisoning of the nonmodern into the void of prememory. On the other hand, a second act of forgetting was necessary, wherein *one forgets that one has forgotten.* The event of erasure will itself have to be forgotten to avoid the first amnesia being memorialized.[38] Nevertheless, this double prohibition can be uncovered by forging psychological and existential connections that link the construction of this event in a past moment with its reappearances in the present. Such links can be crystallized only by allowing what Derrida refers to as a "disorder of identity" to guide one's retrieval of memory.[39] By "disorder" I refer not only to that which resists the imperative to identify oneself by repressing those identifications that are incompatible with the dominant culture (the interdict), but also to events that rupture the ongoing treadmill of nationalist identification. Consequently, what continues to be assumed about or spoken of as "Sikh identity" (either as a property that belongs to an ordered entity or as the work of ordering proper to that entity) is perhaps better referred to as a "disorder." Disorder is therefore constitutive of the very order that manifests as "Sikh identity."

For most Punjabis belonging to my generation and that of my parents, this disorder of identity continues to revolve around a series of events that have scarred the memories of Punjabi Sikhs, Hindus, and Muslims alike, most of whom can attest to the heterological nature of Punjabi identity. Among others one would have to include the following events: in 1947 the partition of Punjab, which not only resulted in the deaths of several hundred thousand Muslims, Sikhs, and Hindus and the dislocation of millions, but also, in the space of a few days of communal madness, eclipsed centuries of coexistence and acculturation through a peculiarly modern form of religious-cleansing; in the 1960s the invocations of shared idioms and identities that characterized the early migration and resettlement experiences of Indian and Pakistani Punjabis in the UK, Canada, and the USA; in 1967 and 1971 the wars between India and Pakistan, which quickly shattered that newfound unity; and in 1984 the acrimonious separation between Punjabi Hindus and Sikhs.

As a Sikh my own disorder derives initially from my family's very different experiences of the 1947 partition. My mother's family members still recall the trauma of being driven one night from their ancestral homelands by their Muslim neighbors in Pakistani Punjab and arriving next morning along with trainloads of other refugees in the predominantly Sikh/Hindu Indian Punjab. My father's family members, on the other hand, who lived in East Punjab, remember Sikh and Hindu vigilantes clearing neighboring villages of Muslims. During the 1960s the specter of communal hatred for the other seemed to have receded in peoples' memories as Punjabi migrants from India and Pakistan found common cause in the face of racial and religious prejudice in Britain.

For many South Asian immigrants in Britain, however, memories of the late sixties revolve less around the pop phenomenon of the Beatles or the England football team's World Cup victory over Germany than they do around the racist overtones of the British social imaginary of this time, a racism that was as equally evident in the scripts of many comedy programs routinely presented on British national television, and the speeches of prominent politicians. One of the most notorious and heavily publicized was the "Rivers of Blood" speech delivered by the conservative cabinet minister Enoch Powell. This was followed less than a decade later by Margaret Thatcher's pre-election television interview in which she pledged that her party would "finally see an end to immigration," thereby heightening the fears of an already defensive British public by suggesting that the British way of life needed special protection as "this country might be swamped by people of a different culture." Speeches such as these drew heavily upon a British social imaginary that had been thoroughly racialized through its experience of empire, but which in the 1960s had begun to experience the trauma of losing its empire. This traumatized racism—what other kind of racism is there?—in turn helped to legitimize the epithet (as well as the practice) of "Paki-bashing," a term that both named the violence perpetrated specifically against South

Asians and aided the rise of the National Front, a fascist fringe party that revived calls for a repatriation of immigrants from the former colonies.

For second-generation South Asians, myself included, much of this racism simply filtered into the school experience, particularly during the 1970s and early 80s; it was something that happened to you at school, necessitating for one's survival either a multiple-consciousness of oneself as South Asian, nonwhite, *and* British, or a form of alienation: either South Asian/nonwhite *or* British. In hindsight, the ways in which these complex identifications were negotiated in the school system more than in any other place, including most of all the acquisition and politics of English enunciation, with or without accents and inflections of all sorts, cannot but make one think of a similar scenario that would have been taking place in the so-called Anglo-Vernacular schools in late nineteenth-century colonial India. If these Anglo-Vernacular schools were in effect factories for manufacturing a new subjectivity for the native elites, a subjectivity that had been religiously, linguistically, and racially corrected according to the English *type*, the question I am forced to ask is to what extent a similar process of subject production—the production of a figure of the native informant—was (and is) going on not only in contemporary English and American school systems but also within the humanities?

During the 1960s and 70s, Indian cinema provided an unlikely place of refuge from British racism. Many South Asian immigrants joined trade unions such as the Indian Workers Association (IWA). The IWA were particularly strong in my home town, Coventry, and some of its members, my father included, bought shares in mainstream cinemas such as the Ritz in Coventry. Well before there were mosques, mandirs, or gurdwaras in Coventry, Sundays belonged to the smoke-filled Ritz on the Foleshill Road, which regularly showcased Bollywood movies and became a social hub for South Asian immigrants, but more importantly a place where Pakistani Muslims and Indian Sikhs and Hindus could gather to experience at least a semblance of communal harmony and seek respite from what seemed like a sea of racism outside. The Ritz indeed created an idyllic moment in the formation of Coventry's South Asian diasporic community. Moreover, it had other implications for communal coexistence, for as I now recall, many Sikhs would rent rooms in their houses to Punjabi Hindu and Muslim families. For a short time at least, and under a common roof, Sikh, Hindu, and Muslim shared cultural practices and recultivated a common idiom that fluidly transgressed the national boundaries associated with Urdu, Hindi, and Punjabi. But when the Indo-Pakistan War broke out again in 1971, tensions arose once more. Alongside other IWA members, my father helped to raise money for India's war effort and eventually the Muslim families moved out in the face of Hindu-Sikh solidarity.

The prevalence of racism in Britain had prompted most Punjabi immigrant families to regularly send remittances back "home" to their village. These remittances allowed relatives back home to purchase modern farming machinery and were in no small way responsible for the Punjab's "Green Revolution"; they also ensured that there would be a safe place to return to if repatriation became a reality. But in the early 1980s, and especially in 1984, the dream of returning was shattered as the seemingly impossible took place. I refer to the violent confrontation between Sikhs and the Indian state, a process in which Sikhs in India lost their image as the "militant auxiliary of the Hindu world"[40] and, in less than a decade, were recast as India's most dangerous internal enemy. The human cost of this process would be very high, but equally painful was the divorce between two communities (Punjabi Hindu and Punjabi Sikh) that had been symbiotically linked since the fifteenth century through common language, culture, and territory, not to mention a shared memory of the Muslim as other.

The early 1980s in India saw the rise of Hindu nationalist parties such as the BJP under the slogan of *Hindutva* (Hindu-ness), a factor that created anxiety both for India's religious minorities and for the ruling secular Congress party. The basic strategy of the Hindu right was to stigmatize non-Hindus (primarily Muslims and Christians), presenting them as a liability to national unity. The emerging BJP presented a threat not only to Congress's diminishing vote bank but also to its claim to be the defender of Indian national unity. In this political tussle between the secular State and a virulent ethno-religious nationalism, the Sikhs soon became easy targets as the main Sikh political party (Akali Dal) was locked in a struggle with Congress over demands for greater political and economic rights for the state of Punjab. Through shrewd political engineering, Congress was able to project ostensibly secular Sikh demands as *religious* demands. Everything the Sikhs did came to be seen as a *religious* politics and therefore as a threat to national unity. Such a move effectively diverted popular attention away from the more tangible threat of the BJP and Hindu nationalism. By 1982 the state-controlled media was regularly reporting incidents of "Hindu-Sikh" violence, which eventually morphed into "Sikh secessionism," which in turn had conveniently found a champion in the militant Sikh cleric Jarnail Singh Bhindranwale. Things came to a head in 1984, when, in an attempt to oust Sikh militants led by Bhindranwale, the Indian army was ordered by Prime Minister Indira Gandhi to storm the Golden Temple complex, the Sikhs' holiest shrine, and the Akāl Takht, the premier seat of Sikh political sovereignty. Three months later Indira Gandhi herself was assassinated by her Sikh bodyguards in revenge for the army operation. In retaliation highly organized and state-orchestrated mobs massacred more than three thousand Sikhs in the capital New Delhi and several hundred more in other parts of India.

Between 1984 and 1993 Punjab became a bloody battleground in the fight between Sikh insurgents, calling for an independent homeland and supported financially by sympathizers in the Sikh diaspora, and the Indian state's counterinsurgency campaign. If anything, the counterinsurgency's massive unleashing of state and popular violence helped to produce the Sikhs as a political minority within the broader Indian nationalist imaginary.[41] Although by the early 1990s the Indian state had effectively crushed the Sikh insurgency, lasting scars were left not only by the thousands of murders, tortures, and rapes committed by the Punjab police and other paramilitary forces, but also by the endless global circulation of stereotypes of "Sikh terrorists" or images of the *amritdhari* Sikh male as the arch-fundamentalist. This mediatization of the Sikhs as a rogue community — a community whose loyalty to the Indian state was always suspect, an instance of countersovereignty to the monopoly and hegemony of the state — profoundly affected the lives of ordinary Sikhs living in India and in the Western diasporas.

While some in the Sikh diaspora took the route of more direct confrontation with the Indian state, others, myself included, attempted initially to intervene in the various public spheres then available to us, before resorting to intellectual activity driven primarily by the desire to understand and circumvent the kind of political response driven by the enunciation of Sikh nationalism and the modes of identification produced by it, which, under the circumstances of the 1980s and 1990s, could lead at best to political marginalization and at worst to political suicide. Partly as a result of this memory of politics in the last few decades, my own theoretico-political position is one that has come to acknowledge that South Asians generally, and Sikhs in particular, continue to be immersed within the effects of imperialism even as "we" refer to "ourselves" and to "our" moment as *postco*lonial. Strictly speaking, therefore, "we" are still neocolonials on the way toward a postcoloniality — this remains a task that needs constant redefining. As I mentioned earlier, that task involves unraveling the link between religion, enunciation, and the political.

A poignant reminder of this in the twentieth century is the representation of political violence as "religious" conflicts between Sikhs/Hindus and Muslims (1947), Hindus and Sikhs (1984), Hindus and Muslims (1992, 2002). Apart from recognizing the physical violence associated with these events, it is necessary to pay attention to the discursive enunciations that accompany these acts: when protagonists claim that "Hinduism/Sikhism/Buddhism is my religion" or "We are not Hindus," or when one presents oneself on an international stage to claim that "my religion has been violated." One can only say "my religion" (implying the link to self and to its repetition as the same) in a Christian-European manner, through a process of "conversion to modernity."[42] To do this, as Derrida rightly notes, would be "to inscribe oneself in a political and intellectual peace dominated by Christianity"[43] and to enter into the struggle for equivocation between nations in which the putatively "universal" value of the concept of religion already derives its meaning from Christianity. More important, insofar as they become attached to particular modes of identification and hence become modes of repetition, such discursive enunciations are marked by the debilitating effects of imperialism.

The project of decolonization, or the kind of work that would allow neocolonials to overcome the debilitating legacies of imperialism, must strive after a different way of life, one that is not ruled by the identitarian mode of enunciation. To construct this alternative way of life, members of a neocolonial society must be able to resist and reinterpret the repetition of the colonial past. A first step toward decolonization is to recognize that nationalist discursive enunciation is premised on a *break* with, or a repression of, the heterological universals embedded within Indian cultures that express themselves via enunciations that nihilize the tendency to make positive ontological statements such as "I am Sikh/Hindu/Muslim." However, in the process of decolonization the neocolonial faces a conundrum. Even as s/he resists and tries to overcome the colonial past, s/he also remains dependent on it. As Kang Nae-hui explains:

The work of decolonization is a de-demystification. It attempts the consequences of colonization, of the modernization of pre-modern societies, which often takes the form of enlightening, disenchanting, and demystifying those communities, ethnic groups and nations forcibly subordinated in the process. We know that colonial subjects are forced to abandon their traditional ways of life since they have been caught up in superstitions, pseudo-sciences or mysticism. Thus they enter into a new discursive space in which Western modernity and scientific reasoning dominate. Decolonization as a critical project functions as a deconstruction of this demystification, hence a de-demystification. De-demystification, however, has to rely on that which it needs to criticize, for it cannot do without the project of enlightenment and modernity. At stake here is a certain solar mythology, for operating in this project is a "darkness of light," a "mythical" space which the enlightenment causes. A "lightened darkness" which the West has seduced the non-West into worshipping, the enlightenment operates as another superstition, but it now consists of scientism and rationalism rather than mysticism and pseudo-science. De-demystification, therefore, is an attempt to get out of the Western system of knowledge which, in the name of modernity and science, has been accusing the non-West of being trapped inside such limitations as Oriental mysticism, historical lag, and the Asiatic mode of production. Although de-demystification thus attempts an escape from capture by the solar mythology of the West, the problem remains that it must depend upon what it has to overcome.[44]

My theoretico-political position is one that therefore actively risks locating my own discursive enunciation not only within the intellectual, theoretical, and political debate over the question of decolonization, but also within the debates over what constitutes "tradition." "Tradition" is of course a problematic and highly contested term. However, I understand the term not as a process for timelessly conserving the past, canonical texts, or values, but in a manner akin to Walter Benjamin's sense of the term: as the coherence, communicability, and transmissibility of experience itself. For Benjamin, "tradition itself is something that is thoroughly alive and extraordinarily changeable"[45] such that "the idea of discontinuity is the foundation of genuine tradition."[46] Tradition is never a secure inheritance but a process of "ceaseless contestation." When it projects itself as a secure transmission, this can have catastrophic consequences.[47]

This kind of catastrophe was experienced by many Sikhs in the early 1990s. Groomed in the nationalist idiom of neocolonial Sikhism, most modern Sikhs have been unable to distinguish between the relatively open process of tradition-ing associated with *gurmat* or *Sikhī,* and the closed and secure *belief system* based on a few fundamental precepts: that Sikhism is an independent religion whose grounding principles are derived from the teachings of its founder, Guru Nānak, and the nine living Gurus who succeeded him; these collective teachings (also known as *gurmat*) are enshrined in the central text of Sikhism, the *Guru Granth Sāhib*; the teachings are centered on a belief in One God from which can be derived the nature of Sikh ethics and *praxis*, that is, a form of repetition (*nitnem*) that pious Sikhs imbibe and follow. Because of the nature of these teachings and hence the distinctly Sikh conception of God, Sikhism can be distinguished from other religions such as Hinduism and Islam. It follows that Sikhism is a separate religion, and that Sikhs have a distinct consciousness of themselves as a community (*quam*) with its homeland in the Punjab. Sikh nationalist ideology thus assumed a direct connection to the teachings of the Sikh Gurus (*gurmat*) as a guarantor of Sikh identity.

For many Sikh nationalists the failure of the Sikh insurgency in the 1990s was a political defeat by the Indian state and precipitated a crisis of identity for which only a limited number of solutions seemed possible. Other Sikhs, however, came to experience the demise of nationalism not as a political defeat but as an opportunity for thinking beyond a narrow ideology and reengaging the political as a process in which those considered the "enemies" of Sikhism—the Indian state, the Hindutva movement—were all locked together in a common struggle of which few were aware. Paradoxically, for these Sikhs, myself included, this new understanding of the political was dependent on releasing the notion of *gurmat* from an ideology that had become both its defense mechanism and its jailor. That is to say, it required not so much a rejection of Sikh tradition as a ruthless reexamination of what is signified by the term *gurmat* (teachings of the Sikh Gurus) and its concomitant *Sikhī* (the process of learning that is necessary to becoming a Sikh), not by going back to some privileged moment in the past, but by engaging the central texts of Sikh tradition, such as the *Guru Granth Sāhib*, and thus opening the tradition from within as a "ceaseless contestation."

Thus the positive thing that could be salvaged from the rupture of the nationalist idiom was the ability to identify the political crisis of Sikh identity with a crisis that is intrinsic to the source of Sikh tradition itself (*gurmat*), and thus one that is central to becoming Sikh (*Sikhī*). What made this particular crisis so meaningful was that both sources targeted a certain fascism that had latched itself to the seemingly innocent modern Sikh enunciation "I am a Sikh." In other words, there was a point of critical resonance between the kind of self-introspection resulting from an engagement with the central Sikh texts and the kind of self-introspection produced by the shattering of nationalist ideology. In order for this resonance to be accessed, however, it was necessary for the textual readings to thoroughly eschew the kind of metaphysics that had been accrued by modernist Sikh understanding. To eschew metaphysics, or to read nonmetaphysically, is to ground the text's meaning in structures of finitude rather than in structures of eternity. The irony here is that this nonmetaphysical interpretation is not only closer to the teaching of the Sikh Gurus within the Ādi Granth, but also a powerful, though repressed, undercurrent of contemporary Sikh thought and practice. To make the shift from a metaphysical framework of eternity to a nonmetaphysical framework based on finitude necessitates an inquiry into the conceptual role of "religion" in relation to the construction of the nationalist idiom. Such nonmetaphysical readings of the tradition texts can therefore be seen as forms of critique that are internal to tradition itself. This perspective enables tradition to function as its own "interruptive unraveling" of a social bond that can become closed and defensive, as in the case of nationalism. In this way such rereadings of the Ādi Granth can be seen to foster a mode of disenchantment or secularization that is inherent in the teachings of the Sikh Gurus. Far from being opposed to what might be termed Sikh spirituality or mysticism, or incidental to the work of reformulating and reinterpreting *gurmat,* such disenchantment or secularization can be shown to be intrinsic to it.

This retrieval of a sense of disenchantment or secularization—which is in every way part of the mystical or spiritual, but which can be glimpsed only through a weakening of normalized identity—has a strong kinship to the risky strategy of developing a theoretico-political standpoint. The risk here is twofold. On the one hand one risks intervening theoretically and politically in certain movements that aim to change the currently nationalized/identitarian modes of repetition that have encompassed Sikh "tradition" in its entirety. To create a position in the battleground of decolonization necessitates a form of theoretical intervention that does more than simply resist the repetition of tradition—what is involved is a rethinking of repetition itself in a way that produces, as one scholar so aptly describes it, a "solicitous mutilation" within the "body of tradition."[48] To intervene in or to mutilate the body of tradition is to accept that the "other" is already within the "self" that normally constitutes "tradition." This intervention refuses distinctions such as secularism versus religion, subjective tradition versus objective History, insider versus outsider, or particular versus universal, preferring instead the risk of transforming, or "solicitously mutilating," the opposition into a mutual contamination of such binaries.

On the other hand, one risks intervening theoretically and politically within the privileged space of secular academic discourse. It is within this space that modes of disenchantment or secularization derived from supposedly "religious" sources such as the *Guru Granth Sāhib* can be seen as problematic particularly from the dominant academic standpoint of liberal humanism and its methodological correlate, the ideal of secular disinterested inquiry. Yet it is precisely this ideal of disinterested humanist inquiry that has been problematized in recent years, and that has shown to be organically connected to the theologism of nationalist ideology.[49] Once its supposedly infallible notion of secular criticism is shown be as much a myth as the standpoint of nationalist ideology, it becomes necessary to rethink the nature of the university as the space from which to begin such interventions. What I have in mind here is Derrida's invocation of the "university without condition . . . the principle right to say everything without condition, . . . and the right to say it publicly, to publish it."[50] This reference to public space invokes an alternative concept of the humanities, the "new humanities," as a space whose formation is underway but not yet arrived at; a space that is part of the university's original project but has almost never been put into effect. The university should thus be "the place in which nothing is beyond question," especially the university's relation to the power of the nation-state and its specter of indivisible sovereignty, for this sovereignty is also "the heritage of a barely secularized theology."[51] The principle of unconditionality must therefore include not only "theory" but the performative discourses of knowledge that produce the event of "the political."[52] One such performative would be to demonstrate that the Sikh subject, *precisely* because of its minoritarian and particular status in a global forum, can nevertheless help to retrieve and reconceive the task of the universal. Paradoxically, however, such a task can only begin by unraveling Sikh tradition's nationalistic self-identification as "religion."

Theology as Cultural Translation

It is from this perspective that the reader must approach part II of this book, in which chapters 3 and 4 treat religion-making (or ontotheologization) as an effect of imperialism but at the same time remain dependent on it in order to make visible the specter of the West in its modern, postmodern, postsecular forms. In the case of Sikh nationalism this ontotheologization occurs via two important events. The first is the imposition of a dominant symbolic order (the colonial idiom) on the indigenous cultures and their subsequent accession to its hermeneutic frame; this is taken up in detail in chapter 3. This new hermeneutic frame—comprising an entire discourse of colonial ethnography (missionary literature, English translations of indigenous literatures and Indological treatises), implemented by a vast network of Anglo-Vernacular mission schools and maintained by a newly imposed capitalist economy—can be regarded as the imperialist technology that prepared the ground for a fundamental transformation in the subjectivity of the native elites.

Chapter 3 illustrates one way in which this transformation of subjectivity happens, by focusing on a concrete instance in the colonial context. The example I refer to is a *language event* that had far-reaching implications for the development of modern Sikh ideology. This event was the commissioning of an official translation of the Sikh scripture (Ādi Granth) by the colonial administration in Punjab, a task that was carried out by the German Indologist Ernest Trumpp. Although it is not generally acknowledged, the language and philosophy informing Trumpp's translation, including his preface on "Sikh religion," effectively demarcated a regime of translation, that is, a hermeneutic frame within which the Sikh texts would be received in future. Despite a vociferous rejection of his work, it is clear that the conceptual vector informing Trumpp's translation helped to catalyze the ontotheologization of the native mindset vis-à-vis the production of the colonial subject as native informant and, inadvertently, its attunement to the political economy of Empire. The greater part of this chapter is devoted to a discussion of the evidence for this theological shift. This evidence is to be found in the works of narrative and scriptural exegesis produced in the late 1920s by native elite scholars belonging to the Sikh reformist movement known as the Singh Sabhā. With regard to the narratives, of particular interest are the philosophical artifices deployed by these scholars to demonstrate that their work "naturally" conforms to the larger master narrative of modernity, and at the same time represents the continuity of indigenous tradition.

One such philosophical artifice reduces Sikhism to a *sui generis* religion by representing tradition as the repetition of an origin or an original event. This move can be traced to two different ideologies of language. One, which was inadvertently adopted by Sikh reformist elites in the nineteenth and early twentieth century, consists of a paradigm of scriptural revelation drawn (less from Islamic sources than) from a tradition of Christian philosophical theology and used to manufacture a "Sikh theology." The early articulations of "Sikh theology" can be traced first to vernacular journals, newspapers, and tract publications that appeared in the last two decades of the nineteenth century, but later on, and more importantly, to the voluminous works of scriptural exegesis in the vernacular composed by scholars such as Kahn Singh Nabha, Bhāī Vīr Singh, Jodh Singh, and Sāhib Singh in the early twentieth century. These were effectively responses to the *economy of lack* incorporated through the project of colonial translation begun by Ernest Trumpp into the framework for receiving (reading/interpreting/translating) the Sikh scripture.[53] The response of the Sikh reformists was to *fulfill* this lack by entering into a dialectical engagement with the colonial translations. But by doing so they inadvertently accepted the equivalence between the colonial idiom and indigenous concepts, and thus entered into a modernizing dialectic driven by the desire for moral improvement. Again, my main task in this key part of the chapter is to account for the philosophical connections between the universalizing logic of modernity and the reciprocity of "meaning-values" that results, notably, in the belief in the equivalence of categories such as "religion" and the colonial elites' enunciation of "Sikh theology."

Close readings of the vernacular commentaries on Sikh scripture demonstrate the way in which the concepts of language and time, as the central ingredients of ordinary human experience, had to be de-ontologized in order for a "Sikh theology" to emerge. This de-ontologization could happen only by imposing structures of transcendence into the exegesis of Sikh scripture, the most prevalent of which was the privileging of eternity over time. This form of metaphysical privileging is best seen in the reorientation of "historical" narratives, which henceforth locate the origin or birth of Sikhism and "Sikh history" in Guru Nānak's mystical experience at Sultanpur (a version of which is located in the *Purātan Janamsakhi*).

However, the most sophisticated theoretical devices for de-ontologizing language/time as dimensions of ordinary human experience are found in the exegetical commentaries on the nature of God. In these commentaries reformist scholars shift the meaning of key terms such as *guru*, *śabda*, and *nām* by transcendentalizing them. Whereas in Sikh scripture each of these terms refers to the immanental force that is synonymous with language, and therefore to the sovereignty of language (i.e., the idea that language itself speaks rather than being a mere vehicle for human speech), within the exegetical commentaries this function of language, and hence the meaning of the terms *guru/śabda/nām*, is reconfigured by way of reference to a personal God conceived as a static immutable Being whose existence is privileged over nonexistence. Indeed the gist of commentaries such as Kahn Singh Nabha's *Gurmat Sudhākhar* and *Gurmat Prabhākhar*, Bhāī Vīr Singh's *Santhyā Sri Guru Granth Sāhib*, and Jodh Singh's *Gurmat Nirnai* consists in the effort to redefine the nature of this existence as a *static immutable One*. This static immutable One comes to define the nature of God's Unity. God's existence and his Oneness come to coincide absolutely in the operation of thinking. The notion of the static immutable One as transcendence of time and world sets a metaphysical standard to which Guru Nānak's own experience itself will be deferred, and becomes a standard according to which human existence in the world, repetition, or subjectivity comes to be measured. This metaphysical distinction between God and world/time is translated into the ethico-political distinction between Sikhs and non-Sikhs (especially Hinduism) and becomes the hallmark of modern Sikh hermeneutics and identity politics.

The idea that *gurmat* is literally "Sikh theology," combined with the notion of a historical origin, can be seen as an ideological formation that enabled these scholars to disguise the work of translation as the "natural" continuity of tradition rather than a *break* with prior traditions. This ideological formation was unwittingly perpetuated by Ernest Trumpp's non-Sikh and Sikh protagonists over the next fifty years. Though rarely considered, however, the regime of translation inaugurated by Trumpp arose out of and reflected some of the key ideological contests in the history of European ideas during the nineteenth century, specifically the religio-philosophical debate between Hegel and Schelling. Central to this debate is the West's reconceptualization of its own comparative imaginary, which emerges at the uneasy intersections between the so-called pantheism controversy and fledgling disciplines such as Indology. By exposing the silent sources and subsequent passage of ideas from Indologists such as Ernest Trumpp and Max Arthur Macauliffe through to indigenous scholars such as Bhāī Vīr Singh and Jodh Singh, the chief exponents of Singh Sabhā ideology, it is possible to read the emergence of "Sikh theology" not only as a transformation of the meaning of *gurmat* rather than an ahistorical continuity, but also, more importantly, as a response to the demand for linguistic and conceptual equivalence and reciprocity, that is, a demand for *gurmat* as a "meaning-value" to enter into the global circulation and exchange of ideas. What allows this to happen is the Sikh reformists' adoption of the ontological proof for God's existence, which, paradoxically, allows an entry into modernity.

By relocating our investigation to the intersections between Indology and the political history of European ideas it is possible to provide a more realistic explanation of how terms such as "Sikh theology" have come to be regarded as native categories (in this case *gurmat*) when neither Sikh experience nor the broader Indic culture from which it is derived can claim to possess a word for "religion" as signifying either a mystical or theological core or a unified faith community. It becomes easier to understand why, even today, something like "Sikh theology" continues to be affirmed as a discursive positivity by believers and skeptics alike. In the case of believers, the credibility of the proposition *gurmat* = "Sikh theology" hinges on the ability of the scriptural commentaries to prove that God exists and that the nature of this existence is an eternally existing identity: again, a static immutable One. Though rarely considered, this static immutable One also constitutes the hermeneutic basis of the political imaginary of modern Sikhism as a belief system. Its invocation underpins the demarcation of the boundary between the Sikh self and its non-Sikh other. From one end of the Sikh social spectrum to the other, the invocation of this static immutable One binds the very structure of personal belief to the representation of identity in the public domain. It may be pertinent to say something here about the nature of identity in relation to the work of nationalization and modernization. In the field of Sikh studies there appear to be at least two contradictory opinions on this subject. These views can be summarized as follows: (i) that there had been a distinctly Sikh identity since the time of the Sikh Gurus; this identity was diluted in the late eighteenth and early nineteenth centuries as a result of the influence of Hinduism, but was revived in the late nineteenth and early twentieth century by Sikh reformist movements; (ii) that there was no distinct Sikh identity prior to the colonial era with its attendant modernization.[54]

By way of clarification I want to stress that the *opposition* between these two views is perhaps misguided. What emerges most clearly in chapter 3 is that the very logic and articulation of identity itself is altered in the colonial period. In other words, the way that we understand Sikh identity in the precolonial period follows a very different logic after the advent of colonialism. Whereas in the precolonial period Sikh identity may have subscribed to a paradoxical logic (e.g., A = B) that fostered relatively fluid boundaries between individuals, social groups, and ideas, during the colonial period Sikh identity began to subscribe to a form of logic that obeyed the law of noncontradiction (A=A). The proof of this alteration resides simultaneously in the social changes brought about by the modernization, imperialism, and the neocolonial reform movements and in the changes in the interpretation of such key texts as the *Guru Granth*. In many ways the *Guru Granth* and related texts of the medieval period provide evidence of a nonmodern logic of identity that continues to exist today even though it has been overlaid by a modern and strictly noncontradictory form. An important consequence of this noncontradictory logic was the production of such ideological formations as "Sikh theology" and "Sikh history," which lay the basis of the dual self-representations of "Sikhs-as-nation" and the later articulation of "Sikhism as world religion." Paradoxically, though, these self-representations constitute not only the intellectual framework of modern Sikh enunciation, but the very mechanism of its noncoincidence with the West, and hence the mechanism by which the formation called "the West" continues to invisibly reproduce and reference itself.

Chapter 4 follows the transference of reformist Sikhism's theological discourse into the discourse of the modern Western university. This transference is best illustrated by W. H. McLeod's classic study *Guru Nānak and the Sikh Religion (GNSR)*, a work that not only oversees the installation of Sikhism into the modern discourse of the history of religions, but also provides a mechanism for rendering at will the essence of Sikh-*ism*, and thus a more-or-less definitive answer to the question "What is Sikhism?." This mechanism—which depends on the scholar's ability to translate from the particularistic discourse of "Sikh theology" to the more universal (because humanistic) discourse of anthropology—in turn governs a complex system of representations that is taken as normative and authoritative by a community of readers and writers in both academia and the media. In this chapter I examine the operations and the political implications of this "generalized translation" by reading it through Derrida's early work on the metaphysics of the "Voice," which is shown to be central to the work of the historian of religion.

What is especially interesting about the operation of the translation from theology to anthropology going on in McLeod's work is its continuity with the very ideology of language that was adopted by the Singh Sabhā reformists in their accession to the discourse of modernity and the translation of *gurmat* to "Sikh theology." The effects of this ideology of language—drawn primarily from the Christian-Platonic tradition of philosophical theology—can be summarized as follows: (i) it accords a metaphysical privilege to figures of Eternity over time, and thereby de-ontologizes the status of language (*śabda*) in Sikh scripture; (ii) by de-ontologizing language, it reduces the very nature of repetition to mimicry of a sacred origin; (iii) consequently repetition, as the mode of one's existing-in-time, and therefore subjectivity, consists in the negation of ego, which is seen as something excessive and opposed to the natural order.

Once these ideologies of language were imported by Sikh reformist scholars (despite their attempts to portray an image of Sikhism as a worldly religion) it was impossible to avoid depicting Nānak's subjectivity, and therefore the origin of Sikhism, in terms of quietist detachment from worldly affairs and politics and the constant repetition of the Name (*nām simaran*). Accordingly, the only true way for Sikhs to exist in the world was to act according to Nānak's subjectivity, which of course takes its meaning from a pacified notion of *nām simaran*—a term that is given the signification of a fundamental passivity or quietism and insofar becomes pivotal to contemporary academic understandings of the nature of Sikhism and "Sikh theology." As a result, modern representations of Sikh theory and practice have been unable to avoid the intractable dualism of religion/secularism or religion/politics. There is no choice but to represent later Sikhism's entry into violence and politics as a *deviation* from the pacifistic subjectivity of Nānak. Hence the ironic injunction that if Sikhs are to exist in modern secular society they must return to its pacifist origin, a move which, in the context of the modern nation-state, imposes a *legal* injunction that effectively forecloses Sikhs and Sikhism from any connection to the political.

By exposing the way in which a certain definition of religion operates in the transference of knowledge about Sikhism from traditional scholarship to the university, chapter 4 also helps to shed new light on several other related issues. These include, on the one hand, the relationship between the construction of mystical experience and the social production of mystics as apolitical subjects, as seen in the long-standing investment by historians of religion in the idea of *nirguṇ bhakti* as a mode of religious interiority or pure mysticism in relation to which any entry into politics is a deviation from "normative" mysticism. And on the other hand it reveals an unmistakable continuity between academic conceptualizations of the relationship between violence and religion, and the engineering of violence perpetrated by the secular nation-state toward minorities. This continuity works through the capture and designation of subjectivity as "religious"—a theme that is routinely transferred to the media with its own constructions of religious violence as opposed to secular nonviolence.

Can a study of the way that scholars conceptualize the relationship between religion and violence offer glimpses into the wider patterns of thought relating to the interplay between religion and politics? Does the historian of religion's understanding *of* or *about* religion itself constitute an ideology of some sort? If so, how does this ideology generally translate from the academy into the discourses of the State, the media, and policymakers? What might be the wider implications of such a connection? My readings in this chapter provide a way of probing and reframing—however obliquely—wider questions, such as the nature of the space called "Sikh studies," the portrayal of religious violence by the media, the relationship between religion and politics, and the question of Sikh sovereignty. The work of this chapter has ethical implications for the representation of stateless minorities such as Sikhs, especially given the negative implications of the portrayals (by the Indian state and the global media) of Sikhs as turbaned fundamentalists, as a threat to Indian democracy, and the corresponding portrayal by academic scholars during the 1980s and early 1990s of political Sikhism as a deviation from true Sikhism. This chapter also highlights the parallels between academic/media representations of Sikhs in 1980s with the post-9/11 portrayal of radical Islam.

Postcoloniality, Theory, and the Afterlives of Religion

One of the key markers that set apart texts such as Jodh Singh's *Gurmat Nirnai* and W. H. McLeod's *Guru Nānak and the Sikh Religion* as classic texts in modern Sikh studies is that they both attempt to provide a certain sense of closure. In the case of Jodh Singh, as with other Sikh neocolonials, closure meant the demarcation and eventual separation between Sikh and Hindu spheres of meaning. The chief ideological agent in this process was to be *gurmat*, or "Sikh theology." By contrast, for W. H. McLeod closure refers to the act of simultaneously demarcating the limits of "theology" in the discourse of the Singh Sabhā, a point beyond which the Sikh reformists could not pass, and passing beyond that limit by providing a truly "systematic Sikh theology."[55] This double act would complete the arc of communication between Sikhism and the

West, thereby fulfilling the Sikhs' desire for theology as a mode of totalizing signification in the domain of European conceptuality.

But as chapters 3 and 4 clearly demonstrate, this closure is never complete. If we have learned anything from the movement called deconstruction in the last four decades, it is that closure can be no more than "a hinge, an opening that articulates the double movement between logocentrism or metaphysics and its other."[56] Given that chapters 3 and 4 apply Heideggerian and Derridean deconstruction to provide a *clôtural* reading of Jodh Singh's *Gurmat Nirnai* and the theological sections of W. H. McLeod's *Guru Nānak and the Sikh Religion*, such a reading could display a potential to disrupt claims to comprehensive unity and self-understanding within the dominant interpretation of these texts, thereby discovering insights within them to which these same texts are blind. My argument is that these disruptions or alterities are moments that open up an afterlife, a mode of survival, that consummates the task of decolonization by helping to create a shift from neocoloniality to postcoloniality. One such disruption or moment of alterity that could not be properly contained within any closure either by McLeod or by the Sikh reformists is the concept of *śabda-guru*—an extraordinarily significant term that has a range of meanings, including, most commonly, that the Guru exists *as* Word, that the Guru *is* Word, and that the Word is revealed by the Guru. The idea here is that even in the event of the death of the human Guru, the Word lives on in the form of Word, or language-in-general.

In one sense, given that it narrowly refers to the physical text of Sikh scripture (the *Guru Granth Sāhib*), the term *śabda-guru* has come to be constituted as the key concept of the belief system that is so central to modern Sikh "orthodoxy." Yet the very same concept is also the most radically subversive in the entire Sikh lexicon insofar as it opens up the very horizon of time and language. My argument is that the term *śabda-guru*—which was transcendentalized by the Singh Sabhā scholars for the purpose of removing any traces of "Hindu" signification, a transcendentalization that is continued in W. H. McLeod's rendering of a "modern Sikh theology"—can be more productively conceptualized as an "empty signifier" or an "absent center of political ontology," to borrow Slavoj Žižek's terminology. As I argue in chapters 4 through 6, the emptiness of this signifier *śabda-guru* comes from its association with ego-loss, which, in theological parlance, corresponds to a divine that is absent, a paradoxical God whose nonexistence (*nirgun*) is the same as his existence (*sargun*). This paradoxical property of the concept *śabda-*

guru—radically conservative yet radically subversive, the very element of "religion" but at the same time the very element of disenchantment, the most religious yet at the same time the most secularizing of principles—can be seen as one of several theoretical and political hinges on which it is possible to stake the task of Sikh postcoloniality, as a question of what it might mean to break with—or to live and think after—the colonial moment, to live within the vestiges of colonialism, the most important of which is the phenomenon and concept of "religion." It will become clear that the project of postcoloniality that I have in mind cannot simply disavow the concept and phenomenon of "religion" as Indian liberal secularists and Marxists have done.

In chapters 5 and 6 I deploy the concept of *śabda-guru* with the intention of re-ontologizing the question of language in order to release two different moments of the political as they relate to the contemporary situation of Sikhs regarding the question of postcoloniality. One such moment might be regarded as "subjective." It consists in revisiting the site of the trauma caused by the entry of Sikhs and Sikhism into the dominant symbolic order of modernity, to reopen the site of original lack and the concomitant act of traumatic repression. This revisitation and reopening is not only a psychoanalytic operation, but also, because the site of the first repression (by Singh Sabhā scholars) revolved around the translation of Sikh scripture into the domain of European conceptuality, an interpretive operation—or, rather, a reinterpretation of Sikh scripture in a way that attempts to release the affects of shame associated with the "scene of colonial surrender" to Western military and conceptual power.

However, the concept of *śabda-guru* can also be used "objectively" to disrupt the subjective technology that perpetuates the effects of imperialism: native informancy, identity politics, the enunciation of culture as religion, and its installation within the discourse of humanism. But even if such a disruption were possible, would it necessarily lead to the freedom that is desired? For example, while the prevailing discourse of secular postcolonial theory inspired by Edward Said rightly targets religion as the source of colonialism, it remains within the parameters of Enlightenment critique. If the subjugation to God (and religion) is simply replaced by a form of subjugation to a human subject that has merely replaced God in the name of liberty, equality, and fraternity, then perhaps what is at stake is (i) the notion of freedom itself and (ii) the language in which we conceptualize that freedom. Maybe the secular notion of freedom itself has to be considered from a completely different perspective in order to effect the desired break?

The idea of such a break is, of course, nothing new. Within the discourse of the social sciences, and specifically within the history of religions, it has taken the form of advocacy of a theoretical shift from traditional ideologies of language based on the primacy of Western writing, the book, God, etc., toward the idea that language is primarily oral/sonic in nature. The adoption of the oral-thesis by two major theoretical schools (ethnology and hermeneutics) testifies to a concern within the Western academy for a more open "living" encounter with previously colonized or non-Western cultures. In defense of the thesis that the ideological shift to language-as-oral implies a *post*-metaphysical, *post*-modernist, *post*-imperialist stance, proponents of these schools have cited the case of Indian tradition as *the* paradigm of orality, and of a civilization where the oral principle has enjoyed an overtly privileged status over writing, resulting in an avoidance of the instrumental and technological consequences of Western writing.

Arguing from the standpoint of minority cultures, however, I attempt in chapter 5 to expose the dangers of implementing the above ideology. I argue that there is a deep-rooted complicity between, on the one hand, the theoretical shift toward the oral or phonemic principle within the humanities propelled by a complicity between hermeneutics and anthropology as the two discourses that are supposedly most open to the other—and, on the other hand, an indigenous ideology of sacred sound derived from the close connection between Veda, Sanskrit, and the structure of caste. According to this ideology, South Asian cultures are governed by a central and unifying principle based on the mystical (because *eternal*) nature of sound, a principle that *ethically* differentiates India from the West. My critique of this Brahmanic economy of sacred sound deploys the motif of translation to reread the relationship between German Indology and the religio-political theory behind contemporary Indian nationalism. Far from being liberating and mystical, the oral principle is shown to be an insidious and ancient power structure that facilitates the preservation of patriarchy and the implementation of ethnic boundaries, as seen in its devaluing and discouraging of multilingualism and cultural intermixing. Seen from this angle, this fixation on Indian orality by a certain strand of structural anthropology exercises a form of the will-to-power. Not only does it allow the anthropologist to escape charges of Eurocentrism associated with writing and thus to retain a certain distance or objectivity in regard to the subject matter of his inquiry, but it also perpetuates one of the most powerful stereotypes about India and Indian nationalism vis-à-vis the West—the idea of India as a nonviolent culture rooted in an authentically Indian spirituality—and, based on this, one of the political motivations for unifying all Indians under a hierarchical principle that also constitutes a boundary of Indian civilization.

Once again, my critique will be formulated vis-à-vis the Sikh notion of *śabda-guru*, which not only utilizes writing and orality without privileging one or the other, but also contests the opposition between them. The radically conservative/subversive notion of *śabda-guru* provides an entry point for a political critique of the essentialized opposition between India and the West. The political nature of the concept *śabda-guru* can be realized in its potential to bring together the subjective and objective aspects of the postcolonial task. My claim is that this task can be consummated through an alternative interpretation of *gurmat* (teachings of the Sikh Gurus) as centered not on eternity and transcendence, as it is in neocolonial interpretations, but around contingency or human finitude. Thus toward the end of chapter 5 I attempt to sketch the barest contours of what an alternative, nonmetaphysical interpretation of *gurmat* might look like. The aim of this postcolonial interpretation is firstly to release the affect of shame that has been associated with the idea and experience of finitude as the universal ground of *gurmat*. The reappropriation of this self-emptying idea constitutes the postcolonial task that makes it possible to break the cycles of repetition that produce identification with nationalized identity politics, world religions, etc. Firmly grounded in structures of finitude, this nonmetaphysical interpretation foreshadows the possibility of writing something like a Sikh philosophy, a task I hope to undertake after this book.

With the release of contingency as a universal (=opening of the political), there would appear to be a convergence between the kind of post*colonial* theory that I have been developing in this book, and what has come to be called post*secular* theory, or political theology. Might this convergence be the place and the occasion for the birth of a new "theoretical matrix" that would be "able to encompass religious and nonreligious or secular systems of thought, practices, and other modes of expression"[57] such as the postcolonial? Could such a "theoretical matrix" serve for something like an equal exchange of ideas in a globalized world? Could the subject of South Asia, normally regarded as a particular (i.e., belonging to a geopolitical area), be regarded as something that actively shares in the universal?

One might think that something like this convergence had been taking place at least since the 1960s. But the reality is quite different. Far from there being any exchange of ideas, I argue that there has been a continuing, albeit more sophisticated, segregation of knowledge formations within the humanities along the lines of universal and particular. The signs of this segregation appear most notably in the unequal effects of theory in regard to Western and non-Western cultures. For example, cultural and critical theory has been used to legitimize the use of phenomena from Judeo-Christian traditions as resources not only for thinking about religion, but for thinking more critically about theory itself, thereby helping to push cultural and critical theory into a "postcritical" phase. Perhaps the clearest indication of this is the conspicuous return of leading thinkers from the left to the religious sources of Western culture in order to revitalize the domain of the political. By contrast, the effects of theory on the study of South Asian "religions" has not only been more modest, but has had precisely the opposite effect. Here the effects of critical theory seem to have reinforced the priority of the secular.

Why, then, do the ideas and phenomena of South Asian traditions not find similar contemporaneity to those of Western traditions? What prevents non-Western traditions of thought and practice (*gurmat, bhakti,* for example) from being used as resources for the "theory-space that is most relevant for the humanities and interpretive social sciences more generally? Why is it that even the idea of non-Western conceptuality, despite its commonsensical justifications, seems theoretically out of place, its 'being' at once anticipated and erased by the logic in which it strives to appear."[58] As Rey Chow reminds us, "this life and death entanglement between non-Western X and Western theory is exactly the juncture (and dead end) at which a rethinking of theory is in order by way of reexamining the way in which Western theory continually references itself."[59] Despite the proliferation of postcolonial critiques, why is it that the humanities and social sciences continue to reconstitute the hegemony of theory as specifically Western and/or the division of intellectual labor between universal and particular knowledge formations? Where does this leave the emancipatory project of postcoloniality? Is the "*post-*" of the postcolonial project doomed merely to follow in the wake of the various "posts" in the humanities: post-modernism, post-humanism, post-secularism, etc.? Is the "post" ultimately a function of the West, and insofar, of the

Enlightenment? Stated differently, in order to make the postcolonial task viable, is it not necessary to distinguish it from the "post-" movement of Western thought itself, which, in its inevitable return to religion, continues to maintain its self-definition as Western? Does the viability of the postcolonial task not depend on interrogating the self-referential "post-" movements that continue to keep theory on what is considered to be its home ground?

Chapter 6 interrogates the mechanism that continues to foreclose the South Asian or non-Western from the supposed ground of theory. I do this by looking more closely at the narratives that write the script of emancipation, the various "post-"'s that aim to liberate us initially from religion, then from modernity, and finally(?) from secularism, in order to arrive at a more nuanced understanding of the political in an era of globalization. What becomes evident is that one of the key links, or philosophical catalysts, as it were, in the construction of the various narratives of liberation is the figure of Hegel. Indeed one could go so far as to say that when cultural theorists distinguish between the various theoretical movements that I shall refer to as modernism (or humanism), postmodernism[1], postmodernism[2], and postsecularism, the very difference between these movements boils down to different ways of appropriating Hegel's thought. But why does the figure of Hegel continue to haunt the site of theory in the humanities? Why is it that intellectual movements as seemingly different as the resolutely *secular* postcolonial theory and postsecular *religious* theory can define their respective projects in relation to Hegel? Why is Hegel so pivotal to the form of theorizing that seeks emancipation in turning away from religion by embracing secularism, and the form of theorizing that seeks emancipation by returning to religion through a deconstruction of the secular? Is it sufficient to simply produce more critical readings of these narratives—in a sense to out-theorize Western theory—in order to confront it with its own foreclosure of this issue? Is it enough to merely acknowledge the inevitability of self-referencing even in the most sophisticated of theoretical undertakings (and this must include deconstruction) in order "to make way for a thorough reassessment of an originary act of repudiation and expulsion [of referentiality] in terms that can begin to address . . . the 'scandal of domination and exploitation of one part of mankind by another'"?[60]

My answer to these questions, by way of conclusion, is to return once again to the question of translation. Rather than trying to outdo Western theory at its own game, I argue that the very effect that makes Western ideas seemingly ubiquitous, namely its globalization, paradoxically, makes the very ground of theory itself unstable. Currently this ground is one on which European languages continue to be privileged despite loud assertions of equivalence, reciprocity, dialogue, interaction, etc. By way of reflection on Derrida's question—"What if *religio* remained untranslatable"—I speculate on whether the power relationship between the West and "the Rest" may not change when changes in the global political economy produce parallel changes in the economy of language (and cultural) relations. When European texts are translated into non-European languages, might it be possible, under a geopolitical economy different from the one that exists now, the one that is slowly but surely running out of breath, as Derrida would say, for non-European host languages to displace the very power differential that keeps theory supposedly on its own ground? What would it mean for thinking to become a thinking-*between*, in which concepts are allowed to compete before they are accepted as universal? Surely, this is the political question that globalization now poses and against which the dominant strands of Western theory continue to barricade themselves even as they run out of breath?

PART I

"Indian Religions" and Western Thought

1   Mono-theo-lingualism

Religion, Language, and Subjectivity in
Colonial North India

The "Failure of Secular Creeds" in Politics and Theory

As late as the 1980s, a period that saw the end of the Cold War
and the spread of free-market global capitalism, many political commentators continued to regard the phenomenon of religion as an anomaly in
the hegemonic narrative of Western secularist modernity. Yet barely two
decades later, faced with the global resurgence of religion, this uncontested self-identification of Western secularism with modernity and postmodernity was forced to see itself as suffering from a crisis, a rupture in
its self-congratulatory narrative. A notable indicator of this change was
provided by the special report and lead article on religion and public life
that was run on November 3, 2007, by the respected journal of political
economy *The Economist*. In his sobering reassessment of religion in public life, the author of the article argued that "in the twentieth century most
Western politicians and intellectuals (and even some clerics) assumed that
religion was becoming marginal to public life."[1] However, the alternative
idea that "religion has re-emerged in public life is to some extent an illusion. It never really went away—certainly not to the extent that French
politicians and American college professors imagined. Its new power is
mostly the consequence of two changes. The first is the failure of secular

creeds."[2] The second is that "religion has returned to the stage as a much more democratic, individualistic affair: a bottom-up marketing success, surprisingly in tune with globalization. Secularism was not as modern as many intellectuals imagined."[3]

Although *The Economist's* special report stopped well short of positing an alternative model to secularism, theorists of religion have argued that the rupture that manifests as the appearance of "public religions" in a previously secular world is one indication among others of a shift from a secular to a postsecular world.[4] The term "postsecular," as Hent de Vries reminds us, is not indicative of a change in historical periodization, nor of any sudden increase in religiosity of those who had held fast to the doctrine of secularism. Rather, "postsecular" is indicative of a change in the mindset of those who previously considered religion to be a primitive relic consigned to history rather than the present, or to the privacy of one's home rather than to the public domain.[5] This rupture, shift, or change in mindset consists in the acknowledgment by secularists and the secular state alike of the continuous presence or survival of religion and religious communities in a world that is becoming more and more disenchanted, more and more secular. Postsecularism is therefore a paradoxical but nevertheless global phenomenon in which religion lives on beyond its preestablished contexts, horizons, and concepts by taking refuge in virtual spaces created by new technologies.[6]

But one could go even further and suggest, as Scott Thomas does, that the term "postsecular" describes something like a loss of faith in the political myth of modernity.[7] According to this political myth, the history of religious sectarianism in premodern Europe has taught us that when religion is politicized or deprivatized it inevitably causes war, intolerance, and perhaps even the collapse of social order; the liberal or secular state is therefore needed to save us from the violent consequences of religion. At the heart of this myth is a conceptualization of religion as the cause of violence. This manner of thinking about religion came into play after the Treaty of Westphalia in 1648 and the rise of Enlightenment reason. The very idea of a postsecularism is therefore inconceivable except as a crisis, an invasion of the secular from the outside. In recent years such invasions have been identified by a variety of markers, such as the " 'problem' of Islam," the Taliban, the veil or headscarf, the "Rushdie affair," suicide bombing, and, of course, 9/11. Crisis, according to this manner of thinking, is the name given to the violence produced by the *return* of religion. Thomas argues that this understanding of religion was invented as part of the political mythology of liberalism and eventually emerged as a universal concept applicable to other cultures. Such a concept of religion has been used to legitimize a form of liberal politics that considers the mixing of politics and religion to be a recipe for violence and therefore dangerous to reason, freedom, and social order. The global resurgence of religion, however, has brought this concept of religion into crisis and challenges the idea that only secular reason can provide a neutral standpoint from which to interpret religion.[8]

Despite its seeming ubiquity, however, the phenomenon in question, which has variously been described as the "return of religion" or the "crisis of secularism," displays revealing similarities and differences in the way it has been received within different geopolitical contexts. In the case of India, for example, the contemporary crisis of secularism can be traced both politically and theoretically. Politically, the crisis can be traced to two very different visions of the secular, advocated by Mohandas K. Gandhi and J. L. Nehru, the respective fathers of the Indian independence movement and the postindependence Indian nation. While Gandhi advocated a religion-inflected version of secularism based on the need for tolerance and pluralism as a means for promoting harmonious coexistence of different religions and ethnic communities in India, Nehru's idea of secularism was based on a strictly rationalistic separation of religion and politics.[9] Unlike Gandhi's idea of secularism, which seemed to be more attuned to indigenous traditions, Nehruvian secularism derived its rationale from the British colonial machinery, which was in large part responsible for creating religious and caste identities as political categories. As Gyan Pandey has pointed out, the British identified "communalism" as an essential feature of Indian society, thereby implying a state of eternal and pervasive conflict between different religious communities: Hindu/Muslim, Śaiva/Vaiṣṇava, Sikh/Muslim, Hindu/Sikh, etc.[10] These communal identities were fixed along lines of caste and religion via (i) census operations, and (ii) separate electorates. This process consolidated competing political identities, which in turn passed into the self-perception of Indians, but, more importantly, affected the policies of the Indian National Congress for almost five decades after independence. Nehru and his successors understood secularism as an instrument that could unify differences by dissolving particular identities under the figure of the Nation. According to Mukul Kesavan, this policy helped to "smelt a citizenry from the ore of a heterogenous population embedded in subjecthood."[11] While this policy clearly succeeded, it nevertheless had to rely on the "colonial predilection" for organizing politics by recourse to communal identities and therefore tapped into and manipulated the self-identification of Hindu and Muslim identities as these had evolved over the last one hundred years. Official (Nehruvian) secularism showed the two very different faces of modernity in postindependence India: modernity as purely secular (universal); versus modernity as religious and communitarian (particular), which in turn was comprised of majoritarian (Hindu) and minoritarian (Muslim, Sikh, Christian, etc.) factions.

In many ways the central problem with the Nehruvian model of secularism was the confident assumption, held by the majority of the Congress leadership, that national solidarity was inherently a quality of India's (Hindu) cultural heritage.[12] This assumption was made painfully evident to the world during the 1947 partition of India as Muslims and Hindus were polarized even further, each community seeing itself as the defender of its own cultural values and integrity. Unlike the Muslims, Sikh politicians cast their lot with Nehru's Congress, which promised to establish a secular state that would defend minority rights. Yet within two decades of partition many Sikhs were regretting this decision as throughout the 1960s and 70s they became locked into one dispute after another with a secular state that was manipulated—invisibly, or so it seemed—by a majoritarian Hindu community.

The "Sikh problem," as it was represented by influential sections of the Indian media and perceived by the Hindu majority, was about a troublesome minority whose secessionist demands challenged the stability and sovereignty of the Indian nation-state. From the Sikh standpoint, the problem was primarily about their need to secure rights as a vulnerable minority in India and about the rights of successively elected majority Sikh governments in Punjab to pursue their own governance free from interference by what was becoming an increasingly centralized government machinery, based in New Delhi. These disputes culminated in the Emergency of 1975 and by the 1980s had grown into a demand for regional autonomy of the Punjab province. It is now well established that Congress policies polarized the situation in Punjab by politically undermining the Akali Dal's nonviolent agitation, thereby promoting the more militant and polarizing elements among the Sikhs.[13] As events seemingly spiraled out of control in 1984, Prime Minister Indira Gandhi ordered the Indian army's invasion of the Golden Temple complex in Amritsar—code name "Operation Blue Star"—to oust Sikh militants occupying the complex, which contained the premier seats of religious and political authority for Sikhs. Barely five months later, Indira Gandhi was assassinated by her Sikh bodyguards, followed almost immediately by several days of anti-Sikh pogroms throughout India but especially in the capital, New Delhi. As numerous human rights reports have made clear, these pogroms were orchestrated once again with the approval of high-level clearance in the ruling Congress party. Operation Blue Star unleashed a vicious cycle of insurgency that lasted until 1996 and was responsible for thousands of deaths, random disappearances, systematic torture, and human rights abuses against a civilian populace by the state police and army.[14]

Congress involvement in what Upendra Baxi has called "state-supported" violence was by no means limited to the "Sikh problem." In retrospect it seems clear that Congress's preoccupation with the Sikhs was to some extent an elaborate smokescreen for the much bigger challenge to Nehruvian secularism: the steady and inexorable rise of the Hindu right under the slogan of Hindutva (Hindu-ness). Led by the Bhartiya Janata Party (BJP) as the publicly elected face of Hindu nationalism, the Hindutva movement had by the late 1980s considerably eroded the Congress's power base. Apart from the sectarian violence that accompanied the rise of the Hindu right, their arrival in 1994 as a democratically elected majority government led by the BJP signaled a watershed in Indian politics: the transformation of Indian democracy from the "pseudo-secularism" of Congress to a secularism defined by the majority Hindu community, effectively a Hindu secularism. So by 1994 India was already being defined by some as a Hindu democracy fueled by a *religious* nationalism.

When we look at the theoretical responses to the various crises of the Indian polity, it is hardly surprising to note how closely they have paralleled political events. Thus until the late 1980s the dominant left-liberal secularist position among Indian intellectuals—most of whom were either Nehruvians or Marxists—identified "religion," "sectarianism," "fundamentalism," and "separatism" (euphemisms for Muslims in Kashmir and Sikhs in Punjab) as *the* threat to a fledgling Indian democracy. This perceived threat was usually instigated from outside the nation by a "foreign hand." Interestingly, Hindu nationalism, though perceived as communalist, was rarely considered a threat to Indian democracy: the threat was always projected as non-Hindu. As the crisis of Indian secularism had set in by the early 1990s, other voices began to make themselves heard. Political psychologists such as Ashis Nandy and Sudhir Kakar and sociologists such as T. N. Madan began to formulate a "communitarian" critique of secularism that advocated decentralizing policies, based on their support for a pluralist democracy rooted in the recognition of the pivotal role of India's religious communities in the makeup of Indian democracy.

For some years the debate between left-liberal secularists and communitarians defined the polarized state of Indian theoretical responses. It was not until the BJP began to redefine Indian democracy in terms of a Hindu secularism and began to influence the writing of Indian history and the entire educational and pedagogical infrastructure of India that a third position began to emerge. This alternative position was defined mainly by disaffected intellectuals of the Indian radical left, many of whom were historians or literary theorists influenced by French poststructuralism and especially by Edward Said's postcolonial theory. Said's critiques of Orientalism and nationalism in works such as *Orientalism* (1978) and *Culture and Imperialism* (1992) and his formulation of a "secular anti-imperialist critique" seems to be the moving influence behind these Indian postcolonial theorists. Central to Said's rethinking of secularism as a safeguard against the injustices of democracy defined by a majoritarian community was the ideological proximity between religion and nationalism. Said's opposition to nationalism is aligned with a notion of the secular as a domain "enunciated from minority positions."[15] When inflected into the scene of Indian polity, Said's "secular anti-imperialist critique" provided a way to think about democracy without succumbing to the myth of national belonging, that is, from the standpoint of those most vulnerable to the vagaries of majoritarian rule. Indian intellectuals influenced by Said—including Ranajit Guha, Romila Thapar, G. C. Spivak, Dipesh Chakrabarty, Homi Bhabha, Partha Chatterjee, Gyan Pandey, and Gyan Prakash, among many others—have in a very real sense helped to establish India as the paradigmatic case of postcolonial theory.

But it is here that we come across an important and revealing difference between the theoretical responses to the crisis of secularism by Western (European-American) and by Indian academics. Much of the critique of secularism by Western academics has been performed mainly by those who are professedly religious, or by those who write from the perspective of the academic study of religion and therefore keep a minimal distance from religion. Nevertheless, Western academics generally share at least a minimal commitment to the idea that religion has been, for better or for worse, part and parcel of the cultural and philosophical frame of the history of the West. By contrast, critiques of secularism by Indian academics come mainly from a strictly historicist perspective and rarely from academics who either profess affiliation to a religion or are part of the scholarly study of religion. Even within critiques of secularism that have been written from a postcolonial/historicist perspective, the absence of discussion about "religion," or any admission that "religion" is an intrinsic part of the Indian cultural frame, is startling.

This point is amply illustrated by Anuradha Dingwaney and Rajeshwari Sundar Rajan in their volume entitled *The Crisis of Secularism in India*. The editors offer the following explanation for the absence of discussion about religion in the discussions of secularism in their book:

> Despite its crisis, secularism bears a normative status within and as constitutive of a modernity that remains the context from which we perform our critique. The critique of secularism is therefore obliged to be self-reflexive, an insider job by secularists themselves. In the contemporary academy it would seem that few exercises of this kind are performed by the professedly religious. Or at least the discourses of the ontotheological and the post-secular today inhabit other spaces than that of the historical, social science, and cultural critiques of secularism such as this one. Writing about a conference on religion that he had convened in Capri in 1994, Derrida defined the (limits of the) participants' position thus: "We are not priests bound in a ministry, nor theologians, nor qualified, competent representatives of religion, nor enemies of religion as such. . . . But we also share a commitment to Enlightenment values." Something of these limits operate in the same way among the essays assembled here, even as a critique of secularism.
>
> Religion, in these essays as well as in the broader discourse that constitutes them, is primarily addressed in terms of historical explanation or as a sociology of religion. . . . The "religious" is a concept that encounters a notable impasse in the work of contemporary post-colonial theorists who attempt to go beyond respectful or wistful acknowledgement of this "other" knowledge.[16]

What Dingwaney and Rajan seem to imply here is that to make a valid critique of secularism, the conceptual terms of this critique must not be tainted with religion or the religious. The terms of this critique, in order to be a critique, must acknowledge a strict separation of the religious and the secular. One cannot think in terms of religious ideas since this would be untrue to Enlightenment values. According to this line of argument, Indian postcolonial theorists see themselves as faithfully adhering to the Enlightenment values because they are able to refuse any contact with religion. Western theorists by contrast have been able to blur the lines of separation between religion and secularism because they "inhabit other spaces" in the humanities, such as theology or the study of religion.[17]

In a sense the attempt to validate the religion/secularism opposition by way of reference to Derrida is a serious misreading not only of Derrida's own position on this subject but of the critical work being done in the field of religion and theology. Derrida and a host of other writers have problematized the very idea that the Enlightenment ever managed to successfully divest itself of religion or theology. As Hent de Vries argues, it is only the uncontested nature of the narrative of Western secularist modernity that has from the outset obscured the fact that the concept of the political (and therefore the secular) "has always been contingent upon a plausible translation and renegotiation of the central categories of this religion's historical belief's, its central rituals and implicit policies."[18]

There is, however, another way of understanding what Dingwaney and Rajan are suggesting. What they and many other Indian postcolonial theorists seem to be alluding to through this disavowal of religion—not only as a political alternative to secularism but as a theoretical influence on the formation of the secular—is that while religion is an intrinsic part of the cultural, historical, and intellectual experience of the West, this may not be valid in the Indian context. "Religion," *as a general concept*, is more likely the result of a transposition from a Christian-European context into an Indian context. Yet it now exists as though it were an indigenous concept. Thus far, the only way for Indian scholars to deal with this problem within the context of the humanities and social sciences has been through the framework of historicism. However, as I shall argue in chapter 2, this move also has a colonial genealogy, which can be traced through Said, Foucault, and Marx back to Hegel. Moreover, because they refuse to read the secular/historical as intrinsically connected to religion, they also fail to see that secularism is as much a colonial imposition as religion. Hence their theoretical stance is no more valid than those who profess to critique secularism from a religious standpoint.

Something similar to this is argued by the Indian sociologist T. N. Madan. Madan points out that "secularism . . . failed to make headway in India since Hindus, Muslims, Buddhists, Sikhs cannot and will not privatize their religion."[19] Secularism for Madan is the "gift of Christianity to mankind and therefore part of the unique history of Europe." Echoing scholars of religion such as S. N. Balagagadhara and Richard King, the question that Madan seems to be raising here is that perhaps

Indians in their encounter with European colonialism have accepted religion (and secularism) as universally translatable and therefore cross-cultural categories. One must therefore differentiate between the gesture of simply refusing to be tainted intellectually or politically by religion, and the rather different gesture of admitting that Indians, even as they describe themselves as secular, have been constructed by their entry into the Christian-European category of religion. Stated otherwise: India's modernization, its entry into Enlightenment discourse, happened by way of a certain politics of religion-making. This is a question that I shall explore further as this chapter progresses and also throughout this book.

In the meantime, however, I want to consider arguments that address these issues while avoiding the negative reaction of conventional postcolonial theory to the appearance of religion, the religious, and religious nationalism in the public domain. These arguments derive from scholars who have demonstrated a more nuanced understanding of the presence of religion in India. I refer to the recent work of Gyan Pandey, Peter van der Veer, Brian Pennington, Kenneth Jones, Harjot Oberoi, Krishna Sharma, and Vasudha Dalmia. Taking the form of detailed micro-studies, their work has, in different ways, traced the colonial roots of this problem to the agency of the Indian native elites who instigated a variety of reform movements during the late nineteenth and early twentieth centuries. In what follows I want to present an overview of the reform movements in order to bring into sharper focus the role of religion-making in the birth of Indian modernity. My aim is to tease out some of the continuities and productive tensions present in their respective presentations of religion. One such tension of particular interest to me consists in the fact that while these studies assume an implicit understanding of religion as a universally applicable concept, they also emphasize the need to take seriously the "interactionist" or "dialogical" nature of the agency of the native elites. Ironically, though, as soon as one opens up the question of agency in this way and begins to probe the specifically *linguistic* nature of the "interaction" or "dialogue" through which agency is formed, it becomes necessary to question the very assumption of a generalized category of religion. Indeed, such an approach opens up the possibility of seeing how a generalized concept of religion, far from being universal, is rather something that *emerges* within native elite discourse. Central to this emergence is the question of language and language acquisition, which I want to bring more into view as this chapter progresses.

Religion and Nationalism in Colonial North India

In his influential study *The Construction of Communalism in Colonial North India,* Gyan Pandey has shown that whereas during the period of the 1870s to 1920 the reform movements mobilized indigenous communities in North India along the clearly defined religious categories of Hindu, Muslim, Sikh (which was obviously in keeping with the idea that what they were reforming or reviving were primordial religious traditions), after the 1920s there is a complete reversal in Indian nationalist discourse, wherein religion and religious traditions are now seen as the basis of division, discord, and disunity. Thus, whereas in the earlier period religion was regarded as the basis of national unity, the period following the 1920s opens up a new era in Indian politics in which nationalism is rigorously conceptualized in direct opposition to religions and religious communities, which are now seen as causes of disunity. The reversal is based on the need to transcend communalism, sectarianism, and religious traditions, which represent primordial elements that are incompatible with modernization and progress. According to this new conceptualization, true nationalism stands above the different religious communities and takes as the basis of its unity not religious communities, but the individual Indian citizen. However, for leading nationalist leaders such as M. K. Gandhi and those Hindus who retained a belief in the centrality of religion and the religious community in India, the search for a "pure" nationalism precipitated significant changes in their analyses of the basis of Indian nationalism. Many of these thinkers now began to emphasize the distinction between the "essentials" of religion—its universal aspect—which could be upheld under all circumstances, and its "nonessential" aspect—singularities that needed to be discarded in the interests of a larger unity.[20]

What Pandey's analysis suggests—but seems unable to follow through on, for reasons that will become clear later—is the prevalence of a discourse between religion and nationalism that is actually guided by ambivalent and competing presuppositions about the nature of religion itself. That is to say, a certain understanding of religion is in fact operative and of crucial importance both (i) for redefining the "new" or "pure" nationalism after the 1920s as secular, democratic, and in tune with the social politics of the citizens, and (ii) for devaluing and marginalizing the earlier, and by implication underdeveloped (because not sufficiently removed from religion/tradition), form of nationalism as communalism. It is the latter kind of politicization of religious communities that has come to be associated with intersectarian conflict and social disunity.

Thus, far from there being any simplistic exclusion of religion from the debate, there continued to reside an ambivalent (and assumed) logic *about* religion—what religion is and how it relates to the Indic context— at the heart of the discourse on nationalism. This ambivalence, as we shall see, not only was responsible for the reversal of the 1920s, but in turn set the pattern for current developments in India, where the secular Indian state has been consistently able to manipulate and engineer sectarian conflict to its own electoral advantage.

Peter van der Veer has taken up this problem in Pandey's early work by developing the idea of "religious nationalism" into a full-fledged thesis in his important study of the intricate relation between religion and politics in contemporary North India.[21] Van der Veer suggests that the seemingly intractable problem of religion and secularism in contemporary India cannot simply be reduced either to the failure of modernizing forces to suppress the primordial forces of religion and sectarianism or to the idea (espoused mainly by communitarians and left-liberal secularists) that "religious nationalisms" of the Hindutva type are a contradiction-in-terms, being no more than a cynical attempt by Brahmin elites to propagate an intolerant sectarian ideology. Despite their apparent unrelatedness, van der Veer argues, both of the above perceptions arise from a cultural discourse of secularization developed in the European Enlightenment that makes a sharp distinction between two incompatible spheres of action: religion and politics. This discourse assigns religion to the private domain as a matter of personal belief; hence any politicization of religion is seen as a transgression of what religion is supposed to be. There is therefore a distinction between "real" religion and politicized religion, and conversely between "real" nationalism and false ("religious") nationalism.

Consequently, religious nationalism of the Hindutva type is no less modern than its secular counterparts in the political arena, given that both participate equally in the material conditions and discursive practices of the modern nation-state. Rather, the reality of religious nationalism suggests a certain uniqueness about India's passage to modernity related to the fact that "for Indians the most important imaginings of the nation are religious as opposed to secular."[22] In India, "religion constitutes a site of difference on which the struggle for alternatives to Western modernity were played out."[23] In that struggle, new religious discourses and practices emerged that can legitimately be termed "religious nationalisms."

The articulations of religious nationalism and the kind of violent intolerance attributed to it cannot simply be regarded as products of a foreign imperial blueprint—i.e., of Orientalist scholarship. Indeed, contemporary religio-political formations that comprise Hindu nationalism are in fact rooted in precolonial indigenous formations, notably the Ramanadi school of Vaiṣṇavism, whose growth from the sixteenth century onward is part of a larger historical process in which *bhakti* has come to define modern traditional Hinduism. Far from being an imported Christian ideology, contemporary religious nationalism has a historical continuity with the devotional traditions of North India, which have a very wide popular base inclusive of caste and noncaste societies.

Given that the terms "crisis of secularism" and "return of religion" are two sides of the same political coin, the only way to unravel the seeming paradox of Indian modernity is to regard concepts such as "modernity," "progress," and "secularity" not as defining tropes of Western self-representation, but as concepts that were minted through the interaction between metropole and colony.[24] The "secular" and the "religious" are more usefully considered as mutually interdependent processes that follow different trajectories in Britain and India. In Britain, for example, the separation of church and state did not lead to a decline in the social and political importance of religion. Rather, "religion" entered the public sphere by becoming nationalized. With the rise of the nation-state there is an enormous shift in the meaning of religion. By contrast, in modern India, precolonial formations were transformed in *opposition* to the state (identified with the colonizer), and religion became the only way of asserting and establishing identity and difference against the colonizer: "Far from having a secularizing influence on Indian society, the modernizing impact of the secular colonial state in fact gave religion a strong new impulse."[25] Consequently, in both India and Britain there was a shift in the location of religion in society, from being part of the state to being part of a new public sphere that emerged in England during the 1790s and, under different circumstances, emerged in India during the 1820s. Let us briefly look at these dual emergences.

"Dialogue" and the Emergence of Public Spheres in Britain and India

In England the relocation of religion to the public sphere is linked to the growth of evangelicalism and the enfranchisement of Catholics as part of the national mainstream. At the heart of the evangelical movement was a broad project conceived by upper-class evangelicals in the heart of the metropole, to convert others *within* England (the lower classes and factory workers, groups that had emerged in the wake of the Industrial Revolution) and others *outside* of the metropole, specifically, non-Christians in India.[26] This project of conversion was undertaken by voluntary societies such as the London Missionary Society (LMS) and the Church Missionary Society (CMS). These missionary societies saw themselves as engaged in a struggle to morally uplift the poor underclass of English society and to save the souls of idolatrous heathens in India. As Brian Pennington has argued, the missionary project was situated at the center of colonial power and conceived by men such as William Wilberforce and Charles Grant in terms of a "comprehensive evangelization of Britain and India alike that would employ the benighted pagan and vulgar factory worker as reflections of each other."[27] Missionary bodies such as the LMS and the CMS not only viewed the British working classes as sources of income and manpower but also as targets of the very proselytization they had in mind for Hindus and other heathens in India.[28]

In India indigenous formations relocated to the public sphere following a different trajectory; nevertheless there are clear parallels with what was happening in England. The causal factors were in fact the same. First was a battle between Orientalists and Anglicists. Orientalists tended to support indigenous traditions of learning and education in India and promoted the learning of Sanskrit and other vernacular languages for English officers in India and the establishment of chairs in Oriental studies in English universities. Anglicists, on the other hand, argued for the replacement of native Indian traditions of learning by English education and Christian civilization. Second was a sustained evangelical attack on the Orientalist image of a civilized and rational Hinduism, an attack that had profound consequences both for policymakers in England and for the East India Company's policy of noninterference in the affairs of Indians. Third, as a reaction to evangelical missionaries and to new British policies in India, was the emergence of indigenous social reformist movements and the rise of a new Indian middle class. However, the impact of and reaction to British colonialism in India involved complexities—demographic, linguistic, legal, theoretical, and religious—that deserve to be considered in more detail. Part of the complexity of the British/Indian encounter, and one that often goes unnoticed, originates in the nomenclature adopted for classifying India's emergence into the public sphere.

While it is now generally accepted in modern Indian historiography that colonialism fostered social groups that collaborated in the task of administering the machinery of the Raj, and thereby in modernizing the indigenous cultures, what continues to be largely misunderstood is the nature of the interactive process between colonizer and colonized. A good example of this interactive process is the very different manner in which the term "religion" was appropriated by different social groups in India. This misunderstanding comes out most clearly in the continued classification of the modernization of these indigenous societies as simply "reformist" or "neo-Hindu" movements that brought about changes in religion, society, and culture. However, closer inspection reveals that these national reform movements were classified in opposition to many other movements, called "revivalist" or "orthodox," whose leaders spoke for traditional socio-religious formations that posited the constancy (*sanātantā*) or unchanging nature of tradition (*sanātana dharma*), and that, by and large, were not centrally coordinated. Even though the spokesmen of these Sanatanist movements articulated and accommodated wide-reaching changes, no documentation appears to have been registered for the simple reason that they chose not to define themselves as modern/izing.[29] Given that the central defining criterion for any reformist movement was socio-religious transformation, scholars throughout the twentieth century experienced difficulty in properly categorizing this group other than as "revivalist," thereby tending to confuse it with the amorphous and unchanging "Hindu" multitude.

To overcome this confusion, changes in nomenclature have been suggested, replacing older terms such as "revivalist," "renaissance," and "neo-Hindu" with the opposition: traditionalist versus reformist.[30] According to Vasudha Dalmia, the differences and similarities between these two categories of social group that contested the public sphere can be summarized as follows. There are two main differences. Traditionalists recognize the authority of both *śruti* (revealed) and *smṛti* (remembered) scriptures, whereas reformists isolate the former (e.g., Veda as revealed) and reject the latter as deviant or degenerate; for traditionalists, institutions such as the *varṇāśrama dharma* (and by implication the *Dharmaśāstras*), temple, and ritual practice are not open to question. Reformists by and large tended to challenge and break with such institutions, which they regarded as corrupt and devoid of universal appeal.[31] The main similarity between the two groups is that both reformists and traditionalists deployed rational argument and cited historical and Indological scholarship in support of their causes. As a result, both groups tended to brand popular religious practice as mere "superstition." This point notwithstanding, it is important to note the nature of the similarity and the difference.

Differences between reformism and traditionalism refer to how they access the precolonial domain—in other words, how they interpret or relate to what they regard as their "own" or the "authentic," i.e., the domain of the self. However, similarities between them refer to their individual *interactions* and *responses* to the domain that they both regard as alien, other, and imposed, namely the colonial and the missionary.

Given, then, that what divided reformists and traditionalists is an internal dialogue over issues such as tradition and authenticity, and what joined them was an external dialogue or contract with the other (colonizer), it seems clear that one cannot simply speak of self/other polarizations such as indigenous/colonized versus foreign/colonizer. Rather, one must speak, on the one hand, of the self's relationship to the self, or how traditionalists and reformists each negotiated between themselves as to what constituted the indigenous, authentic, or self; and on the other, of the self's relationship to the other, or how traditionalists and reformists each negotiated what constitutes the alien/other. It is through these separate but ultimately linked negotiations that the differences of these two groups came to be articulated in the public spheres and manifested as different social identities. In other words, what are often posited as polarities were in fact interactive.

If it is true that interaction was the basis on which the self/other relationship was constituted over a period of time, this raises a different set of questions. How is the work of this interaction to be conceptualized, given that it is not simply a historical problem, something that happened in the colonial past, but a process that is very much ongoing in contemporary politics? In what sense, then, are the legacies and strands of older reformist and traditionalist movements reincarnated as contemporary political constellations that continue to vie for dominance not only in the public sphere (whether in India or the West) but for the very nature of this sphere as religious or secular—and that, indeed, continue to determine the nature of the public domain in relation to the religion of the nation? The question therefore becomes: how and why did the conceptualization of the "interpretive process" central to the work of interaction become essentially linked to the conceptualization of religion, and how did its conceptualization as religion come to determine the relationality between self and other as exclusive religious identities (Hindu, Muslim, Sikh)?

The above questions bring together several dimensions—religion, language, subjectivity, and power—that are necessary for understanding the colonial context of nineteenth-century North India and how imperialist structures instituted at that time repeat themselves in contemporary political formations. Until relatively recently the debate on this issue was dominated by neo-Marxist or by Foucauldian theory, which harbors two fundamental misconceptions about the nature of interaction between colonizer and colonized.[32] The first misconception is that language is immaterial and that as a result discursivity plays a secondary role in the interactive process. Second, is that the origins of power and shifts in power are located only within individual unified subjects. In contradistinction I want to argue that the nature of the interactive process cannot be envisaged without reference either to the material conditions under which power is instituted by the colonial state, or, given that power is also assumed by the colonized, to a psychological dimension relating to shifts in power. We could say that the work of interaction/interpretation/dialogue between metropole and colony is a causative factor in the "colonization of psychic space."[33] If language is material, as I show later, and if power is an effect of language's materiality, then subjectivity is both an instrument and an effect of power. This suggests that regulatory norms are internalized by the subject concerned. I intend to show that the internalizing mechanism—the means by which power is accepted and assumed by the subject—works within the discursive and specifically linguistic realm, and is constituted both in discourses that objectify language and by the discourse of religion.

In order to develop such a conceptual model for analyzing the interactive process, I shall begin by adopting two important insights from the subaltern historian Ranajit Guha, whose work provides a useful conduit between the neo-Marxist historicism and the Lacanian/Derridian theory that I begin to develop toward the end of this chapter and deploy in later chapters. Following Antonio Gramsci, Guha argued that the articulation of power in colonial North India in both its institutional (political) and discursive aspects could be conceptualized in terms of the interplay between dominance and subjection. Thus, dominance consists of persuasion (essentially discursive) and force (political). Subjection consists of resistance (political/institutional) and collaboration (again essentially discursive).[34] The central point in Guha's thesis is that these interacting pairs offer a framework for locating the relationship between colonizer and colonized in a way that accounts equally for the political and the discursive aspects but does not simplistically reduce this relationship either to the imposition of a Western colonial framework on a much weaker native mindset, or to the equally simplistic notion of a facile interchange, a cultural blending of ideas between East and West.[35]

Bearing in mind this inseparability of the political and the discursive, it is possible to reconstruct the colonizer/colonized relation in terms of a hierarchical differentiation between the colonizer's idiom (or the "first idiom") and the idioms that come to be articulated by the colonized through interaction with the colonizer (second and third idioms).[36] The first idiom is provided by the British. It comprises the institutions, concepts, language, and intellectual heritage of the colonizer—not to mention the terms of their critique of native traditions, given through Indological, ethnographic, and missionary literature. The first idiom was made accessible to urban classes newly confronted with colonial institutions—law courts, schools, and colleges, etc.—mainly through the new print media: i.e., English newspapers, English textbooks, and missionary tracts. The second idiom—the "classical" Indian—was derived from the precolonial tradition of the colonized. It was deliberately constructed through a collaboration between indigenous elites and colonial scholars (Orientalists), for the purpose of legitimating the (then)-contemporary Hindu restructuring of sociopolitical and religious discourse by reducing the multiplicity of classical traditions on the subcontinent to a unifying tradition, which for ideological purposes amounted to the Aryan-Hindu. In the course of time these first two idioms overlapped, crossed, subverted each other, and eventually coalesced into the third idiom. This third idiom, which included both traditional and reformist formulations, articulated itself as the nationalist or modernist.[37]

In the following discussion this threefold hierarchical schema serves as a convenient device for tracing the emergence of native elite subjectivity (reformist and traditionalist) through their discursive interactions with the British and with each other. For present purposes, I shall focus on three historically distinct periods corresponding at the same time to three distinct geographical areas in which the interaction took place: 1780–1820s in Bengal; 1840s–1860 in Banaras; and 1870s–1920 in Punjab and the Northwest Provinces. The purpose of this somewhat broad sweep is to provide an overview of the encounter between Indians and the British that highlights the emergence of the concept of religion as a product of the collaborative interaction between the colonial idiom of the colonizer and nationalist idiom of the colonized, as opposed to its being assumed as a universal. To discern this concept's emergence it is necessary to follow the movement and transformation of the terms "Hindu" and "Hinduism" in the battle between the Orientalists and the Anglicists over the three time periods and geographical areas noted above. By tracing the fate of the terms "Hindu"/"Hinduism" in this way, it will be possible to relocate the concept of religion in relation to the question of discursivity and hence language. The link between language and religion will be crucial to formulating an alternative model of discursivity—which in effect performs the essential work of forming colonial subjectivity—later in this chapter.

The Colonial Idiom: The Anglicist
Reversal of the "Hindoo" Stereotype

As Richard King has noted, the two prevalent stereotypes in the Western characterization of India—the image of Hinduism as an exemplar of the "mystic East" and therefore as a tolerant and peaceful civilization versus the image of India as a land torn by religious divisions and militant fanatics—is part of a representation that has a considerable ancestry, going back to "older colonial myths about Oriental despotism and the irrationality of the colonial subject."[38] The ambivalence of this image epitomized the two sides of the British debate over the true nature of Hinduism, which Thomas Trautman has termed "Indomania" and "Indophobia" in his book *Aryans and British India*. The term "British Indomania" refers to the cumulative effect on the British mind produced by the work of the Calcutta Orientalists William Jones, Charles Wilkins, Francis Wilford, and H. T. Colebrook, who collectively pioneered the field of Indology through research published in the Asiatick Society's journal *Asiatick Researches* between the late 1780s and 1815. The journal was founded by William Jones as a tool for presenting the antiquity of Indian culture and civilization and as a way of influencing East India Company policy.

"Indomania" is also a misleading term, however, since the early Orientalists' passion for India was always underpinned by an even stronger commitment to the expansion of the colonial state, which conceived itself as the instrument of Christian morality.[39] More importantly, the ambivalence of the stereotype of Hinduism was already part of the Orientalist image of Hinduism. At the risk of simplification, this Orientalist image can be reduced to the following characteristics and assumptions[40]:

(i) Each religious tradition in India has a specific place on the conceptual map of Indian cultures. Each tradition is comprised of mutually exclusive entities, of which Hinduism was one. Being the largest tradition, it constituted the default identity of non-Muslims. Thus the Orientalists' conception of religious diversity in India was based on the primacy of communalism and competing sectarian conflicts.

(ii) The contemporary state of India's religions was a condition of the naturally polymorphic ecology of India. Thus the term "Hinduism" implied not a religion of rational subjects but a process of overproduction and excess that fascinated the Orientalist.

(iii) Contemporary Hinduism's polytheism, with its irrationality, gross idolatry, and priestly excesses, appeared to differ sharply from the elegant monistic philosophy of the learned classes represented in the classical texts, especially the Upaniṣads and commentaries on the Upaniṣads known as Vedānta. In line with prevalent theories of natural religion and human society as originally monotheistic and rational, William Jones and his colleagues postulated the idea of an Indian Golden Age, from which Hinduism had fallen due to Muslim incursions. The idea of an "original" Hinduism also presented a moral task for contemporary Hinduism, which was a fallen, illicit, and immoral entity compared to the "original" Hinduism, for which the central principle was the rational adoration of the one true God.

(iv) In later publications and on the basis of the linguistic researches for which he is perhaps best known, Jones developed the theory of a shared ancestral linkage between Europeans and Asiatics. Central to Jones' construction was the idea of an original state shared by all men who possessed reason. More important, this was a state that the colonizer was committed to retrieving on behalf of its subjects, which in turn justified the British presence in India.

By the first decade of the nineteenth century, however, this Orientalist image of India and Hinduism had come under concerted attack from Anglicists in both England and India. Riding on a new wave of scientifically grounded race theories, Anglicists singled out for attack the idea of an Indian Golden Age and the notion of a proximity between Europe and the Orient. India had not merely fallen into idolatry and polytheism, they argued, but was by nature idolatrous and therefore beyond retrieval. What it needed was stronger Christian intervention. The lynchpin in the Anglicist strategy was the new and supposedly more accurate fieldwork of evangelical missionaries, notably the Serampore Baptists Joshua Marshman, William Carey, and William Ward. As Brian Pennington observes, these missionary preachers pitted themselves not against the Hindu devotee or the Brahmin priest, but against the material object of Hindu devotion, namely, the idol, which more than any other factor subverted the human capacity for reason and piety:

> This epic formula pitting the missionary against the Hindu idol quickly assumed a pre-eminent place in popular Christian literature, feeding the British appetite for outrageous stories from the colonies. Antipodal to the piety promoted by the missionary spinning it, this tale of brazen, archetypal idolatry contributed to India's overshadowing all other colonies in the British popular imagination. In the manifestation of the strongly nationalist religious subjectivity . . . the evangelical missionary's confrontation with the Hindu idol encoded so many other contrasts critical to the crystallization of a British sense of national self: reason vs. irrationality, Christian vs. pagan, mind vs. body, freed vs. enslaved, and so forth.[41]

The work of William Ward is exemplary of the missionary literature that became a centerpiece of the Anglicist construction of Hinduism. Unlike the Orientalists, who presented an image of Hinduism as refined and poetic, an image derived mainly from textual sources, Ward was "an observer in the field of actual Hindu life and culture."[42] Ward's proto-ethnographic technique, which presented detailed descriptions of actual Hindu practices, was widely acclaimed not only by a Christian public but by politicians and bureaucrats who determined British policy toward India. For Ward, the essence of religion lay not in texts but in actual practice. It was "living Hinduism" that really mattered. Ward's central work, the four-volume *View of the Hindoos*,[43] hinged on one crucial argument: that Hinduism's fallen state is due to its polytheistic idolatry and specifically to its conception of deity. The basic fault of the "Hindoo system" was that it had "no one principle," "no one operative principle" that could provide ethical uplift. Hindu religion was devoid of moral theology. Ward's connection of Hinduism's idolatrous practices to the sexual immorality of Hindus had a major effect not only on the way that Britons and Europeans conceptualized Hinduism, but on the way in which they configured their own sense of national (British) identity in the nineteenth century:

In pamphlet wars, sermons, public meetings and political speeches, one finds a British public constituted out of discourse about Hindu religious practices. Lurid in nature, this material invited children, the working poor, and the middle classes to join the elites in debates over Britain's relationship to idolatry. Their common scrutiny of the colonial government's policies concerning temple maintenance and patronage, sati, missionaries helped forge a common national identity in which Hindu and Christian religion were deeply implicated.[44]

In addition to its popularity in the public sphere, Ward's work was avidly read and cited by British and European scholars, notably James Mill and G. W. F. Hegel. As we shall note in the next chapter, Ward's combination of ethnography and theology influenced James Mill's historical placement of Hindus in relation to the British Empire, and Hegel's conceptualization of the relationship between religion and history, which in turn led to his retheorizing the concept of religion in relation to the placement of India and Hinduism. Once the concept of religion was reconceptualized in this way, the standpoint of Indologists and the discipline of Indology, which had been the stronghold of the Orientalists, would eventually be transformed.

Over the forty years or so during which the battle between Anglicists and Orientalists had raged (1790s to the 1830s)—a battle in which the Anglicists emerged victorious and which ended with the British parliament's endorsement of Thomas Macaulay's 1835 *Minute on Indian Education* as the basis of official policy on India—the East India Company also changed its policy from giving patronage to Hindu temples and promoting knowledge of indigenous languages and cultures among British officers, to dissolving that connection through the formation of committees for supervising and managing temples and other indigenous institutions. In the early decades of the nineteenth century these committees promoted the growth of a new public sphere, which fostered at the same time a "colonial politics of representation" not only between Hindus and Muslims, but between Hindus and Hindus and Muslims and Muslims. These policies, which entailed a certain degree of interference in indigenous affairs and an effect on belief systems that was perhaps unavoidable, set off a series of reformist reactions among Hindus, Muslims, and, in the latter decades of the nineteenth century, Sikhs.

While these reformist reactions were responses to colonial modernity, they were equally the products of precolonial discursive traditions.

Fueled by advancing print media such as newspapers, the creation of new vernacular languages, and new methods for acquiring education (Anglo-vernacular schools), these reformist movements helped to transform Indian consciousness and identity in the colony in much the same way that evangelicals had transformed Christian consciousness in Britain. Indeed, insofar as these transformations/revivals involved the creation of newer public spheres in both England and India, they can be regarded as parallel to each other.

Indian Public Responses to the Colonial Idiom

Reformists

Broadly speaking, there were two different kinds of "Hindu public" response to colonial modernity: reformist and traditionalist. The earliest and best-known example of the modernist/reformist "Hindu public" response is the work of Rammohan Roy (1772–1883), the "father of the Bengal renaissance," and his organization, the Brāhmo Samāj. Born into a wealthy Brahmin family, Rammohan Roy was unlike other Indians. Wealthy and privately educated in English, he came into close contact with British officers and administrators during the last decade of the eighteenth century and the first decades of the nineteenth century.

Strongly influenced on the one hand by early Orientalist literature on India and Hinduism, and on the other by English and American Unitarianism, Roy founded the Brāhmo Samāj, which propagated a deist/universalist religion based on certain Hindu sources, notably the *Veda* and specifically the Upaniṣads and the Vedānta commentaries, which Orientalists had invested with the status of the "central theology of Hinduism." In various publications and through his own newspaper (*Sambad Kaumudi*) Roy tried to formulate a "rational Hinduism" that could become the basis of a universal religion (and therefore as a perfect example of a natural religion, whose basis was not "God" but a notion of reason shared by all men).[45] Roy was, however, careful to establish his views by isolating certain textual sources as exclusively authoritative (e.g., *Veda* as opposed to *Puraṇā*) and by shifting interpretive authority away from living gurus toward one's own private, rational judgment. It was therefore a laicized or secular humanistic Hinduism insofar as it was available to all men and was beyond the religious, racial, and sectarian divisions that characterized other religions in their concrete particularity, including popular devotional Hinduism. Reflecting this point of view, Roy's politics was centered around establishing a version of Hinduism shorn of priesthood, ritual, caste, superstition, and idolatry.

The presence and activities of the Brāhmo Samāj were not limited to Bengal. Branches of the Brāhmo Samāj were set up throughout North India as Bengali officials moved with the British Empire into Banaras and eventually into the Northwest Provinces. By the 1860s branches of the Brāhmo Samāj had been established at Lahore, Rawalpindi, Amritsar, Shimla, and Dera Ghazi Khan, among other places. Initially at least, Punjabi elites eagerly embraced the Brāhmo message, which helped them come to terms with the cultural forces and social transformations let loose by the Raj. In 1876 the Brāhmo Samāj established a functionary to translate its ideology into Hindi, Punjabi, and Urdu. During the 1870s the Lahore Samāj was visited by prominent Bengali leaders of the movement, such as Keshabchandra Sen, Debendranath Tagore, and Majumdar.[46]

Punjabi Sikhs also began to join the Brāhmo Samāj, especially after the wealthy aristocrat Dyal Singh Majithia staked his fortune on their cause.[47] Because he had been educated at a mission school and brought up by an English governess, Dyal Singh's upbringing was ideally suited to the Brāhmo message. He became friends with leading Hindu and Muslim reformers of the day, such as Swami Vivekanada and Syed Ahmed Khan. In 1881 Dyal Singh began publishing *The Tribune*, a weekly English newspaper that became a powerful instrument for broadcasting Brāhmo ideology in Punjab. However, the influence of Christianity on Brāhmo ideology made it too much of a target for rival and more powerful reformist movements in Punjab, notably the Ārya Samāj and the Singh Sabhā.

The Ārya Samāj was in many ways North India's most effective and important reformist movement. Founded by Dayananda Saraswati, an itinerant teacher from the prestigious order of Śaivite Daśnāmis, the movement began in Maharastra but succeeded mainly in Punjab and the Northwest Provinces. Dayananda's vision was to return contemporary Hinduism to a pristine Aryan religion (*Āryā Dharma*) based on the *Veda*, which he considered the ultimate source of knowledge. As the original Vedic religion, Ārya Dharma was a rational universal religion of a particular group of people (the Āryās), and as such was the crucible of civilization. Through extensive Sanskrit commentaries on the *Veda*, Dayananda sought to show that Western scientific knowledge was anticipated and superseded by the Veda.[48] Dayananda's emphasis on Vedic rationalism seems to be derived from Brāhmo teachings, with which he had had extensive contact. For Dayananda, Vedic revelation was monotheistic, and in his commentaries he shunned all references to polytheism in the Veda. Moreover, this Vedic monotheism was philosophically compatible with the monism of Advaita Vedānta, particularly the version of Advaita taught by Śankara, the founder of the Daśnami order, to which Dayananda belonged. These two strands—the monism of Advaita Vedānta and the monotheism of Śaivism (in which Śiva is both supreme being and personal God)—have a long tradition. However, the rejection of image worship and caste entailed in these teachings could find widespread acceptance only in Punjab, where there was a long tradition of imageless devotional worship and anticaste teachings.

Not surprisingly, many of Dayananda's early adherents in Lahore in 1871 included Sikhs, who did not have a taste for Brāhmo teachings. One of the Ārya Samāj's most important innovations was the establishment of what were known as Dayananda Anglo-Vedic (or D.A.V.) schools and colleges, which, partly because English teaching as well as Sanskrit was part of the core curriculum, attracted Ārya and non-Ārya Hindus and provided a popular alternative to the Anglo-vernacular schools run by Christian missionaries.[49] Through these schools and their extensive networks, the Ārya Samāj brought the debate on the nature of Hinduism to the public, helped to create a public sphere in which Hindus could voice their opinion, and very effectively mobilized "Hindu" consciousness throughout the twentieth century.

As noted above, many Sikhs, at least initially, found common cause with what eventually became identified as "Hindu" reformist movements such as the Brāhmo and Ārya Samāj. Part of the reason for this is that the boundaries demarcating Sikh from Hindu were not yet based on the category "religion"—understood as a monolithic and unified community of believers—and continued to remain fluid. Nevertheless it is possible to identify several distinctly Sikh responses to British rule that anticipate the formation of a public sphere among the Sikhs. These responses came initially from the Nirankārī and Nāmdhārī sects. The Nirankārīs, founded by Baba Dyal Das (1783–1853), took their name from their condemnation of idolatry and their participation in Hindu rituals that had become prevalent among many Sikhs. The Nāmdhārīs, founded by Baba Ram Singh (1816–84), came to be regarded as a separatist movement when they instituted a separate baptismal ritual and code of conduct. Ram

Singh advocated strict vegetarianism, the wearing of all-white dress, and loud chanting—because of which they were nicknamed *kūkās* (lit. "howlers"), on account of their spontaneous outbursts during devotional trances. In 1871 the Nāmdhārīs came into conflict with the British when they violently opposed the colonial administration's reintroduction of cow slaughter (previously banned by Maharaja Ranjit Singh), in the process killing Muslim butchers in Amritsar and Ludhiana. The British ruthlessly suppressed the uprising by tying sixty-five Nāmdhārīs to the mouths of cannons and blowing them to pieces.

By far the most influential Sikh reformist movement was the Singh Sabhā, founded in 1873 under aristocratic patronage. By 1879 the movement had suffered an internal schism that led to the formation of the conservative Amritsar-based faction led by Baba Khem Singh Bedi, and the more radical (and ultimately far more successful) Lahore-based faction led initially by Giani Ditt Singh and Principal Gurmukh Singh, and subsequently by such names as Kahn Singh Nabha, Teja Singh, Vir Singh, and Jodh Singh. Through its political functionary, the Chief Khalsā Diwan (CKD), a body set up in 1902 to jointly conduct the affairs of the Amritsar and Lahore factions, the Singh Sabhā movement achieved the most successful reinterpretation of a Sikhism adapted to modernity, one which continues to exert a hegemonic influence on Sikh self-consciousness. Their reformulation was based on the colonially inspired distinction between, on the one hand, a monotheistic-historical Sikhism centered on the authority of a clearly recognizable scripture and embodied by the Tat (authentic) Khalsā ideal, and, on the other hand, a pantheistic ahistorical Hinduism. Crucially, the Singh Sabhā redefined the means by which the tradition was communicated. By making use of British colonial patronage and new forms of transportation, commerce, and communication (especially the printing press), the Singh Sabhās were able to develop an extensive network of chapters across Northern India. Through the combined effect of tract publications and more systematic works of theology and history, the leading Singh Sabhā scholars redefined the doctrinal foundations of Sikhism in a way that would have been unimaginable only a few decades earlier.

While it is well established that reformist movements like the Singh Sabhā had a major impact on the enunciation of Sikh identity in the late nineteenth and early twentieth century, there continues to be a mistaken impression that a distinctly Sikh self-consciousness began when scholars associated with the Singh Sabhā movement began to insist all

of a sudden, as it were, that Sikhs were not Hindu. The 1898 tract publication entitled *"Ham Hindu Nahin"* ("We Are Not Hindus") by Kahn
Singh Nabha is usually cited as evidence of this.[50] Initially written in
Hindi (thereby indicating the audience being targeted), *"Ham Hindu
Nahin"* did indeed create a watershed in Sikh-Hindu relations, but it
would be factually more correct to say that this publication was written
as a response to the reformist and traditionalist Hindu formations that
had begun to claim that Sikhs were "Hindu." Roughly at the same time,
several tracts were published with the title *"Sikh Hindu Hain"* ("Sikhs
Are Hindus").[51] Clearly the late nineteenth-century debates concerning
the inclusion or exclusion of Sikhs were dependent on what exactly was
meant by the term "Hindu."

Although indigenous use of the term "Hindu" by Hindus themselves
can be traced to well before the fifteenth century, its usage is derived
from Persian Muslim influences and was primarily indicative of a distinction between people who were "native" and people who were foreign
(*mleccha*).[52] Specifically, the word "Hindu" is a Perso-Arabic variant on
the Sanskrit term *Sindhu*, which referred to those people who lived near
the river Indus in northwest India. The Arabic derivative of *Sindhu* is
Al-Hind, which refers to the people of the Indus region. Although these
broad connotations were never discarded, by the beginning of the nineteenth century the term "Hindu" had accrued strongly religious connotations that had been developed under Orientalist influences. By the late
nineteenth century, through the interactions between Orientalists, native
elite scholars, and missionaries, the term "Hindu" had become a master
signifier of a specifically religious identity.

From this perspective, Kahn Singh Nabha's *"Ham Hindu Nahin"* can
be regarded as a refutation of the nationalized/religionized version of
Hindu identity. Though regarded as a classic statement of Sikh identity,
"Ham Hindu Nahin" is not an outright negation of the term "Hindu" but
rather a negation of the term "Hindu" as a master signifier. There is a
subtle but important difference, for what changes is the logic of identity
itself. This crucial change in the understanding of identity had implications for the way in which Hindus and Sikhs could enunciate their identities both in the colonial period and today. As a consequence, one cannot
say that the articulation of Sikh identity began in the colonial period. If
what changed was the way in which identity was conceived, then it is
necessary to consider the possibility that identity enunciation, when it is
associated with or translated through "religion," becomes something else

entirely, with tangible consequences in the social domain. This thesis will
be developed in greater detail over the next two chapters.

Traditionalists

In practical terms the reformist articulation, which projected itself as a laicized humanistic Hinduism, had clearly discernible impacts.
Insofar as it was an indigenous confirmation of the Orientalist image of
Hinduism, it clearly frustrated missionaries and Anglicists, who considered Hinduism to be incapable of adopting a universalist standpoint and
unable to qualify as a proper religion. In addition, the projection of a laicized Hinduism left reformists isolated from mainstream Hindu society,
whether this was in Bengal, Banaras, or Punjab.

The vast majority of non-Muslim society in Northern India had since
the fourteenth century become associated with one or another of the various strands of devotional practice known as *bhakti*, and particularly with
Vaiṣṇava *bhakti*, which eventually became the face of contemporary
Hinduism. Traditionalist Hindus who belonged to one or another of the
Vaiṣṇava *bhakti* strands defined themselves according to the following
tenets and practices: (i) that *Veda* and *Purāṇā* (*śruti* and *smṛti*) are both
legitimate authorities; (ii) that the *Dharmaśastras* remain authoritative as
sources for formulating religious and civil law, and *varṇāśrama dharma*
is not open to change or questioning; (iii) that temple and ritual practice as
well as the role of gurus and mahants is central; (iv) that the central mode
of practice consists in devotion (*bhakti*), normally to a deity or idol.[53]

In order to protect these long-running traditions and practices, traditionalists responded by forming *dharma sabhās* (lit. "associations bound
by duty to caste"). Like the Orientalists, the missionaries, and their reformist counterparts, traditionalists also utilized vernacular print media
and founded newspapers to help galvanize public opinion in India. In
order to do so, however, they ended up professing a version of a homogenized Hinduism with a centralized authority. The earliest example
of traditionalist public response corresponds to the appearance of indigenous newspapers such as the *Samācār Candrikā,* published as early as
1822 by Bhabhanicaran, and the formation of the Dharma Sabhā in Calcutta. The combination of print and community organization helped to
fuel popular resistance to British rule, to missionary proselytization, and
to those considered native turncoats, such as the Brāhmos. Early issues

of the *Candrikā* discussed popular Hindu practices such as idol worship, the institution of caste, the status of Sanskrit versus vernaculars, and female education, among other issues. Grounded in Vaiṣṇava practice and theology, the main cause was to preserve the pristine and perennial tradition of the Hindus (*sanātana dharma*) in a modern age. Articles and editorials aimed to "craft a public image of Indian religion but also to promote openly Hindu unity and identity by patterning religious activity for Hindus while decentring potentially divisive issues of belief and Hindu sectarianism."[54]

By December 1829, however, the issues at stake had reached a crisis point, after the governor-general of India, William Bentick, outlawed the practice known as *sahamarana* (dying along with), which had been labeled by British observers as "*satī*." Bentick intervened to prohibit women from burning themselves on the pyres that consumed their husbands' corpses. By doing so, Bentick effectively rejected a promise — in place since 1793 — that the colonial government would not attempt to regulate religious practice.[55] Evangelicals and Anglicists in England had long since been lobbying Parliament to outlaw *satī*. This issue, more than any other, brought to a head the conflicts brewing among different groups in India, for *satī* came to assume iconic status for Christians, who opposed it, and traditionalist Hindus, who sought to defend it. One of the first projects undertaken by the Calcutta Dharma Sabhā, formed in 1830, was to collect signatures to repeal the law, a move that ultimately failed to make any headway.

In the decades following the formation of the original Dharma Sabhā in Calcutta, many similar *dharma sabhās* sprang into existence all over North India. Of these it was the Kāśī Dharma Sabhā that eventually became the most important. Kāśī is the earlier name of Varanasi (Banaras), one of the seven sacred cities for Hindus, and the center of sacerdotal tradition. Because of its association with Kāśī, this particular *dharma sabhā* came to exert immense influence on the self-representations of the *dharma sabhā* — the center of Vaiṣṇava *bhakti* — as *sanātana dharma*. Vasudha Dalmia identifies two key elements that enabled the consolidation of the position of Vaiṣṇava *bhakti* as broadly representative of the homogenous entity we know today as "Hinduism."

One element is the manipulation of the public sphere by traditionalist spokesmen such as Hariścandra Bhāratendu. As with the Calcutta Dharma Sabhā, the formation of public opinion in Banaras took place primarily on the platform provided by the vernacular newspapers and journals edited by Hariścandar. The formation of public opinion in the vernacular medium can be regarded as a counterresistance to the Western colonial idiom.[56] The second element is the identification of Vaiṣṇava *bhakti* within the public domain as representative of the religion of the Hindus. The process by which this happened is again clearly defined in the vernacular press. To do this it was necessary first to identify a particular tradition (the Vaiṣṇava) as the proper "religion" of the Hindus by amalgamating the various other strands of Vaiṣṇava tradition (*sampradāyas*) into a homogenous "Hinduism" of pan-continental dimensions; second, to link these traditions linguistically to the mainstream Sanskritic tradition; and third, to link them racially to Aryan Hindus.

According to Vasudha Dalmia, there are several distinct stages in the evolution of this homogenized "Hinduism," which can be outlined as follows.[57] The first stage was the shift in sensibilities of Hindus, from a precolonial ease with heterogeneity and multiplicity of Hindu traditions to what might be called a *dis*-ease with this very same constitutive heterogeneity or multiplicity. Prompted by Orientalists, missionaries, and reformists, this dis-ease took the form of a self-questioning: What exactly holds Hindus together at the level of belief? What forms the *unifying* core or center of Hindu tradition? What forces are inimical to the formation as a whole? Clearly, questions such as these prompted the need for internal consolidation and, in order for this consolidation to happen, the need for formation based on unity rather than multiplicity. Such internal consolidation could be brought about only by a unifying ideology. Consequently, there was a widening of boundaries to include other Vaiṣṇava traditions through a manifesto that set out rules for membership in this unified entity. This manifesto stressed two central items: (i) the monotheistic nature of the overarching Vaiṣṇava formation, and (ii) the propagation of *bhakti* as the essence of Vaiṣṇava practice. Both of these elements became central to the traditionalist formulation of Vaiṣṇavism as the "religion of the Hindus."[58]

But how was this intimate connection between *bhakti* and monotheism forged? In the construction of *bhakti* as the essential component of the "religion of the Hindus," Dalmia notes that the stand of traditionalist spokesmen like Hariścandra and his contemporaries concerning the Vaiṣṇava tradition in their conception of Hindu *dharma* and the increasing emphasis on *bhakti* as a transcendent category

> was by no means an isolated attempt to legitimize their own local and
> regional position. Their views coincided with a dominant stream of

thought and research as it was crystallizing in the nineteenth century, so that the two mutually reinforced each other and, to some extent, even expressly sought mutual legitimation, though admittedly with variations and some inevitable contradictions.[59]

In Hariścandra's writings there is, for example, a new focus on monotheism as natural to Vaiṣṇavism, a move that was made easier once the *Bhāgvata Puraṇā* and the *Gītā* were emphasized as canonical texts. To further solidify this stance, Hariścandra produced exegeses and translations of the *bhakti sūtras*. The key move in these exegeses was to oppose Advaita Vedānta to *bhakti* in order to uproot the former and make room for the love of a personal God as well as advocacy of the erotic, emotional, and ritual aspects of *bhakti*, even though this was against the intellectual tide of the time. Hariścandra's strategy was in tune with works such as Schlegel's *Über die Sprache und Weisheit der Indier* (1808) which, against the early Orientalists, had identified Viṣṇu as the central deity of a sun-worshiping Ur-monotheism that was prevalent in the Vedic Aryan peoples. Also, by 1846 the leading British Indologist H. H. Wilson had begun to represent *bhakti* both as a form of religion and as an innovative development on "primitive forms" such as Vedānta. This was effectively the start of the theory of *bhakti* as a reform movement internal to Hinduism that had received its impetus for reviving its dormant monotheistic tendencies from the presence of Islam in India.

Rather more difficult for Hariścandra, however, was the task of creating a pan-Indian unity and coherence of various Hindu sects around Vaiṣṇavism. This was accomplished by narrating the origin and spread of other Vaiṣṇava sects in relation to each other and within a historical sequence that excluded Śaivism, Vedāntism (or *jñāna*), Jainism, and Buddhism. By doing this Hariścandra was further able to argue that monotheism was indigenous to South Asia, although it had remained dormant and dispersed; it was not imported through either Islam or Christianity. In the nineteenth century, the multiple monotheistic Hindu sects coalesced into the dominant Vaiṣṇava stream headed by the Kāśī Dharma Sabhā. In her work *Bhakti and the Bhakti Movement*, Krishna Sharma argues that this particular move was to a large extent dependent on and in a sense reinforced by a series of new developments in the field of Indology during the latter half of the nineteenth century. These moves were instigated by names such as Albrect Weber and Friedrich Lorinser working in Germany, and Monier Monier-Williams and George Grierson working in England.[60]

These developments began in 1868 with the publication of Albrect Weber's *Über die Kṛṣṇajanāshṭamī*, which linked the Krishna myths with Christianity. A decade later Lorinser translated the *Bhāgvata Gītā* and identified it specifically as a *bhakti* text. However, it was Monier-Williams who argued that Vaiṣṇava *bhakti* was the only cultic formation in India that possessed the ingredients of monotheism.[61] This was achieved by overcoming the polytheistic trinity of Brahma-Viṣṇu-Śiva and absorbing it into the figure of Viṣṇu. Monier-Williams then articulated a dialectical schema that purported to demonstrate how Hindu sects had evolved into "religions." The grand narrative in this dialectical schema involved a loss of religiosity, or a fall from the Ur-monotheism of early Vedic culture into the monistic philosophy of Brahmanism, followed by a further degradation into Śaivism, ending with a revival during the Islamic era in the form of *bhakti*.[62] This revival of *bhakti* was of course reinforced by the presence of the Aryan British race and Christian religion in India since the early eighteenth century. Monier-Williams was responsible for one of the most prevalent schemas for understanding Hinduism, namely, the progression from *karma mārg* (ritual path), to *jñana mārg* (path of wisdom/philosophy exemplified by Vedāntic monism), and ending with the *bhakti mārg* (path of devotion to a personal God, or Hindu monotheism).[63] The corresponding philosophical categories governing this evolution are monism, polytheism, and monotheism.

Thus it is the collusion or interaction between Indologists and native elites (both traditionalists and reformists) that helped to crystalize a pervasive theory of *bhakti*, which subsequently passed into the *Religionswissenschaft* and from there into modern South Asian studies. Krishna Sharma has drawn attention to three factors that define this "*bhakti* theory." The three factors that constitute the meaning of *bhakti* are: (i) a belief in a personal God, or "personalistic faith" as opposed to "impersonalistic philosophy"; (ii) a non-monistic view of reality; (iii) the negation of *jñāna* (knowledge/philosophy) as enabling wisdom. However, as Sharma rightly points out, *bhakti* is a generic term indicative of *bhāva*, which is a condition or mood of existence, a state of mind governed by sensuous feeling or emotion rather than nonsensuous intellect. *Bhakti* has never suggested any theology or doctrine, nor any exclusive reference to a personal God. As such the current "academic definition of bhakti is not corroborated by Hindu evidence. It is entirely a modern formation and can be traced back to the nineteenth century," particularly to the work of the Indologists mentioned above.[64]

According to this academic definition, *bhakti* was identified with Advaita Vedānta, and thus defined as antagonistic to "philosophy" and any path of true contemplation or wisdom. It was instead defined as a determinate "religion" based on devotion to a God whose central attribute is existence—being—a God to whom the devotee could relate herself through emotion and the senses.[65] Hence its designation as *saguṇa-bhakti*—a form of devotion or love toward a being that can be predicated. Through its further identification with the tradition of Vaiṣṇavism, which in turn comes to be seen as "Hindu monotheism," *saguṇa-bhakti* was made to appear incompatible with *nirguṇa-bhakti*—a form of devotion or love toward a being whose central attribute is nonexistence, a being that cannot be predicated. Yet throughout Indian history *nirguṇa-bhakti* was given due recognition by all *astika* groups—those who broadly subscribed to a doctrine of existence or being as opposed to pure nothingness. Similarly, the central ideas of Advaita Vedānta (the impersonal nature of the divine, nondualism between man and God) are also constitutive of the multidimensional *saguṇa-bhakti* traditions. In fact Hindu thinkers and practitioners almost never kept *jñāna* ("philosophy") and *bhakti* ("devotion") apart.

In a sense Sharma goes too far in attributing the current academic definition of *bhakti* solely to the work of the Indologists. It is more useful to suggest that the academic theory of *bhakti* arose from the ideological interaction and collaboration between Indologists and traditionalist native elites. This is in turn led to the coining of a new nationalist idiom that purports to speak in the name of tradition even as it overcomes the heterological tendencies implicit in Hindu tradition prior to the colonial encounter. It is precisely because of this collusion between Britons and Indians that the theory cannot be called a *misrepresentation* of *bhakti*—it is rather a *transformation* of the idiom of *bhakti* into a nationalist idiom.

Nevertheless, Sharma's assessment points to an aspect that is often underemphasized by historians of religion or specialists in modern South Asian studies. This is the fact that the transformation of the heterological tendencies of *bhakti* prior to colonialism—what Sharma calls "misrepresentation" or "bias"—is determined by two fundamental principles, derived from Western sources. One is the separation between religion and philosophy and the second is the dictum that theism (or "true religion") implies belief, specifically belief in a personal God. Indeed, the real value of Sharma's work lies in its having pointed to an issue that continues to be overlooked: namely, that although the current "*bhakti* theory" was shaped by Indologists, their own formulations were in turn subject to some very important intellectual changes going on in Western thought at that time. Particularly important in this regard is the relationship between religion and philosophy (or between theology and philosophy). Indeed, the conceptual relationship between the categories monotheism/monism/ pantheism is sharpened and determined by intellectual and political battles going on in the European academies. At stake in these intellectual and political battles was a major shift in the concept of religion, that was itself due to the pluralization of knowledge about other "religions." This shift had consequences for how missionaries and Indologists represented not only Christian religion but the "religions" of other cultures. And inadvertently, through these colonizers' interaction/encounter with the native elites, this specific representation impacted the way native elites in India understood the meaning of "religion."

Although Sharma does not acknowledge it, what helps this shift is a link between the mechanics of representation (the nature of thought or thinking as the work proper to the domain of philosophy) and the resulting definition of "religion." The definition of religion, in other words, cannot be taken for granted as something given by Christian missionaries, for they too were subject to the forces that helped to change the definition of one's own religion or the religions of others. Rather, philosophy—as the domain that makes the rules for thinking, conceptualizing, and categorizing—was itself being reformulated in this battle. As we shall see in chapter 2, the result of philosophy's reformulation in the nineteenth century is the incorporation of the idea of God's existence into the act of thinking itself, and therefore into the very constitution of reason.

Rethinking the "Interactionist" Model of Colonial Agency

Krishna Sharma's thesis is an important contribution to our understanding of the colonial encounter insofar as she discerns, albeit indirectly, a shift in the relationship between philosophy and religion. She does this by highlighting an important difference between the notion of religion deployed by early Orientalists and philosophers during the 1770s to 1820s, and that deployed by Indologists and philosophers after the mid-nineteenth century. Sharma's work indirectly suggests the need to reassess the nature of the colonial idiom as the medium of thought and as the medium into which translation occurs into the target language. It is therefore necessary to reassess the interaction between colonizer and colonized, to which many social scientists too easily attribute a "dialogical" status.

At stake here is a theory of translation that coincides with a theory of religion, and vice versa. Social scientists too easily assume that notions like dialogue or interaction necessarily involve some aspect of communication, but rarely consider that this very idea of communication also involves an obfuscation of translation. It has become something of a conventional wisdom to conceptualize this interaction as a dialogue among concerned and interested persons and groups in colonial North India who had stakes in producing a certain kind of reading and who colluded in the creation of a modernist discourse. This collusion resulted in an accommodation and assimilation of Western ideas, offered resistance to the colonizer by making connections to classical or precolonial traditions, and ultimately helped the native elites to make a transition to the modern nationalist idiom. But this particular understanding of colonial interaction depends on an implicit model of communication in which both parties are assumed to be capable of speaking and thinking freely with each other. In short, this model considers the indigenous elites to be agents who collaborated of their own free will and were equally responsible for shaping the face of modern Hinduism, Sikhism, etc.

Far from clarifying the issue, however, this implicit model of communication actually raises further questions. For example, although it is empirically correct to say that the native elites "freely" collaborated, a problem arises when we probe the nature of this "freedom" and its motivations. To put it differently: What is agency, and how is it defined in such instances? Must not a particular type of subject/agent as *sovereign* already be assumed in order for the "dialogical" model to be established? Given that the evidence for agency/freedom is largely empirical (the notion that the native elites were able to enter into conversation with the colonizer, or that they could read, understand, and translate into the colonizer's language) isn't the nature of agency determined in advance by epistemological considerations? Isn't the nature of agency, then, already presupposed as epistemic: that the speech of native elites would be deemed successful, that it produced the required result, namely, the achievement of recognition by the colonizer? Yet what seems to be forgotten here is that the success of this communication was contingent on achieving a break with their own language horizons. As I shall argue below, behind the assumption of "dialogue," or free interaction, is the assumption of intersubjective and therefore *unhindered* communication between colonizer and colonized, which in turn is linked to a predetermination of translation as an apolitical process of exchange of speech and ideas. The idea is disavowed that the colonial state always already both determines the conceptual framework of communication and, as a result of this, determines the nature of translation in a way that closes the field of the political. To pose the idea of unhindered or intersubjective communication as a question or a problem is to think about this issue from a political perspective, or to think about translation as the opening of the political.

From a political perspective, therefore, it could be argued that the interactionist thesis has relatively limited purchase. For what is much less clear is the status of the central category, namely "religion," that for scholars such as Pandey, van der Veer, Dalmia, and Pennington constitutes the site of the encounter/interaction/transformation. Unlike Marxist accounts of coloniality in which religion is equated with primitivity and thereby written out of history, these scholars have strived to make religion more visible both as a concept of modernity and as the site of historical interaction between India and Britain. Nonetheless, the category "religion" still continues to be an unresolved issue in their studies. The main problem seems to be that "religion" is assumed to be a cross-cultural and generalizable category that is always already there, and that can be unproblematically affirmed by both Christians and Hindus, something they can both recognize and respond to despite the fact that they have different cultural histories. The problem seems to reside in the presumed symmetry between religion and response (as unhindered communication), between religion and intersubjectivity. Related to this assumption of intersubjectivity is the notion of what counts as a subject or agent.

In contradistinction, a more useful form of questioning might ask how a modern Western understanding of religion became dominant in the nineteenth century, and how it was willingly accepted by other cultures as a universal concept. How does the project of modernization provide a new conceptual framework in which colonizer and colonized mutually recognize themselves as subjects? At stake here are the legitimacy of the category "Hinduism" and, directly related to this, the legitimacy of subjects who respond affirmatively to it and in doing so ground their identity as primarily religious. Part of the problem here is the lack of attention to the category "religion" *as a question*, that is to say, a matter not only that can be theorized, but that tells us something about the nature of theory itself.

Let me clarify what I mean by the phrase "religion as a question" by way of reference to the current debate regarding the label "Hinduism" (or for that matter "Sikhism"). The main issues in this debate are usefully summarized by Brian Pennington in his book *Was Hinduism Invented?*. The central issue seems to be something like this: given that the term "Hindu" has signified regional, cultural, and religious identifications, and from the twentieth century onward comes to be associated with nationalist connections, is there any set of pan-Indic practices and identities that one can meaningfully gather under a single label like "Hinduism"? Scholarly opinion seems to be divided into two main camps: there are the "constructionists" (influenced by Said's strand of postcolonial theory), who claim that entities such as "Hinduism," "Sikhism," etc., never existed in their current form and are relatively recent constructs that emerged primarily as a result of the encounter with colonialism and modernity;[66] and there are the "naturalists," who argue that however diffuse or multivalent the term "Hinduism" might be, it is nevertheless identifiable and therefore meaningful as an analytical category and as a descriptive label, and, moreover, it is true to observed social and historical reality.[67]

For Pennington, the debate over the "appropriateness of the term 'Hinduism' is also an aspect of the larger question about the genealogy of the concept of religion."[68] Thus for naturalists, even though there isn't a direct linguistic equivalent for "religion" within Indian languages, religion is a totally translatable and therefore universal concept that exists naturally through correspondence or analogy in Hindu culture and language. For the constructionists, however, religion is a concept specific to Western culture and history. It became associated with Hindu traditions because of Western imperialist hegemony and is neither legitimate nor useful for looking at Indian cultures.

While acknowledging the cogency of constructionist claims, Pennington points out that Hindus themselves never really contested the clearly developing category of "Hinduism." The absence of indigenous self-critique suggests that the category "Hinduism" made sense to Hindus and that it corresponded to certain elements of Indian self-understanding. Without some prior self-understanding, with which the "emergent concept Hinduism resonated," there could have been "no basis for an intercultural debate (i.e., between British rulers and Indian subjects) or an intercultural one (between opposing Hindu groups) on issues related to

Hindu teaching without some implicit acceptance of the very category already in place."[69] Pennington's argument does attempt to mediate the gap between constructionists and naturalists by reiterating van der Veer's argument that the collectivity of formations known today as "Hinduism" had a precolonial continuity of *longue durée*, but these formations were undeniably altered as a result of the encounter with European imperialism, which resulted in discursive interactions between Britons and Hindus that contributed in turn to the growth of the homogenized entity known as "Hinduism."

Again, all this really achieves little more than to reaffirm the idea that religion was always present in India although it changed in the nineteenth century, an affirmation based on the assumption that religion is a generalizable and therefore elastic concept that can be stretched to cover the contingencies of each age.[70] Moreover, the logic of presupposing that "religion" can, however minimally, be applied to precolonial indigenous formations elides other crucial issues. Although Advaita Vedānta had become more or less established as the "central theology of Hinduism" by the first decade of the nineteenth century, and Hinduism had been made characterizable as a monistic philosophy of the learned classes rather than as a popular religion in the proper sense of the term, the element that is central to popular Hinduism today—namely, *bhakti,* or Hindu devotionalism, identifiable with its sects or *sampradāyas*—had yet to achieve recognition as "religion" in the sense that "religion" was perceived in the nineteenth and twentieth century. In fact, as noted above, the practice known as *bhakti* had to struggle to become identifiable with the category "religion," and this process took a period of time. It cannot simply be assumed, therefore, that indigenous precolonial formations were constituted as "religion," which in turn suggests that we cannot take the term "religion" to be as readily translatable as is assumed by many historians and social scientists.

But perhaps the debate between constructionists and naturalists is not as polarized as it seems. It may actually be more helpful to suggest that the process of *transformation*, which occurred as a result of the "discursive interaction" between Britons and Hindus, has not yet been rigorously conceptualized. I suggest this because there are clues in Pennington's own analysis that point to a different solution. At several points in his argument against the constructionists Pennington makes reference to the term "Hinduism" as a *"clearly developing category,"* suggesting that "Hinduism" is an *"emergent concept"* and that *"the idea of Hinduism slowly took shape*" (italics mine).[71] Although Pennington doesn't seem to be aware of it, these assertions give an important clue to an alternative direction in which the debate could be taken, for they imply that the idea of "Hinduism" did not have shape or form *before* the colonial encounter. The *idea* came into form and therefore into existence only after this encounter.

Accepting that the idea of "Hinduism" *slowly took shape*, was this not because, prior to this happening, the category of religion itself needed to take shape in the Hindu imagination? It needed to attain form, which means that it may have been formless or nonexistent as a regulative idea for Hindus prior to colonialism. The way in which notions such as "interaction," "discursive relations," and "dialogue" seem to elide the operations through which an idea takes shape, and therefore the operations of thought through which the Hindu mind is eventually transformed, should alert us to the fact that the question of language is central to this entire issue. An idea can take shape only in the mind, and only through the process of thought. Thought itself takes a universally recognizable shape or form only through words or language. Yet what seems to be assumed in the "interactionist" model is (i) that the concept(ualization) of religion is independent of language, that it has an objective or universal meaning(s) independent of language (more precisely, it is objective and universal *because* it is independent of language), and (ii) that, if language is somehow necessary to the process of subject formation, religion is independent of subjectivity.

But what if the concept of religion were allowed to remain in question, as something that cannot and perhaps should not be decided upon? Such a possibility arises if we take language to be pivotal in the transformation of Hindu consciousness during the colonial encounter, and consequently central to the *slow taking shape* of the idea of "Hinduism." Although precolonial Hindus may not have possessed a linguistic equivalent of the term "religion," the transformation helped to manufacture a nationalist subject capable of *enunciating* his or her subjectivity through the concept "religion." Stated differently, the central issue can be framed in the following terms: what if the so-called fact or datum of "religious" identity is connected to the possibility of the concept of religion *being enunciated*, and therefore, to the possibility of there coming into existence a proper linguistic medium, a medium that allows a certain kind of universalization of language, and that may not have existed prior to the colonial encounter? To be more specific, what if the datum of "Hinduism" comes into existence only when Hindus, who previously did not possess such a term, *slowly come to enunciate* it as if it were their own, as if it had always existed within their language and culture? What if the convergence between religion and language is so close that the taking shape of the idea of religion is not only a taking shape *within* language but, at the very same time, the taking shape *of* a language? Furthermore, what if religion and language are indissociably linked to the birth of a new subjectivity, specifically in this case the subjectivity of the nationalist elites, which mistakenly comes to be represented as a (secular) linguistic identity as opposed to a religious identity, as if these were two different things?

This intimate proximity between language and religion suggests a different way of approaching the phenomenon—which has variously been termed "transformation," "conversion to modernity," and "colonial interaction"—than the common desire among scholars to give agency back to the colonial subject, whether it is through religion or history. What these now-standard methods of imputing agency overlook is that transformation is first and foremost a transformation of agency, and therefore a reforming or recreation of it. Moreover, the emphasis on agency fails to recognize that the proximity between language and religion constitutes what I would call the peculiarity of Indian decolonization. This peculiarity concerns the situation in which Indians and Britons engaged with the public sphere by enunciating identities that were *brought into existence* through a process of mutual configuration that is simultaneously linguistic and religious.

It is important to note here that this is not just theoretical conjecture. For some time now it has been recognized that language and religion have both exerted enormous influence on the development of nationalism in South Asia. Events such as the partitioning of India in 1947 into the apparent reality of an Urdu-speaking Muslim nation, Pakistan, and a Hindi-speaking India, populated mainly by Hindus; the inauguration of linguistic states in India in 1955; the anti-Hindi agitation in South India in 1965; and the inauguration of a Punjabi Suba in 1965 following mostly Sikh agitation—all testify to the empirical manifestation of these two symbols in recent years. But most scholarly treatments of these events have taken "language" and "religion" not only to be conceptually distinct entities, but as conferring distinctness on languages and religions that comprise these two fields. However, in the nineteenth century neither the standardized "religions" Hinduism/Islam/Sikhism nor the standardized languages Hindi/Urdu/Punjabi that now are taken to correspond naturally to them had yet "found expression in the consciousness, actions and cultural performances of the human actors they describe."[72] What eventually came to be accepted by the late nineteenth and early twentieth centuries as religious identity and/or linguistic identity was not to be found before this time.

In his study *The Construction of Religious Boundaries*, Harjot Oberoi observes:

> It is not without reason that Indian languages do not possess a noun for religion as signifying a single uniform and centralized community of believers. If the work carried out in linguistic cognition is correct, the absence of such a term is most revealing. . . . From the time of the so-called Sapir-Whorf hypothesis, it has become widely recognized that language plays a pivotal role in our construction of reality and the way we act on that reality. This insight has been further consolidated in the field of ethnosemantics, whose proponents assert that all culturally significant phenomena tend to be reflected in lexical, grammatical or synthetic structures.
>
> If one were to follow these propositions, then it is hard to conceive of an organized religion in the absence of an indigenous taxon confirming its existence, for the more central a cultural form is to a people, the more reason for it to find concordance in an overt category of their language.[73]

It is interesting to note that Oberoi's observation concerning the construction of religious identity in colonial India finds equal cogency in the case of language identities in India during the same period. As the work of different scholars seems to imply, what most language speakers regard as their "mother tongue"—signifying a distinct linguistic identity and a definite origin that applies to a uniformly single, homogenized, and centralized community of language users (Urdu, Hindi, Punjabi)—is also the result of a certain constructive imagining that cannot be separated from the construction of religion in the nineteenth century. Rather, the prevalent language situation even up to the mid-nineteenth century was a very fluid one. Following the work of cultural theorist Naoki Sakai, it could be suggested that the normative mode of address between language users in precolonial India was what might be described as "heterolingual," a term that reflects not only the coexistence of a multiplicity of languages on the subcontinent but a kind of mutual interaction and transformation that is best described as *co-contamination*. By the late nineteenth century, how-ever, the heterolingual language situation had given way to a mode of address that Sakai calls "homolingual"—a term that can be used to describe the homogenization of native Indian languages according to a particular standard. That standard was English.

Modes of Address: English and the Purification of Native Speech

It will be helpful here to elaborate on Sakai's notion of heterolingual and homolingual address and how these terms relate to the language situation of precolonial India. "Homolingual address" signifies a manner of relating to other speakers in which the addresser adopts the stance of being a representative of a homogenous language community and addresses others whom s/he believes also represent an equally homogenous language community.[74] This is not the same as having a common language and belonging to the same language community. Rather, people can belong to different languages—say, English and "Hindustanee"—and still address themselves homolingually. In homolingual address the collectivity "we" corresponds to a commonality built on an assumed assurance of immediate and reciprocal recognition between two distinct subjects A and B. These subjects understand each other because there is reciprocal transparent communication between them in a homogenous medium. That is to say, there is no need for translation between subjects A and B.

In contrast, heterolinguality can be described as a mode of address that resists conformity to the typically modern notion of communication understood as the successful transfer of meanings and information.[75] In heterolingual address such transfer of meaning and information is not necessarily the central criterion. Translation therefore takes place at every reception. Though several languages may encounter one other, there is no reciprocal apprehension nor is transparent communication guaranteed between addresser and addressee. The "we," or commonality, of heterolingual address is based on a disparity not only between addresser and addressee, but of addresser/addressee within himself. There is an otherness or foreignness that is intrinsic to addresser and addressee. The "we" of heterolingual address therefore designates a nonrelational relation, that is, a relation that is performative in nature irrespective of whether or not "we" communicate.[76]

These two modes of address imply two different attitudes with regard to the otherness of the addresser/addressee. In homolingual address the self is self and other is other. Self cannot be (with/in or part of) the other and disparity exists only *between* subjects, not *within* subjects. In heterolingual address, the boundaries between self and other are more blurred. Because self can contain other and vice versa, subjectivity is indeterminate and fluid. It moves back and forth, or, to use Sakai's term, "oscillates" between self and other. Consequently, in heterolingual address, the movement of translation is normal to the constitution of self. In homolingual address, translation is replaced by the *representation of* translation, that is, by an economy of translation as unhindered communication. This representation of translation results from the operations of the imagination, a process whereby the mind creates an imaginary schema or diagram onto which the two language unities A and B, corresponding to the unified subjects A and B, are located. Being thus spatialized onto a representation, the indeterminacy proper to languages is erased, and as a result the personality or subjectivity is fixed as its temporality is erased. Sakai goes further and draws out the implications of this operation, stressing that

only in the representation of translation can we construe the process of translation as a transfer of some message from "this" side to "that" side, as a dialogue between one person and another, as if dialogue should necessarily take place according to the model of communication. Thus the representation of translation also enables the representation of ethnic or national subjects, and in spite of the presence of the translator who is always in between, translation, no longer as difference or repetition but as representation, is made to discriminatorily posit one language unity against another (and one "cultural" unity against another). In this sense the representation of translation transforms *difference in repetition* into *species difference* (diaphora) between two specific identities, and helps constitute the putative unities of national languages, and thereby reinscribes the initial difference and incommensurality as a specific, that is, commensurate and conceptual difference between two particular languages within the continuity of the generality of Language. As a result of this displacement, translation is represented as a form of communication between two fully formed, different but *comparable*, language communities.[77]

In many ways the term "heterolingual" usefully describes the state of language/speech relations prevalent in precolonial India. On their arrival in India the British found a very complex and confusing language situation. The commonly spoken language of North India first encountered by the British was an undifferentiated blend of tongues. This was a composite language comprised of several vernaculars, with a varying admixture of Sanskrit, Persian, and Arabic, depending on the region and social context in which this language was spoken. The British initially referred to this language as "Moors," "Indostan," and later "Hindustanee," but it was commonly known to its native speakers as *Khari-boli*. Despite its complexity, its fluidity, and the fact that it defied classification, the British quickly recognized three levels or styles in "Moors."[78] The highest level was the "High Court or Persian Style," which was the "pompous and pedantic language of literature and politics" that drew heavily on Arabic and Persian vocabulary. The lowest level was the "vulgar" component, which the British believed was spoken by the "Hindoos" and the lower order of servants. Referred to as "Hinduee," this "vulgar" level had the smallest admixture of "foreign" words and was thought to be the pristine, though rustic, language of the Hindus prior to the Muslim invasions of India. The fluidity of this language was due to the fact that, compared to languages such as Sanskrit, Persian, and Arabic, it had no written grammar and was often thought of as a kind of "jargon" or "pidgin" than a proper language.[79]

The heterogeneity of Hindustanee is attested to by the observations of the first Orientalist scholars and employees of the East India Company. Men like William Jones, Charles Wilkins, and H. T. Colebrook began the process of mapping the linguistic and cultural terms ("manners and customs") of the Indians as a preparation for administrative measures soon to follow.[80] Although Jones and his colleagues had no interest in Christianizing the Indians, he nonetheless expressed surprise and disappointment over the currently hybridized state of Indian languages and religions, which to him had fallen during the last nine hundred years or so from a former state of purity (the so-called Indian Golden Age) through the corrupting influence of Islamic rule. A jurist by profession, Jones expressed frustration at his local native informants for their blending of tongues, resulting in "insincerity," "infidelity," and a high frequency of perjury in the native speech. The "oath of a low native" had little value, for they committed perjury "with as little remorse as if it were proof of ingenuity, or even a merit."[81] These observations were echoed by administrators and missionaries, who were constantly thwarted in their attempts to address the natives "in their own language"; the natives appeared not to recognize a single language that they could call their own, nor as a consequence of this confusion could they register a satisfactory response to the question "What is your religion?." The goal of conversion to Christianity could not be realized unless there was first a correspondence of concepts, one language : one religion, both of which were simply lacking in their present state; even before that, however, there needed to be found a ground or horizon upon which such a translation/conversion could happen.

The only way the British could hope to achieve such correspondence was to rectify what they perceived as the damage done by Islamic corruption, by removing its influence from the presently common language, called *Hindoostanee*, or Moors, by early European observers and spoken by Hindus and Muslims alike. For the British this could only be accomplished by classifying and codifying the hybridized mess that constituted the spoken language, and this had to be effected through the efforts of grammarians like William Jones, Nathaniel Halhed, and especially John Gilchrist.[82] The work of these early grammarians was generally guided by the prevailing perception of the essentially "religious" difference between Hindus and Muslims and fostered by a suspicion of any process that breached the boundary between self and other. Despite the blending of languages over time to form the prevalent *Hindoostanee*, this perceived difference was institutionalized through educational bodies such as the Oriental Seminar at Calcutta, founded by John Gilchrist. Following Jones and Halhed, Gilchrist designated the popular (vulgarized and degraded) speech of the country as *Hindoostanee*, a term thereby denoting all the inhabitants of India. Insofar as it was the language of the multitude, Hindustani stood in need of correction. The rectified form of Hindustani, designated *Hinduwee,* would then correspond to the language of the Hindus before the Muslim invasion:

> We should invariably discard all other denominations of the popular speech of this country, including the unmeaning word Moors and substitute for them *Hindoostanee*, whether the people here constantly do so or not, as they can hardly discriminate sufficiently to observe the use and propriety of such distinctions, even when pointed out to them. *Hinduwee,* I have treated as the exclusive property of the Hindoos alone, and have constantly applied it to the old language of India, which prevailed before the Moosulman invasion; and in fact now constitutes among them, the base or ground work of the *Hindoostanee,* a comparatively recent superstructure, composed of Arabic and Persian, in which the two last may be considered in the same relation, that Latin

and French bear to English, while we may justly treat the *Hinduwee* of the modern speech or *Hindoostanee*, as the Saxon of the former.[83]

Gilchrist gave up his army post in the 1790s and took upon himself the job of learning and codifying this spoken language, insisting, to the chagrin of his Indian collaborators, that it must have had a grammar at one time. In his writings Gilchrist often castigated his Indian informants and collaborators for failing to take their own mother tongue seriously. He seemed genuinely surprised by the negative tone of their responses to his queries, when they even asked whether "it was ever yet known in any country that men had to consult vocabularies and rudiments for their own vernacular speech?."[84] This resistance notwithstanding, Gilchrist and others knew that the need to codify and create grammars was a task whose outcome would be immensely beneficial to the British, given that the spoken language represented nothing less than the *lingua franca* of the country and a command of the language meant an acquisition of the language of command. Gilchrist's publications, including *A Grammar of the Hindoostanee Language* (1796) and *The Oriental Linguist* (1798), had two major effects. First, they accelerated language acquisition among first-language users such as military personnel and administrators. Second, they provided the impetus for "fixing" the hybrid and fluid nature of the spoken languages and the creation of modern standard languages such as Hindi and Urdu, a point I shall take up in more detail below.

Naturally the model adopted for standardizing the spoken languages of the subcontinent was the English language, and in Gilchrist's case the currently extant version of Johnson's *English Dictionary*. As Bernard Cohn notes, "Gilchrist would explain the English term as best he could to the Hindustanis, who would then 'furnish the synonymous vocables in their own speech.'"[85] The sheer presence of English, as the fixed standard according to which the fluid spoken languages would be reformulated, cannot be overemphasized. Whereas prior to the colonial encounter the norm for the Indian languages was translation as a mode of being constantly exposed in encounter to the incommensurality of different languages, soon after the initial contact between English and North Indian language forms, the earlier kind of encounter was displaced by another: the encounter between the unity and fixed identity of English versus the fluid Indian, which would soon receive a corresponding unity and identity.

What grammars and dictionaries did was to stabilize the naturally translational *existence* of the spoken languages by means of the *representation of* translation. To have a representation of translation means that there is in advance an idea of what translation is, and that the Englishman is already assured of the nature or thing-ness of the language encountered. Despite the Englishman's assurance, it is only the representation of translation that gives rise to the possibility of figuring out the unity of his own language against the supposed unity of the Indian. The discursive apparatus that gives rise to the representation of translation is an operation of thinking according to what is variously known as the law of noncontradiction or the principle of reason. This prior determination of translation as representation consists in the displacement of encounter as mutual contamination of self and other, toward a stance where the other is ordered by making it knowable to the self. What therefore happens in the representation of translation is that the threatening chaos of the other's fluidity is secured. It is made stable and fixed. This securing of stability demands that what is overwhelming be transposed or translated into something that stands as identical. From this moment on translation is shifted onto the ground of representation as a procedure through which something is made present to the self as an object.[86] Thus the standard (English) is based ultimately on the self-certainty of one's own cultural form or horizon, namely, the English self or character. This already-formed horizon is the essential part of what Sakai calls the "schema of co-figuration," which is the discursive apparatus whereby a community constitutes itself as the self or the standard, by making visible the figure of an other—in this case the imagined purity of Indo-Aryan-derived Hindi from the hybridized melange of Hindustani languages. Hence the fixing of heterolingual Hindustani into homolingual Hindi occurs only when the other is perceived as constituted by a contamination that requires purification. The two imagined unities, English and the Hindi in the process of being purified, resemble each other in an operation that is almost entirely spectral.

This helps to clarify the nature of the "first," or colonial, idiom. The first idiom not only represents the material force of the colonizer (laws, military strength, institutions, etc.), but refers just as much to the immaterial force implicit within the already formed horizon of cultural identity or self-certainty invested in English character. It is the immaterial force of this first idiom that brings about change in the mode of translation, which in turn results in the shift from a heterolingual to homolingual domain where translation becomes fixed and meanings are specified. Even before it became legally institutionalized in 1835—thereby displacing Persian as the official language of the colonial state—the presence of English was central to the operations of governance. Its presence was manifest from the beginning in the sense that it changed the meaning of translation and, in so doing, brought colonizer and colonized together onto an imagined common platform or grid, and thus into a particular mode of social relation.

All of this brings into question the supposed ideological opposition between Orientalists (who wanted to continue patronage of indigenous languages and modes of education) and Anglicists (who wanted to replace them wholesale with English language and education). From this perspective not only were the language policies of Orientalists and Anglicists ideologically closer than is often thought, but their language policies in fact reflected and provided a frame for their religious policies. Thus the idea that Orientalists were pro-Hindu whereas the Anglicists were anti-Hindu is far too simplistic. In reality the only difference between them was the way in which policies were to be implemented rather than any religious or linguistic persuasion, for, as I have already noted, the Orientalists were still staunchly Christian and British. A good example of this is the controversy that had raged between Orientalists and Anglicists as to whether the money made available by the Charter Act of 1813 (which made £10,000 available for the purpose of educating the natives in India) was to be used for indigenous education or for English-style education. This dispute was finally settled when Thomas Macaulay's *Minute on Indian Education* became part of state policy. Macaulay, like Charles Grant and other Evangelicals before him, strongly advocated education in English and the replacement of indigenous education. Practically this meant endorsing higher education (post–age eleven) and leaving indigenous primary education to its own devices. As schools and colleges were set up by the British after 1835, Persian and other languages gave way to English as the medium of learning and as the language of Law.

My point is that even before it was officially instituted by the Anglicist lobby, English was already, thanks to the efforts of the Orientalists, performing the role of the language of Law. Not the Law of British government, but the language-as-Law because of its self-definition as the proper, because universal, language of thought, speech, and writing, as compared to the improper spoken languages of India. In other words, through the efforts of Orientalists, a regime of translation was instituted in which English was assumed to provide the very law of translation. The operation of this law depended on the presence of the Englishman or Orientalist who could bring Indian languages and English into virtual "contact" through the schema of co-figuration. Once this virtual "contact" was created, it was necessary for all linguistic relations and transactions to begin with a silent invocation of English as standard, before returning to English. English had therefore already assumed its place as language-in-general, and therefore as the origin and end of every transaction, compared to which other languages could only be particular languages. The spoken languages of India were charged with the task of recovering their mother tongues *as compared to English*. This was the task set for them by the Orientalists well before the Anglicists legally instituted English.

Fabrication of the "Mother Tongue(s)"

> *How, then, stands the case? We have to educate a people who cannot at present be educated by means of their mother tongue. We must teach them a foreign language.*   —Thomas Macaulay, "Indian Education"[87]

The institutionalization of *Hindustanee* (which continued to be written in Perso-Arabic script) and *Hinduwee* (henceforth written in Devanagri script used for Sanskrit) as two autonomous linguistic entities came about with the founding of Fort William College in Calcutta in 1800 for the purpose of training young British civilians. With Gilchrist driving the college's policy on language, the task of teaching the newly created *Hinduwee* (later to be called Hindi and designated as *bhakha*, or the people's true language) was given to a Gujrati Brahmin, Lallujilal, who was hired to teach it to the native Hindus in the Devanagri script. A similar service was performed for Hindustani (later known as Urdu) by a Muslim from Delhi, Mir Amman.[88] Despite the composition of a number of texts in Hindustani and *Hinduwee* by the early 1800s, it wasn't the natives themselves (for whom the language of everyday use by Muslims and Hindus alike still existed in undifferentiated or heterolingual state) but the missionaries who solidified the use of *Hinduwee* as the language of the Hindus (today's Hindi) through the composition and propagation of extensive missionary literature in *Hinduwee* and the implementation of the first printing presses in India in South Asian languages.

The following example is commonly cited to illustrate the discrepancy between official British declaration and desire for a rectified Hindi to become the standard vernacular, and the actual state of native speech, especially in Banaras, the traditional heartland of orthodox Hinduism.[89] In 1846, almost five decades after the founding of institutions such as the Oriental Seminary and Fort William College, when James Ballantyne, the newly appointed principal of Banaras Sanskrit College, asked the students to use the newly created Hindi in their written exercises, he found the results to be very poorly executed, with students showing no enthusiasm for rectifying the everyday use of language. Several students formulated reasons for this apparent disregard toward correction:

> We don't clearly understand what you Europeans mean by the term Hindi. . . . If the purity of Hindi is to consist in the exclusion of (Muslim) words, we shall require to study Persian and Arabic in order to ascertain which of the words we are in the habit of using everyday, is Arabic or Persian and which is Hindi. . . . What you call Hindi will eventually merge in some future modification of the Urdu; nor do we see any great cause of regret in this prospect.[90]

Far from being dissuaded by these protests, however, Ballantyne argued that the task of forming the national language, of retrieving the true identity of the Hindus' mother tongue, couldn't be left to "peasants." It remained the duty of the religious orthodox elites of Banaras "to endeavour to get rid of the unprofitable diversity of provincial dialects by creating a standard literature in which one uniform system of grammar and orthography should be followed. The Pandits of Banaras, if they valued the fame of their city, ought to strive to make the dialect of the holy city the standard for all India by writing books which should attract the attention and form the style of all their countrymen."[91]

Ballantyne's remarks turned out to be almost prophetic, as a new generation of native elites educated during the 1850s–1870s in Anglo-vernacular institutions such as Banaras Sanskrit College took on this task with great zeal. Exposed to English language through the Anglo-vernacular school, these new native elites were instrumental in politicizing Hindi as an autonomous national language of the Hindus by purging their lived heterolingual experience of the foreign effects of Islam and Perso-Arabic. To propagate Hindi as the national language of the Hindus, it was necessary to enunciate a *one* of Hindi, Hindi as *one*, and the Hindus as the subject of the enunciation "I am Hindu," in which the previously disparate "I" of enunciation and "I" of existence were unified.[92] Of the native elites educated in the 1860s through the 1870s, the most avid propagator of Hindi was Hariścandra Bhāratendu. More than that of any other single figure, his literary output effected the religio-cultural schism between modern standard Hindi (Hindus) and Urdu (Muslims), ironically while being linguistically and culturally steeped in those traditions whose influence he was helping to cleanse.

Despite the publicizing of Hindi, however, it is clear that even by the 1890s public acceptance of Hindi was very limited. As late as 1889 the Indologist George Grierson could therefore comment that Hindi was still limited to a "prose form in one uniform dialect, the mother tongue of no native born Indian, *forced into acceptance by the prestige of its inventors*" (emphasis added).[93] Grierson's comment reveals more than just the colonizers' hubris about their own role in manufacturing Hindi. It begs certain other questions. If virtually nobody spoke Hindi in 1889 except a few elites and if the linguistic state of the populace was still predominantly heterolingual—a polysystem that intrinsically resisted differentiation into the language of "familiarity" versus the language of the "foreigner," indeed resisted the demarcation between native/foreign or self/other, and therefore resisted the process of "othering" or of making the other—why did the schism happen for native elites such as Hariścandra, who in every way belonged to the heterolingual domain? What made them convert to a belief in the autonomy of Hindi, a belief in the certainty of the representation "I speak Hindi (therefore) I am a Hindu," which is effectively a "conversion to modernity"?

The term "conversion" seems more apt than the more prevalent notion of "dialogue" for several reasons. First, and as discussed earlier in this chapter, the term "dialogue" suggests a mutual exchange of ideas between colonizer and colonized for which the native elites had been prepared through the acquisition of English in the Anglo-vernacular schools. It suggests that their entry into modernity, and by implication colonization, was beneficial for the native elites insofar as it helped them to retrieve their true identity from what the British regarded as the false multitude of languages and cultures. Only such an identity could provide a basis for building bridges or dialogue between past and present, between a passive East and an active West, thereby enabling a revitalization of the colonized mind. However, it is difficult to square this idealistic notion of dialogue—and the attendant notion that the Anglo-vernacular elites were heroic individuals who built bridges between different civilizations— with the fact that they were instrumental in fabricating new boundaries that helped to shut out part of the body of lived experience.

The term "conversion," by contrast, evokes a certain violence of transformation in one's intellectual-existential horizon. "Conversion" suggests the less heroic activity of bringing about a decisive break, a breaking away from the old—in the sense of elevating oneself above the multitude although acting as its representative—that is achieved by an active forgetting of the old. This break/forgetting is necessary for erecting an identity as a locus of the self-same, the new that is certain of its self-representation. The erection of this identity must be accompanied by modernity's trademark: to forget that one has broken with the old, the multitude, that is to say, a second forgetting *in which one forgets that one has forgotten.*

The term "conversion" is also more in tune with George Grierson's comment that the belief in Hindi as an autonomous mother tongue of the Hindus was "forced into acceptance." This particular phrase resonates, ironically, with Derrida's remarks about the nature of the interdict as the mechanism of colonial law that forbids the nonidentical, nonlocatable experience of heterolinguality from coming-to-words. For Derrida, the interdict is never set down, never enacted as an official decree. Its mechanism is not a passive forgetting but an active repression (where one *automatically* forgets that one has forgotten). It is something that "happens to you at school," a "pedagogical mechanism."[94] For the native elites, in the face of colonial censorship, the one and only option for accessing something called "Hindi" was the Anglo-vernacular school, where one had to learn English and Hindi together. It is this institution that takes on a silent and insidious role in forming the new experience and character of the native elites who were subjected to its "pedagogical mechanism" as opposed to those native elites who were schooled in traditional schools, the *gurukuls*, *madrassas*, and *pathshallas.*

Given (i) that the force of English was responsible for the shift from hetero- to homolingualism, and (ii) that this linguistic shift occurred at the same time and parallel to the process by which hetero-religiosity gave way to the formation of distinct religious boundaries catalyzed by the redefining of *bhakti* as the "real religion of the Hindus," two questions arise. First, how did Indians come to willingly accept a mode of identification that effectively broke with the previous (precolonial) mode of expression/thought/action? Second, is it possible to speculate on a way to theorize the linguistic and the religious together, at the same time? What would be the use of such a model or theory today? One way to think about this would be to return to a question I posed earlier. How does the acquisition of English—which is the only thing that separates the Anglo-vernacular elites from other elites—precipitate the kind of schism in the minds of those who were educated in these institutions? After all, the concept of education was not new to Indian culture. Nor, it would appear, was the addition of another (dominant) language to a context in which heterolingualism and linguistic hierarchy were not mutually incompatible. What, then, was peculiar to the English education, and specifically to the acquisition of English?

The English Orthopaideia: "Generalized Translation" and the Transition to the Global Fiduciary

Our subjects have set out on a new career of improvement: they are about to have a new character imprinted on them.
    —*Charles Trevelyan*, On the Education of the People of India[95]

Clearly referring to a desired psychological alteration, one that would make them break willingly with the indigenous systems of speech and education, Charles Trevelyan, brother-in-law of Thomas Macaulay, envisaged that such an alteration would be brought through the agency of English literature, which would result in Indians being "educated in the same way, interested in the same objects, engaged in the same pursuits," thereby ending up "more English than Hindu . . . since the summit of their ambition is *to resemble us*."[96] The crucial element in this strategy was the Anglo-vernacular institution, which was part of a hierarchical network of schools and colleges modeled on the English university, with its representative abroad being Calcutta's Oriental College. Education in these Anglo-vernacular (A/V) institutions combined an education in English and in vernacular languages. It was imparted initially at mission and state schools set up by the British administration and later at institutions set up and run by native elites themselves, a good example of the latter being the network of Dayananda Anglo-Vedic schools run by the Ārya Samāj.

Although this new-style A/V education was pioneered in Bengal during the 1830s, it had quickly spread to Banaras by the 1840s and to Punjab by the 1860s. Biographical data suggest that students were not normally admitted to the A/V schools until the age of eleven. Before this they would typically be tutored at traditional centers of learning. It is therefore likely that students would acquire no more than a modest grounding in English by their late teens, some even acquiring English much later. What this suggests is that the discursive context of the students educated in A/V schools—their relationship to English and their "own" languages—was far more complex than is suggested by the terms "interaction" or "dialogue." It involved existential and psychological dimensions that are usually forgotten.

At the heart of the A/V school's program was a paradoxical procedure wherein the process of learning one's own mother tongue (say Hindi) was just as dependent on the work of learning the foreign language (English), as the learning of English is dependent on the invention of the mother tongue (Hindi). This peculiar interdependence can be traced to the colonizer's mis-cognition of the heterolingual field as something that the native *lacked*: "We have to educate a people who cannot at present be educated by means of their mother tongue. We must teach them some foreign language."[97] Macaulay obviously believed that the natives' relation to language was promiscuous and immoral because they had lost recognition of the essential nature of language—its oneness and ownness—and therefore its identity and self-sameness. Because of this lack of identity they needed to be taught a foreign language, English, representing the figure of the "other" that would help them to rediscover their own.

Hence the basic strategy adopted by the A/V schools, in which English (other) and vernacular Hindi (own) are juxtaposed, helped to delineate a power relation into the practice of language instruction, whose basic form was dictation followed by memorization of English words. Through dictation the learner of English imitates, memorizes, and attempts to reproduce utterances not in order to say what he means, but to say what one is expected to say without meaning it. This kind of instruction and teaching of English was prevalent in the early decades of nineteenth-century India. To quote Sivanath Sastri: at first "attention was limited primarily to the teaching of English words and their meanings. The greater the number of words and their meanings memorized by a person, the higher was his standing as a man vastly learned in English. . . . There were many schools where at the end of the day the pupils were made to recite English words much in the same manner as they recited multiplication tables."[98] At this stage of language instruction, neither English as foreign language nor Hindi as mother tongue had fully constituted themselves as individual languages. The fullness of English meaning could not be acquired because the native speaker/learner was still in the heterolingual state. In an instance such as this, failing to constitute itself as "proper" speech, the native learner's speech remains mimetic. Even so, such mimetic speech can be regarded as a process wherein a speaking subject is constructed. It is in effect a subjective technology that transformed the speaker and brought about fundamental changes to the world that the speaker has previously inhabited.

The interesting thing here is that the technology that inscribes or imprints the "new character" is driven by a constitutive lack, which can be described quite simply as the native's nonknowledge of the foreign language (English) and of his own mother tongue (Hindi), indeed his constitutive nonknowledge of the horizons native/foreign or self/other. This constitutive lack defines the heterolingual state. But if that is the case, how does one come to know the foreignness of a foreign language (the very concept of otherness is that which establishes the difference between other and self) when one doesn't already have a mother tongue, that is, when one's own world is the *khoric* nonplace of the heterolingual? Indeed, how can I make any assertion at all about something I declare I have no knowledge of, e.g., English as a foreign or unknown language, whose meaning is not already available to me either as an object of empirical knowledge or as an implicit understanding (even a vague horizon) because it is not in proximity to me? It is as yet far beyond my reach.

Interestingly, Sakai finds a resolution to this problem in a somewhat obscure section of Kant's *Critique of Pure Reason*. In the section entitled "The Final Purpose of the Natural Dialectic of Human Reason," Kant argues that "there is a great difference between something being given to my reason as an *object absolutely*, or merely as an *object in the idea*. In the former case our concepts are employed to determine the object; in the latter case there is in fact only a schema for which no object, not even a hypothetical one, is directly given, and which only enables us to represent to ourselves other objects in an indirect manner, namely, in their systematic unity, by means of their relation to this idea."[99] If Kant is right, it may be possible to make assertions about an unknown or foreign language that is not available to the native learners. For in such a case the "objective reality" of the unknown language is not to be taken as referring *directly* to an object. Rather, it should be considered only as a "schema constructed in accordance with the conditions of the greatest possible unity of reason—the schema of the concept of a thing in general."[100] The purpose of this schema is to secure the "greatest possible systematic unity in the empirical employment of our reason."[101]

Following Kant, Naoki Sakai suggests that because I am deprived of the English meanings, the only relationship I could possibly have towards the foreign language would be something akin to the kind of certainty that comprises belief in the unknown, the mystical or the transcendent.[102] What belief does here is to fill the lack of meaning by providing some kind of guideline, a figure or schema through which I can at least relate to the unknown language, which cannot be given to me as an empirically verifiable object of knowledge. The figure of the unknown, however vague initially, makes it possible for me to desire to know what it represents. It is this desire that directs me to the unknown. This figure is given to me via language instructors as a configuration of languages that are institutionalized in the disciplinary taxonomy by which foreign language learning is facilitated. In the colonial context of India the configuration of languages referred to here would be the one created by the line of linguists and grammarians going back to William Jones, Nathaniel Halhed, and John Gilchrist and reproduced by native teachers such as Lallujilal and Mir Amman. This schema is seamlessly transferred from the canons of Orientalist grammars, through the pedagogy of native and other language instructors, and then to the native elites who subject themselves to the authority of the language instructors' dictation.

In this process of language instruction, the figure of the unknown language is at first vague and abstract since one's own language has not yet been formulated. As one learns it, however, it gradually becomes more concrete, while at the same time one's own language emerges as a contrasting figure. Thus the already familiar mother tongue is figured out, is given solidity in contrast to the unknown (English). The whole process is transparent, though. Over time, as I become more aware of the foreign, I am informed of the figure of a mother tongue that I have lived and experienced but never known. I am made to believe that there is a mother tongue that really exists. My linguistic identity, as articulated through enunciations such as "I speak Hindi," is therefore given to me through the availability of terms for comparison in which the familiar and foreign, self and other, are rendered re-presentable through figures that are imagined all along. English was never learned through the mother tongue. Rather a mother tongue had to be invented as a specter or mirror image that corresponds to what Sakai calls "homolinguality" and to what Derrida calls the "monolingualism" of the English other. The paradox here is that the idea of the unity of "one's own" had to be invented in order to break with what was *actually* one's own, namely, the heterolingual.

Although Sakai's Kantian model of co-figuration provides a persuasive account of the subjective technology underpinning language acquisition, it nevertheless falls short of explaining key questions relevant to the context of the A/V school. For example, how did the native elites freely choose to break with the heterolingual domain? Why is the subject who enunciates a linguistic identity ("my mother tongue is Hindi") at the same time a religious subject ("I am Hindu")? In other words, why in the moment of its formation, is the mono*lingualism* of the other also the mono*theism* of the other?

Whereas Sakai merely hints that the native learner's decision to approach the unknown other "requires a sort of bet" or "commitment" to the schema that is given to me by language instructors as a "hearsay devoid of original evidence,"[103] Jacques Derrida's diverse writings on language point more directly to the theological underpinnings of the process that Sakai terms "co-figuration." Two essays in particular—"Theology of Translation" and "Faith and Knowledge Beyond the Limits of Reason Alone"—address seemingly unconnected themes such as translation, faith, and knowledge formation, but on closer inspection reveal how co-figuration repeats a past imperialism within contemporary discourses.

In "Theology of Translation" Derrida speculates on a particular moment in German Romanticism, suggesting that "a certain thinking about *Bildung*," indeed, "all the modifications of *bilden* [form, formation, figure, co(n)-figuration, schematization, etc.], are inseparable from what one could call precisely the imperative of translation."[104] There is, Derrida suggests, an "ontotheological dimension, a problematics of ontotheology that is located at the founding of a certain concept of translation."[105] This ontotheological dimension of translation can be found in the very operation of co-figuration, which appears innocuously as the Kantian scheme of the imagination (*Einbildungskraft*) but is in fact nothing more than the process of objectification of translation, the "totalizing gathering together" of the imagination into an "art of generalized translation."[106] This "generalized translation" corresponds to an assumed "originary unity" of the imagination, the assumption that there is but "one world" into which two languages, or language speakers, are thrown together in the schema of co-figuration. But it is precisely because of this assumed "originary unity" that "generalized translation" is already a disavowal of translation as such. As a result the "generalized translation" that takes place in any schema of co-figuration, any schematization as such is in fact a representation of translation, that is, the objectification of translation. The final destination of this objectification is to think the inaccessible and in so doing, to give expression to what cannot be accessed, namely, the Unknown. This kind of translation, Derrida suggests, is no different from theology's notion of "communion with the divine."[107]

The theme of "generalized translation" is broached again, albeit in a different context, in the essay "Faith and Knowledge: The Two Sources of

'Religion' at the Limits of Reason Alone." This essay gives us a glimpse of how the assumption of "generalized translation" is at work in colonial institutions such as the A/V school. In "Faith and Knowledge" Derrida points to the theological underpinnings of the social contract involved in all linguistic acquisition and encounter, indeed in all human addressivity.[108] Crucial here is the role of a certain kind of prohibition, for which Derrida uses the term "interdict."[109] Objectively the interdict corresponds to the regime of translation imposed by the prestige of English language as "official," as Law, mediated through the agency of language instructors in the A/V school. From the standpoint of the native elites subjected to this Law, the interdict operates as a self-censorship that comes into effect by prohibiting a certain kind of speech from being articulated. Instead the interdict specifies access to uncensored identifications while in that very moment actively repressing other identifications. It can be regarded as the native's willing agreement to submit to language as Law (or to the Law as language). Through such submission one responds to the other and in thus responding will have entered into a relation with the other.

However, the very possibility of this response is premised on a confidence trick. One responds to the other as if one had already mastered language, and as if, in responding, one is in control of meaning or communication. Although Derrida doesn't reveal his source, he is clearly indebted to Lacan's notion of the Unconscious structured like a language. We could therefore say, in a pastiche of Lacan, that the subject cannot *acquire* language but only *accede* to it. In effect this is another way of saying that one does not master language—rather, one is mastered *by* language. Which of course begs the question: Why does one's subjection to language/Law *appear* as a freely given response to the other? Lacan would say that the subject has to let himself into the other's word by investing a certain degree of faith in the other simply on the basis of the words he speaks, and that without any correspondence between facts and proofs, this creates a minimal social relation between speaking beings.[110] But what guarantees the investment of belief or good faith in the other? Stated differently, what guarantees that the native's response will be recognized by the other, and through such recognition be deemed by the other a response-able subject, a subject who has a similar self-consciousness to his own?

For Derrida the very fact that we require language to speak to another and for another to respond means that speaking/responding is unavoidable insofar as speech/response provides the possibility of the social bond or what might be regarded as the minimal form of community:

the self in relation to an-other (the not-self). Thus the subject cannot respond and there can be no responsibility unless there is first of all an agreement already:

> No response without a principle of responsibility: one must respond to the other, before the other and for oneself. And no responsibility without a *given word*, a sworn faith, without a pledge, without an oath, without some *sacrament* or *ius iurandum*.[111]

There was, it seems, no question of the native's *not* responding. By responding the native promises to tell the truth and asks the other to believe that he is also an other. But a promise cannot properly take place even though promising is inevitable as soon as the native opens his mouth: "From the moment I open my mouth, I have already promised; or rather . . . the promise has seized the I that promises to speak to the other. . . . This promise is older than I am."[112] Language, like Lacan's symbolic order, precedes those who speak it or those through whom it speaks. For the colonized native subjected to the law of English as Law, there could never be any question of not responding to the other, for "language has started without us, in us and before us. This is what theology calls God, and it is necessary, it will have been necessary to speak."[113]

The connection between God and the possibility of speech/response is better explained in the text of the "Faith and Knowledge" essay, where Derrida provides an important clue as to what is really going on. He warns:

> Before even envisaging the semantic history of testimony, of oaths, of the given word (. . . indispensable to whomever hopes to think religion under its proper or secularized forms), before even recalling that some sort of "I promise the truth" is always at work, and some sort of "I make this commitment before the other from the moment that I address him, even and perhaps above all to commit perjury," we must formally take note of the fact that *we are already speaking Latin*. We make a point of this in order to recall that the world today speaks Latin (most often via Anglo-American) when it authorizes itself in the *name of religion*.[114]

What Derrida seems to suggest here goes beyond the issue of Latin's linguistic hegemony. The reference to Latin is a pointer toward a structural principle around which an entire tradition (religious, intellectual, cultural, and political) continues to gravitate. At the core of this structure is enshrined a sacred principle that Derrida calls an "*a priori* ineluctable," or inescapable presupposition: that at the very moment of our coming to speech, at the very moment that an "I" addresses or responds to another "I" (and therefore to an other), the self engenders the figure of God as a witness, "quasi-mechanically," as it were. The very emergence of our speech presupposes that God can be called upon as a witness, albeit the Supreme Witness, who testifies to the legality or correctness of the self's relation to an other, indeed to the inviolability of the *distance* between self and other: "Presupposed at the origin of all address, coming from the other *to whom it is also addressed*, the wager of a sworn promise, taking immediately God as its witness, cannot not but have already . . . engendered God quasi-mechanically."[115]

According to this model of language, speech begins by presupposing the existence of God, which is also the condition for his absence or nonexistence. Without God, or with a God who is nonexistent, there is no absolute witness and therefore no ground for a proper relationship between self and other. With God, or a God who exists, we have the existence of a third who guarantees even the minimal social bond between self and other, even when—and perhaps most importantly—the self/I commits perjury, when I lie to the other, or when the pledge is at its most secular. Derrida refers to this fiduciary structure as a "transcendental addressing machine."[116] As such the fiduciary is effectively a mechanism that allows God to be invoked as an "originary unity," the transcendent One, but does not stop Him from being called upon at will and put to good use.

Quite simply, the fiduciary can be regarded as a "performative experience of the act of faith," without which there can be no address to the other. Constituted on the "soil of bare belief"[117] the fiduciary not only underlies everything to do with religion or the religious, but insofar as it is also a principle of "fundamental translatability," it underpins the generalized "institutional translation of the theology of translation" into the secular domain. Consequently, the fiduciary translates into the objectification of knowledge in the humanities according to the "rhythm of techno-science," and because State structures depend essentially and concretely on the performativity of sciences and techno-sciences, it also translates into "what has rightly been called the military-industrial-complex of the modern State," and extends even beyond that to the economic rationality of capitalism.[118]

Yet contrary to the prevalent idea that belief/faith is central to all religions, Derrida argues that the fiduciary is rooted in a peculiarly Christian concept of the world. As such the fiduciary can only be spoken of universally in relation to other cultures through the phenomenon of Latinity and its globalization, or "globalatinization," to use Derrida's neologism.[119] The intimate connection between religion and language signified by "Latinity" is echoed by Daniel Dubuisson, who asks how "we Westerners" can claim to conceive of the idea of religion or of any religious fact when "we (our very selves, our ways of thinking, our most common perceptions) are immersed in a language in which there pre-exists the concept of religion and, along with it, a multitude of often very ancient connections and semantic networks, even if they have been ceaselessly revised?"[120] It is impossible for the West to avoid this impasse:

> Our language is also our world, the two coextensive with each other (the aspects of the world that our language does not know do not exist and, symmetrically, what exists for our language exists equally for us in one way or another). The ultimate paradox is probably this: does something that does not exist but that we can name, thanks to our language (the soul, angels and so on), not still exist in a certain way for, or in, our minds, actually more than what truly does exist but that our language ignores?[121]

Globalatinization in all of its manifestations is the result of presupposing a "concept of fundamental translatability [that] is linked poetically to a natural language"[122] that itself *resists translation*. Today globalatinization enables the fiduciary, the core mechanism of Christianity and its language, to retain its hegemony due to the conceptual apparatus of international law, global political rhetoric—which is also a "generalized rhetoric or translatology"—and (though Derrida doesn't specifically mention this) the various modes of multiculturalism. It can be seen as the global re-Christianization of the planet through the discourse of secular conceptuality. Though rarely acknowledged, wherever the conceptual apparatus of international law and politics (and multiculturalism—to which I shall return in chapter 4) dominates, it speaks through the discourse of religion. As a result of its implicit "theology of translation" religion is peaceably imposed (or violently *self*-imposed) on all things that remain foreign to what this word designates.

Though not always obvious, the process of globalatinization repeats a mechanism—the "theology of translation"—that was put into play at the micro-level in the Anglo-vernacular school, a mechanism variously described as the manufacture of consent, native-informancy, or mimicry. I cite these three modes of cultural interaction only to indicate what has been missed by theorists on the left, namely, the inseparability of contemporary globalatinization even in its most secular forms from the value tradition of Christianity. One must note here that although this event had been anticipated by Nietzsche, who connected the death of God (atheism) with Christian values, and in Heidegger's essay "The Age of the World Picture," Derrida goes further in pointing out the implications of globalatinization and/or the "generalized translation" of religion for non-Christians.

Indeed, what the term "globalatinization" highlights is the indissociability of language and religion, a "fundamental translatability" between these two spheres, both of which figure prominently in the native elites' acceptance of and resistance to the colonial symbolic order in India. And more important still is the centrality to both language and religion of the structure of the fiduciary, which is organized around the figure of the other. The term helps us to understand why, in the context of nineteenth-century colonization, the reform movements were simultaneously movements for reforming spoken language and for reforming religion; why these two movements resulted in the emergence of a unified subject in whom the formerly heterolingual/heteroreligious experience becomes centralized through enunciations such as "I speak Hindi (or Urdu, Punjabi, etc.)," "My religion is Hindu (Muslim, Sikh, etc.)"; and why these enunciations, once they become synonymous with the nation, worked to destroy the subject's own otherness, its radical heterogeneity.

I have tried in this chapter to problematize the idea that colonial interaction could have been based on anything like a dialogical or intersubjective communication. I argued that the nature of the colonial idiom is far more problematic than is normally acknowledged, not only for its role in the emergence of a certain kind of subjectivity (a religious identity), but because its effects continue to be repeated in the contemporary discourse of the humanities. In later chapters (4, 5, and 6) this repetition of a past imperialism will be tracked in more detail. First, though, it is necessary to delve more closely into the nature of the colonial idiom. This will be the work of the next chapter.

2 Hegel and the Comparative Imaginary of the West

The Orthodoxy of Secular Anti-Imperialist Critique

Arguably the most important theoretical movement to have influenced postcolonial studies of India stems from Edward Said's critique of Orientalism. Now built in to the very fabric of discourse on South Asia, the central thrust of "post-Orientalist" critique is directed at the static understanding of "area" as an object of scholarly inquiry, and more specifically at the versions of Orientalism spawned by the intimate relationship between Indology and British colonialism. In hindsight, though, Said's influence on South Asian studies may seem surprising, given that he has not specifically engaged the major source of Orientalism in the case of India, namely German Indology.[1]

The problem with Said's "redefinition of Orientalism as more or less the whole of Western authoritative pronouncements on Asian societies"[2] is that it is simply unable to account for the changing nature of Orientalism itself. Problems also arise in translating Said's thesis into the Indian context, even though the case of India provides a better example for Said's Foucauldian thesis of power/knowledge than does the Middle East. As Thomas Trautmann argues, newer and older meanings of the term "Orientalism" become confused with each other in discussion about India. Following Trautmann, it is more helpful to distinguish between two different senses of the term "Orientalism" (Orientalism[1] and Orientalism[2]) both of which, as we noted in chapter 1, are in fact forms of Occidentalism.

Orientalism[1] refers to knowledge produced by scholars who knew Asian languages. In the case of India this group consists primarily of the early British Orientalists such as Sir William Jones, Charles Wilkins, Nathaniel Halhed, and H. T. Colebrook. These scholars constituted the core of a distinct policy group that had existed since the time of Warren Hastings, the first governor-general of India. This group promoted education about India in the vernacular languages of India. However, Orientalism[1] was not restricted to British scholars. It included thinkers and administrators in Europe, especially in France and Germany, who read translations of the works of Jones and his colleagues. These included Voltaire, Herder, Schlegel, Schelling, Novalis, and many others. Together these groups embodied a tendency to represent knowledge about India in a positive light, using it as a means for critiquing contemporary forms of Christian orthodoxy and understandings of European modernity. At its height (between 1780 and 1810) this tendency came to be caricatured by its opponents as Indomania.

Orientalism[2], on the other hand, refers to European representations of Asia that arose out of a disaffection and anxiety produced by the comparative valuations of new knowledges of India produced by Orientalism[1]. Fueling this disaffection were the often convergent movements of Christian revivalism, national identity, and scientific racism. Advocates of Orientalism[2] promoted European languages and therefore the primacy of a European, as opposed to an Asian, conceptual medium as sufficient for knowing the Orient. As we shall see later in this chapter, the focus of Orientalism[2] on the European representation of Asia is itself an indicator of deeper philosophical and theoretical concerns in the encounter between India and Europe, specifically: (i) the place of Christianity as central to European identity, and as a consequence of this, (ii) the need to work out the relationship between representation and religion. The latter is a pointer to the *mediatic* nature of religion itself.[3] As this nexus of problems is worked out, the definition of religion itself changes.

One of the problems with post-Saidian scholarship in South Asian studies is the tendency to ignore the second aspect, namely, the relationship between religion and representation, and to assume that the idea of religion operating in colonial discourse since the English Enlightenment is effectively unchanged. As a result, British Orientalism, with its emphasis on empiricist, anthropological, and historicist surveys of India and its inhabitants, is regarded as the exemplary colonial discourse on India. In contradistinction, German Orientalism is regarded as overly fixated on philosophy, bereft of empirical contact with India and therefore caricatured as overly idealistic. This caricature of idealism has in some ways contributed to the relative neglect of the German contribution. Yet as Sheldon Pollock notes, "No serious encounter with Orientalism as it relates to traditional India can avoid the case of Germany," given that the German effort alone surpassed the combined European and American forms of Orientalism.[4] It is the German connection, Pollock argues, that continues to nourish one of the most venerable Orientalist constructions, namely, the idea that non-Western cultures are firmly in the grip of religion (India being the paradigm of this Eastern "obsession with religion"), whereas Western cultures overcame this tendency in the wake of the European Enlightenment. More important, though, the case of Germany also "directs attention away from the periphery to the national political culture and the relationship of power and knowledge at the core,"[5] by which Pollock means the often unacknowledged relationship between the demarcation of European identity and the emerging vision of *Wissenschaft*, which together comprised the basis of the European conceptual framework.

In recent years a growing number of postcolonial theorists specializing in South Asia have begun to remedy Said's omission by giving more prominence to the German connection.[6] In what seems to have become a consistent narrative, these studies have independently gravitated around the figure of G. W. F. Hegel, and specifically have come to regard Hegel's influential *Lectures on the Philosophy of History* (*LPH*) as the Ur-text for colonial and neocolonial representations of India. The genius of the *LPH* texts was, of course, that while perpetuating the myths of a "religion-obsessed India" and a uniquely "Indian transcendental wisdom," they keep India politically and intellectually consigned to this very representation outside history. At the risk of oversimplifying: this narrative expresses the hope that once the conceptual matrix of the *LPH* text is dismantled, it will be possible to generate not simply a "post-Orientalist" critique of the more blatant forms of Eurocentrism, but, following Said, a *secular* anti-imperialist critique. Any movement beyond Orientalism must therefore go through a secular purge, the desired aim of which is to guard against the return of religion or any form of repressed religiosity in its various guises.

By removing the religio-spiritual underpinnings of the *LPH* it becomes possible to conceptualize agency on behalf of subaltern groups
whose rights were usurped by the religious nationalism of neocolonial
elites. Once historicism (minus religion) safely underpins the study of
South Asian cultures, we have a neutral zone that distances South Asian
culture from the harmful and divisive influences of colonialism and neo-
colonialism, both of which are religious in orientation. The concepts
of area and historicism thus converge in a mutually beneficial alliance
that allows scholars to properly conceive postcolonial agency. Since the
mid-1980s versions of this secular anti-imperialist paradigm have been
accommodated within discourses of modern South Asian studies, both
as an area specialization and as part of the humanities disciplines—religious studies (comparative religion/history of religions), anthropology,
history, international studies, politics, etc.—that utilize South Asia as an
archival resource.

However, if this form of critical theory was supposed to provide a corrective to the West's continuing will-to-power, it has, through a somewhat
simplistic disavowal of the question of religion in favor of historicism as
a critical source, simply reinstated the very Hegelianism that it set out to
remove. The idea that historicism in itself can provide the proper element
for thinking about postcolonial agency fails to account for several things.
First, it fails to acknowledge the extent to which the conceptualizations of
religion and history are mutually imbricated in Hegel's thought (a problem that will be more fully explored later in this chapter). Second, as
Dipesh Chakrabarty rightly points out, it overlooks the deep ties that bind
historicism as a mode of thought to the formation of political modernity
in India—a political modernity that is no less religious than it is secular.[7]
Consider for example the almost cathartic return of religion and religious
traditions as legitimate and democratic vehicles for voicing cultural, political, and existential concerns—indeed, in some cases as the only means
for articulating life-worlds that were colonized and translated as religion,
repressed by secular modernity, but continue to simultaneously adopt and
resist the aporetic space created by the (un)translatability of religion as a
concept. Historicist thought can conceive of this return of religion only as
an inherent failure or incompleteness of the transition to capitalism and
modernity that is characteristic of countries like India.

Third, there is growing evidence of what might be called a cultural
identity crisis in the humanities and social sciences, a crisis that revolves
around the interminable opposition between religion and historicism.

Two seemingly different examples can be cited to illustrate this crisis. On the one hand, is the effects of demographic changes on pedagogy and research. Whereas in the 1960s and 70s theorists who also specialized in the field of South Asia were drawn largely from the host communities in Europe and North America, the field today is populated by increasing numbers of South Asian theorists. The difference this makes is that their interventions in the academy are governed by an understanding of a life-world that, far from representing a South Asian particularity, is in fact inscribed by a desire to contest existing forms of universality. Hence the increasingly vocal demand from South Asian academics to be regarded as more than mere producers of empirical data broadly fits the kind of secular decolonization that results from exorcizing the "religious effects" of Hegelian ideology.

On the other hand, following the retreat of Marxist thought and the rampancy of neoliberalism after the end of the Cold War, there has been a conspicuous return to the religious sources of Western culture by leading thinkers of the Left. I refer to the recent work of theorists such as Slavoj Žižek, Alain Badiou, and Gianni Vattimo, among others. Faced with the triumphalism of American global power in the 1980s, the massive return of religion into the heart of national and global politics (indeed into the project of democracy itself), and the conspicuous failure of the traditional Left, these thinkers have, in different ways, called for a renewal of European political thought. For them, European thought is endangered not only by American globalization but also by the medley of third-world cultures ("New Age Mysticisms" and "paganisms"), which exploit the political void created by the postmodern relativism that has afflicted the European mind.[8] The resurrection of Hegel figures prominently in this push to return theory to its Christian roots. As this theme will be dealt with more thoroughly in chapter 6, it should suffice to note here that the very idea of such a "renewal of left Eurocentrism" simply illuminates the presence of a crisis that has always been at the heart of theory itself, which today begs the question as to whether theory can move beyond its craving to identify with a particular culture that has always been *religious*, even when it denies religion or portends to have overcome religion.

This chapter argues for a reexamination of Hegel's texts on India and Indian religion from the perspective of his *Lectures on the Philosophy of Religion* (*LPR*). For it is these texts, rather than the more widely read *LPH*, that allow us to discern a possible connection between the idea of a "generalized translation," the law of thinking and the conceptualization of religion and history in light of the West's encounter with Indology. This connection in turn helps to sheds light on the crisis of theory in relation to the problem of cultural pluralism, particularly the way that this plays out in the disciplinary organization of the humanities. Although postcolonial theorists such as Ronald Inden, Gayatri Spivak, and more recently Pheng Cheah have attempted to locate this conceptual matrix in Hegel's *LPH*, these texts merely reveal its outer contours. Its inner mechanism remains remarkably resistant to exposure as the result of a belief that underpins the very means by which these scholars seek to conceptualize the break with imperialism. As William Hart has argued, this belief, attributable in the first place to Karl Marx, also provides the impetus behind secular postcolonial theorizing.[9] Marx neatly summarized it as follows: "The criticism of religion is the premise of all criticism." Stated otherwise, critical thinking can begin only with a displacement of religion or the religious by historicism. What secular postcolonial theory fails to acknowledge, however, is that Marx's standpoint was not only anticipated by Hegel but in fact was problematized in the *LPR from the standpoint of religion*! Indeed, Hegel's perpetual struggle to theorize what Chakrabarty calls the "transition to capital" revolved around the question of the *difference* between religion and history.[10] The evidence for this can be found in the relatively neglected second part of the *LPR* (which deals with determinate religions) and specifically the transition from the 1824 to the 1827 *LPR* text, where Hegel can be found attempting to articulate the problem of transition from universal to particular in terms of a transparent relation between religion and history, but more significantly as far as this chapter is concerned, in the context of a discussion on the proper place of India and Indology within the emerging discourse of *Wissenschaft*.

Though largely overlooked by the dominant narratives in the humanities, the discourse of Indology is more closely linked to the reconceptualization of religion and history in the nineteenth century—and more importantly to the continuing disengagement between theory and Indic phenomena—than is given credit for. To properly examine this link it will therefore be necessary to question the accepted narratives of Indology and to resituate them in relation to the coemergence of universal and particular knowledge formations. In this chapter I want to trace the connections between the historical development of Indology and the diverse plethora of cultural and intellectual debates that contributed to the making of the European conceptual framework, or what was termed in chapter 1 as the first, or colonial, idiom. Though rarely acknowledged in postcolonial and modern South Asian studies, at the center of these debates was the discourse of religion, specifically in the shape of new disciplines such as philosophy of religion and history of religions. As a result the prevailing opinion fails to register the philosophical nuances in the construction of the field of Indology, or the extent to which Indology is part of the history of ideas in the nineteenth century.[11] As indicated in chapter 1, Indology underwent significant changes during the nineteenth century, as a result of which we can differentiate between two phases of Indology: a pre-1840s and a post-1860s Indology. The split between these phases calls for a different genealogy, one that takes into account Indology's reformulation in the light of the reconceptualization of religion in terms of ontotheology. Such a genealogy could act as a more sensitive seismograph to the different currents that have contributed to the construction of the colonial idiom and later Indian nationalist discourses.

In the approach I am suggesting, events such as the interaction between Indologists, missionaries, and native elites, far from being peripheral to Western intellectual currents, must be read through key moves in the debates between theology and historicism, art and religion, religion and philosophy, etc. I do not intend here to chart these debates individually, or to exhume empirical evidence as such. My intention, rather, is to question what came to be invested in the intellectual and institutional efforts to identify origins and demarcate boundaries in art, religion, and philosophy in relation to the growing knowledge of Oriental cultures. In contradistinction to the conventional trend of postcolonial studies that takes "religion" as a predefined category and incompatible with critical thought, I shall adopt a Heideggerian tone and treat religion as a *question*: "What is?"—a question that has a certain ontology as well as a genealogy that helps to deconstruct religion's normally transparent relationship to metaphysics, thereby pushing the limits of critique even further. Such an approach is necessary if we are to understand the relationship between the colonial idiom and the often-ambivalent psychological mechanisms by which the colonial administration in India achieved one of its main objectives: the formation of a *modern* identity for Indian elites, an identity that is, paradoxically, religious in essence. What is at stake therefore—and in asking this we are already touching upon questions that will be explored at length in the next two chapters—is how and why the thinking of the native elites came to be expressed in a theological idiom, or why Indian nationalist scholars have persisted with and found it necessary to continually revert to asserting a coevalness between Indian religion and monotheism. Why are theological concepts, far from being specious, pivotal terms in the historical encounter between India and Europe that motivated all future movements for reform and national identification?

Cultural Nationalism and the "Intellectual Rekindling of Christianity"

Whether or not the phenomenon of nationalism actually originated in the period spanning roughly the 1770s to the 1830s, there is now an overwhelming consensus among scholars that this happens to be the period in which the self-consciousness of national identity grew and flourished throughout Europe.[12] It was in this period that the nation became a metaphysical entity as well as a political unity based on accumulated historical experience. Independent studies[13] have pointed to three main factors within the intellectual context of this period that contributed to the gathering force behind national identity and self-consciousness: Christian reaction and revivalism, the rise of the concept of "progress," and the parallel growth of racism and Romantic Hellenism. To the extent that Europe can be identified with Christendom, all three movements can be regarded as intrinsically connected. Moreover, the growth of national consciousness is associated with an intellectual resurgence of Christianity, both Protestant and Catholic, that had no parallel since the middle ages.[14]

In an era dominated by advances in secular science, Enlightenment rationalism, and increasing awareness of non-Christian religions and cultures, criticism and hostility toward traditional Christian dogma and the role of the Church were widespread. As Robert Rosenblaum argues, many leading Christian intellectuals and artists, particularly in the Germany of the 1790s, felt an intensely personal need to "revitalize the experience of divinity in a secular world that lay outside the sacred confines of the traditional Christian iconography" and thus to respond "to the eighteenth century's repeated assaults upon traditional Christianity"[15] by resurrecting or replacing the stagnant images of the Church. Relying on the liberating force of "Higher Criticism" on the one hand, and the development of a new metaphysics within German philosophy on the other, the intellectual proponents of this revitalized Christianity—including names such as Schleiermacher, Herder, the Schlegel brothers, Novalis, Fichte, Schelling, and Hegel—hoped to reinterpret the spiritual core of Christianity in nontraditional terms. In their new philosophical, theological, and artistic insights these thinkers found ways to reconcile themes such as revelation with the normally opposed faculties of critical thinking and artistic sensibility.

Closely connected to the "intellectual rekindling" of Christianity was the concept of "progress." This word signifies a new understanding of time, specifically European man's relationship to his past, present, and future, reflecting a transformation throughout the early eighteenth century of Europe's image of itself in relation to other cultures. Beginning with the defeat of Islam (the fall of the Ottoman Turks) and the acceptance of Newtonian physics, by the eighteenth century the concept of "progress" had become increasingly associated with a feeling of European cultural superiority, a notion that grew with European economic, industrial, and territorial expansion. The clearest statements of the idea of progress in the eighteenth century are exemplified by Condorcet's *Sketch of a historical Table of the Progress of the Human Spirit* (1793) and Turgot's *On the Successive Progress of the Human Spirit* (1750). According to this new paradigm, human freedom and natural law interacted in the production of human history, which was now recognized as an unavoidable reality with implications for all areas of inquiry, particularly those relating to the knowledge of non-European civilizations. Non-European cultures had to be viewed in an ascending order as the human spirit "progressed." In an ultimately circular argument it was asserted that Europe was "now" more further advanced than any other continent, or that whenever Europeans imported or borrowed techniques, concepts, aesthetic tastes, then some ineffable European quality was added to whatever was borrowed, making it more perfect: "Those arts which had their invention among other races of man have come to perfection in Europe."[16] It is possible to discern here a close parallel with the ancient Greeks' disavowal of foreign influence: "Whatever the Greeks acquire from foreigners is finally turned by them into something better..."[17]

As mentioned earlier, what reinforced Christian revivalism and the paradigm of "progress" was a combination of racism and Romantic Hellenism. Historians of European colonialism generally accept that a clearcut racism based on skin color became widespread in late seventeenth-century Europe as a result of the increasing importance of the American colonies, with their twin policies of exterminating native Americans and the enslavement of black Africans. Both of these policies presented moral problems to Protestant societies, in which the equality of all men before God and personal freedom were central values. What eased their discomfort was that a variety of writers, classical and contemporary, could be drawn upon to justify slavery and the adoption of racist attitudes. Aristotle, for example, argued at length in favor of slavery on the belief that Greeks were inherently superior to other peoples, particularly the Asiatic races, who, "though they possessed brains and skill, were yet lacking in courage and willpower; so they have remained both enslaved and subject." By contrast, "the Hellenic race . . . has to have the best political institutions and to be capable of ruling others."[18]

More important, however, is the fact that this kind of *conceptual* racism also pervaded the thought of more contemporary Enlightenment thinkers such as John Locke, David Hume, and Immanuel Kant. Indeed, as Robert Bernasconi has convincingly argued, the first proper articulation of race as a *concept* can safely be attributed to Kant and cannot be separated from his philosophical work.[19] "Race" it seems, has been part and parcel of the philosophical tradition itself. In this way prominent philosophers not only helped to reinforce certain attitudes and perspectives in centers of learning such as Göttingen that were at the time pioneering the establishment of modern disciplinary scholarship and source criticism, but also helped to provide a cultural bridge between English and German intellectual Protestantism and its relationship to non-Christian civilizations such as Egypt, India, and Africa. To give one important example: disciplinary studies and source criticism came to be regarded as the academic face of the new Romantic concern with ethnicity and racial origin that was current in British and German circles at the time. Typical sentiments included the notion that races and ethnicities are naturally tied to particular geographical areas and climates, or the belief that European temperate climates are better than those of other continents in regard to creating courageous and free character.

Despite its pervasiveness throughout the eighteenth and nineteenth centuries, color racism was not as important as what might be termed "cultural xenophobia"—a term that more often than not appears in its more sanitized form, "cultural nationalism"—the belief in Greece as the origin and youth of modern Christian Europe. The possibility of such an alliance between ancient Greece and Christianity first occurred during the Renaissance with Erasmus's defense of Christian religion against magic. During this period Germans were also becoming aware of similarities between the German and Greek languages, resulting, after the Reformation, in the powerful image of German and Greek as the two languages of Protestantism pitted against a decadent and corrupt Latin as the language of Roman Catholicism. Greek thus came to be regarded as a sacred and more authentically Christian language than Latin. Luther, after all, not only fought the Church of Rome with the Greek Testament but also laid the foundation for the Protestant emphasis on individual freedom to locate its origins in Greek sources.

During the eighteenth century the most ardent proponent of Greece was the art historian J. J. Winckelmann. For Winckelmann Greek influence was not limited to philosophy but could be found in something more important: aesthetics. The effect of Winckelmann's work on the Hellenization of German intellectual culture during the late eighteenth and early nineteenth centuries was enormous, helping to replace the dominant Latin humanistic tradition with an entirely new humanism based on classical Greece, and thus reaffirming what the Germans came to regard as their special relationship to Greek sources, philosophical, literary, and artistic. Winckelmann's idealized image of the "divine Greek" became central to the new discipline of classics (*Philologie*), better known in its "scientific" form as *Altertumswissenschaft,* or the science of antiquity. Through these institutionalized disciplines it fostered an attitude among European scholars that regarded the Greek language and culture as beyond historical and linguistic laws, indeed, more worthy of veneration than critical analysis.

The influence of Winckelmann notwithstanding, one must also take into account that it is during the intensely conservative period between 1815 and 1830—coinciding with the outbreak of the Greek War of Independence, when all Western European nations were swept by anti-Oriental, anti-African, pro-Hellenic feelings—that Humboldt introduced his educational reforms into the German academy, instituting the new University of Berlin, where these reforms would be implemented. Based on the model of *Bildung* (civilizing, enculturation) and a core curriculum of *Altertumswissenschaft,* these reforms were instrumental in making the Greek paradigm, with its alliance to Christian revivalism, central to the study of other disciplines, including the more established ones such as mathematics, philosophy, and theology as well as newly emerging disciplines specializing in the study of non-European civilizations, namely the disciplines of Egyptology, Sinology, and, importantly as far as this chapter is concerned, of Indology.

A point that needs to be noted particularly in relation to Indology is that Britain was a key participant in the whole process that fueled the nationalist movements in Europe during the period 1780–1840. The reason I suggest this is the tendency of historical surveys of Indology to disproportionately emphasize the difference between the kinds of Indology that came from Britain and Germany in a way that mirrors the popular distinction between empiricism and idealism as the philosophical characteristics of the two nations. Yet this distinction is exaggerated insofar as it ignores evidence to the contrary that suggests that there was a long-standing transmission of ideas between the two countries, not to mention an importation of German Romanticism, philosophical idealism, and educational ideology into Britain during the early decades of the nineteenth century. This fact clearly challenges the standard view, which minimizes the German contribution by asserting that the colonial idiom in relation to India is mainly a British construction.[20] Rather, during the course of this chapter I aim to highlight the pivotal role of religion in reversing the orientation of Indology during the early decades of the nineteenth century. This role can be understood only by acknowledging the importance of strategic supra-national alliances between seemingly different schools of thought—British/German, empiricism/idealism, secular/religious. These supra-national alliances were driven not so much by the need for an exchange of ideas but by much deeper and overriding religious concerns, which prompted the forging of political solidarity based on a Euro-Christian civilizational unity in relation to its Oriental and African others. Moreover, it is these supra-national alliances that, in terms of ideology and administration, coin the dominant perspective of the colonial idiom, and are reflected in the directional shifts in discourses of religion and Indology. It is to the overlap between these two discourses that I now turn my attention.

Monogenesis: Race, Reason, and Monotheism in Orientalism[1]

The accepted narratives depicting the rise of Indology credit men such as Sir William Jones and his contemporaries Charles Wilkins, Nathaniel Halhed, and H. T. Colebrook with the institutionalization of Orientalism as a "scientific" research tradition. It is often forgotten, however, that these men straddled and worked within the intellectual parameters of two major movements in European cultural thinking: the tail end of Enlightenment deism and the birth of racial theory for classifying the human species. Thus, well before they had embarked on their Orientalist endeavors, Jones et al. were already heir to a considerable body of isolated writings and accounts of India and its natives, produced mainly by Jesuit missionaries such as Robert de Nobili (1577–1656) and Abraham Roger (1663), the Lutheran missionary Bartholomaus Ziegenbalg (1683–1719), the British diplomats Alexander Dow and J. Holzwell (1761–1767), and one of the contemporary readers of Dow and Holzwell, the French *philosophe* Voltaire.[21] Their remarks are clearly influenced by the generally benign deistic outlook of the late seventeenth and early eighteenth centuries.

Running like a thread through these reports is the idea that Indians, despite their fall into idolatry and superstition, once possessed a monotheistic belief in the One highest and most perfect being. Constant references to the "natural light of reason" or "basic human reason," which they felt the natives possessed, were necessary for the missionaries, serving both as a bridge and as the basis for the possibility of receiving Christian revelation. As Ziegenbalg states in his main work *Genealogie der malabarischen Götter*: "These heathens recognize from the light of nature that there is a God, a truth which they did not need the Christians to teach them,"[22] a view that is echoed by Voltaire, who took a more radical stand, professing that India is the home of religion in its oldest and purest form: "the Brahmins . . . could establish religion only on the basis of universal reason."[23] Nevertheless—and again there is broad unanimity in this theme—the Indians had fallen from the pure religion of natural reason, of which they were the first possessors, into the degenerate religion represented by the Purāṇic tradition: "In spite of the knowledge that there is only one single divine being, these heathens have nonetheless allowed themselves to be seduced by the devil and their ancient poets into believing in a multitude of gods."[24] Thus Jones and his colleagues inherited a long-prevalent view of India that had been used to illustrate a key motif of deism, namely, the fall and decline of civilization via the eclipse of the "natural light of reason" through superstition, dogma, and ritualism. Stated differently: the decay of religion from a state of pristine (Vedic) monotheism into heathen polytheism occurred by a loss of reason.

Far from challenging the inherited view of an original Indian Ur-monotheism, Jones' work in comparative linguistics, for which he is chiefly remembered, actually appeared to confirm this view. On the basis of an affinity between the verb roots of Sanskrit, Latin, and Greek, Jones postulated "a common ancestral origin" for these languages. From this Jones conjectured that the European and Indian races sprang from a common source. The question of the origins of the European peoples had been the subject of intense speculation, no more so than at academic centers such as Göttingen, where, at about the same time that Jones' work was published, Blumenbach was expounding his new classification of human races. Blumenbach's work was not only based on Linnaeus' earlier typology of natural life forms, as is often thought. More importantly, Blumenbach was indebted to Kant for a conceptual articulation of race in terms of teleological principles.[25] When translations of Jones' work reached a German readership, it was but a short step to link the idea of an ultimate proto-language (Indo-European) with Blumenbach's theory of an Aryan Caucasian proto-race from which are descended the Indian Brahmins as well as the modern European races. In another important paper, "On the Origin and Families of Nations," Jones was able to bring this new element of linguistic precision to racial speculation, arguing that there was

> incontestable proof . . . that the first race of Persians and Indians, to whom we may add the Romans and Greeks, the Goths, and the old Egyptians or Ethiops, originally spoke the same language and professed the same popular faith.[26]

It would appear that for Jones and other Orientalists of his generation, there was no real contradiction between *religious* ideology based on monotheism and the natural light of reason, and an overtly *racial* ideology centered on the belief in pure and original stocks of languages/peoples. In other words, not only were race, religion, and the possession of reason seen as compatible, but each was able to justify the other. Although the existing idea of an Indian Ur-monotheism/language/race blended well with Orientalist translations of Sanskrit classics to generate the myth of an Indian Golden Age, Jones could not easily avoid the contradiction between the once-glorious past of the Hindus and their present "degenerate" and "abased" state, except by distinguishing their "primitive religion and languages," which had not changed and which "prevail to this day with more or less their ancient purity," from their "arts," "government," and "knowledge," which have become debased. Jones' belief in an Indian Ur-monotheism and language thus came close to a version of monogenesis—the belief that humanity and therefore civilization came from a single source—that was shared by philosophers such as Kant. For Kant the appeal of monogenesis lay not only in its conformity to the Biblical account of the beginnings of humanity, but that it lent itself, via the notion of universal reason, to discussions of "human fraternity." Ironically, therefore, the facile overlap in the monogenetic hypothesis between the concepts of race, Ur-monotheism, and an *Ur-sprache* became, in the context of the late eighteenth century, a resource for liberals who needed to justify colonialism.

As is well known, Jones' translations of Indian classics generated enthusiasm in England and in Germany. The academic results of this enthusiasm were the establishment of many chairs of Sanskrit and Oriental Studies, and the creation of a disciplinary base that, in alliance with Germanic studies, might have threatened the monopoly of Latin and Greek studies as the only ancient languages deemed relevant to the European identity and its conceptual framework. Although these new academic studies were based initially in Britain, it seems that before the 1820s the more "liberal" Orientalism[1] inspired by William Jones was replaced by a more aggressive style of representing the nature of the Hindus (Orientalism[2]) that entailed a more "progressive"—i.e., historicist—frame of narrating non-Western others, as exemplified by James Mills' enormously influential *History of British India*. Mill's *History* and his espousal of utilitarian ideology coincided with and reflected the new mood of economic and military expansion of British interest in India. Jones' translations also engendered a new wave of uncompromising missionary activity, led by the Serampore Baptists William Ward, Joshua Marshman, and William Carey, who produced new translations and more comprehensive empirical work, the most influential of which was Ward's monumental *Mythology and Religion of the Hindoos*.

What needs to be noted for the purposes of our study is that although these new developments in the early nineteenth century provided a serious challenge to the prevalent deistic notions of an original Indian monotheism and an Indian Golden Age, these developments alone were not sufficient to displace the deist paradigm. Although it is rarely acknowledged, the displacement of deism in relation to Orientalist studies was achieved through the kind of ideological/political alliance that I mentioned earlier: in this case, a supra-national alliance between English utilitarian historiography and missionary translations on the one hand, and on the other, new developments in German philosophizing on the nature of language and religion. The ideological bridge for this alliance was a combined British-German (Protestant) opposition to monogeneticism. That is to say, this was an alliance between *historicism*—which supported the opposite ideal of polygeneticism, or the belief in multiple and distinct origins and evolution of the races of man—and *a new theory of religion.* This debate is reflected most powerfully by the way in which Indology was developed and reformulated within the leading German academic institutions, such as Jena, Heidelberg, Göttingen, Tübingen, and of course Berlin.

The German reshaping of the "Oriental Renaissance"[27] found powerful expression among a remarkable group of philosophers and thinkers who flourished between 1790 and the 1840s, a lineage running from Herder and the Schlegel brothers, through Schelling and Hegel, to Schopenhauer. What distinguishes these thinkers is that they were at the heart of intellectual debates and responsible for reshaping the direction of many different disciplines, including philosophy, theology, religion and culture, history, and, significantly for us, Indology. Indeed, developments in Indology mirrored many of the key debates in these other disciplines, particularly philosophy and religion.

The single most influential figure in the overlap between German Indology and philosophy was Hegel. Hegel's reputation is owed mainly to the fact that his intellectual output straddled most if not all of the key changes in European thinking from the 1790s to the 1820s, effecting far-reaching changes in a wide variety of disciplines, including philosophy of religion, theology, art, history, and culture, not to mention Indology itself. Hegel's writings on Hinduism and Indian culture form short but consistent parts of his encyclopedic surveys of the philosophy of art, history, and religion as well as his lectures on the history of philosophy. However, it is in the posthumously published *Lectures on the Philosophy of Religion*[28] that Hegel provides his most sustained engagement with Indology and Hinduism. Of special importance here is the fact that Hegel presents Hinduism in relation to the "concept of religion" as such, which he unfolds in some detail. What emerges therefore is not just a descriptive stereotype of Hinduism, but an ontotheological schema—Hegel's own reworking of ontotheology—which ensured that a stereotyped version of the terms "Hindu"/"Hinduism" would be received not only within mainstream disciplines such as philosophical theology, Indology, and the emerging science of religions, but also, mediated by future Indologists, by the native elites themselves. Within recent critiques of Orientalism the *Lectures on the Philosophy of Religion* are generally neglected in favor of the more accessible *Lectures on the Philosophy of History.* It is often forgotten, however, that some of the key ideas in Hegel's *Philosophy of History* are derived from the transition between the 1824 and the 1827 lectures, that is, as a result of Hegel's mature philosophy of religion.[29]

Indeed the final version of the *Philosophy of History* was not delivered until the 1831 semester, the year of Hegel's death.

The import of what is stated in these lectures is best appreciated in the light of Hegel's earlier writings, his disagreements and departures from Jena Romanticism, but most importantly his long-running philosophical feud with his former friend and roommate, F. W. Schelling.

Indology and the Pantheist Controversy: Herder, Schlegel, and Schelling

Compared with notable contemporaries such as Herder and Schlegel, who had begun writing on India as early as the late 1780s and the 1790s, Hegel's writings on Hinduism appear relatively late in his career (1820s). Even at that stage they appear within lecture courses on the historical systematization of the realms of art, religion, and philosophy.

By the 1790s J. G. Herder—one of the pioneers of the Romantic movement as well as of the early German interest in India—basing his work on William Jones' linguistics, initiated two important and at the time controversial themes concerning Indian culture. The first of these was the notion of India as ancestral home of European races.[30] Herder was of course a beneficiary of some of the most profound changes in the intellectual climate of Europe, in particular the notion of the *aesthetic* as it developed during the late eighteenth century, bringing with it a shift away from the purely rationalist (Enlightenment) focus on the nature of the object toward the quality of the experience evoked, and the corresponding articulation or expression of this experience in a given environment. Initially a reaction against deistic notions, this new phase of expressivism[31]—the outward manifesting of man's inner potential as seen in art for example—carried the implication of a newer and fuller individuation: man's autonomy from nature. Reflected in the potentiality to create or bring forth something original, this autonomy brought man closer to the divine. Connected to this is the idea that each individual is different and original. With Herder this notion of originality extended to individual cultures, nations, and peoples (*Volker*). Each *Volker* has its own way of being human. It was therefore considered justifiable to view Oriental cultures as autonomous entities in their own right and, because of their greater antiquity, as the source of Europeans' historical being.

While the link between the notion of the aesthetic, nationalism, and ethnicity clearly helped to locate questions on the origin of European cultural identity at the heart of Romantic philosophy even as they spoke of the East as different, it also raised a problem that would continue to rankle in the minds of those philosophers who had studied Oriental cultures. If the dialect of the aesthetic gave rise to a realization of freedom, then this freedom was inevitably linked to a revaluation of the role of sensuous experience as opposed to abstract intelligence. Since Oriental cultures were known to value sensuous experience, this clearly created a dilemma for philosophers and theologians committed to a Christian tradition that had long linked the role of the sensuous to paganism and idolatry. Suspicion of the sensuous created an essential divide between European philosophers, a divide that is perhaps best illustrated by the so-called pantheism controversy.

Pantheism was in fact the other main theme in Herder's characterization of India, although it was by no means peculiar to Herder alone. As the expression of a shift in religious sensibilities—a shift from the deistic notion of God as the cause, and therefore existing outside of man and world, to the idea of a universal soul encompassing the world as One and All that was arising in the late eighteenth century—it is associated with a revival of interest in Spinoza. Instigated primarily by Lessing (though covertly shared by Goethe, Hölderlin, Fichte, Schlegel, and Schelling), Spinozism provided, initially at least, a secret refuge for the Romantic yearning for an all-embracing unity that could heal the inherent separations and divisions of modern existence, with its attendant dichotomies of thought such as faith/knowledge, God/World, tradition/modernity. But inasmuch as this German variety of Spinozism provided a focus for criticizing orthodox Christian religion and, therefore, a bridge to non-Christian Oriental cultures, it also became a focus for opposition from committed Christian thinkers such as Jacobi, Schleiermacher, and, as we shall see, Hegel himself. In other words, "pantheism" became a polarized term, an intellectual football as it were, in debates concerning the existence of God on the one hand, and the ultimate source of self and cultural identity (European vs. Oriental?) on the other. The path from Herder to Hegel, however, passed through the contributions of two important personalities connected with the Romantic movement: Schlegel and Schelling.

Schlegel's early articles, published in *Europa* and *Athenaeum* (1800–1803), betray a period of flirtation with a romantically glorified conception of pantheism, one that is very much in keeping with a sharp criticism of the European present with its loss of unity, harmony, and capacity for religion:

> Man has indeed come very far on the art of arbitrary division or, what amounts to the same thing, in mechanism, and thus man has almost become a machine. . . . Man cannot sink any deeper. [32]

His general philosophical outlook during this period was governed by a fascination with the Orient: "For the pinnacle of Romanticism we must look" primarily to India. "Here is the actual source of all languages, all the thoughts and poem of the human spirit, everything, without exception comes from India."[33] It seems, however, that these early notions were shaped largely by readings from secondary sources, in particular Jones' work on Indo-European language affinity and Wilkins' descriptive accounts of the "deistic Hindoos." By 1808, however, having acquired a training in Sanskrit and Persian and converted to Roman Catholicism, Schlegel's initial enthusiasm had turned to outright criticism. With the publication of his book *On the Language and Wisdom of the Indians*, the once-cherished motif of pantheism became instead the focal point of his criticism of India. Primarily a philosophical statement, the work was intended to demonstrate the profound affinity between European philosophy and the new discipline of Indology.

In the second part of this work, entitled "On Philosophy," Schlegel defines the different systems of Indian thought under the titles "emanation," "naturalism," "dualism," and "pantheism." Although the religion and philosophy of the Hindus were still glorified for their antiquity, the authoritative Indian texts were no longer regarded as providing evidence of an undistorted pristineness but were considered to be distortions and misinterpretations of the original teachings, which were now lost. The original revelation given to Indians soon fell into a state of "philosophical error" called emanation. Defined as "a rise of error," the loss of simplicity of divine knowledge and a falling away from natural reason, emanation was considered "the most ancient error . . . a misuse of the divine gift (of revelation) resulting in wild fabrications . . . a result of the first fall from God." Nevertheless, emanation according to Schlegel was not to be confused with pantheism, which was the most recent and degenerate of all the Indian teachings:

> The most important epochs of Indian and Oriental philosophy and religion in general are the following: first the system of emanation,

which eventually degenerated into astrological superstition and fa-
natical materialism; the doctrine of two principles, whose dualistic
system eventually changed into pantheism. The human spirit has not
sunk deeper in Oriental philosophy than into pantheism, which is just
as pernicious for morals as materialism and, moreover destroys the
imagination as well.[34]

The critique of pantheism not only forms the philosophical heart of the
work but is also a direct pointer to a perceived ethical difference between
Europe and the Orient. For Schlegel, pantheism was an abstract, negative
concept of the infinite, devoid of any inner content, a concept that leads
to indifference, leaving no room for individuality or moral discernment, a
"destructive influence on life." What makes this later critique philosophically interesting is that Schlegel considers pantheism to be "the system
of pure reason" and yet at the same time to be the greatest failure in the
history of human thought. Borrowing what had become a key weapon in
Christianity's dual counteroffensive against the Enlightenment and early
Romantic "atheists," the concept of pantheism was connected to an irreligious egoistic disposition.

By far the most frequent and important target of the Christian philosophical invective against pantheism was Friedrich Schelling, who, along
with his predecessor Herder and younger contemporary Schopenhauer,
formed the core of a group of European philosophers who came to be associated with a defense (against Hegel in particular) of philosophical and
religious pantheism and the importation of Oriental ideas into Europe.
However, part of the problem in trying to gauge Schelling's exact role
in these debates are the dominant narratives in the history of modern European philosophy, which tend to portray Schelling simply as part of the
group of thinkers responsible for the development of German idealism.
It is a story that begins with Fichte's reworking of Kant's critiques, continues with Schelling's *System of Transcendental Idealism*, and culminates in Hegel's system. Hegel is then superseded by Marx, who inverts
Hegel's speculative logic into a form of materialism.[35] Clearly, though,
the story carries a logic of development that is already Hegelian. This
narrative was further consolidated in the twentieth century by post-Hei-
deggerian modes of recounting the history of philosophy as a history of
metaphysics that comes to an end with Nietzsche and Heidegger. The
overall result is a series of well-known caricatures of Schelling's philosophy as propagating: (i) pantheism derived from a monistic Absolute

Identity as the real ground of existence, with the world being regarded as a fall from the Absolute and therefore illusory, a position that ultimately leads to the errors of dualism; (ii) the annihilation of self, which ultimately dissolves any basis for ethics, knowledge, and religion; (iii) onto-theology[36]; (iv) Indomania, along with its attendant aspects: the belief in an Indian Ur-monotheism, and the glorification of Indian antiquity, which would ultimately lead European philosophy to become adversly affected by primitive, pagan ideas from India.

The problem with these caricatures, even the seemingly anti-Hegelian ones, is that they represent strictly European concerns inasmuch as the self that is recounted is still clearly Western. Clearly, therefore, there is a vested interest in maintaining such a narrative insofar as it maintains the self-representation of European consciousness. As Andrew Bowie and Manfred Frank have pointed out, these caricatures misrepresent what was actually at stake in the intellectual debates that took place during the early decades of the nineteenth century.[37] More important, what is often forgotten is that these debates took their impetus not so much from the polarized perspective of Occidentalism versus Orientalism, but from a common concern, namely the individual thinkers' relationship to the Christian foundations of the European conceptual framework and identity. Indeed, the alleged "Indomania" of figures such as Herder, Schelling, and Schopenhauer was in fact secondary to their desire to present a very different way of perceiving Europe, a difference that does not necessarily come from a foreign source, but is already at the heart of European traditions.

Nowhere are the nature and implications of this debate better demonstrated than in the battle for intellectual supremacy between the respective systems of Schelling and Hegel. This battle, which began in the early 1800s with Hegel's critiques of Schelling's *Identitätsphilosophie* and *Naturphilosophie*, heated up considerably in the early 1820s, following Hegel's arrival at the University of Berlin and the dissemination of his lecture courses on aesthetics, history, and religion. With Berlin at this time being recognized as one of the two premier institutions of European thinking, the stakes for rivals like Schelling and Hegel could not have been greater. Given the very different orientations of their philosophy, it was imperative as to which philosophy would succeed, particularly since Schelling's thought had already exercised considerable influence beyond Berlin and beyond the field of philosophy. The stakes of this battle amounted to nothing less than the future political direction of European identity. Although the debate between Schelling and Hegel can be viewed from different perspectives—those of art, history, theology, etc.—I want to narrow the focus to the relationship between Indology (as the production of knowledge about Oriental religions and cultures) and the theorization of religion, or how the nature of religion came to be redefined through an encounter with Indology, given that what was at stake (for European philosophers) in (re)defining "religion" was the place and status of European self-consciousness as essentially Christian.

Rather than presenting separate readings of Schelling and Hegel on these issues, I shall focus on Hegel's text, notably the 1824–1827 *Lectures on the Philosophy of Religion*. By reading Hegel's argument from within, I hope to demonstrate how much his reworking of the concept of religion in relation to Indology is dependent on a systematic and parallel undermining of Schelling's *Naturphilosophie* and *Identitätsphilosophie*. As will become apparent even through the Hegelian lens, Schelling's ideas emerge as a dangerous alternative that must be marginalized or repressed; I say "dangerous" because Schelling's theory opens a space for the encounter between Indian and European ideas that is neither dedicated to maintaining a superior vantage point for Christian-European self-consciousness nor reducible to the relationship between colonizer and colonized. In many ways Schelling's system is an important and overlooked precursor to the late twentieth century's postmetaphysical, postcolonial approaches, especially in the field of the study of religions. As we shall see in chapter 6, elements of the Schelling and Hegel debate are evident in the contemporary crisis of theory in the humanities.

Although Hegel had been writing at length on religion since his early education at the Tübingen theological seminary, his famous discussions on world religions and on Indian/Hindu religion in particular only appeared toward the end of his career, as part of the 1824–1827 Berlin *Lectures on the Philosophy of Religion*.[38] Contrary to received opinion, however, the Berlin lectures are more than simply an extension of leading ideas from *The Phenomenology of Spirit*.[39] The Berlin lecture course in its published form represents a deepening of his critique and consequent philosophical estrangement from the Jena Romantics, and Schelling in particular. But more important, it represents the clearest articulation of a new form of classification based on the connection between two interconnected themes: *race/ethnicity/nation* and *ontotheology*. The former refers to a desired separation of the European/Greek/Christian group of religions from the Oriental and African groups on racial grounds. According to this racial classification, non-European cultures had to be excluded from the history of philosophy and from the possibility of their ever having received a revelation in the first place. Revelation was linked to historico-spiritual evolution. Ontotheology refers to a way of thinking about determinate religions in terms of their classification within a particular order of civilization, a process that is entirely governed by theologico-political considerations. The interconnection between these two themes is elaborated within a long discussion of the proper constitution of the first two stages of the dialectic: the stage of Primal Unity as we see it in natural or immediate religion, and the stage of Representation as seen in artistic or determinate religions, i.e., religions as they are manifested in history.

For Hegel, accounting for the difference between these two stages of the dialectic will be pivotal not only to his placement of Indian "religions" in relation to the concept of religion-in-general, but to what constitutes the boundary between the West and the "Rest" or between history and prehistory. What becomes clear as we read Hegel's text closely is that the concept of religion-in-general is being fleshed out in tandem with the simultaneous inclusion/exclusion of India within history. Furthermore, this fleshing out of a concept of religion as universal is simultaneously the fleshing out of a mode of thinking in which the operation of thought becomes indistinguishable from a "generalized translation"—the ability to translate infinitely and at will between the universal and the particular.[40]

Naming the Origin: Hegel's Critique of Deism and Natural Religion

"The first thing," according to Hegel, is "to classify these determinate, ethnic religions."[41] Yet the very idea of classification implies the need to constitute an order of things, indeed a need to order the religions of different nations or ethnicities. Not only are race and nation already presupposed as the basis on which religions exist, but Hegel's first act revives an ancient theme wherein the act of naming sets one apart from the other. At stake here was not simply the idea of a beginning, an origin, the original condition of religion, but the *identity* of that origin. To whom—which nation, culture, or ethnicity—did the earliest condition of religion belong? To whom belonged the ability to *name* the origin and, as a consequence, the *value* of the origin in relation to what comes after:

history as what is past, and modernity, the present, as signaling the end of history? For Hegel this classification could not be taken lightly, in a "merely subjective way." Rather it had to be a "necessary classification" that followed objectively from the nature of spirit,[42] and the mode of existence assumed by spirit as it proceeded dialectically from the lowest stages of existence (the origin/original condition) to the highest stage (the present moment).

Thus "according to our classification, nature religion is the lowest level, the most imperfect and thus the first, while according to the other way of viewing it is not only the first but the truest."[43] This "other way of viewing it" is a thinly disguised allusion to Schelling's *Identitätsphilosophie*, which provided the strongest philosophical grounding for the idea of the Absolute (One) as the perfect origin and therefore the "original condition of mankind and religion."[44] According to Hegel's reading of Schelling, this notion of absolute and primal identity that excludes all difference suggests both that humanity had been in a state of innocent perfection, a pristine state of being in which spirit is clairvoyant, a free fantasy already in possession of artistic and scientific knowledge and that in this state humanity could see God directly.[45] Moreover, Schelling directly connected his philosophical notion of absolute identity (*Indifferenzpunkt*) to a mythic golden age: "I firmly believe that the earliest condition of the human race was a civilized one and that the first states, sciences, arts, religions were founded simultaneously, . . . [i.e., they were] not separated but perfectly fused, as they will again be in their final form."[46] Even more unpalatable for Hegel was Schelling's suggestion that ethnicities or nations other than the Greeks could have existed simultaneously in a state of perfection, or had access to anything resembling science or scientific knowledge: "What if already in Greek mythology (not to mention Indian and other Oriental mythologies) there emerged the remains of a knowledge, indeed even a system, which goes far beyond the circle drawn by the oldest revelation known through scriptural evidences?"[47]

From Hegel's point of view it was entirely contradictory to hold on to the notion of a perfect origin (the Absolute One) and yet continue to represent it as a state *in time*, that is, a state that once existed, but was lost by chance:

> On the one hand . . . [this state as represented] . . . includes the necessary idea of divine self consciousness, . . . But on the other, this idea is represented as *existing*, i.e. as a state which has occurred in time or is

now over. . . . This is in fact the crux of the matter. It is imagined then that the oneness of humanity with nature, and then with God, is original in the sense that this original is what comes first in existence.[48]

Two issues are at stake here for Hegel. First is the conception of time, and related to this the criterion whereby truth/reality is measured. The question here is whether the original condition (of man and therefore of nature religion) is what comes first *in time*, in which case "original" implies a natural unity, that is, a coincidence in a center, a paradise, an identity of the human and the divine as the only true state of religion. For this original condition and for humanity's divine state to have been lost, however, could mean only one of two things: either that time and contingency had intruded into the divine life from outside, or, that time and contingency were a divine necessity. The latter possibility clearly implied an origin that admitted difference. Clearly perfection and original difference were incompatible ideas. In either case time and history could not correspond to the notion of the divine as Absolute, but would sink to the status of the single mythic, and therefore eternal, moment in the divine totality—"a moment that cannot be absolute and truthful." In the sections on "Hindu Religion" Hegel will compare this moment to the legendary "Moment" of Brahma's existence in the divine totality (the Hindu Trimurty), in order to explain how this "mythic moment" is at the heart of the pantheist notion of time that is the seed of illusion (*maya*), falsehood, and error. Clearly, Hegel is looking for a notion of time and history in which (i) the divine becomes involved in and as history, the history of mankind, and (ii) humanity being initially imperfect must evolve historically toward the present state.

This brings us to the second issue, one that is of course directly related to the conception of time, namely, the *value* of the European present, as a universal criterion of truth or reality—or rather, the possibility of this present being *devalued*. For Hegel, the potential for such a devaluation clearly lurked in the Schellingian representation of the original condition "as *existing*, as a state which has occurred in time and is now over." If so, there was always the dangerous possibility of it existing again. It could, philosophically, be resurrected! Alternatively there was the specter of coeval-ness. An origin that admitted difference could allow different cultures to coexist. If such coexistence were shown to be not only philosophically but empirically viable, there was clearly no moral justification for European dominance over the Orient. The dangers were plainly obvious.

What began as theological speculation could end up creating unnecessary political dilemmas. Coeval-ness threatened to ground otherwise disparate cultures in the same world, in the context of a living present, this present being a threatening site of existential encounter between colonizer and colonized. The only real question, therefore, was how to maintain distance from the Orient under the gaze of a tactile eye. Hegel no doubt found this scenario somewhat disconcerting, for until the 1820s European writings on Indian religion had never really threatened the notion—long cherished since the missionary accounts, strengthened by Jones' linguistics, and fostered by the Jena Romantics—of the ambiguity and primacy of the Oriental religions among the religions of mankind. If anything this view had provided a strong counterbalance to European (largely French and British) pride in the achievements of modern science. Only with the availability of a new wave of empiricist and utilitarian ethnographic historiography[49] did Hegel venture into properly Indological territory, which until then, among the philosophers, had belonged almost exclusively to Schlegel and Schelling.

This newer ethnographic data on Oriental religions appeared to be in tune with Hegel's earlier evolutionist reasoning—the progressive movement from plants, through animals, to humankind. In a clear reversal of the Romantic theories, mankind's original state was posited as a state of natural unity or immediacy with the plant and animal kingdom, where the only awareness is of an instinctive kind, much the same as that possessed by animals, or in the case of humans, the kind of awareness possessed by sleepwalkers.[50] However, this private state of being has nothing to do with spirit or the spiritual, since in nature religion's "rational consciousness has been stilled." What Hegel defines as "the spiritual," on the other hand,

is not in immediate unity with nature, but on the contrary *it has to cross* the infinite gulf that separates it from the natural; unity first comes into being as a reconciliation that is brought about; it is not a reconciledness that is there from the outset, and this genuine unity is achieved only through *movement*, through a *process*, through first *getting away from* one's immediate existence and then returning to self.[51] [emphasis added]

If indeed further clarification for this point were needed, Hegel provided it in an updated version of the 1827 lectures by making a clearcut distinction between his own "Nature Religion" and the deistic notion of "Natur*al*

Religion," which might easily be confused. "The first form of religion is . . . what we call nature religion . . . [but] in this modern period this term . . . has for some time had a different sense; we have understood this to mean what human beings are able to cognize through their reason, through the natural light of their reason."[52] Thus according to the Hegelian classification, "natural reason" is an erroneous expression. "Natural" is understood to mean "the immediate." It has to do with the *sensible* or the "uncultivated," as opposed to the *super*-sensible or "metaphysical":

> "Natural religion," as the term has been employed in more recent times, has also referred to mere metaphysical religion, where "metaphysics" has had the sense of "understandable thought." That is the modern religion of the understanding—or what is called "*deism*," a result of the Enlightenment, the knowledge of God as an abstraction . . . to which all definitions of God are reduced . . . it is the final extreme position of the abstract understanding that results from the Kantian critique [53]

The preceding argument is targeted as much at the *Naturphilosophie* as it is against Enlightenment deism, given that Schelling's argument, which appealed to an "original dualism in nature," implied the exact opposite to Hegel. For Schelling nature and spirit, sensuous and supersensuous are not absolutely different—they are fundamentally related. Nature always already contains within itself the seed of its own motion or activity vis-à-vis the principle of the negative, i.e., inhibition (*Hemmung*). Nature evolves by means of this original repression of the sensible. Of course the problem for Schelling is that this cannot be considered from the standpoint of metaphysics or reason but only by means of a mythologizing or aesthetic reason, which for Hegel is self-defeating. Hegel, by contrast, appropriates the principle of the negative on behalf of reason. By virtue of the negative not only is reason a "liberation vis-à-vis the natural but [it is] the subjection of the natural to itself, making it fit the measure of, and be obedient to, itself."[54]

Thus by contrast to Schelling's *Naturphilosophie*, reason alone is the self-elevation of the natural, and the term "spirit" refers precisely to such a self-extrication from nature:

> Because of this ambiguity we should avoid the term "natural reason." The genuine sense of natural reason is "spirit or reason according to the concept." Yet the "concept"—what is *truly* rational—is accessible

only to someone with a *scientific* education, whose mind is liberated from immediate intuition. . . . This rationality and knowledge emerge only . . . with the last stage of human existence; the first stage of human existence is as an animal.[55] [emphasis added]

If the desired effect of Hegel's polemic was to salvage for European civilization the value of the present as the culmination of spirit's progress through history, this was achieved by demarcating true science as strictly belonging to European heritage alone, that is, by providing empirical evidence—*real* proof as opposed to the idealizing speculation of the Romantics and deists—for the backwardness, stultification, and therefore intrinsic inferiority of the Oriental present. Referring indirectly to Schelling:

Attempts have been made to demonstrate historically the view that the human race began from and enjoyed a pristine state of perfection. There are numerous peoples among whom have been found relics of art, of phantasy and sometimes also of scientific knowledge, which seem to be incompatible with their present state. From this evidence of a better mode of existence, people have inferred an earlier state of perfection, a state of completely ethical life. . . . Among the Hindus a wisdom of knowledge has been found which is so great that it is not consistent with their present educational and cultural level.[56]

Of Passage and Installation: The Question of Spirit

Having thus introduced the following ideas: that the "original condition"—the stage of primal unity—is not only the earliest but the lowest stage of mankind and religion, and that the "boundary" separating the stages of primal unity and determinate religion corresponds to the process of becoming conscious, that is, to the attainment of the representative function, Hegel proceeds to elaborate one of the major themes of his lecture course: to demonstrate *"what spirit is"* by charting its historical progress as manifested through the religious experience of mankind, beginning with the Oriental religions as "those furthest removed from the truth" and ending with Germanic Christianity as the fully developed (revealed) concept of religion in general. The phrase *"what spirit is"*[57] refers to the appearance of spirit at various stages in history. The story that accompanies each appearance—its phenomenology—thus corresponds to the concrete forms of the *ethnic* religions. As Hegel himself states, "the elaboration of what spirit is [phenomenology] forms the entire content of the philosophy of religion."[58]

An important issue arises at this point. It concerns the relation between the representation of religion as a concrete phenomenon (the "what spirit is"), and the *operation whereby* religion is represented (the "what is" *of spirit*). Putting this another way: although the "what spirit is" is given by a particular representation of religion (its determinate manifestation in the form of an *ethnē*), spirit is not simply *given* as being-there, but is always already presupposed within the framing question "what is?" and therefore within the conceptualizing operation itself. What this clearly suggests are two very different ways of speaking about or relating to spirit: the epistemo-phenomenological ("what spirit is") and the ontological (the "what is" *of spirit*), rolled into a single operation of conceptualization.[59]

What seems to be at stake in uncovering the ontology of the question—the operation of thinking about spirit—is the problem of passage or transition, or how spirit, which by definition is innermost, can fall into time (i.e., be objectified as an external phenomenon) and yet remain spirit. Hegel does not formulate the problem in quite these terms, but the terms in which he does present the problem are of far-reaching importance to understanding how Indian "religion" comes to be represented under the category of pantheism, and even more so to the very project of thinking about religion(s) within the field of the question "what is . . . ?" Indeed the question "What is religion?" becomes for Indologists, philosophers of religion, and most importantly the native elites, not only a grounding question, but equally, a necessary assumption in the translation and reception of Oriental culture *as religion*. To the present day the question "What is religion?," now little more than a formulaic definition, remains the basis on which the plurality, diversity, and difference between cultures is thought.

The difference between these two ways of articulating religion is undertaken by Hegel in the two separate parts of the *LPR*. Part I, "The Concept of Religion in General," focuses on the operation through which religion is conceptualized or thought about (the "what is" *of spirit*). In contrast to the mainly theoretical first part, part II, "Determinate Religion," presents the empirical proof, i.e., the phenomena corresponding to the religious experience of the diversity of nations, ethnicities, or races of mankind ("what spirit is"). Although Hegel's aim was to project total correspondence between part I and part II, the achievement of such correspondence, as we shall see below, proved far more difficult in the earlier lectures, leading eventually to a shift in emphasis from the 1824 formulation toward a more conducive formulation in 1827. I shall begin by elaborating some of the problems in part I of the 1824 lectures.

The Temporality of Movement

One of the central themes of part I was to develop the basis for exchangeability among the terms "God," "religion," and "spirit." For Hegel this translatability between God/religion/spirit derives from the speculative definition of religion outlined initially in the lecture manuscript and explicated more fully in part I of the 1824 lecture course. At this stage the definition that Hegel presents is more or less straightforward. In the lecture manuscript Hegel begins by arguing that the speculative definition of religion is an antithesis of two essential moments: (i) the subjective side, based in the element of absolute universality exemplified by pure thinking; (ii) the objective side, consisting in absolute singularity, pure sensibility. Religion consists essentially of the relation between the two. The speculative element holds together religious consciousness and its object (God or religion as a concrete form):

> This speculative [element] is what comes to consciousness in religion. Otherwise, God is an indeterminate, empty name. This is the religious standpoint . . .
> Accordingly religion itself as such exists as this speculative element.[60]

But while it is all very well to say that this speculative element enables unhindered passage between the two antithetical moments of religion, the "concept" of religion nevertheless remains nothing more than an abstract definition unless one can prove that the concept is *necessary*—necessity here meaning what cannot be mediated by anything else. In order for there to be a concept of religion, religion itself must be necessary, which begs the question, what is it that is necessary about religion? Hegel answers this clearly in section B of the 1824 lecture course: "Since . . . the necessity of religion occurs within religion itself it is also the case that the concept of religion will be generated within religion itself; the syllogistic outcome of religion, the true religion, is what produces consciousness itself, the one which has for its object *what religion is*."[61]

If the establishment of a general translatability between God/religion/
spirit seemed relatively straightforward in part I, where thought operates
in an unhindered environment, this process of translation becomes much
more problematic in part II, where Hegel is confronted with empirical
knowledge of real religions and needs to enact a movement or passage
between theoretical concept and empirical fact, between "religion,"
which is self-generating, and religions, which cannot simply be assumed
to have generated themselves. Thus in part II Hegel argues for the need
to begin with a correct definition of the "concept" before enacting the
passage to empirical religions. In part II, however, Hegel proceeds more
cautiously, his definition of the "concept" being preceded by way of reference to the "metaphysical":

> To begin with, we must discuss the *concept* of this metaphysical and
> explain what is meant by it.[62]

Accordingly, the name "God" can be understood as the "metaphysical concept" of religion and therefore as the subject of religion, which means that
the "metaphysical concept of God" is necessarily implicit in any and every
conceptualizing of religion. This, Hegel reminds us, is the familiar form
of thinking that appears as the theological proofs for the existence of God.
What needs to be noted for our purposes is the circular relation between
(i) the nature of "the concept" as metaphysical and (ii) "the metaphysical"
as the nature of the concept that now becomes the defining criterion for
what counts as religion, indeed for the possibility of an unhindered passage or translatability between theory and empirical fact, between concept
and phenomenon. The entire matter thus hinges on how the "metaphysical" accounts for this mediation. Resorting to a very traditional argument,
Hegel argues that the truth of "the metaphysical" resides in its being a mediation whose essence is *movement* or *pure activity*, i.e., movement as the
self-negation of the merely finite or empirical, the negation of negation:

> Such mediation is contained in the divine idea itself, and it is only
> when it is understood in this way that it becomes a necessary determi-
> nation, a necessary moment.[63]

In other words, the transition between the two moments of religion,
between the speculative and the concrete, is simply a "necessary moment
of the concept, a *going forth* of mediation, an *activity* on the part of the

concept itself." The admission that notions such as the "metaphysical" and the "concept" must be presupposed ("contained in the divine idea itself . . . where we must discard the form of the understanding") clearly indicates that the work of the " 'concept' of the metaphysical" is reductionistic. This admission is the first, though tacit, acknowledgment on Hegel's part that the desired formulation for a "Concept of Religion" (part I), which would be mirrored perfectly by the empirical proofs in part II, is still eluding him. It signals early on in the 1824 lectures a failure to come to terms with the problem of the "Original Condition"—the problem of trying to conceptually determine the origin of religion. The problem, as it turns out, is how there can be knowledge of the other (how the other can be classified or located in a system of knowledge) without the knower being involved in time and therefore in a necessary relation to the other. By reducing the danger of actual movement (which would entail a movement of the self and therefore a fall into time or the subject's being related to the object of study) to an *idealization*, all further encounters with the empirical will have been rendered safe through a decontaminating operation. The object as other must never be able to present any danger in being encountered. It should be able to be encountered from a distance, by remote control, as it were.

What Hegel clearly recognized was the centrality of time to any project of systematic classification. This is particularly evident in Hegel's continued efforts to prove that the nature of movement as the essence of "what religion is" remains the same in parts I and II. The statement in part I reads as follows:

> Religion is the consciousness of the true in and for itself as opposed to sensible, finite truth, sense perception, etc. This is the precise definition of religion that we are acquainted with initially from representation.
>
> Consciousness of the true that has being in and for itself without limit and universally: this is an *elevation*, a *rising above*, a reflecting upon, a *passing over* from what is immediate, sensible (for what is sensible is what is first and not therefore the elevation); and thus it is a *going out* and on to an *other*. . . . This is the process of spirit in general and since it is the absolutely universal, therefore this activity is *thought*, and God is the highest thought. . . . At this point God and religion exist in and through *thought*—simply and solely in and for thought.[64]

Compare this with the corresponding statement in part II:

Humanity *rises* from the finite to the infinite, rises above the singular and *raises itself* to the universal, to being-in-and-for-itself.

Even when we speak of religion in these speculative (abstract) terms, we already have here the relation of *transition* from finite to infinite.

. . . this *progress* (of consciousness in religion) is necessary, it is contained in the concept . . . The process of *elevation to God* is just what we have seen: this finite self-consciousness does not remain bound to the finite; it relinquishes the nature of the finite, jettisons it, and pictures to itself the infinite; this is what happens so to speak, in the process of elevation to God, and this is the rational element in that process. This *progression* is the innermost or purely logical element. [65]

The link between parts I and II relies on the following argument: thus far in the existence of mankind every experience or appearance of religion has revealed itself as relative or transitory. As such the kind of thinking that is proper to the religious standpoint cannot simply be another version of prior attempts to ground religion in an absolute (universal) principle, which would be merely subjective. Instead it must be grounded in pure movement, negation of negation, whose essence is expressed by the term *Aufhebung*, which has the triple meaning of negating something as a partial reality, of preserving its essence, and of elevating it to a universal sphere of meaning. As such, *Aufhebung* is an onto-economic term that describes the process of absolutely retaining something as it slips away.[66] However, the attempt to think in pure thought would itself be *intransitive*. The transition proper to the *Aufhebung* can have no beginning in time.

Co-Origination; or, The Difference Between Religion and History

On the other hand, from the standpoint of knowledge about other religion*s* (phenomena), in this case Oriental religions, there appears to be a completely different kind of movement, one that is involved in the progression of consciousness to the first stage of religion (hence the need to classify Indian religions), the primal unity that appears *in* history and therefore in the time of human religious experience. By Hegel's own criteria, to be classifiable as religion Indian culture had to have progressed from a stage where it was *not yet* religion. Inasmuch as the antiquity of Indian religion was regarded as unchallenged even by Hegel, the real problem, therefore, was that the emergence of history, or the first "moment" of the *Aufhebung,* appeared to coincide with the emergence of Indian religion.

The dilemma for Hegel was how to classify Indic culture *as* religion and yet keep it outside of history, which properly speaking belonged to the West. There were two obstacles here. First, there was an abundance of seemingly compelling evidence relating to the antiquity of Sanskrit as the source of Indo-Aryan languages and race. Backed by the philological authority of Sir William Jones and the philosophical arguments of Schlegel and Schelling, among others, this evidence tended to suggest that Orient and Occident shared the same origin, given which there could then be no moral justification either for the colonization of India or for placing Indian religions outside the pale of history.

The second obstacle was more complex in that it stemmed from Hegel's attempt in part 1 ("The Concept of Religion in General") to define "what religion is" in and through thought itself. According to this definition, "Religion is the consciousness of the true that has being in and for itself without limit and universally."[67] In other words, the kind of thinking that is proper to religion had to be grounded in a principle that was not subjective but objective and universal. Thinking about religion had to be grounded in a *pure* movement, a *pure* transition ("pure" in the sense that such a movement must not leave any trace in time). It must be an occulted movement that could not rely for its movement on anything outside of itself. Such movement, which is effectively the definition of transcendence, also comprises the essence of historicism, the impulse to historicize, which belongs to the West. Transcendental historicity—having history, being able to define "what history is" and yet to remain outside of history in the sense of not being affected by it—defines what it means to be Western as opposed to Oriental.

But here was the problem. Inasmuch as the antiquity of Indian religion was regarded as unchallenged even by Hegel, the real problem was that the emergence of history, or the first moment of the *Aufhebung*, appeared to coincide with the emergence of Indian religion. By Hegel's own definition, Indian culture, insofar as it could be defined as religion or religious, also showed a progression in consciousness (i.e., movement, elevation, transition), thus allowing it to be demarcated at the stage of primal unity, which corresponds to the "moment" when history begins. To his distaste, Hegel was confronted by the possibility of a *coincidence* between the origination of religion in India and the origination of history. It was clearly difficult to avoid the necessity of a "first moment" of the *Aufhe-bung*. Which is to say, however, that the essence of transition necessary for Indian religions to emerge and the essence of transition necessary for history to emerge appeared to be the same. Moreover, both appeared to have definite origins *in time*.

This was not merely incidental to the 1824 *LPR* course. It was also an issue in his vastly more popular *LPH* course, which Hegel had formulated and delivered a year earlier than the religion seminars. In one of the key chapters of the *LPH* Hegel tackles head on "the topic of how the origin of history is to be conceived." The problem, which he contests, is that the discovery of Sanskrit projected as an incontestable fact the idea of a bond between Germanic and Indic peoples and cultures. But for Hegel this event had to be kept outside history. Whereas the seemingly more secular *LPH* text manages to sidestep the issue of Indian religion's origination, the 1824 *LPR* text finds itself entangled in the issue of the *co*-origination of history and religion. Two possibilities now suggested themselves. Either the origin is contaminated by cultural difference, in the sense that two or more cultures share the same origin, in which case the *Aufhebung* is supplementary to nature (from which it follows that domination, as the work of the *Aufhebung,* belongs not so much to the domain of nature as it does to the domain of culture). Or, there is coexistence of two different *Aufhebungen*, two different essences of transition: one that corresponds to the continuum of transitions that we call history or historical knowledge, and one that corresponds to the *original transition* from nature that defines "what religion is."

Certainly within the 1824 lectures little or no indication is given of any qualitative difference in the nature of transition. In fact Hegel takes care to emphasize that the nature of transition as it occurs in the history of religions is not only the same as, but is in fact grounded in, the concept:

> This transition, however, is not simply a factual one, but is grounded in the nature of these determinations as well; that is to say it is grounded in the concept, . . . [hence] there is no need for us to advance beyond this definition of the transition. Considering it in more detail, it is possible to grasp it in two ways: first as a transition from the finite to the infinite as a beyond—this is a more modern relationship. But secondly it can be taken in such a way that the unity of both is maintained and the finite is preserved in the infinite. This is how it is in nature religion. *But to define this relationship more precisely, whether the infinite is [already]*

separated from the finite, or whether there is a transition from the finite to the infinite . . . this need not concern us.[68] [emphasis mine]

Hegel's nonchalance—*"this need not concern us"*—is misplaced, given that any project of systematic classification requires there to be a basic distinction between (i) a state of primal unity where religion/history/consciousness have *not yet* emerged, and (ii) the *first* emergence of religion as nature religion. Between the "not yet" and the "first" lies the origin of history and religion as self-caused. But it is this very co-origination of history and religion, motivated by the *Aufhebung*, that creates the dilemma for Hegel in regard to the classification of Indian culture as religion.

Although both choices are distasteful to Hegel, the second is potentially more threatening as far as the construction of systematic knowledge is concerned. For any knowledge to count as scientific there must be consistency between the continuum of transitions that corresponds to historical knowledge of religions, and the *original* transition that corresponds to the concept of religion. The essence of the two *Aufhebungen*—the concept of religion versus the history of religions—must be qualitatively consistent throughout, which of course derives from the very definition of essence as that which is unique, one, and only one.

To entertain the possibility that there are different kinds of essences would mean that the concept of *Aufhebung* itself is flawed. An imperfection in the *Aufhebung* would not only jeopardize the basis of knowledge itself, but bring Indian religions unbearably close to the origin of history. Hegel needed to keep India as far as possible from this origin in order to protect not only the West's claim to superiority in conceptual knowledge (what we today call Eurocentrism) but also the central mechanism behind its conceptual superiority: the idea of unhindered or "fundamental translatability" between cultures. Logically speaking, the latter simply collapses into the former. An imperfect *Aufhebung* implies an imperfect origin: original *co*-existence, the original plurality of cultures. What is especially interesting about the 1824 course is that Hegel will opt for the second choice and will try to qualify the very definition of *Aufhebung* rather than allow India into history. Clearly what was at stake in demarcating history in relation to India and religion was the conceptual purity of European identity.

From a political perspective alone he needed to place Hinduism within a comparative context of historical development. Any task of comparing or classifying requires a possession in advance of a metaphysical concept that allows the knower to simultaneously relate to and transcend the known. Yet, Hegel argues, this is precisely what Oriental religions *lack*. Compared with European religions, they do not possess a metaphysical concept of God. Possession of such a concept would qualify them for a place within the defining boundary of the history of philosophy, thus bringing the Orient uncomfortably close to the birthplace of philosophy, Greece. At play here is the bitter war of cultural politics between the respective protagonists of Orientalism[1] and Orientalism[2] over the origins of civilization and the true roots of European cultural identity. At this stage of the 1824 lectures, Hegel's main counteroffensive against the Orientalist thesis of an Indian Golden Age that could also have been the possible origin of European identity was to align his readings of the Hindu concept of God with Schelling's notion of the Absolute, and to argue for a proximity between the Hindu notion of Brahman as substance and the notion of substance in Schelling's *Identitätsphilosophie*. From here it was but a short step to label both as pantheistic and atheistic.

The result, however—certainly in the 1824 course—was far from satisfactory. The conflation between Hinduism and pantheism was problematical in itself. Hegel effectively consigned pantheism (and by default Schelling's system of *Identitätphilosophie*), along with atheism, outside the boundary of religion. There can be "in 'true' pantheism and atheism no talk of elevation, of transition, of the metaphysical/rational." To speak of elevation, of some kind at least, in Hinduism is clearly contradictory to this. Furthermore, although Hegel manages, by placing Hinduism as near as possible to the level of primal unity, to maintain a qualitatively large gap between the Orient and Greece, this is in effect undermined by the fact that the essence of transition in nature religion is necessarily the same as in artistic religion. A quantum gap between two cultures is hardly justifiable if the activity of spirit going on within them is essentially the same!

Thus the difference between inconsistent and consistent elevation signifies the need for a reliable mode of differentiating between nature religion as a stage of prehistory and artistic religion as a stage of history. What is rarely acknowledged, however, is that the designation "inconsistent/consistent" actually rehearses moves made in a similar discussion in the *Phenomenology of Spirit* where Hegel is trying to establish the transition from inorganic nature to the kind of consciousness whose ultimate expression is achieved in the family.[69] What Hegel regards as the definitive transition is played out in the passage from animal desire to human desire, which is able to fulfill itself in labor, work, or art. What properly distinguishes animal and human desire is the degree to which each exhibits the essence of transition vis-à-vis the dialectic of the *Aufhebung*. Once again, as Derrida suggests in *Glas*, it is a question of time. In animal *Aufhebungen* the moments of the *Aufhebung* are dissociated and external, "separated in time." Inhibition and consummation do not occupy the same moment: "In the animal there is no dialectic of the *Aufhebung* present to the animal."[70] Its desire is—to use the language of the *LPR*—inconsistent. Animal dialectic announces itself as the not-yet, as prehistorical. The animal as such does not have history. By contrast, in human desire the *Aufhebung* properly relieves itself in the present. It is present to man. The *Aufhebung* is history. The result: no religion or history for animals. Man has religion and history. Yet Indians have religion but no history! A strange ambivalence on Hegel's part toward Orientals, or simply an irreconcilable contradiction?

Clearly a task opens up for Hegel in the middle of the 1824 lectures: to reformulate the definition of the *Aufhebung* as an answer to the question "What is religion?" and to achieve a proper installation of Hinduism such that Hinduism is viewed as histori*cal* but always outside history. This reformulation takes place in the 1827 lectures, which represent Hegel's mature philosophy of religion. Space prevents me from undertaking a detailed reading of these texts. I shall therefore restrict my remarks to the way in which Hegel's revised definition of the metaphysical helps to create a stereotypical version of "Hindu" and Hinduism—consigned to the past but never *in* history—that became pervasive in later discourses of Indology, comparative theology, and philosophy.

Linking *Aufhebung* to the Ontological Proof for God's Existence

Perhaps the major difference between the 1824 and 1827 lectures is that in 1824 Hegel's formulation of "the metaphysical" and his notion of God as an abstract universal, the "self-enclosed" substance, could too easily be confused with the God of Spinoza, with Schelling's *Identitätsphilosophie*, and not surprisingly with the pantheism of the Hindus. Hegel's solution in part I of the 1827 lectures was to introduce two newly titled sections, "[A]: The Concept of God" and "[B]: The Knowledge of God," in part I of the 1827 lectures, neither of which had a parallel in the earlier lectures. As before, the success of Hegel's strategy would depend on persuading his audience of an absolute correspondence between the two sections [A] and [B], without dissolving the reality status of "empirical religions." Hegel's argument goes something like this.

Far from being abstract, God's substantiality is such that it always already includes subjectivity and the possibility of knowledge. This is so if we accept that substance is not merely one moment in the concept of God, an undifferentiated monad, but rather that this first moment—divine universality—is an "*abiding unity*" that already includes distinction or difference within itself. The second moment—distinction in general—is therefore already implicit within primal unity. Thus while it is perfectly valid to presuppose God's existence from a conceptual or speculative viewpoint, God cannot be considered alone (as is the case in natural theology, which begins from the proofs of God) but is always already considered in conjunction with the knowledge of God, which in turn presupposes a primal cleavage between God and the consciousness for which God is an object. Thus from the standpoint of knowledge all that needs to be shown is that humans have religion: "All we need to do is to prove that religion exists."[71]

Yet as Hegel recognizes, "to prove that religion exists" is no straightforward task. One cannot get around this issue by simply "appealing to the (empirical) fact that all peoples have religion."[72] The expression "all" itself is misleading, since "there are peoples of whom it can hardly be said that they have religion."[73] The empirical plurality of religions is unreliable when it comes to *proving* that such and such a religion exists. What Hegel is after is a criterion for judging and classifying the *being* of a religion, the "what is" or objectivity of a religion, the extent to which God appears as an object of knowledge for a particular religion. However, the particular object "God" can be grounded only in a "soil that is suitable to it." In which "soil" could God be an object of knowledge? Hegel scarcely pauses to consider the irony of his metaphor for the ground of knowledge. The soil for religious knowledge—knowledge of God—is *thinking*. God can be obtained only by thought. This is based on the "ancient preconception that human beings are thinking beings and that by thinking and thinking alone they distinguish themselves from the beasts. . . . Human beings think and they alone have religion. From this it can be concluded that religion has its inmost seat in thought."[74]

In section [B], "Knowledge of God," thought continues to command closest attention: "Only in thought is the object properly grounded."[75] The implication here is that thinking, compared with other elements that constitute a "Knowledge of God," such as feeling, faith, or representation, is more closely connected to objectivity, to the reality status of the object of religion, that is to say, the being-status of God, or what amounts to the same thing, the status of God as being. If thought must concern itself with the reality/being/truth status of its object, if what is at stake is the being of God, then the primary task of thought is to prove the necessity of God's existence. Such proof constitutes the cognitive dimension of the "elevation to God" and by implication "the *meta*physical," the activity of spirit. Thus whereas Hegel had discussed the three main proofs—the cosmological, the teleological, and the ontological—separately, in part II of the 1824 lectures, in the process failing to properly demonstrate the necessity of proof for the concept of religion, we find in the 1827 lectures that Hegel's treatment of the three main proofs is gathered under part I: "The Concept of Religion." In Hegel's reformulation each later proof passes beyond while at the same time assuming and preserving—or, to adopt Derrida's neologism, *relieving*—its predecessor. Thus in relieving the earlier proofs the ontological proof assumes the role of the *Aufhebung* itself.

The real impact of this measure is seen in part II, in its direct application to determinate religions. The three proofs are shown to constitute a series of historical "elevations to God." These elevations now correspond to the evolution of different forms of thinking and consequently different attainments of subjectivity within these cultures. Hegel's new schematic ordering of the three proofs in part I corresponds in part II to an improved classification wherein each religion's ability to prove God's existence is a measure of its proximity or distance from the ultimate criterion for thinking, namely, the ontological proof. Compare for example the following statements:

> We could indeed say that proof is not needed, by appealing to the fact that all peoples have religion. But that is only taken for granted, and in general we do not get around the issue [simply] with the expression "all." For there are also peoples of whom it could hardly be said that they have religion. . . . There is also the phenomenon of a cultural extreme where the being of God is denied altogether, and where it is likewise denied that religion is the most genuine expression of spirit.[76]

> It can be said of all religions that they are religions . . . but at the same time, in that they are limited, they do not correspond to the concept.

And yet they must contain it, or else they would not be religions. But the concept is present in them in different ways. At first they contain it only implicitly. These religions are only particular moments of the concept, [but] they do not correspond to the concept, for it is not actual within them. Thus while humanity is of course implicitly free, Africans and Asians are not, because they do not have the consciousness of what constitutes the concept of humanity. The principle by which God is defined for human beings is also the principle for how humanity defines itself inwardly. . . . An inferior god or a nature god has inferior, natural and unfree human beings as correlates.[77]

In addition to providing empirical proof for the validity of the ontological proof, statements such as these serve to usher in a resolution to the main problem that dogged the 1824 lectures, namely, the contradiction in the definition of the *Aufhebung* as it applies simultaneously to the origin of religion and to the origin of history *as* the history of religion*s*. The resolution consists in being able to qualitatively differentiate two different natures of "elevation" in the nature religions and artistic religions. We have therefore something akin to the following scheme. At the bottom of the scale are African religions—also termed the religions of magic—comprising Egyptian religion and religions of the "Negroid" races. At this stage there is "no inward cleavage of consciousness."[78] Such a cleavage would indicate the ability to make a distinction between sensuous matter and spirit: "Here, the moment of religion . . . and therefore the moment of elevation is still shut up in the natural state. Only where there is distinction/cleavage can religion first originate."[79] Such cleavage first occurs in Oriental religion, specifically in its Asiatic form. But even at this stage God is defined only as absolute power or substance, within which "the natural will, the subject, is only something transient, an accident, lacking selfhood, devoid of freedom. The highest merit of humanity here is to know itself as something null."[80] Hegel qualifies this stage as "*inconsistent elevation*," which has its historical existence in the three Oriental religions of substance: Hinduism, Buddhism, and the Chinese.

If we speak here of "the elevation of spirit" this must be defined more precisely, for even within nature religion we will find an elevating of thought above mere natural powers. . . . *But this elevation is carried out inconsistently, and it is just this monstrous and terrible inconsis-*

tency . . . this mixture of nature and spirit that [defines] the content of this stage.[81] [emphasis added]

If the qualification "inconsistent" allows Oriental religions to be included within the boundary defined by the "concept of religion" and at the same to be kept at a safe distance from European religions, this is done by contrasting the inconsistency against the quality of essence that belongs to the stage of religion above it, namely, *"consistent elevation,"* which applies specifically to the artistic religions Greek/Roman: "Set against [Oriental religion] is the second stage of determinate religion, at which the elevation is carried through consistently"[82] — the term "consistent" here implying that spirit is the ruling or dominant aspect, where nature is mastered completely.

Hegel's Schema as a Diagram for the Production of History

The indissociable link between the reformulated *Aufhebung* (consistent versus inconsistent elevation) and the ontological proof comes into play more clearly in the phenomenological sections in which Hegel describes Hinduism. As stated earlier, the most far-reaching effect of the reformulated *Aufhebung* in the 1827 lectures, as far as the classification of Oriental religions is concerned, was that thinking — more precisely, the degree to which a particular culture was capable of thinking God's existence — becomes the central criterion in the classification of historical religions. That is, the ontological proof determines the distance that is to be placed between the history of European religions and the prehistory of Oriental religions. The determination of this distance is given shape within the narrative of the section entitled "Determinate Religions." Hegel's narrative in this section can be regarded as a classificatory/comparative schema that is being fleshed out as the narrative progresses.

To fully appreciate the link between the ontological proof and the fleshing out of this schema it is necessary to understand the proper relationship between Hegel's restatement of the ontological argument as a way of thinking about God/religion, and the occulted principle that underpins the expression of the argument itself. To better understand the ontotheological architectonics of Hegel's schema, it will be helpful to draw upon two of Martin Heidegger's lecture courses: the lecture course entitled

The Will to Power as Knowledge and as Metaphysics, which comprises the third of his four-volume *Nietzsche* lectures, and a separate set of lectures published under the title *The Principle of Reason*.[83] The former text takes the question "What is knowledge?" outside the realm of epistemology and resituates it in relation to the "will to power," thus anticipating one of Foucault's major themes. In the text of *The Principle of Reason*, Heidegger interrogates one of the basic themes in Western philosophy, namely, the notion of ground, which was expressed initially as God and subsequently as reason. At the intersection of these two lecture courses is a shift from God to a specific human disposition that grasps the world and takes it over in a gesture that is justified as a "practical need" for humanity, or better still, a form of praxis called knowledge. It is precisely this shift that is evident in Hegel's deployment of the ontological proof.

In light of Heidegger's lecture courses, Hegel's reformulation of the ontological argument can be read as an ingenious reformulation of a tradition that had an early statement in St. Anselm's *Proslogion* ("God is that than which a greater cannot be thought . . . He who understands that God exists cannot think of him as non-existent") and a restatement by Descartes, who argued that reason itself holds only insofar as God exists.[84] In Hegel's further restatement, to think properly is to think the identity of all things in God and God in all things. In proper thinking, therefore the thought of God is both necessary and unavoidable. The only way to avoid (thinking about) God is *not to think*. Thinking is therefore impossible apart from the implicit and explicit thought of God. And so, the argument goes, insofar as God exists, God cannot *not* be thought. Which is to say that God cannot be identified with nothingness. God is not nothing.[85]

But to say that *God is not nothing!* is not the end of the matter. For as Heidegger argues in *The Principle of Reason*, hiding behind this manner of rendering the ontological argument is another, and more insidious, presupposition: *nothing exists without reason*—known to the Western theological and philosophical tradition as the principle of reason. Stated differently, everything that exists necessarily has a reason. The logic of this principle goes something like the following. The reason things exist rather than not-exist resides in their cause. It follows that the first cause must also be the highest cause, or the highest existing reason, God. Yet although God is conceived as the highest being He is nevertheless being thought of from within the totality of everything that exists, which means that God, as with all other things that exist, remains subject to the principle of reason. Going a step further, God exists only insofar as the principle of reason holds.[86]

According to Heidegger, what this circular form of thinking reveals is a specific human disposition called *knowing* in which man relates himself to a world of things he encounters through his perception of them.[87] This perception is initially and fundamentally experienced as "chaos." Chaos is a key term in Heidegger's explication and signifies a fundamental experience of "the world" prior to its being regulated and governed by the categories of the imagination. "Chaos" therefore implies unregulated experience, the experience of the world as motion, time, fluidity, sensuousness, multiplicity. In other words, the experience of the world as yet unknown, what is not-yet regulated by our perception.

Following Nietzsche, Heidegger argues that in any encounter with the world our standpoint is not one of knowing but of schematizing. To schematize is "to impose upon chaos as much regularity and as many forms as our practical needs require."[88] By "practical needs" Heidegger means something like praxis, the fundamental activity of man that distinguishes him from an animal. Our "practical need" is to stabilize any encounter with the world, to render stable the element of multiplicity, time, fluidity, or motion that is inherent to the unknown. Hence our "practical need" demands the schematization of chaos. Schematizing is thus an active process enabled by the "forming force" of reason, which imposes order on chaos according to a particular standard. That standard is either the notion of God as a static immutable being or the unchanging essence of reason that in turn underpins the absolute certainty of the self-representing (knowing) subject. Whatever is encountered in knowing is known when it is cognized as fixed and stable in relation to the absolute stability of God/reason/subject. In this way, the unknown is installed, made secure in standing before the subject (as knower). Such installation is necessary for knowledge to count as knowledge.[89]

The relevance of the Heidegger's lectures for exposing the architectonics of Hegel's "practical need" now becomes clearer. The need for Hegel was to simultaneously compare and classify the growing knowledge of Oriental religions according to a set standard. With the ontological proof providing the law or the standard for thinking about religion—*God cannot not be thought, therefore God cannot be nothing*—Hegel's narrative description of Hinduism sketches out a schema in the reader's imagination. Schematization can be seen as an *a priori* operation of sketching out a visual frame or time chart. Upon this time chart are gathered together the ontological proof and what is encountered as the object of knowledge—in this case Hindu religion. This gathering together of the ontological proof and Hinduism is a process through which each is automatically compared and, through comparison, is automatically set in its proper place. What goes on in this automatic comparing/classifying is none other than the process of co-figuration, in which the figure and place of the West are reestablished and reconfirmed each time the narrative makes reference to Hinduism (or any other Oriental religion). Initially an unknown quantity, a stabilized figure of "Hinduism" itself is fleshed out in this encounter. This co-figuration is of course an improved version of Kantian co-figuration. The main difference is that the work of co-figuring is now carried out on a visual time chart—that is to say, it is marked out onto an historical grid. Hegel's version of co-figuring is the historicization of knowledge. More accurately, the time chart is the history or phenomenology of religions whose primary axis is drawn automatically by the Hegelian narrative itself.

As Gayatri Spivak points out in her perceptive reading of Hegel on the *Srimadbhagavadgita*, "Hegel places all of history and reality upon a diagram." By reading off the diagram, "the laws of motion of history are made visible as, concurrently, the Hegelian morphology is fleshed out."[90] The active reading of the time of this law has the effect of producing history itself. Moreover, as Spivak rightly suggests, "what we have in Hegel's narrative is not an epistemology [an account of how individual subjects produce religion] but an epistemography, a graduated diagram of how knowledge comes into being."[91] The Hegelian schema is a dynamic epistemograph wherein each new configuration steps forth in the sublation of earlier stages of the struggle. So, whereas in the West the proof of God's existence provides the (ontotheological) law for thinking about God/religion as the exclusion of the nothing, Oriental religions by *comparison* (i.e., by automatically reading off the epistemograph) have not sufficiently evolved or received the required "elevation" to this stage of thinking. Oriental thinking remains at the level of nothingness. Hegel's "proof" for his assertion that Hindus cannot think, and thereby his justification for the "practical need" to maintain a suitably safe distance between India and Europe, is given by typical Hindu representations of God—characterized by their incapacity to present coherent, noncontradictory representations—and therefore, an inability to obey the law of thinking itself:

These alterations with sometimes the One, sometimes with the differentia as the complete totality[92] — this is what constitutes the inconsistency of this sphere; but it also the inconsistency of reason vis-a-vis the understanding.[93]

This confusion marking the Hindu presentation is notable in that this inconsistency has its ground in the very content of these determinations, in their necessary dialectic; [thus] the necessity of the concept becomes apparent initially only as deviation or confusion, as something that has no internal stability within itself, and it is only the nature of the concept that brings a solid foundation into this confusion.[94]

The contradictory nature of the Hindu representation, its inability to erect a secure (fixed and immutable) image that can be rendered back to a subject, in turn gives rise to a certain relationship between their concept of God and the *cultus*. The precise standpoint of Hindu religion is the "One substance — Brahman." From such a standpoint, however, God cannot be said to exist or to have determinate being, since this one substantiality is merely present as pure being-within-itself that remains abstract, purely by itself. At this stage thinking is the substance, the in-itself. It is a thinking that cannot yet be applied, not yet grasped in categories,[95] unable to say anything objective about God, e.g., that he exists. In such thinking God is merely an abstractum. This kind of being, Brahman, exists in self-consciousness only in the abstraction of the understanding as posited by me. The subjective "I" is the only affirmative element that is present when the Hindu says in and to himself: "I am Brahman."[96]

As Hegel argues, this form of thinking could not have progressed any further than the stage exemplified by the statement "I am Brahman." To do so, thinking would have to determine itself internally and then sublate this determination in order to become concrete. Thinking would then be "what we call reason."[97] But such concrete unity, reason, and rationality are not consistent with the Hindu Brahman. Hegel therefore equates this naive stage of thinking — "natural thinking" — with the subjective and objective vanity of present-day reflective thought (*Identitätsphilosophie*) and thus with the pantheism of Jacobi and Lessing, which asserts that we know nothing of God; that the ego has no affirmative relation to God; that God is for the ego a nothing, devoid of content.[98]

Consequently the highest manifestation of its *cultus* is a state of being dead to the world;[99] a renunciation in which Hindus relinquish all consciousness and willing, their goal being total indifference to action.[100] "In this state, devoid of thought, . . . the human being is Brahman itself."[101] Hindus have no category for what we articulate by the phrase "there is" or "there are." Stated differently, the Hindus' inability to erect a stable image that can be rendered back (represented) to a subject, and thus their inability to mediate the process of thinking, *is itself proof that Hindus cannot prove that God exists*, from which "it follows that there is no ethics to be found, no determinate form of rational freedom, no right, no duty. The Hindu people are utterly sunk in the depths of an unethical life."[102] Indian cultures that cannot properly differentiate being from the *nihil* (= chaos/time/nature) are unable to account for the ontological difference between being and beings. As a result, Indians can only think God in *not* thinking, or in *thinking nothing*. As such they remain incapable of proving that God exists, thereby devoid of any sense of history, fated inevitably to remain subject to an external power. For Hegel, then, it would follow that the enforcement of imperial/empirical time in the cultural-political interests of maintaining the ascendancy of European identity is both justified and lawful.

Influences of Hegel's Schema

Although it is often overlooked, the ontotheological nature of the Hegelian epistemograph exerted a theoretical and political influence with important consequences for future intellectual encounters between India and Europe. Much of this influence was mediated through a variety of different channels. For our purposes the two most relevant ones are (i) a division of knowledge in the emerging humanities between theory and empiricism (see chapter 6), and (ii) a reconstitution of the nature of Indology. As we shall see, these measures effected an exclusion of India from any meaningful engagement with the domains of "theory" and "the political" even as India was included within the plurality of world cultures as "religion." This double effect, of excluding India through its inclusion is operative even today. Let me briefly consider these two phenomena in turn.

One of the key sites where the division of knowledge took place is the emergence of a science of religion (*Religionswissenschaft*) firmly centered on the political economy of European imperialism. As I will show later in this chapter, through its adoption of the figure of "world" or the "global" as a figure of plurality, Hegel's schema can be considered an *onto-theo-ideo*-logical panopticon that parallels the political economy of empire. Although the term "science of religion" is commonly associated with the work of Friedrich Max Müller, references to this concept were in fact made more than half a century earlier in Hegel's *Lectures on the Philosophy of Religion*.[103] In fact Hegel's deployment of the words "science of religion" in the *LPR* anticipates the simultaneous genesis of two subdisciplines, the philosophy of religion and the history/phenomenology of religions, both of which evolved into full-fledged disciplines in their own right. These two disciplines and the theoretical distinctions between them have, in one form or another, dominated the study of religion in the Western academy. To this day Hegel continues to exert an often invisible but powerful influence on current debates in the study of religion.

Related to the division of knowledge is the ontotheological reconstitution of Indology, which in turn influenced a new phase of Indological activity that focused on the translation and exegesis of North Indian devotional texts and traditions by European scholars, followed by the response to these Indological works by native elite scholars and the subsequent "dialogue" that ensued between them. This in turn resulted in the transference of leading European-Christian ideas into the ideology of the religious reform movements in the late nineteenth century and, related to this, the postcolonial reproduction of native informancy through the enunciation of imagined "religious" traditions. I shall discuss each of these points briefly below. This chapter will conclude with a short discussion highlighting the way in which Hegel's ideas continue to be relevant to current debates in modern study of religion(s), a theme that will be explored in greater detail in the chapters to follow.

The Political Economy of Empire and the Making of "World Religions"

Hegel's efforts to (i) define the nature of the impulse behind the origination of history, (ii) avoid the problems of cultural co-origination, and (iii) thereby head off the very possibilities of intellectual borrowings between cultures can be seen as part of his anxiety about an originary diremption, or crisis of identity, at the heart of the intrinsically linked concepts of Europe/Modernity/Christianity. In other words, Hegel's metaphysics was politically motivated at the deepest level, a point that is echoed by Michael Hardt and Antonio Negri in their influential work *Empire*.[104] According to Hardt and Negri, modernity is not a unitary concept but rather appears in two modes. The first mode was a radical revolutionary process that broke with the past and declared the immanence of world and life, posing humanity and desire at the center of history. For Hardt and Negri the philosophy of Spinoza provides a good example of this tendency toward immanence. Opposed to this, however, was a second mode of modernity, which deployed a transcendental apparatus to suppress the potential for liberating the multitude. In the struggle for hegemony between these two modes, victory went to the second and hence to the forces of order that sought to neutralize the revolutionary effects of modernity. This internal conflict at the heart of European modernity was simultaneously reflected on a global scale in the form of external conflict. The same counterrevolutionary power that sought to control the potentially subversive forces within Europe also began to realize the possibility and necessity of subordinating other cultures to European domination. Eurocentrism, as exhibited in the formation called Orientalism[2], was born as a reaction to the potentiality of a newfound human equality.[105]

In many ways Hegel's metaphysics epitomizes this second mode of modernity. As Hardt and Negri point out, Hegel's project "could not but take place against the backdrop of European expansion . . . and the very real violence of European conquest and colonialism."[106] However, the real threat for Hegel from the colonized was not physical but intellectual—a threat to the very design of the *concept*. Hence the ontotheological schema can be considered a diagram of power that at the same time provided a means for controlling the constituent and subversive forces within Europe that championed a revolutionary plane of immanence, as well as a "negation of non-European desire." During Hegel's tenure the thought of his archrival Schelling and his later antipode Schopenhauer must be considered good examples of such "non-European desire." Hegel's diagram was a mechanism of power for imposing order on the multitude within Europe and the potential multitude in the colonial spaces that were brought to Europe's doorstep through empirical knowledge of Oriental cultures.

Hardt and Negri are quite correct in suggesting that the theoretical solution offered by Hegel in the form of the ontotheological schema "demonstrates the profound and intimate relationship between modern European politics and metaphysics." But their suggestion that contemporary postcolonial and postmodern theory is limited to a critique of Hegel's dialectic, and therefore complicit with the form of power they criticize, is more problematic (as I shall show more fully in chapter 6). Hardt and Negri in fact share the very same blindspot in their analysis of contemporary global power that they call "empire." Their mistake is to conflate secular neo-Marxist postcolonial critique (Said, Bhabha, Spivak, etc.) with postmodernist critique per se, when the two can be quite different things, as demonstrated by the preponderance of postsecular modernity. The latter variety offers a critique of conventional secular modernity from a nontheistic position, thereby breaking the stereotype that forces critical theory and religion to stand apart. Part of the problem of those committed to a purely secular modernity—and this would include many postmodernists and postcolonial theorists—is that they fail to see the survival of Hegel's spirit in empire/globalization due to their reluctance to engage with the question of religion. The problem, as I alluded to earlier in this chapter, is their consistent failure to pose religion as a *question* or as a source for critical thinking, seeing it only as the ultimate barrier to true critique. Indeed, what they seem to miss is the inseparability of religion and history in Hegel, which makes it possible for there to be more than one kind of modernity. To reiterate, part of that problem consists in failing to see the polyvalent nature of the Hegelian schema as a diagram of power that exerted a theoretical and practical influence on colonial, neocolonial,[107] and now postcolonial/globalized formations of power. To understand the nuances of this, it will be helpful to relate Hegel's diagram to a certain strand in the formation of the humanities and social sciences that informs modern and now postmodern discourses of pluralism. I refer to the discourse of "world religions."

Although it is often overlooked, the ontotheological nature of the Hegelian diagram whose form Hegel had sketched in the *LPR* text, was almost seamlessly incorporated into the newly created curriculum of the human sciences, whose blueprint had been laid by Wilhelm Humboldt at roughly the same time that Hegel was appointed as professor of philosophy at the University of Berlin. The key to the emergence of the human sciences was the reconstitution of history both as a scientific discipline in its own right and, more important, as the foundational methodology for the study of human and social phenomena. Following this reconstitution of history, the early decades of the nineteenth century saw the rise of three new social scientific disciplines: political science, economics, and sociology. While these three sciences were deemed adequate for the study of the European society, it was quite a different matter for the study of non-European societies. As a consequence of this imbalance two additional disciplines came into being for studying non-European societies: anthropology, in the case of small, tribal societies without writing, and Orientalism, in the societies with venerable civilizations and illustrious written traditions. Because these two disciplines were perceived to be most preoccupied with "religion" (the non-European societies who had not yet reached a level of historical maturity were deemed to be thoroughly in the grip of religion, or had lost an originally pure religion due to hybridization and racial mixing), these in turn gave rise to another discipline, called the science of religion (*Religionswissenschaft*), later renamed as comparative religion or history of religions, from which emerged the discourse of "world religions."[108]

In her recent study *The Invention of World Religions*, Tomoko Masuzawa notes that "when religion came to be identified as such . . . it came to be recognized above all as something that, in the opinions of many self-consciously modern Europeans, was in the process of disappearing from their midst"[109] Meanwhile, the two new sciences corresponding to non-European worlds, anthropology and Orientalism, promoted and bolstered the presupposition that those who were supposedly unlike them, namely non-Europeans, continued to be obsessed by this thing called "religion." The emergence of the category "world religions" therefore allowed Europeans to "do the vital work of churning the stuff of Europe's ever-expanding epistemic domain and of forging from that ferment an enormous apparition: the essential identity of the West."[110]

Masuzawa traces this intellectual development, which took place in the German academy and involved prominent German intellectuals, from the mid-nineteenth century through to usage in the humanities and social sciences curriculum today. Her trajectory encompasses the early modern taxonomy of religions (notably the shift from national religion to universal religion), the legacy of comparative theology, the discovery of Buddhism as an Aryan religion, the rise of philology and Max Müller's linguistic classification of religions, and the classification of Islam as a non-Aryan religion. It ends with the legitimization of "world religions" discourse through the work of prominent German intellectuals such as Max Weber and Ernst Troeltsch in the twentieth century. Through the influence of Weber (a sociologist) and Troeltsch (a theologian-cum-historian) the category of "world religions" provided a means for Europeans, on the one hand, to acknowledge the diversity and plurality of human cultures, but crucially, on the other hand, to maintain the subject position in the unfolding of world history. It was a way to "preserve European universalism in the language of pluralism."[111]

Though not directly acknowledged by Masuzawa, the conceptual engine necessary for the world religions discourse to emerge was Hegel's revision of Kantian co-figuration into an ontotheological diagram that precedes many of the developments outlined above by almost half a century. Hegel's schema anticipates the logic of the transition from ethnic/ national religion to universal/ world religion, while retaining the uniquely particular hegemony of Europeans as a race or civilization, and of the religion proper to that race (Christianity). As demonstrated earlier, what Hegel bequeathed to the European scholars engaged with the study of non-European cultures was the ability to make the transition from particular to universal and yet give the impression that no transition had actually occurred. This move in fact anticipates not only the process of bracketing, or transcendental epoché that Husserl made the basis of his phenomenological method, but also the formation of the two main approaches to the study of religion in the late nineteenth and early twentieth century, namely, the philosophy of religion and the history of religions. This move is worked out and relies upon an imaginary comparative grid of "world religions." Seen from this angle, the comparative grid is little more than a process of bringing other religions onto a grid sketched out in advance, a way of installing the difference and diversity of other religions. More importantly, though, the comparative grid also coerces those who read off the grid into believing that being installed in this manner, and the image or picture of diversity that results from this being gathered and placed together, is an entirely innocuous, if not benign, procedure.

Hegel's Panopticon: The Concept of "World" as a Figure of Plurality

Although it is not immediately obvious, the success of this procedure revolves around a collective understanding both of the term "world" and of the retention of an individual sovereignty in the plural term "religions." Thus when Hindus, Buddhists, Jews, or Muslims read the comparative grid (irrespective of whether it is in its earlier *LPR* version or in its later Weberian format, since the conceptual logic behind them is the same while only the empirical detail is different), their immediate anxiety about plurality, or about one's relative place in the schema is dispelled because the diagram does not obliterate contradictory, amorphous, ahistorical otherness from the centralized vantage point of the "world." Rather, the diagram seems to acknowledge the other's claims as constitutive of the larger self-identical whole (the "world"). The diagram differentiates the identities of others into discrete phenomena and attributes autonomy to them. This giving of individuation to other religions conveys a sense of sovereign integrity, but obscures the fact that identities are dependent on belief in a dominant totality: "the world." To acquire validity the other must accommodate its partiality by objectifying itself, thereby subordinating itself by taking its assigned place on the grid. If fulfilled, such accommodation results in a peaceful truce with the "world" and between the various "religions" of the world. The peace works because each sovereign entity is given a value associated with its fixed place. It is rendered useful within the economy of "world religions." Yet the commodity it produces (namely its "religious identity") has a value that benefits the economy. The very idea of such an economy is the seductive ruse that maintains a political peace between the diversity of religions. The Hegelian epistemograph is also the essential figure of a political economy.

This peace is entirely superficial, however. For without understanding its mechanism of power, its readers are likely to be pacified into accepting the appearance of peace as its truth. The real engine behind this political economy is the concept of "world," which signifies plurality and which is figured out by Hegel as the comparative grid of cultures, religions, etc. Even though it is not explicitly named by Hegel, the concept of "world" serves as a panopticon that translates European hegemony into the language of pluralism. But how so? To understand what is going on in this concept of "world," I want to draw upon one of Martin Heidegger's later essays, "The Age of the World Picture," a work whose arguments are connected to the earlier lecture courses *The Will to Power as Knowledge and as Metaphysics* and *The Principle of Reason*.[112] Although the text of this essay does not refer to Hegel or to religion per se, its argument nevertheless exposes the insidious manner in which Hegel's panopticon continues to embed itself in the human and social sciences, which in turn justifies itself as the official window for viewing a global humanity.

One of the main targets of Heidegger's critique in "The Age of the World Picture" is the relationship between history and science, or the way in which history comes to define itself as objective, i.e., scientific. For Heidegger, history becomes objective/scientific only when it is able to represent the past as that which is fixed and stable:

What is stable is what is past, that on which historiographical explanation reckons . . . the comparable. Through the constant comparing of
everything with everything, what is intelligible is found by calculation
and is certified and established as the ground plan of history.[113]

To reiterate what Heidegger means by this statement: only what is fixed
can be compared, and only through constant comparing does history become scientific. The key phrase here is "constant comparing," which simultaneously points to the essential activity and to the essential danger
that is part and parcel of the operation of historiographical explanation.
The danger manifests itself more clearly if we trace the word "compare"
back to its Latin roots, whence *com-parare,* "to couple," which gives the
connotation of co-appearing, of the appearing together of multiple things
in the same time and space. The danger resides in the originary being-
together or coexistence of difference in all things. Historical science reduces this difference to a stable identity that can be measured (compared)
against others. But such measurement is possible only because science
(the process of constituting knowledge through measuring and calculating) is redefined as "ongoing activity."[114] From within this new definition
modern science appropriates movement to itself even as it fixes and stabilizes everything it encounters. Science itself therefore has a metaphysical
or transcendental essence: "ongoing activity" in contradistinction from
activity that is no longer going on, past. Science therefore defines itself
as a self-elevation. It is an *activity* that by definition is always already
elevated in relation to that which it encounters as knowledge. According
to Heidegger, this definition of science has enabled it to become institutionalized within the modern university as a mode of knowing that we
call "research." "Research" is ongoing activity.

But, Heidegger goes on to ask, "what conception of beings and what
concept of truth, grounds the fact that science becomes research?"[115]
The answer, in short, is truth conceived as representation (*Vorstellung*),
in which everything is objectified and secured in its objectivity for the
human being as a knowing subject. Science is transformed into research—the essential phenomenon of the modern university—only when
the essence of truth is transformed into the certainty of representation—a
move first identified in Descartes' *Meditations on First Philosophy.* Contrary to the medieval scholastic doctrines that considered the human's
becoming subject as a self-liberation, Heidegger claims that subjectivity
entails a transformation of human essence into an entity that assumes the

role of *subjectum*: that being which becomes the "relational center" of everything else in the world.[116]

As a consequence of this transformation, everything becomes a "world picture" for man, who takes his place as its "relational center." Where world becomes picture everything that exists is set before man as something familiar and ready to be used or acted upon; everything becomes a "standing reserve," to use Heidegger's term. The "world picture" comprises a peculiarly modern configuration in which "observation and teaching about the world change into a doctrine of man, an anthropology. It is no wonder that humanism first arises where the world becomes picture."[117] Humanism, for Heidegger, is "nothing but a moral-aesthetic anthropology," or, better, a theo-aesthetic that signifies that man's fundamental standpoint is now a "worldview" (*Weltanshauung*). Yet this "worldview" is not something given once and for all. Instead, the very nature of modern representation is that "man contends for the position in which he can be that particular being who gives, measure, and draws the guidelines for everything else in the world."[118] In other words, there can be no relations between "worldviews." A plurality of "worldviews" is merely epiphenomenal. It can exist only as a confrontation of worldviews in which there must be an eventual winner. And there can be only one winner in this confrontation between worldviews, namely, that portion of humanity that has a hold on the definition of science:

> For the sake of this struggle of worldviews and in keeping with its meaning, man brings into play his unlimited power of calculating, planning, and molding of all things. Science as research is absolutely necessary for establishing of self in the world.[119]

What Heidegger effectively uncovers is the mechanism behind Hegel's panoptical diagram, which is at work in any survey of knowledge grounded in a historicist vector. The trick is not simply the representation of the all, of diversity, plurality, difference, time, other(s) through the configuration of "world," but more accurately the preservation of the particular constellations "European" and "Christianity" through the language of universalism. It is this move that allowed Hegel, and, following Hegel, a host of Indologists, philosophers, historians, religionists, etc., to transmute Christianity's theological transcendence into the secular transcendence of the human sciences, and which continues to enable the circulation of Hegel's panoptic schema within the contemporary curriculum of the human sciences. The human sciences are in turn legitimized because they can historically transcend theology and religion. Clearly, though, any move that attempts to establish secularity through the transcendence of history/science/modernity is itself minimally theological. It is because this move is disavowed that the problem of race and religion is more closely intertwined than is often given credit for, and why they are indissociable from the formation that designates itself "the West."

Following Talal Asad, it could be said that it is this very disavowal of the historical transcendence of religion that "allows us to think of religion as 'infecting' the secular domain or as replicating within it the structure of theological concepts. The concept of 'the secular' today is part of a doctrine called secularism."[120] The genealogy of the secularism doctrine can be traced partly to a post-Reformation concept of humanism, partly to the Enlightenment concept of nature, and partly to Hegel's philosophy of history.[121] As I have argued earlier, within Hegel's philosophy historicism generates religion. This mutual imbrication of religion and secular historicism was particularly evident in the ideological reconstitution of Indology in the decades following Hegel's death.

The Ontotheological Reconstitution of Indology

We noted in chapter 1 that a broad shift in the nature and development of Indology took place after the 1860s. This shift was partly the outcome of the rise of Indophobia (Orientalism[2]), spurred in turn by the rise of evangelicalism, historicism, and race science, and partly brought about by the final phase of British imperialist expansion and consolidation of its conquered territories, especially in Punjab and the Northwest Provinces. Hence the second phase in the development of Indology was initiated by notable German Indologists such as Albrecht Weber, Friedrich Lorinser, Ernst Trumpp, and Friedrich Max Müller. These men received their training at institutions such as the Tübingen Stift, Göttingen, and Berlin, where, through the influence of his students, Hegel's ideas continued to set the tone for thought long after his death. Within these institutions a sound theological training combined with the study of the *Altertumswissenschaft* constituted the core curriculum of the humanities programme (*Geisteswissenschaften*). Indology would normally be taken as a specialist graduate option in addition to the core curriculum and would be limited to graduates undergoing training for missionary and administrative work in British India. Inevitably the ontotheological presuppositions of the Hegelian schema passed seamlessly into the discipline of Indology.

To quickly illustrate this shift: the early phase of Indological research (pre-1840s), which had its beginnings with the work of William Jones, Charles Wilkins, and H. T. Colebrook, posited Advaita Vedānta as the central philosophy and theology of Hinduism.[122] According to this particular representation—which continued to be propagated throughout the nineteenth century by "Indophiles" such as Schelling, Schopenhauer, and Max Muller—Hinduism could in essence be considered a philosophy but not a true religion as the term was understood in the West. The nearest thing to "genuine religion" in India was the mélange of cults and sects based on the worship of chthonic deities. If Hindus had had a true religion it could only have existed in the remote and ancient past, a Golden Age from which the originally Aryan race of Hindus had fallen into their present state through centuries of domination and racial mixing.[123]

After the 1860s, however, the work of a new generation of Indologists—among them H. H. Wilson, Albrect Weber, Friedrich Lorinser, Ernest Trumpp, Monier Williams, and George Grierson—began to "discover" what soon came to be regarded as the "*only real religion of the Hindus*" within the various forms of devotion (*bhakti*) to personal deities, but particularly within Vaiṣṇava *bhakti* or the tradition of devotion to the deity Viṣṇu.[124] Not surprisingly, this view received intellectual support from orthodox Hindu scholars and publicists, which led during the last two decades of the nineteenth century to the integration of the various *sampradāyas* (sects) under the all-encompassing political leadership of the Vaiṣṇava *sampradāya*.[125] As a result, *bhakti* as a devotional form common to all true Indian religiosity and monotheism as proper to it crystallized as the essential feature not only of Vaiṣṇavism, but of pan-Indian Hinduism.[126]

This important shift in perception was made possible by a new framework for thinking about religions that was at the same time *ontotheological* (allowing the Indologist access to Indian thinking about God's existence) and *phenomenological* (allowing them to introduce a degree of historicization to different phenomena). An important consequence of this new standpoint was that it allowed Indologists to remain committed to a Euro-Christian standpoint, given that many of them were also active missionaries, and yet claim secular status for their work. Consequently, for the first time in Western intellectual history, terms such as theism, monotheism, and pantheism became standardized *world-historical* categories (or secularized categories, if we follow Talal Asad) for classifying non-Western cultures. They became formulaic concepts imposing a logic of the stereotype into the activity of thinking about religion and religions. Historicism becomes the foundation for thinking about religion as such.

Although the new distinction between pantheism and monotheism overtakes earlier traditions of distinguishing between heathens and Christians, and the use of these terms by the seventeenth- and eighteenth-century deists,[127] a more important issue arises here than merely an improved procedure for classification. Given that this world-historical categorization (mono- versus pantheism) is part of the colonial procedure for managing the multiplicity of new religions that were flooding the knowledge market—one that finds its most comprehensive expression in Hegel's various Berlin lecture courses and will only be refined in Husserl's version of phenomenology—is there not a transparent slippage in its application from religion versus religion*s* to the secular concept of culture versus culture*s*? That is to say, isn't the mono- versus pantheism distinction, as it comes to be understood after Hegel, effectively also the basic measure of what counts most as culture in the multicultural frame despite its supposedly secular-humanist framing?

If these world-historical categories are simply part and parcel of the evolution of metaphysical thinking, this brings into visibility the historico-comparative (or phenomenological) enterprise as an apparatus that has continued to protect Western secular-humanism either from a cross-fertilization of ideas or a radical questioning of its ground, both of these possibilities being caricatured as the approach of "Eastern" nihilism. Eric Alliez points to precisely this problem in his important work *Capital Times*. Alliez qualifies the notion that historico-comparative phenomenology as a tool for encountering non-Western cultures is a purely modern development reflecting the separation between religion and secularism. Instead, for Alliez, phenomenology must be regarded as a continuation of the tradition of distancing non-Christian otherness inaugurated by St. Augustine's treatment of time and consciousness in Book 9 of the *Confessions*. As a result, our modern sense of phenomenological positioning, as elaborated in the tradition of comparativism that runs from Augustine through Hegel and Husserl to Eliade, "in its most dynamic effects must be considered the ultimate process of covering over the Christian conception of the world."[128] If Alliez is right, then the positioning of cultural multiplicity can be conceptually traced to the manner in which Augustinian theology has distanced and installed its non-Christian interlocutors.

Several consequences of the Hegelian schema can be discerned in the work of these Indologists. For example, while the early phase of Indology tried as far as possible to espouse a religiously neutral approach to Oriental culture, this very neutrality caused considerable hindrance to the proselytizing agenda of the early missionaries in India. By contrast, the work of post-Hegelian Indologists inspired a new generation of missionaries fully conversant with Indological materials, scientific in their methodology, but above all, fully committed to the Euro-Christian standpoint. This was due largely to the reformulated and more coherent standpoint of religion. Insofar as Western thinking completely effaces the possibility of contradiction and manages to distance itself sufficiently from the *nihil*, chaos, thinking about religion is absolutely metaphysical, which means, properly speaking, theoretical.

With aboriginal pantheism and contemporaneous monotheism at opposite ends of the Hegelian epistemograph, history is now coextensive with the progression of theism. Stated differently, history consists in the progressive conquest of time and correspondingly with the conquest of nature, the *nihil*, chaos—which means that the origin of history coincides with the consistent sublation of pantheism. This historico-ethical sublation of time, the effort of keeping the *nihil* at a safe operating distance, effectively rendered the discipline of Indology as politically harmless. After Hegel it was ethically and politically correct to be a Christian and an Indologist. As an ethico-political standpoint the ontotheological schema allowed the Indologist simultaneously to be a theologian/philosopher as well as an anthropologist. It allowed Indology to remain rooted within the element of Western religio-philosophical tradition and in the same moment to be empowered to transcend this very tradition infinitely and at will—*the attainment of a perfect, or "generalized," translatability.* This is a standpoint in which theology (the standpoint of divinity) and anthropology (the standpoint of historicism) coincide in translating other cultures according to an onto-theo-logical—i.e., metaphysical—mode of thinking. The Hegelian epistemograph therefore provided an ambivalent rule for translation. While it empowered Indology by positing the law (*Gesetz*) for thinking about Indic culture as religion, the actual operation of the law remained invisible. To put this law into operation becomes the task of the post-Hegelian Indologist theoretically empowered as an *Übersetzer*, the translator who will never need to move, having always already gathered-together (co-figured) subject and object in the work of the imagination.

Theosophy, Indology, and the Religious Reform Movements

The most famous of the Indologist-translators in the late nineteenth century was of course Max Müller, the man regarded as the progenitor of disciplines variously called the science of religions (*Religionswissenschaft*), comparative religion, or history of religions.[129] Max Müller's achievements notwithstanding, this attribution may be somewhat exaggerated. Peter Harrison, for example, questions why "most accounts of the history of comparative religion or of *Religionswissenschaft* have the "dispassionate" study of the religions beginning in the nineteenth century with such figures as Max Müller and C. P. Tiele."[130] For Harrison it makes more sense to locate the empirical beginnings of the science of religion in the English Enlightenment, which provided the groundwork for the later emergence of the *Religionswissenschaft*, whereas the philosophical antecedents of Müller's work are squarely located in nineteenth-century German philosophy. Thus, while Müller is mainly remembered for his contributions to the emerging science of religions and comparative philology, and for his translations of the *Rig Veda*, an important and pervasive strand of his thought continues to be neglected. I refer to his attempts to write a philosophy of religion informed by—or better still, grounded in—the historical study of religions.[131] His doctoral thesis, it should be remembered, was not in linguistics or Indology, but in philosophy. Müller's philosophy of religion distinguishes between two branches in the science of religion that he called the "comparative and the theoretic theology."[132] The first was devoted to an impartial—i.e., scientific—study of the religions of mankind; the second (which Müller referred to as his philosophy of religion) would be based on comparative theology and its purpose would be to investigate the nature and development of religion and its hidden purpose.[133]

The most comprehensive account of Max Müller's philosophy of religion can be found in the Gifford Lectures that he delivered between 1888 and 1892, well after his better-known publications on comparative language and the *Rig Veda*. In a manner reminiscent of Hegel's Berlin lecture course on the philosophy of religion, Müller used his Gifford Lectures to work out a philosophy of religion that could begin to answer the religious crisis that had gripped Europe throughout the nineteenth century. This crisis was deepened partly by the historical and critical study of religion inaugurated by such scholars as Burckhardt and de Wette, and partly by the growing influence of Darwinian evolutionary theory, which had shifted the emphasis from language to biology as the defining factor for determining race. Müller's aim was to show that the central tenets of religion, such as belief in God, the soul, and an afterlife, did not necessarily depend on an original revelation specific to Christianity. In contradistinction to revelation Müller posited the idea of natural religion, a religion that is "in the head, in the heart, in the sky, the rocks, the rivers, and the mountains."[134] Although Müller's notion of natural religion had clear affinities with the thinkers of the Scottish Enlightenment, particularly Locke and Hume, who stressed the autonomy of the human mind in its reflection on God, the influence of Herder, Humboldt, and Hegel is more marked, as a result of which "religion could be treated as a necessary outcome of the mind of man and therefore be studied in its historical development."[135]

Consequently, revelation belongs to the history of religions, not to a specific religion. Müller's natural religion manifested itself as a progression through three different perceptions of the infinite: nature, man, and self. The first of these was physical religion, corresponding to natural phenomena as the starting point for reflection on the infinite. The other two manifestations of the infinite were anthropological religion (which implies various aspects of the infinite and man as objective and subjective reality) and psychological religion (also called theosophy, the wisdom of God, which dealt with the man's highest achievable conceptions of God). In other words, the concept of the infinite had to progress through distinct stages of historical evolution, from the negative to the positive, corresponding to these three forms of religion, "beginning with the simple negation of what is finite and the assertion of an invisible Beyond, and leading to a perceptive belief in that most real Infinite in which, to quote the words of St. Paul, 'we live and move and have our being.'"[136]

Müller considered his meditations on the third stage of natural religion's historical evolution (entitled "Psychological Religion, or Theosophy"), which he delivered as the final part of the Gifford Lectures, as the culmination of a lifelong meditation on religion. For Müller, the term "theosophy" (which he believed had been misappropriated by Madame Blavatsky and Colonel Olcott and presaged into the service of occultism) expressed the highest possible conception of God achievable by the human mind. This highest possible conception of God constituted the final consummation of all religion and was to be found in the "oneness of the objective God and the subjective soul." For Müller, the essence of theosophy consisted in the notion that "the subject and the object of all being and knowing are one and the same."[137] This was the highest summit of thought the human mind had reached, and the clearest expression of this could be found not only in the texts and teachings of the last part of the *Veda*, known as the Upaniṣads or Vedānta, but in Christian sources such as the later theology of St. Paul and St. John, as well as in the mystical traditions of Christianity, notable the writings of Eckhart.

As we saw earlier in this chapter, more than half a century before Max Müller, Hegel had also tried to articulate an evolution of religious ideas by reinterpreting the three successive stages representing the historical development of the proofs for God's existence. Within Hegel's system as a whole there was a progression from the cosmological, through the teleological, and to the ontological argument for the existence of God. This succession corresponds respectively to the transition from the religion of nature, through the religion of individuality, to the religion of the absolute. Philosophically this transition corresponds to the movement from the philosophy of nature, through the philosophy of spirit, to the philosophy of logic (which is in fact a supplement to the philosophy of religion). Hegel saw the earliest condition of religion as the most primitive and therefore as a form of finite negativity that must be overcome and somehow preserved in the higher and more advanced forms. Müller on the other hand retained a similar notion of progressive religious evolution but designates the Vedānta as the earliest expression of the original unity between God and man, and manages to evaluate it positively.

At first glance, their penchant for historicism notwithstanding, Hegel and Müller seem to be conceptually opposed to each other. Moreover, such an opposition seems to support the established narratives in the history of religions, which locate Müller squarely within a long line of Indophiles generated and sustained by the kind of "liberal" Orientalism[1] espoused by Sir William Jones a century earlier. This narrative suggests, furthermore, that by articulating a "universal religion" that was not tied to Christian revelation, but focused more on the "love of God," it brought Christianity close to Vedānta. Along with his belief in monogenesis and a "universal brotherhood" implying a racial kinship between European Aryans and Indian or Hindu Aryans, it presented a challenge to Christian orthodoxy and British racial supremacy. Consequently, despite his appeals to Kantian philosophy,

Müller's ideas were eclipsed by the rise of the Christian right in the form of evangelicalism in England and Hegelian philosophy of history.

Scrutinized more closely, though, the opposition between Hegel's Occidentalist philosophy of religion and Müller's Orientalist philosophy of religion turns out to be somewhat superficial. Both men tried to use the same criterion to underpin the scientific status for their projects, namely, history. In order for Müller's alternative philosophy of religion to count as truly scientific or impartial it was necessary for Müller to place himself within the dominant theoretical current of his time and specifically in conversation with Herder, Humboldt, and especially Hegel, to whom he makes numerous references, despite criticizing the latter's reading of Indological materials and his lack of respect for the facts. In other words, despite his Romantic tendency for going back to the pure origin of language, religion, or race, he had to accede to a belief in historicism and become a full-fledged member of the historicist school. It is not surprising, therefore, that he should regard his study of the evolution of religious ideas as the most important part of his science of religion.

Ironically, though, Müller's aspiration for scientific status is also the cause of the irresolvable tension in his work between his conception of religion and his conception of history. It is the irreconcilability of these things—the Romantic yearning for the pure origin and the dedication to historical evolution of ideas—that led to the eclipse of his work on language, myth, and especially religion.[138] Müller's conception of religion (the most sophisticated statement of this being his Gifford Lectures on theosophy), as we have seen, gravitated back to the Romantic notion of a pure origin, a monogenesis that subsequently degenerates in history. He used this idea to critique orthodox forms of Christianity and modernity. At the same time, though, he also holds fast to an evolution of race and religion that culminates in the present moment of German/British imperialism as the flowering of Aryan Christianity. In contrast, while the Veda and Vedānta are the lifeblood of natural religion in India and of theosophy, the Indic contribution was limited to being a mere "historical record of the highest value in the history of religion."

Wilhelm Halbfass makes the important observation that while Müller included and privileged Vedānta *within* the history of religions and comparative study of religions, he never spoke of "comparative philosophy."[139] The reason for this should by now be clear from our earlier discussion. Properly speaking, philosophy gives the reason/law/concept for history as such. History and philosophy are conceptually inseparable.

While Müller can acknowledge the movement of history and evolution as foundational for any science, history itself is philosophical. It is underpinned by a transcendental condition, and thus belongs to the West, to a Christian Europe. As with Hegel, there exists an unspoken condition of historical difference between India and Europe. Because of this historical difference, Hegel's and Müller's respective philosophies of religion differ in degree but not in kind. They represent two different varieties of a broadly Occidentalist standpoint that constructs the Euro-Christian West through its Oriental other. This helps us to understand why Müller was supportive toward the efforts by indigenous Hindu reformist movements to modernize Hinduism. For in reforming Hinduism, the Brāhmo Samāj and other reformist groups were not simply returning to and thus reclaiming a lost origin (Vedānta as the central theology of Hinduism), but, ironically, in reclaiming the notion of the One taught by Vedānta, the reformists were approximating toward Christian doctrines of unity. Hence the only possible end for Hindus was to become *like* Christians— but, of course, never the same! In becoming like Christians they would automatically, though surreptitiously, dethrone the Vedānta.

Although Max Müller tried unsuccessfully to distance his theosophy from Hegel's philosophy of religion (though clearly not his concept of history), another example of Hegel's influence on East–West translation can be seen in the development of the theosophical movement, which has by and large been relegated to debates on New Age movements, occultism, and perennial spiritualisms. In the intriguing essay "Iconoclasm," Mark C. Taylor brings to light some of the hidden connections between ontotheology (or "theoesthetics," to use Taylor's own term) and the core principles of theosophy.[140] Taylor argues that the roots of modern ontotheology, especially in its Hegelian version, lie deeply buried in the Western mystical traditions, the word "theosophy" itself referring to the wisdom of God necessary for salvation. First mentioned by Dionysus the Areopagite (fifth–sixth century), theosophy also finds important expressions in the writings of medieval mystics such as Jakob Böhme, whose influence was openly acknowledged by Hegel and the Jena Romantics.

The distinctively modern version of theosophy can be traced to Helena Blavatsky, whose writings profoundly affected many artists and thinkers in the late nineteenth and early twentieth century. Blavatsky's lasting achievement was to syncretize Western esoteric ideas with those of ancient Egypt and particularly with what were assumed to be the central teachings of Vedānta. But as Taylor points out:

> While tracing her spiritual lineage back to Alexandrian, Neo-Platonic and Indian philosophy, Blavatsky also recognizes more recent anticipations of her vision. Hegel in particular appears at critical points in Blavatsky's exposition of Theosophy. In the opening pages of *The Secret Doctrine* she invokes Hegel in an effort to clarify the fundamental principles of her position:
>
>> The ABSOLUTE; the *Parabrahm* of the Vedāntins, or the One Reality, SAT, which is, as Hegel says, both Absolute Being and Non-Being. . . .
>>
>> THE ONE REALITY; Its *dual* aspects in the conditioned universe.
>
> Summarizing the loss and return involved in all spiritual development, Blavatsky writes: "We believe in a Universal Divine Principle, the root of ALL, from which all proceeds, and within which all shall be absorbed at the end of the great cycle of Being." The "great cycle of Being" reinscribes the circular rhythm of Hegel's dialectic. As the "Universal Divine Principle" emanates from the spiritual domain to the material world, lingers, and then returns to its origin, so Hegel's "Absolute Spirit" proceeds from the realm of Logic (*Science of Logic*, which Hegel describes as "the mind of God before the creation of the world"), into nature (*Philosophy of Nature*) and history (*Philosophy of Spirit*), and eventually returns to the sphere of "the Absolute Idea."[141]

But despite her usage of some of Hegel's ideas, it is also clear that Blavatsky was not simply a Hegelian. This can be gleaned from her statement on the most basic belief of theosophy—"*all men* have physically and spiritually the same origin"—which was something that Schelling also argued in his early work and which constituted one of his main differences with Hegel. For Hegel the origin is precisely *not* shared by all men. Moreover, for Blavatsky the origin, being Absolute Unity, is an "Unknowable deific essence"—it cannot be represented.

More important than the nature of this disagreement with Hegel, which brings her close to Schelling's understanding of Advaita Vedānta, is the timing of Blavatsky's statements. In 1879 Blavatsky moved to India, where she led the Theosophical Society until her death in 1891. The period of twelve years or so that Blavatsky spent in India coincided with the height of the religious reform movements of North India and points to a collaboration and exchange of ideas between theosophists and the most influential Vedāntins of the age, such as Swami Vivekananda. After Blavatsky's death the leadership of the Theosophical Society fell to Annie Besant, an English woman who continued to propound Blatvatsky's basic ideas while at the same time increasing the degree of collaboration with the native elites. One of Annie Besant's most important but overlooked achievements was to decisively shape the form and ideology of the text- books of *sanātana dharma*, or Hindu traditionalism, that evolved from Banaras Sanskrit College (now Banaras Hindu University) to achieve pancontinental influence throughout the twentieth century. Bringing the earlier claims of Hindu reformists such as Debendranath Tagore, Keshabchandra Sen, and Vivekananda into line with the principles of theosophy, Besant and her Hindu collaborators outlined a thesis of "*sanātana dharma* as the universal religion" with a view to presenting "an outline of the basic principles of religion, which all Hindus, of whatever special sect, would be glad to see in the hearts and heads of their children."[142] Annie Besant's closest collaborator was Bhagvan Das, whose main work, *The Essential Unity of All Religions*, evokes the underlying unity of all religions from a neo-Hindu perspective. The organizational proficiency of these college textbooks helped to spark a series of other major studies centered around the *sanātana dharma* as the "eternal Vedic dharma" or the all-encompassing Indian religion.[143] In short, at the center of this particular brand of *sanātana dharma* ideology was the idea of the *Veda* not only as the source of all religious experience in the Indian context, but of all historical religions.

This kind of ideology, which can be seen as a mode of neo-Hindu self-assertion against the Christian West, is a good example of the way in which the ontotheological schema was not simply imbibed but actually inverted by the natives elites in order to redefine a principle of unity necessary for enunciating a nationalist identity. It is worth remembering, however, that the rising power and pancontinental influence of Hindu self-assertion of this type also helped to spawn reactions against it from other Indian elites, and not only Muslim elites but, surprisingly, Sikh elites. As I shall argue in the next chapter, the eventual self-assertion of Sikhs as a nation and as a "world religion" distinct from Hinduism by neo-Sikh formations was influenced by a reconstituted Indology (Orientalism[2]) and indirectly by the spectral presence of the ontotheological schema.

PART II

Theology as Cultural Translation

3 Sikhism and the Politics of Religion-Making

This chapter investigates how the category of "religion" was transferred from the first ethnographic reports of the Sikhs in the late eighteenth and early nineteenth centuries, to the cultural, theoretical, and political projects of the Sikh elites in the late nineteenth and early twentieth centuries, giving rise over a period of about fifty years (1870s to the 1920s) to the ontotheological underpinnings of the modern Sikh imaginary. Such a transformation was enabled by the imposition of a dominant symbolic order on the indigenous cultures, followed by the appropriation of this symbolic order by the native elites. As we noted in chapter 1, the appropriation of this symbolic order—an order exemplified by an entire discourse of colonial ethnographies, missionary literatures, and translations, implemented by a vast network of Anglo-vernacular mission schools, and maintained by a newly imposed capitalist economy—prepared the ground for a fundamental shift in the receptive psychology of the native elites in the late nineteenth and twentieth centuries.

In the case of the Sikhs, if one event could be singled out for its consequences, it would be the commissioning of an "official" translation of the *Ādi Granth* by the colonial administration in Punjab. The task of creating this "official" translation was entrusted to the German Indologist Ernest Trumpp. Although it is not generally acknowledged, the conceptual terminology underpinning Trumpp's translation, including his infamous preface to the Sikh "religion," effectively demarcated a field of translation (to use Bourdieu's term), that is to say, a discursive regime that provided the conceptual framework within which the future discourse on modern Sikhism would be received. This regime of translation contained an ideology about religion and theology that makes translators imagine their relation to what they do in translation as a "dialogue" or an exchange of guarantees. Despite the vociferous rejection of his work, the conceptual vector underpinning Trumpp's translation helped to catalyze the theologization of the native elite mindset, and, inadvertently, its attunement to the economy of empire.

The first part of this chapter will look at the *re*-presentation of indigenous thought and culture under the signifier "religion." Such a *re*-presentation begins with what are effectively the first encounters between Sikhs and Europeans in the late eighteenth century. These early encounters had the effect of sketching out the contours of what was to become a regime of cultural translation. This regime is effectively a heuristic device for delineating cultural difference. I begin by showing how the regime of translation starts to take shape in the archive that comprises precolonial knowledge of the Sikhs. The term "precolonial" refers to the fact that during this early period, from the 1780s to about 1849, the Sikhs and their dominion had not yet been annexed under the inexorable movement of the British Empire from Bengal (in eastern India) to the Punjab and the Northwestern Provinces. Annexation took place after the British-Sikh Wars in 1849.

The chapter then moves on to look at a major shift within the earlier (precolonial) regime of translation. This shift was prompted by publication of the first English translation of the *Ādi Granth* in 1877. The main part of this chapter is devoted to discussing the nature and effects of this shift. I argue that central to this alteration in the regime of translation is the work of ontotheology, which plays a crucial role in the interpretive work of two Indologists (Ernest Trumpp and Max Arthur Macauliffe) and their interaction with leading Sikh reformists of the late nineteenth and early twentieth century. Closely scrutinized, the shift in the regime of translation is not an entirely unanticipated event, but arises out of what Jeffrey Cox has termed "imperial fault lines" that run through colonial discourse. These fault lines, which represent points of conflicting and divergent opinion over cultural signifiers such as "religion," highlights the intellectual contradictions of the colonial idiom. I argue that not only are such imperial fault lines present in the precolonial accounts of Sikhs and their "religion," but, importantly, they echo some of the key ideological contests in the history of European ideas during the nineteenth century, specifically Orientalism[1] and Orientalism[2], which in turn arise out of the religio-philosophical debate between figures such as Hegel and Schelling. Closely tied to this debate is Europe's reconceptualization of its own comparative imaginary, which emerges at the uneasy intersections between the so-called pantheism controversy and the emergence of fledgling disciplines such as Indology.

The latter parts of this chapter will attempt to track the passage of key theological ideas from the work of these Indologists into the historical narratives and the commentaries on scripture produced by leading Sikh reformist scholars, such as Bhāī Vīr Singh and Dr. Bhāī Jodh Singh, writing in the early decades of the twentieth century. Of particular interest are the philosophical devices adopted by these native elite scholars to demonstrate that their work "naturally" conformed to the larger master narrative of colonialism, and at the same time represented the continuity of indigenous tradition. Such devices enable these scholars to disguise the work of translation (and hence the disparity between colonial and colonized cultures) as the "natural" movement of tradition, and thus to represent the central teachings of the Sikh Gurus (*gurmat*) as "Sikh theology."

Early Colonial Accounts of Sikhs and Sikhism

That the first European accounts of the Sikhs were documented and published within a few years of each other during the 1780s attests to the growing anxieties over the rise of Sikh power in the Punjab initially in the shape of the Sikh *misls*,[1] shortly followed by the rise of the Sikh ruler Ranjit Singh, and thus to what was forecast as the looming possibility of a British-Sikh encounter in the not-so-distant future. A. L. Henri Polier's short article "The Siques"[2] represents the earliest report of the Sikhs. This was followed by equally sketchy, though better-informed, accounts written by George Forster (1783) and James Browne (1785).[3] These were primarily ethnographic accounts relating to the "manners and customs" of a relatively unknown people. All three accounts were commissioned either by Indian nobles such as the Nawab of Oudh, who had commissioned Polier's account, or by Warren Hastings, then-director of the East India Company. The rationale behind these investigations was to provide the Company with an archival base on which the colonial state could draw in regard to the nature of Sikh polity and the territory over which they were steadily establishing control.

Even at this early stage there emerges a remarkably consistent picture of the Sikhs. For example Polier, Browne, and Forster all showed a concern to give reasons for what they perceived as the "rapid progress" of the Sikhs in relation to other inhabitants of the Indian subcontinent. Thus Browne notes that "their manners and conversations [were] very unlike the other inhabitants of Hindustan, owing no doubt to the *freedom of their government*" [4] (my emphasis), and furthermore, that the Sikhs "appeared to bear that kind of relation to the Hindoo religion, which the Protestant does to the Romish." The reasons for their "rapid progress," he maintains in the same introduction, are to be attributed to "their polity which contained in its *original principles* so much internal vigour" (emphasis mine). Likewise, Polier and Forster independently speak of the "*democratic elements* in Sikh society," and suggest that the secret of their success is due to "unparalleled activity."

An interesting variation on these accounts was the publication in 1788 of "Seeks and their College" by Charles Wilkins, the leading Sanskritist of the time, in the journal *Asiatick Researches*. At a meeting of the Asiatick Society of Bengal Wilkins presented the "Seeks" as a third distinct community, a "sect of people who are distinguished from the worshipers of Brahm and the followers of Mahommed by the appellation *Seek*."[5] Wilkins' short report depicted the Sikh tradition as a foil to the fantastic store of Hindu belief indicated in Jones's and Francis Wilford's contemporaneous reports on Hindu texts. By providing an example of an indigenous resistance and protest against the pervasive influence of Hindu ideas and institutions, Wilkins's account of the Sikhs can be seen as part of a growing literature that enabled the alterization of Hinduism.[6] Wilkins describes a temple in which men treated certain books with a religious reverence. What particularly impressed Wilkins was the unassuming piety inspired by a recognition of the unity, omnipresence, and omnipotence of the deity, thus giving the place an almost scholarly aura. For Wilkins, Sikh veneration of a central sacred text (presumably the *Guru Granth*) indicated a rational religion of the book. He described the founding Sikh teacher, Guru Nānak, as a Hindu apostate whose chief concern was moral virtue. To Wilkins the Sikhs' ethical and scriptural concerns reflected Christianity more than Hinduism. This image of a rational reformist sect was presented in bold contrast to the Asiatick Society's representations of Hinduism.

These early accounts not only presented a somewhat contrasting picture to Jones's characterizations of the "indolent and submissive Hindus," who were "incapable of civil liberty." They also provide insights into the nature of judgment at work in what are ostensibly proto-ethnographic writings. Apart from its stark empirical realism, this judgment is informed by some of the new currents dominating European thinking at the time—the emergence of Enlightenment humanism, the idea of religion and rationality as cultural universals, and the relationship between Protestantism and nationalism in Britain and Germany, to name but a few—and therefore sees the presence or absence of these principles in the "history" and "nature" of other races.

The next opportunity for a close observation of the Sikhs within their own territory came in the first decade of the nineteenth century, a time when they were becoming firmly entrenched as a military power under Ranjit Singh. This opportunity was taken by Colonel John Malcolm, who published his influential *Sketch of the Sikhs* in 1812. For more than thirty years Malcolm's *Sketch* provided the only substantial introduction available, until the publication of J. D. Cunningham's *History of the Sikhs* in 1848. John Malcolm's *Sketch*, while it echoes the earlier observations of Browne and Wilkins, provides more substantial information regarding the "religion" of the Sikhs. Malcolm had a considerably longer contact-time with the Sikhs during the first decade of the nineteenth century, which allowed him to elaborate on the "reasons for their rapid progress." However, there is an interesting tension in Malcolm's categorization of the Sikh religion: "There is no branch of this sketch . . . more curious and important, or that offers more difficulties to the inquirer than the religion of the Sikhs." He continues: "We meet with a creed of pure deism . . . grounded on the most sublime general truths, [yet] blended with the . . . absurdities of Hindu mythology and the fables of Muhammedanism." [7] This tension, which reappears in future European accounts of Sikhism, is an example of the kind of "imperial fault lines" that hold together divergent opinions over the meaning of terms such as "religion" within European intellectual culture.[8]

Unable to place the Sikhs into a category of their own, Malcolm, in line with his predecessors, opts for the reformist (Protestant) model: "Nanac professed a desire to reform, not destroy, . . . to conciliate Hindus and Muslims." [9] As to their "original principles," the reasons for their "internal vigour," Malcolm is able to go further than either Browne or Forster, who were content to merely pose the question. This "internal vigour," the secret of their success, is the outcome of changes brought about by the last Guru:

> It was reserved for the last Guru, Govind, to give a new character to the religion . . . by the complete abolition of a system of civil polity . . . [i.e., the *varnāshramadharma* "code of the Hindus," a decision that was] "calculated to preserve a vast community in tranquility and obedience to its rulers, . . . [but] which made the country . . . an easy conquest to ever more powerful foreign invaders.[10]

J. D. Cunningham's *History of the Sikhs* (1849) was the last significant (i.e., monographic) contribution to the precolonial phase of literature about the Sikhs.[11] Its importance lies in the fact that its publication bridges not only the demise of Sikh rule and the annexation of Sikh dominions by the British, but also the decline of the intellectual formation Orientalism[1] and the dominant assertion of Orientalism[2]. Cunningham deploys a narrative strategy that translates the colonized culture as religion in the very process of subsuming it under "history." This narrative repeats earlier suggestions that the precursors of India and England are Greece and Rome—where a once glorious, but now fallen, civilization is conquered (for its own benefit) by a more vigorous race. The colonized natives are thus rescued from their stultified past and inserted into the narrative thread of an imperial history in which England, as the mother country, is the location of civilization:

> The condition of India from remote ages to the present time is an episode in the history of the world inferior only to the fall of Rome and the establishment of Christianity. . . . The well-being of India's . . . millions is now linked with the fate of the foremost nation of the West, and the representatives of the Judean faith and Roman polity will long wage a war of principles with the speculative Brahmin, the authoritative Mullah and the hardy believing Sikh.[12]

Cunningham was thereby able to bridge the difference between Orientalism[1] and Orientalism[2], but at the same time leave room for the arrival of the Sikhs almost as a new phenomenon in the history of India. Compared to the present state of the Hindu and Muslim as representative of the Indian native's backwardness, stultified religion, and morals, Cunningham argues that "Sikhism is an *active and pervading principle.*" Whereas the "observers of ancient creeds quietly pursue their way, self-satisfied and indifferent about others . . . the Sikhs are converts to a *new religion.*"[13] This "active principle," or the "reason" for "their vigour," is ascribed to the Sikhs' conversion to a "new religion," rather than its previous description as a reformed version of Hinduism. For Cunningham, Sikhism was a "living faith," a "species of pure theism" as opposed to the "dead ritual and priest craft of the Hindoos." Because of this conversion to a "new religion" the Sikhs "now preach the unity of God and the equality of man . . . [and consequently have] succeeded to sovereign power."[14] Cunningham's conviction about Sikhism's novelty seems to have inspired his book's main objective, which was to "give Sikhism its place in the general history of humanity."

But how could Cunningham justify the colonial presence and at the same time present an apparently sympathetic portrayal of the Sikhs? How was he to explain their obvious, though short-lived, political success without having to admit that there was anything intrinsic to the nature of Indian culture in its present state that could have effected this? The trick was to provide an explanation for the characteristics of the Sikhs that made them appear so obviously different from the "Hindoos," and yet to avoid giving them an identity in the European sense. To circumvent this problem, Cunningham developed a historical narrative in which *religion* played a dominant part in the making of *nations*. The cornerstone of his discourse is the polarity between Sikhs and "Hindoos," which he develops and exploits by means of a phallocentric logic that differentiates Sikhs from "other natives," but only to the extent that they display the qualities that the West already has in abundance. Thus the Sikh and "Hindoo" are related as spirit is to body, or male to female. The Sikhs have a religion that is "active," "enthused by a living principle" that "breathes a new spirit," which fertilizes the passive, barren body of the "Hindoo multitude."

To avoid equating the Sikhs with the West, however, he constantly reminds the reader of the organic connection between the Sikh spirit and the "Hindoo" body. Thus the Sikhs cannot be the same as the West or aspire to its position, but can resemble it by cultivating similar qualities. Ultimately, for Cunningham, the British-Sikh encounter reaffirms the Protestant ethic of justifying colonial experience in terms of moral obligation, by using the Sikh story as an indigenous example of success — albeit a success that cannot be maintained from within its own cultural resources.

Cunningham's discourse therefore reinforces the self-image of the colonizer as well as the otherness of the natives. Psychologically, the effect of the discourse is to say that the natives can become what they once were, if they mimic and imbibe the characteristics of colonial culture, which brings with it the opportunity of revival, as both gift and necessity.

While these early accounts of Sikhs and Sikhism, from Browne's *Tracts* (1788) through to Cunningham's *History* (1849), give the impression of a more-or-less uniform representation of the Sikhs in colonial literature that is formed within the purview of the intellectual formation Orientalism[1], closer scrutiny reveals the presence of prominent dissenting voices — among them the Serampore missionary William Ward, historian James Mill, and Indologist H. H. Wilson — who tended to view Sikhism from a perspective that was strongly attuned to the standpoint of Christian evangelicalism. William Ward's short "Account of the Shikhs" (1815) actually refutes John Malcolm's interpretation of Sikhism as a deism. Relying on the testimony of a native informant ("a learned Shikh employed in the Serampore printing office"), Ward offered what was probably the first Western rendering of Sikh doctrine based on Guru Nanak's authoritative hymn, the Japji.[15] For Ward it seemed obvious that the Sikhs were "Hindoos," which is why his account appears within his broad survey of the *History, Literature, and Mythology of the Hindus* (1821). The historian James Mill was more forthright in dismissing the idea that Sikhs were deists. Thus in his review of John Malcolm's *Sketch* published in the influential *Edinburgh Review*, Mill concluded that the Sikhs were "mere Hindus," "an unenlightened people" who nevertheless lived in a prosperous land. In the same article Mill gives a hint of what was to become certain policy: "If a conqueror would dominate over the whole of India, the region of ground now covered by the Sikhs must be controlled." [16]

A more detailed exposition of Sikh belief and practice appeared in the *Journal of the Royal Asiatic Society* (a successor to *Asiastick Researches*) in 1828 authored by H. H. Wilson, the leading Indologist of his day. Wilson's article "Civil and Religious Institutions of the Sikhs" relies on the testimony of a "Nirmalā Sikh priest" of Banaras who allowed him to witness certain Sikh ceremonies and explained some key doctrines of "Sikh faith." From his encounter with this particular native informant Wilson was able to surmise that the "Sikh faith, if anything so vague deserves the appellation of a faith,"[17] is derived from the *Ādi Granth*, which is "a large volume but contains no systematic exposition of doctrines — no condensed creed — no rules for ritual observances. It is an unconnected compilation of verses of a mystical or moral purport."[18] In the light of what he had witnessed, Wilson argued that "the Sikh religion scarcely deserves the name of a religious faith. A vague notion of a Creator and source of all things, . . . pervades the poetry of Nānak and his fellow bards, but is little else than a poetical acknowledgement of a deity who is defined by negatives—without form, without time, without attributes."[19] Evidently, for Wilson, Sikhism as an "experiment has not been very successful," as there appeared to be "very little difference between a Nirmalā Sikh and an orthodox Hindu of the Vaiṣṇava sect."[20]

Even at this relatively early stage of British-Sikh encounter, these conflicting opinions about the nature and identity of Sikhs and Sikhism seems to corroborate the argument that there were distinct fault lines running through the colonizing culture and its intellectual idiom. These fault lines can be traced to philosophical and political battles raging within the Western academy and in the public sphere about the place of Oriental knowledges in relation to an emerging sense of European and British nationalist sensibilities. One of the prime catalysts in this battle was the shift in the concept of religion: from natural religion (informing Orientalism[1]) to a historicist concept of religion (informing Orientalism[2]) that eventually gave rise to the notion of "world religions," a configuration that is responsible for silently replicating the figure of the West.

The shift from natural religion to historicist religion is more than a change in concept. It also signals an alteration in the regime for translating colonized cultures from a reliance on the native informant to the role of the translator as Indologist/theorist of religion. As we have seen in chapter 2, this alteration is not so much a reversal but a retuning of the colonial machine to meet the growing need for accommodating Orientalist knowledge production to the requirements of European cultural and political identity. It is a need to center European identity, a figure of the West, in the very act of translating other cultures. It will be helpful to briefly elaborate on the philosophical underpinnings of this regime of translation as it relates to knowledge formation about Sikhs and Sikhism.

I argued in chapter 2 that the deist paradigm along with the concept of natural religion was furthered by using knowledge of Oriental cultures as a foil against the claims of Christianity. One implication of the concept of natural religion, with its implication of universal rationality, was that it broke the seemingly normative link between Christianity and European self-perception. Thus for the early reports of the Sikhs by writers influenced by deism (Browne, Wilkins, Malcolm), the category "religion" is based not just on what it means to be Christian as opposed to non-Christian, but on a more universal definition that had arisen in view of an increased awareness of the existence of Oriental cultures, which for them represented Christianity's other. Such awareness necessitated the defining of a lowest common denominator, namely the substantive definition of "natural religion." Religion is "natural" because it exists in all societies. It is conceived of as a set of propositions to which believers can give their assent, and these propositions thereby become the basis on which different religions can be judged and compared.

The term "natural" is linked to a major philosophical shift in the late seventeenth century, away from revelation—typified by forms of interiority and God's writing as scripture mediated by the authority of the Church—to the outside world, or God's writing as nature. Mediated by figures such as Voltaire, Locke, and Hume, this philosophical shift was an important step in the formation of the modern concept of the rational self—a self that is epistemologically central to the purview of what lies outside it, i.e., nature. The "natural" is therefore a metaphor for a realist mode of rational selfhood. The first versions of this shift are enshrined in the theories of Enlightenment deism, for which a religion is "natural" if it can commend itself to the human mind by means of its intrinsic rationality. The arbiter of this rationality is the epistemic self. A culture other than Christianity can be defined as a "religion" if it is rational. To be rational it must affirm something about the fundamental nature of reality. In other words, its propositions should be meaningful statements about reality, and thereby add not only to knowledge per se (science) but to self-knowledge.

"To affirm meaningful statements about reality" meant that any statement that conforms to "common sense" (reality as "out there" and affirmable by all rational beings) is a basic premise of early Enlightenment humanism. More important, it is a variant of the classical concept of the mimetic relationship between "reality" and "knowledge." And insofar as this "knowledge" is mediated by language—propositions, or truth-statements—this is a naive form of the representational theory of language. Thus a form of cultural translation exemplified by travel reports and other ethnographic literature, insofar as it mimetically represents the truth of what is observed, reflects the experience of reality. It should be clear how the categorization of a culture as a "religion" is not just a simple mapping, but involves a process of translation that in turn presupposes a certain philosophical notion of the relationship between language and reality. Ultimately such translation—what is normally portrayed as the transparent crossing of different cultures—becomes a cornerstone of the civilizing mission and the ideology of liberal humanism. It follows, therefore, that when the early ethnographers make statements such as "With Sikhism we meet with a creed of pure deism" (Cunningham), or "It was on a principle of pure deism that Nanac entirely grounded his religion" (Malcolm), or that Sikhism is a religion of "pure deism uncluttered by priestcraft" (Wilkins), conceptual categories such as "deism," "theism," and "religion" are not available to the native informant, whether that informant is a Sikh or a Persian document.[21]

A prerequisite of the early moments of colonial encounter was the political expediency of gaining knowledge of other cultures by learning their language—the act of crossing over into the linguistic and cultural domain of the other. To make such knowledge available to the European world, however, the information gathered needed to be translated back into English. The language of thinking, or more specifically the language in which judgment takes place, is necessarily English. My point is that the native informant has relatively little effect on the process of judgment itself.[22] What is transported back into English must affirm something if it is not to be characterized as non-sense; it must make sense. Making sense means conforming to "nature" as seen by the European self, but more importantly, sense or meaning must be confirmed intersubjectively by other rational beings; this can only be done in the language of European society. Propelled by a major shift in the concept of religion during the second half of the nineteenth century, this model of translation undergoes a radical change by the time it was appropriated by leading Indologists such as Ernest Trumpp.

Demarcating a Regime of Translation: Trumpp's "Odium Theologicum"

It may seem surprising, though it would hardly be an exaggeration, to suggest that Ernest Trumpp's basic thesis concerning the Sikhs' religious system—summarized in twenty short pages—remains historically the most influential document concerning the question "What is Sikhism?" The brevity of this prefatory chapter, entitled "Sketch of the Religion of the Sikhs,"[23] belies the profound impact it has exerted on the reception and representation of the Sikh scriptures. Despite the vociferous rejection of this work by Sikhs ever since its publication in 1877, it would not be far from the truth to suggest that the vector informing the Sikh response—and consequently over the next fifty years their adoption of "theology" as a conceptual framework for translating Sikh scripture— is largely a response to Trumpp's translation and, more important, to his schematization of the Sikh religion. Why did Trumpp's work have such an influence? Why was there felt such a need to refute this work? Let me begin by recounting some of the basic themes put forward by Trumpp and the influences that caused him to write in such a manner.

Viewed from the perspective chalked out in the preceding chapters, Trumpp's "Sketch" presents remarkable similarities to the ideological construction of Vaiṣṇavism as the "only real religion of the Hindus" by Indologists such as Monier Williams, Weber, Grierson, and Lorinser, all of whom were Trumpp's contemporaries and peers. Moreover, Trumpp was not writing for the lay reader. His work was instigated and funded by the Punjab Administration, who apparently wished to gain a more authentic understanding of the Sikhs, a task that would be facilitated by gaining access to their sacred scriptures. Trumpp's primary audience would therefore have consisted of influential policy makers and, because of Trumpp's renown in Europe as a scholar of Oriental languages, the growing market of Orientalists, philosophers, and missionaries who had had, until then, little or no knowledge of Sikhs except as a "sect of the Hindus."

At the outset of the "Sketch" Trumpp informs the reader that what he is about to present is an attempt to remedy a prevalent bias in the received view of the Sikhs and their religious system. Trumpp's indebtedness to the well-established Orientalist traditions can be immediately discerned from the nature of his remarks.[24] He conceived his task not merely as a work of translation, but as the work of a benefactor endeavoring to impose a semblance of systematic unity and the principles of speculative philosophy, which the Ādi Granth apparently lacked:

> Nānak was not a speculative philosopher who built up a concise system of scientific principles; his thoughts were uttered in a loose way, . . . now scattered throughout the Granth, and must first be patiently searched out and collected into a whole, prior to forming an idea of his tenets .[25]

Trumpp's inheritance of German and British Orientalism led him to compare the "chief point in Nānak's doctrine"—namely, the "unity of the Supreme Being"—with the Hindu philosophical systems, which were "already more or less familiarized with this idea."[26] In reality this Being alone exists:

> It is the ground or root of all things, the source, from which all have
> sprung, the primary cause; in this sense it is called the *creator*. But we
> must not misunderstand this appellation, for no creation out of nothing
> is thereby intended. When Absolute Being is styled the creator, the *ex-
> pansion* of the same into a *plurality of forms* is thereby meant. . . .
> [T]he whole universe and all things therein are identified with the
> Supreme. . . . All the finite created beings have therefore no separate
> existence apart from the Absolute, they are only its various forms and
> appearances. . . . All creatures are therefore alike with the only differ-
> ence that the Absolute becomes self-conscious in man. . . . No teleo-
> logical principle whatever is assigned for the production or destruction
> of the created beings.[27]

Unable to find reasonable grounds for specifically differentiating the notion of "Supreme Being" in the Ādi Granth from the orthodox Hindu philosophy, Trumpp proceeded to classify the Granth's central philosophy as "pantheism," albeit one that leaned toward a degraded "dualism":

> We need hardly remark that this whole definition of the Supreme is
> altogether *pantheistic*. The Hindu way of thinking comprehends in the
> Absolute both spirit and matter, as the creation of material bodies out
> of nothing is totally incomprehensible to the Hindu mind.[28]

What for Trumpp appeared to be a contradiction—that Indians were not concerned to separate the *unity* of the Supreme Being from a *dualistic* pantheism—becomes part of a general strategy on his part to show that the Ādi Granth is an incoherent document full of contradictory statements. Unable to fully account for this contradiction, however, Trumpp resorts to distinguishing between two different varieties of pantheism within the Ādi Granth: a "grosser" as against a "finer." This move is strongly reminiscent of Hegel's problem of defining the difference between religions by means of a distinction between consistent and inconsistent elevation, found in the 1827 *Lectures on the Philosophy of Religion*.

> The grosser Pantheism identifies all things with the Absolute, the universe
> in its various forms being considered a part of it. The finer Pantheism on

the other hand distinguishes between the Absolute and the finite beings, and borders frequently on Theism. . . . [In the finer Pantheism] God . . . remains distinct from the creatures . . . [and] creation assumes the form of emanation from the supreme; the reality of matter is denied.[29]

Trumpp then proceeds to give an indication of the intellectual and ideological pole against which he measures his interpretation of the Granth:

That an Absolute thus-defined cannot be a self-conscious spirit endowed with a free will and acting according to teleological principles, seems never to have struck their minds. For after the strongest Pantheistic expressions the Supreme is again addressed as a self-conscious personality . . . with whom man endeavors to enter into personal relations. Contradictory statements of this kind we find a great many in the Granth.[30]

These remarks are of more than simply passing interest. They allow us an insight into the main intellectual influence upon Trumpp's thinking, and consequently, the orientation of his translation, both of these being particularly dependent on the passage of ideas between the philosophy of religion and Indology. Discernable here is the influence of Schlegel's distinction between emanation and pantheism, according to which the latter, as found mainly in Vaiṣṇava strands of Vedānta, represents the most degenerate form of all Indian thinking. There can be little doubt, however, that Hegel's writings on the philosophy of religion provide the main ideological influence behind Trumpp's distinction between "fine" and "gross" pantheism. By the mid-nineteenth century, when Trumpp was receiving his theological training at Tübingen, Hegel's reputation as a leading European thinker had been firmly established for some time. His influence on theology, history of religions, and Orientalism was particularly marked. Prompted by personal attacks from influential pietist theologians such as Thöluck on what was perceived to be a closet pantheism within Hegel's own philosophy, Hegel himself had begun to distinguish between the "genuine pantheism" that he attributed to Schelling and the early Schlegel, and "Spinozistic pantheism," which had certain similarities to Oriental pantheism. Indeed, by 1827 we find that Hegel had begun to differentiate the nature of pantheism within Oriental religions, a move that was tied up with his failure in the 1824 lectures to formulate a suitable definition for the standpoint of religion.

It thereby allowed him to differentiate between the outright atheism of Buddhism from the kind of pantheism specific to Hinduism, which differed only in the sense that "a countless number of incarnations" are adopted, although, as Hegel states, these incarnations are "merely a mask that substance adopts and exchanges in contingent fashion."[31] Hence, implicit in many of Trumpp's remarks is the historically oriented grading of religions according to their proximity or distance from the theoretical standpoint of religion, namely, the "metaphysical as such," or the "Absolute" as "self-conscious spirit" that is peculiar to the Hegelian schema.[32]

In regard to ethics in the Ādi Granth, Trumpp asked the following questions: "What is the relationship of man to the Supreme? [and] How did it happen that [the individual soul] fell into impurity or sin?"[33] The answers to these questions are provided in several short passages, which deserve to be reproduced here because they provide, in short, the central themes around which the future response of Sikh reformist scholars will be organized:

[The aim of existence] . . . is the total dissolution of individual existence by the reabsorption of the soul in the fountain of light . . . i.e. Nirbān[34], the total cessation of individual consciousness and reunion with the vacuum. If there be any doubt on the Pantheistic character of the tenets of the Sikh Gurus regarding the Supreme, it would be dissolved by their doctrine of Nirbān. Where no personal God is taught or believed in, man cannot aspire to find communion with him; his aim can only be . . . individual annihilation. We therefore find no allusion to the joys of a future life in the Granth. The immortality of the soul is taught only as far as the doctrine of transmigration requires it. . . . The Nirbān . . . was the grand object which Buddha . . . held out to the poor people. From his atheistic point of view he could look for nothing else; personal existence . . . with the evils of this life . . . not counterbalanced by corresponding pleasures . . . appeared as the greatest evil. Buddhism . . . like Sikhism . . . is unrestricted Pessimism, unable to hold out . . . any solace. . . .[35]

From the foregoing remarks it is plain enough, that in a religion where the highest object of life is individual existence, there can be no room for a system of moral duties; we need therefore hardly point out, how wrong the statement of some authors is, that Sikhism is a moralizing Deism.[36]

These passages are important for a number of reasons. First there is Trumpp's implicit rejection of the prevalent view among the Punjab administration officers, of the un-Hindu-like character of the Sikhs. It implies that the Western hope and desire to find within the central texts of the Sikhs reasons for their outwardly "deistic" or "moral" being were misguided. On Trumpp's account the contents of the Ādi Granth were not a good indicator of the Sikhs' present character and position, since the tenets expressed therein could only lead to a pessimistic nihilism—which from a European standpoint could only lead to an immoral existence. Thus the answer to what made them tick must be located not within the contents of their sacred scriptures, but rather in their historical evolution. The reasons for their apparent difference from "degenerate Hinduism" had no necessity, but were purely arbitrary or incidental, the result of historical accident caused by external factors outside their control, rather than being the result of something located in the teachings of the Ādi Granth, which conveyed only "a lack of teleological principles."

The rejection of Sikhism as a "moralizing deism," replaced instead by the view of it as a cross between pantheism and atheism, represented a considerable dilemma to the emerging Sikh elites in the years following the publication of Trumpp's work. Under constant threat from Christian missionaries, Hindu reformists (particularly members of the Ārya Samāj), faced with internal opposition from those Sikhs who envisaged Sikh tradition as a strand of the *sanātana dharma*, or "orthodox" Hinduism, Sikh elites saw that Trumpp's work posed a very serious challenge to their chances of gaining political recognition and patronage for their cause.[37] The import of passages such as the above threatened to undermine the very basis of Sikh reformists' claims for recognition from the administration, and, in a wider context, their claims to possess an individual self-consciousness: the moral basis for any future claims that the community be regarded as a nation and that they were its legitimate representatives. It would certainly have undermined their efforts to reconstitute the *rahit*[38] tradition, which would be fundamental to the project of nationalizing Sikh traditions by cementing its religious boundaries.

Backed by the authority of the colonial administration, Trumpp's translation and accompanying "odium theologicum" toward the Sikh religion put several far-reaching classificatory moves into operation. For the first time Sikhism was installed into a position on the graph of historical evolution of religions that was even lower than the position of Hinduism. In fact, Trumpp placed Sikhism on a par with atheistic Buddhism. Leaving aside his discernment of the lack of proper theological character—its incoherence, multiple, and contradictory conceptions of God and self—within the Ādi Granth, this is an interesting and potentially fruitful observation on Trumpp's part, although the implications of this cannot be explored here. The real implication of this move was to invalidate, on the basis of empirical observation and from the evidence of their own scriptures, the prevalent view that the Sikh religion was a "moralizing deism" or that it possessed any historical or "leavening" impulse of its own.[39] As a result, prevalent notions about Sikhism—that Sikhs were not really "Hindoos" but had been wrongly identified with them on account of their own "fall," or that their "fall" was due to the incursions of Brahmanism, which had crept in as a result of Maharajah Ranjit Singh's opulence (hence their defeat at the hands of the British), or that their encounter with the British would help to revitalize the original spirit of Sikhism—all stood to be undermined. According to Trumpp's reading, Sikhism, like Hinduism, was always already "fallen" in the sense that it was outside history. Or to use Hegelian terminology, Sikhism did not possess any *Aufhebung*—that essential extrication and elevation from gross nature into history that only Western religions possessed. It was therefore a mistake to say that Sikhism had "fallen" but could be resurrected.

More important perhaps was the displacement of the discursive field of translation and interpretation of the Ādi Granth into an order of things governed by oppositions such as theism/atheism and chaos/order. In other words, the conceptual terminology in any future debate or discourse concerning Sikhism was shifted into the domain of ontotheology: where all propositions and statements on the Sikh religion were automatically rerouted through the question concerning the existence of God as the ground of rational thinking. As a result, indigenous Sikh and Western interpreters were presented with clearly defined tasks. For Sikhs, this was to prove their commitment to the idea of God's existence, which meant a commitment to prove that their central texts could provide a suitable concept of God, if they hoped to receive political recognition and patronage from Europeans as a *valuable* and *useful* religion. For Westerners, having determined the nature and essence of Sikh religion in terms of its conception of God and the self, the path was cleared for the only real task that remained, that is, comparative and classificatory study.

Whether one liked it or not, Trumpp's demarcation of conceptual boundaries for the study of Sikhism provided a framework that future interpreters could contest but never remain outside of. Indeed, as we shall see, in order to refute Trumpp, both Sikh reformists and Western scholars of Sikhism needed first to engage with the terminology and framework he had imposed. Yet in doing so they were inadvertently forced to adopt its very premises. What Trumpp had effectively inaugurated was a framework for the future politics of religious language that was centered on a rigorous conceptualization of God's being; this would become instrumental not only in refiguring boundaries between religions but also in constructing a Sikh national consciousness.

Pincott and the Politics of Classification

While Trumpp's opponents could dismiss his work on the bases of its purported bias and inaccuracies, what they were unable to dismiss was the fact that Trumpp had managed to move the ground of future discourse on Sikh scripture to the purview of the Western intellectual and religious tradition, and specifically into the context of current debates in theology and philosophy. This is due partly to Trumpp's credentials as a philologist, but, more important, to his formal training in theology and philosophy at the Tübingen Stift. Compared to his predecessors, who had presented mainly observational travel accounts or histories without any real knowledge of the central Sikh texts, Trumpp was, intellectually speaking, on relatively safe ground. Perhaps the best indication of this is the ineffectiveness of attempts by Sikhs and non-Sikhs alike to refute the central aspects of Trumpp's programme.

A good example of this is provided by Frederic Pincott's two articles, "Sikhism" and "The Arrangement of Hymns of the Ādi Granth," both of which were originally published in the *Journal of the Royal Asiatic Society*.[40] Against Trumpp's argument that there was only an accidental relation between Islamic and Sikh concepts of God, Pincott in his article "Sikhism" tried to adduce a greater influence of Persian Sūfism, and thereby of Islamic monotheism, on Sikhism. By the end of this article, however, Pincott ends up reaffirming Trumpp's basic thesis: that Sikhism *is* pantheism "based on Hinduism, modified by Buddhism," but merely "stirred into new life by Sūfism."[41] What is noteworthy in Pincott's essay is his inadvertent accession to historicist premises, which seems to lead *logically* toward the need to demonstrate an adequate conception of God and the moral qualities of Sikhism.

Even more revealing is the fate of the later article, "The Arrangement of Hymns in the Ādi Granth," in which Pincott attempts to undermine one of Trumpp's main complaints about the Sikh scripture, namely the lack of a "leading principle" within the Ādi Granth.[42] For Trumpp this lack of a "leading principle" is clear evidence that the compilers of the *Granth* seem to have paid less attention to the proper organization of its contents than to attaining a "bulky size." By thus "jumbling together whatever came to hand without any judicious selection, the Granth has become an exceedingly incoherent and wearisome book," a "mere promiscuous heap of verses." Pincott's main corrective was to argue that the Ādi Granth could be shown to be "arranged on a definitive plan from end to end." This order or plan is based on the system of North Indian *rāg*, or musical measures, whose "characteristic peculiarity is that it is based on the theory that each musical sound corresponds to some emotion of the human heart. When any particular sound predominates in a tune, that tune is supposed to give rise to a peculiar rāg, or emotion."[43]

What Pincott failed to show, however, was the *sense* in which the arrangement was methodical—specifically that the "ordering principle" here was not in fact based on rational or intellectual principles but on a "nonsystem" that emphasizes the primacy of mood or emotion related to a particular *rāg* as a necessary prerequisite for any understanding of the words of the hymn. What this indicates is that the original composition of these hymns by the Sikh Gurus may have been dictated by aesthetic sensibilities centered on mood/emotion as opposed to conceptual thought alone.

The fact that Pincott's essay was rarely ever referenced again either by Indologists or by Sikh reformist scholars is not only an indicator of Trumpp's influence, but, more important, a consequence of the war of cultural politics going on within the European academy, a war that was characterized by the two very different ways in which European intellectuals conceived of the relationship between India and Europe or, more broadly, between the West and the non-West. As I argued earlier, the contrast is perhaps best represented by the ideological battle between Hegel and Schelling.[44] As discussed in chapter 2, the battle between these two figures centered on the status of proper conceptual thought based on a reflective self-consciousness in contradistinction to the kind of thinking that resists purely conceptual or reflective thinking. Grounded in transience as opposed to the stasis of the concept, the latter kind of thinking arises in the encounter with the domain of art and the sensuous and finds its prime example in wordless music. Interestingly, the respective attitudes of these ideologues toward artforms such as music are mirrored by their comparative attitudes towards Indian and Western religions. Thus whereas Schelling valorized music, pantheism, and Indian religions in that they resisted the rigorously conceptual thinking promulgated by Hegel, for Hegel art, the sensuous, and pantheism epitomized the very reasons Indian religions had never been able to achieve the freedom of history. It therefore justified his theoretical positioning of India outside the pale of history.

Judged from this perspective, it is not difficult to understand why, first, claims such as those Pincott was making—that there is an "ordering principle" based on emotion and mood as opposed to metaphysical conceptuality—would, like the views of Schelling, be swimming against the tide of his time. Second, this view helps to explain why the *decisive response* to Trumpp's work from reformist Sikhs came as late as the 1920s and 1930s, almost half a century after the publication of Trumpp's Ādi Granth translation. Third, it explains why this response, which came mainly in the shape of short narratives on Sikh history and longer, more systematic works of scriptural exegesis (*ṭīkās*) of a broadly theological nature, tended to implement the very distinction that Trumpp had accused the Ādi Granth of lacking, namely, the metaphysical distinction between literal and figural. As a result, the ontotheological schema will take priority over *rāg*, so that in future *rāg* will be treated either as a "mere superscription," or nonintellectual adornment to the proper literary work, or, as is still commonly thought, as no more than an identity card that ensures correct oral transmission from generation to generation. The length of time required by reformist Sikhs to finally come up with such a response indicates that their enunciation needed to evolve from a phase characterized by a lack of "proper" theological expression, to the phase in the 1920s–1930s wherein this desire is fulfilled through a process of intercultural mimesis, resulting in what can be described as the production of an "adequate" articulation of systematic narrative and a theological concept of God.

Although it is not generally recognized, the evolution of reformist discourse from prenarrative to narrative,[45] or from pretheology to theology, centers on two things: (i) a perceived difference between Indic and European notions of time and ontology—one of the issues that fueled the philosophical divergence between Schelling and Hegel; (ii) the mimetic co-figuration of this difference as identity—the identification of new discourses called "Sikh theology" and "Sikh history" and of course the iden-

SIKHISM AND THE POLITICS OF RELIGION-MAKING   195

tity of a subject who learned to enunciate via these discourses. Although this process continues to be unproblematically projected as a "dialogue" between two respective agents, colonizer and colonized, what needs to be remembered is that the agency of the colonized cannot exist outside of his enunciation within a particular regime of discourse *to which he had to accede without choice*. What this tells us is that agency cannot simply be ascribed through a mode of epistemological certainty. Rather, new forms of agency or subjectivity will have been generated through this very process of accession and enunciation. Yet this will never have been the process of transparent linguistic and cultural exchange that is indicated by the word "dialogue," but rather will have involved a fundamental fissuring and transformation of the indigenous temporal and ontological perspective. In the case of reformist Sikhs this process was catalyzed through the "dialogue" with the Orientalist scholar Max Arthur Macauliffe. Let me turn to a reassessment of this "dialogue," which prefigures the emergence of "Sikh theology."

Manufacturing Native Informancy: Macauliffe's "Dialogue" with the Sikh Reformists

Since the early period of colonial rule one of the prevalent assumptions about Indian and specifically Hindu civilizations was that they lacked a sense of history.[46] Hindus, it was generally argued, showed disdain for historical narrative of the type Europeans had come to expect from "civilized" cultures. The most obvious reason for this deficiency was their cyclical conception of time, in which the passage of time was viewed negatively. Through their belief in cyclical time, individual existence came to be regarded as unreal since it was only one link in a continual chain of existence. Without a definable origin of time there could be no clear distinction between nature and history, good and evil, and consequently no proper ground for either subjectivity or nationhood. As shown by representations that emphasized the annihilation of the self as the highest object of religion, Hindu time and existence became a metonym for decline and nihilism. In practice this resulted in the rejection of a unified corporeal existence (one body, one soul) in favor of the promiscuous existence of hybrid identities.

The colonial assumption that Hindus lacked history was never unitary, however. As I have argued in the previous chapter, it could be traced to two competing Western models of history and therefore two different ways of conceiving the Hindu lack of history. On the one hand was the model of history—conceived and propagated in the work of Hegel and James Mill—according to which Hindus lacked history absolutely (Orientalism[2]). And on the other hand was the model of history—which had its intellectual roots in Enlightenment deism (notably Kant) and was propagated by a long line of Indologists, beginning with William Jones—according to which Hindus had fallen from an original state of monotheism and reason to their present condition (Orientalism[1]). Although the possibility of a Hindu revival is held out in Orientalism[1], it is ironically the second phase of Indology (Orientalism[2]), informed by the new philosophical speculation about the nature of "religion" along a Hegelian model of history, that led to the "discovery" of *bhakti* and the idea of a "*bhakti* movement" as the platform for the revival of the Hindu mind.

As outlined in chapter 1, this idea of a "*bhakti* movement" gave the impetus for Indologists to reconceptualize two divergent accounts: (i) of *bhakti* as the "only true religion" of the Hindus, one which included Sikhs and could be traced back to an imagined Aryan Hindu race as it existed before the Muslim incursions; and (ii) of *bhakti* as no more than a precursory movement that, "leavened" by the influence of Islamic monotheism, merely prepared the way for the advent of the Sikh religion.[47] What concerns us here is that these accounts invited opposing responses from Hindu and Sikh reformists to the representation of *bhakti* either as a continuity with Hindu time and tradition, or as a fundamental point of departure from the body of lived Hindu experience. But whereas Hindu reformists used the *bhakti* movement as a means of hearkening back to a mythic origin, Sikh reformists appropriated the idea of the "*bhakti* movement" as the precursor of a new time, a new origin, the foundation for a Sikh narrative representing a true elevation and extrication from the Hindu body.

For Sikh reformists this quest to extricate themselves from the negative stereotype of contemporary Hinduism was inextricably connected, as we have seen, with Trumpp's thesis that Sikhs, according to the testimony of their own scriptures, were Hindus, and that they shared ideologically, theologically, and ontologically a Hindu time and space. Trumpp's work served to accentuate the crisis for reformist Sikhs, leading them to articulate their search for identity with questions such as: Were Sikhs Hindus? If not, what in fact were they? How could they provide evidence that would demonstrate what they claimed? On what basis could they redraw cultural boundaries that had become blurred?

In the absence of any systematic theological speculation, which had yet to evolve, Sikh reformists in the late nineteenth century were able to distance themselves from the negative "Hindu" stereotype by drawing upon two very different sources, indigenous and foreign. Indigenous sources included *janamsākhīs*, or hagiographical literature, consisting mainly of narratives of the lives of the Sikh Gurus and specifically Nānak; the eighteenth-century *Gurbilās* literature, which consisted of narratives of the lives of the sixth and tenth Gurus, stressing their roles as warriors; and the eighteenth-century *rahit nāmā* literature, which dealt with codes of conduct and the moral behavior of Sikhs initiated into the Khalsā order.[48] On the other hand was the foreign corpus, comprising early and contemporary European narrative accounts that portray Sikhism as a "new religion."[49] The primary distinction that can be drawn between these two groups of sources is that the narrative structures of the indigenous sources remain firmly rooted within an Indic system of time. There is no evidence either of a break with a broadly Indic ontology, or of the idea of a "*bhakti* movement" as the necessary precursor to a break. By contrast, the Orientalist narrative accounts, based on the work of Indologists such H. H. Wilson, Albrecht Weber, F. Lorinser, George Grierson, and Monier-Williams not only develop the idea of *bhakti* as a "movement," but, more important, seamlessly incorporate precolonial narratives into the properly historical narrative of imperial history grounded in the priority of the present.[50]

The real importance of European (Orientalist[1]) narratives lies in the fact not only that they provide an antidote to Trumpp, but also that they will become reference points for Sikh reformists within indigenous constructions of an authentic "Sikh history" and "Sikh theology." That is to say, Sikh reformists aligned the *timing* of the Indic narratives and their own lived experiences with and within the historical present of the Orientalist narrative, thereby effecting a "conversion to [the time of] modernity." The kind of interaction whereby this alignment is achieved, namely "dialogue," is particularly revealing, irrespective of whether such "dialogue" is between persons or between persons and texts. The work of Max Arthur Macauliffe is illustrative of the way in which "dialogue" between Sikh reformists and the British helped to effect a convergence and eventual concordance of ontologically distinct narratives.

Macauliffe's role, personally and pedagogically, in the overall project of late nineteenth- and early twentieth-century Sikh reformism is of singular importance for a number of reasons. His main work, the monumental six-volume study *The Sikh Religion: Its Gurus, Sacred Writings, and Authors*, is a work of translation and at the same time a historiography. Its publication by Oxford University Press in 1909 gained for it significant credibility and sympathy from a European readership, and in that sense alone provided a major corrective to Trumpp's potentially damaging work. Moreover, its lucid narrative style and contextualization of traditional Sikh materials proved to be highly popular with reformists and continues to be eulogized even today by many Sikhs. However, what concerns us here is not Macauliffe's reception as a historian, which is adequately treated elsewhere.[51] Of greater relevance to us is the way in which his work and close personal contacts with leading reformist scholars of the day helped not so much to overcome Trumpp's thesis, as is often thought, but simply to *invert* it, thus remaining within the very space of cultural translation that Trumpp had opened.

Macauliffe's work has often been eulogized for reflecting "mainstream Singh Sabhā theology"[52] or the "moral and religious purity of original Sikhism [, which was] in danger of being lost,"[53] primarily through maintaining a close collaboration with a retinue of well-known *giānīs*, whose opinions he would consult extensively and to whom he would submit his manuscripts for a final examination. But there is a problem with this viewpoint. First, during the period of Macauliffe's research there was strictly speaking no form of literature that could be regarded as a Sikh "theology." As W. H. McLeod has argued, the earliest systematic articulations of Sikh "theology" did not appear until the late 1920s.[54] Any "theology" at this time can be spoken of only as implicit: a form of expression that the reformists desired but were not able to enunciate. Indeed, evidence that the reformists were unable to formulate anything like a "theology" is given by Macauliffe himself in the preface to *The Sikh Religion* and elsewhere. On the one hand Macauliffe stresses that unlike his predecessor, Ernest Trumpp, he (Macauliffe) "worked very closely with the assistance of the few *gyānīs*, or professional interpreters of the Sikh canonical writings, who now survive."[55] On the other hand, he seems convinced that of these "few or none is capable of giving an English interpretation. They generally construe in tedious paraphrases in their own dialects. But more than this there is hardly any one Sikh who is capable of making a correct translation of his sacred writings."[56] This somewhat ambivalent statement made after the publication of

The Sikh Religion corroborates similar sentiments expressed by Macauliffe during the period when he was still engaged on the translation:

> I could have wished the translation into English was made by a Sikh, but—and it may be as well to put the matter clearly to prevent error and disappointment—there is not as yet, so far as I am aware, any Sikh sufficiently acquainted with English to make any idiomatic translation into it; and another translation such as Dr. Trumpp's would only cast further ridicule on the Sikh religion. The work therefore, if done at all, must be done by an Englishman. In a few generations there will no doubt be Sikhs who can write literary English, but it is hardly likely that such will be well acquainted with the Granth Sāhib, seeing that there are now hardly any Sikhs who have made an advanced study of English, and at the same time acquired a complete knowledge of their sacred writings.[57]

These statements are interesting for several reasons. In addition to postulating why there were no systematic works of theology or history forthcoming from Sikhs at the time, he also exposes one of the major limitations of the early Anglo-vernacular education: that English could not be appropriated by the native elites to the level required for equal intellectual exchange, i.e., to a level where the native elites could *think* in English. This of course raises further questions regarding the nature of Macauliffe's "close collaboration" with traditional native experts. Were these native experts (including such prominent reformists such as Kahn Singh Nabha, who authored and published the polemical and influential tract entitled "*Ham Hindu Nahin*" ["We Are Not Hindus"] in 1899) involved as equal partners in some form of "dialogue" with Macauliffe? If these experts were "totally unacquainted with English," could they adequately *judge* the valuation and wider import of the form and meaning given by Macauliffe, other than its potential for gaining access to a space that they desired to occupy but remained beyond their reach, a space to which access was interdicted?

Seeming to anticipate this problem, Macauliffe further states: "I have also whenever practicable engaged English-speaking Sikhs to read my translations, and invited them to offer me their comments and suggestions."[58] But this seems to contradict the suggestion made in the previous paragraph, that "there are now hardly any Sikhs who have made an advanced study of English." What could be the point of engaging someone to read and comment on an English translation if that very reader was unlikely to have made a sufficiently advanced study of English? What kind of interlocution would it be where one party (the Sikh) is not naturally inclined to speak and think in English, and where the other party (Macauliffe) would not be naturally inclined to speak and think in Punjabi? The question as to which language the "dialogue" is conducted in becomes moot once it is recognized that the target language—the language in which there must be a consensus or agreement between the two parties for any dialogue to have occurred—is English.

This can be considered in two ways. In the case of the *giānīs* who have no English, Macauliffe, as with any other European translator, will have acquired an ability to cross over from his native English into the foreign idiom of Punjabi. For the meaning of the Punjabi idiom to remain anything but "private" there must already be in place an automatic agreement between the two parties to the effect that private meanings (corresponding in this case to the Punjabi idiom) must be rendered transferable into the public—that is, universally intelligible—idiom of English. Clearly the distinction between private and public manifests the interdiction of a certain law—in this case imperial law—as to which language counts as "official." If this law is adhered to by colonizer and colonized, then neither the crossing into Punjabi nor the act of transference back into English will have distorted the private experience of the native experts. While both parties will have agreed in advance upon the "meaning" of any particular word or phrase, the natives will have had no say in determining the appearance and location of this meaning in the public domain: English. I refer of course to the act of judgment. According to Macauliffe, those who specifically possess the power to locate the meaning of the foreign idiom within English only include himself and other "such eminent scholars who have permanently settled in England and who can write English *like Englishmen*" (emphasis mine).[59] Because, by inference, one cannot adequately locate meaning outside of a certain native land or by becoming native to the land in whose language one writes, the kind of acculturation to English implied by Macauliffe could not have happened in India.

Consequently, in the case of Macauliffe's collaboration with "those learned Sikhs acquainted with English," it is again the Sikhs who must make their Punjabi idiom (consigned as a result of the colonial interdict to the realm of private meaning) *conform* to the target language, English. The oppositions private versus public, native Indic knowledge versus European knowledge, etc., are of course based on the distinction between the native and the foreign, which can in turn be regarded as a "natural" projection of the *a priori* distinction between self and other. Although "common sense" dictates that this distinction can be bridged by the heroic effort of a translator, the act of translation itself will have been elided to give the impression of a communication or dialogue. The key point, however, is that the final authority in determining the transference and relocation of the native meaning not only happens in English, but rests with whatever conforms most closely to the English self. Meaning as such is therefore determined from within a properly English context, which necessarily means an English social context.

In his thought-provoking essay "The Concept of Cultural Translation in British Social Anthropology," Talal Asad has argued that this kind of cultural translation is a matter of determining implicit meanings.[60] The term "implicit" suggests not only the meanings the native speaker actually acknowledges in his speech, or the meanings the native listener necessarily accepts, but those he is "capable of sharing" with scientific authority.[61] What seems to be evident here in the implicit/explicit, private/public oppositions is the replacement of the *un*translatable or the *im*plicit by a *representation* of translation, that is, an economy of translation-as-dialogue where the act of enunciating is elided. If Asad is right, it is this economization of translation into successful communication or "dialogue" that gives rise to the idea of implicit meanings or the untranslatable as that which resists fluent and silent transferal. As Naoki Sakai further reminds us, the notion of the implicit or untranslatable is "testimony to the sociality of the translator," his prior determination as a representative of the English state and the society of those who speak proper English.[62] Yet it is this very sociality of the translator that erases the ontology of the implicit/untranslatable in order to replace it with a *homolingual* communication: English as the Law for translation. Whichever way we look at it though, the final outcome—an outcome that is already presupposed—will always be the simultaneous installation and reproduction of the figure of the native informant, the native who can enunciate properly only insofar as his speech renders into English correct knowledge or information, a process that it will be necessary to keep disguised as "dialogue."

Reinstalling Sikhism Within the History of Religions

In accordance with Asad's suggestion, the works of colonial translation exemplified by both Trumpp and Macauliffe can be considered as simultaneously psychoanalytical and theological exercises. "Psychoanalytic" because "implicit" suggests unconscious meaning, something that the native does not yet know but only desires, because he is as yet incapable of enunciating in a form recognizable to the society that is supposed to know, the purveyor of truth. "Theological" because his narrative retelling presents Sikhism as the essence of reform, an exemplary story of indigenous self-extrication from the Indian fall and the awakening to the "consciousness of intellectual and ethical responsibility."[63] This awakening is best illustrated in Macauliffe's "Introduction" to *The Sikh Religion*, where he sets out what can be regarded as a "theoretical" framework for the book as a whole—the "theory" being a concise but "necessary" presentation "on the origin and progress of religion until it received its monotheistic consummation, accepted by Guru Nānak."[64]

Thus for Macauliffe—as also for his better-known peers and contemporaries who collectively shaped what I have elsewhere termed the second, and post-Hegelian, phase of Indological research—the origin of religion is an imperfect state where, in his immediacy to nature, "miserable and resourceless primitive man felt the inclemency and fury of the elements."[65] Religion then progresses with civilization, following a series of well-known stages—each stage corresponding to an extension of man's intellectual condition—from primitive polytheism and the worship of minor deities, the subordination of minor deities to a single supreme deity, which lead in turn to a more exalted concept of divinity, namely the idea or concept of the One: "For many centuries thinking men in India have . . . made no secret of their faith in the sole primal creator."[66] This is the high point of Hinduism, its Golden Age. But at this stage an "important question arose (as to) how the Supreme Being should be represented."[67] Although primitive representations were initially anthropomorphic, eventually, as "man's conception of God extended . . . the belief arose that God is diffused through all matter, and that it (matter) is a part of him: this belief is known as Pantheism."[68]

Macauliffe's view—that, properly speaking, pantheism is the "creed of intellectual Hindus"—can be traced through a long line of Indological scholarship, going back to H. T. Colebrook. In Macauliffe's text pantheism, being considered as unsuitable for thinking about true religion, is therefore used to distinguish Sikhs, "who believe in a personal God," from Hindus. Hindus, in other words, do not have religion but philosophy, as a result of which they remained in a prehistorical state, a state of "mental darkness" until the fifteenth century, that is, when "a great cyclical wave of reformation spread over India and Europe, resulting in the awakening of the Indian mind "to the consciousness of intellectual responsibility."[69]

Two things need to be noted in Macauliffe's theoretical presentation of the progress of religion. First, it differs from that of his contemporaries, such as Weber, only in that they ascribe "monotheism" to *bhakti* in general. For Macauliffe, who essentially follows Cunningham, Sikh monotheism requires *bhakti* as a precursor—that is, as a prehistorical phase— in order for Sikhism to be designated as a proper or historical religion. Hence the idea that Sikhism is a *new* or living religion. The distinction between life and death, sleep and awakening is subtle but crucial to the distinction between *bhakti* and Sikhism. Second, and what is more relevant to our argument, notwithstanding his attempt to reverse Trumpp's charge that Sikhism is mere pantheism, Macauliffe admits failure in dissociating Sikhism from pantheism:

> No religious teacher has succeeded in *logically* dissociating theism from pantheism. In some passages of the Guru's writings pantheism is, as we have seen, distinctly implied, while in other texts is made distinct from the creator.[70] [emphasis mine]

Given that Macauliffe attributes this inability to the failure of logic, it needs to be asked whether in continuing to maintain the clear distinction between Hinduism and Sikhism in terms of the oppositions pantheism/ monotheism and pre-history/history—and therefore classifying one in relation to another *historically*, i.e., as historical identities—the thinking behind such classification does not itself partake of the very essence and function of metaphysical logic? Moreover, insofar as the work of such logic consists in the (self)-movement from chaos to order by referring to oneself as an origin, is this movement not the very definition of *transcendence* in the sense of moving over and beyond? What Macauliffe describes, therefore, is not the mere distinction between two entities Sikhism and Hindu-ism. In faithfully mirroring what reformist Sikhs say, he identifies the self-movement of Sikhism as a transcendence of Hinduism, grounded in a self-consciousness that is indissociably linked to the concept of God proper to Sikhism.

In other words, the possession of historical origin is linked to the ability of Sikh "subjects" to conceive a particular idea of God. The point here is that Macauliffe's response to Trumpp's *odium theologicum* is imbricated in the same ontotheological framework as Trumpp's work. From this perspective the only real difference between them is the position and status that each attributes to Sikhism on the ontotheological schema called the history/ progress of religion(s): *either* a full-fledged theism, as in Macauliffe's case, *or* a pantheism/atheism, as in the case of Trumpp. While Trumpp denied Sikh reformists what they desired (an authentically Sikh origin, subjectivity, and a "sufficiently exalted idea of God"), Macauliffe helped them to satisfy their desire for precisely these things. As I shall demonstrate later in this chapter, the desire of Sikh reformists to conceive a "sufficiently exalted idea of God" could only be fulfilled by accounting for the concept of God in their own scriptures. This was the task that befell the writers of the exegetical commentaries that came almost fifty years after the publication of Trumpp's work. It is in these commentaries, and in the task of proving God's existence with which these commentaries open, that the beginnings of the formation called "Sikh theology" are to be located.

Reconstituting *Gurmat* as "Sikh Theology"

Macauliffe's efforts notwithstanding, the definitive response to Trumpp, coming almost fifty years after his translation was first published, appeared in the form of short treatises on Sikh history and longer, more systematic works of scriptural exegesis (*ṭīkās*) that were of a broadly theological nature. One of the more far-reaching effects of these commentaries is that they helped to crystallize a new and distinctive way of representing the central teaching of the Ādi Granth. The central teachings (*gurmat*) came to be projected from a standpoint of a systematic concept of God or Ultimate Reality, based on which "*gurmat*," "theology," and "tradition" come to be seen as synonymous. The idea that *gurmat* (= theology = tradition) is synonymous with a proper concept of God came to exert a hegemonic influence on the modern Sikh imaginary.

Surprisingly, however, the suggestion that the prevailing concept of God in modern Sikhism evolved under historical circumstances goes against the grain of conventional wisdom about Sikhism—both traditionalist and historical[71]—which assume that the commentaries of the Singh Sabhā simply extracted and reproduced a theological hermeneutic that is intrinsic to the teachings of Guru Nānak as found in the central Sikh scripture, the Ādi Granth. The familiar narrative of traditionalist scholarship, for example, assumes that at the heart of Sikhism lies the mystical experience of its founder, Guru Nānak, an experience that is articulated through his own poetic compositions (*gurbānī*) and the teachings that follow from these (*gurmat*). The nature of this teaching conforms to a revealed theology grounded in the concept of a transcendent and immanent God. By way of comparison, the prevailing perspective in historical (and by self-definition "critical") Sikh studies, as articulated by its most distinguished exponent W. H. McLeod, considers Guru Nānak to be part and parcel of the devotional tradition of North India and specifically within the Sant lineage. The basis of Sant religiosity is *nirguṇ bhakti*, or devotion to the Name of an ineffable transcendent being. Speculating elsewhere on the possibility of a Sikh theology for modern times, McLeod argues that although strictly speaking theology is a Western discipline, Sikh tradition "as it has evolved" under the Singh Sabhā is rendered "eminently suitable to a theological treatment."[72] The idea of a Sikh theology can therefore be justified because theology encompasses both the "natural theology of Nanak's *bānī*" and the evolution of a Sikh exegetical tradition in the hands of the Singh Sabhā. Hence the word *gurmat* as used by the Singh Sabhā is a suitably pragmatic translation for "theology." The only requirement today would be to modernize its mode of reception. Since this perspective is likely to be echoed by traditionalist scholars, there appears to be a consensus on one of the central points about the Sikh religion.

However, I would argue for a degree of vigilance to be exercised at precisely the point where there appears to be a fundamental link between these two otherwise divergent schools of thought. The link consists in a certain understanding of transcendence that refers simultaneously to the idea of a transcendent being and a method of inquiry. In this sense both narratives adhere to a preconceived notion of transcendence as universal or transcultural, which enables it to be used as both a theological and an anthropological tool in the conceptualization of religion. Though rarely understood, however, both "critical" and "traditionalist" narratives deploy two very different models of transcendence: epistemological transcendence and theological transcendence.[73] Despite differences, these two models have come to be confused and entangled with each other, resulting in a dialectical illusion that pretends to achieve its own self-transcendence. This illusion has been most pervasive in movements such as phenomenology, systematic theology, and, through them, the comparative study of religion.[74] The result, broadly speaking, has been a confusion between the conditions of possibility and their products. Such confusions commonly conflate the transcendental with the transcendent, performing a gesture that can be described as metaphysics or ontotheology.

Following Heidegger's pregnant suggestion that the basic constitution of metaphysics is ontotheological[75]—which means that far from being a term that can be applied without prejudice to all cultures, ontotheological metaphysics is rooted in a specific religio-cultural tradition whose contours reveal themselves through the combination and continuity of the Greek (*onto-*), medieval-scholastic (*theo-*), and secular-humanist (*-logical*) traditions—it is possible to uncover a somewhat uneasy intersection between postcolonial theory and recent continental philosophy of religion. This intersection questions the belief in the unhindered translatability and/or universality of themes such as religion/God/theology into non-Western contexts. For cultural traditions such as the Indic, which have no exact referents for "religion"/"God"/"theology," one cannot simply make such assumptions as "Sikh theology" unless one also assumes the existence of a transcendental subject—a subject who invokes the desire for "Sikh theology," and one that is necessary for there to be any historical, i.e., epistemological classification of Sikh theology as a phenomenon. It follows that the unhindered translatability or universality of terms such as "religion"/"God"/"theology" cannot simply be assumed. It is precisely through assumptions such as "Sikh theology," or a subject who naturally corresponds to the desire for "Sikh theology," that a metaphysical violence can be discerned at the heart of the hermeneutic that reconstitutes *gurmat* as a theological transcendence proper to the Sikh tradition. The term "violence" is appropriate here because the consensus over the existence of Sikh theology rests, it will be argued, on a failure to recognize a metaphysics that disguises the processes of change and transformation as the *continuity* of Sikh tradition. Violence, in other words, refers to the erasure of time and temporality in the reconstitution of *gurmat*.

The issue, therefore, concerns the precise status of transcendence. Should we take for granted the gesture of transcendence that is generally deployed in the comparative study of religions, particularly if the predominant usage of this term can be traced to a genealogy that is specific to the history of Western philosophy? A hallmark of this gesture, as Eric Alliez reminds us, is that "*the objectivation-subjectivation of being and of time* [what Alliez calls the "conquest of time"] *is in no way carried out in the Orient. Western Europe is where that 'very pestilineal disease' germinates.*"[76] Never carried out, one should add, prior to the event-horizon of colonial translation!

Thus the idea of relating transcendence to the event of translation is not to dismiss transcendence, but rather to ask what comes to be invested socially and politically in the meaning of transcendence. For the purposes of this chapter it will be helpful to delimit its meaning according to the following questions, which at the same time will guide the critical vector of our questioning: (i) Is transcendence to be understood as the *overcoming* of time, of sensuousness, and therefore of alterity—an understanding that bears the hallmark of Western metaphysics or ontotheology? (ii) Or can transcendence be understood *as* time and alterity itself?—Not the transcendence *of* time, which is no more than its conquest, but transcendence as *timing,* as existence beyond the static moment, the process of becoming. Clearly the difference between these radically opposed approaches to transcendence is based on their respective relations to time.

It should be clear that my approach does not attempt to dismiss phenomena such as "Sikh theology," "Sikh mysticism," etc. Rather, by using strategies developed independently by Jacques Derrida and Martin Heidegger, and indicated by the difference between the two questions above, I propose to outline an activity of "double reading." A "double reading" is such that on the one hand it pays close attention to the texts of a particular tradition, but on the other hand, *in that very attention* it discloses a rupture in these texts that requires a radically different reading of it, thus destabilizing it, and, in the undecidability thereby created, opens the possibility of thinking differently. Although it may not be immediately obvious, the notion of transcendence provides one such rupture, allowing us to steer between the extremes of third-world traditionalist theologism and first-world phenomenological historicism (i.e., between theology and secularism), neither of which is sufficiently skeptical of its own epistemological (and therefore egocentric) foundations. It may therefore be possible to open an alternative space for thinking about the history of religions otherwise than the dominant "world religions" approach—a space that would be more in tune with the postcolonial diasporic struggle for *dis-identification.* By "dis-identification" I refer to a critical space that allows one to think at the limits of established pedagogical disciplines, as well as to a critical subjectivity that is more attuned to the task of creating a postcolonial and postnationalist global diasporic Sikh imaginary. For such a departure to take place, however, it is necessary first to understand the theoretical underpinnings of the neocolonial Sikh imaginary, which continues to exert a stranglehold on contemporary Sikh thinking.

In order to open this particular space I shall trace the complex interweaving of time and ontology in the enunciation of authentic Sikh narrative and theology by leading Sikh reformist scholars such as Bhāī Vīr Singh, Principal Teja Singh, Kahn Singh Nabha, Sāhib Singh, and Jodh Singh, whose respective works are widely regarded as the basis of modern and "orthodox" Sikh thinking. An extended survey of their works is beyond the scope of this chapter. My focus will therefore be restricted to the discussion of two aspects that become central to future treatments of modern Sikh ideology. In the first section I touch briefly on a typical Singh Sabhā narrative—in this case Teja Singh's *Growth of Responsibility in Sikhism*—outlining the emergence of Sikhs as a nation ("Sikh history") in relation to the term "Hindu," which, by the latter part of the mid-nineteenth century, had been transformed into the master signifier of Indian religious identity, culture, and civilization. As I mentioned in chapter 1, it is in relation to the identity politics organized around the master signifier "Hindu," and specifically the claim made by some that "Sikhs Are Hindus" ("*Sikh Hindu Hain*"), that Kahn Singh Nabha felt it necessary to publish his polemic reply: "We [Sikhs] Are not Hindus" ("*Ham Hindu Nahin*"). What interest me specifically in Teja Singh's narrative are the conceptual moves deployed to engineer breaks in the temporal structure of tradition. Such breaks effectively reconstitute self–other relations through the creation of a *sui generis* "religion," Sikhism, that is fully attuned to the political economy of empire.

In the second section, which comprises the main part of this chapter, I focus on the construction of a systematic concept of God ("Sikh theology") in the vernacular commentaries, which was necessary for creating the proper distance between the signifiers "Sikh" and "Hindu." Linking history and theology is the conceptual dynamic of transcendence, which becomes foundational to both. As a conceptual tool the dynamic of transcendence is specifically outlined according to the following threefold process: (i) the historical justification of the reformist project as the fulfillment, i.e., nationalization, of Sikh tradition, (ii) the reconstitution of *gurmat* as "Sikh theology," i.e., the construction of a systematic concept of God within the vernacular commentaries, (iii) and the enunciation of a peculiarly modern Sikh subjectivity, a move whose consequences are as much theoretical as political. Each of these will be treated in turn.

Nation and the Time of *Novitas*: Teja Singh's *The Growth of Responsibility in Sikhism*

Although its thesis can hardly lay claim to originality in any real sense,[77] Teja Singh's influential monograph *The Growth of Responsibility in Sikhism* is otherwise exemplary in revealing how a narrative of the nation articulates a certain ambivalence that informs all reformist projects of this period that attempt to make the repetition of tradition contemporaneous with the time of modernity. To plot the narrative of the nation will require accession to a notion of history as the fundamental horizon for projecting a Sikh "world." This "world," which refers to the viewpoint from which the separation of self and other can be visualized, is in fact borrowed almost verbatim from J. D. Cunningham's 1849 *History of the Sikhs*:

> [I]f studied from this [i.e., Cunningham's] point of view, all apparent contradictions of Sikh history would disappear. There would seem to be no break, no digression in the programme of Sikh life. . . . *Its principle of life remained the same, though it underwent a constant transfiguration*, assuming a great variety of forms, caused solely by local and occasional circumstances.[78]

As chapter headings in *Growth of Responsibility* indicate, Sikh self-hood is to be visualized in terms of a stepwise development of moral virtues, each bequeathed by successive Sikh Gurus in a manner that reveals "the gradual making and development of a nation in the hands of its ten successive leaders." Thus the ideals of "enlightenment," "obedience," "equality," "servitude," and "judgment" culminate in the final virtue: "full responsibility." What the narrative plots is the blueprint for moral living, a praxis whose end is achieved by attaining "devolution," or political autonomy, the recognition from the imperial administration that Sikhs have at last reacquired the ability to govern their own body and society: "The nation that has reached this stage is fit for all the responsibilities of self-government."[79] The timeliness of this statement can be gathered from Teja Singh's opening remark, "Every politically minded Indian is thinking of self-government and feeling big with the prospect of India's coming pretty soon into her own."[80]

Yet the very attempt to narrate the Sikh nation in concordance with the time of modernity will always be haunted by the "distancing presence of another temporality that disturbs the contemporaneity of the national present."[81] This "other temporality" is of course what the narrative of the nation had sought to overcome, in the sense of historically surmounting, namely the *past*, or the *pre*-narrative corresponding to the period when the *bhakti* reformers, who came before Nānak, were still struggling to extricate their ideas from entanglement within the Indic womb.

A nation . . . [m]ust first cleanse itself of impurities accumulated in the
course of centuries of ignorance and apathy. Then, to subdue the disruptive tendencies of different prejudices inherited from the past.[82]

With regard to the work of the *bhakti* reformers we are told that "the mere
preaching of principles . . . does not create nations."[83] While these "good
and able reformers" did much to "purify religion and enrich literature
. . . [t]hey appear to have been so impressed with the nothingness of this
life that they deemed it unworthy of a thought to build a new order of
society."[84] In a move that is typically modern, *bhakti* will be construed as
consciousness but not yet as *self*-consciousness, which is only achieved
with the advent of Nānak. Only Nānak can give *bhakti* the particular impulse that enables the passage from consciousness to the beginnings of
self-consciousness. In line with Cunningham and Macauliffe, this impulse is to be located in the concept of God (theology) that is specific to
Nānak's experience of the divine: "The guiding concept at this stage of
their progress is the fear of God."[85]

Thus the movement from the prenarrative stage of the *bhakti* reformers to the narrative stage of Nānak and his successor Gurus indicates a
new beginning. This new beginning represents a break with what comes
before, a break that must, in the process of breaking, efface the memory
of having broken from and, therefore, of having been connected to a
tradition. With the advent of Nānak "worldly life became the field . . .
for action."[86] As such, in the movement from prenarrative to narrative
the origin corresponds to the movement from immoral chaos to a moral
order. The moral order is the re-presentation of the origin. Because the
origin unfolds as the *worldly activity* of Nānak, this narrative can be
imitated and repeated. By contrast, the *quietism* of the *bhakti* reformers
(because it is prenarrative) does not allow for a repetition in the sense
of being able to participate in a moral order. The underlying message
here is that Nānak is not a mere reformer within an ongoing "Hindu"
tradition, as were the *bhakti* saints. Rather, the figure of Nānak provides
the prototype, a new beginning, where "new" is not simply a break with
tradition. Any hint of having broken with tradition would be to recall the
memory of this break, which means that Nānak might, on the testimony
of a recalled memory, have been a "Hindu." This might imply that his
teaching (*gurmat*) could only have arisen from within the "Hindu" tradition. To avoid this dangerous possibility, the figure of Nānak had to be
made to coincide with the origin and thus with the essence of divinity

itself. From this point on the Singh Sabhā scholars will studiously avoid translating the word "*guru*" as "*avatār*," preferring instead to translate it as "Prophet" to whom God spoke and revealed his Word. Nānak must therefore *hear* God's voice, which in the event of revelation effaces itself, leaving no worldly trace.

The narrative strategy clearly revolves around the ambivalent force of the "new" as that which simultaneously partakes of divinity and modernity. In the figure of Nānak the "new" represents, on the one hand, the divine (nonhuman) origin. On the other, "new" represents the prototype that modern Sikhs can thereby imitate. Thus the moral quest for modern Sikhs would be regarded as consisting in the praxis of imitative action, correct or orthodox conduct; in practicing this conduct one becomes part of the new order, simultaneously partaking of the origin itself. Such correct action, the praxis that pertains to authentic Sikh living, is presented as the continually unfolding plot of Sikhism. But insofar as it represents the origin, this tradition is a *mimetic praxis* inasmuch as it produces or creates the organization of events by the process of emplotment. The problem with this scheme was that Nānak's coincidence with the origin effectively made him a deity. To overcome this problem the reformists had to reinterpret the *janamsākhī* legend of Nānak's consecration as God's representative in terms of a pseudo-theory based on revelation and embellished with suitable quotations from the Ādi Granth.

The success of the nationalist narrative, its ability to inculcate belief and acceptance by a wide range of readers, depended on whether it could be projected as a model of concordance in view of the historical events of colonial domination and the decline of Indian civilization. Sikh and non-Sikh readers had to be persuaded that this narrative represented both continuity and break with tradition, a standpoint that was also being contested by the Singh Sabhā's *sanātanist* opponents. But which tradition? And what kind of a "present" is it that constantly needs to resort to the process of surmounting and transcending the time of repetition? From a psychoanalytic viewpoint the idea of surmounting or transcending a past is associated with the repression of a cultural "unconscious," namely, the "Hindu" as the past, the night, or the womb of Sikhism. The emergence of this "other temporality" is disconcerting to the desire of Sikh reformists to present Sikhism as coterminous with modernity, which consciously projects only the separation between Sikhism and the Hindu/Indic womb, or the successful jettisoning of the latter. Clearly what the need for transcendence discloses is not so much the emergence of narrative from pre-

or nonnarrative, but the site of a struggle between ontologically different types of narrative. Traces of this struggle cast doubt as to whether the emergent "nationalist" perspective—of an elite or subaltern culture— within a culture of social contestation can ever articulate its "representative" authority in that fullness of narrative time and visual synchrony"[87] of the imagined nation.[88]

Transcendence and the Overcoming of Lack

Let us return to the question of how "Sikh theology" comes to be produced within the commentaries on Sikh scripture. From a postcolonial perspective it is more instructive to treat invocations of "Sikh history" and "Sikh theology" as a kind of "performative utterance." Adapted from J. L. Austin's speech-act theory, the idea of "performative utterance" signifies a certain enunciation that may not necessarily have found articulation prior to the event of colonial translation, but which comes to realization after the imposition (and acceptance) of a certain regime of translation, in this case, the publication of Ernest Trumpp's "official" translation of the Ādi Granth in 1877.[89]

As explained above, Trumpp's work not only threatened to displace the image of Sikhism in the minds of colonial administrators to well below that of other Indic religions, it also propagated the idea that Sikhs were "merely Hindus" and that Nānak's teaching was essentially pantheistic, suggesting thereby that early European accounts of Sikhs, as a separate monotheistic or deistic religion within the Indic context, were largely mistaken. According to Trumpp's evidence, the pantheistic nature of Sikhism could be found within Guru Nānak's own hymns, which fundamentally *lacked* an adequate concept of God and consequently an adequate notion of the self. More important than the mere distinction between the categories "monotheism" and "pantheism"—what is in effect the *condition* for the validity of such categories—was that Trumpp managed to displace the conceptual framework for any future discourse about Sikh scripture into the domain of ontotheology, that is, toward a field of translation in which all statements and propositions about the teachings of the Sikh Gurus were automatically routed through the question concerning the existence of God. Thus the task for the Singh Sabhā scholars was to disprove the reading of *gurmat* as pantheism and therefore the signification of *lack* that pantheism implied.

In contradistinction to the view that Singh Sabhā ideologues simply retrieved Guru Nānak's original intentions and seamlessly relocated
them into a modern idiom (implying thereby the propriety of theological transcendence to the Ādi Granth), I propose to read the emergence
of Sikh theology in terms of a struggle to overcome the signification of
lack. In this reading the notion of lack becomes a critical hinge for any
postcolonial reading of Sikh scripture insofar as it points to a fundamental resistance within the teachings of the Ādi Granth—and therefore
within any conceptualization of gurmat—to what is known as metaphysics in Western philosophy and religion. Inevitably such resistance
also points to one of the more important though unresolved tensions
in modern (neonationalist) representations of Sikh religiosity, namely,
that *modern* Sikhism could only have come into being by repressing
what is essentially nonmodern. The "nonmodern" refers to that which
is incommensurable with modern consciousness, such as contradictory
and paradoxical notions of nonduality, identity, and the self—modes
of subjectivity that do not conform to the "*ego cogito*" of the broadly
Cartesian type.

Some important clues about this resistance can be gleaned by comparing the meanings of nonduality, self, and identity as we find them in the
hymns of the Ādi Granth with the meanings that come to be delineated
in the commentaries. Consider for example the following verses from
the hymn *Siddh Goṣṭ*, which depicts a debate between the Siddhās (expert practitioners of Yoga belonging to the Gorakhnāth sect) and Guru
Nānak. Here we find Nānak evoking themes such as nonduality, self/ego/
identity, and freedom but at the same time avoiding a direct metaphysical
response to questions posed by the Siddhās:[90]

SIDDHĀS:
What's the origin of the self?

Where does it go? Where does it remain when merged?

The teacher who can explain this mystery has indeed effaced all trace
   of desire.
How can one love a reality that has no form or trace?
Of itself the Absolute is the knower and the doer. How do you explain
   this, Nānak?   22

NĀNAK:

Originating from nature's order, one returns to this order, remaining
   always indistinct.

Through the *guru*'s instruction one practices truth to gain a measure
   of divine form.

As for the beginning, one can only speak in terms of wonder, for the
   One was absorbed in void.

Think of the earrings as the uncontrived nature of the *guru*'s wisdom:
   that all existence is real.

By means of the *guru*'s word one spontaneously attains the limitless
   state and merges into it.

O Nānak, one who works and inquires genuinely will not take another
   path.

Wondrous is the divine way. This truth is known only to those who
   walk in its way.

Consider him a *yogī* who becomes detached by effacing self-love and
   enshrining truth within.   23

As form arises from infinite multiplicity, so existence becomes nonexistence.

Through inner wisdom imparted by the *guru* one becomes attuned to
   the Name.

The ego's sense of difference is removed by recognizing the One truly
   as One.

He alone is a *yogī* who understands the *guru*'s teaching and lets his
   lotus-mind bloom within.

Dying to the self everything becomes clear and one finds the source of
   all compassion.

O Nānak, by realizing the self's connectedness to all beings, honor is
   attained.   24

The *gurmukh*'s self arises from truthful existence, then merges into its
   source, becoming identical with the One.

The self-centered beings come into this world yet find no place of rest.

Attached to a sense of otherness, their coming and going continues.

Blessed by the *guru*'s instruction, one learns self-discrimination and
   this ceaseless wandering ends,

Man's congenital sickness is attachment to duality through which one
   forgets the Name's real taste.

He alone is aware who is becomes aware without self-effort.
Through the *guru*'s Word he is liberated.
Nānak, the mortal who effaces duality by stilling the ego,
Swims and helps others to swim across.

In verses such as these, the tenor of which is repeated throughout the Ādi Granth, the nonduality of the Absolute is conceptually inseparable from the notion of freedom exemplified by the polar themes of fusion and separation. In conformity to broadly Indic patterns, knowledge of such an Absolute is grounded in a state of existence that has realized this nonduality by relinquishing the individuality of the ego and merging itself into the Other. In this state of being one instinctively resists representation and conceptualization in terms of subject-object duality. An individual who is able to realize this state of existence (*gurmukh*) no longer represents the Absolute to himself since the distinction between self and other, I and not-I, disappears into a knowing that knows without immediately splitting into subject and object. Though caricatured on the one hand as annihilation, dissolution, or depersonalization, and on the other hand as an impractical ideal, the figure of the *gurmukh*, and the kind of freedom associated with it, is better seen as an intensely creative form of existence through which the world is perceived not as something outside of ourselves, to be recognized in detail, adapted, complied with, and fitted into our idiosyncratic inner world, but rather as an infinite succession of creative acts.

The resistance posed by such meaning reveals what could be termed the "middle ground" that is constantly evoked in the compositions of the Sikh Gurus and the Sants. This is a ground which, in the absence of a certain metaphysical violence, refuses a systematic *concept* of God—indeed, refuses conceptualization as it is understood in the Western philosophical traditions. Yet it would be a mistake to think of this middle ground as some kind of "original" Sikhism historically prior to colonialism and the nationalization of Sikh traditions. Whereas the term "original" remains connected to some kind of authorial intention or psychological state that can be retrieved from a standpoint of present self-consciousness, or perhaps a form of Sikh religiosity that was historically displaced, the term "middle ground" points to idioms, practices, forms, and strata of experience that are different from but also broadly continuous with those of the wider North Indian devotional traditions. One could cite, for example, practices such as *kīrtan* and *nām simaran*, themes such as *rāg* and *rasa*, which evoke feeling and mood, or again themes relating to personal time and destiny such as *muktī*, *karmā*, and *saṃskāras*. Despite the temptation to treat them as exotic or mystical, these themes comprise what de Certeau called the "practice of everyday life" in Sikh traditions. Yet with the emergence of a rationalized idiom characteristic of modern monotheistic Sikhism, accompanied by its demand for uniqueness and clearly defined religious and cultural boundaries, the articulation of these nonmodern modes of thinking and experience have undergone—indeed, continue to undergo—a certain repression. In what follows, the term "middle ground"—insofar as it refers simultaneously to a nonduality and subjectivity that is nonrepresentational, nonconceptual, that cannot be theorized in terms of a subject that knows itself as an object nor reduced to the cognitive or the ethical—will provide a means for demonstrating continuities and transformations in the emergence of a "Sikh theology."

Not surprisingly, from the Western colonial perspective of translators such as Trumpp, this perspective on nonduality that I term as the "middle ground" came to be projected as a *lack* of a proper concept of God, a *lack* of ethical standpoint, and a *lack* of freedom in the religion of the Sikhs. In the vernacular commentaries one finds a treatment of nonduality that responds to these accusations of lack, and for this reason begins to distance itself from the middle ground of the Ādi Granth. Perhaps the best examples of this are the commentaries on the opening line of the Ādi Granth, which will be closely analyzed in the following section of this chapter. This opening line is better known as the *mūl mantar*, or the root mantra of Sikhism. For Sikhs the *mūl mantar* serves as the creedal statement that expounds the central attributes of God:

Ik oaṁkār
satinām, karta purukh, nirbhau, nirvair,
akāl mūrat, ajūnī, saimbhaṁ, gurparsād

One God exists
truth by name, creative power, without fear, without enmity, timeless
    form, unborn, self-existent, by the Guru's grace.[91]

In an effort to satisfy the perceived "lack" of an adequate conceptualization of God, Singh Sabhā scholars invested a disproportionate effort to enunciate a precise and consistent meaning for the twelve or so words of the *mūl mantar*, because its meaning would reflect the meaning of the *Ādi Granth* text as a whole. In what follows I undertake a deconstructive[92] reading of the way in which *gurmat* (lit. "teaching/instruction of the *guru*") is constituted as theology, that is, as a system of knowledge about God, a process that is linked to the work of imagining God's existence in a particular way. To illustrate how this new imagining is produced it will be necessary to pay close attention to the hermeneutic strategies deployed by the various Singh Sabhā scholars,[93] in particular their complex weavings of time and ontology. Of the main vernacular commentaries, the commentary on the *mūl mantar* by Bhāī Vīr Singh (hereafter BVS) is by far the longest, running to some thirty-six pages of dense exegesis. Unlike all other preceding commentaries in the Sikh tradition, BVS's text reads unmistakably like a systematic philosophical argument for the existence of God—indeed a redefining of God's attributes "according to the *guru*'s own instruction." My analysis in the next section will therefore focus mainly on BVS's text and, for reasons that will become clear, on three words in the *mūl mantar*: *ik oaṁkār* (One God exists), *satinām* (truth by name) and *akāl mūrat* (timeless form). I conclude this chapter by arguing that the Sikh reformist mode of thought, far from restating an original Sikh monotheism, actually makes a shift from previous patterns of nonduality by importing a version of the ontological proof for God's existence.

Refiguring Time as Eternity: The Eclipse of Nonduality in the Vernacular Commentaries on Sikh Scripture

The Paradoxical Divine: ik oaṁkār

A short and rather innocuous-looking footnote to the *mūl mantar* by Teja Singh in his principal commentary, the *Śabdarth Sri Guru Granth Sāhib*, summarizes the conceptual drive behind the reformists' exegetical project:

Ih vārtik rachnā sikhī da "mūl mantar" hai. Arthāt is vich oh bunyādī galāṁ dasīāṁ hoīāṁ han jinhāṁute Sikkh dharam de nemān dī nīhṁ rakhī gai hai. Ih niṁh vahigurū dī hastī dī hai, jīs dā sarūp inhāṁ lafzāṁ vich ditā hoiā hai.

This verse composition is the "*mūl mantar*" of Sikhī(sm); that is to say, within it are expounded those basic things upon which the foundations of religious faith [*dharam de nemān dī nīhṁ*] have been built. This foundation is the being or existence of God [*hastī*], whose configuration [*sarūp*] is given in these words . . . [of the *mūl mantar*].[94]

In three short points this statement outlines the circular hermeneutic of Singh Sabhā theology: that scripture grounds the religious faith called Sikhism; that this ground is the existence of God; and that God's existence is configured or represented by the words of scripture. Yet the circularity of the statement also reveals a fissure that prevents any intended closure. This fissure is the difference between the being of God *as God* and the being of God as he comes to be *configured* or imagined in the commentary (*sarūp, hastī, homd*)—a configuration that in turn points beyond its portrayal in scripture toward a logic of self-retrieval from which it originates. It is to the strategies of self-retrieval—disguised as an effacement or interiorization of the self—that my reading will pay constant attention.

What is immediately noticeable about the commentaries on the meaning of the *mūl mantar* and specifically the first syllable, *ik oaṁkār*, is that they are rendered as a cleansing of authentic Sikh meaning by removing from it any association with the root mantra of Hinduism, namely the syllable *oṁ*. Each of the Singh Sabhā exegetes presents short summaries of the syllable *oṁ* as it has been understood in the *sanātana dharma*—i.e., in the Vedic and Purāṇic traditions—before contrasting it with the "true" Sikh interpretation, which begins with the countering phrase: "But according to Gurmat . . . " (*par gurmat vic . . .*). The Sikh reformists justify their opposition to Vedic meanings by making a fundamental distinction between the Vedic *oṁ* and the Sikh *ik oaṁkār*. The Sikh syllable is differentiated from the Hindu by the numeral 1 (*ik*), which, they argue, is evidence for the monotheistic nature of Sikhism, i.e., its emphasis on the oneness of God, whereas in Sanātan tradition *oṁ* symbolizes the pantheistic nature of the Hindu trinity of Brahma, Viṣṇu, and Śiva.[95]

For Sikh reformists, however, it seems that the actual target of their critiques was not Vedānta as such. There is, for example, no sustained engagement with any Vedāntic system. It is rather the influx of Vedāntic ideas from the Udasī and Nirmalā schools throughout the nineteenth century and its effect on the interpretation of Sikh scriptures that appears to have been their real concern. Under the patronage of Maharaja Ranjit Singh many within the Udasī and Nirmalā sects managed to establish themselves as readers of the Ādi Granth or as attendants of Sikh *dharmsālās*.[96] Notable Udasī scholars, such as Anandghān, who had trained at centers of Hindu learning such as Kāśī wrote influential commentaries on the Japjī. Despite certain differences with the Udasī sect, Nirmalā scholars of the early to mid-nineteenth century, such as Kavi Santokh Singh, Pandit Tarā Singh Narotam, Gianī Gian Singh, and Gulāb Singh, were equally inclined towards Vedāntic interpretations of *gurbānī*, maintaining that *gurbānī* was essentially an expression of ancient Vedic teachings in the current vernacular.[97]

Paradoxically, though, the efforts of Sikh reformist scholars to remove Hindu influence led them to construct a system that, though outwardly monotheistic, could not avoid denegatory references to the ancient Vedāntic metaphysics. Consider, for example, the interpretations of Kahn Singh and Jodh Singh, which happen to be virtually identical: "But according to *gurmat* the numeral 1 is placed before the word *oṁ* in order to clarify that the creator is one" (*par gurmat vic oṁ de mudh ekā likhke sidh kītā hai ki kartār ik hai*).[98] Here the Hindu word *oṁ* is the same as the Sikh word *oaṁkār*, except for its qualification by the numeral 1. Similarly, for Jodh Singh the matter is relatively straightforward—the numeral 1 serves to emphasize the essential quality of the being of God as unity: "that Being which is one only" (*ōh hastī keval ik hai*).[99]

Bhāī Vīr Singh's interpretation is more complex than either of the above. He comments at length on the separate components of the syllable *ik oaṁkār*. According to Vīr Singh the numeral 1 is not a quality that can be attributed to a being: "this '1' has not been used as a numerical attribute/quality but as a denotative" (*Ih 1 'sankhyā vācik vishesan karke nahīṁ vartian par "saṁgyā" karke vartaion hoi*).[100] The numeral "1" stands for "that which signifies his configuration, his name" (*jo us de sarūp dā likhāyak us dā nām hai*).[101] By naming the essence of God's being as oneness or unity (*ektav*) the numeral "1" is not the same as any other attribute. This "1" qualifies but cannot itself be qualified by any other quality except itself. By referring only to itself "1" denotes absolute identity and unity, pure oneness: *ektav*. Ironically, though, in the very first line of his commentary Vīr Singh is forced to speak about this ineffable "1":

Oneness exists (the formless, who is in a state of indeterminate void)
There is existence (manifesting as form yet still oneness).

ektav hai (niraṁkār, jo nāntav vic)
oaṁkār (rūp hoke phir ektav) hai.[102]

In other words, Bhāī Vīr Singh's need to account for the coming-into-form as a transition from pure oneness or indeterminate void illustrates the *aporia* of any beginning—namely, that the primal act is an act of translation, the translation from formlessness to form, from void to existence. Yet no sooner is the act of translation revealed than it must be denegated or foreclosed lest the movement of this translation be revealed as a movement of thought and therefore as an imperfection within this "One." I borrow the terms "denegation" and "foreclosure" from the vocabulary of Lacanian psychoanalysis. They refer to a peculiar strategy of repression in which, according to Lacan, "the ego rejects [an] incompatible idea together with the affect and behaves as if the idea never occurred to the ego."[103] The affect in question here is an anxiety concerning the disclosure of time at the heart of God's identity, his Oneness. The anxiety points to a potentially serious obstacle in any attempt to present a systematic theology and an ethically responsible subject, that is to say, a subject that is capable of successfully separating itself from the maternal (in this case "Hindu") body. In Vīr Singh's text the work of denegation centers mainly around the polysemic nature of the word *nāntav*, which occurs at key moments in the explication of *ik oaṁkār* and specifically in the work of delimiting the precise nature of the Oneness (*ektav*). Derived from the root *nan*, meaning "nothing" or "negative," the term *nāntav* refers to what is abstract, indeterminate, or devoid of form. At the same time, indeed later in the very same commentary, *nāntav* will also carry the meanings of multiplicity, differentiation, and diversity within the created expanse.

For Vīr Singh: "this One which we speak of in periodic time as beyond the reach of mind or intelligence . . . without form, without sign or mark . . . [also happens to be] that which we perceive as abstract or indeterminate. . . . [B]y further contemplating this aspect we perceive this aspect as diffused through all existent beings. What this means is that within His own oneness he always exists as one" (*thit duārā updēsh karde han man buddhī dī paunch to parai hai . . . us dā rūp koī nahīn, chhin koi nahīn . . . Ki jo nantav vic dekh rahe ho, is vic khoj kardian asī ghat ghat vic us nū dekhiā hai. Bhāv ih hoiā ki oh apnī ektav vic sadā ik hai*).[104]

The word "always" indicates a refiguring of time that serves to suture any perceived difference between God's oneness and existence that may be implied through the polysemic term *nāntav*: "When there is but the One then [He] exists as one. When perceived as indeterminate then he exists as diffused, but though diffused, his existence is not eclipsed by nonexistence. In the state of abstraction also he remains but one" (*jad ik hai tan ik hai. Jad nāntav vic dekho, tan ghat ghat vic hai, par oh ghat ghat vic hon karke prānchin nāhīn ho gia. Oh nāntav vic bī āp ik dā ik hī hai*).[105]

Clearly, Vīr Singh's anxiety is linked to the possiblity of misperceiving God's paradoxical oneness as a duality: there/not-there; existent/nonexistent. Yet for Vīr Singh the very suggestion that the "1" could signify nonexistence is anathema, tantamount to an imperfect concept of God. Indeed only a few paragraphs later we come across an even stronger disavowal of nonexistence: "According to the instruction of the (Tenth) Guru the ground [*mūl*] of this infinite [*anokhā*] or abstract [*nāntav*] or created [*sriṣṭī*], '1,' whatever we call it, is not a zero or void [*shūn*]. It is not nonexistence or negation [*anhoṅd yā manfiat nahīṅ*], rather [its ground] is existence which is '1' [*par homḍ hai jo ik hai*]. The visible and invisible [*drishya andrishya*] are manifestations of this 'one' unmoved being ['*iko*' *thir hastī*]."[106] To reinforce this a revealing footnote states:

> The meaning of "*shūn*" is nonexistence [*shūn dā artha "anhoṅd" hai*]. But according to the teaching of the Guru "1" stands for "true existence" ["*yatharth hastī*"]. Nothingness or nonexistence ["*shūn mātar yā anhoṅd*"] is not *gurmat*. . . . Sometimes, though, the idea of "nothingness" has been used in explanations of the existence of the Supreme Being [*shūn pad kai ver paramātmān dī hastī de arthān vic āyā hai*]. Consider for example, Sankara's saying :

> "*ghambīr dhīram nirvāna sūnyam/sansāra saram nācha pāpa punyam.*"

> Compare this to the Guru's own saying: "*Ghat ghat shūn kā jannai bheo//ādi purakh niranjan deo*," [in which] *shūn* does not refer to nothingness or nonexistence [*oh anhomḍ nahin*] but to the primal being [*ādi purakh hai*] who manifests to us as configuration/form [*prakāsh sarūp hai*]. . . . But here the meaning of *shūn* is the Supreme Deity without sign or mark [*ithai shiin dā arth niramjan parmātman dev hai*].[107]

The strategy of denegation is just as evident in the explication of the letter *oaṁkār*, which comprises the linguistic half of the symbol *ik oaṁkār*. Thus we read:

> From antiquity *oṁ* has been a symbol for the supreme being [*paramesvar*], **but in gurmat** it is pronounced as *oaṁkār*. It is the proper manifestation of the Supreme Being in which [his] Nirguṇ aspect and Sarguṇ aspects are indiscriminately present and in which the dynamic and causal aspects are united.
>
> In the Upaniṣads *oṁ* is the basis of the Nirguṇa and Saguṇa aspects of Brahman. The Purāṇic writers split [the word *oṁ*] into the letters *a u m*, indicating the threefold division of the Hindu pantheon. **But in gurmat** there is no such division. *Oṁ* is one letter and its meaning is Supreme Being. In its written form it conveys that Nirguṇ, in becoming Sarguṇ, yet remains one.[108]

Despite his efforts to the contrary, the central issue that arises in Bhāī Vīr Singh's treatment of *ik oaṁkār* is the unmistakable tension between desire and fact. On the one hand is the desire to know and therefore to present God's identity as Absolute (as God exists in himself), an identity that cannot be represented except through number (*ek, ektav*) and negation (*nirguṇ*), which do not admit either attribute or relationality. On the other hand is the fact that in speaking about God duality and contradiction cannot be avoided. Indeed the very movement toward speech about God must be represented as a difference between non-language and language, nothingness and existence, *un*knowable and knowable, non-time and time. To acknowledge this difference, however, is to imply that time and movement relate "essentially" to God's Absoluteness—which means, paradoxically, that God cannot be Absolute.

It is therefore the contradictory logic of this idea—where difference grounds the very possibility for presenting the identity of God—that Vīr Singh and his fellow ideologues will be careful to avoid. Consequently, for them, number ("1") and word (*oaṁkar*) cannot be admitted as different or as representing a difference in God's identity, which is pure oneness (*ektav*). To admit such difference would inaugurate a translation from one mode ("1" = Nirguṇ = nonexistence = unsayable) to another mode (*oaṁkar* = Sarguṇ = existence = the sayable). The very idea of a passage from one to another would introduce contingency, nihilism, and indeed uncertainty at the ground of existence. God's identity might not then be Absolute. If so, could the entire message of the Sikh scripture (*gurmat*) have been unfolded on a nihilistic ground? Could impermanence be the proper ground of *gurmat*? A ground that, in its unfolding, automatically undermines itself?

It is to avoid this dangerous possibility that Vīr Singh and others attempt to overcome the paradox at the heart of *ik oaṁkar*. This is done by implementing a metaphysical assumption: that identity (*ektav*, "oneness") is the condition for existence, and conversely that existence is the condition for identity. The intrinsic bond between identity and existence ensures that the division between *Nirguṇ* and *Sarguṇ* will have been overcome through a classic deployment of the law of noncontradiction (A = A). Thus, *Nirguṇ*—normally translated as ineffable—comes to be *represented* by an identity (the identity of *Nirguṇ* and *Sarguṇ*) that is logically prior to the difference between them. However, the very resource for this identification can come only from the definition of being itself. This move—a move where the possibility of *Nirguṇ* as void /nonexistence is circumvented by assuming that the identity of *Nirguṇ* and *Sarguṇ* grounds any difference between them—actually takes place in the commentary on *sat(i)nām*.

Dynamics of Transcendence: sat(i)

Although the conventional translation for the compound word *sat(i)nām* is "True Name," "Whose Name is Truth," etc., the commentaries begin by separating its two component terms *sat(i)* (=being, existence) and *nām* (=name), and then focus almost completely on *sat(i)* so that the meaning of this term becomes determinative for *sat(i)nām*. The commentaries read as follows:

"that being who remains of constant essence through the three modes
   of time"
tin kāl vic ik ras hoṇ vālā pṛsidh pārbrahman.   —Kahn Singh[109]

"that (being) which endures as existing forever"
sadā kaim rahīṁ vālā.   —Teja Singh[110]

"whose name is the existent being"
jis dā nām hai hond vālā.   —Sāhib Singh[111]

"that being/existence who always remains"
sadā rahiṇ valī oh hastī.   —Jodh Singh[112]

"That (being) which in time and eternity always remains stable/immu-table" [*jo kāl akāl sadā hī thir rahe*], or: "that oneness which being an immutable oneness, whose name alone exists; '*satya*' in other words is that self-conscious being that remains always stable/immutable" ([*oh ektav*] *sadā thir* [*ektav hai, us dā*] *nām hī hai* [*sat(i) arthāt sadā thir rahiṇ vālā chetan vajūd*]).   —BVS[113]

Consider the word "*sat*" to be an exposition of "1." The meaning of "1" is the one primal form which is one in every state of being, that is, which is immutable. Thus the meaning of the word "*sat*" is that eternal (without break) form which remains always stable through the three states of time. (*is vic sat pad* "*1*" *dā hi māno ṭīkā hai | "1" dā arth hai— ek hai mūl hastī jo har hāl "1" hai, arthāt jo sadā abdal hai. So 'sat" pad dā arth hai—trai kāl abādh rūp jo sadā thir hai*).   —BVS[114]

Two things immediately strike us about these commentaries. First, there is almost complete unanimity in the way that exegesis on "the Name" is subsumed into questions of time and ontology. Second, and what follows from the first move, is the repeated use of words that stress a particular mode of time where continuity is valued above change: "always," "always fixed" (*sadā, sadā thir, sadā hī thir*); "of singular essence" (*ek ras*); "al-ways remaining fixed" (*sadā thir hai*); "always existing without change" (*sadā abdal hai*); "eternal form" (*abādh rūp*).

Contrary to appearances, these innocent-looking phrases suggest that the exegesis on *sat* is more than simply an extended exposition of the nature of "1," as Vīr Singh himself seems to suggest. In fact the exege-sis on *sati* is used to justify a particular reading of transcendence—one where the very meaning of transcendence is redefined in relation to the refiguration of time as eternity. The implication of this move can be use-fully explained by way of a comparison to Platonic metaphysics. Such a comparison is revealing in view of the dominant Western metaphysical context in which all Indian thinkers of the time were operating.

Plato's key statement on this matter derives from his theory of naming, as given in the *Cratylus*.[115] His theory of naming is concerned with two issues: (i) the distinction between name and thing, and (ii) what is named in the thing. As a measure of correctness, the name names the essential being within a thing. This essential being is the locus of the thing's meaning and by nature it must be fixed and of permanent duration. The very activity of naming, as the giving of a proper name, is therefore dependent on the assumption that what is named—essence as such—is "always such as it is." In turn, however, existence that is "always such as it is" depends on the distinction between two modes of temporality: the temporality of eternity against the temporality of the present moment. This distinction is valid because things come into existence (they are created) and pass away (have a finite lifetime). But that which is *essential* being, and thus "always such as it is," cannot by definition come into existence or pass away. It is eternal. There is no prior and no after to the creative event. The Platonic essential being, the "always such as it is," refers to the fact that what is named cannot be subject to change. Rather, what is named must be self-referring, always the same as itself, always identical. Hence the identity of the eternal: the eternally self-same as that which is always self-present.

Bhāī Vīr Singh's exegesis follows a very similar logic. For example, the distinction between time (*kāl*) and not-time (*akāl*) is effectively dissolved by grounding it in a being (*hastī, hond*) that is always stable (*sadā hī thir*); stable because it admits of no change in essence. The point of difference between *kāl* and *akāl* (namely the not, or the negative) is sublated into a moment that is eternally self-present. Governing the relation between time (*kāl*) and not-time (*akāl*) is the identity of God as eternal self-presence—which is indistinguishable from the notion of transcendence as absolute stability.

Ironically, though, the very possibility of division and duality raises further issues. If, as the commentary suggests, the truth of God's identity lies in its eternal self-presence, how is this identity to be conveyed to those who read the commentary? How is this Being of God, when God is *being* God, to be presented? What is the link between that which is to be *presented* (Truth, identity of God) and the *form* of the presentation? Will any presentation of the truth/identity of the divine not itself admit of an invasion of time into the eternal moment? Will there not have been a movement or transference from one moment to another, the well-known fall into time and contingency? Or, if the eternal moment must be preserved, will any presentation not be a virtual presentation, no more than a reflection of what is always-as-it-is? Will this transference not risk the danger of being *mis*perceived, *mis*understood—which from the beginning it was the projected aim of these commentaries to avoid?

In short, the duality between the presentation and what is presented reveals one of the classic problems of religious knowledge: that there is an unavoidable discrepancy between the time of divinity (which the commentary seeks to present directly) and the time of the exegesis (which can at best re-present the divine). This discrepancy can derive only from a finite cognitive process, an act of imagining. The dilemma for Vīr Singh was how to efface any link to time and contingency by shifting attention away from the operation of the imagination and by co-implication the identity of the thinker. He attempts to overcome this problem (still within the exegesis of *sat(i)*) by deploying a three-step strategy of self-effacement.

Step 1. Vīr Singh distinguishes two different kinds of cognition: the cognition of God as he is perceived (*lakh laiṇ vale dā lakhyā lakh laiṇa*)[116] and the kind of cognition that is proper to the *being* of God as Absolute, the nature of which is intrinsic to the nature of the word "being," or *sat(i)*. Thus *sat(i)* is the first word that follows the numeric symbol *ik oaṁkār*, which had established the identity of God as oneness:

> Now through words the same perception is given of that One always-
> stable being. After *ik oaṁkār* the first word is *sat*.
> *huṇ padān yā lafzān duārā use iko 'sadā hī thir hastī" nū lakhaunde
> han. Ton magron pahilā pad "sat(i)" lahinde han.*[117]

Sat(i) is therefore a privileged word in that it is a verbal manifestation of "1." There is **no change or variation** in going from "1" to *sat(i)*. *Sat(i)* is therefore not based on a cognition *of* God, but constitutes the ground for cognition as such. That is to say, God's existence must first be guaranteed in order for there to be any possible cognition *of* God. This division of cognition is not entirely successful, however. Problems arise once we move beyond the essential word to a multiplicity of words, and consequently to the manifold ways of perceiving and describing God. The *mūl mantar* itself is an example of this since the words *kartā purukh, nirbhau, nirvair*, etc., can be regarded as different attributes of the same divine being.[118]

Step 2. Yet, the commentary goes on, these should be regarded only as qualities (*lacchan*), "because they are all different ways of cognizing that existent being" (*kionke us sat(i) hastī de eh sāre lakhāyak han*). But these qualities (*enhāṁ lacchaṇā yā guṇā*), which have been elaborated at length in the sacred text (*jo inhāṁ de visthār vic gurbānī vic uchāre han*), are not to be cognized through everyday thinking because such thinking will prolong the duality of a perception that perceives difference or multiplicity as a characteristic of the divine identity."[119] Instead of a thinking based on empirical sense perception, which also causes the mind to be dispersed and can only give rise to multiple perceptions of God, "we" must cultivate the kind of cognition that stabilizes the manifold into a unity. Because thinking based on sense perception always remains within the element of time and will always give rise to anxiety, it must be displaced by a more elevated form of cognition, such as meditative repetition (*jāp*) and remembrance of the divine name (*simaraṇ*), which *transcend* time:

> When we shall begin to meditate upon these perceived qualities, then the tendency of consciousness to be dispersed will be reduced, unity will come about, and, with attention fixed on the one eternal Being, union will be attained (*Jad asīṁ inhāṁ lakhāyak lacchaṇ dā, yā inhāṁ vicoṁ kise ik dā yā gurmantra dā jap simaran karāṁge tāṁ chit dī birtī dā vikhep ghaṭegā ekāgartā āvegī te ik akāl purakh vic birtī dā tikāo hoke mel parāpat hovaigī*).[120]

Again, the kind of transcendence implied is one that immobilizes time, thus making it accord with the absolute immobilization of the eternal being of God. But as Vīr Singh realizes, the trace of the imagination cannot be effaced so easily. In order to argue for a shift toward repetition and remembrance, must he himself not rely on the very thinking he wishes to suppress? Doesn't the need to speak about God in terms of qualities and the fact that "we" can only perceive in multiple qualities (*guṇ/lacchaṇ*) contaminate the divine with time?

Step 3. Once again, though, a way is found to avert the impending danger, by resorting to yet another distinction, only this time it is the notion of quality (*lacchaṇ*) itself that will be divided. The argument goes something like this. For some time there has been a consensus among philosophers that there are two different types of qualities (*lacchaṇ do prakār de vidhvānān ne manne han*). Those qualities that give direct knowledge and understanding of the form are called "*sarūp lacchaṇ*." These are qualities that can be configured (*sarūp nū siddhā jnāṇ vale lacchaṇ nū sarūp lacchaṇ kahiṁde hun*)—as, for example, when we say: "that white house" (*jaise kahiṁde hai sāhmaṇā cittā ghar*).[121] The other type of quality is called "*taṭsath lacchaṇ*," where the description of what is perceived abstracts from or transcends the form (*dūsare taṭsath lacchaṇ jo pās de padārthān karke yā horṇān ton bhinta viśheśhtā ādi karke lakhā deṁ*). Alternatively, *taṭsath lacchaṇ* are those qualities regarding which one can make direct statements not in terms of their form but in terms of their grounding principles (*yā tatsath lacchan oh hai jō sarūp nū laike nahīṁ sagon us de guṇ dharm ādikān nū laike varṇan kītā jāi*).[122]

A problem arises here, because although strictly speaking the word for being (*sat[i]*) is a *taṭsath lacchaṇ*, it has a tendency to be wrongly mistaken for a *sarūp lacchaṇ*, given that words such as *sat(i)* /*asat(i)* (being/nonbeing) and *sac* / *jhūṭ* (truth/falsehood) remain subject to an oppositional duality and therefore to the work of a finite imagination. For any word to qualify as a *taṭsath lacchaṇ* the word or attribute in question should allow one to speak about God, or allow God to be configured, but, in the act of configuring, must also *automatically* negate or overcome any relation to the sensuous. However, the word *sat(i)* manages to escape being mistaken for a configurable quality (*sarūp lacchaṇ*) because its true referent is the divine as formless (*niraṁkār*): "Thus the word '*sat(i)*' refers to the 'configurable quality' of the formless divine (*so 'sati' niraṁkar dā 'sarūp lacchaṇ' kahīdā hai*)."[123] However, even the word "formless" is not *absolutely* transcendent insofar as it will still remain in opposition to form, image, and therefore the work of imagination. What Vīr Singh needs is a *taṭsath lacchaṇ* that is able to cognize formlessness without this cognition being compromised. Fortunately such a *taṭsath lacchaṇ* par excellence is found in the word *kartā*, meaning "Creator," which he introduces toward the end of the commentary on *sat(i)*:

> Now the transcendent [in the sense of quality-less] quality [*taṭsath lacchaṇ*] that enables us to cognize the form of the formless divine is called "creator" [*kartā*].
> *huṇ niraṁkār de sarup nū lakhāṇ vāle taṭsath lacchaṇ kahinde hain "kartā.*"

> Where this word "*kartā*" is found in the *mūl mantar* it gives the sense of the transcendent quality of the formless divine and operates as a causative name [*kirtam nām*].
> *jithe ih pad mūl mantar vic piā hai uthai ih niraṁkār dā taṭsath lacchaṇ hokai āyā hai te kirtam nām hokai piā hai.*[124]

The progressive movement of the foregoing argument toward the transcendent qualities (*taṭsath lacchaṇ*) is crucial for the purpose of projecting a "pure" presentation of the divine being. As we have seen, the word *sat(i)* cannot directly present this formless divine without resort to *sarūp lacchaṇ*, or configuring qualities, that in turn are rooted in the sensuous and therefore in the operation of human imagination as the faculty that configures the sensuous. By contrast, a *taṭsath lacchaṇ* such as *kartā* signifies a causation whose agency is not dependent on, or affected by, anything other than itself. Hence *kartā* cannot simply mean "Creator," but "*un*caused cause," "*un*moved mover." It conveys direct understanding of the divine form, an ability to go beyond limitations of form by providing insight into that which gives the possibility of there being such form. The causativity intrinsic to *kartā* signifies that which is self-caused, made from its own self. It implies that (God), who in giving remains unaffected by the giving—or that which in moving or causing to be moved itself—remains *un*moved, always-as-it-is.

The aim of these *taṭsath lacchaṇ* is clearly to neutralize any threat to the transcendence of the divine by trying to remove—through a process of dematerialization—any link to time and world, to the other, to the sensuous. By thus depriving any link to anything external, including being itself, what is ultimately effected is a pure self-positing, the self-movement of the form that is the subject. This pure subjectivity that defines the identity of God tries to efface every trace of the operation of imagining that might even hint at the existence of an *other* subject, that is, of alterity per se, since the presence of alterity would threaten the pure transcendence of this One.

Traces of Idolatry: Akāl Mūrat, or Image of the Eternal

The commentaries on the phrase "*akāl mūrat*" point to a convergence of the main anxieties outlined above. Briefly, the commentaries on "*akāl mūrat*" read as follows:

"(that being) whose installation/representation is not subject to time"
jis dī sthāpanā samai de bhed karke nahī.   —Kahn Singh[125]

"(that being) which is unaffected by time"
us hastī pur samai dā asar nahī.   —Jodh Singh[126]

"that being whose form [*sarūp*] is beyond time, i.e., whose body
[*sarīr*] is not subject to destruction"
jis dā sarūp kāl to pare hai bhāv, jis dā sarīr nās rahit hai.
       —Sāhib Singh[127]

He is outside of time, yet being unaffected by time he is not nonexistent,
he exists as form/shape/image (i.e., He is in existence), meaning thereby that he has form [but] that form is not affected by time (*Oh akāl = kāl
rahit hai, akāl hokai oh anhoṁd nahīṁ, oh mūrati (=hoṇd hai) arthāt
us dā vajūd yā sarūp hai jo sarup kāl to rahit haī*).   —BVS[128]

In view of the previous effort to prove that God, though existent, cannot be limited by form or figuration, the presence of the word "*mūrat*" —
which conveys the meanings of image, shape, form, picture, painting,
idol, body, likeness, etc. — might have presented a more direct challenge
to the reformists, not least because one of the most important sociopolitical factors behind the divergence between reformists and traditionalists
in colonial North India centered on the issue of the worship of images
and idols (*mūrtī pūjā*). As the Sikh reformist commentaries clearly admit,
even within the *mūl mantar* the word "*mūrat*" cannot easily escape a connection to time and world. But if the presentation of the formless divine
"according to gurmat" was to avoid any association with "Hindu" idolatry, it would be necessary for the reformists to show: (i) that the word
"*mūrat*" as used in Sikh scripture, and being qualified by "*akāl*," has a
very different signification to the "Hindu"; (ii) that there is no contradiction or inconsistency in placing "*akāl*" and "*mūrat*" together.

On the first count Vīr Singh's remarks are fairly self-assured. "*Akāl
mūrat*," he argues, takes its final meaning solely from the *mūl mantra*.
It does not correspond to images painted on paper, on cloth, or on walls
(*kāgaz ke kapṛai te kandān te chitaritān mūrtīāni*) nor does it correspond to idols engraved in stone or cast in metal (*patharāni te ukāṛiāni te
dhātūāni vic dālīāni mūrtīāni*).[129] According to the *mūl mantra* these are
forbidden (*mūl mantra de lakṣ hoṇ to varjit ho gaīān*).

On the other count, regarding the consistency of meaning between *akāl*
and *mūrati*, there seems to be less certainty. The problem revolves around
the semantic ambiguity of *kāl* (time), which can have two different meanings, depending on whether it is perceived subjectively or objectively.
Thus *kāl* can be perceived subjectively as duration (*samā*), according to
the threefold division of time (*trai vaṇḍān vic*) as beginning, middle, and

end or past, present, and future (*ādi, mad, ant*).[130] This is time as it is
ascertained by the self, or, to be more faithful to Vīr Singh's text, it is the
sense of time as the self *believes* time to exist (*āp nū partīt karoūṁdā
hai*).[131] Alternatively time can be perceived objectively, as when it shows
itself to our self from the perspective of the end of time, i.e., teleologi-
cally (*kal jo "ant" vic apnā āp nū dikhāldā hai tā arth maut ho jandā
hai*).[132] Thus if *kāl* is taken objectively as "death" then *a-kāl* can take
on the meanings of immortal, eternal, that which always remains as it is.
Hence *akāl mūrati* must mean the eternal form, the form that transcends
time, and, because it transcends time, that which is able to transcend form
itself. But, as Vīr Singh explains, because the objective meaning of time
as "death/end" is already contained within the subjective notion of time
("*kāl*" *pad dā arth "maut" arth "kāl" pad de "samā" arth de antargat
hai*), it is already part of a typically human understanding of time as a
figure that is represented to a self who is always already present to itself.
It follows, though, that the negation of this human time (*kāl* as being-in-
time) into *a-kāl* might imply a negation of the very mode of time whereby
we conceive existence in general and the existence of all things; in other
words, the logic of negation intrinsic to *akāl* could be misunderstood as
nonexistence. However, it is, finally, to avoid this very possibility that Vīr
Singh will stress that it is perfectly correct to write "*akāl murat*" ("*akāl*"
kahkai murat pad nāl likhnā is vāstai sahī hai). By being "*akāl*," which
also implies the negation of subjective human time, God does not become
nonexistent ("*akāl*" *hoṁ karke oh "an-hond" nahin ho jāṁdā*).[133]

His efforts to find conceptual closure notwithstanding, Vīr Singh's
argument reveals gaps at the very point where claims to extreme transcendence appear to be strongest. An obvious flaw is the reliance on the
metaphor of the sun to conceptualize divine transcendence of a sensuous
form and quality. Yet even this seemingly innocuous use of the metaphoric imagination is not enough to preserve the effect of sensuous imagery
while eliminating the threat posed by linking the sensuous to the divine.
As one scholar (writing about a similar issue, although in the very different context of early Christianity) has astutely noted: "In the all or nothing stakes implied by the extreme transcendence of the One, . . . even
this tiniest residue [of the sensuous image] to which it inconspicuously
but necessarily looks for support is enough to compromise its avowed
independence."[134] What begins as an assured strategy of the concept's
upward movement turns into a rather uncertain trade-off: good metaphors
for bad idols, good concepts for bad images; *akāl mūrat* for *mūratī*, the

external form for the perishable supplement. Yet the valuation of the "good" image of eternity will have been generated within a subjective standpoint, produced by a self whose primary mode of relationality is auto-affection—the production of the self by the self. Given that auto-affection is ultimately premised on a failure, in the sense that it can work only by subjecting time to a metaphysical figure of eternity, so also for Bhāī Vīr Singh, the eternal form (*akāl mūrat*) can be presented only by thinking in and through form itself. It can only be imagined as a form in time: *sarīr, sarūp, hoṁd, hastī*.

Ironically, then, attempts by the Singh Sabhā writers to overcome idolatry and idolatrous notions of God by means of the elevated concept have to admit the "tiniest residue" of idolatry into the process of cleansing *gurmat* (and therefore Sikhism) from any contamination by Hinduism. All along, it seems, the Singh Sabhā reformists were doing in their exegetical works precisely what they accused Hindus of doing in practice—which of course means that the project of constructing religious boundaries is compromised from the very outset. The question, however, is why, in a presentation where form simply replaces form, the trade-off could ever have been considered profitable? What is it that the reformists desired to gain? Or, inverting the question: What is it that the reformists thought they *lacked*?

From the Ontological Proof to the Formulation of Sikhism as a "World Religion"

To read the history of neocolonial reform movements such as the Singh Sabhā as the history of a perceived lack is to question some of the foundational assumptions on which modern knowledge about Sikhism is based. Sikh scholars in the reformist tradition have unanimously disavowed the relevance or necessity of formal theological proofs to Sikhism, preferring to argue that God and theology are naturally present in the Ādi Granth. Writing within the conceptual framework set by Trumpp's translation, the Singh Sabhā scholars needed to prove that Sikhism was not Hinduism by proving that the Sikh concept of God was not pantheistic but monotheistic. In short they need to prove that God exists, that God's Name names this existence, and that the nature of this existence is an eternal identity, a static immutable One.

In view of its form and conceptual dynamic, however, it is difficult to deny that Bhāī Vīr Singh's exegesis aspires to the status of a theological proof. Given that his commentary is structured not only by a dialectical chain of propositional statements about the nature of God, but also by a conceptual dynamic that moves from the Oneness of God (*ektav*), through the Being of God (*sat[i]*), to the Eternal as the Identity of God (*akāl*), the *form* and *logic* of his presentation bears a striking resemblance to the scholastic doctrine of *scientia dei*, the importance of which lies in its inseparability from the ontological argument.[135] However, one would need to qualify the statement that Vīr Singh's exegesis on the nondual One *is* an ontological proof for the existence of God. Indeed, the appearance of such a proof is surprising for several reasons. First, although he received a secondary education in an Anglo-vernacular mission school, there is no indication that he had detailed knowledge of Western philosophical theology and specifically not the history of the ontological proof. Second, prior to the Singh Sabhā movement there is nothing akin to the ontological argument in the Sikh hermeneutic tradition.[136] Third, in the broader Indic context, although there are venerable traditions of analysis and argumentation about the nature and reality of "God," all of these traditions differ from the ontological argument as it is known in the West, in regard to at least one crucial point, which can be explained in the following way.

Ordinarily the ontological argument in its various statements revolves around the definition of God as "that Being than which nothing greater can be thought. . . . He who understands that God exists cannot think of Him as nonexistent." In short, God cannot be identified with nothingness. God is *not* nothing. Yet the matter can never end there. For hiding behind this rendering of the ontological argument is the presupposition that nothing exists without reason, known in the Western philosophical and theological tradition as the principle of reason.[137] The logic of this principle goes something like this. The reason things exist rather than not exist resides in their cause. It follows that the first cause must also be the highest cause, a cause that towers above or transcends all others, namely, God. God's being thus transcends in the sense of being over-against and exceeding all conditioned beings. But although God is conceived as the highest being, such transcendence is still conceived from within the totality of all that exists. Which means that God, as with all other things that exist, remains subject to the principle of reason. God exists—indeed knowledge about God exists—only insofar as the principle of reason itself holds. Stated differently, God exists only insofar as there is first a self-grounding cognition, a self-knowing-itself, which is able to present itself in the mode of an *"ego cogito."* It belongs to this self-presenting subject, which first and foremost *knows* itself, that it certify itself continually, which means as an identity.

In his *Metaphysical Foundations of Logic* Heidegger argues that the subjective basis of theological knowledge (i.e., self-consciousness) remains hidden due to a long-standing confusion between two different ways of conceiving transcendence: the epistemological and the theological.[138] Though seemingly opposed, the standpoint of epistemology is in fact taken for granted in all theological reasoning, resulting in the confusion between "the transcend*ent*" (the highest Being, first cause, God etc) and "transcend*ence*." The latter term is crucial since its signification of passing beyond limits can be understood in very different ways. There is, for example, the metaphysical sense of being absolutely unaffected by time, in which case the meanings of transcendent and transcendence are conjoined to give what is known as ontotheology. Though it is largely absent from Indian and other Oriental forms of thinking,[139] this notion of transcendence has been characteristic of the various presentations of the ontological proof in Western religious and philosophical thinking, that is to say, the kind of thinking that continually grounds itself on the field of self-consciousness, whether this is in the form of Descartes' *"ego cogito,"* Kant's transcendental subject, or Hegel's panoptical schema of determinate religions, outlined in the *Lectures on the Philosophy of Religion*, that allows the subject to observe everything from the transcendental vantage point of world history.

My point here is that irrespective of whether the context is Aquinas' *Summa Theologica* or Bhāī Vīr Singh's commentary on the *mūl mantra*, the work done by the ontological argument for God's existence gives us theoretical purchase into the relationship between, on the one hand, the construction of a figure of God as a static immutable One that is therefore also the definition of origin as such (insofar as this origin is synonymous with God's creative activity [*kartā*] as the transcendence of the *nihil*), and on the other hand, the construction of modern Sikh identity, which is fleshed out, takes on form, incarnates itself, in the light of the former. As long as this identity reproduces itself in *modern* Sikh enunciation as "Sikh sovereignty" or as the "Sikh people," it never ceases to resemble the figure of God as "sovereign cause of itself and end for itself."[140] This resemblance is mutual, however. What becomes clear from Vīr Singh's commentary is that the figure of God and the figure of Sikh identity do not exist independently. They are mutually *co*-figured in the dialectical movement of propositional statements about the nature of God that is the commentary itself. As Derrida reminds us with reference to Aristotle's *Metaphysics*, this co-figuring in terms of the "semblable," the like or the similar, this movement of "resemblance never ceases to motivate thought, pure Actuality. . . . Neither moving nor being itself moved, the actuality of this pure energy sets everything in motion, a motion of return to self, a circular motion" that is always cyclical. "And what induces or inspires this is a desire. God, the pure actuality of the Prime Mover, is at once erogenous and thinkable. He is, so to speak, desirable, the first desirable as the first intelligible thinking itself, as thought thinking itself, as thought thinking thought."[141] Hence the self can be co-figured as an identity because it desires this energy of the Prime Mover and by so desiring it partakes in a certain pleasure: "A taking pleasure in the self, a circular and specular auto-affection that is analogous to or in accordance with the thinking of thought."[142]

Does this suggest then, despite the elaborate arguments about God's identity in Bhāī Vīr Singh's commentary, that the true motivation behind the project of "Sikh theology" is neither God nor knowledge about God, but a desire to constitute a subject? A desire that is therefore political? The important point here is that we cannot separate the question of desire and pleasure from the question of the political as the domain of "calculation and incalculable to which desire and pleasure give rise."[143] What the commentary presents, therefore, is the working of a very human desire to project *gurmat* within a particular horizon: the ontotheological framework of the history of religions, and through this to the tautological form of modern Sikh enunciation, "I am a Sikh," because this Sikh "I" cannot be non-Sikh. From within the ontotheological framework the relation that Sikhs entertain to others will be governed by their respective degree of access to a transcendent God.

In effect the presence of the ontological proof within the vernacular commentaries inaugurates a cycle of political theology whose hermeneutic core binds the very structure of what is called "Sikh belief" to the enunciation of identity in the public sphere. From within this ontotheological framework the relation that the Sikh entertains to himself and to others will be governed by its degree of proximity to the static immutable One. According to this logic, the desire for Sikh identity to conform to the attributes of a transcendental being must ultimately abolish anything that does not accord with this identity. As such it must transcend the alterity of the other through a politics of identification, since the difference that constitutes the other (in this case Hindu or Muslim) undermines the self-presence of the

Sikh by co-appearing at the origin. Which means, of course, that if the origin is from the outset contaminated by the other, the other must be reduced to the same or cast out of humanity altogether. In this manner the logic of transcendence deployed by Singh Sabhā reformists has collectively refigured discourses involving such topics as the following:

Individual and collective identity. The question may arise as to whether my analysis and argument above suggest that Sikh identity was created in the colonial period. I have already alluded to this problem in chapter 1 in relation to Kahn Singh Nabha's provocative publication *Ham Hindu Nahin* ("We are not Hindus"), which refutes the term "Hindu" as a master signifier—a signifier that also purports to give meaning to the term "Sikh." But if this is the case, did Kahn Singh initiate a break between Hindus and Sikhs that led to the development of the Sikh identity? The answer to this question must be an unqualified no! The enunciation of a Sikh identity does not begin in the colonial period, and it would be wrong to adduce this from my analysis above. A Sikh identity, however amorphous it might have been, had already emerged in the sixteenth and seventeenth centuries. Rather, what changes in the colonial period is the way in which identity was conceived. As I stated earlier, it is the *logic* of identity that changes in the colonial period. In the precolonial period the articulation of Sikh identity was never articulated though the dualistic logic of either/or (e.g., A=A, B=B, but A≠B). The logic of Sikh identity (indeed of Hindu identity) prior to colonialism, and as far back as the sixteenth century, was articulated in terms of a complex or relational logic, according to which it would be perfectly valid to suggest that A=B, the implication of which would be the existence of relatively fluid social and individual boundaries. In other words, the logic of identity changes from complex or relational to dualistic. And this change resulted from of a politics of religion-making driven by ontotheology—the first victim of which was the signifier "Hindu." It is therefore interesting to note, as J. S. Grewal argues, that despite the provocative tone of *Ham Hindu Nahin*, "Bhāī Kahn Singh Nabha had no objection to Sikhs being called Hindu if the term meant simply Indian, *without bringing in any religious dimension.* The crucial question about the Hindu-Sikh debate is why at that particular juncture *so much importance came to be attached to religious identity*" (emphasis mine).[144]

Sikh ethics. Even a cursory glance at the post–Singh Sabhā writings on Sikh ethics shows that virtually all discourse on ethics is made to conform to a metaphysical ideal, namely, the attributes of a static immutable God, which in turn define a moral standard to which all Sikhs must somehow conform. Such conformity is best attained through inculcating correct belief. Not surprisingly, the modern Sikh Code of Conduct (*Sikh Rahit Maryāda*)[145] begins the definition of a Sikh as "[a]ny human being who faithfully believes in One Immortal Being."[146] Though rarely considered, one consequence of locking the discourse of ethics into a belief system[147] is that it has prevented contemporary Sikhism and individual Sikhs from adequately responding to the complex variety of ethical questions now being raised.[148]

Topologies of death and necrophilia (martyrdom, war, self-sacrifice, and the image of the tortured Sikh body).[149] I refer here to the fact that the static immutability of the divine is best described — because of its stasis — as death. Little wonder then that the kind of unity with divine stasis sought by reformists as the ultimate goal of their religious philosophy can be attained only through an identification with death. This necrophilic tendency of the modern Sikh imaginary underlies the reformists' investment in the production of martyrologies,[150] the promulgation of the image of the tortured Sikh body of Sikh tradition and the more recent images of what Brian Axel has aptly termed the "nation's tortured body,"[151] and the preeminence given to the male warrior Sikh in modern Sikh art.

Systematic eradications of myth and mythic art. Appearing to follow logically from Bhāī Vīr Singh's commentary on *akāl murat*, there has been within many historic Sikh places of worship, including the Harimander complex, and particularly since 1984, a program of whitewashing over, or cleansing away, what is considered to be "Hindu" imagery in which Sikhism is clearly depicted as having shared a tradition.

Partition-parturition. What tends to have been overemphasized by the dominant area studies approach in contemporary Sikh studies is the imagining of an exclusively Sikh homeland/territory/space. To what extent is the notion of an exclusive Sikh territory, and ultimately the partitioning among nations/peoples/religions, a logical consequence of a theo-aesthetic principle based on the static immutable One in relation to which time is configured as space or area?

In the history of Western thought the ontological argument for God's existence has — paradoxically, through its failure to prove the existence of God — also established the conditions of modernity itself, of modern critical thought. In Brayton Polka's words, it comprises the "unconscious hermeneutic" of modernity, a hermeneutic whose critical principle is a specific form of ontology in which God's identity (Eternal Being) serves as a measure of difference between God and world, and the separation between God and world in turn is a surrogate for the self versus other.[152] Moreover, insofar as the ontological argument implies a desire for the universal, it is intrinsically connected to all political thought. Indeed, within the Western tradition any and every transition from particular to universal, and therefore political theory, has been underpinned by this ontological argument (e.g., Anselm, Aquinas, Descartes, Kant, Hegel, Marx). As I have shown in this chapter it is precisely this unconscious hermeneutic of modernity that Bhāī Vīr Singh and his colleagues appropriated and internalized, even though it remains antithetical to Indian devotional and philosophical traditions and to what I have called the nondual ground of Sikhism.

But while the ontological separation between God and world is merely implicit in Bhāī Vīr Singh's commentary, it appears explicitly for the first time in the work of his younger colleague and protégé, Jodh Singh, whose major work of 1932, *Gurmat Nirnai*, is probably the first systematic work of what came to be called "Sikh theology." In *Gurmat Nirnai* Jodh Singh lays out chapter headings in a way that reproduces the ontological separation at the foundation of his treatise: (i) *akāl purukh* (God), (ii) *sriṣṭī rachnā* (world), (iii) *manukh* (man), ... (vi) *Guru* (the Guru), ... (ix) *Śabda* (word), (xiii) *Bhāīchārak Baṇtar* (brotherhood), (xiv) *Khalsā* (community of the elect).[153] Jodh Singh's interpretive schema is neither novel nor analytically exhaustive. At best it transfers and condenses the philosophical rigor of Bhāī Vīr Singh's work into a more accessible idiom. Nevertheless its effect and hold on postindependence Sikh scholars, particularly those writing in English, has been, and remains, pervasive. After 1932 its schema became a blueprint for modern Sikh thought. There are two reasons for this. First, it provides a very succinct and accessible schema that is reproduced with equal facility by Sikhs writing in Punjabi and in English. More important, however, *Gurmat Nirnai*, particularly after the late 1950s, provides for Sikh scholars, clerics, and politicians a transition to the category of the universal, specifically in the shape of the rapidly developing "world religions" discourse.

As we shall see in the next chapter, this faith on the part of Sikh scholars in the world religions discourse, exemplified by the academic discipline of history of religions, was misplaced. But once Sikh elites had internalized the mechanism of using God as a measure of cultural ideology and therefore political difference, what naturally follows from this is the idea of a Sikh "world," i.e., a view of the world and a view onto the world, that is at the same time a metaphor for the diversity of religions that exist in this world. That is to say, the elite "club" to which Sikhism demands entry was subsequently taken up by a postindependence generation of Sikh theologians, philosophers (such as Sher Singh, Jodh Singh, G. S. Talib, Kapur Singh, Daljeet Singh, Gopal Singh, and Jasbir Singh Ahluwalia), and historians (such as Khushwant Singh).[154] These writers simply assumed the historical narrative and theological proofs that the Singh Sabhā writers had so painstakingly worked out. Because their works were written to an increasingly Anglophone audience both within and outside India, they can be regarded as the group that truly popularized the idea of Sikhism as "world religion."

What needs to be remembered here is that the postindependence (1947) political context of these writers is somewhat different from that of the early Singh Sabhā writers. While Hindus achieved independence through the creation of India as a nation-state, Sikh hopes of achieving a separate nation-state were dashed. Moreover, they had agreed to live with the very nation/culture from which they had previously sought ideological separation during the period of British occupation. Consequently the idea of Sikhism as a "world religion" becomes more explicit after 1947. In each of these later works the enunciation of two principles central to Sikh doctrine (belief in an authentic origin of Sikhism, and belief in something called "Sikh theology" as an adequate translation for the teachings of the Sikh Gurus) becomes a means of automatic comparison with, and separation from, Hinduism—a separation that provides the possibility for Sikhs to enter into interfaith dialogue with Christians, Buddhists, Muslims, and Hindus. Interestingly, this enunciation of a "Sikh theology" by these scholars is taken up and assumed by Western anthropologists during the 1960s and 1970s and becomes part of a Western world religions frame in religious studies. In other words, the discourse of Sikhism as "world religion" has its beginnings in the colonial discourse of British and German Indologists and historians, from where it is appropriated and internalized by the proto-nationalist Singh Sabhā reformists and the post-1947 generation of Sikh nationalist writers, and ultimately passes back into the writings of post-1960s Anglo-American anthropologists and religion scholars (the teachers of an official world religions discourse in the Anglo-American academy), who, as we shall in the next chapter, in turn read it back to the current generation of Sikhs in the late twentieth century.

4   Violence, Mysticism, and the Capture of Subjectivity

In this chapter I continue to trace the movement of cultural translation designated by the term "Sikh theology" into the humanities program of the modern Western university, specifically the discourse of the history of religions. To do this it is necessary to determine how the subject of Sikhism, or the Sikh subject, came to be determined as a distinctly "religious" subject. I argue that a certain understanding of violence, or, rather, a set of unexamined assumptions about the relationship between religion and violence, is necessary for the construction and deployment of this subject as "religious" in the modern academic study of religions. In the case of Sikh studies this *doxa* is cemented by the appropriation of neocolonial constructions of "Sikh theology" (such as those examined in the previous chapter) and their systematic translation into the broadly anthropo-historicist or secular frame that constitutes the task of the historian of religion.

The first part of this chapter is devoted to unraveling the theoretical mechanisms responsible for framing the essence of the "religious" subject (Sikh "religiosity'" or mysticism) by one of its most capable scholars, the historian W. H. McLeod. This involves a continuing transcendentalization of key terms such as *śabda-guru*, such that the radically emancipatory potential of this term is captured and given a rigidly metaphysical signification.

The second part of the chapter demonstrates how such theoretical mechanisms, which draw on an unexamined set of assumptions about the relationship between religion and violence, can be transferred, often unintentionally and unreflectively, on the one hand, into the discourse of media journalists and academic experts specializing in the study of "religious violence," and on the other hand, by the secular state in its efforts to politically manage religious pluralism. When this process is examined more closely, it becomes clear that state, media, and academia, while subscribing to a doctrine of secularism, are linked through a process of "generalized translation" that allows them either to frame the very possibilities of thinking about violence (in the case of media and academia) or to socially and politically engineer violence (in the case of the state) ironically through discourses that construct religion and religious subjects.

Wars of Scholarship

Responses to the regime of colonial translation by Sikh scholars belonging to the reformist Singh Sabhā movement produced some of the enduring themes of modern Sikh ideology. The ideological impulses created by the Singh Sabhā movement, impulses that were at once religious and linguistic, continued through the early decades of the twentieth century, fueling various political agitations. Notable among such agitations was the Gurdwara Reform Movement, which aimed to wrest control of Sikh places of worship from the British. These theo-ideological impulses came to fruition in the 1920s with the formation of a body to oversee the functioning of Sikh places of worship (the S.G.P.C.[1]) and a Sikh political party (the Akālī Dal) to represent Sikh interests as Indians jostled for influence during the final decades of the struggle for independence. This was followed soon after independence by agitations for a Punjabi-speaking state, which, given that Sikhs had lost out in the struggle for a state of their own, would ensure some measure of Sikh political autonomy.

One of the crowning achievements of the postindependence Sikh agitations was the creation of several new universities based in Punjab during the 1960s. Two of these new universities, Guru Nānak Dev University (Amritsar) and Punjabi University (Patiala), incorporated and projected key ideological concepts of modern reformist Sikhism: the idea that Sikhs are a nation, that Sikhism is a "world religion," and that Punjabi is the national language of the Sikhs. In some ways the creation of these two

educational institutions during the 1960s compensated for the disappointment that many Sikhs felt in not achieving a separate nation-state during
the partition of India in 1947. Their establishment also coincided with a
spate of events that allowed Sikhs to begin representing themselves as a
"world religion," a representation that had remained implicit within the
Singh Sabhā's dominant narrative of "Sikhs as a nation."

However, such attempts to universalize the image of Sikhism never
achieved currency until the representations of Sikhism as a "nation" or
"world religion" returned to their place of origination, namely the West,
and until Western scholarship intervened, however subtly, in its reconfig-
uration. According to the anthropologist Verne Dusenbury, "despite the
efforts of the Singh Sabhā writers and sympathizers (such as Macauliffe)
to represent the Sikh religion to the English-speaking public, world-religion textbooks and comparative religionists (all based in the West) largely ignored Sikhism. . . . It was not until the late 1960s and early 1970s
that a number of convergent events allowed Sikhs to effectively make the
claim that Sikhism is a 'world-religion' rather than a parochial faith."[2]
Dusenbury cites events such as the three-hundredth and five-hundredth
birth anniversary celebrations of Guru Gobind Singh and Guru Nānak respectively, and the one-hundredth anniversary of the Singh Sabhā movement as well as the global dispersion of Sikhs from Punjab and the mass
conversions of non-Punjabi Westerners to Sikhism. More important,
though, Dusenbury emphasizes the fact that "renewed scholarly attention
from Western academics—especially the work of W. H. McLeod (beginning with *Guru Nānak and the Sikh Religion* in 1968) . . . made Sikhism a legitimate topic of intellectual contemplation and discussion in the
West. . . . Having a chronicler of McLeod's stature (however critically
his work may have been received in some quarters) has ultimately helped
legitimate Sikhism as a religious tradition worthy of academic study in
Western universities."[3]

This is an interesting statement that requires some expansion and examination. It suggests, first, that despite the development of discourse
about Sikhism in the hands of the Singh Sabhā scholars, Sikhs themselves
were unable to present their tradition as a *legitimate* object of study for
the West. In order to gain *legitimacy*, Sikh tradition would require the
aid or intervention of Western scholarship. In other words, and second,
it suggests that there is yet another, and perhaps final, phase in the encounter between Sikhs and the West—involving the circulation of knowledge about Sikh tradition back into the purview of the university—that

will close the arc of communication between Sikhs and the West. As we have seen, this arc of communication began with the West's encounter with Sikhs in the nineteenth century, developed with the Singh Sabhā, and enters a period of "closure" with the return of the Sikh object (Sikh-*ism*) back to where it was generated: the space of the West's "intellectual contemplation." It is in this latest phase of encounter that we see the emergence of the master narrative of "Sikhism as world religion," which focuses more on the "universal appeal and relevance of the Sikh Gurus' teachings."[4] Third, there is the intriguing possibility that the space in which the Sikh object comes to be properly installed as a "legitimate topic of intellectual contemplation and discussion in the West"—a space that has since come to be loosely termed as "Sikh studies"—is intrinsically linked to the full and proper articulation of the master narrative of "Sikhism as a world-religion," a narrative that is itself based on the idea that the teachings of the Sikh Gurus constitute the formation that has come to be known as "Sikh theology."

There is a certain irony in this as it suggests that the secular space of Sikh studies is grounded on something akin to "Sikh theology." Moreover, there is the question of legitimacy. Sikhism as a religious tradition is not legitimate by itself. Something else, a certain kind of representation or advocacy, is necessary to make it "worthy of academic study in Western universities." In other words, without this advocacy Sikhism as a religious tradition might appear illegitimate, and so its appearance in the university would not be lawful—which of course points to the operation of censorship in relation to the representation of religion or religious tradition. As one might expect, there is nothing remarkable about the operation of censorship by the university in regards to certain kinds of knowledge formation. After all, the university's secular vocation is based on the need to maintain objectivity in regard to the subject under scrutiny. But in the case of Sikhism questions of censorship, legitimacy, representation, and religion have become deeply entangled with the scholarship of one man, W. H. McLeod, the very person who, as Dusenbury points out, has done more than any other scholar to ensure the transmission of knowledge about Sikhism into the university and its representation from there to the outside world. Consequently, it would not be too farfetched to suggest that the site of the university, and McLeod's scholarly works in particular, may be considered exemplary of the third phase of encounter between Sikhs and the West. Indeed, as N. G. Barrier writes in his foreword to W. H. McLeod's autobiography:

The encounter between Sikhism and the West has helped frame the Sikh institutions, ideas, and controversies that abound today. Over the last century, scholarly study of Sikh traditions has become part of the Sikh efforts to understand themselves and their past. At various times, the fusion of religion and politics has involved intellectuals, but generally on the periphery as groups and organizations vied for power and control of new political parties and institutions. This has now changed dramatically.

Just as American politics, metaphor, and public discourse were altered by the attacks on September 11, 2001, so the growing militancy and turmoil that culminated in the attack on the Golden Temple and the Delhi riots in 1984 reshaped the relationship between religion and politics among Sikhs. Academic research and authors quickly became enmeshed in the ensuing debate over controversial elements in Sikh public life. No individual Sikh or Western has been more pivotal in the resulting wars over scholarship and Sikhism than Professor W. H. ("Hew") McLeod.[5]

Barrier's statement inadvertently provides the faintest glimpse of an almost intangible connection between the wars of scholarship over Sikhism and events that reshaped the relationship between religion and politics among Sikhs.[6] On the face of it even the suggestion of such a connection seems preposterous! W. H. McLeod specialized not in South Asian politics but in the history and religion of the Sikhs. He has neither written on nor professed interest in contemporary Sikh or South Asian politics. Even his recent autobiography is mostly silent about the sociopolitical situation in South Asia, suggesting that there was never any connection between his avowedly historical, even ivory tower, approach to scholarship and wider political concerns.[7] It seems that the only possible connection would be the vastly different receptions of McLeod's work in the university and the Sikh community respectively.

On the one hand McLeod had established by the late 1970s and 80s a solid reputation within the academy as the foremost Western interpreter of Sikh religion and history. Bearing in mind the relative paucity of knowledge about Sikhs at the time, it seems inevitable that students, scholars, teachers, media journalists, and policymakers would turn to the substantial and growing corpus of scholarly publications by McLeod for understanding Sikhism and the social and political activities of Sikhs. On the other hand, many Sikhs—including those who sympathized with the political and armed struggle against the Indian state, but also many others frustrated by their inability to resist the consistently negative stereotypes of Sikhs and Sikhism circulating in the media as well as in academic works during the 1980s and 90s—bitterly opposed McLeod's writings and vented their anger against the work and personalities of scholars associated with him.[8]

This state of affairs is most evident in the controversy over the establishment of Sikh studies programs in North American universities. At its peak this controversy appeared to echo the deepening impasse between advocates of Sikh nationalism and those who advocated secularism. Media coverage of this dispute tended to focus on the "Sikh problem" as solely due to the intransigence of a small but vocal minority of "fundamentalist" Sikhs who appeared incapable of adjusting to secular democratic ideals espoused by Western universities. Having hijacked the Sikh community's agenda on education, these "fundamentalists" were bent on destroying any Sikh studies program that did not conform to the narrow ideology of Sikh religious nationalism.

The opposing perspective from the Sikhs paints an equally grim picture. In their eyes, Western academics (and by implication W. H. McLeod and his students) contrived to distort the true message of Sikhism as reflected by "Sikh ideology" and have thus misrepresented Sikh history and its traditions to the outside world. Sikhism, they argue, is endowed with all the ingredients that would enable it to be regarded as a "world religion." It has a well-documented history, a community, life-cycle rituals, and, most important, a sacred scripture, the *Guru Granth Sāhib*, whose contents were revealed to perfected beings such as the Sikh Gurus. Thus, they argue, we can do justice to the study of Sikhism only if we recognize the nature of the object of our study as a "religion" and that religion is "a reality to which history and historical intellectual analysis alone is ill-suited. Only in part can history and the intellect measure the intuitive reality that transcends both."[9] The study of Sikhism, like the "proper study of religion, involves a study of the spiritual dimension and experiences of man. . . . The study of religion requires sharp insights into the totality of life, including transcendental knowledge concerning God, the universe, and the human spirit."[10] The assumption here is that Sikhism is a religion and that its nature is *sui generis*.

McLeod's most succinct rebuttal of these criticisms appeared in the text of an article entitled "Cries of Outrage: History Versus Tradition in the Study of the Sikh Community."[11] McLeod's constant thesis in this response is that the disagreement comes down in the final analysis to a difference between two approaches to history. On the one hand are "traditionalist historians," who trust traditional sources and view them with the certainty of religious belief, and on the other are critical historians, who view traditional sources with skepticism. While traditionalists can claim to take cognizance of "a higher level of reality" or to have "transcendental knowledge concerning God," the critical historian claims to be "devoid of any such religious or spiritual experience" or "devoid of that spiritual sense which traditionalists claim access to" (p. 132). Rather, the critical historian claims to work through a "free intelligence," as a result of which he is "uninhibited by the constraints that shackle the understanding of the traditionalist" (p. 128). The implications of this distinction is obvious: critical historians are true historians, their work can claim strict impartiality, whereas traditionalists, because they are tied to a religious/nationalist ideology, can only aspire to a pseudo-history, an ultimately false history that can never claim scientific status. Moreover, this distinction arises not only from epistemic difference but from an ontological difference between the two kinds of historian. They lead "separate existences," argues McLeod. Although McLeod's language is more conciliatory than that of his antagonists—he alludes to his "limitations" as a historian—his analysis in fact perpetuates similar binary oppositions to those used by the media. Even the self-deprecating talk of "limitations" in fact turns out to be a valorization of secular historicism over religious tradition. In the end, the two approaches are totally opposed and cannot be reconciled. The academic historian values the scientific credentials of his work and cannot mix "scholarly analysis" with the "piety of believers" (p. 124). As McLeod repeats several times, he is "quite unable to enter into their belief" and therefore "devoid of any pretence to that spiritual sense. . . . I simply do not possess it" (p. 133).

While this episode, and McLeod's explanation of it, attests to a serious disagreement with certain members of the Sikh community, it suggests almost no link (or even the need to make a link) to the sociopolitical context in which the "wars of scholarship" were taking place. The implication here seems to be that the connection to politics is something internal to Sikhs themselves. It is essentially a "Sikh problem" and one that stems historically from their involvement in politics. As such it has unnecessarily implicated a reputable and innocent scholar.

It is difficult, however, not to be suspicious of the terms of McLeod's critical moves, specifically the simultaneous affirmation of his identity as a critical historian and his disavowals of religion, religious belief, and traditionalist history. My suspicions are aroused partly by Dusenbury's endorsement of McLeod's work as having helped to make Sikhism recognizable as a "world religion" in textbooks and scholarly opinion. To achieve this McLeod would need to present an understanding of Sikhism that conforms to a universal definition of religion. Yet the only element that allows such conformity is a narrative that presents the teachings of the Sikh Gurus as transcending the particularity of the North Indian context in which they emerged, and therefore as relevant to the rest of humanity. In other words, McLeod would have to assume the existence of some minimal "theology" at the heart of Sikhism and that the teachings of the Sikh Gurus constitute a "Sikh theology." In fact, when we look closely at McLeod's oeuvre, despite his emphatic denial of interest in or connection to the religion or the spiritual, the element of the theological, and specifically an understanding of "Sikh theology," is unmistakably present.

But why would the historian need an understanding of "Sikh theology"? More important, if as we have shown in the previous chapter, "Sikh theology" is not natural to the teachings of the Sikh Gurus, but was constructed by Singh Sabhā scholars as part of their accession to the regime of colonial translation of Sikh scripture, why would a critical historian such as McLeod even need to assume its centrality to Sikhism? Does the assumption that "Sikh theology" is natural rather than constructed not implicate McLeod's work in a peculiar *relationship* with Singh Sabhā ideology and scholarship? Can it therefore not be located in continuity with the neocolonialist reproduction of Sikhism? If so, how is it that one kind of theology can be disavowed as ideological when it is in the hands of traditionalists, but be rendered nonideological, hence safe and useful, in the hands of the historian? Is it possible, then, that the theological constitutes the very hinge upon which are based both Singh Sabhā theology and McLeod's construction of the secular anthropology and history of Sikhs and Sikhism? In what way is theology crucial to modern Sikh studies, to the modernity and professed secularity of this space, and yet how is it then the disavowed element in the very discipline that McLeod's works help to create?

I believe there are grounds for suspecting that perhaps the oppositions—university versus community, nonideological historian versus ideological traditionalist, etc.—are themselves misleading. Perhaps the oppositional terms in which the "wars of scholarship" and the resulting impasse have been represented are themselves misleading? Is the valorization of one term over another part of a deeper and invisible ideology that is assumed but denied by the historian? In order to understand this impasse and the "wars of scholarship" it is necessary to look more carefully at the understanding of or about religion that is part of the academic contract. We need to look at the definition of religion that is operative in the transference of knowledge about Sikhism from traditional scholarship to the university. Can a study of the way that historians theorize and conceptualize religion offer glimpses into the wider patterns of thought relating to the relationship between religion and politics? Does the historian of religion's understanding *of* or *about* religion itself constitute an ideology of some sort? If so, how does this ideology affect or influence the wider representation of Sikhism as the object of knowledge, beginning in the academy but moving then to its eventual deployment by the media and by policymakers? What might be the wider implications of such a connection?

To begin answering some of these questions I want to focus the greater part of this chapter on a study of W. H. McLeod's understanding and presentation of "Sikh theology." Because McLeod as a critical historian both affirms history and denies a connection or involvement with religion as its other, yet cannot help but practice "Sikh theology" in order to construct his object, his work provides a rich resource and a useful sounding board for exploring issues related to the foregoing questions. I shall therefore focus on McLeod's presentation of "Sikh theology," which, for him, constitutes the heart of Sikh religiosity, the basis of Sikh religious experience as found in the teachings of Sikhism's originator, Guru Nānak.[12] My reading will provide a way of probing and reframing—however obliquely—wider questions concerning the nature of the space called Sikh studies, the relationship between religion and violence and its portrayal by the media, the relationship between religion and politics, the question of authority and sovereignty in the Sikh Panth, and, most important, the possibility of tradition as a repetition *without* return to the self of the nation. Part of my agenda in this study is to shift the emphasis away from the personality of individual scholars such as McLeod, who in my opinion has been unfairly targeted by some Sikhs, and to resituate his work in relation to wider debates in the theoretical study of religions and in relation to the question of ideology in the humanities and social sciences. Central to this is the issue of the representation of violence in relation to the "theological" core of religious traditions.

I shall begin by looking at two of McLeod's key statements on Sikh theology (or Sikh doctrine, as he calls it), which are separated by three decades. These texts are *Guru Nānak and the Sikh Religion*, published by Oxford University's Clarendon Press in 1968, and *Sikhism*, published by Penguin in 1998. Let me begin with the 1998 text before coming back to look at a central section in the last chapter of the earlier work.

How Sacred Origins Construct a "Critical" History of the Sikh Religion

Although references to Sikh religiosity can be found scattered throughout W. H. McLeod's works beginning with his 1968 monograph, *Guru Nānak and the Sikh Religion*, his clearest statement concerning the basis of Sikh religious experience can be found in the 1998 volume *Sikhism*. My interest in this book lies in the hermeneutic connection between the two central, though seemingly independent, sections, on history and religion respectively. McLeod's narrative goes something like the following.

Insofar as it is possible to speak of the beginnings of any religious tradition, the religion called Sikhism originated through the teachings of the man Guru Nānak, who can be justly regarded as part of the lineage of the North Indian poet-saints commonly referred to as the Sants. Unlike the Sants who preceded him, however, Nānak founded a community of followers (the early Nānak-panth) comprised mainly of high-caste Hindus (*khatris* and *brahmins*) and passed on the title and status of Guru, which represented spiritual and temporal authority, to a succession of nine living Gurus. Under the first three of these successors, Angad, Amardas, and Ramdas, each of whom consolidated the early Nānak-panth, there was no conflict either with the majority Hindu and Muslim communities or with the rule of the early Mughal emperors Babur, Humayan, and Akbar. Things changed with the accession of Jahangir to the throne in 1605. The fifth Guru, Arjan, appears to have incurred the wrath of Jahangir. This was brought about in part by the expansion of the Nānak-panth under Guru Arjan's tenure, and in part by the fact that this Guru had been inadvertently pulled into the politics of succession to the Mughal throne by giving hospitality to Jahangir's nephew, Amir Khusrau, who was also a rival claimant to the throne. Amir Khusrau raised a rebellion against the emperor, for which he was declared an outlaw and pursued by Jahangir's army toward the northwestern parts of India. During his flight took he refuge at Amritsar, where apparently he was blessed by Guru Arjan. For this transgression Guru Arjan was summoned to Lahore, tried for treason, tortured, and finally executed. Thereafter tensions between the Sikhs and the Mughal empire continued to increase, as Arjan's son and heir, Guru Hargobind, began the process of transforming the peaceful early Nānak-panth into an overtly militarized movement, a process that was facilitated by an influx of lower-caste *jats* (workers, peasants), who helped to swell the ranks of the mostly *khatri* and *brahmin* members of the early Nānak-panth. This process of change and response to the "disturbed circumstances" of the time culminated in 1699 with the founding of the Khalsā under the tenth and last Guru, Gobind Singh. The growth and expansion of Sikh(ism) from the death of the tenth Guru to the present day demonstrates the continuing effects and blueprint of transformation in the shape of militarization.

Insofar as it relies on a well-worn methodology based on historical source criticism, in contradistinction to the traditionalist interpretations, McLeod's narrative can be regarded as academically sound. It reads like any other work within the academic history of religion. It is, in other words, a "critical" history of religion. Its vocation as "critical" precludes it from trusting or taking for granted traditional sources. To make up for this, academic courtesies and apologies will be offered in advance for subjecting tradition to strict historical analysis: "The task must be undertaken with due concern for the feelings of believers." Indeed, "we must take heed of such feelings by expressing ourselves as prudently as possible."[13] But closer scrutiny of McLeod's historical narrative reveals something altogether more interesting. At key junctures the narrative appears to be underpinned by certain assumptions regarding the nature of the Sikh religion in relation to the nature of religion in general. That is to say, the basic historicity of the narrative — its claim to being an historical narrative that presents the *development* of the early Sikh religion (the passage or movement from Guru Nānak to his successors) — is structured not only on the basis of definitive knowledge about the meaning of Guru Nānak's message, but in terms of assumptions about the meaning of religion as such. The passages are worth repeating here since the appearance of the term "religion"/"religions"/"religiosity" reveal a certain urgency in McLeod's narrative:

PANTH OF GURU NĀNAK

What is not based on assumption is the nature of the Panth thus formed. What was the message that Nānak consistently preached, the doctrine that was at the heart of all he said in the works he has left? The message which Nānak preached . . . was love of the divine Name. . . . It was, in other words, an *explicitly religious* message and the people who acknowledge him as Guru did so for *religious reasons*. The Panth was therefore a *religious organization*.   (p. 9; emphasis added).

This body of loyal believers constituted his Sikhs, expressing their oneness by gathering as a *satsang* (a congregation or "fellowship of true believers") for *kīrtan* (hymn singing). The body constituted the Panth, or . . . the Nānak-panth. . . . And *it was a religious* Panth.   (p. 11; emphasis added)

When we go back to the time of Guru Nānak *that message is virtually the sole reason for the existence of the Nānak-panth; and the Nānak-panth is accordingly a religious community* which bound together people who affirmed belief in Nānak's conviction of the all powerful, all-liberating divine Name.   (p. 11; emphasis added)

But Nānak, we must repeat, was the Master of a *religious* community and it is *a strictly religious community* which he passed on to his chosen successor.   (p. 12; emphasis added)

GURU ANGAD

The Panth which Guru Angad had received from Guru Nānak he passed on to his successor, the third Guru, Amar Dās, *essentially unchanged.*   (p. 19; emphasis added)

That it was *still a religious* Panth is beyond question.   (p. 20; emphasis added)

GURU AMAR DĀS

The Nānak-Panth Guru Amar Dās handed on to his successor was therefore the *same as he had received.* . . . It was *still a religious* Panth preaching the message Guru Nānak had taught. . . . Clearly the Panth was continuing on the manner Guru Nānak had left it and clearly *it was the same* Nānak-panth.   (p. 25; emphasis added)

GURU RAM DAS

In 1581 Guru Ram Dās breathed his last. It was still the Nānak-Panth which he passed on to his successor; *that Panth still upheld the divine Name* as the means to liberation.   (p. 27; emphasis added)

GURU ARJAN

The Nānak-Panth was *still a religious* Panth, a Panth with all the features of developing maturity surrounding it, but *still a religious* Panth. It was however, just about to begin the process of change into something more and tradition marks the close of Arjan's life as the hinge of change.   (p. 32; emphasis added)

With the phrase "still a religious Panth" being repeated more than ten times in the space of a few pages, the author could hardly make his point more forcefully! Why such emphasis on the *religious* nature of the early Nānak-Panth and on the *continuity* of the Panth as the same? What is the link between McLeod's deployment of "religious"/"religion" and the continuity of the same (identity)? These questions may seem somewhat banal, especially in view of the fact that both traditional and historical narratives agree on the idea of change and transformation after Guru Arjan's death. At stake here are a nexus of issues that can be fully understood only once we have determined the critical force behind the terms "religion" and "religious" in McLeod's historical narrative. This can be achieved with relative ease by turning to McLeod's chapter on "Sikh Doctrine" in his *Sikhism* (1998), which not only details Nānak's essential teaching about the Name but also gives some clues about McLeod's understanding of the nature of religion and the religious in relation to history.

The Sant Ideal: *nirguṇ bhakti* [14]

According to McLeod, Nānak's teaching can be located broadly within the devotional traditions of Northern India and belongs specifically to the Sant lineage, which stressed the need for interior religion as opposed to external observance. Sant religiosity is based on experience of the divine as ineffable, wholly without form or quality (*nirguṇa*). The *nirguṇa* concept of God contrasts with the notion of God as *saguṇa* found in Vaiṣṇava Hinduism. Although in Hinduism there has always been an unresolved tension between *nirguṇa* and *saguṇa* notions, the contribution of the Sants was to resolve the distinction between them by means of a conception of God that transcends the difference between the two terms.[15] In their practice and teaching the Sants favor a concept of God whose primal aspect is *nirguṇa* and whose secondary aspect is *saguṇa*. A *nirguṇa* deity is essentially a supreme or transcendent God. While devotion to a *nirguṇa* transcendent deity would normally be a logical impossibility,[16] in the case of Sant tradition such devotion is directed toward the transcendent One through the vehicle of the Name. Consequently the experience of such *nirguṇa bhakti* (devotion to the formless divine) is one that is absolutely subjective or interior. Unlike *saguṇa bhakti,* which relies on form, sensuality, worldliness, and time, the experience of *nirguṇa bhakti* involves a permanent stilling of all sensory aspects, culminating in the peace of eternal stasis. This state of immutability characteristic of a *nirguṇa* deity translates on the social level as a retreat into absolute interiority, involving withdrawal from the outside world, and a rejection of worldly activity, especially politics. As such it is an entirely subjective or mystical state. This mystical state defines the nature of true religion itself. As we had occasion to note in chapter 3, *nirguṇ* gives the meaning or essence of religion as such, and religion by definition is nonviolent, nonpolitical, nontemporal.

As others have observed, this correspondence between the eternally static quality of the immutable transcendent One (*nirguṇ*) and the mystical experience of the devotee as absolutely interior can be traced to the Enlightenment tradition of defining mysticism in opposition to the "rational."[17] Thus defined, mysticism comes to represent the preeminently private, the nonrational, and quietism.[18] Moreover, the ascription of mysticism to the Sants is part of a dual strategy, one which (i) ascribes identity to the nature of Sant religiosity so that one can posit it within a comparative history of religions and religious experience, and (ii) simultaneously denies that a Sant could be involved in time, world, and politics. The religious ideal of the Sants, and therefore of Nānak, is a purely contemplative, nonworldly, nonviolent, interior experience (a subjective state of absolute peace, etc.). The very idea that a Sant could become involved in worldly politics would be to transgress the very identity ascribed to Sants and, as a result, the meaning of *nirguṇ bhakti* itself. As such it would transgress the meaning and identity of God as static immutable One. What makes this theory so attractive is the availability of convenient empirical evidence for the characteristics of the Sant ideal. McLeod thus points to the social characteristics of the early Nānak-panth, which happened to be of an entirely peaceful nature, avoiding confrontation and involvement in politics, and composed of mainly conservative-minded devotees belonging to the mostly high-caste *khatris* and *brahmins*, who had little reason to complain about the social and political order they were born into.[19] According to this model, the ideal of *nirguṇ bhakti* and the quietist practice of *nām simaran* associated with it constitute the religious norm of Nānak and the Sants.

If we continue this line of reasoning, however, we find a marked contrast between the practice and teaching of Nānak and the succession of Gurus who came after him, particularly Gurus Amar Dās, Arjan, Hargobind, and Gobind Singh. Judged by the evidence of their actions, these Gurus appear to have *deviated* from the religious norm created by Nānak and the Sants. The later Gurus instituted changes, entered the worldly realm of politics, and even resorted to violence in order to resist the Mughal state. Within McLeod's narrative, these deviations from the religious norm are exemplified by (i) the third Guru, Amar Dās, who further developed the social infrastructure for the Nānak-panth, (ii) fifth Guru Arjan's compilation of a central scripture (the Ādi Granth) and his indirect involvement in the politics of succession by giving refuge to Amir Khusrau, resulting in his martyrdom, (iii) sixth Guru Hargobind's donning of the twin swords, symbolizing the doctrine of *mīrī-pīrī* (the inseparability of spirituality and politics) and his violent confrontation with the state. Lastly and perhaps most famously there is tenth Guru Gobind Singh's creation of the Khalsā, a religio-military order that effectively sets the tone for the historical evolution of Sikhism as a politicized religion with distinct boundaries.

McLeod's narrative utilizes a form of mimesis that is foundational to a conceptualization of religion as *sui generis*. According to this narrative, the *origin* of Sikhism can be located within the religious experience of its founder, Guru Nānak. During Nānak's own lifetime the *quality* of that original experience, and the degree to which his followers could *participate* in the interiority of that experience through *nām simaran* and thereby exclude all externalities, determines the nature of the early Nānak-Panth. As we pass from Nānak to his successors, however, the quality of the original experience becomes diluted, and is further weakened by the active involvement of later Gurus in practical affairs and worldly politics. By the time we get to the Khalsā (two centuries after Guru Nānak's death) the original experience has been well and truly corrupted. According to this mode of interpretation, only Nānak and the members of the early

Nānak-panth remained true to the Sant ideal and can therefore be described as *truly religious*. Accordingly, the Gurus who came after Nānak can only have been imitations or weaker copies of the original.

Despite the obvious differences between "traditionalist" and "historicist" narratives, it becomes abundantly clear that these two narratives are more closely linked than it would first appear. What links them is the conception of an absolute beginning or origin of religion—religion as *sui generis*—in relation to which the narrative evolves. As we have seen in the previous chapter, the "traditionalist" narrative, represented by the Singh Sabhā, locates the origin of Sikhism in Nānak's revelatory communion with God and in the qualitative elevation of this mystical experience above the Hindu/*bhakti* religions. The "traditionalist" origin effectively constitutes a break with and jettisoning of the Hindu maternal womb. The quality of this elevation—or, stated differently, the degree of *originality* of Nānak's experience—was maintained by the succession of living Sikh Gurus and remains intact today within the message of the sacred scripture of the Sikhs, the Ādi Granth. The "traditionalist" narrative has a well-defined teleological and comparative trajectory. While it does not project anything like the end of time or history, it is nevertheless future-oriented. Furthermore its origin as elevation is an extrication from Hinduism as that which is *not yet* properly religion and *not yet* properly history.

Similarly, McLeod's "historical" narrative also locates the origin of Sikhism, which means the truth, or essence, of Sikhism, in Nānak's mystical experience. But unlike the traditionalist narrative, the nature of origin is conceived in accordance with time-honored patterns of Indic religiosity characterized by interiority, stilling of emotions, ascetic detachment from time and world, etc. Unless this origin is maintained through the unadulterated practice of repeating the divine Name (*nām simaraṇ*), the result will be a fall into time, a degeneration of the purity of the religious ideal. Insofar as the development of Sikhism necessarily entails involvement in time and world, both secular historical and religious traditional narratives of Sikhism continue to revolve around a mimesis of the origin. As a result, all phenomena, all events and future "religiosities," are merely supplemental to the origin. Once again McLeod alludes to the plausibility of this theory by citing empirical evidence along with the logical inference that can be reasoned from it: "Our inference is the manner in which people practice *nām simaraṇ* today."[20] In other words, there are definitely some people today who continue to practice *nām simaraṇ* in much the same way as it was practiced four or five hundred years ago.

This mode of practice is based on the vocal repetition of a sound or name, a process that may be internalized with sufficient practice. The aim of this repetition is to be able to repeat the original event and thereby *reproduce* the religious ideal of Sikhism. Upon closer examination, however, it follows that the idea of *nām simaran* as a religious ideal is encoded into the customs and habits of Sikhs today. Those people who most closely conform to this religious ideal today are more likely to be *khatris*, who continue to be regarded as conforming to peaceful, nonviolent, and detached traits of the early Nānak-panth, or Sant ideal. By way of contrast, the *jats* and other lower-caste subgroups, have always had a more relaxed and ambivalent attitude toward the religious ideal and are more likely to deviate from the norm, such as becoming involved in politics or other forms of violence.

Two issues emerge from the above analysis. First, the task of the historian is not as empirical as it might seem. McLeod's protestations to the contrary notwithstanding, any claims for "objectivity" and "disinterestedness" in secular historiography are clearly compromised by even the minimal intellectual transaction with religious theory or theology.[21] The task of historically defining and classifying empirical data or social phenomena within history cannot be done without minimal reference to its other, namely theology or some religious ideal. Whenever the historian claims a certain secularity for his object (Sikh society or any other phenomena), it will always already have been defined in relation to and from within a mimetic representation of time that legitimates its object as secular in terms of its distance from a religious origin. No matter how great this distance, though, it constitutes a minimal *connection* to religion or the religious.

Related to this is the second point, which concerns the nature of change and transformation within the historical narrative. At first sight change/transformation appears to occupy a prominent place in the historical narrative hinging especially on the life and death of the fifth Guru, Arjan. Indeed McLeod contrasts the relatively slow pace of change that occurred up to the fourth Guru with the kind of "radical change" that occurred after the death of the fifth Guru.[22] But what exactly is the difference between "change" and "radical change," when the concept of time that underpins "change" is already determined as a mimesis of the origin? That is, if the historical narrative cannot avoid reference to a concept of time as mimesis, a time that is grounded in the absolute *originality* of Nānak's mystical experience, then "change" will always be supplementary to stasis, where stasis gives the *identity* that governs this mystical experience or origin of Sikh religion. Since "change" is already a break with—a loss or degeneration of—this *identity* (of the essential religious experience of Nānak), then "radical change" merely signifies a greater degree of loss or degeneration rather than a change that occurs in kind.

In and of itself this may not be particularly consequential. But because the question of time (what time *is*) is intrinsic both to the historian's task (of presenting the object of knowledge as past) and to his own identity as a historian (being disinterested and distanced from the object of knowledge), then evidence to the contrary that shows that the historian in fact participates in more than one conception of time, or where there appears to be a discrepancy between the historian's time and the time of his(tory's) object, must be taken seriously since this constitutes a problem for the premises of knowledge formation. If we recall from chapter 2, this was also the problem that dogged Hegel. And as Tomoko Masuzawa has shown, it also continued to plague historians of religion such as Mircea Eliade.[23] Of course, if we simply follow Eliade's lead and discern not one but two distinct strands in McLeod's discourse, then many of the above anxieties simply vanish. One strand is the history of religion(s), that is, the routine practice of producing, presenting, and explaining historical data or phenomena that pertain to entities that project themselves as religions, such as Sikhism. The other strand corresponds to what Eliade calls creative or religious hermeneutics—the discourse in which the historian, contrary to his academic vows of abstinence, participates in the task of thinking or working through the "creative" aspect of religion. Within this strand the historian participates in the "religious" world of his objects like a religious thinker, a philosopher, or a theorist of religion.

In common with most historians of religion, then, McLeod situates the second strand so that it is never overtly present within his corpus of works but rather always below the surface of the properly historical task of presenting phenomena. This second strand of the task of the historian of religion is repressed, kept as far out of sight and earshot as possible. Only in two of McLeod's texts does the religious hermeneutic appear in anything like an overt form: one is the edition of *Sikhism* we have discussed up to now; the other—and in many ways, formative—text in McLeod's corpus is the fifth chapter of his 1968 magnum opus, *Guru Nānak and the Sikh Religion* (GNSR), which attempts to give a definitive overview of what Sikhs call *gurmat*: lit. "the teaching or message of Guru Nānak," what modern Sikhism has termed "Sikh theology." A reexamination of this chapter, entitled "The Teachings of Guru Nānak," is warranted for several reasons. First, this chapter marks a watershed in the modern study of Sikhism in the sense that there will be no significant work of religious hermeneutics or "Sikh theology" after the publication of *GNSR*. Indeed all other explanations of Sikh religiosity since *GNSR* read as footnotes to it. Second, the writing of this fifth chapter signals the "closure," if not the end, of Western academic interest in "Sikh theology." Thereafter most of the academic work in Sikh studies will be focused on Sikh society and its history.

My reading of this chapter will be guided by the following questions. Why does academic research into religious hermeneutics or "Sikh theology" stop so suddenly in modern academic Sikh studies? What exactly is the nature of Guru Nānak's religiosity when this is, on the one hand, valorized and defined by the historian's singular preoccupation with the practice of *nām simaraṇ,* and yet on the other hand, devalued in relation to the proper vocation of the academic researcher in Sikh studies, which is to focus on history? What, then, is the role of the "creative-hermeneutic" for the historian, given that the essential task of modern Sikh praxis is also to recuperate the valorized origin through *nām simaraṇ,* although this mode of praxis is devalued as traditional(ism) or nonmodernity? And, through this devaluation, must the traditionalist defer to the historian when it comes to questions of truth value, etc.? Why, on the one hand, is a working definition of *nām simaraṇ* valorized while, on the other, the attempt to participate is not considered to exist in real time, that is, not to be truly historical, and therefore cannot be part of the academic task? This brings us back to the question: Why does the academic historian himself indulge in the theorization of religion while stating his freedom from it? What exactly is at stake here? Given that the historian can do both tasks yet disallows religious practitioners from participating in both tasks, how does the historian manage to translate between two worlds? To what extent is McLeod's policy repeating the moves of Eliade and Hegel's exclusion of India outside theory and politics by determining the origin in terms of prehistory and history?

What Is Modern Sikh Theology?

W. H. McLeod's equivalent term for what Eliade refers to as "religious" or "creative hermeneutics" is simply "theology." Though well aware that this term is rooted in the Western intellectual and religious tradition, he nevertheless argues that "theology" can legitimately be applied to the Sikh context. For McLeod, Sant doctrine, and more explicitly Guru Nānak's doctrine, gives priority to the *nirguṇ* as opposed to the *sarguṇ* character of God. God's Oneness and transcendent character (*nirguṇ*) are intrinsically connected. Consequently "it is theology we find in the *śabads* and *śloks* of Guru Nānak." Moreover, "[t]heology is the correct word to use in this connection for the whole of Guru Nānak's thought revolves around his understanding of the nature of God."[24] In addition, the fact that "Sikhism is an evolved tradition," with a doctrine that was developed by the Singh Sabhā, renders it "eminently suitable to theological treatment."[25]

McLeod's confidence is misleading, however. For as we saw in the previous chapter, the birth of "Sikh theology" and its equation with the word *gurmat* (lit. "teachings of the Guru") must be considered a pragmatic response or "performative utterance" to a colonial regime of translation that demanded representation in its own conceptual categories, especially the category "theology" (understood broadly as a systematic and coherent doctrine of God), which was seen to be fundamentally lacking in the Sikh scripture. Accordingly the discourse that comes to be regarded as either the "evolution of a tradition" (McLeod) or the "revival of tradition" (Singh Sabhā) is better considered a cultural translation brought about by conditions of colonial rule. As I argued in the previous chapter, the critical move that equates "theology," *gurmat*, and tradition effectively denies that translation took place or, alternatively, affirms that terms such as "theology"/"God"/"religion" are universally translatable across cultures.

Interestingly, McLeod seems to acknowledge this when he asks why the Singh Sabhā scholars, whose discourse had evolved to the point where it could be regarded as "suitable for theological treatment," did not take the theological quest to completion and develop a more integrated and systematic theology.[26] One answer might be that their primary objective was political. It was to inculcate a sense of national identity, of belonging within well-defined boundaries, and in doing so to consolidate the Sikh community as an entity that is sociopolitically distinct from Hinduism. Due to this preoccupation, the Singh Sabhā approach to scholarship remained strong in certain areas, such as scriptural commentary and history. But, for McLeod there remains a significant gap:

Theology, however, was largely neglected. The one major work of theology produced by a Singh Sabhā scholar is Jodh Singh's *Gurmati*

Nirnay, yet even this justly popular work stands at the edge of the discipline rather than within it. *Gurmati Nirnay* is a brief work consisting largely of quotations from scripture, and it presents a series of isolated concepts rather than a closely reasoned statement of the Sikh tradition. Arguably, it should be regarded as an addition to the several commentaries of the period rather than as a contribution to Sikh theology.

The example set by *Gurmati Nirnay* has been followed ever since, with the result that the theological analysis of Sikhism remains undeveloped. Brief studies of individual concepts occasionally appear, but the effort is seldom made to build these blocks into a single integrated structure. Even when several concepts are treated in sequence, the result typically remains a series of discrete items, with little evidence of a developing pattern or unified result. A theology of Sikhism, integrated and comprehensive, has yet to be written.

... Singh Sabhā scholars put considerable effort into identifying and defining specific features of the tradition. The problem arises from the fact that they generally stopped at that point, leaving the integrated analysis to a later generation.[27]

McLeod's comments are both interesting and insightful, as they reveal the limits of the scriptural commentaries produced by the Singh Sabhā. However, the delimitation of "Sikh theology" as the proper domain for any essential thinking about the teachings of the Sikh Gurus, or the religious experience proper to Sikhism, is more problematic and needs to be considered more carefully. Especially perplexing is that toward the end of the article McLeod calls for the production of a systematic Sikh theology, a "Sikh theology for modern times," in order to complete the task that Singh Sabhā scholars like Bhāī Vīr Singh and Bhāī Jodh Singh left unfinished. Yet two decades earlier McLeod had himself attempted just such a completion in chapter five of *GNSR* ("The Teachings of Guru Nānak"), through a close reading of Jodh Singh's *Gurmati Nirnai* followed by an attempt to go beyond that work, that is to say, an attempt to fill the "significant gap" left by the Singh Sabhā scholars. What interests me is why a historian who professes no connection to the questions that motivate adherents of a religious tradition would himself attempt such a thing. What is at stake in the attempt to transgress the limits of a tradition? To find out let us continue to follow the trajectory of McLeod's fifth chapter in GNSR.

As we have seen, Bhāī Vīr Singh and Jodh Singh attempted, in different ways, to ground Sikh doctrine on the basis of a rigorous conceptualization of the transcendent One using indigenous sources and language. At the outset of his exposition of Sikh theology McLeod closely follows the Singh Sabhā model insofar as his first move is to define the central attributes, or the "nature of God." For this purpose the *mūl mantar*, or opening statement, from the Ādi Granth "serve[s] both as a starting point and as a final summary," as it is accepted by Sikh tradition as a declaration of the unity of God. The unity of God is therefore the central defining attribute of God's nature. This is followed by several pages of exposition that reiterate the classic Singh Sabhā theme affirming that Sikhism is neither Hinduism nor pantheistic, and that God is ineffable (*nirguṇ*) but revealed through his phenomena (*sarguṇ*). However, the expression of God's absolute unity, or transcendence, is the *nirguṇ* aspect, even though this attribute "receives little attention, for beyond the mere affirmation there is nothing man can say of it" except when the devotee experiences it "in the ultimate condition of absolute union."[28] Hence the *realization* of this unity and transcendence, the actual *path* to God, and therefore the means of achieving release or salvation, must be concerned with God's immanent, or *sarguṇ*, aspect. What this means, therefore, is that God dwells *within* the human heart. McLeod makes much of this point: "Here we are at the crucial point, the point at which there can exist communication between God and man." Through such communication, the normally unregenerate nature of man can be transformed and man can be saved. This "communication between God and man" is in effect the expression of God's saving activity: "Here, in the divine Order (*hukam*), is the inscription of His will for all who are able to read it. Here it is that the Word (*śabda*) and the Name (*nām*) acquire the substance which renders them meaningful to the human understanding. And here it is that the Guru's voice is to be heard."[29]

As McLeod rightly emphasizes, however, none of the Singh Sabhā scholars were able to develop this specific point, that is, the connection between God and man, or how God communicates with man. In fact they never managed to go much further than to demonstrate the nature of God's unity. Despite a recognition of the doctrine of immanence, what these scholars failed to do was to go beyond transcendence (Bhāī Vīr Singh) or to go beyond merely stating the equivalence of Guru and Word (Jodh Singh). The result, as McLeod notes, "has been an inability to give a satisfactory, coherent answer to the question of *how* in the thought of Guru Nānak, God communicates with man. The question has been allowed to remain a mystery." Referring directly to Jodh Singh's analysis of these terms in *Gurmati Nirnai*, McLeod goes on to say that "it is not sufficient to state that the Guru is God, that *hukam* is His will, that the *śabda* is the divine Word, and that the *nām* represents the sum total of all God's qualities. Not all of these definitions can be accepted without qualification, and even if they could be so accepted the basic question would still remain unanswered."[30] In fact it appears from this statement that this was the very question that the Singh Sabhā scholars were incapable of articulating. The real question remained a mystery until McLeod rearticulates it on their behalf: "In what way is the divine word so presented to the human understanding that it can be recognized, accepted, and followed. This is the fundamental question."[31]

By framing the question in this way McLeod shows an acute awareness of the limits of Singh Sabhā discourse, notably their "inability" to explain the age-old problem of the "movement" between the transcendent (*nirguṇ*) and immanent aspects (*sarguṇ*) of the divine. Stated differently, this movement refers to the going-out/mediation/ expression of the divine into the world that is experienced through time and language. Within the Sikh scripture the possibility of such expressive movement is closely associated with the interlinked notions of *guru, śabda,* and *nām,* all of which refer to language as simultaneously divine and human, and ultimately to the question of sovereignty as it emerges in Sikh thought.

The fact that these terms refer simultaneously to language, to the divine, and to the question of sovereignty should already alert us to the possibility of an intriguing connection between the teachings of the Sikh Gurus (and of course other related movements in Indic traditions) and recent "death of God" strands of continental philosophy of religion that have explored such themes in detail. But as I shall try to show below, McLeod's creative hermeneutic, which unfolds in the important subsection of the fifth chapter entitled "Divine Self-Expression," has served to shift attention away from the terms *guru/śabda/nām* as a nexus that might invite further and deeper reflection on the relationship between language and sovereignty in Sikh thought.

In order to explain how and why this occurs, it is necessary to analyze the interrelated nexus of the terms *guru/śabda/nām* in some detail. I shall proceed by pointing out some aspects of the concept of "guru" in Sikh tradition prior to its reinterpretation during the colonial period by notable Singh Sabhā scholars such as Jodh Singh. While it may seem like a digression, it will help to highlight some important nuances and conceptual continuities between the precolonial, colonial, and postcolonial understandings of the term "guru." This in turn will be useful for introducing themes such as orality and writing in the South Asian context, which will be discussed at length in the next chapter.

My discussion will begin by looking at Jodh Singh's rendering of these terms in his *Gurmati Nirnai* before returning to McLeod's account of this particular nexus of words. True to his claim, McLeod's account will read as the most theologically systematic and lucid. Paradoxically, however, in his attempt to be more systematic, McLeod's account also allows us to see how and why terms that refer to language become transcendentalized or deontologized (to use Michel de Certeau's term) within his rendering of "Sikh theology." My interest, to repeat what I stated earlier, is not only to ascertain what is at stake in such a deontologization of language, but, following Martin Heidegger's later thinking about language, to determine how it may be possible to *re*-ontologize the question of language. I want to ask, in other words, what possible theoretical and sociopolitical consequences might follow from regarding language as radically immanent.

Guru, Śabda, Nām: Language and the Location of Author(ity)

Precolonial Period

During the lifetime of the Sikh Gurus, the Guru-Sikh relationship remained largely within the Indian tradition of oral mediation. The question "What is a guru?" did not arise.[32] A living guru's spoken word and personality were taken as marks of authority. This continued during the lifetime of the ten Sikh Gurus. Prior to his death, however, historical sources suggest that the tenth and last living (*dehdhārī*),[33] or human, Guru declared that all authority (and thus the role of Guru itself) would pass to the Ādi Granth, or sacred scripture of the Sikhs, which henceforth would be known as Guru Granth, and to the corporate community of the Khalsā.[34] Hence the doctrine of dual authority: Guru Granth (Guru as text) and Guru Panth (Guru as Khalsā).[35]

Although there does not appear to have been a consensus over the acceptance of dual authority in the early decades of the eighteenth century, historical sources do suggest that the dual doctrine of Guru Granth and Guru Panth had a direct impact on Sikh polity in the later decades. According to J. S. Grewal, "what was needed most was a sense of solidarity and unity of action."[36] Hence the belief that the Guru was present among the Sikhs both as text (Granth) and as community (Panth) aided the evolution of a related institution known as *Gurūmatā,* which played a pivotal role in the political struggle of the Sikhs at this time. The word *matā* in Punjabi means a decision agreed upon by common consent. Hence a *Gurūmatā* was seen by the majority of Sikhs as both a morally binding resolution and a medium for the expression of political authority and sovereignty.[37] Given that the Khalsā Sikhs were mainly preoccupied with survival during this relatively unstable period, and could not manage their shrines and other centers of learning, the management of Sikh shrines, and as a result most of the exegetical and interpretive work on texts considered sacred by the Sikhs, passed into the custodianship of the Udāsī and Nirmalā ashrams throughout North India.

In the early decades of the nineteenth century with the establishment of Sikh rule under Maharaja Ranjit Singh, the lands occupied by the new Sikh ruling class were redistributed and administered among his followers, many of whom belonged to the former Sikh *misls.* As Khalsā Sikhs became more politically settled and as Ranjit Singh's rule became more autocratic, the *Gurūmatā* was effectively abolished, thereby ensuring that the doctrine of Guru Panth would lose its efficacy.[38] At the same time, however, Ranjit Singh continued to patronize Udāsī and Nirmalā ashrams. The single most important result of this was the more pronounced diffusion of Vedic and Purānic concepts into existing Sikh interpretive frameworks, especially the framework for understanding the teachings of the Sikh Gurus (*gurmat*). One of the concepts that begins to affect the understanding of *gurmat* is the notion of time as an eternally recurring cycle associated with the figure of the Hindu deity Viṣṇu. As one of the three principal gods of popular Hinduism, the figure of Viṣṇu, being associated with the sun, with light and luminosity, represents the fundamental life instincts of preservation, sustenance, growth—in general the desire for an enhancement of and increase in life, indeed for eternal existence. At the popular level this notion of time is interpreted in terms of the eternal avatārs (incarnations) of Viṣṇu, and on another level through the Brahmanic notion of *sanātana dharma,* or the continuity of tradition without beginning or end.[39]

In the Sikh context the consequences of this doctrine were twofold. First, the Sikh Gurus could be represented as incarnations of Viṣṇu. The conflation of the attributes of Viṣṇu—eternal light and life—results in the banishment of death, a refusal to accept the death of the Sikh Gurus, indeed a refusal to accept death as such. Death is forever delayed in the sense that the principle that authorizes the notion of "what is a guru," that is, the *essence* of a guru, is none other than the Viṣṇu principle, which can be incarnated in a variety of other human or nonhuman forms. One of the consequences of this is the proliferation of *dehdhārī* gurus and other ascetics, all claiming to be avatārs of Viṣṇu.

Second, and what is not so much a consequence, but probably the enabling factor for the proliferation of *dehdhārī* gurus and the avatār paradigm, is the predominance of the oral context for the reception and transmission of Indian culture as a whole. If what marks the post-guru period is the loss of the living guru, the guru as a face-to-face speaking being, then this loss is the loss of the immediate presence associated with the guru's *voice*, and as a result the status of his *spoken* word as divinely inspired. If so, the following equation can justifiably be thought to represent this particular situation: GURU = AUTHORITY = VOICE OR SPOKEN WORD. Due to the all-pervasive oral paradigm, for any written text to be accepted as guru, the belief had to be inspired that the text was still animated by the living presence of a human voice.

In effect there is a convergence here between (i) the paradigm of orality (i.e., sound as the privileged element of eternity and the sacred) and (ii) the paradigm of the avatār (with its conceptualization of time as an endlessly recurring circle).[40] This convergence between circular time and sacred sound finds expression in the role of the human voice as that which under*pins* the temporal and spiritual authority of a *dehdhārī* guru, and at the same time under*mines* the written text. What needs to be unraveled here is the connection between time, the oral, and the written in the Indian context. A fuller discussion on this crucial topic will be deferred till chapter 5. It should suffice to note, however, that the pervasive influence of a Brahmanic metaphysics of sound helped the Sikh community to make a psychological transition from the *death* of a living guru to the *birth* of the written, but only at a cost. For at the same time it acts as an instrument of cultural censorship on a massive scale.[41]

Colonial Period: Jodh Singh's Gurmat Nirnai *and the Problem of Shared Idioms*

By the mid-nineteenth century, the oral domain had begun to give way under colonial influence to the dominance of the printing press.

Perhaps more than any other single factor, what distinguishes the inter-pretative situation of the Singh Sabhā scholars is their mastery of print culture.[42] As a consequence of this new technology the Singh Sabhā elites were able to standardize the text of the Ādi Granth, a move that effectively eradicated controversies over the acceptance of this particular text as well as rival manuscripts. Despite the shift to a standardized text, the continued popular appeal of personal living gurus as well as the reli-ance on the metaphysics of sound—hence the continuity of the avatār paradigm—could not be easily eradicated. As is evident from their po-lemics, commentaries, and exegeses on the notion of guru, there seems to have been an abiding preoccupation with removing all vestiges of what was regarded as "Hindu" influence.

It is within this context that Jodh Singh takes up the issue of authority in his *Gurmat Nirnai* by suggesting that the word *sat(i)-guru*[43] should be regarded as a referent of ultimate authority. For Jodh Singh and other Singh Sabhā ideologues the central question was: "Who is the 'True' Guru?"[44] After reproducing a series of quotations, he argues that wher-ever the word "guru" is used in Sikh scripture, it is intended to replace the sanātan notion of avatār.[45] Traditionally it had been held that an avatār comes into existence from out of the void (nonexistence) in order to rees-tablish *dharma* (moral order):[46]

> But according to *gurmat* [the teachings of Sikh Gurus] God is never in-carnated. Accordingly, the Sikh belief is that at such a time it is a Guru that appears. It is evident that in Sikh usage the word "guru" assumes those meanings originally associated with "avatār." As such it refers to those special beings sent by God to reveal the path of truth again. It does not possess the meanings that Hindus ordinarily attach to the word "guru" . . . (in which case) . . . each Hindu would attach himself to some exalted person whom he regards as a guru, in order that he might develop spiritually. Even within a single family (not to mention the country as a whole) there might be several preceptors. Such people may not actually claim to have been sent by God . . . (but) . . . failure to realize this difference has led some Sikhs astray.[47]

To further emphasize this contrast with the Hindu understanding of "guru," Jodh Singh pushes the meaning of "guru" toward the notion of prophet or God's personal messenger sent to reveal the path of True reli-gion.[48] This line of reasoning bears some obvious validity as far as living gurus are concerned. But for the Singh Sabhā scholars the only physical guru was the written text, which made it somewhat easier to borrow more directly from Middle Eastern religious traditions and so to move away from the sanātan sphere of influence.

That this logic did not always result in the desired consistency of argument is best illustrated by Jodh Singh's exposition of *śabda* (word or sound), which is treated under the chapter heading "*Anhad Śabda* (unstruck word or sound)."[49] Much of this chapter consists of an attempt to show that the Sikh version of *anhad śabda*[50] owes nothing either to the prior Nāth usage of the term, or to its prevalence within the theory and practice of Haṭha-Yoga. Much of the rhetoric is directed at Nāth-Yogic conventions, which place emphasis on the hearing of a mystical sound (*anhad śabda*) by those who have mastered certain physical techniques.[51] It would appear, though, that the target of Jodh Singh's criticisms is not so much the efficacy of the physical exercises, but the metaphysical doctrine of sound (*nād*) that underpins Nāth and Yogic usage.

The argument itself revolves around the meaning of the word *anhad*. As Jodh Singh reads it, the dominant metaphysical doctrine of sound comes from Patañjali's Yoga-Sūtras. In keeping with the primacy of the oral domain within Indian tradition, the essence of *śabda* is *nād*, i.e., sound or vibration. Without the qualifier *anhad,* the terms *śabda* and *nād* represent conventional or physical sound that can be heard by all and sundry. *Anhad nād*, however, cannot be heard via the physical organ of the ear. It can only be "heard" (in the sense of heard-understood) by those who have mentally and physically prepared themselves for it, that is, by those who have cultivated the "inner organ" by means of which alone it is possible to attain union with the *anhad nād*. Possibly because the target of this theory is the mind, and therefore has a psychological undertone, when translated into philosophical/theological terminology, it is best rendered by a monistic concept of divinity. By contrast, Jodh Singh elaborates a somewhat simpler theory where *śabda* is not any sound, mystical or otherwise, but quite simply the divine Word that mediates knowledge of God to man.[52] *Śabda* is *guru-kā-śabda* (Guru's Word) and *gurbānī* is the utterances of the Guru as recorded in scripture.[53] But in trying to explain what *anhad* means, Jodh Singh's interpretation inadvertently falls back on the very metaphysics he is trying to eliminate. To further define *anhad* Jodh Singh uses terms such as "eternal/undying" and "unbroken/continuous" in order to characterize the connection between *śabda* and the mind or memory (*mn*) of a listener or reader.[54] This connection is clearly also psychological and meant to attune the senses in a certain way.[55] Given that his aim was to demarcate the boundary between the Sikh and Hindu positions on a firmer basis, the resulting definition is not entirely convincing: *anhad* refers to a state of mind achieved by inculcating the teaching of the Guru (*gurupdesh*), a state of mind in which there is unbroken attachment to (and knowledge of) God's Name. Clearly, both positions ultimately depend on a similar principle: a metaphysics of eternity, the eternality of the present moment, of continuous attachment to God, a state of undivided being, and therefore, a suppression of temporality.

My point here is not to prove that Jodh Singh is right or wrong but to point out the paradoxical nature of the problem. The Singh Sabhā scholars made strenuous efforts to show that Sikhs are not Hindus by undertaking to prove that their cultural texts represent a break with, and therefore belong outside of, the Hindu tradition. Ironically, however, they are able to articulate their nonidentity only by differentiating idioms that were shared by many other North Indian cultures.

There is a further complication in the Singh Sabhā's attempt to mark out a definitive boundary between themselves and the "Hindu." This complication appears in their attempts to authorize a separate identity, a move that required them to transcendentalize or deontologize the very language they were using by demarcating the ownness and oneness of the Punjabi language. By their doing so, Punjabi language is removed from its heterolingual ground and becomes homolingual. By thus breaking with its own cultural difference, the very difference that allowed idioms to be shared, Punjabi language loses its being and becomes instead a mere marker and carrier of identity whose ultimate referent is a theological principle, a static immutable One. Ironically, however, the very authority that was required for establishing an alternative (i.e., *non-Hindu*) metaphysical basis for the fundamental words of "their own" tradition (words such as *śabda/guru/nām*) comes not so much from Punjabi—which, as stated above, provided a gritty resistance to the establishment of strictly metaphysical boundaries—but from the Western theological tradition and, specifically, in Jodh Singh's case, from the English language. A good example of this can seen by comparing Jodh Singh's enunciations on the same topic in his native Punjabi (for example, in *Gurmat Nirnai*) and in articles written by him in English (such as "Theological Concepts in Sikhism" or "Sikh Philosophy").[56]

If we take *anhad śabda* or *śabda* within the Punjabi text of *Gurmat Nirnai* as our example, what becomes quite clear is the impossibility for Jodh Singh and others to avoid metaphors of sound, despite the fact that the *śabda* as guru is a written text. This is the result primarily of the strength of the oral tradition itself, but also derives from the musical structure of the Ādi Granth. References to *rāg*, *dhun*, and *nād*[57] are therefore consistently used when referring to union with "God" and to describe the state of mind concerned.[58] The only way for Jodh Singh to establish anything like a concrete difference between Sikh and Hindu idioms is to negate references to sound as mere figures of speech. Once the references to sound are seen as metaphors, they lose their "reality" status; they become deontologized. On the other hand, within his English texts, explanations of *śabda-guru* take on a very different emphasis. References to *anhad* are conveniently dropped, there being no firm basis for comparative assessment of this term except, as I have said, as "mere" metaphor. *Śabda* on its own is much easier to explain: "The guru communicates his ideas through the Word . . . it is the Word of the guru that is the guru."[59]

For our purposes, the main point is that the notion of authority, and therefore the whole idea of how *śabda* in itself can be authoritative, carries a different connotation in Punjabi and English respectively. The indigenous Punjabi terminology is governed by an impersonal notion of reality as sound. Consequently there is neither author nor origin as such. *Śabda* as sound is the ultimate principle, though this does not mean that this notion of reality is materialistic. When Jodh Singh tries to differentiate the Sikh version of *śabda* by referring to it as unbroken/continuous/eternal, he is unable to escape the grasp of the metaphysical principle irrespective of whether it is Vedāntic monism or Patañjali's *yoga* theory. This metaphysical principle is the cyclical notion of time,[60] which inevitably favors avatārs and *dehdhārī* gurus.

When Jodh Singh's idiom switches to English, however, *śabda* is interpreted by way of reference to a once-and-for-all act of creation *ex nihilo*, a once-and-for-all communication between God and man, where the Guru plays the part of messenger. There is a more concrete sense of authority here grounded and guaranteed by God. For the Singh Sabhā scholars it was easier to counter the influence of *dehdhārī* gurus by adopting these overtly theological concepts. Hence God's communication is now revealed in Guru Nānak's word as recorded in the Ādi Granth, which meant that the written text is invested with sole authority. As a rhetorical principle this is perfectly defensible. In practice, however, the written text remained a collection of dead letters unless it could be made to speak, unless, that is, some living presence could be found to inspire the text. It is to fulfill this requirement that Singh Sabhā scholarship, and following it modern Sikh interpreters, settled for a Christianized understanding of the notion of guru as an "Eternal Verbum," though without a full awareness of its political implications.

This brings our discussion back to McLeod's earlier observation: that this is precisely the point where the Singh Sabhā's interpretative project stopped. They did not, indeed could not, go past this particular point. As McLeod has correctly noted, what the Singh Sabhā scholars failed to do was to show *how* God communicates with man. In other words, they failed to show *how* the Word-as-Guru or Guru-as-Word (*śabda-guru*) is authoritative. Despite stating the rather obvious analogy between the Punjabi and English terms, that "Guru is God, that Hukam is His Will, that *śabda* is the divine Word, and that Nam represents the sum total of all God's qualities," the result remained an inability to give a satisfactory coherent answer to how in the thought of Guru Nānak God communicates with man.[61] As if to remedy this shortcoming, McLeod presents a modified version of Jodh Singh's *Gurmat Nirnai* schema in the fifth chapter of *GNSR*. It reads as follows: (i) nature of God, (ii) nature of unregenerate man, (iii) Divine self-expression, and (iv) the discipline. This schema is perhaps closer to what McLeod would consider as the systematic discipline of theology and the best way to represent Nānak's teachings. For our purposes the section entitled "The Divine Self-Expression" is most relevant, for it is here that McLeod attempts to remedy the basic shortcoming of the Singh Sabhā scholars, the point beyond which they could not go. Their main shortcoming was that they could not universalize the meaning of *śabda or nām*. Let me therefore turn to the key section in McLeod's own rendering of "Sikh theology," entitled the "Divine Self-Expression."

Reading the "Divine Self-Expression"

Presence: The Guru as Voice

McLeod's conceptual schema for presenting Guru Nānak's teaching differs only superficially from Jodh Singh's. The most obvious difference is that McLeod condenses three of Jodh Singh's chapters, on *satguru* (Guru), *nām* (the Name), and *anhat śabda* (Word), into a single section called "The Divine Self-Expression," thereby allowing it to take precedence over the discussion on "discipline" and eliminating the need for a chapter on creation. However, the central question motivating both McLeod's and Jodh Singh's discussions tended to revolve around the same basic issue: namely, the problem of authority or sovereignty in contemporary Sikhism. For McLeod specifically this problem has to be mediated via the following questions: Who is a (true) Guru? Who was the *guru* of Guru Nānak? What kind of authority is passed on between a dying human guru and his living successor? How are we to understand the passage of authority from the succession of living Gurus to scripture (the Ādi Granth)? What does it mean for words of scripture, indeed, a "mere" text to be Guru? What does it mean for Word to be Guru? And for the Guru to be Word?

Clearly the question of authority revolves around the presence or absence of a living guru. Implicit within McLeod's reading is that Jodh Singh and others could not effectively answer this question, as they were preoccupied with contesting the "Hindu" paradigm of the avatār. Given that the Indian paradigm devalued the written word/text, the issue of divine authority could not be taken beyond the living oral word, the word of face-to-face communication, the passage of words from the mouth of the guru to the ear of the disciple. Once this circuit linking mouth and ear had ceased with the death of a living Guru, the Singh Sabhā were unable to show how the sense of divinity that animated the living Guru was transferred to the written word. According to McLeod, they failed to show how *communication could survive* beyond the living presence of spoken words, that is, beyond the context of speech and orality. "Communication" is the key term here, because not only does it signify survival, the living on beyond death and time, but it also explains the manner in which the divine Word is so presented to the human understanding that it can be recognized, accepted, and followed.[62]

For McLeod this communication is part of the self-expression of the Divine. It constitutes the creative impulse of God, a going-out from void or absolute self-absorption. To say that it is creative suggests something like God's absolute nonreliance on anything else, anything outside of God. "Divine self-expression" is therefore a principle of self-empowerment, that which enables the divine to be incarnated within a human body. The divine is communicative or communication in that it provides the substance that renders meaning to human understanding as opposed to nonmeaning. It is this understanding that differentiates humans from animals. And it is within human understanding "that the Word (*śabda*) and the Name (*Nām*) acquire the substance which renders them meaningful to human understanding. It is here that Guru's voice is to be heard."[63]

In other words, the substance of communication is voice. As we shall see, the notion of voice is pivotal to McLeod's presentation of systematic Sikh theology. To discern its role more fully, however, it is necessary to ask *how* communication occurs and what is being communicated to the human understanding. To answer this question McLeod turns to an analysis of several key words — including *śabda* (word), *nām* (name of God), *guru* (spiritual preceptor), and *sach* (Truth) — that can be summarized as follows. *Śabda* (word) has a reformative — as distinguished from an ontological — function in Nānak's poetry. It functions as the "vehicle" of communication and "provides the means" for soteriological release. Further, although *nām* and *śabda* are synonymous, *śabda* is the "medium of communication" whereas *nām* is the "object of communication."[64] Accordingly *śabda* and *nām* can be distinguished with regard to their roles: *nām* is the object of worship. It constitutes the referent or signified of the *śabda*, which is merely the carrier or receptacle of *nām*, and therefore secondary. The supplementary nature of *śabda* becomes more apparent in its connection to the term *guru*. In this case, *śabda* is qualified by *Guru*: it is the Guru's word (*gur-kā-śabda*). The linguistic term *śabda* therefore merely points to *guru* as its nonlinguistic referent. Strictly speaking *śabda* is always the *medium* whereas *guru* is that which communicates or animates *śabda*.

This line of reasoning is fairly evident when the Guru in question happens to be a living and fully present personality, someone who is regarded as a creative and perfect personality and who stands as guide and exemplar.[65] But what happens when the Guru is no longer present in body and voice? Or when there is no longer a possibility of reliance on a living voice or body, as is the case when the Guru is a text or scripture? The obvious example of this is the event following the death of the tenth and last living Guru of the Sikhs, Guru Gobind Singh. According to Sikh tradition, just before his death Guru Gobind Singh passed on his personal authority not to a human guru but to the scripture (that is, to the text known as Ādi Granth, which thenceforth became known as the Guru Granth Sāhib) and to the community of those initiated into the order of the Khalsā.[66] In the absence of the living Guru, Sikh tradition has held the text of the Guru Granth to be the Word of the Guru and therefore the final authority ever since.

But this transfer of authority of the Word of the Guru to text is not as radical as it might sound. As McLeod rightly argues, the Sant tradition (and Guru Nānak, who followed suit) had already made a "major modification" to the traditional Indian doctrine of guru. The Sants did not acknowledge any human guru as the source of their wisdom. For the Sants and for Nānak the real guru is the *satguru*, which is effectively a nonhuman principle. The term *satguru* is meant to designate the idea that enlightenment for both the Sants and for Nānak was nonmediated. It did not come from a human source but from their own experience. Guru Nānak himself states that *his* guru, *his* authority is the Word (*śabda guru surat dhun chelā*: the Word is guru, my consciousness attuned to it is its disciple[67]). McLeod refers to the *satguru* principle as "an inner voice." It is the "mystical movement" or "light of God" found in the innermost recesses of the human soul." However, a strict identification between Guru and God is also to be avoided because the Guru, strictly speaking, is the *agent* of revelation whereas God is the *object* of revelation. Consequently the Guru can be identified with the "Voice of God." The "Voice" is accordingly "the means whereby God imparts truth to man."[68]

With the idea that "Voice" is the privileged substance by means of which God communicates with man, and that what is communicated by "Voice" is truth, McLeod underscores the conceptual circularity of his formulation. Indeed all of these words (*śabda/nām/guru*) are simply different aspects of an all-embracing concept of Truth (*sach*) which gives them their fundamental identity.[69] That identity can be neatly expressed in the formula:

> The Guru accordingly *is* God; the Guru *is* the Voice of God; and the Guru *is* the Word, the Truth of God.[70]

Absence: The Guru as Writing

With extensive quotes from the Ādi Granth to support its argument, McLeod's exegesis on "Divine Self-Expression" gives the impression of having consummated the desire of Sikh reformist scholars to formulate *gurmat* as a "Sikh theology." In one sense this is true. While the Singh Sabhā scholars collectively struggled to extricate *gurmat* from an Indian orality that privileged the human context of living gurus as face-to-face communicators of truth, McLeod easily connects the notion of authority directly to the "Voice of God" as the ultimate principle that underpins the communication of truth. However, if the properly critical move that takes place in McLeod's work, namely, the transmutation of the living Guru's voice into the "Voice" of God, can be shown to be a case of cultural translation, the question that then arises is whether it is possible to comprehend the terms *śabda/guru/nām* from an entirely different perspective—one that does not conform to the desire for ontotheological presence.

Though not generally recognized, such a possibility presents itself if we allow ourselves to take seriously—that is to say *literally*—the traditional Sikh belief that just prior to his death, spiritual authority was transferred by the last living Guru, Gobind Singh, to the text of the Ādi Granth, which henceforth became known as the Guru Granth. In other words, after the death of the living Guru, a radical absence of the signified (which represents meaning in the moment-to-moment presence of the living Guru) becomes concomitant with the written word or text. One could also argue that within the modern Sikh context, manifestations of this absence include a bibliolatry or idolization of the Ādi Granth (often portrayed as Khalsā "orthodoxy") or the hankering for personal gurus (anti-Khalsā "heterodoxy"). Both of these phenomena can be regarded as a sign of the community's psychological repression of the immediate implications of absence. Whatever the merits or demerits of such an argument, it is possible to show that the idea that the Guru is *literally* the Word, and that the Word is *literally* language—nothing more and nothing less than language—may be far more radical than is generally given credit.

Such an argument, however, counteracts the reversal that has taken place in modern man's relationship to language, the so-called deontologization of language wherein language loses its being and becomes a mere vehicle for communicating ideas and concepts between human beings who possess the same self-consciousness. When language is thus deontologized, man presumes to be the originator and thus the owner of the words he speaks. This manner of thinking about the relationship between man and language has come to be regarded as completely natural, a way of thinking that can be universally affirmed according to a common sense that is shared by all humanity. According to this way of thinking, the essence of humanity is bound up with the notion that man is a self-conscious thinking being who stands above animals because he is able to think and express his thoughts.[71]

In the context of Guru Nānak's teaching, however, one might need to explore a rather different set of propositions. For example, if Word, or *śabda*, is literally language (as written and spoken) and if such language corresponds to an absence of human presence (as voice), then language *of itself* is the preceptor or guru. Language *of itself* is the giver and that which is given. Stated otherwise: the "origin" of Word is language itself! Such a thesis is not far removed from the notion of *satguru* as a nonhuman form of mediation. From an ontotheological perspective, however, one that is also central to modern "Sikh theology," such a thesis is unacceptable. How can mere language authorize itself? How can language, a mere supplement or medium, be guru? If one is to take these questions seriously it is necessary to transgress the usual scenarios of *śabda* as medium of "revelation," or as the medium for communication between God and man. It involves questioning the order of signification that we regard as natural or as a matter of common sense, and that subordinates language to transcendental concepts such as "Voice" (consciousness), "God," or "Truth."

One of the most sustained attempts to invert the ontotheological order of signification can be found in Jacques Derrida's readings of Edmund Husserl in texts such as *Speech and Phenomena* and *Edmund Husserl's "Origin of Geometry."* Husserl's philosophical texts not only provided one of the most lucid modern reformulations of ontotheology, but also provided the philosophical basis for the phenomenology of religion, a discipline that inherits ontotheology in the guise of secular historicism. What this inversion means and how it relates on the one hand to the scenario of absence — the empty place of authority that was previously occupied by a living guru, exemplified in Sikh tradition by the phenomenon of the guru as writing or text — and on the other to McLeod's theological hermeneutics needs to be spelled out more fully. In the theoretical digression that follows, I argue that Derrida's retrieval of the ontology of language in his readings of Husserl can be usefully deployed to show what is going on in the reduction of language (and hence the function of Guru) to the metaphysical concept of "Voice" in W. H. McLeod's text. More important, though, it allows us to situate McLeod's determination of Guru-as-Voice within a broader realm of signification that is intrinsic to the phenomenological experience and to the operation of phenomenology within the study of religions.

Voice, Language, Subjectivity: A Theoretical Digression

It would not take great powers of advocacy to show that McLeod's exegesis on the "Voice" taps into an order of signification — one that has come to be regarded as normal, natural, a matter of "common" sense—in which the central position is occupied by Man. According to this "common" sense way of thinking, which by self-definition can be universally affirmed by all like-minded individuals, the essence of what it means to be human, as opposed to animal, consists in the idea that man is the *zoon logon echon*—the animal who has the capacity to talk, or to say something about something. In contrast to the animal, man possesses the *logos* (from the Greek verb *legein*, to say or talk), which means that man alone is able to think logically. Logical thinking therefore presupposes the following components: (i) the assertion of something about something, (ii) the necessity of words or language as the vehicle of this assertion, (iii) a subject about which the assertion is made and which is somehow immediately and continuously present.[72] Thus if man is defined in terms of his capacity for thinking, this thinking is realized only in its coming-to-words, i.e., in the capacity for language. Insofar as language not only facilitates the "materialization" of thinking but happens to be the very matter of thinking, language is ontological. Language has being.[73]

But if language, just like man, has being, if language exists, how does it lose its being and come to be regarded as some*thing* that man possesses? Or to use de Certeau's term, how does language come to be deontologized? Heidegger's answer to this points to the interpretation of Being as presence. Derrida, who follows Heidegger's initial lead, argues that this interpretation of being finds its clearest and most influential articulation in the tradition of phenomenology represented by Husserl. For Husserl the determination of being as presence takes two forms: (i) objective: something *is* insofar as it presents itself as an objectivity presented to thought; (ii) subjective: a subject *is* only insofar as it is self-present. It must be present to itself in the immediacy of any conscious act. These two forms provide phenomenology with its axial concept, namely, apodictic evidence: the call for objects to be presented or brought forth to an immediate and self-present intuition, a transcendental consciousness, the realm of what is primordially "my own." By contrast anything that is empirical, worldly, subject to time stands opposed to this realm of self-present own-ness. It constitutes the sphere of otherness, that which is mediated and which is therefore different from self-present conscious life. The distinction between these spheres—the sphere that is "my own," which implies immediacy, as opposed to the sphere that denotes "otherness," which implies the necessity for mediation—underpins Husserl's account of language.[74]

The purpose of language, for Husserl, is to function as a tool. Language is basically an instrument for recording and transmitting meaningful statements that can thereby serve scientific thought, to set down bodies of doctrine or to enable communication between people to take place. Communication, here, is the correct passage of proper knowledge, that is, knowledge that makes sense. Language that makes sense is meaningful. However, meaningful language has its own rules and purpose: to express meaning in the form of reference to an object. Thus conceived, language serves the cause of scientific objectivity, whose highest manifestation is seen in logical predication. To do this language deploys two types of sign—indicative and expressive—of which only the latter is meaningful. With indication (*Anzeichen*) "we usually feel the connection" of the sign vehicle with the simultaneously present object.[75] But because this "feeling" is no more than a kind of anticipation, there is no meaning-content as such in indication. An expression (*Ausdruck*), however, *carries* meaning-content with it. Expressions presuppose an intentional meaning-endowing act that takes place in the immediacy of a self-present consciousness, the sphere of "solitary mental life" or "transcendental consciousness" or "interior monologues." In other words, expression requires a signifying medium in order to communicate a pregiven sense or intention that is presumed to be directly present to oneself and which one seeks to indicate to others. Within this process of signification, language is conceived of as a transparent or self-effacing medium for conveying meaning from one interiority to another. The basis of expression is an ideal communication: interior dialogue or the dialogue of the soul with itself.[76]

"Real" communication, by contrast, can happen only as an abandonment of this privileged sphere of interior dialogue. It involves a going out into the world. For Husserl communication can only be a representation, an exact mirroring of what primordially takes place in the inner sphere. The inner sphere alone guarantees the infinite repeatability and meaningfulness of the communication. The ideal inner sphere involves a realm of identity between acts: a present act and any act that lives outside present consciousness. The role of language in this kind of communication is fundamental to *phenomenological experience* and to the operation of phenomenology. According to this pervasive model, communication is first of all an "I think *to myself*" (my own subjectivity or self-constitution as a subject or self consciousness) and only subsequently a maintenance of identity between one subject and another who must mirror the identity.

> *Communication . . . in effect implies a transmission charged with mak-*
> *ing pass, from one subject to another, the identity of a signified object,*
> *of a meaning or of a concept* rightfully separable from the process of
> passage and from the signifying operation. Communication presup-
> poses subjects (whose identity and presence are constituted before the
> signifying operation) and objects (signified concepts, a thought mean-
> ing that the passage of communication will have neither to constitute,
> nor by all rights, to transform). A communicates B to C. [77]

But this normative model of communication depends crucially on (i)
the paradigm of self-consciousness, the idea that a subject can be present to itself in a realm of interiority and (ii) the notion that language effaces itself in the signifying operation. According to Derrida, who analyzes these assumptions in *Speech and Phenomena*, these two processes
are completely interdependent. The former, the paradigm of thinking in
terms of self-presence, is based on the system of "hearing (understanding)-oneself-speak" through the phonic substance—which presents itself
as a signifier that is nonexterior, nonempirical or nonworldly, and noncontingent.[78] Summarized in the concept of "voice," thinking is thema-
tized in the manner of hearing-oneself-speak. This is the so-called interior dialogue. Derrida problematizes this inner speech:

> When I speak, it belongs to the phenomenological essence of this op-
> eration that I hear myself at the same time that I speak. The signifier,
> animated by my breath and by the meaning intention, is in absolute
> proximity to me.[79]

Now the medium of the interior speech ("I-hear-myself-speak/think) is
the "voice." The voice is the signifying substance, the medium given to
consciousness. From this perspective voice is consciousness itself. Thus
when I speak I am conscious not only of being present for what I think,
but also of keeping as close as possible to my thought (I hear the voice as
soon as I emit it) or to a signifier such as voice that not only does not fall
into the world, but seems to erase itself or become transparent in order to
allow the concept to present itself. The operation whereby the self/subject
is constituted and then constantly regenerated through the I-hear-myself-
speak/think, is what Derrida calls "auto-affection." The "I" comes into
being, it affects itself, by hearing-itself-speak/think in so-called normal
speech or communication with others. The nature of language itself is

already predetermined as "voice" and so is presupposed as belonging to the self—i.e., language is subordinated to the self, "I," or ego. Normal speech relations are therefore based on the function of the ego, which is thought to generate language or to use language for its own purposes as a tool for transferring information.

If auto-affection can be recognized as a mechanism for generating self-sameness through the subordination of the signifier/language, it becomes possible to destabilize this privilege of the voice-ear circuit. Once this de-stabilization occurs, auto-affection is no longer seen as the source of individual identity, but rather as the very means of alienation of the self from the world in general. More important, by deconstructing the privilege of the voice, a different kind of speech can be heard, one that is no longer generated by or from the conscious self or ego, but from an unconscious other (although this is not the other *of* the ego). For Derrida, if the signifier of the ego/self is "voice," then the signifier of this unconscious other is writing-in-general (*écriture*)—a much-misunderstood term that simply means language liberated from the privilege of the voice, and therefore, from the privilege accorded to ideality. What Derrida means by writing is that from the standpoint of this other, *language itself speaks*, and that this happens only when the ego-self is silent.

To suggest that language speaks rather than ego/I speaks is not only to destabilize the normative model of communication but also to point to a different model of the mind,[80] wherein language is the source rather than the instrument of communication. Language as the voice-of-the-other directs the hearing subject to another signifier rather than to what Derrida calls a transcendental signified such as "God," "Voice," "Truth."[81] Once language as unconscious directs the mind in this way, the "object" of one's existence is not a transcendental signified, but rather something like a path, or a way of existing in time.

Derrida's notion of writing as released from the transcendentalizing/deontologizing effects of "voice" finds greater clarity in Lacan's psycho-analytic theory of language and subjectivity, which I shall explore in the next chapter. Nevertheless, the foregoing analysis allows us to discern more clearly the intricate links between voice/truth/communication in McLeod's "Divine Self-Expression" and to the task of reconceiving the nature of the absent guru, the guru-as-writing. Normally, a written text that happens to be concomitant with the absence of an author(ity), divine or otherwise—such as the Ādi Granth—implies the impossibility of communication. For there to be communication what needs to be guaranteed

is the proper conveyance of truth. But the very idea of properly conveying truth also suggests that truth may be conveyed *im*properly. It begs the
question as to whether there is a difference in the being of truth as Truth
and the being of truth as communication.

Stated otherwise: does the essence of Truth change in its being communicated or conveyed? This possibility arises from the metaphysical definition of truth as that which is "universally valid," which in turn means
that which is always and everywhere valid, is itself immutable and eternal, transcending time. Truth as such cannot admit of any change, which
means that the signifier that conveys truth can admit no relationship to
anything worldly, exterior, in time. For truth to be presented as truth and
at the same time to be communicated (represented), the relation between
signifier and signified must be one of perfect transparency, absolute identity, where the signifier effaces itself in the act of communication. As we
have seen, "voice" is the signifier par excellence that maintains the essential identity of truth insofar as it leaves no trace or impression of having
been related to anything outside, to anything worldly or in time.

But what is it about the notion of voice that on the one hand gives the
impression of maintaining absolute ideality of self-presence, but at the
same time *presents itself* as the nonexterior, nonmundane, nonempirical,
or noncontingent signifier? Stated differently: what is it that gives voice
its seemingly divine characteristic? For Derrida, this peculiar quality of
the voice lies in its

> being immediately proximate to that which within "thought" as *logos*
> relates to "meaning," produces it, receives it, speaks it, "composes" it.
> If, for Aristotle, "spoken words are the symbols of mental experience
> (*pathēmata tes psychēs*) and written words are the symbols of spoken
> words" it is because voice, product of the first symbols, has a relation-
> ship of essential and immediate proximity with the mind.[82]

Unlike all other signifiers—which by definition leave their imprint or
trace on the mind, and thereby constitute a derivative or conventional
form of signification—voice leaves no impression, because it signifies
"mental experiences" that themselves reflect or mirror things by natural resemblance: "Between being and mind, things and affections, there
would be a *relationship of translation or natural signification* between the
mind and the *logos*, a rapport of conventional symbolization" (emphasis
added).[83] The reference to "translation or natural signification" refers to

a movement of signification in the mind that effaces itself. Such translation is transparent. Since voice is the *archi*-signifier, voice and translation are intrinsically linked in that they constitute the basis of a universal language that is available to all men who have "mental experiences." As Aristotle writes:

> Spoken words are symbols of mental experiences and just as all men
> do not have the same writings, so all men do not have the same spoken
> sounds. Yet the *mental experiences* are the same for all, as also are
> those things of which our experiences are the images.[84]

According to this classical logic, translation and translatability are not primarily conventional. They do not primarily belong to the order of the signifier. Rather, they belong primarily to the intimate order of the speech and voice, and occur naturally within the mind. Furthermore, since "all men" by definition have "mental experiences" (*pathēmata*) that constitute a kind of universal language, it follows that translation is also primarily a universal process of signifier effacement. What's implied here is not only the possibility of a universal language, but the assumption that the work of moving between different cultures can be reduced to a "generalized translation."

This last point has important implications for our reading of the "Divine Self-Expression," which appears to be theologically transparent. For what becomes much clearer in the light of the above explanation is the basic point in McLeod's "creative" hermeneutic: that the body of signifiers known as Ādi Granth and regarded as Guru is no more than a vehicle not only for communicating God's truth to man, but for *translating* God's truth to all men. Moreover, once this vehicle is understood to be a supplement for God's Voice-Mind, for whom no translation is necessary, it can eventually be discarded. In other words, McLeod's theological or creative hermeneutic serves primarily as a building block for a broader project of anthropology. The effacement of translation that is part of Sikh theology's truth/message is not necessarily unique to the Sikh scripture but should be considered part of a universal signification belonging to all humans. The idea of transparent translation is precisely what makes it possible to conceptually demarcate any culture in terms of its "theology." Valorized under the designation "anthropology/science/methodology," such a process of universal or generalized translation is based on the ability to efface the movement of signification proper to it and effectively turns the focus of inquiry toward humanism—that is to say, toward the real *act* of translation that results from a process of cultural encounter in which subjectivity and identity cannot remain immune or immutable.

By any standards McLeod's explanation of voice in the "Divine Self-Expression" is a masterful piece of creative hermeneutics. It shows how the written text/scripture can be a Guru/author(ity) only if the text or written signifier (as guru) can be reduced conceptually to the operation of metaphor or natural signification. Accordingly, the text can be guru metaphorically but not literally. Insofar as Voice (of God) *represents* the signifier, which means that it effaces the body of signifier to allow spirit/meaning to pass, one can conveniently forget that translation has taken place. To bring translation to mind would bring unnecessary attention to the medium of communication. Hence the written text of the Ādi Granth is portrayed as a vehicle for "God's communication with Man," which is a communication of Man with other Men. In itself it is nothing. Its meaning can only be given/understood by way of reference to Voice as the transcendental signified. Voice eliminates translation because it seems to suggest that we are all now communicating to each other. We are all living and thinking in a medium we all share. Because we share the *same* world, the work of translation is generalized to the operation of metaphor.

Translation and the Normalization of "Religious" Subjectivity

The above explanation might be easily accepted as a contribution to a cross-cultural theological hermeneutics were it not for the presence of several innocent-looking statements that immediately precede the main body of the creative hermeneutic. Closely scrutinized, these statements reveal a very different perspective on the creative hermeneutic. It may seem a little harsh to subject only a few lines from McLeod's corpus to such close scrutiny. But it must be remembered that these seemingly innocent exergues serve to disguise what has become a paradigmatic practice of cultural translation within the humanities and social sciences. At stake, therefore, is not the work of an individual scholar, but a practice of writing about non-European cultures under the categories of "religion" or "theology." Valorized under the names "science," "methodology," and specifically "phenomenology," this practice of writing continues to hide the very movement of signification proper to such terms. This practice of writing institutes a normative way of thinking about the separation between religion and violence, religion and politics, religion and secularism. One way of demystifying this occultation is to attend to the operations of translation going on within such foundational texts in the study of religions. Contrary to appearance, then, the shift toward translation in our discussion on the "Divine Self-Expression" was not a supplementary exercise but in fact central to the demonstration of an underlying unity to the seemingly unrelated issues that I mentioned at the start of this chapter: the deontologization of language, the relationship between religion and violence, the defining of religious experience and hence of *sui generis* religion, and the portrayal of religious violence by media and policymakers.

Viewed from this perspective, such prefatory statements serve to disguise the operations of thought that underpin a particular work. Bearing this in mind, let us return once more to McLeod's exegesis of Sikh thought by way of the following exergues (emphases mine):

For no one is the injunction *to tread softly* more relevant than for the historian, whose study carries him into regions beyond his own society.

This book is a study of *the man* Guru Nānak. A reference to the Sikh religion has been included in the title because the adherents of that religion quite rightly regard *Guru Nānak as a determinative formulator of the beliefs* which have ever since constituted the primary basis of the Sikh religion.

This study is intended to discharge a threefold task. In the first place it seeks to apply rigorous historical methodology to the traditions concerning the life of Guru Nānak; secondly, it attempts *to provide a systematic statement of his teachings*; and thirdly, it endeavors to fuse the glimpses provided by the traditional biographies with the personality emerging from the teachings.

For the section dealing with the teachings of Guru Nānak the methodology adopted is much simpler. . . . [A]n effort has been made *to gather into a systematic form the various beliefs which we find dispersed through his works*. This can be done with relative ease, for it is clear that *such a pattern was present in the mind of their author*.

If we are to indicate a more general purpose beyond the threefold task pursued in this study it could perhaps be expressed in terms of a *quest for creative understanding* . . . [Such a task of creative understanding] . . . requires a *prior understanding of the man* whom Sikhs own as their first Guru.[85]

Now compare the above with the following statements, which immediately precede the exegesis on Sikh theology. For McLeod, the teachings of Guru Nānak can have meaning only in light of a developed understanding of "Guru Nānak's beliefs, of what may properly be called his theology."[86]

Theology is the correct word to use in this connection, for the whole of Guru Nānak's thought revolves around his understanding of the nature of God. . . . It is theology we find in the *śabdas* and *śloks* of Guru Nānak and it is theology of a refined quality.

This theology is not, of course, set out in any systematic form. Guru Nānak's writings bear witness to his experience of God and the characteristic expression of that experience is the hymn of praise which it engenders. Neither Guru Nānak nor Guru Arjan, who compiled the Ādi Granth, sought to set out his beliefs in an integrated pattern and we should not expect them to have done so. Theirs was essentially a religion of experience, the "real" as opposed to the "notional." The latter can, however, do much to impart an understanding of the former. "Theology" as Professor Basil Willey reminds us, is "the notional formulation of what the experience seems to mean." For the purpose of our understanding an integrated pattern can do much to clarify the nature of Guru Nānak's belief.

Guru Nānak produced a coherent pattern of thought and one which . . . is followed to this day by orthodox Sikhism. In his own way Guru Nānak was also a mystic and . . . the climax of his thought is to be found in an ineffable union with God, the Formless One. The climax itself was beyond analysis or expression.[87]

The hermeneutic trajectory within these statements seems fairly clear and might go something like this: the quest for creative understanding of Sikhs and Sikhism requires an understanding of the man Guru Nānak. To understand the man one must first understand his teachings or intentions as given in his writings. To understand the text one needs an understanding of Guru Nānak's "beliefs," and his beliefs in turn constitute his theology, which is never direct but a merely notional formulation of the "real" experience of the ineffable One.

But hidden behind these seemingly innocuous statements—and linking the terms "understanding," "the man Guru Nānak," "his beliefs," "his theology"—are two distinct moments of creative interpretation, which constitute acts of translation. Two operations are occurring, yet no evidence of either is presented or acknowledged, for both operations of thought present themselves in the guise of transparent or natural signification—hence a different meaning can be discerned for the author's injunction "to tread softly." Excessive noise, unwanted discussion, seems unwelcome here for it may dislodge the veil, or complicate matters unnecessarily.

The first moment of interpretation, as we have already seen, concerns the relation of the man Guru Nānak to his own writing. The matter is not clearcut, though, for the question of authorship is far from settled. Nānak's writing is a representation, a reformulation in the medium of ideas, of a prior experience of "ineffable union." If this primary experience can be considered to be the original impression, and Nānak's psyche is the receptive pad upon which the impression is stamped, then Nānak cannot be the true author or writer. Nānak is merely the vehicle for the true author. Consequently, as the foregoing discussion showed, the status of scripture attributed to Nānak's name, his *bāni*, is purely metaphorical as it does no more than carry the original impression of the "ineffable union" with God. And as we have already seen, the only medium that could carry the impression of ineffability is one that is able to efface itself in the very moment of its impression. That medium is the voice.

Hence the first moment of creative interpretation by McLeod is the postulation of a passage from the divine to the human, from eternity to time, formlessness to form, immediate to the mediated. Yet this passage from nothingness into language, which is ordinarily called "communication," entails an act of translation. But who is the translator? For the "Divine Self-Expression," as we have seen, annuls the act of translation through the work of metaphor/Voice, which presents a transcendental signifier (voice/sound) in the moment that we begin to think of the impression of ineffable union. And insofar as it effaces the impression, and therefore the act or the deed of translation, McLeod's interpretation conveys to the reader the impression of his own invisibility. Through the replacement of one impression by another, he simply aids the representation of what is naturally there; the only impression he conveys is the divinity of the Voice.

But things are not quite as they seem. There is a second moment of interpretation in McLeod's exegesis that is far less obvious but that inadvertently reveals the creative hermeneutic of the act of translator and the identity of the true translator. One reason this move is less conspicuous is the quest for creative understanding embedded within McLeod's other central project: the *ethnographic* project of providing a "systematic statement of Nānak's teachings" in the English language and to a global community of readers.

Although it might seem counterintuitive, the second moment of interpretation and the true act of translation is McLeod's attribution of Nānak's passage from the ineffable experience of God to his notional formulation of the experience (his *bānī*), i.e., from the mystical experience to the language of theology. By designating Nānak's writing as "theology" or "beliefs and intentions," McLeod presents Nānak as a translator who successfully negotiated the passage from nothingness to existence, from the noncommunicational void of mystic experience to the realm of conventional language. This move therefore inverts the order of signification in which experience is prior to language, where language is a mere vehicle for communicating the experience. As such there is no language prior to the experience. Language is therefore concomitant with coming-into-consciousness, with the reflective act of a self-conscious being. According to this move, having thus translated the gap between unconscious ineffable experience and self-consciousness, Nānak, *unlike* other mystics, shows himself to be a competent language user, properly in control of language. Nānak's ability to formulate or express the ineffable shows that he exercised the faculty of rationality without which he would not be able to communicate with others in the world.

On the one hand this move imputes to Nānak a position of responsibility for his words. This is clear from McLeod's attribution to Nānak of the terms "belief" and "intentions" in the sense that Nānak holds such and such a belief, etc. Moreover "belief" is synonymous with Nānak's thoughts and his theology. Insofar as "belief"/"theology" refer to the meaning-intentions behind the writing, it is clear that these terms valorize the self-consciousness of the "man Guru Nānak." They ascribe to Nānak a normalized subjectivity. On the other hand, the move simultaneously renders invisible McLeod's ethnographic ascription of theology. In the very act of shifting responsibility and subjectivity to the other, McLeod succeeds in effacing his own subjectivity and in so doing suspends the very evidence for involvement in this interpretive move.

I shall return to the issue of this suspension shortly. Contrary to their alleged function in the "Divine Self-Expression"—which was to show how Guru Nānak explains "God's communication with man"—terms such as "belief"/"thought" say little or nothing about this communication. Rather, terms such as these should be regarded as heuristic devices that allow the ethnographer-translator on the one hand to ascribe a unique "religious" subjectivity to Nānak, and on the other hand to conceal his own identity as translator. This technology, which allows the historian of religion to simultaneously ascribe and conceal subjectivity, or to define Sikh religiosity as *sui generis* and at the same time absolve the historian of responsibility for this act, is of course the phenomenological *epochē*—the scholar's self-conscious suspension or bracketing of his own historical being, which also entails a suspension of the faculty of judgment. McLeod's reliance on such a move places his work within a well-established tradition of scholarship in religious studies associated with such names as Rudolf Otto, Mircea Eliade, Huston Smith, Wilfred-Cantwell Smith, and Ninian Smart, to mention but a few. Indeed McLeod's *Guru Nānak and the Sikh Religion* can be regarded as a specialized example of the wider school of thought institutionalized under the title of the phenomenology or history of religions.

In order to further elucidate what is going on in the second moment of McLeod's creative hermeneutic, I want to draw upon two rather different, almost opposed, theoretical strands in the study of religion, to be found in the work of John Hick and Russell T. McCutcheon. John Hick is a philosopher of religion whose later works turn to phenomenological issues in order to develop a theory of religion that is able to respond to the problem of religious pluralism. Hick's work provides theoretical support for the central thesis of the phenomenology of religion associated with Mircea Eliade, W. C. Smith, and Ninian Smart—namely, that religion is *sui generis*. In contrast, McCutcheon is an outspoken critic of the discourse of *sui generis* religion. Despite their very different backgrounds and orientations toward the *sui generis* category, the work of both of these scholars revolves in very different ways around the implications of religious pluralism for representing non-Western cultures in the discourse of the humanities and social sciences. Before returning to the above discussion, I want to briefly trace this vexed connection between the category of *sui generis* religion and the question of religious pluralism in order to better relocate this question in McLeod's text.

Sui Generis Religion and the Question of Pluralism

John Hick's major work of the 1980s, *An Interpretation of Religion: Human Responses to the Transcendent,*[88] represents a fusion of the two major theoretical currents that informed the study of religion during the nineteenth and twentieth centuries. One is the modern academic construction of mysticism, which derives mainly from Friedrich Schleiermacher's attempts to circumvent the Kantian stranglehold on epistemology, which effectively rendered any genuine religious experience impossible. In Kant's view human knowledge can never extend to knowledge of the thing or the object itself. The best we can hope for is a descriptive knowledge of the thing as it appears to the human subject. Yet the price of locating the human subject as the foundational center of all knowledge is that we are debarred from knowledge of any transcendent reality. Schleiermacher tried to retrieve religious and mystical experience from Kant's critical theory by viewing such experiences as unique, intense, subjective states of consciousness, thereby escaping Kant's main stricture. In the twentieth century William James became the most notable and enduring exponent of this focus on mystic experience as centralized in an intense subjective state of interiority.[89]

The other theoretical current is concerned with the translatability of the mystical core of religious experience to its occurrence in history, and thus of its applicability to a plurality of cultural forms. In doing so it provides a corrective to Schleiermacher's ideas, which were directed primarily at a European Christian readership; because his theory remained fixated with the subjective or interior state of consciousness, it was unable to pass over into the historical-empirical domain, which — as Hegel (and later Husserl) was to show — needed to incorporate the historical evolution of cultures. Indeed Hegel's critical reworking of Schleiermacher's earlier ideas on the aesthetic of religious experience continues to inform the modern phenomenology of religions associated with Otto, Scheler, van der Leeuw, Eliade, and John Hick. Of these John Hick's *An Interpretation of Religion* provides the most philosophically sustained attempt to locate a theory of religious experience (religion as *sui generis*) within the wider religious experience of mankind, which is to say, the historical context of social and cultural pluralism.

Hick basically subdivides mystical experience into two types: unitive and communicative. Unitive mysticism is described as a state of absolute absorption/union with the Real. A state of pure interiority, it does not admit of any relation between the mystic and the external world. Communitive mysticism, by contrast, is described as a "form of encounter" between the Real and the mystic that is subsequently relayed or translated as dreams, visions, or auditions to society at large in a language that is commonly understood. The "encounter" is further described as an impact of the transcendent Reality on the mystic's psyche, which is then expressed in forms supplied by his own mind.[90] However, this division between the "unitive" and the "communitive" is more problematic than appears at first sight. The problem—one that is shared by other scholars of "pluralism" who rely on the same basic philosophy—is the need to posit this distinction between unitive and communitive as entirely natural.[91] The question here is whether this distinction results from the valorization of a particular ability that the mystic may or may not possess, this valorization being a way of classifying mystics and mysticism in terms of their success or failure to communicate that which is experienced. Thus the measure of mystic ability would be "the mystic's own mindset," his ability to "express in forms supplied by his mind."[92] Mystics who remain wrapped in the unitive state are unable to communicate with others, and are therefore of little use to society at large.

Later in the same book Hick states that "even in the profoundest unitive mysticism the mind (of the mystic) operates with culturally specific concepts and what is experienced accordingly is a manifestation of the Real rather than the Real-in-itself." The measure of the mystic is his ability to transform the unitive experience of the Real-in-itself into the communitive. Clearly the distinction between unitive and communitive reflects not only the Kantian opposition that Hick (and others) wishes to maintain between the Real-in-itself (i.e., the Real as transcendent, beyond the external world, beyond time and space, etc.) and the Real-as-manifested (i.e., the Real-as-qualified by attributes/predicates of culture, form, time/space, i.e., the human), but also the privileging of the Real-in-itself within this opposition. A cursory overview of the discourse of phenomenology of religions will show that variants of these two philosophical presuppositions—(i) the privileging of the unitive state of the Real and (ii) the movement of the Real into the phenomenal or the communitive—

are routinely used to explain pluralism and cultural diversity in terms of the essence of religious experience.

This point is not lost on one of its most outspoken critics, Russell Mc-Cutcheon. In recent works, such as *Manufacturing Religion: Sui Generis Religion and the Politics of Nostalgia*,[93] McCutcheon argues that the foremost concern of the comparative study of religion as it has developed within the confines of the discourse on *sui generis* religion is the problem of religious pluralism. According to this viewpoint—a viewpoint that is deeply indebted to the efforts of such scholars to situate religiosity as a fundamental element of all human experience—"from the outset all people are considered, to whatever degree, to be religious, and the problem for the comparativist is simply to document or assess the great diversity of beliefs and rituals."[94] "Sadly," McCutcheon continues, "comparative religion practiced in this manner is more akin to a theology of religious pluralism." It becomes part and parcel of religious dialogue rather than the critical study of religion. Hence the discourse on *sui generis* religion, preoccupied with the problem of religious pluralism, has come to dominate the field as a whole. Why then does this subjective category, which somehow transcends communication, continue to dominate research as well as the production of textbooks for the classroom?[95] Citing Wayne Proudfoot, McCutcheon gives the answer that the discourse on *sui generis* religion is popular precisely because it is "an efficient and powerful means for cloaking other theoretical and political concerns."[96] Although the task of the comparative religionist is projected as disinterested knowledge of man himself, this "new humanism" is in fact deeply ideological. It serves a specific sociocultural function for scholars of religion by providing an effective protective strategy for their social judgments, thus giving them autonomy from contextual influences. This protection privileges certain kinds of judgments made by the scholar of religion and simultaneously excludes other competing methodologies.[97]

I am in considerable agreement with McCutcheon's critique of *sui generis* discourse and its enabling of a certain kind of pluralism. However, I think he is right for rather different reasons. McCutcheon's alternative to *sui generis* discourse is what he considers to be "an oppositional, or naturalist, discourse which can generate explicit and testable theories of religion."[98] For example, it is not enough to say that *sui generis* discourse is theological. Rather, it is necessary to show that possible relations exist between the kind of decontextualization/idealization made possible through the use of this protective strategy and the larger sociopolitical world. A naturalist discourse must address potential linkages with other concrete political issues and events. In other words the kind of polytheoretical and multidisciplinary discourse being advocated must ultimately be grounded in history as the "context in which human action takes place."[99] McCutcheon's model is therefore inspired by a belief in history. It is grounded in a belief in secular humanism similar to the kind that in different ways inspired Marx, Foucault, Said, and, I would like to add, Husserl.

As I pointed out at the start of this chapter, W. H. McLeod's methodological defense also relies on values of secular humanistic critique and therefore to history as the antidote to theological/*sui generis* assumptions with which he charges the insider perspective. What seems to be left untouched by the apparently more radical nature of methodologies grounded in history is the complicity between history as an unquestioned ground of sociopolitical critique and practice and the ideological formation of the doctrine of secularism. As de Certeau, Derrida, Talal Asad, and Hent de Vries remind us in different ways, and as we have noted in our own critique of Hegel in chapter 2, history and the historical are always minimally tainted with theology in the moment of their genesis. The secular is always already based on the religious. In short: though McCutcheon points out the necessary, though problematic, connection between subjective states of consciousness and religious pluralism, he does not adequately attend to the question that really concerns us: Why and how does the translation of the mystic-unitive state into the phenomenal-communitive come to be elevated into a principle of "humanity" at large, which is itself the law of secular liberal humanism?

A more probing insight into this problem is provided by Derrida's reading of Husserl's essay "Origin of Geometry." Husserl, we should remember, laid the philosophical foundations for the phenomenology of religion, a discipline that takes its point of departure from the following problem: how to make the transition from intrasubjectivity ("geometrical ideality"), which if left to itself would remain ineffable, a purely mystic-unitive and noncommunicative state without historicity, to the intersubjective state of historicity ("ideal Objectivity"), which is "omnitemporal" and "intelligible to all"? Husserl's answer is that "geometrical ideality" translates into "Objectivity" by means of language, "through which it receives, so to speak, its linguistic flesh."[100]

But how does this occur? How does language produce the "Objective" from the "merely intra-subjective"? For Husserl, this "how" is achieved by a return to the speaking subject through an argument that is entirely circular. The conditions of objectivity are those of historicity. Since historicity is humanity's essential horizon, its "living present" that provides the vital movement of coexistence (i.e., humanity as a community of speaking beings, speech being the element of life), then this means that the transcendental ground of historicity is speech, which is transcendental because it is able to efface itself in the moment of its production. History therefore establishes itself as the possibility of its own appearing, and this possibility is "language in general," that is, the infinite translatability of language.[101]

As Derrida notes, however, speech is no longer simply the expression of "ideal Objectivity." Rather "*speech constitutes the object of a concrete juridical condition of truth*" (emphasis added). Stated differently: speech doesn't just constitute an ideal Object, it produces and reproduces it as a common object because speech also constitutes humanity's consciousness of itself as "an immediate and linguistic community," "a community of speaking beings" that exists "in one and the same world."[102] "Intersubjectivity" is therefore a community of speaking beings who share a world because they have at their disposal a universal (infinitely translatable) language. Voice and intersubjectivity are not merely connected: they frame the concept of "world" as a figure of plurality. But for Derrida speech/voice is primarily an "I hear myself speak," that is, an ego, which produces in itself the identity and ideal permanence of an object in order to be able to communicate it to another ego. Consequently intersubjectivity consists primarily in the communication of ego to other egos, exactly the same as itself.[103]

Although this notion of intersubjectivity sounds like an acknowledgment by Husserl of radical pluralism and equality at the heart of his "community of fellow mankind," it is far from this. The problem with Husserl's model is that the communication that would make community possible can happen only in certain kinds of mankind—specifically, those portions of mankind designated "mature," that is, those whose egos have achieved a normalized development. Only such egos can effect the passage from the mystic-unitive state to the communitive, from "geometric ideality" to "ideal Objectivity." In other words a law of exclusion is operative in this model of normalized development, a law that casts out "madmen" and "children"—metonyms for mystics and religious types and non-European peoples, those who are not "historically advanced."[104] This law of exclusion, underwritten by the circular relationship between voice, historicity, and intersubjectivity, is the "ultimate juridical instant [which] announces the most radical unity of the world."[105]

In a manner not dissimilar to Hegel's designation of consistent and inconsistent "elevations," this law of exclusion operates by designating a proper or improper transition of humanity—from mystic to communitive, intrasubjective to intersubjective, from solitude to pluralism—that is basic to phenomenology. True to its primary vocation as the science of ordering, phenomenology can therefore be considered a disciplinary microtechnology that works by simultaneously segregating humanity *in the name of pluralism* and accommodating any possible emergent differential constituencies to a humanist core. Yet while this microtechnology is central to the operation of the humanities, it is by no means limited to the work of scholars. For as Derrida so astutely notes, this benign pluralism of the humanities is inseparably tied to the power of the state. What links the university with its poetic logic of uni-formation of knowledge to the structure of the state is a movement of invisible translation that configures knowledge into action.[106] The world of knowledge (university) in its fully objectified form is the world of action (state). This totalized "objectification" is in effect *"an art of generalized translation"*[107]—it is a trick or a ruse that, through the deontologization of language, enables the "truth discourse" of humanism: the modern doctrine in which the world is transformed into a phenomenon for man, who becomes its relational center.[108]

Thus if the terms "humanism" and "generalized translation" can be regarded as essentially synonymous, then "phenomenology," as the performative art of generalized translation, traverses the entire lateral continuum of being, from the representation of being itself, through language and cultural production, into the very fabric of sociopolitical formations. One place where this phenomenological law or doctrine of humanism circulates, often in dialogue with the study of religions, is the state's mediatic representation of religious violence, to which I turn my attention below.

Translating the Theory of Religion
Into the Liberal Imaginary

At this point it is useful to pull together the various threads of this chapter. It is possible to trace the problematic of cultural translation that goes under the rubric of "Sikh theology" to the metaphysical distinction between (i) Guru Nānak's original mystical experience and (ii) the translation of that experience into the temporal domain that begins with the production of Guru Nānak's *bānī*. According to this distinction the word "theology" names the desire of Sikh reformists and nationalists to recuperate and repeat the origin through the practice of *nām simaraṇ*. In a sense McLeod's text can be viewed as completing the arc of communication between Sikhs and the West, an arc that was instigated by British colonial reports about the Sikhs, continued by the Western educated colonial elites who imbibed the language and terms of the conversation through Trumpp and Macauliffe, and finally closed when the conversation returned almost full circle to its home base: the Western university.

The invisible but central consequence of this arc of communication was to shift all discourse on or about *gurmat* back onto to the field of the ego. Yet this was precisely the domain the Sikh Gurus have consistently critiqued throughout their writings. One consequence of systematizing the Sikh Gurus' teaching was to shift the discourse of *gurmat* from its "middle" ground, which, as we shall see in chapter 5, consists of a heteronomic dialogue between non-ego and ego, and transplant it onto the homologic ground of ego ("Sikh theology"). Through this transplantation, which for the most part remains invisible, an "art of generalized translation," all discourse of or about Sikhism is brought under the purview of liberal humanism, which masquerades as the benign pluralism that holds together the "collection of separated individualities"[109] known as the "world religions."

McLeod's success in sealing this arc of communication can be measured not only by the fact that his *GNSR* is able to package Sikh-*ism* as an essence that can be installed and supervised and therefore enter the circulation of knowledge in the discourse of humanism. More importantly, it signals the definitive closure of theological discourse about Sikhism even as its own theological operations remain "beyond the free play of criticism." I use the term "closure" in Derrida's sense, where it points not to the literal closure, but to the defining of the limits of a discourse, the demarcation of a boundary that separates "Sikh theology" (whose spokesperson is the Sikh traditionalist) from humanistic inquiry (whose spokesperson is the historian of religion). A cursory glance at scholarly output on Sikhs and Sikhism after the 1968 publication of *GNSR* will show that the topic of "Sikh theology" will never be broached again in any detail. And the reason for this is not far to seek. It has to do with the fact that from the standpoint of humanistic inquiry, both the original experience of Guru Nānak and the translation of this experience into time and history are deprived of ontological status.

This might seem to contradict my earlier reading of McLeod's interpretation of the origin(al experience). But according to the same interpretation, however rapturous the height of the mystical experience might have been, the origin would have remained inconsequential, effectively useless, if Nānak had not moved out of it and into the world of time and writing. According to this mimetic logic, at the very moment that Nānak breaks with the immediacy of the origin(al moment), there is an unavoidable fall into time. All that comes after the origin—evolution, development, religion, faith, etc.—is merely an aftereffect, an echo of the original event, which can exist as such only in the recuperative memory of Sikh tradition. The logic of mimesis dictates that what comes after the origin(al event), the course of events regarded as "tradition," is from the historian's point of view contingent upon the truth of the origin(al event), and insofar, inherently doubtful, a false or pseudo-reality about which nothing can be affirmed unless evidence to the contrary is presented.[110] As I have already indicated above, however, the implications of this logic go further. Although the phenomenon called Sikhism corresponds to a degenerative evolution, it is nevertheless possible to get an indication of its level of spiritual creativity by determining to what degree it corresponds to or imitates this origin through certain prescribed practices, such as *nām simaraṇ*. The presupposition here is that formations designated as religions necessarily demonstrate a desire to repeat the origin.

How then are we to understand McLeod's ambivalent stand toward the question of the origin? On the one hand he voluntarily renounces the pursuit of the origin, claiming to rely on a purely "intellectual analysis" based on reason alone, one that "lacks the intuitive reality that transcends both history and the intellect," that is to say, lacks the element called the "religious" or the "spiritual":

> For those of us who are largely devoid of this religious or spiritual experience no amount of explaining can ever succeed in communicating what is meant by these terms. . . . But I approach Sikhism as a historian, one who is devoid of any pretence to that spiritual sense which many Sikhs (and many Christians too) assure me is vital to its understanding.[111]

As Tomoko Masuzawa points out, this kind of renunciation—where the historian of religion denies that what happened at the beginning or founding moment of a religion is a problem for him—is a standard phenomenological move. Yet on the other hand, continues Masuzawa, "the same 'science' admits, or rather presumes, that the question of origin is of the utmost concern for some other people."[112] Indeed, historians of religion routinely impute a desire for knowledge of the origin to all religions and "religious" peoples. Religion, by definition, is said to be essentially concerned with origins and with the need to repeat the origin, to re-present it, to make that origin present again and again, here and now. Insofar as they attempt to repeat the origin, "religious" people thereby demonstrate a level of spiritual creativity that is specific to each religion. But because this repetition occurs in time, here and now, and because it can never recreate the origin, they end up merely contributing to a progressive weakening of the initial experience that is memorialized by some as "tradition," and by others as "history." The creativity of these repetitions of the same is ultimately limited as it "remains stubbornly fixated on the *arche.*"[113] It can therefore never achieve the level of creativity or elevation required to transcend itself. Ironically, though, this ultimate level of creativity or transcendence is part of the historian's vocation and identity since he can at the same time give meaning to the original experience (in this case of Guru Nānak) and successfully translate this meaning into the text of history, and as if by magic, efface any sense or trace of having translated. Yet an absolute desire for the origin *and* the failure to translate will be imputed to the Gurus who immediately succeeded Nānak as well as to those who follow the Sikh tradition today.

Once again, the mechanism revolves around the nature of repetition. For as long as religions and religious peoples remain stuck in the loop of "dreamtime" they remain unconscious of their historicity. Such repetition—which attempts to imitate a conception of the origin via a certain practice of *nām simaraṇ* as the reproduction of what is absolutely nonviolent (namely the absolute stasis of a divinity that is defined by its eternality)—is privileged repetition. As long as this continues to happen the historian is relatively unconcerned. The problem arises, however, when practitioners of religion show signs, for whatever reason, of breaking out of the static ontology of "dreamtime." This might happen when such practitioners refuse conformity to a repetition of the same by assuming their historicity and in so doing determine sovereignty in a different way. Such repetition, which transgresses the boundary of its "dreamtime," would constitute an entry into the political, and will therefore be represented as violence. Violence here would mean not simply a deviation from the religious ideal of the original experience, but the kind of change that challenges the ontological order itself. Such repetition, along with its associated violence, will by its very definition be deemed unlawful.

Once the rhetoric of disinterestedness is exposed as little more than a masquerade, the political underpinnings of the work of the historian of religion become more obvious. I am not suggesting here that the historian of religion has a left- or right-leaning tendency, but rather that the logic that s/he deploys is part of an older tradition of political philosophy presupposed by the left and right alike. This is the tradition of liberalism or liberal humanism.[114] Liberalism entails a position, at once theoretical and political, that understands humans as (i) individual moral agents who strive to free themselves of oppressive constraints that shackle those who are not yet free or incapable of elevating themselves above such constraints, (ii) reducible to a form of interiority exemplified by the properly individuated ego. Moreover, this form of individualized interiority is universal, which also means fundamentally translatable across cultures.

In the hands of the historian of religion, this "fundamental translatability" results from ceding the sovereignty of language to the sovereignty of human speaking. Man speaks because he controls language. Man speaks because he controls (i.e., effaces) the work of translation that is intrinsic to the being of language. Thus controlled, language becomes generally translatable. As alluded to in the foregoing discussion, the logic of "generalized translation" is simply a different term for the universalizing tendency of liberal humanism. Though rarely considered, the logic of such translation as deployed by the historian of religion closely resembles the logic by which the state machinery functions in the fabric of modern liberal societies. This is perhaps most evident in those liberal societies governed by the rationale to maintain a sharp dividing line between the rule of law and order and the threat of chaos represented by that which is radically different or other. Just as the historian of religion, armed with an overwhelming theoretical advantage, exercises judgment *about* violence as a deviation from the proper definition of religion (which is always defined in relation to the propriety of law), so the state, armed with its overwhelming material advantage, reserves for itself the exercise of violence as legal (where law and legality is defined in relation to the definition of religion). The link between them is the conformity of law to the figure of the divine as absolute stasis. Given that absolute stasis represents absolute order, anything that perturbs the stasis of the divine threatens the rule of law.

In their recent work on war and democracy, Michael Hardt and Antonio Negri analyze this link between violence, the law, and state machinery.

Hardt and Negri argue that once the state reserves for itself the exercise of violence as legal, all other social violence is deemed illegitimate.[115] Although religion doesn't specifically figure in their argument, it is not difficult to see that a perfect example of social violence would be the violence attributable to religion. "Religious" violence has by definition deviated from its proper place, namely the domain of privatized interiority that, as I have shown above, corresponds to divine stasis, which in turn is the truth of religion. Although the state's legitimation of violence is grounded in the structures of law, an adequate notion of legitimate violence is in turn dependent on the law's claim to morality. Violence is legitimate if it can be morally justified, but illegitimate if its basis is immoral.[116] This is of course a circular argument, for the law's claim to morality is itself justified by the state's presentation through the media of an enemy with its attendant threat of indeterminate chaos. Ultimately, then, it is the presence of the enemy that legitimates the violence of the state. The figure of the enemy can be seen to function either as a schema of reason or as a schema of mythologization. Either way the schema sketches out in advance the very horizon on which are constructed the sphere of one's own (self) versus the sphere of what is radically different (other). Within the triangular nature of the schema that connects the representation of chaos-religion-enemy: (i) chaos names that which has fallen from the state of order, (ii) the guarantor of order is the state of divine stasis exemplified by the truth of religion, and (iii) the enemy is a figure of chaos that deviates and tempts into deviation from the truth of religion.

While this schema serves to demonstrate the state's need for maintaining security, it is in fact based on the two sources that, as Derrida argues, constitute the phenomenon called "religion." These two sources are, on the one hand, the notion of sacredness exhibited by the experience of remaining unscathed or untouched by anything exterior, and, on the other, the experience of belief (the fiduciary-*ity* of confidence, trustworthiness, faith, credit, etc.).[117] Thus the signification of religious violence as radically different from the state's use of violence, which is justifiable, depends on the very same fiduciary structure. That is, when the other or enemy is confronted as other, the pure relation to other *is* faith. The state simultaneously *suspends belief* in the name of knowledge (religion must remain unscathed, untouched by violence by remaining privatized—religious identity must be conformed to!), and *reinforces it* (believe in the purity of public space that guarantees the structure of society!). By thus endorsing religious identity as the only state in which religion can exist socially and at the same time manipulating knowledge about the fiduciary structure of religious identity, the state demonstrates an almost transcendental ability not only to monopolize violence, but, more insidiously, to manufacture violence and then switch it off at will.

In short, liberal humanism entails a theoretical and political position that in turn maps out into a very real correspondence (or "generalized translation") between the domains of academic theory and state politics insofar as they are both able to manipulate the relationship between religious identity and violence. This ability to translate between theory and politics, and hence the ability to switch the flow of violence on and off (which would also imply a seemingly facile connection to constitutional law), is clearly illustrated, in contexts as different as India and the United States, by the recent mediatization of "religious" conflict between Hindus and Muslims (Ayodhya in 1992, Gujarat in 2002), Hindus and Sikhs (Punjab and New Delhi in 1984) Buddhists and Hindus (in Sri Lanka), Muslims and the West (post–9/11).

The term "mediatization" effectively names the mechanisms whereby academic theory fluidly translates into state politics and from there into the global circulation of the stereotype. Despite their different geographical and cultural contexts, it is not difficult to demonstrate parallels between the media representation of these conflicts in India during the 1980s and 1990s and the representation of religious violence in the U.S. media post–9/11. For one thing both India and the United States are large democratic states with legal constituencies framed in the name of secularism but governed in reality by overwhelming religious majorities—Christian in the case of the U.S. and Hindu in the case of India. Second, the main ideological vector in U.S. and Indian media and academia during the 1980s and early 90s with regard to the representation of religious violence largely echoed state policy, not only by attributing violence to some enemy of the state (turbaned and bearded Sikhs or Muslim fundamentalists with regard to India, Muslims with regard to the U.S.) but also by narrating and displaying the spectacle of violence as a deviation of these troublesome minorities from the "truth" of the religions they purport to represent, where "truth" is contained in some kind of fiduciary structure. Of course, the "truth" of these religions, as both the media and academia have been so keen to portray, is peace, or nonresistance to the law of the state. It is the ultimate measure of a religion's compatibility with democracy. Clearly, what is elided in this representation is that the definition of religion in terms of peace/nonresistance is also a legal definition. It is framed by a juridical process that has predetermined the definition of religion as a renunciation of violence, and violence as a deviation or fall from religion's truth.

Third, there is an interesting, though relatively unexplored, convergence between India and the United States during the early 1980s in their respective representations of religious violence. The early 1980s witnessed the development of an academic forum on terrorism and media to consider the growing problem of "terrorist theater"—a staged performance of violence in which the "terrorist" had become the "master of ceremonies at a media spectacle."[118] The major international forum for this was the *Second International Conference on Terrorism* held in Washington, D.C., in 1984. This was an important policymaking event in which a new public figure, the "terrorism expert," joined with policymakers, journalists, and politicians in articulating the phenomenon of media terrorism. In a deft series of moves this conference, along with its published output, aptly named *Terrorism: How the West Can Win*, translated a broad understanding of terrorism as: (i) the broad targeting of civilians with a focus on an international event such as hostage taking that made extensive use of the media, (ii) an infection whose main site and source was the Middle East, (iii) having a special relationship to "Islam," such that the "world of Islam" effectively invented religious terrorism.[119]

Particularly interesting was the timing of this high-profile conference and the way its central message was adapted by the Indian state and media before and especially after 1984. During this period the Indian state invested heavily in propagating the idea of an imminent threat to the nation, primarily by Kashmiri Muslims, but increasingly after 1982 by Sikh separatists, whose imagery was effortlessly reinvented as the new international terrorists sponsored by India's Muslim neighbor, Pakistan. This is an iconic episode in recent Indian politics that demonstrates the state's ability to switch violence on and off, seemingly at will. Let me briefly elaborate on this ability to manipulate the relationship between religious identity and violence by referring to the secular Indian state's careful crafting of the phenomenon of "Sikh terrorism" and how this phenomenon was seamlessly incorporated into the academic domain. I will end this section by making reference to the post–9/11 wave of hate crimes in the U.S. motivated, again, by an overinvestment on the part of the state and popular imaginary in the connected signifiers, religion and violence.

Violence and the Mediatization of the Sikhs, 1984 to 9/11

The Indian state's creation and successful deployment of the image of "Sikh terrorism" between 1982 and 1992 was dependent on its ability to recognize and manipulate the relationship between two key signifiers of identity. The more important one was the master signifier "Hindu," which was central to the fantasy of the national imaginary that formed the basis of identification with an image of totality: Hindu/Hindustan/Hinduism as a nation, a civilization, and a religion. A master signifier, as explained earlier, is any term that operates through the logic of identity—where identity in turn is defined as religious identity and as the condition for difference. Once the master signifier is defined and accepted as a universal, all other signifiers (e.g., Sikh or Muslim identity) work as particulars and in opposition to the master signifier. Thus within the symbolic order of the nation, "Sikh identity" had to be enunciated by way of a subaltern relation to the master signifier, for example, "We are Sikhs *because* we are not Hindus." I shall come back to this in a moment.

This complex interplay between signifiers, perceived either as acceding to or as resisting assimilation to the "national symbolic" that operated at the level of language and law, is aptly illustrated by the political strategies of the ruling secular Congress Party and its think-tank organ, the National Integration Committee (NIC), which was mainly responsible for manufacturing the fantasy of national unity and integration after 1958 and particularly in the early 1980s.[120] This was a period when Congress had to counter a dual threat to its electoral bases at the national and provincial level. The main threat came from the religious activities of the Hindu nationalist movement, the BJP, RSS, and VHP. During the 1980s the VHP successfully organized its networks along religious lines by taking measures such as: (i) mobilizing *sādhūs* and other notable activists and patrons, by integrating the main strands of devotional Hinduism—Vaiṣṇavites, Śaivites, and Tantrists—under a common slogan of Mother India, (ii) organizing a series of unity conferences to highlight the dangers to Hinduism from "proselytizing" religions such as Islam and Christianity, and (iii) holding a series of high-profile nationally televised marches, such as the "sacrifice for unanimity" march (*ekatmatā yajna*) in 1983.[121] Emboldened by the success of these earlier measures, the VHP convened a large gathering of Hindu religious figures in April 1984 in the capital, New Delhi, for the purpose of issuing a resolution for the "libera-tion" of three temple sites in North India, at Mathura, at Varanasi, and in Ayodhya. This temple liberation project was designed to link the calls for Hindu unity with an anti-Muslim rhetoric. To define and mobilize a Hindu religious identity, the VHP decided that it was necessary to iden-tify an enemy. From then on "Muslims would be cast as violators of the sacred homeland."[122]

Besieged by vocal minorities such as the Sikhs at the provincial level and by Hindu fundamentalists at the national level, the ruling Congress seemed be caught in a serious dilemma. Muslims were part of an impor-tant vote bank for Congress as the self-styled party of "unity in diversity," but they could not afford to alienate mainstream Hindus, who comprised the vast majority of Indian voters but were increasingly affected by the upsurge of BJP/RSS/VHP activity and rhetoric.

Congress' solution to this dilemma was to divert the attention of the Hindu voting bloc by creating the figure of an alternative enemy: the Sikh. Ever since the imposition of emergency rule by Indira Gandhi in 1977, the main Sikh political party, the Akālī Dal, had been a major thorn in the side of the Congress due to its sustained nonviolent campaign directed against the suspension of democratic rule. Throughout the early 1980s the Akālī leadership had kept up a series of economic and territorial de-mands designed to gain a certain measure of autonomy for the state of Punjab. These included a demand for increased water rights for Punjabi farmers, the return of Punjabi lingusitic territories given to the neighbor-ing state of Haryana, and demand for more open Center-State relations.[123] The Akālī opposition had succeeded thus far mainly because their tactics and conduct had remained within the limits of constitutional law and was therefore perceived to be entirely secular. In addition it was backed by an alliance with the Janata Party, a mainly Hindu political party and pre-cursor of the future nationalist Bhartīya Janata Party (BJP). Congress' master stroke was to religionize the Akālī Dal's ostensibly secular and nonviolent stance. They did this by promoting controversial and extrem-ist elements within Punjab and in the Punjabi diaspora, whose combined presence would communalize the nature of the political scene. Among these elements was a new extremist Sikh political party (the Dal Khalsā), a former Congress minister and expatriate, Jagjit Singh Chauhan, who instigated the demand for a separate Sikh state (Khalistan), and notably the militant cleric Sant Jarnail Singh Bhindranwale. All of these elements were covertly supported by high-profile members of the Congress Party.

As the head of a Sikh missionary institution, the Damdami Taksaal, Bhindranwale was brought into Punjab's state politics by prominent Congress figures such as Giani Zail Singh, then president of India and a former chief minister of Punjab,[124] with the sole purpose of undermining the popular support base of the dominant Sikh political party, the Akālī Dal. The combined presence of the Dal Khalsā and Sant Bhindranwale was intended to further catalyze an already communalized scene.[125]

Although Bhindranwale quickly discovered Congress' true motives and turned against his former promoters, party officials soon found a new role for him. Because they portrayed him through the media as the archetypal "Sikh fundamentalist" representative of the aspirations of all Sikhs, Bhindranwale's name became synonymous with the image of secessionism and as chief instigator of what was termed as the "Hindu/Sikh conflict." Through the neat conflation of the image of Bhindranwale as the arch–"Sikh terrorist" with the "Punjab problem" within India, and the demand for Khalistan, which came mainly from outside India, the Sikh community as a whole came to be perceived as the "enemy within," ready at any moment to collude with the "foreign hand" of Pakistan and undermine the unity of the Indian nation. In this way Congress found an effective way of undermining a key component of the BJP's campaign strategy during the early to mid-1980s to project itself as the only party that championed the cause of the Hindu majority and national unity. Following the death of Bhindranwale and his supporters at the hands of the Indian Army in 1984, the state machinery continued to project Punjab as a chaotic or "disturbed region" infested with Sikh terrorists whose resistance was evidence of a deviation both from the essentially peaceful nature of Sikhism and from a key principle of the democratic state, namely, that it alone exercised a legal mandate to deploy violence for the protection of the peaceful majority.

In hindsight what remains most disturbing about the Indian state's handling of the "Sikh problem" is not so much the number of people who were killed over a twelve-year period, nor even the controlled precision with which the state allowed the chaos of insurgency to proliferate before brutally and clinically exterminating it almost at will. What continues to disturb is the degree of unison—one might even speak of a circular relationship—between the secular state, the national and global media, and the academic domain that was generated in the aftermath of the events of 1984, and could easily be generated again, as was so evident following the events of 9/11.[126] I refer to the manner in which an avowedly secular democratic state was able to bet on the close fiduciary connection between the enunciation of religious identity (in this case Sikh identity) and the law as enshrined within the nation's constitution. Implicit within this constitution, and thus within the structure of Indian law, is an overlap between the signifier "Hindu" and national identity. In both secular and religious versions of Indian nationalism the signifier "Hindu" names the closest proximity between the "I" of the nation and its "Oneness" or unity, hence its truth value. Understood in this way, the signifier "Hindu" becomes the guarantor of a *Pax Indica* that is enshrined within the constitution. But, when the "I" and the "One" coalesce in this manner, all other named identities, hence all manner of pluralism, must be deemed not-true, or not *as* true. According to this logic, something like the enunciation "Sikh identity" will always be deemed suspect, an affront to the true identity of the nation. The state is always able to bet on this fiduciary structure, and more importantly to win every time! The state's covert policy, it would seem, was to trap Sikhs (in this case the Akālī Dal leadership) into enunciating their being as a *religious* identity. To remain within the *Pax Indica*, however, Sikhs can enunciate this identity only privately. Expression or enactment of this identity in the public sphere would constitute a violation of public space—and this public space is clearly defined by the nationalist master signifier "Hindu." It would seem that Sikhs have been constituted as violators of the *Pax Indica* ever since Bhāī Kahn Singh first enunciated "*Ham Hindu Nahin*" ("We Are Not Hindus") as a retort to an earlier publication "*Sikh Hindu Hai*" ("Sikhs Are Hindus") back in the late nineteenth century.

Once the fiduciary structure of this trap was set back in the colonial era, it continued to be used by the Indian state at various times, but with devastating consequences for Sikhs in the 1980s. Once confronted with the figure of the Sikh as "enemy," Hindus reacted by differentiating themselves from it, while Sikhs were forced into a dilemma: *either* to reject this "enemy," thereby (i) affirming that militancy is a deviation from "true" Sikhism, and (ii) renouncing the right to resist the state (a principle historically and "theologically" inscribed in Sikh tradition); *or*, to identify with the "enemy," thereby (i) affirming that Sikhism itself is not a true religion and by nature incompatible with democracy, and (ii) affirming that Sikhs and Sikhism can never rightfully belong within the ambit of the Indian nation, hence justifying separatism—which inevitably invites the morally sanctioned violence of the state. The moral of the story is that as long as minorities respond to the demand for religion in a predictable way, the state continues to keep its finger on the fiduciary structure of religion. Consequently the fiduciary can be turned on or off at the whim of the state and milked not only to produce violence when and where needed, but ironically to *legitimize* state violence by creating a *spectacle* of violence in the eyes of international law.

But for Sikhs the story does not finish there. Most people in Punjab who had experienced the horrors of the 1980s and early 90s breathed a sigh of relief with the cessation of the Sikh insurgency and the "normalizing" of the political scene in Punjab heralded by the return of an Akālī Dal–BJP coalition government in 1996. After the events of 9/11, however, things took a very different turn for diaspora Sikhs. The attacks of September 11, 2001, on the United States by radical Islamists linked to Osama bin Laden resuscitated the association of religion with violence, which was then brought into the forefront of public debate by the global media. With the U.S. media's massive and overt sensitization of the American mindset with the image of a bearded and turbaned Bin Laden, the events of 9/11 created an unexpected and deadly problem of "mistaken identity" for many Sikhs and South Asians living in the U.S. and Europe. Mistaken for Muslims, turban-wearing Sikhs were targeted in a wave of hate crimes, which began with the murder of fifty-two-year-old Balbir Singh Sodhi who was shot five times in the back at a gas station in Mesa, Arizona, on September 15, 2001. The media quickly absorbed and distilled the dangerous religious and racial rhetoric deployed by the U.S. political establishment, which was initiated by George W. Bush's televised speeches to the nation. In laying out a fundamental civilizational divide between the secular West (but based on Christian ethical values) and the "Axis of Evil," which referred to those nations, regimes, and individuals who stood against the rule of Western democracy (implicitly referring to the Taliban, Al Qaida, and other Islamist groups connected to the Palestinian struggle, Saddam Hussein, Iran, and North Korea), these speeches deployed the fiduciary nature of religion.

Within hours of the 9/11 attacks a frenzied U.S. media was awash with images and posters of a bearded and turbaned Osama bin Laden. One newspaper front cover in particular—carrying a photograph of bin Laden with the title "Wanted: Dead or Alive"—was displayed by many Americans on cars and even on the front doors of their homes. Within this heightened atmosphere, male Sikhs in particular very quickly became substitute embodiments for "bin Laden" and "Islamic terror" and as such represented a socially and politically sanctioned hate crime target. Once labeled in this way, Sikhs were a legitimate target for a "socially appropriate emotion" of revenge and retributive justice that was expressed in "socially inappropriate ways."[127] As Jasbir Puar notes, "these hate crimes became normalized within a refashioned post 9/11 racial landscape, but more significantly, they became immanent to the counter terrorism objectives of the state, operating as an extended arm of the nation, encouraging the surveillance and strike capacities of the patriotic populace."[128]

While Puar rightly brings attention to the heteronormative frame of white middle-class America, which endowed the turban-wearing man with a terrorist masculinity, what seems to be underplayed in her analysis is the religious grounding of this frame, a grounding that equally motivates liberal and conservative sentiments. Within this religio-heteronormativity, the turbaned man is not just a patriarchal figure who presents "a resistant anti-assimilationist stance" but a deviant figure of monstrosity, a barbaric evil that refuses to become civilized: "The turban both reveals and hides the terrorist, a constant sliding between that which can be disciplined and that which must be outlawed."[129] Not surprisingly, the turban, in its capacity to invade the visual public space of an American citizenry of both religious and secular persuasions, becomes a source of contagious affect that continues to cause anxiety.

Sikh responses to the post-9/11 hate crimes were nothing if not predictable. One manifestation of the domestication demanded of those ethnic groups that did not conform to American-ness was that large numbers of Sikh men, particularly the children of new immigrants, chose to disrobe their turbans. In such cases turban removal "functioned as a reorientation into masculine patriotic identity."[130] Other Sikhs who refused to disrobe their turbans adopted different types of self-preservationist but ultimately assimilative tactics. Candlelight vigils accompanied by group singing of the U.S. national anthem became common. This was a way in which Sikhs could mark themselves as patriotic but victimized citizens. Sikhs increasingly began to hang American flags outside their homes, on their cars, or outside *gurdwara* premises. Public relations firms were hired and Sikh advocacy groups sprang up to try to educate fellow Americans about Sikhs and to alleviate their anxieties about the turban. The real irony here is that many of these same Sikh organizations had been petitioning the U.S. government about human rights abuses committed by the Indian state against Sikhs, insisting that Sikhs were a religious identity separate from Hindus.

A common response among Sikh communities throughout the United States was to engage in interfaith dialogues with neighboring Christian and Jewish communities. This was clearly driven by a desire to correct the "mistaken identity" and to inhabit the normative religious space that is part and parcel of American patriotism. A key component of these dialogues was the emphatic enunciations that: (i) Sikhs were not terrorists, (ii) that Sikhs were not Muslims, (iii) that Sikhism was a "world religion." Identification as a world religion ensured two coveted prizes: an admittance into the moral space governed by Christianity and, as a result of this, a safe passage and proper placement within secular public space. The idea here is that being seen to be like Christianity accrued both religious and secular benefits.

However, in 2004, such attempts to negotiate the Scylla of religion and the Charybdis of secularism caused a different kind of dilemma for Sikhs living in France in the wake of the French government's widely publicized ban on the wearing of "religious symbols" in public — a ban that included the turban. For French Sikhs the problem was exacerbated by the fact that the American and British Sikh groups advocating on their behalf were divided about how to actually contest the French government's ban. While the London-based Sikh Human Rights Group opted for a more pragmatic argument (that Sikhism was not necessarily a religion but a culture, and that it had become a religion through its entry into the colonial frame), the New York–based group United Sikhs continued to argue that Sikhism was a religion, that the turban was a mandatory religious item, and that the French government was in violation of their fundamental religious rights. The secular nature of the British group's argument may have favorably impacted the French government had it not been for a well-publicized legal battle that was going on in New York at roughly the same time. Shortly after September 2001, a Sikh traffic enforcement officer, Jasjit Singh Jaggi, employed by the New York Police Department filed a law suit against his employer alleging that the NYPD had denied him numerous requests for a religious accommodation, that is, the right to wear a turban while on duty on the grounds of religious discrimination against turban-wearing Sikhs. In April 2004 the presiding judge ruled that traffic agent Jaggi had been discriminated against on the basis of religious beliefs when the NYPD ordered him to remove his turban and beard or face dismissal.[131]

What seems to be noteworthy about the French and American cases respectively is that in order to argue their case for wearing turbans in public space, and thus to be integrated into secular liberal society, Sikhs found it necessary to formulate two different kinds of language that in turn recognize and negotiate between two seemingly different kinds of public space—the *religious* space of American secularism and the *nonreligious* space of French *laïcité*. Despite the apparent differences between Indian, American, and French forms of secularism, Sikh identity ended up being cast as a violator of both forms of public space. This violation was due to nothing more than the desire of many Sikhs to assert a secularization—the ability not only to be within the world but to make and remake this world in ways that allow them to move beyond the limits of an installed and interiorized subjectivity and to escape a mode of repetition that keeps them confined within the loop of their "dreamtime."

In this chapter I have attempted to show a connection between several different discourses of religion-making—the production of "religious" identity by the historian of religion and its utilization by experts on "religious" violence and media journalism, and the management of religious pluralism by secular states—all of which subscribe to the doctrine of secularism, and in doing so rely on the static ontology of a privatized (in this case Sikh) subjectivity. Furthermore, I have tried to show that the connection between these discourses is a process of "generalized translation" that helps to create an unholy alliance between academia, media, and the state. My intention here has not been to exonerate the actual violence perpetrated by militants, or by those of a narrow persuasion who have unnecessarily targeted academic scholars for one reason or another. Rather, I have tried to highlight the problem of adopting "a secularist position that privileges its own standpoint as *uniquely* positioned to promote tolerance, pluralism and protection of minorities in a modern society."[132] The irony here is that in the various attempts to exclude "religious" discourse from the public arena, the pluralistic ground championed by the secularist doctrine is itself undermined. The blindspot of secularism appears when it dogmatically sets itself up as the *doxa* and thus the authoritative center of public discourse. Central to this *doxa* is the oppositional discourse of "religion" and violence, and the process of identity politics that in turn serves to maintain a strict dichotomy between "religious" and "secular" worldviews.

What cannot be lost sight of is the need for political and theoretical interventions that can change this system and, more important, enable those "captured" neocolonial subjectivities to break out of the repetitions of identity in order to salvage a different mode of repetition that does not respond to the politics of identity. But how does one break the circle of repetition and make a new mode of repetition which repeats not identity but identity-in-difference? It is to this question that the next chapter will give attention.

PART III

Postcolonial Exits

5   Ideologies of Sacred Sound

In chapter 4 we glimpsed the possibility of pulling away one of the key terms in the Sikh lexicon, namely, the concept of *śabda-guru* (the Word as Guru), from the grasp of an ontotheology imposed on it by Sikh neocolonial and modern Western interpretations. Yet the question remained whether, once disentangled from the colonial metaphysics, the term *śabda-guru* could then be relocated into some indigenous context. During the late 1970s and 80s, in the wake of a postwar crisis of humanism that seemed to have afflicted the humanities and social sciences, different versions of this very move were implemented by scholars specializing in the history of religions. Central to this move was a distinction between literate (Western) and oral (Indic) cultures that was transmuted into a desire to give some form of agency back to the colonized by returning them to their original precolonial modes of repetition, i.e., to some kind of authentic subjectivity. This chapter seeks to expose the deeply problematic nature of such moves in the history of religions project, especially when they speak in the name of anti-imperialism. I shall argue that the move in question actually reproduces a technology of domination implicit in the distinction between the oral and the literate.

In what follows I use the concept of *śabda-guru* as a foil for interrogating the metaphysical underpinnings of orality, or what I have called ideologies of sacred sound, that have embedded themselves within various discourses in the humanities and social sciences. Such ideologies of sacred sound can be traced to several interlinked sources. First is a certain historical complicity between Orientalism and Brahmanism, which resulted in a regeneration of what I have termed the Vedic economy, an economy that continues to ideologically underpin one of the most powerful strands of the Indian nationalist imaginary. Second is a surreptitious entry of the Vedic economy into the discourse of the history of religions, ironically in the guise of a linguistic critique of modernism and imperialism. Far from breaking with past imperialisms, such moves have helped to cement the concept of religion as *sui generis*, in the process making it ever more general and global in its scope. The ideological function of the metaphysics of sacred sound can be seen in its capacity to rigidly determine the possibilities of repetition (i.e., modes of subjectivity) as forms of mimesis.

Following these multiple interrogations I shall return to the concept of *śabda-guru* in order to pose the question as to whether Sikhs today can exit from cycles of repetition that return to some kind of origin. It is this desire to exit such cycles of repetition that provides the possibility of a genuinely postcolonial move.

Language and the Crises of Humanism

In his book *The Discipline of Religion* Russell T. McCutcheon argues that historians of religion based in a postwar U.S. academy forged "an institutionally autonomous, humanistically based, study of religion" and reestablished the history of religions as a "credible academic pursuit."[1] As reflected in their rhetorical strategies, the task of staking out the boundaries of this new discipline, called "history of religions," was unmistakably linked in the minds of these scholars to the broader shifts in global and national politics, specifically, the role of the United States as a future mediator between "European culture and the culture of the Asian nations." In other words, the rebirth of the study of religions at institutions such as the University of Chicago was conceived as "a politically neutral force for mediating Europe and Asia"[2]—a barely disguised allusion to the demise of the old world order (European), the birth of a new world order (American), and a recognition of a possible danger to the hegemony of the old and the new orders from a decolonized and rapidly industrializing Asia.

In some ways the reemergence of the history of religions as a discipline that exemplified the new humanism can be seen as a response to the "crisis of humanism" diagnosed by Hegel and Husserl, among others, for which their various forms of phenomenology were meant to be correctives. Others, such as Hardt and Negri, have theorized this "crisis of humanism" as an ongoing political battle between two conflicting visions of humanity at the heart of European modernity. In the history of the modern West, this battle was between the revolutionary philosophies of immanence (represented by Spinoza, Schelling, etc.) and the counterrevolutionary philosophies of transcendence (represented by Descartes, Kant, Hegel, Husserl, etc.), each of which successively bequeathed the imposition of an ontotheological apparatus that was the distinctive trademark of European Enlightenment thought. As Hardt and Negri see it, this second mode of modernity "needed above all to guarantee its control over new figures of social production in Europe and in the colonial spaces in order to rule and profit from the new forces that were transforming nature."[3] The idea was to maintain the effects of domination in a transcendental and seemingly neutral form—the *anthropologos*—which would enable the production of the new humanity.

Jacques Derrida notes a similar manifestation of this "crisis," along with the attempt to suppress its radical implications. In his influential essay "Sign, Structure, and Play in the Discourse of the Human Sciences," Derrida comments that the postwar period, especially the decade of the 1950s, was marked by well-documented global changes on the political and academic fronts.[4] On the one hand was a broad geopolitical dislocation: the end of imperialism, itself marked by the displacement of Europe from center stage and its insertion into a global melting pot of alternative cultures, along with the uprooting, mass migration, and resettlement of excolonials within the West. On the other hand, and mirroring the geopolitical dislocation, we find similar dislocations within the Western academy that constitute a "rupture" or "disruption" in the structure of the human sciences, whose primary theme has been the determination of being as permanent presence, or the redefining of identity as the condition of difference. More simply, the Western tradition of education, despite its apparent variations, of which the humanities is the latest variant, has been an ontotheological one, based on a philosophy of presence, the mystified assumption of an original Identity that has been dispersed with the "fall" into time.[5] It is this grounding theoretical principle of metaphysics that has enabled the transcendental apparatus of humanism. If the rupture of this tradition can be associated with three seminal movements in European thinking—Nietzsche and Heidegger's critiques of metaphysics and the Freudian critique of self-presence—the force of the rupture crystallizes around two key moments. First is the "moment when language invaded the universal problematic," that is, "the moment when everything became discourse."[6] Second, and related to this, is the birth of a privileged human science: ethnology. This event arrives with multiple possibilities, which make themselves felt in the proliferation of self-delimiting discourses within the Western academy such as hermeneutics, structuralism, poststructuralism, neo-Marxism, etc. In relation to these new discourses, ethnology operates like a sounding board, helping to make visible and audible the universalist and ethnocentric pretensions of Western "self-understanding."

This rupture in the history of Western metaphysics takes on a special and wider significance for the representation of South Asian texts and cultures. This is best illustrated by way of reference to the birth of ethnological discourse on Indian culture within the American academy, which also reflects both the geopolitical and the academic aspects of the rupture. On the one hand, a declining British political interest in India is replaced by American interest in the mid 1950s in the "South Asian" region (the change in geographical designation is not unimportant here), which, as events have proved, was merely an extension of American imperialism in East Asia as a whole, not to mention the corresponding expansion of the English language to an unprecedented global level. On the other hand, in contrast to trends within the British academy, it would appear that within American universities the newly emergent discourse of ethnology (ethnoscience) has been more receptive to the rupturing influence of language. In the American academy research on South Asian culture has been pursued under the ambit of two seemingly distinct schools of thought, which, for the purposes of this discussion, will be referred to as the *hermeneutic* as opposed to the *anthropological* approach. Despite the obvious differences between these two cultural paradigms, a shared concern has begun to emerge, centered largely around the events of decolonization and globalization.[7] Before joining the main argument in this chapter, it will be helpful to introduce each insofar as they are relevant to the genealogy I am tracing here.

The Phonemic Principle in Hermeneutics and Ethnology

Hermeneutics has become a sort of *koiné*, the overall context or common idiom of Western culture,[8] and its influence on the human sciences is illustrated by the following statements by Wilfred Cantwell-Smith, a leading advocate of the comparative study of "world religions":

> The nineteenth century saw the rise of a great attempt to give this matter serious and disciplined consideration: searching out material, recording it carefully, scrutinising it systematically, interpreting it. This was the task of the universities, which gradually enshrined Oriental and anthropological studies, and here and there established chairs of *Religionswissenschaft*. In our day a new development in these studies is to be discerned, inauguarating a second major stage. . . .
>
> In the first phase there was amassed an imposing knowledge about other people's religions. In the second phase it is those peoples themselves that are present. The large-scale compilation of data of the nineteenth century . . . has in the twentieth century, and particularly since World War II, been supplemented by a living encounter—a large-scale face-to-face-meeting between persons of diverse faith. . . .
>
> The traditional form of Western scholarship in the study of other mens' religion was that of an impersonal presentation of an "it." . . . The next stage is a dialogue, where "we" talk *to* "you." If there is listening and mutuality, this may become that "we" talk *with* "you." The culmination of this progress is when "we all" are talking with each other about "us." . . .
>
> [Thus] the present position is an encounter. When persons or human communities meet, there arises a need to communicate. What had been a description is in the process of becoming a dialogue.[9]

Though written in the context of the "history of religions," Cantwell-Smith's statement reflects the influence and concerns of a postwar generation of European philosophers and cultural anthropologists for a more open—"living"—encounter with "other" non-Western cultures.

The shift from *Begriffe* to *Gesprache* highlights the better-known aspect of hermeneutics: as a philosophy of intersubjective communication that in its most influential form (exemplified by the philosophical hermeneutics of Heidegger and Gadamer) centers on the problematic of understanding as the discursive basis for rethinking the relationship between self and other in a global context. Hence the desire for "living encounter" takes the form of a "dialogical framework" for cross-cultural understanding, a kind of flexible "conversation" between minds, texts, and cultures that differ from one another. If in the attempt to rethink self–other relations, understanding translates the problematic distance between self and other into the question of movement (how "we" can or should approach or encounter the "other" who belongs to a distant world), then the question of movement, and everything involved with it, is itself transformed by the operation of the understanding into a particular relation between self and language. From that point on, the methodological element at the center of history of religions discourse became the problematic of self-understanding (*Verstehen*), where the modern study of religions replaces the earlier colonial/missionary tendency to *confront* the Other, with the desire to *understand* the other.[10] Once the Other is constituted as other, hermeneutics dissolves itself into a more universal cultural anthropology, a "new humanism," and insofar as it dethrones sectarian theology it reconstitutes itself as the birth of a new modernity.[11]

The broader political ramifications of hermeneutics as the main theoretical paradigm of the humanities cannot be explored here.[12] Instead I want to focus on the way in which ethnology similarly forecloses the political work of enunciation through a move that constitutes the other as radically incommensurable. Central to this operation is the deployment of an ideology of language as essentially phonemic in nature, an ideology that helps to (i) construct an authentic South Asian object, and (ii) demarcate the authenticity of South Asian religions as a valid object/area within the history of religions, ironically, through an anti-imperialist critique of the Western concept of religion. One of things that interests me, and about which I shall try to remain vigilant, is why and how the positing of radical incommensurability by way of reference to a belief in language's essentially phonemic nature comes to be justified as an anti-imperialist stance.

In the study of South Asian cultures this school of thought takes as its primary objective the construction of an ethnosocial science based on South Asian "first principles." According to the ethnosociology developed by McKimm Marriott, people in South Asian contexts can be characterized by a monistic rather than a dualistic mindset.[13] The traditional dualisms of Western metaphysics—morality/nature, sacred/profane, mind/body, matter/spirit, etc.—do not have the same relevance in South Asian cultures, which work according to their own, nondual, logics.[14] Because of this nondual logic, South Asian contexts do not distinguish between a sociocultural world and a biophysical world. For Marriott, South Asian ideologies are characterized by a "cognitive non-duality of action and actor, code and substance."[15] Within such an ideology language does not transcend the natural world but stems from a perfect (divine) substance that is embodied not only in minds and bodies but also "in substances that may have physical attributes, such as sound, shape, matter, force, etc."[16]

This argument, put forward in the heyday of area studies, takes its basic premises from the European and American schools of structural linguistics and anthropology.[17] Stated briefly, the movement of structuralism, which arose independently in America and Europe, was based on a reaction against the dominant mode of epistemological realism during the nineteenth and early twentieth centuries.[18] Structuralism holds that the world is not made of independently existing things or objects, but rather is constructed via the fundamental relationship between knower/known, man/world, etc. Some structuring principle—namely language—orders this relationship to reality. As the constitutive structure of human reality, language operates by means of a structuring principle that overrides the objective epistemological certainty of the realist ethnographer. The important implication for the ethnologist is the realization that his own language provides the explanation for and on behalf of the native language, and, since language is structured by its cultural context, that each language has a structure or logic that is proper to it. A more important implication perhaps is that the structure of language is determined at the level of the phoneme since the phoneme comes into presence at the very moment when language emerges as speech. The phonemic principle can therefore be regarded as the fundamental structural concept itself. Hence the basic postulate of structuralism: that language is fundamentally subject to phonematic production, which is to say that language is fundamentally oral in nature.

Closely linked to this form of structuralism—and taking its impetus mainly from Lévi-Strauss' linking of writing to Western ethnocentrism—is a group of political and theoretical critiques of classic anthropology that can briefly be described as a rejection of "visualism." In different though complimentary ways Walter J. Ong, Jack Goody, Marshall McLuhan, and Johannes Fabian have argued that the truth status accorded to vision in Western literate cultures, as also to writing and the book in general, has predominated over other sensory forms, in particular the evidences of sound and interlocution (speech, dialogue, conversation).[19] As Ong points out, the decontextualized nature of the written word has contributed to its greater universalizing and/or imperializing tendency. On a similar note, Jack Goody has argued that the development of literature effectively allowed certain religious worldviews to spread beyond their particular and local context and become "world religions."[20] Indeed Walter Ong adds to Goody's argument the suggestion that the inherent dualism of writing, with its separation of knower and known, subject and object, has contributed to an "increasingly articulate introspectivity," which has enabled the interiorization or privatization of religious traditions such as Buddhism, Judaism, Christianity, and Islam.[21] As a result the taxonomic imagination in the West is strongly visualist and maps cultures as spatialized arrays.

During the 1980s a number of North American scholars working broadly in the history of religions appropriated the earlier insights of Ong and Goody to the study of sacred texts and scripture of "world religions." Works such as William A. Graham's *Beyond the Written Word: Oral Aspects of Scripture in the History of Religion* (1987), followed closely by Harold Coward's *Sacred Word and Sacred Text* (1988), Miriam Levering's *Rethinking Scripture* (1989), and more recently Wilfred Cantwell-Smith's *What is Scripture?* (1993), have effectively combined the critique of Western writing and print culture with the basic structuralist principle of language as phonemic production, arguing that sacred scriptures are fundamentally oral/aural in nature and only secondarily textual. Scholars such as Guy L. Beck took this approach a step further, arguing that the oral/sonic constitutes in similar ways the dimension of the sacred as that which is proper to the monistic or nondualistic South Asian "first principles."[22]

In the light of the above, a commonality can be seen to emerge independently between the hermeneutic and the ethnological strands that comprise the reconstituted discipline of history of religions. Insofar as both strands posit themselves as a thinking-after or a thinking-beyond the epoch of imperialism and Orientalism, this thinking corresponds *in practice* to the adoption of a more self-reflexive mode of accounting, where the native as the previously silent object of study is transformed into a discursive respondent—it is a recognition, in other words, of the decolonized status of the Oriental subject as an equal partner in a democratic dialogue. *In theory* it corresponds to an inversion in the former ideology of language based on the primacy of Western writing, the book, etc., toward the idea that the structure of language is provided by the phonemic/sonic principle.

In defense of this thesis that language as oral constitutes an exit from Western imperialism, scholars have often cited the case of Indian tradition, as the paradigm first of orality in general, and second of a civilization where the sonic principle has enjoyed an overtly privileged status over writing. As a consequence of the sonic principle, ethnologists have been able to argue that South Asian cultures have managed to avoid the tyrannies of writing, metaphysics, and science, which in turn accounts for why they manifest the more tolerant and less repressive attitudes toward other cultures characteristic of Hindu civilization.[23] In addition, scholars professing a more hermeneutic vocation have been able to claim that the category of sound gives direct and immediate access to the sacred core and origin of Indian religiosity, its "central mystery," and thus to the essence of Indian culture, i.e., that which most properly differentiates it from the Western dualistic logic or metaphysics.[24]

In this sense, not only have these schools endorsed a continuation of what is believed to be the traditional and therefore authentic structure of South Asian (and specifically Hindu) society and culture, for which the property of sound "most fully characterises and represents the ineffable and irreducible character of the divine," but, more important, Indian neocolonial elites have reciprocated these citations, thereby sanctioning their validity. What is being suggested here is that Indian and Western cultures perceive the orality/writing distinction in different ways. The West perceives the distinction in terms of a rationalistic ideology with an inherent "bias toward vision as the noblest sense and toward geometry qua spatial conceptualization as the most exact way of communicating knowledge."[25] Indians (and Hindus specifically) perceive the distinction in terms of the underlying category of sound as the "category most expressive of the numinous" in addition to its being the "most productive in terms of understanding and unity, the most personally human, and in this sense closest to the divine."[26]

One implication of this is that these distinctive perceptions of orality and writing constitute two different cultural universals that operate respectively within South Asia and the West. In view of the fact that this universal aspect of South Asian culture has been ignored or marginalized within the humanities and social sciences, the history of religions project has tried to give agency back to what it perceives as the oppressed victims of the colonialist and neocolonialist legacy. And it has done this by presenting oral traditions as sites of struggle of an undifferentiated subaltern consciousness which strives to make its voice heard against the overwhelming dominance exerted by the neocolonialist legacy of Orientalist scholarship and the scholarship of neonationalist elites who adopted Western textuality in the form of print capitalism.

Orality, Texts, and the Nationalist Imaginary

A rather different account regarding textuality and orality is given by Peter van der Veer in his book *Imperial Encounters: Religion and Modernity in India and Britain*. While van der Veer accepts that orality plays a significant role in Indian culture and that oral traditions are often a site of resistance against domination by groups or individuals, he nevertheless warns that "this should not lead us to the romantic notion that orality provides direct access to, for instance 'subaltern consciousness.' . . . We should be equally wary of an interpretation of the Orientalist archive as marking a total transition from self-identifying, authentic speech, to imperialist textuality."[27]

The situation, in van der Veer's view, is more complex. In fact the idea of an opposition between Orientalism (with its implications of a nonnative imperialist textuality and print capitalism) and an authentic Hindu orality is due in part to an uncritical adherence to Benedict Anderson's theory of nationalism. According to Anderson, the rise of all true nationalisms required a privileged connection between printed scripture and a unifying concept of nation. In order to achieve the connection to printed scripture out of a culture that was predominantly oral, Indian nationalist elites adopted the German *Wissenschaft* made available to them through Max Müller's critical text editions of the Rig Veda. Müller's pioneering first printed edition of the Veda was in some ways a culmination of the search for the Ur-text of Hindu civilization as a key to a lost Golden Age, a project initiated by William Jones and the early Orientalists. Müller's first text edition of the Rig Veda induced a sense of shock and crisis among orthodox Brahmins, who had for centuries adhered to the oral tradition of transmitting and receiving the Veda within the paradigm of Sanskrit as sacred sound. As native elites began to edit and produce printed versions of their own tradition-texts, such as the Mahabharata and Ramayana, the possession of a text-based Indian national heritage finally allowed Hindus to gain entry into the elite club of "world religions" and fulfilled Hindus' desire to be represented alongside Christians, Muslims, Jews, and Buddhists as a "People of the Book." Such a designation was the primary marker of nationhood and civilization.

Compared to that of other forms of nationalism, however, the creation of an Indian nationalist heritage can be seen as anomalous. For the print-based nationalist heritage of India would never have been accepted by Hindus had it simply contradicted the two underlying principles of Hindu orthodoxy that legitimate authority, namely, the Veda as orally transmitted, orality as grounded in the divine language of Sanskrit, and ipso facto, the prohibition against writing.[28] The new print-based nationalism therefore had to link itself to the Brahmanical need to ground nationalist texts in the authority of the revelatory experience of Vedic ṛṣis, i.e., in what they had "heard" (śruti) at the time of origin. Far from being a simple accession to Western modernity via Orientalism, what happens to be unique about Indian nationalism is its ability to combine the Brahmanical need for orality, as the grounding principle of power and law, with the Orientalist search for the Golden Age of Hindu civilization (which was in effect a search for a lost Aryan people) and ultimately a racial link between India and the West. In other words, to properly understand the vicissitudes of Indian nationalism, one must attend to the creation of an ideological link between Orientalism and Brahmanism. Notwithstanding the obvious though stereotyped difference between these two cultural forms—Indology's penchant for writing versus Brahmanism's orality—there is, as van der Veer suspects but does not probe, a more deep-rooted complicity between the two schools during the colonial period, an alliance based on the principle of sound as the ontological principle that grounds not only each culture's sense of identity, but also its ethos and, ultimately, its ethnocentrism.

Although the charge of a complicity between Orientalism and Brahmanism seems surprising at first, van der Veer finds support for his claim in the work of Jacques Derrida, who questions the facile distinction between "societies without writing" and "societies with writing." Since his earliest publications Derrida has demonstrated that Western intellectual traditions (including Orientalism and print-capitalism) have covertly regarded speech as preceding writing and thus as closer to reality. In this privileging of speech Derrida sees a desire for origins, a nostalgia for pure presence. Despite the outward dominance of writing and print-culture in the West, for Derrida it is orality—the sonic principle—that has enjoyed a covertly privileged status over writing, and has done so precisely because of a continued belief in the proximity of the oral to the divine/the metaphysical/the transcendent. In effect, Derrida's thesis complicates the simplistic picture of opposed universals and the supposed ethical difference that they represent:

on the one hand, the ethnocentrism of Western textuality and the openness of Indian orality, and on the other hand, Western hermeneutics and ethnology as anti-ethnocentric paradigms suitable for liberating the victims of colonial oppression. There is, as van der Veer contends, a hidden convergence between nineteenth-century Indology and the ancient Brahmanic ideology of sacred sound. What Derrida's work suggests is that this link also finds a strong resonance in the contemporary humanities and social sciences, especially within the hermeneutical and ethnological strands that have affected the history of religions.

Part of my task in this chapter will be to examine how this ideology based on the primacy of sound is transferred from Indology/Brahmanism to the contemporary discourse of the humanities and social sciences. Given that a certain privileging of orality seems to be the "glue" that links these two domains, a useful strategy for this task is to recontextualize the question of orality and specifically the ideology of language as fundamentally phonemic, in terms of a domain that poses resistance to its viability as a universal. The context that I have in mind is that of translation, and specifically the translation of Sikh scripture. For on the one hand, Sikh scripture severely complicates the issue of opposed cultural universals as it possesses equally strong oral and written dimensions, placing it both within and outside the South Asian mold described by Marriott and others. On the other hand, because of the rapidly changing context of its reception, Sikh scripture today faces the problem of translation into multilingual global diasporas dominated by English as the target language, thereby evoking memories of the first translation by Ernest Trumpp in 1877. My aim, however, is not to dismiss the question of universals but to rethink it through the anomalous case of Sikh scripture.

Ethnoscience and the Problem of Translation:
The Case of Sikh Scripture

In a challenging article published in the journal *History of Religions*,[29] Verne Dusenbury usefully reinterprets McKim Marriott's substance theories according to the following structuralist premises: (i) a belief in the existence of "first principles," or "conceptual logics," proper to South Asian civilization that mirror and are mirrored by the traditional Hindu doxa of sacred sound; (ii) this peculiarly South Asian conceptual logic finds its locus in the fundamentally nondualistic ideology of language that in turn derives from a privilege accorded to the nature of sound; (iii) this ideology applies to all languages and cultures of South Asia and thereby represents a cultural universal. Assuming that these three intrinsically connected points hold, it would be fair to suggest that the issue of translation—specifically the translation of South Asian languages into European languages governed by a dualistic metaphysics—poses a fundamental challenge to the continuation of the traditional ideology of sacred sound as well as to the structuralist premises of ethnosocial sciences of South Asia.

This challenge is particularly evident in the ongoing controversy over the translatability of Sikh scripture into dominant pancontinental contexts such as South Asia or Europe. The controversy stems from a single fact: that in the absence of a living Guru (preceptor) Sikh tradition has taken a written text to be its Guru, the source of its authority and the central focus of its cultural organization. But the language of the text is becoming increasingly unintelligible to Sikh worshipers within both their native Punjabi and Western diasporic contexts. To counteract this growing distanciation between the written text and its reader reception, and to retain Sikhism's image as a living world religion based on the perception of it as a "religion of the book," some reformist Sikhs and non-Sikh scholars of Sikhism have suggested that the scripture should be translated into languages intelligible to Sikh worshipers and to potential converts. Indeed, they argue, resistance to the introduction of English translations amounts to a "bibliolatry" or "idol worship" of a linguistically dead original.[30]

To illustrate their point scholars such as Owen W. Cole and others point to the prevalence in contemporary Sikhism of ritual practices such as *akhaṇḍ pāṭh*—uninterrupted oral recitation of the Ādi Granth from beginning to end, usually within a set time period of forty-eight hours.[31] For Cole, the very meaning of the text (Word) as Guru resides in its ability to transfer meaning—presumably correct semantico-referential, and therefore theological, meaning—to the reader or listener. From such a standpoint the idea of unbroken cover-to-cover recitals of the Guru Granth taking place in a diasporic context governed by Anglophone reception, where listeners would have little or no understanding of the words, might seem purely performative and ritualistic. One does not have to agree with Cole's assessment, but in recent years the shift toward pure performance and ritual has also become a major aspect of the Punjabi context, where the majority of listeners are more familiar with the language of the text. Due to an increasingly busy lifestyle for most members of the Sikh community, *akhaṇḍ pāṭh* has become not only a key feature of village and city life in Punjab, but also the major contributor to performative ritual in the central Sikh shrine, the Golden Temple complex at Amritsar. Here it is possible to observe multiple *akhaṇḍ pāṭhs* going on in different rooms spread out across the temple complex, but very often one can also see multiple *akhaṇḍ pāṭh* taking place in the same room. As a performative ritual, the *akhaṇḍ pāṭh*, and more specifically the visual imagery of the Guru Granth as a book and of Sikhism as a "religion of the book," has received greater prominence in the last decade or so due to its being projected through the medium of live television into Sikh homes throughout the world. The increasingly rich dialectic between visual and the sonic aspects of the Granth calls for a thorough and searching analysis of ritual theory and its relationship to existing Sikh doctrine, which cannot be attempted here.[32]

Other scholars, including Verne Dusenbury, have challenged what they perceive as Cole's theological bias, which seems to converge conveniently with the propagandist zeal of some mainstream Khalsā Sikhs, pointing instead to the fact that in "actual practice" Sikh scripture occupies a middle ground between Western monotheistic and Indian monistic traditions.[33] Applying McKim Marriott's structuralist theories to the phenomenon of Sikh worship, Dusenbury argues that Sikh scripture "implicitly challenges analytic dichotomies that rigidly oppose oral and written texts or sound and meaning. . . . Most Sikhs appear to live quite comfortably with a written text retaining crucial oral usages, in which the sacred sound properties of the words have not been subordinated to their meanings." Thus for Dusenbury the translation controversy resides in the fact that Sikhs actually hold a rather different understanding of the properties of language and, as a result of this, a different way of thinking about the question who or what is a Guru. It is an understanding dictated by the fundamental nonduality of the prevailing South Asian cosmology, "which recognizes the material as well as the cognitive properties of language (especially articulated speech)."[34] To illustrate what he means by material properties of language Dusenbury uses the term "physiological engagement" (adapted from A. L. Babb), which refers to the "Word of God" as an effect transmitted by the Guru and embodied forever in the Ādi Granth:

> During the lifetimes of the ten living human Sikh Gurus, physiological engagement with Akāl Purakh (the divine) came directly through the person of the Guru—for example by incorporating his *darśhan* (vi-

sual emanations) or *charan amrit* (foot water), as well as singing his hymns (*kirtan*). Since the ascension of the Granth (the Holy Book) and the Panth (the corporate assembly) to the status of co-Guru following the death in 1708 of Guru Gobind Singh, exact repetition of the *gurbāṇī*, the natural sacred sounds of the Ādi Granth, and performance of *sevā* (selfless service) to the Panth, appear to be considered especially efficacious in incorporating the Guru's divinely coded substances.[35] [underscoring mine]

Although Dusenbury's analysis of "worship substances" relies too heavily on structuralist theory, it nevertheless usefully draws attention to the phenomenon of the *exact reproduction of sacred sound* of the Gurus and the Ādi Granth, which has become, especially since the late nineteenth century, a crucial feature of all distinctively Sikh life-cycle rituals and therefore of modern Sikhism. This exact reproduction of sacred sound is particularly closely associated with the practice of *akhaṇḍ pāṭh*. During the *akhaṇḍ pāṭh* practitioners will take meticulous care to ensure that the sacred sounds are replicated exactly as they might have been enunciated by the Sikh Gurus and the other poets whose inspired utterances are collected in the Ādi Granth. Great emphasis is laid today on correct pronunciation and intonation in reciting the Granth and, in the case of *akhaṇḍ pāṭh*, ensuring that recitation is passed from one reader to the next without any break in the words themselves. To ensure that the recital remains unbroken, each new reader picks up the words from the line on his or her predecessor's lips. The two readers will continue in unison until the new reader has properly adjusted herself into the rhythm of the recital.

A very similar principle of exact sound reproduction can be adduced in routine liturgical practices (*nitnem*), at the heart of which is the theory and practice of *nām simaraṇ*. To remind ourselves, *nām simaraṇ* is a form of repetition that in its wider sense refers to a variety of methods of contemplation, repetition, and remembrance of the Name (*nām*). In a narrower sense it relies on two nondiscursive interlinked techniques (*sādhanās*) performed individually or in a group. *Nām simaraṇ* begins with the technique of voiced repetition, where the practitioner chants aloud a fixed word (such as *vāhiguru* or *satnām*), repeating this over and over until the voiced word becomes interiorized as a soundless and spontaneous repetition (*ajapā jāp*). Understood purely as a technique, *nām simaraṇ* (and *akhaṇḍ pāṭh*) involves the exact reproduction of the word-sounds supposedly heard and then uttered by the human Gurus. As another ethnologist,

Kristina Myrvold, explains, the purpose of this exact replication is to reproduce the sacred words originally revealed phonetically to Guru Nānak and subsequently composed as a written text. It is assumed here that orality chronologically precedes writing.[36] Hence "worship acts" such as *akhaṇḍ pāṭh* or *nām simaraṇ* are "modes to reproduce divine messages or to communicate the true teaching of the Gurus."[37] From her analytic viewpoint Myrvold regards these "worship acts" as

> meta-pragmatic discourses which reveal the existence of a "performativist language" ideology which does not only value what the sacred sounds are saying but also what they are capable of doing. When the sacred gurbānī hymns move into performance they are attributed power and agency to accomplish things in the social world.[38]

The idea of a "performativist language" is borrowed from J. L. Austin's speech-act theory, which holds that an utterance is not merely a means for communicating referential content (and therefore neither true nor false) but an act that makes something happen in the social world. For Myrvold the emphasis on exact sound reproduction in worship acts such as *akhaṇḍ pāṭh* and *nām simaraṇ* is performative insofar as it enables Sikhs to evoke and manifest the agency and presence of the Guru. In fact Myrvold goes so far as to suggest that there is a "Sikh model of revelation," one which takes place in a diachronic schema that links different historical agents in a hierarchical arrangement: God as Speaker, Guru Nānak as listener, the Guru Granth as text, and finally Sikhs today as listeners and speakers:

> Unlike ordinary speech events, the Sikh model implies a hierarchical evaluation of the different speech chains involved: the original speech events that took place between God and the human Gurus belonged to a higher order. The Gurus were both listeners of these words and authors of compositions that were later incorporated in the Sikh scripture. After the scripture's status was transformed to *Guru* Granth Sāhib, the sacred text became a personified speaker of divine words. Through each step in the chain of speech events, the originally divine words descended to humans in history and are made perpetually manifest in present worship context.[39]

The differences between them notwithstanding, there are some resonances between the structuralist and speech-act approaches. First of these is the idea of a transcendental domain of speech that is mimetically reproduced by pious Sikhs in the social domain through ritual. Second is a common interest in giving agency back to "religious" Sikhs, an agency that is, again, dependent on correctly reproducing a transcendent origin. Third, despite these approaches' acceptance of the notion that *śabda-guru* (the Word-as-Guru) authorizes agency, and despite their desire to locate the agency of "religious" Sikhs within the secular world of the here and now, the locus of authority (manifest as the Guru's agency) is itself projected back onto a sacred origin, which is sacred because it transcends the worldly domain. If so, the agency that these ethnologists desire to give back to pious Sikhs is always a "religious" agency that descends from its sacred origin into a transaction with the worldly domain (and of course, nothing could be more worldly than human language). Thus although pious Sikhs use the medium of language to transact their connection of agencies, the worldliness of that language must be repressed by invoking the domain of orality, which has a more pristine connection to the sacred.

Whichever way we look at it, there will always be at work here a fundamental opposition between the religious and the secular. Given that their aim is to justify the existence of Sikh piety and ritual as something that takes place in a secular world, it actually ends up doing precisely the opposite. If the distinction between sacred and secular remains, what could be the purpose of giving agency back to the Sikhs? What role does agency play? Moreover, if repetition is central to the notion of agency, what kind of repetition is involved?

One way of approaching these questions (which I will confront more directly later in this chapter) is to look more closely at those scholars against whom both of these groups of ethnologists, structuralist and speech-act, are arguing. Both target the claims, on the one hand, of Western scholars who argue that translations of the Guru Granth Sāhib can adequately and safely replace the original text, on the grounds that English translations would not necessarily undermine the authority of the Guru as Word (*śabda-guru*). On the other hand, they target Sikh "propagandists" — presumably those trained in the modernist Singh Sabhā mold and sanctioned by the Shiromani Gurdwara Parbandhak Committee (SGPC) to become spokespersons for the Panth, and who preach against the increasing ritualization in the Sikh community. By targeting the explicit theologism of Western scholars and the implicit theologism of the "propagandists," the ethnologist, by giving agency back to the indigenous subject (thereby censuring the neocolonial impulse in modern Sikhism), covertly stakes a claim to anti-imperialist and anti-Orientalist credentials. One could have a certain sympathy for this desire to liberate pious Sikhs if it did not at the same time derive its legitimacy from the claim that their ethnoscience enables the indigenous subjects to represent themselves through their own universals, such as the nondualistic ideology of language proper to orality. This in turn would allow them to represent themselves through their difference from the West, a difference that the "propagandists" so much despise. Clearly, though, this ascription of absolute difference from the West simply propagates the West/non-West binary that has always been central to imperialism and Orientalism in its various forms.

In one sense, both kinds of ethnologists are justified in calling attention to the theological and Orientalist bias of those who ask for a replacement of the original *gurmukhī* text with European translations and, what follows as a result of this, the eradication of excessive ritual. What remains problematic, however, is the privileging of orality, which allows both for the "agency of the Guru" to be made present in the social world by correct intonation, and for the recuperation of an authentic South Asian lifeworld through the monistic ideology of sound. Several reasons can be adduced for this.

First, as I have argued in the previous chapter, even the most theologically orientated of the Singh Sabhā scholars could not easily avoid using the language of sonic monism even as they were eradicating "Hindu" influence from the prior exegesis of the Ādi Granth. This is partly because they, like other North Indians, were culturally embedded within a hegemonic cultural matrix based on the paradigm of orality. Far from being neutral, however, this oral matrix was governed by its own structural grammar, best seen in the form of rules applying to kinship lineages (*birādaris*), clans (*got*), and castes (*zāt*). In the nineteenth century this cultural matrix came to be identified by traditional elites as a tradition without roots in linear time, i.e., *sanātan*. Within this context the oral mediation of societal norms by elites such as *brahmins*, *pīrs*, *sādhus*, and other living (*dehdhārī*) gurus was a sustaining pillar of *sanātan* culture. And the reason for this is not difficult to seek. The finite and temporal nature of sound, along with the sense of proximity and personal agency engendered by voiced mediation, had significant social implications—in particular greater fluidity across linguistic and religious boundaries.

Nevertheless, as Harjot Oberoi clearly recognized, the term *sanātan* and the seemingly idyllic culture associated with it that he refers to as an "enchanted universe," which prevailed prior to colonialism and the rise of reformist Sikhism, derives from the Sanskrit term *sanātana dhar-ma*, which alludes to traditions and practices that are ancient, existing in mythic time and created at the origin of time.[40] In the nineteenth century the term *sanātana dharma* was reappropriated by orthodox Hindu elites to characterize their social order as the "unshakeable, venerable order" which is at the same time an all-encompassing order that required no reforms or innovations because it had never changed. Closer inspection, however, reveals that its supposed eternality referred to norms and rules of life laid down by the "Brahmanical paradigm of *varnāśrama dharma* according to which there are four *varnas* and four *aśramas*, or stages of life."[41] But once the Brahmanical connection is acknowledged, greater caution must be exercised in equating orality with the heterolingual context of precolonial North India, or in plying it with anti-imperialist credentials. I shall return to this issue later in this chapter as it has implications for the construction of any history of (Sikh) religion. My point here is simply to register the fact that the oral paradigm is intrinsically part of an ancient indigenous power structure, namely the Brahmanic ideology of sacred sound, which was socially institutionalized through the framework of caste. It is this power structure that the teachings of the Sikh Gurus, and in a different way the scholars of the Singh Sabhā movement, remained resistant to.

Second, there is no credible evidence that any ideology of sacred sound—which refers to a technology of reproducing exactly correct sound(s) in order to gain access to the sound-words originally heard and enunciated by the Sikh Gurus—was ever sanctioned by the Sikh Gurus, nor indeed part of the oral transmission of scripture practiced by the early Sikh community. Arguments to the contrary notwithstanding, it can be shown that the technology of sonic replication is fundamentally at odds with the teachings of the Sikh Gurus and also with various traditions of *gurmat sangīt* or *kīrtan*, which have little to do with a belief in sacred sound. I am not denying that this model lives on even within orthodox Sikh practices, indeed, it has even been adopted by many Western converts to Sikhism. Rather I am trying to point out that there is a much stronger and more pervasive strand that resists these practices both within historic and contemporary Sikh exegetical traditions and within the writings of the Sikh Gurus.

The concerns I have outlined above should at the very least evoke suspicion about the underlying assumptions and sociohistorical effects enabled by the nondualistic ideology of language with its attendant concept of transcendent sound. If a certain ideology of language based on sacred sound constitutes something like an essential pan–South Asian property that is responsible for structuring the oral tradition and the cultural logic of an entire geographical region, and if it is in fact derived from a specific cultural tradition (the Brahmanic or Vedic tradition of *varṇaśrama dharma*), what is it about this property (the sacredness of sound) that justifies its claim to being a universal as well as a grounding, origin(al), and unifying center of South Asian culture? Going back to Peter van der Veer's earlier question: if there is an historical complicity between this Brahmanic ideal of sacred sound and the rise of knowledge formations that specialize in the study of ethnic cultures, how does this South Asian universal feed back into the discourse of the history of religions (in its hermeneutical and ethnoscientific versions)? If this unique property (that is, the transcendence or sacredness of sound) is invoked by the nationalist imaginary as the basis of some of the typical characteristics of Hindu civilization (its cultural tolerance, inherent pluralism, nonviolence, etc.) why has there been, ever since the birth of Hindu nationalism, an explicit tendency toward an assimilatory, monocultural, monolinguistic, monoracial monotheism that takes its authority from the Veda? Is there within this property and its reappropriation by Hindu nationalist elites an implicit metaphysics that gravitates around a particular ethnic consciousness—specifically the institution of caste?

Moreover, if, as I have suggested above, the dominant strand of Sikh spiritual practice, as based on the teachings of the Sikh Gurus, is firmly resistant to the notion of sacredness or transcendence of sound, is it possible to find from within the sources of Sikh tradition, such as the Guru Granth Sāhib, a very different concept of language/Word, something like a cultural singularity, that simultaneously resists the Singh Sabhā's ontotheologization of the Word and the reconsolidation of a pan–South Asian universalism in the shape of *sanātana dharma* or caste Brahmanism? To put it more bluntly, is it possible to argue that there is latent within the teachings of the Sikh Gurus and within strands of Sikh tradition an understanding of language/Word that resists two different kinds of transcendental metaphysics: on the one hand, the metaphysics borrowed by the Sikh reformists from Christian philosophical theology, which allowed Sikhism to be identified as a "religion of the book"; and on the other hand, the metaphysics of sacred sound deriving from what I shall call the Vedic economy?[42] While the former interprets the Word of Sikh scripture as directly revealed by a monotheistic God, etc., the latter interprets the Word of scripture monistically as part of an eternal cosmic Wisdom, an eternal vibration without beginning or end. Although it is rarely acknowledged, the two are not necessarily the same or even close. Either way, the concept of language in the teachings of the Sikh Gurus is deontologized, which is to say that it is presaged into the service of an origin that is *sui generis*.

My argument is that there is such a principle which not only resists the transcendentalization (monotheistic and monistic) of language, but also moves us beyond the notion of sovereignty associated with the nationalist imaginary, toward a notion of sovereignty that is, paradoxically, free of it*self*. As I had begun to outline in chapter 4, the concept of *śabda-guru* (lit. "the Guru as Word or language") is such a principle, able to resist complete assimilation both by the Sikh reformists and by the model of humanism in the history of religions project. As a cultural singularity the concept of *śabda-guru* can be regarded as sovereign because it can be universalized even as it remains singular. Insofar as it represents the *difference within Sikh tradition itself*, a difference that connects Sikhs and Sikhism to its other, it can be envisaged as the "middle ground" of Sikhism. Residing at the intersection between language and self (it is both yet neither of these), this paradoxical principle simultaneously underpins the conservative form of Sikh identity (e.g., the Khalsā's tendency toward religious affirmation: monotheism, religion of the book, etc.) and the most radically deconstructive aspect of Sikh tradition, *its tendency to resist becoming a religion*. This tendency resides in the sovereignty of language, which questions the very idea of what it means to be human.[43]

Although it was possible in chapter 4 to pull the concept of *śabda-guru* clear from the contours of Christian metaphysics around which the Sikh reformist and history of religions discourses gravitated, what could not be explained in sufficient detail was the way in which the concept of *śabda-guru* differs from and therefore resists the Vedic paradigm of language. As Jodh Singh and other reformists knew only too well, this has always been a problem, made doubly difficult by the fact that the terms used in both traditions are similar if not the same. Part of what I attempt to do below is to show that although the notion of *śabda-guru* is rooted in South Asian traditions of thinking about language and reality, its doubly conservative-radical gesture—of self-affirmation/self-deconstruction, enchantment/disenchantment, and consolidation/dissemination—fundamentally resists the Vedic economy. Indeed, the nonmonotheistic, nonmonistic conception of *śabda-guru* that I shall be exploring, far from being yet another idiosyncratic product of modern Sikh ideology, resists ideology as such. Consequently it works as a foil for interrogating the broader themes central to this chapter: (i) the historical complicity between Orientalism and Brahmanism (what I will refer to as the Vedic economy) in the making of the nationalist imaginary; (ii) the question of language in the discourse of the humanities, and the becoming ever more general and global of the category "religion."

In order to elucidate these issues it will be helpful to briefly sketch out a political critique of the concept of sacred sound that is central to the Vedic economy. This critique can be considered political insofar as it focuses on the question of repetition, defined quite simply as a way of repeating or reproducing one's existence in the world, a way of being in time. Repetition is intrinsically political because it involves engagement with time, the world, and other(s), rather than a reproduction of eternity that fosters a mimetic reproduction of self. Though rarely acknowledged, this difference between two possible types of repetition in the South Asian context derives from very different notions of word or language (śabda). One of my aims in what follows below is to bring attention to the depoliticization of the concept of language in certain influential strands of Indian linguistics, or how it is that the physical signifier in language is conceptually dematerialized in relation to the nonphysical. This distinction between the physical and nonphysical runs through much of early and modern Indian linguistics. What follows, then, is a somewhat unconventional attempt to trace the contours of the concept of sacred sound as it runs through early Vedic texts, evolves into the main strands of Indian linguistics, transmutes itself into the language philosophy of nationalists such as Ananda Coomaraswamy, and eventually finds its way into the discourse of history of religions. My aim here is not to provide a history of the concept of sacred sound but something far less ambitious. My aim is simply to track the continuity of certain metaphysical operations—particularly the role of mimesis—within some well-known strands of Indian linguistics. This exercise is necessary for the task of working out a more coherent understanding of the Sikh concept of śabda-guru as a universal within the postcolonial context, which I shall undertake at the end of this chapter.

Sounding the Vedic Economy

Let me therefore begin with the following question: what is this property that gives coherence to a pan–South Asian universal? What, in other words, justifies the description of this property in terms of the sacred or transcendental nature of sound, which frames, however loosely, a certain kind of cultural unity and coherence that is sociologically associated with the institution of caste?

The answer to the first question is fairly straightforward. In the sense of a "defining or essential quality" or "predicate" the word "property" refers to *dharma* [44] — a term whose translation as "religion" is by no means an insignificant event in the intellectual encounter between India and Europe. Thus although *dharma* in its original Vedic etymology refers to the principle of stability,[45] or the power that upholds and maintains an established order, its subsequent history tells of a pragmatic adaptation by the Vedic Aryans to designate and differentiate the sociocultural boundaries of their own community from those who were defined as foreigners or outsiders.[46] In other words, *dharma* — in its signification as "custom" or "propriety" — became the central concept of a rigorously ethnocentric self-assertion by Vedic culture, a demarcation of Aryan identity from the non-Aryan (*mleccha*: "foreigner"). *Dharma* represented a unique and exclusive norm of one particular society (the Vedic Aryan). As such it provided a framework of "correctness" and "orthodoxy," and consequently the set of beliefs and relationships that legitimized the position of the Brahmins as official guardians of *dharma*.

But in this sense of "property" or "predicate," *dharma* was also inseparable from that of which it was a predicate, namely Veda, as well as the linguistic vehicle of Veda: the Sanskrit language. By the time of the *Dharmaśāstra* literature the relationship between these three entities, Veda, Sanskrit, and *dharma*, had become a circular one.[47] If the sacredness of Aryan *dharma* was fundamentally grounded in the idea of only one privileged language (other languages being impure or "fallen" variants), then Sanskrit in turn received its sacred sanction from Veda.

According to Madhav Deshpande, what kept the circular relationship between identity, language, and scripture (corresponding to Ārya/Sanskrit/Veda) intact — thereby allowing it to maintain, preserve, and support what was most proper to a particular community — was an ideology based on two interlinked ideas: (i) the notion that the essence of language is sound or voice (*vāk*), and (ii) the idea that *vāk* is eternal and therefore intrinsically sacred. Together these two notions comprise what Deshpande calls the "Theology of Eternal Sanskrit," an ideological framework in which Brahmin scholars were rigorously primed.[48]

Equally important in reinforcing the eternity paradigm was the characterization of Veda as *śruti* (lit. "that which is heard"), as opposed to non-Vedic sources, which were characterized as *smṛti* (lit. "remembered" or "recollected"). Although I shall return to this distinction, the point to note is that the *śruti*/*smṛti* distinction is based on a particular understanding of the notion of experience. According to this concept of experience, the Sanskrit language—which by definition means "perfected"—is "heard" (*śruti*). It speaks in a mode of immediacy or timeless presence that needs no support or mediation. By contrast, non-Vedic languages, which are termed Prakrit—implying fallen, "earthy," imperfect, corrupted, etc.—require recollection or the use of memory, where memory involves a reliance on or mediation via human languages subject to temporality or sequencing. The difference between having "heard" (*śruti*) and having "recollected" (*smṛti*) is crucial. *Śruti* refers to a nonsensory "hearing," one that cannot be heard with the physical organ, but only by the cultivation of an "inner ear." It refers to a mode of being in which the *ṛṣi* (the one who is privileged to hear-understand the original sound) is at one with the nonempirical element of sound, which is also the element of ideality, that is, of an experience that is not in-the-world or in time.[49]

The major consequence of this "Theology of Eternal Sanskrit," based on Eternal Sound (*vāk*), is the suppression of the empirical signifier—that is to say, a suppression of "physical" writing and "physical" sound, which in turn means a suppression of the element of time and difference. Concomitant with this suppression is the production of cultural identity—the Vedic Aryan *dharma*—based on the essentially circular identity of Veda/Sanskrit/*dharma*.

With the textual evolution of the Veda, the concept of eternal *vāk*, which is present mainly in the Rig Veda, merged in the later Brahmanas section of the Veda with another evolving concept: *Brāhman*. Although in the early stages of its development the word *Brāhman* (from the Sanskrit root *Bṛh*, implying a sacred force or power) referred to the power of speech sounds in Vedic mantras, it became merged with *vāk* to give the earliest meaning of *Brāhman* as "sacred Word" or "Sacred formula," which referred ultimately to the Veda itself. With further evolution the term *Brāhman* developed during the Upaniṣads period (800–500 B.C.) into the ontological dualism between eternal and temporal knowledge. The important point as far as this chapter is concerned is that in the Upaniṣads *śabda-brahman* replaces *vāk* and becomes the focal point for post-Upaniṣadic speculation on the nature of sound and its relation to—that is, its capacity to "reveal"—reality (*Brāhman*).

During the post-Upaniṣadic period (500 B.C.–A.D. 500) the earlier ideas were taken over and developed into rigid systems of theoretical linguistics, with a particular emphasis on the elaboration of grammar (*vyākarana*) and phonetics. The most important works in the early development of this field are the *Aṣṭādhyāyī* of Paṇīni (500 B.C.)—a comprehensive grammar of the Sanskrit language that included both Vedic Sanskrit and classical "Laukika" Sanskrit—and Patañjali's *Mahābhāṣya*.[50] The linguistic speculations of both of these early scholars exerted a profound and lasting effect on the future development of this field, to the extent that they can be regarded as direct forerunners of the philosophical schools that specialized in developing theories based on the relationship between *śabda* (word/sound) and *Brāhman* (eternal ground). Especially significant are the two opposed schools: the Mīmāṃsā (or the Varṇavāda) school, expounded by Kumārila, and the Grammarian (or Sphoṭavada) school, whose chief exponent is Bhartṛhari.

A detailed historical treatment of the subtle differences between these linguistic schools is well beyond the scope of this present section. I shall therefore limit myself to some brief remarks concerning their collective contribution to the continued predominance of orality in Indian traditions, but from a viewpoint that remains somewhat ignored in most accounts of Indian linguistic tradition (as also in the history of ideas), which tend to idealize their contribution to a venerable tradition that continues to this day.[51] What I have in mind is a materialist viewpoint that not only takes account of, but starts from, the sociopolitical context of these thinkers, as determined by the encounter between cultures that in turn gave rise to an overall mood of anxiety and insecurity rather than of settled existence, which would favor philosophical speculation. To reiterate the questions that concern me: (i) What is the connection between the philosophical justification for controlling speech/sound production in the reception and transmission of culture and the simultaneous preservation of *dharma* (cultural identity), which results in the suppression or exclusion of the foreign? (ii) How does the element of sound generate the metaphysical scheme that consciously promotes the oral paradigm while at the same time consciously suppressing writing, understood not only as physical inscription, but as temporal experience?

Deontologizing the Word (*śabda*): Metaphysics of "Eternal Sanskrit" and the Production of a Sonic Mimetology

It is a well-known fact that the predominance of orality in Indian tradition was not the result of the Indians' inability to write, but was a *conscious decision*, sustained over a long period, to orally reproduce knowledge that derived initially from literate sources.[52] The oral medium, which was overtly privileged over writing, was considered to be the element par excellence for preserving the purity of Aryan *dharma*, or sociolinguistic identity, which, certainly up to the time of Pāṇini (500 B.C.) had been largely centered around the correct performance and transmission of the Vedic ritual mantra and fire sacrifice. For several centuries before Pāṇini the inevitability of increased cultural and linguistic contact and competition from competing non-Aryan cultures had forced the Vedic Aryans to carefully review the relationship between the Sanskrit of the Vedic texts and the kind of Sanskrit that was actually spoken.

In his study of the social implications of the relationship between Sanskrit and Prakrit, Deshpande makes an important connection between the suppression of multilingualism and the suppression of multiple identities in the social culture of the Vedic Aryans.[53] Despite strict social restrictions, however, it is likely that Brahmins could not have avoided linguistic contact with non-Āryas. The only way to do this, however, and at the same time the only way to avoid "polluting" Sanskrit, was for Brahmins and other Āryas to adopt the (Prakrit) languages of non-Āryas in order to speak to them. In this way at least they could prevent Sanskrit from being spoken by non-Āryas—which they were prohibited from doing in any case. Over time the Āryas had in fact become *bilingual*, although they could never admit to this: hence the suppression of the Prakrit language as their "own."[54] The important point, however, is that even this suppressed bilingualism would have been instrumental in the generation of new vernacular languages (and also identities), in which Aryans had always participated, but which, in the interests of preserving the purity of Veda/Sanskrit/*dharma*, they conveniently forgot by the ingenious mechanism of devaluing the role of human memory or, better stated, by technologizing the role of human memory. This last point will be further developed toward the end of this chapter. The end of this stage appears to be marked by the *Aṣṭādhyāyī*, in which Pāṇini formulated the "rules" (*Prātiśākhyas*) for the correct usage of Sanskrit, which had the dual purpose of (i) enabling a correct oral reproduction of Veda, and (ii) prohibiting or minimizing "speech contact" between Aryan and non-Aryans. [55]

While language—specifically Sanskrit—had been recognized as a central criterion for the definition of "Ārya," it is not until Patañjali (150 B.C.), the famous exponent of the "Sanskrit renaissance," that the study of grammar (vyākarana) became the criterion for determining *ethos* in terms of foreignness and propriety simultaneously. This association between language (Sanskrit) and *dharma* (Vedic-Aryan) is perhaps the essential step in the extraordinary future development of the philosophical schools of language that promoted both orality and a suppression of writing to the extent that writing was positively tabooed. Indeed, as we learn from several of the early Upaniṣads, writing was considered pollution. It was an act that violated *dharmic* boundaries: "(A) Brahmin should not recite or orally transmit the Vedas after he has eaten meat, seen blood or a dead body, had sexual intercourse, or engaged in writing."[56] This hostility toward writing is more easily appreciated in the context of ongoing socioeconomic, political, and linguistic conflicts, and religious competition and encounters.[57]

While the taboos against writing certainly helped to foster a culture of oral transmission and reproduction, it is in fact a combination of the phonetic nature of Sanskrit and the rigid system of rule-governed techniques for implementing the phonetics (known as *Prātiśākhyas*) that enabled incredibly large portions of the Veda to be memorized and reproduced correctly. Indeed, phonetic language and memory technique functioned in tandem, allowing the internalization of human speech, that is, its removal from the externalizing influence of time. Given that the primary interest at this time was to preserve the sacred speech sounds of the Veda in a disciplined and pure form, it is not surprising that the *Prātiśākhyas* was the first branch of Indian linguistics to attain independent status, followed closely by the study of phonetics in its own right.

Thus by the time the two main schools of Indian linguistics had established themselves as authoritative modes of speculation, the use and transmission of Sanskrit in relation to Vedic text had already become a strictly internalized discipline premised on two fundamental assumptions: (i) a relationship between *śabda* (sound/word) and *artha* (meaning) based on the notion of *nitya*, i.e., the word or sound as eternal and proper to itself; (ii) following the already prevalent and mutually inclusive paradigms of eternal Veda, eternal Sanskrit, and eternal *dharma, the direct connection of* artha *(meaning) to consciousness*, which, by implication, referred to the currently extant domain of speech activity within the community.

In other words, consciousness of oneself as Ārya depended on a direct correspondence between the meaningfulness of Vedic stanzas and the correct speaking of Sanskrit. Moreover, the externally spoken *śabda* must correctly reproduce the memorized/internalized *śabda-artha* within the here and now of the present moment. The key point here is the attainment via correct reproduction within a moment of full presence of an absolute identity between the external signifier (=articulated/voiced *śabda*) and the internal signified (*artha*=memorized word as meaning).[58] Stated differently: *śabda,* as the sound/word of Veda, and *artha,* the meaning as given or authorized by Vedic community or social elites, coincide properly only in a certain *type* of humanity.

That *śabda* (signifier) and *artha* (signified) can remain in absolute proximity—the very aim of Varṇavāda theory is to reproduce perfectly the internal "unstruck" sound—is underwritten by a theory of phonetic writing in which the letters of the alphabet (or individual phonematic units) are differentiated according to their relative degree of "voiceness." What I have termed here as a theory of phonetic writing in Mīmāṁsā is thought to be based on positions found in some of the earliest phonetic texts such as the *Paṇīniya Śikṣa*[59] and the *Ṛk-Pratiśākhya.*[60] In the latter text the idea of phonetic writing is succinctly developed by way of a discussion that focuses on the differing roles of breath and voice in the production and classification of speech sounds: "Breath is emitted in the case of the voiceless consonants, and voice in the case of voiced consonants and vowels." Further, all vowels, semivowels, and "voiced" consonants contain descending degrees of "voice," or what is called "glottal resonance" (*nāda*) by the phoneticians: "The air which retains *nāda* 'voice, resonance' on account of the closure in the glottis is viewed by this tradition as constituting pure *ghosa* 'voice, resounding, reverberating' and is represented by the sound *a.*"[61] Since each consonant contains the letter *a* in combination with either a voiced or unvoiced consonantal prefix, the various letters of the alphabet are distinguished and categorized according to "voiceness," with vowels at the forefront.[62]

The tendency throughout these classical texts on phonetics is to highlight the role of voiced sound, or *nāda,* as the means of interiorizing language. Yet the real issue in these texts concerns "speech production," or the origin of language itself: is language created out of nothing or does it exist eternally? If language is created out of nothing—a view propounded by opponents of the Vedic economy, particularly the Buddhists—and is therefore conventional or manmade, would this not undermine the privilege of speech/sound over writing? If on the other hand it existed eternally,[63] then the very question of language would have to begin with the primacy of speech or sound.

Clearly, by allocating a degree of "voiceness" as measured by the proximity of different phonemes to the sound a, these early phonetic theories provided the basis on which the spoken word—in this case the re-produced or re-cited Vedic speech sounds—could correctly, i.e., absolutely, reproduce the original unstruck sound (*anhad nāda*) and thereby enter into the immediate and privileged inner unity of meaning. This inner unity of meaning is the articulated unity of sound and meaning within the voice. There is, in other words, a complicity between voice and meaning, between voice and the operation of internalizing, and between voice and notions such as *ātman* and *śruti* that pertain to present the domain of interiority as such and in its immediacy.

Indian linguistic theory, then, did not stop at the purely material difference between speech and writing. Its fundamental premise, the eternality/propriety (*nitya*) of sound, provided from the outset the metaphysical impetus behind the split between signifier/signified, *śabda-brahman/ Pārabrahman*, and *śabda/artha*. The way in which metaphysics operates in this split can be usefully illustrated by means of a comparison between the Platonic system, as given in the *Cratylus* and *Phaedrus*, and Bhartṛhari's *sphoṭa* theory.

Traditional Indian linguistics has laid stress on the proposition that articulate sound (*śabda*) is eternal, forever the same, and that the connection between an articulate sound (*śabda*) and its meaning (*artha*) is not due to convention, but is by nature inherent in the sound itself. Plato deals with a similar problem in his *Cratylus*: whether the relation between sound and meaning is essential or accidental. Plato maintains, for example, that a true name applies to that thing which has a natural meaning, where meaning refers to imitation or the likeness of a name to the thing, i.e., the participation of the thing itself in terms of sound. But since vocal imitation (i.e., naming via speech) is imperfect at recollecting the likeness of the thing, the formation of words in speech must be aided by art:

> As an artist imitates a figure, so we make speech by the art of the name . . . or some other art. [64]

This art of naming must have an artificer,[65] where the artificer is the cause or reason why anything has a name—this reason being none other than mind, for which Plato uses the metaphor "the beautiful," i.e., the form or ideal:

> Is not mind that which called things by their names, isn't mind the beautiful? . . .
> Then mind is rightly called beauty because she does the work we recognize and speak of as beautiful.[66]

Earlier in the *Cratylus*, Plato indirectly identifies art (*technē*) with the "possession of mind,"[67] giving the impression that "art" and the "beautiful" could be metaphors for the technique of engraving or inscribing within the mind or within memory: *the art of memory, or mnemo-technic.* If so, it means that Plato considers the signifier, or sound-as-inscribed-in-memory, to be secondary, merely an aid to *perfect* recollection. What is primary is that which is eternal, namely the *ousia*, or essence, in a particular thing. Consequently the *ousia* in a spoken name is the original (or eternal) sound itself, the ideal or "unstruck" sound, that underlies what is spoken in normal utterance, which because of its exteriority is only imperfectly remembered.

In a similar sense to Plato's *Cratylus* (though one can clearly overdetermine the comparison), Indian linguistic philosophy has interpreted the terms *śabda* and *artha* in terms of the perfect and inseparable union of sound and meaning, the unity and totality of essence and nature. Such an interpretation is a specialized variation on the more general philosophical theme of *nāma-rūpa*—a term that encapsulates one of the perennial problems of the Indian religious and philosophical tradition. *Nāma-rūpa* represents none other than the problem of "exemplarism," which has been expounded in a variety of different ways: the One and many, God and creation, mind and world, identity and difference, reality and phenomenality. These different ways of expressing what is essentially the same problem reflect the centrality of the fundamental question of metaphysics to all of them: the difference or identity—which is to say, the *relation*—between time and eternity, between beings and Being.

In addition to its standard metaphysical connotations, *nāma-rūpa* is also directly linked to the problem of language. The Sanskrit term *nāma/nāman*, which corresponds to the English "name/naming," can be defined as an internal linguistic potential for thinking that is prior to any possibility of exterior manifestation (*rūpa*) of that thinking as speech. *Nāma* is considered to be the eternal substance that underlies the very possibility of speech, while *rūpa* (lit. "color, shape, figure") is the outer and finite counterpart of *nāma*.

Despite the broadly Platonic distinctions that are used to describe the *nāma-rūpa* relationship, the idea of a *metaphysical* analogy between the Greek and the Vedic is not unfounded.[68] Such an analogy is expounded, for example, in the work of the Indian philosopher/art historian Ananda Coomaraswamy.[69] In his translation of the following line from Sankara-charya's *Svātman-nirūpana*, Coomaraswamy would appear to be perfectly justified in interpreting it not only via the thematics of *nāma-rūpa*, but also by way of comparison to the Platonic Type/token distinction, or to the scholastic distinction between *imago imaginans* and *imago imaginata:*

> The Primal Spirant (*paramātman*) sees the world-picture (*jagac-citra*: lit. "the picture of what moves") painted by itself upon a canvas that is nothing but itself, and takes a great delight therein.[70]

Notwithstanding his assimilation of Judeo-Christian creationism to refer to the origin in terms of Spirant/breath and for which he conveniently finds an even earlier Rig Vedic equivalent in order to justify his interpretation, the key move in the above passage is Coomaraswamy's translation of *ātman* not as self, which too easily links to the later Vedic and Western visual thematics of knowledge (*darśana/vidyā* and *episteme*), but rather his translation of *ātman* as speech,[71] and of *paramātman* as the primal sound/spirant—a move that brings the word *ātman* back into the domain and problematic of language. *Nāma* therefore corresponds to the Primal Sound in the sense of naming—an active naming that *gives* phenomenal being (*rūpa*) to time and world and therefore to an order of things that is merely contingent upon the eternality of the primal act of naming (*nāman*).

What is being suggested in Coomaraswamy's translation by way of reference to Platonic and Scholastic metaphysics is that *nāma*, the divine eternal substance, gives rise to the conception of a single living language that is the sum of all imaginable articulations. The interchangeability of light and sound metaphors[72] merely testifies to the fact that they are simply different aspects of a fundamental metaphysical principle that is common to the Greek and Vedic view of language, namely a conception of time in which eternity is privileged over "any temporal succession of events":

The name or form of the thing is thus prior—prior, that is, in hierarchy rather than in time—to the thing itself, and is its *raison d'etre*, whether as pattern or as name.[73]

As a result, all existing determinate languages are merely partially remembered, more or less fragmented echoes of the universal divine sound *nāma*, just as all modes of vision are more or less obscure refractions of the world-picture *(jagac-citra)*, or eternal mirror.[74] Hence the metaphysical doctrine of a single, and by implication eternal and universal, sound, as opposed to groups of sound uttered in succession (which, of course, is what is meant by spoken language), lies behind the notion of a universal language.

Such a thesis finds its clearest and most influential expression in Bhartṛhari's *sphoṭa* theory of language.[75] The importance of Bhartṛhari's theory resides in (i) his reestablishment of the authority of the Brahmanical oral tradition, particularly in building upon the work of Patañjali, (ii) the direct and indirect influence it has exerted upon popular religious traditions, especially Kashmir Śaivism and the Yoga tradition of Gorakhnāth. Thus the Yoga theory of "internal," or unstruck, sound *(anhad nāda)*, the hearing of which is supposed to be obtained as the culmination of Yogic *āsanas*, is largely indebted to the grammarian school, and particularly to the figures Patañjali and Bhartṛhari, although the latter's influence on the Nāth tradition is largely inherited through Kashmir Śaivism. It is through these popular traditions that the Vedic paradigm has continued to exert influence on Sant and Sikh practices such as *nām simaraṇ*.[76]

The main contribution of the *sphoṭa* theory was its construction of an ontological basis for language, which it accomplished by reinterpreting the Vedic notion of eternal *vāk* in a manner that was quite different from the Varṇavāda school. This was done by proposing that *vāk* (sound) reveals itself as a linguistic absolute, the *sphoṭa* (= unity of *śabda-artha*), which happens to be internal to "normal human consciousness." For Bhartṛhari the locus of meaning is in the mind. A distinction is made between the being of an object in the external world—and therefore in time—and its being in the form of a mental cognition. It is the *internal relation* between language (*śabda*) and its mental cognition (*artha*) that ensures its eternality. Ontologically, all meaning resides within human consciousness, where, in being related to sound on various distinct levels, it also aspires toward an ultimate unity, namely the *sphoṭa* as the *śabda-Brahman*, which Bhartṛhari regards as the essence of Veda.

The success or failure of the above thesis really depends on how it answers the question "What is language (*śabda*)?" given that *śabda* is equally comprised of: (i) *nāda*, the physical vehicle for communicating meaning publicly, i.e., "in the world" (also known as the "noisy realities," *nāda* refers to speech sounds or written letters that are sequentially uttered or read); (ii) that which is communicated, i.e., meaning, or *sphoṭa*.

Bhartṛhari's answer is somewhat problematic: *śabda* "is" *sphoṭa*, and *sphoṭa* "is" the real vehicle of meaning,[77] or the substance that underlies and is the basis of meaning. As such *sphoṭa* is an undifferentiated unity, a partless, sequenceless, eternal entity. *Sphoṭa* is language in its preverbal potential state; a potentiality that can be actualized by means of physical *nāda*, i.e., sequential utterance. More importantly, though, the theory reveals the basis for its claim to universality—the idea that *sphoṭa* is inherent and internal to consciousness, "in the mind" of speakers and listeners. The reason is that in order to *think* of *sphoṭa* as an undifferentiated, sequenceless, meaning-bearing symbol, it is absolutely necessary to already presuppose the *ātman* in its omniscient, transcendental aspect, on the basis of which (or within which) any thinking-as-such can occur.

Sphoṭa theory's circularity is in part due to the above transcendental presupposition. More importantly, though, the transcendental framework of *sphoṭa* theory closely matches the *nāma-rūpa* thematic, and this is especially evident in the analogies given by Bhartṛhari to illustrate his point. For example:

> The potentiality (*kratu*) called language is like the yolk of a hen's egg. It develops (being articulated) into the form of an act where it obtains parts and sequences.[78]

A more telling analogy from the *Vākyapadīya* repeats the age-old distinction between the painter and painting:

> Just as a figure is grasped by the painter's unified consciousness, and is painted on the canvas as another, complete, unified figure, likewise language (*śabda*) possesses all these three stages.[79]

As the examples given above clearly show, and as Coomaraswamy is at pains to demonstrate in his essays, there is more than just an accidental resemblance between the Platonic and Vedic traditions. Thus on the basis of the following: (i) a dual temporality: *eternity* = perfect language (*nāma*) versus *time* = everyday language (*rūpa*), and (ii) a coincidence of light and sound metaphors in a transcendental signified (i.e., a divine unchanging substance), one could argue that Coomaraswamy is justified in naming metaphysics as the site of a "proper" convergence between these two traditions. By "proper" I mean that the Platonic and Vedic share a similar operation, which Coomaraswamy identifies variously as "reflection," "mirroring," "echoing," and, in several instances, "mimesis":

> In what manner the ideas are causal with respect to their contingent aspects will be apparent when we recall that the central consciousness is always thought of as a Light or Sound, of which the contingent forms . . . are projections, reflections, expressions, or echoes, thrown as it were, upon the wall of Plato's cave, or upon the screen of a theatre.[80]

Coomaraswamy might here be accused of importing a subjective desire—the desire of the Oriental to mimic the Western medium in order to attain for the Vedic sources (his "own" tradition) the kind of stature enjoyed by Plato. But this would overlook the fact that Coomaraswamy was already aware of the difference between the Platonic, which expresses itself through metaphors of light (reflection/mirroring, etc.), and the Vedic, which expresses itself through both sonic and visual metaphors ("Not that light and sound are strictly speaking synonymous [for though they refer to one and the same thing, they do so under different aspects]").[81] Thus the terms used to describe a convergence of the two traditions—"mirroring," "reflection," and most importantly "mimesis"—refer less to the equivalence of the *aspect* namely light and/or sound, than they do to the *form* or *ideal* in which they inhere, namely eternity.

But even this—the identification of metaphysics as the site of cultural convergence—is not the real point that Coomaraswamy seems to be making. His real intention always remains below the surface of his text on "Vedic Exemplarism," which can be read superficially as an investigation into the role of mimesis in Platonic and Vedic theology. If the intention surfaces at all, it does so not within the "Exemplarism" essay, but, interestingly, in another essay, "*Nirukta = Hermenia*," which, not surprisingly, is also concerned with the role of mimesis, but this time in its relation to a universal language and by implication the only language, that is, a single underlying Sound:

The assumption more immediately underlying the traditional science
of hermeneutics (*nirukta*) is that there remains in spoken languages a
trace of universality, and particularly of natural *mimesis* (by which of
course we do not mean a merely onomatopoetic likeness but one of
true analogy) that even in languages considerably modified by art and
convention, there still survives a considerable part of a naturally adequate symbolism. It is assumed in other words that certain assonances,
which may or may not correspond to the actual pedigrees of words,
are nevertheless indications of their affinities and meanings, just as we
recognise family likeness, both of appearance and of character, apart
from the line of direct inheritance. All of which is anything but a matter of "folk etymology"; it is not a matter of etymology at all in the
narrowest sense of the word, but rather of significant assonance, and
*in any case the "folk" tradition is a matter of the folk only in respect
of its transmission, not its origin; "folklore" and Philosophia Perennis
spring from a common source.*[82] [emphasis added]

Coomaraswamy's real intention, though cloaked under a discussion
of one of the perennial issues in classical theology, is in fact to lay the
groundwork for a particular mode of repetition that takes its example
from a Vedic life-world. The mode of repetition is, of course, mimesis—
in other words, the possibility for Indians to repeat their existence, to
engage the world, even a colonial world, and their possibility for being
political are tied to an origin that is Veda.

Mimesis operates in such a way as to invert the order of signification
between man (self) and language, such that language is deontologized.
From being an ontological ground of thinking language is displaced to
a secondary instrumental function, i.e., an art or technique, for the use
of man. As Phillipe Lacoue-Labarthe argues in his important essay "Typography," in the case of the Platonic heritage this inversion is part of
an elaborate ruse, a trick of the light, a play of shadows as it were, that
diverts attention away from the *subject/author who produces mimesis*,
and toward a notion of mimesis as a self-grounded or authorless operation, an eternal repetition of the same. The trick that inverts the order
of signification therefore consists in shifting the emphasis from the subject "*who* produces mimesis" to the metaphysical question: "What is mimesis?"—the answer to which will be disguised behind theological and
mythological explanations.[83]

In this economy of sacred sound, mimesis—here a "sonic" mimesis—is again the central mechanism that brings about the inversion in relation to language. Although its paradigmatic case is the patronymic transmission of Veda from Ārya to Ārya, this model is transferred by means of the hegemony of the oral paradigm to other text-based cultures (e.g., Sikhism), where perfect recitation, the exact reproduction of sound, has taken root. Here the vocation of the reciter or ritual specialist is to preserve the sacred (eternal) form of the original sound. The sacredness of this form consists in its being *śruti*: the most authoritative and original form of experience, a pure and direct intellectual intuition that is heard-understood, that is, revealed immediately. However, the authority of *śruti* is founded on a denial of any connection to *human* experience. Humans can certainly experience things/objects/meanings, but are nevertheless committed to verbally articulating what they know, thereby entrusting such knowledge to memory. As inherently temporal, human experience is always already distanced from the actual moment of experience. Such distancing, which is simultaneously a timing, makes the object slip into the past. At most it can be recollected, remembered, and thereby preserved as tradition (*smṛti*). The fundamental dilemma for the ritual specialist is the need to preserve the language of the gods in the world of men (to borrow the title of Sheldon Pollock's recent book). The dilemma is of course that of being human or simply having to live and then die with other men. It is not simply a technique that is at issue here but what that technique represents: a way to live, the standard according to which one lives (*ethos*), and therefore the boundaries of a particular community (*ethnicity*).

Within any economy of sacred sound that refers to an origin—irrespective of whether it is Vedic recitation, the *akhaṇḍ pāṭh*, or the practice of *nām simaraṇ*—the central dilemma is that the site of origin(al hearing or revelation), and hence its eternality, must be preserved. Yet the very operation of preserving the origin works only by *denying* or *forgetting* that the act of preservation involves the temporal activity of remembering. Thus the central dilemma—how eternity can be guaranteed in a temporal medium—is overcome by resorting to a mnemotechnique by means of which the reciter claims to ensure flawless transmission of the text by perfectly imitating the eternal ("soundless") sound (*nām*). Yet this mnemotechnique denies being merely a mnemonic aid—that is, it denies any reliance on memory, which would involve a detour through the world and time of *human* experience. This is to say that the operation of memory is devalued at the very moment that a mnemotechnique is deployed in order to project a privileged access to the origin as such. A perfect con trick! But how does the illusion work?

As we have seen in chapter 4, Derrida, in his *Speech and Phenomena*, analyzes a process very similar to Vedic transmission in his readings of the master metaphysician Edmund Husserl. According to Derrida, this kind of strategy succeeds because of an "unfailing complicity" between sound (as voice) and idealization, a complicity between the words or signifiers, which are recited, and the illusion that these same signifiers participate in the ideality that is projected as *śruti*, or origin. The ideality or pure interiority that characterizes *śruti* can be expressed only through an element that does not appear to have worldly form. This element is voiced sound, or *nāda*. At the same moment that he recites, the reciter interiorizes the recited signifiers. Interiorization refers to the sort of operation in which when I speak (or recite), it belongs to the essence of this operation that I hear-understand myself in the same moment that I speak.[84] "In the same moment" refers to the fact that the signifiers (words recited/spoken) and the signified (meaning-intention that becomes immediately present to, is revealed to or is understood by, the speaker) remain in absolute proximity. Interiorization implies that the spoken signifier is by nature transparent — again an illusion, since the signifier's "body" seems to efface itself in the same moment that it is produced. The spoken signifier — sound or voice — does not linger in time. It is not subject to the worldly conditions of birth, decay, death. Transcending time and world, it is ideal.

The "unfailing complicity" between sound and ideality thus comes from the moment of coincidence between sound and meaning, signifier and signified, in the moment of production and effacement. This moment does not extend forward or backward. It is absolutely present, now, eternal, eternity itself. Further, because the eternal moment remains in the absolute proximity of the privileged communicative arcs — speaking/hearing-understanding, recitation/revelation (*śruti*), voice/meaning — then not only what is revealed as such (meaning-intention), but also that *for-which* and *to-which* revelation occurs — namely subjectivity, consciousness, or self-presence — can be infinitely repeated as the same: *repetition* as the production of identity, of the subject as identical to itself.

This relation is perhaps better illustrated by the proximity of the Sanskrit term *śruti* with its more recent cognates, the (Prakritic) terms *surat/surati*:[85]

Śruti

1. "That which is heard"; Eternal Word or Sound that has been seen and heard by the *rsis*;
2. Vedic revelation; the Vedas and Upaniṣads

Surat/Surati

A. 1. Memory/mind; mystical faculty (*antahkaran*) that functions to interiorize the outer, or cognitive, senses, and thus create memory.
2. Pure concentration; the mystical faculty as cultivated by *sants* (saints), as opposed to everyday calculative thought.
3. Pinnacle of lover-beloved relationship.
4. *Śruti*: Veda or Vedic revelation.
5. Listening; mystical state of listening in which revelation occurs.
6. Proper (= one's own) attunement.
B. 1. Consciousness; awareness; understanding.

It is evident even with the Prakritic cognates *surat(i)* that an otherwise strong relationship between memory as technique and the nature of sound is nevertheless qualified by a distinction between a lower, or human, memory based on everyday calculative thinking, and a higher memory cultivated by superhumans, or mystics and saints, those who have accessed the occult faculty of the *antahkaran*—the faculty of interiorizing, of inner spacing, or idealizing. Hence, two moves—the simultaneous privileging of sound/hearing while suppressing their sensory or worldly nature, and, as a consequence of this, the devaluation of memory—constitute the illusory mechanism of the con trick deployed by ritual specialists to preserve cultural boundaries. The trick consists in shifting our attention away from the fact that the correctly recited word, the "perfectly" imitated phoneme, is only an imperfect copy, a *mimeme*, of the eternal sound, and toward a view of "external" language as mnemotechnique for correctly voicing/imitating/sounding the original single sound. It works to make us forget that "external" sound (*nāda*) and internal, "or unstruck," sound (*sphoṭa, anhad nāda*) are both intrinsically dependent on memory, and that the boundary between internal/external, sacred/profane, eternity/time, etc., is from the outset fissured and polluted.

In view of the above, Coomaraswamy's intention becomes clearer. As we have seen with regard to memory, it involves a division of mimesis: privileged/devalued, proper/improper/, sonic/visual. Since what is at stake is the possibility of infinitely reproducing the origin, all models of repetition based on the Vedic economy of sacred sound will be (and will always have been) privileged. Better still, Vedic repetition is (and will always have been) the exemplar, the model, or type—*varṇa*[86]—of the original "unstruck" sound or phoneme—*varṇa*. The original sound, let us recall, can never have been struck, since its strike, its impression, or—dare one say it—its *inscription* will always already have been annihilated in its coming-to-be.

In a manner complimentary to this sonic mimetology, the appropriation (hearing/understanding) of this pure sound by the listener is also interiorized. Aural reception, being the other half of the communicative arc, must also maintain the purity of the origin. *Vocal* transmission and *aural* reception maintain the proximity to the origin. Since the entire aim of the oral-aural tradition is to "imprint" sameness or ideality of the original sound on all minds that are attuned to hear this sound (those who possess the correct *dharma*), such proximity reinforces the boundaries of the listening community. Historically speaking, the continuity (*sanātanta*) of *dharmic* boundary has been maintained through the rigorous institution of caste denominations (*varṇā dharma*) so that the boundary of those not privileged with correct birth/*dharma* cannot pollute the *dharma* of those privileged with the eternal sound. Proximity to the original sound echoed by proximity to one's type or kind (determined largely by distance from or proximity to the exemplary caste) not only minimizes any leakage to the outside, but prevents the outside leaking in. These concepts help to underpin a typically Indian "xenology" that reflects a Brahminical worldview:

> The Indocentrism developed in "orthodox" Hindu thought transcends by far what is ordinarily called "ethnocentrism." It is not simply an unquestioned perspective or bias, but a sophisticated *theoretical* structure of self-universalization and self-isolation. Seen from within this complex, highly differentiated structure, the *mlecchas* are nothing but a faint and distant phenomenon at the horizon of indigenous tradition. They do not possess an "otherness" against which one's own identity could be asserted or in which it could be reflected.[87]

It is difficult to deny the essential continuity even of seemingly secular neonationalist Indian scholars[88] with the central themes of Vedic tradition, and specifically with the grammarians Paṇini, Patañjali, and Bhartṛhari. The notion of universal language as a single eternal sound testifies to this. Given that this is so, the underlying intention behind Coomaraswamy's philosophy of language and art is not difficult to spot. It is to demonstrate that that which is proper to Indian civilization, namely Vedic orality, is universal and at the same time analogous to universals in the Greek or Western tradition. Parallel to this eternal property (*sanātana dharma*) is the community that has continued to uphold and imbibe it. This eternal property(=eternal Veda=eternal Sanskrit) has engendered a specific type of community, one which finds its modern variant in the secular and religious forms of Indian nationalism. It is the continued will to preserve this economy and its revitalization—ironically, through the textualization of the nationalist imaginary initially via Indological and theosophical literature—that has resulted in the identification of *sanātana dharma* as the "universal religion" of India. It is this very universal that has been routinely deployed by secular and religious Hindu nationalists to try to subvert the Western distinction between secularism and religion. Hinduism, they argue, is not like other religions in the sense that it is eternal and therefore universal. As universal, it corresponds to religion-in-general. And because it is universal, it is also the basis for the notion of the secular, specifically an Indian or Hindu secularism. Within this universal frame, minority cultural formations that resist this universal—for example, Sikhism—will be defined as nothing more than a variant of the secular Hindu universal, which is also the definition of religion-in-general.

Sonic Hermeneutics as an Ethnology of Sikhism

Given the ideological continuity between the ancient Vedic economy, *sanātana dharma*, Indology, theosophy, and Hindu nationalism, it is somewhat surprising that scholars, inspired by what they believe to be "postmodern" and "postcolonial" ideals, have continued to transfer this ideology into the contemporary history of religions. I have already cited the case of ethnologists such as Verne Dusenbury (and, in a rather different way, Kristina Myrvold), whose approach seems to disavow the role of orality not only as a hermeneutic of power, but also as a paradigm that conforms to a *sui generis* model of religion.

A less obvious example of this can be found in Harjot Oberoi's otherwise innovative book *The Construction of Religious Boundaries: Culture, Identity, and Diversity in the Sikh Tradition*. The main thread of Oberoi's historical narrative, indeed the very force of his thesis concerning the rise to power of Khalsā Sikhism and the concomitant decline of (what he regards as) "sanātan" Sikhism, is crucially dependent on an interpretation of South Asian religion and history determined by the distinction between orality and literacy, according to which the following historical *epistemes* can be identified.[89]

1. *Guru Nānak to Guru Ramdās*.[90] This period concerns the evolution of the Nānak-Panth, which for Oberoi and others is the "original" Sikhism because it is rooted firmly within indigenous North Indian religious culture. Its typical characteristics include pacifism, a rejection of religious externality, and the nondelimitation of religious boundaries, with the consequent fluidity and pluralism of identities among its adherents. For Oberoi, Nānak-Panthis are essentially "sanātan" Sikhs.

2. *Guru Arjan to Guru Gobind Singh*.[91] A period dominated by the birth and evolution of an essentially different type of Sikh(-ism); one that is governed by the introduction and adoption of writing—i.e., the Ādi Granth text—as the main definer of religious boundary. As Oberoi himself states:

> The production of the Ādi Granth (by the fifth Guru) turned the Sikhs into a "textual community," that is, a group of people whose social and religious activities are centred around a text, and who seek to order their everyday life in close correspondence with what the text actually prescribes.[92]

Textuality (or writing) thus becomes coterminous with the fixity and delimitation of religious boundaries, indeed of religion itself, in the sense that "those who are beyond the pale of the text begin to be viewed as outsiders." During this period, what Oberoi—following Brian Stock's *The Implications of Literacy*—calls "textual Sikhism" continues to evolve until it reaches completion with Guru Gobind Singh's Khalsā and the Guru Granth/Guru Panth doctrine.

3. *The late nineteenth century*. The distinction between Khalsā Sikhs and "sanātan" Sikhs reemerges and is once again resolved, with the Guru Granth as the boundary marker.

Within this hermeneutic, orality, as representative of the natural, primal, and pluralistic popular state of Indic culture (and of which the early Nānak-Panth is a part), is usurped by a textual culture, both in the early days of the Guru period and again during colonialism. At key stages in Indian history the *violence of writing*—initially the violence of the Islamic "book," and subsequently the combined violence of Western colonial print culture and the Christian "book"—is committed upon an innocent indigenous culture. In other words, orality is *prior* to textuality in the same way that indigenous Indian religion (sanātan culture) is prior to the landing of Islamic and British/European religions on Indian soil. Orality is synonymous with nativeness, ahistoricality, pacifism, and plurality, whereas textuality is foreign, violent, bringing with it a linear history of decline and the construction of boundaries.

The problem here is not just Oberoi's tacit acceptance of the Vedic economy, which remains invisible within his text. It is not the oral signifier in itself that is the problem, but rather that writing is not understood as an operation that is intrinsically temporal, as the *form* of temporality, and therefore as the very condition of orality. Instead writing is interpreted in terms of an *a priori* metaphysical distinction: the difference between orality and writing and the consequent privileging of the former over the latter. It is this tacit accession to metaphysics as such that not only upholds the Vedic economy—the *proper* "South Asian first principles"—but the history of religions discourse within which Oberoi represents the sanātan culture as a *concept of religion* proper to the culture and civilization of India.[93]

What needs to be noted is an insidious relationship between this form of metaphysics and the conceptualization of religion that continues to inform Oberoi's narrative even as, earlier in his book, he rightly calls for a questioning of the category of religion. Far from being questioned, however, his oral hermeneutic already presupposes religion as a generalizable category. By maintaining a grip on the concept of religion—where religion is simply assumed as an origin that maintains itself as unpolluted, safe, sacrosanct, nonviolent—the historian can separate religion from politics (identified with violence, writing, and hence a deviation from the universal religion). Once this *sui generis* ideology is internalized it becomes impossible for the Sikh subject to escape the "dreamtime" loop since "authentic" Sikh subjectivity or repetition will already have been defined in terms of quietist detachment from worldly politics through a constant remembrance of the Name (*nām simaraṇ*) performed in conformity with the timeless Indian universal.

The problem with this hermeneutic, however, is that it carries well beyond theoretical debates in the study of religions. Indeed, its implications are positively dangerous, given the recent resurgence and the various self-representations of Hindu nationalism—as an ethnic identity based on caste consciousness, or as a universal religion, or even as an authentically Indian/Hindu secularism—all of which claim India as their own. These congruent self-representations reflect traditional forms of hegemony that have refused to acknowledge cultural differences, regarding Jain, Buddhist, and Sikh traditions as mere streams flowing into a broader Hindu ocean. As Cynthia Mahmoud has argued, "the domination of a Brahmanic/Hindu center throughout Indian history is replicated today in the Hindu resurgence, which claims that being Hindu simply means being Indian, a stance which sounds like an aspect of tolerance but is taken by non-Hindus as exclusionary,"[94] as it equates resistance to the Brahmanic universal as a betrayal of Indian unity. Moreover, during the 1980s and 1990s many Indian liberals and self-styled secularists simply failed to recognize that it was not the "intransigence of minorities but the appropriation of Indian identity by the majority Hindu community" that constituted the central threat to Indian democracy. During this time period, we see this same lack of recognition in both scholarly and journalistic narratives about Sikhism in relation to the crisis of Indian unity. As we have seen, most of these narratives portrayed later Sikhism's entry into violence and politics as a *deviation* from the pacifistic subjectivity of Guru Nānak. From this followed the ironic injunction that if Sikhs are to exist in modern secular society, irrespective of whether this is Western or Indian, they have to maintain their repetition (that is, subjectivity or agency) as a reproduction of their pacifist origin.

Let me briefly recount the gist of one particular strand of thought that runs through the last three chapters. The form of repetition recounted above, the one that creates and reproduces sacred origin, creates a vicious cycle derived from the following sources. First is the Sikh reformists' encounter, collaboration with, and appropriation of the colonial idiom, which ironically brought them closer to the very object of their critique (so-called sanatān Sikhism or Hinduism) through their internalization of forms of metaphysics, resulting in the deontologization of language. Second, this metaphysics that

356   POSTCOLONIAL EXITS

results in the deontologization of language is transferred to and replicated by the modern history of religions even as this discipline speaks in the name of anti-imperialism articulated as the desire to give agency back to the colonized by returning them to their original precolonial modes of repetition.

The question I want to pose in the final part of this chapter is whether it is possible for Sikhs today, first, to recognize this form of repetition as a vicious cycle and, second, to exit this cycle. Furthermore, is it possible to reenvisage this exit by thinking about the question of repetition in a way that avoids the return to origins? Might the *avoidance* of this return to origins constitute a properly *post*colonial exit from the dialectical cycle within which modern reformist Sikhism has become trapped? In what follows I will try to find ways of answering these questions. To do this I want to take a fresh look at the relationship between the notion of lack and the possibility of reappropriating universals in a way that avoids the Asian/Western binary. Specifically I shall be asking whether it is possible to accept lack as inherent to the formation of subjectivity and repetition, and thereby reontologize the question of language.

Revisiting the Site of Lack

The conventional understanding of the postcolonial move has been to follow the "secularization thesis," which entails a straightforward negation of religion, or a negation of what Said called the "religious effects" of nationalism. As I have shown throughout this book, modern Asian studies and the discipline of history of religions have by and large internalized this particular standpoint by focusing its intellectual activity on the secular practice of historicism as the grounding principle for all other disciplines in the humanities and social sciences. One way of going beyond this conventional understanding is to return to the site where the dialectical cycle was first generated, namely, the site of Sikh scripture's translation into English and the subsequent transfer of *gurmat* into the categories of Western conceptuality. But before we can make this kind of postcolonial move, let me clarify once again the nature of the interaction between colonizer and colonized, which led to a very different kind of transformation during the colonial period, one which resulted in the reification of repetition in terms of transcendental (sacred) origin.

The term "transformation" as I use it in the colonial context implies a "conversion to modernity" and therefore implicates both *material* and *psychological* changes in the nature of agency that are motivated by a dialectical interchange between colonizer and colonized. As we saw in chapter 3, central to the movement of this dialectic was the constitution of lack. The colonizer observes that what is missing in the colonized's accounts of themselves and their culture (God, religion, nation, self, transcendence, freedom, etc.) is the element of the universal. In place of this missing element the colonizer posits a lack. This in turn gives rise to a desire in the native elites for the fulfillment of this lack, a desire that is consummated through a process that simultaneously mimics and negates the colonizer's universal, resulting in the emergence of the nationalist subject, followed by the nationalization of tradition, and culminating in its representation as "global religion" (Sikh "theology"/"history" → Sikhs as nation → Sikhism as world religion). What keeps this dialectical engine from stalling is a mode of identification that, by invoking transcendental structures and *sui generis* religion, continues to govern the modern and postmodern forms of Sikhism, and therefore limits their possibilities of repetition, that is, the manner in which they relate to self and world. In other words, the engagement of Sikhs with the modern and postmodern world is limited to revivals, reforms, and returnings to an essence that is *sui generis*. In this phase the political process set off by lack is purely *reactive*. It simply negates the colonizer's universals (God, religion, freedom, etc.) by setting up closed boundaries driven by the logic of identity (or pure difference). The problem with this form of identity politics is that it leaves the form of oppression unchanged.

Now, if the negation of this perceived lack constitutes the colonial subject, it follows that any attempt to exit the colonial repetition must negate the first negation of lack and thereby invert the colonizer/colonized relationship "in what it has of universality." As Ernesto Laclau notes, this inversion must take place at the level of universal reference so that the identities of both colonizer and colonized are radically altered.[95] The second inversion must negate the principle of identity or boundary formation as such. In our case, however, the postcolonial move cannot be a mere operation of logic that would then effect yet another transition to a new phase, while all along the very presupposition of linear historical movement remains in place. As we recall from earlier chapters, the nationalizing process involves a traumatic entry into modernity as History, a trauma that involves a repression of nonmodern meanings and understandings of self, time, and world. The repression of these nonmodern meanings and understandings constitutes *an affect of*

shame. That is to say, if the negation of lack involved a psychological repression of themes, subjects, and meanings in Sikh scripture and modes
of existence that are incompatible with modernity, then the negation of
the first negation of lack cannot be performed by logic alone (since this
logic remains incompatible with the repressed content) but only by *revisiting and reopening the site of the original lack and the concomitant
act of traumatic repression, i.e., by releasing the affect of shame*.

Not only would this revisitation and reopening involve a psychoanalytic operation, but, since the site of the first repression (by the Singh Sabhā
scholars) revolved around the enactment of a translation in response to a
regime of colonial translation (imposed by Trumpp et al.), but they would
require an act of *re*reading and *re*interpretation of Sikh scripture. However, the purpose of this *re*reading of scripture would be to rescue forms
of signification that were deemed incompatible with colonial modernity
and that were thought to have been exorcized long since by nationalist/
modernist reason and repressed into the precolonial past. These nonmodern forms of signification survive as an undercurrent in certain strands of
Sikh oral exegesis and in the lives of many Sikhs and even manage to occasionally manifest themselves in certain reappropriations of the political
that haunt the modernist/nationalist mindset.[96]

But doesn't this call for rereading and reinterpretation of scripture
sound like yet another hermeneutic process? And was hermeneutics not
involved in both the production and the installation of the nationalist
subject as the subject of "Sikh theology" or of the "religious" Sikh that
constitutes the object of the history of religions? While this cannot be
denied, my aim here is to resist the notion of hermeneutics that reduces
the heterolingual mode of address proper to the work of translation to the
homolingual address proper to the work of representation. Heterolingual
translation reduced to homolingual representation involves: (i) the metaphoric transport of meanings from a self-conscious subject A to another
self-conscious subject B, followed by (ii) a circular return to subject A,
thereby (iii) retaining the distinction between self and other (A and B)
even in its most radical forms. As we have seen, such a hermeneutic sustained the illusion of a closed circle linking the horizon of the nationalist
subject and scripture (transparency of theological meaning based on an
omniscient God). The circular return to self is precisely what closed the
gap (i.e., filled in the *lack* of understanding) between reader and text.

Against this notion of hermeneutics I prefer to read the idea of lack
(following Slavoj Žižek's readings of Lacan) as the discrepancy between

nationalist enunciation (the *said*) and the *saying* of the text, a discrepancy that continues to haunt the nationalist subject. To revisit the scene of this lack/discrepancy is to reopen the trauma of encounter and to enact, via re-translation, a *different kind of repetition*. Such a repetition can only be an engagement with the world and time (a focus on the theme of immanence or what was wrongly understood as "pantheism" within the Ādi Granth) rather than a seeking of security through structures of transcendence and eternity. Such a repetition cannot latch onto any master-signifiers from the dominant symbolic order: God, nation, religion, freedom, etc. Rather, such a reinterpretation can only proceed through the gesture of *disidentification*, which works by acknowledging that lack is not primarily external but rather *internal* both to the subject and to the political process as such. Central to this reinterpretation is a recognition that the universal itself is fundamentally lacking, that the universal is always constituted by empty signifiers.[97] If lack or emptiness is constitutive of the universal, this allows for that universal to be shared. By allowing for other oppressed particulars to stand in for that universal but without negating it, reinterpretation will aim to be part of the broader process of signification and therefore has an inherently political function.

However, in order for this project of retranslation/reinterpretation to begin again, it is necessary to accept a certain (nonmodern) notion of language that is prevalent within the Ādi Granth (and texts of a similar nature). Philosophically this notion can be expressed by saying that language is sovereign prior to the formation of self-as-ego. Or in terms that Heidegger might use, language speaks prior to its being spoken by man, that is, prior to its becoming an instrument of human communication. In the Sikh context, the same notion is expressed by saying that the text *is* Guru (implying that its function is to teach or to instruct the reader/listener's mind). One must accept the primacy and sovereignty of the text as *śabda-guru*, the word/language-as-guru whose function is to instruct and transform the self-ego of the reader/listener. In this instance, the term *śabda-guru* has to be seen as an empty signifier rather than a signifier of fullness or presence.

This kind of retranslation will in every way be a performative, a mode of repetition that engenders a certain action or performativity on behalf of the reader/translator. But it is at the same time an act of repetition that, in a manner of speaking, takes us back to the moment of the colonized native elites' "original" entry into the symbolic order imposed by the colonizer, in order to relive that moment as though it had not yet taken place in order to consider and translate what is lost by it.[98] This gesture should not be mistaken for the illusion of time travel that accompanies historiographical exercises. Rather what we glimpse here is the moment before we enter the symbolic order, as though we could somehow choose whether to recognize the master-signifiers God, religion, etc., by means of which we became a subject. To do this is to repeat what Žižek, following Lacan, calls the "forced choice": to recognize that for the nationalist subject who accedes to the dominant symbolic order as a subject, there never was and never will have been a real choice. The repetition of this "forced choice" resembles a psychoanalytic exercise insofar as it helps to break the transferential relation that led to the colonizer's self/language/culture and to the position he occupies, and that today leads to the position occupied by the historian of religion as the creative hermeneut, the master of meaning.

Ultimately, the aim of revisiting and retranslating the site of lack is to read lack otherwise by retracing the steps trodden by Trumpp and the Singh Sabhā, in order to interrupt the enunciation that follows from it. The interruption of this Orientalist-nationalist enunciation has the effect of "render[ing] visible the distance that separates the master of meaning [colonial Indologist/neocolonial scholar/historian of religion] from the place he occupies."[99] Once introduced, this noncoincidence of the master's meaning and the place he occupies can be seen as a rupture in the discourse of metaphysics (or ontotheology) that facilitates the transparent movement of Sikh culture/texts initially under the sign of "theology" to their installation within the liberal humanist framework of the modern university (the domain of the "history of religions"). It is this rupture of enunciation that makes possible the kind of repetition that does not repeat origins, and therefore a different way of speaking, thinking, acting that not only renders possible any exit from colonialism, but at the same time changes the very meaning of the "post-."

Reclaiming the Nondual Ground of the Guru Granth

This reinterpretation, I would like to suggest, must take into account two things: first, the fact that postcoloniality is as much a *promise* as it is a *predicament* for Sikhs;[100] second, the fact that the teachings of the Sikh Gurus in Sikh scripture conform neither to ethical monotheism espoused by the Singh Sabhā, which reproduces the dualistic structures of

Western metaphysics, nor to the Vedic theo-ideology of "eternal Sanskrit." Indeed, if one looks closely at the nature of the hymns in the Ādi Granth one encounters two stark empirical facts: (i) the organizational structure of the text according to music and (ii) the *reiteration* of key themes throughout the text—themes that do not obey any theological or transcendental structure. Let me consider each of these in turn.

Music and the Temporal Structure of the Guru Granth

As far as the organizational structure of the Ādi Granth is concerned, the vast majority of the hymns are organized into thirty-one "chapters." These "chapters" are *ragas*, or classical measures of North Indian music. That the Sikh Gurus relied on aesthetics to organize the text should not be surprising, given that all of the Gurus were well versed in contemporary styles of Indian music and wished their hymns to be sung according to the *rāg* (measure) and *tāl* (rhythm) that properly express the emotions within a particular hymn and in a performance style compatible with the meaning of the hymn. Contrary to a certain view, the role of *rāg* and *tāl* is not supplementary to the text, but central, since according to Indian aesthetic theory each musical *rāg* evokes a particular mood that has its own distinct flavor (*rasa*), which may vary across a spectrum that ranges from adoration and rejoicing to desolation and entreaty. To render the *rāg* correctly in performance (*kīrtan*) is to correctly express one particular mood and not another. In order to reproduce a certain mood, traditions of Sikh musicology (*gurmat sangīt*) stress the performance rules and melodic material as the best way of maintaining the individual properties of a *rāg* and of preserving the broad message of a particular hymn.[101] Each hymn is therefore set to a predefined *rāg*, and when it is sung, the feelings and emotions associated with this *rāg* affect the lyrical interpretation of the text.

The organizing function of the *rāg* and *tāl* cannot simply be reduced to a decorative or ornamental function that makes them supplementary to the literary aspect of the text. This was the very reason for its dismissal by Orientalists, and for its continued marginalization by the dominant form of representation in the humanities. Rather, *rāg/tāl* perform a function that is in every sense "philosophical-political" (or perhaps "theologico-political") insofar as their very presence has to do with a form of subjectivity that resists being reduced to the operations of reflective consciousness and conceptual thought. Indian philosophical aesthetics has long recognized the resistance posed by the self/I to grasping itself, to making itself into an object for reflection. Self-conscious reflection was considered to be dependent on prior sensory feelings or intuitions. Unlike reflective thought, feeling cannot return to itself and thereby affect itself, given that its pure form is time. Because of this, the "I," or reflective subject, is inherently lacking, meaning that it cannot be adequately represented in a language dependent on concepts and reflection alone. Nevertheless, unlike its Western counterpart, Indian aesthetics did not simply reject nonreflective or nonconceptual thinking and subjectivity, but rather articulated them through media other than language, notably music and dance, in order for this lack to be articulated, so that what was lacking could be gestured. Music, especially music linked to poetic language, has always been considered the most appropriate medium for this because the very form of music is time, and time is inherently lacking. It disappears continually. Hence, unlike language, music is not subject to auto-affection and is better able to articulate the nature of existence in time.

Again, though, it is important to stress that music's advantage is that it does not dispense either with subjectivity or with thought. Instead, in order for *rāg* and *tāl* to be expressed and objectively understood, there must exist a different kind of subjectivity, a subjectivity that resists representation. The kind of subjectivity proper to music, based on the movement of self-erasure proper to its temporal element, avoids the metaphysical operation that splits the sensuous from the intelligible. In doing so it brings different aspects of subjectivity together: sensuous (unconscious) and intelligible (conscious).

It is for this reason that the performance of Sikh *kīrtan* is not merely ornamental/decorative and therefore supplemental to the text. As art, it provides rules for a kind of thinking that resists being reduced to representation, or self-reflective thought. According to various traditions of Sikh musicology, the purpose of setting the Guru's words to a *rāg/tāl* is to make an impression on the self-conscious aspect of the listener's mind, in such a way that it is forced into dialogue with its unconscious aspect (emotions, drives, feelings). When the two different aspects of subjectivity speak to each other, as it were, the mind is said to be brought home. The Gurus aimed to convey expression through feelings and moods because they comprise an aspect of consciousness that *resists the conceptual production of figures of eternity.*

Apart from determining meaning and subjectivity, the co-primacy
of music and textuality, orality and writing, aesthetic and intelligible in
the structure of the Ādi Granth helps us to understand another, largely
misunderstood, aspect of Sikhism—what is variously expressed as the
"mystical experience" of Guru Nānak, or "God's revelation" to Nānak,
but which would more accurately be termed as the emergence of Nānak's
subjectivity, a subjectivity that, far from being passive and quietistic, is
excessive and *sovereign* insofar as it resists the return-to-self (or self-conscious thinking and representation) that characterizes everyday notions of
self. Sovereignty in Nānak's writings is therefore linked not to subjectivity as self-accumulation but to a form of subjectivity that erases the self's
tendency to return to itself (an aspect of auto-affection). I shall return to
this theme shortly.

Temporal Themes in the Guru Granth

The second empirical fact that one encounters in reading the Ādi
Granth is the constant reiteration within the text of certain key themes.
That is to say, there are leading ideas that are repeated over and over
again, and more often than not these ideas exist together in a single hymn
so that their interconnectedness comprises a single overall teaching that
is known as *gurmat*. However, this interconnectedness also presents one
of the most formidable obstacles to the task of translating and representing the contents of Sikh scripture. Nevertheless, such a task was recently
undertaken and published under the title *Teachings of the Sikh Gurus:
Selections from the Sikh Scriptures*.[102] The themes selected were: (i) one-
(ness), (ii) time and contingency, (iii) mind (self/ego), (iv) action and
grace, (v) word as Guru, and (vi) fusion/love/nonknowledge. There is
meant to be no hierarchy or order among these themes. Each contains
or is internally connected to every other. These thematic titles are meant
to signal a shift from the tightly organized schema adopted by the Singh
Sabhā scholars, which imbibed and mirrored the Western conceptualization of religion. The themes are interdependent and fluid, and they cannot
be considered "categories" of thought or judgment as understood in the
Western philosophical tradition. Categories are ways in which reality is
organized according to certain divisions, and they require some sort of
transcendental apperception, the presumed unity of a transcendental self.
For the Sikh Gurus, however, because categories can exist only within

the horizon of a reflective self-conscious mind, the very idea of horizon itself must be broken if we are to understand and experience the notion of unity that underpins and connects all the other themes. Categories are no more than mental constructs subject to something more fundamental: the passage of time.

The writings of the Gurus are by contrast radically intercategorical, emphasizing the fluid interplay and crossings of different themes within any other theme. There is therefore no hierarchy or progression from one theme to another. Each theme could easily provide an entry to all of the others. The connection between them—and the clue to the nonherme- neutical interpretation that I am attempting here—can be envisaged as a spiraling thought that does not return to any self or subject who may have produced that thought. This would be opposed to conceptual or cat- egorical thought, which returns full circle to its starting point in the ego, thereby recuperating and accumulating the ego in a process of repetition, so that this repetition becomes ego-repetition. Nevertheless, the above nonhermeneutical arrangement suggests a possible movement: from the experience of One as an experience of time and contingency (1), which manifests as an existential awareness of one's own mortality (2), which in turn deepens reflection on the nature of mind (3), and leads to a way of acting in deed, word, and thought that is spontaneous (attachment-in- detachment) (4). This twofold movement of renunciation–attachment of ego is attained through a submission to language (*sabda/nām*) (5), which enables the emergence of an "authentic" subject (*gurmukh*) who not only cultivates the highest states of bliss but shows a profound will to share and communicate this bliss to others (6).

The Word as Guru: Toward a
Materialist Sketch of Nānak's Teachings

The foregrounding of these themes in the Ādi Granth makes it possible to propose a rather different reading of Guru Nānak's teach- ings (*gurmat*) that breaks with the dialectical cycle of return to origins that governs the modernist (both academic and neocolonial) understand- ing.[103] The irony of course is that the possibility of such a break was still there in the modernist approaches, only it remained repressed under an affect of shame (neocolonial), or under the narrative of dominance/prog- ress (Orientalist/history of religions). All that was required for this break was a shift in the intellectual and existential perspective from which the Granth is received, namely, the shift from eternity to time. Such a shift in perspective could even be discerned from within the traditional hagiographies, in particular, the scene of Nānak's nomination as Guru, the point at which Nānak receives the Word. However, I prefer to start at a point slightly before this: the scene of his childhood or adolescence. This scene is recounted—albeit in a more muted fashion—by the literature known as the *janamsākhīs*. The most important of the *janamsākhīs* is the *Purātan*.

The *Purātan janamsākhī* generally presents Nānak in typically hagiographical fashion as a perfected being who produced miracles from an early age and whose latent divinity was activated by God's call at a certain point in his life. However, a short section in the *janamsākhī* seems to be punctuated by the emergence of a darker side to Nānak's developing personality, a phase that begins in early adolescence and continues until the scene of nomination at around the age of thirty or so. It is an account that stands in stark contrast to the image of Nānak as superhuman miracle producer that characterizes much of the narrative. According to the *Purātan janamsākhī*, during this period symptoms of an existential malaise, a depressive illness, began to manifest themselves as Nānak began to withdraw more and more from society and worldly activity. He refused to speak to family and friends, refused all manner of work, and spent his time mainly with *fakirs* (renunciants). Despite the fact that he was married at this time and had two sons, Nānak's condition only seemed to deteriorate, to the extent that members of his family lamented that he had become "a crazed fool," that he was "out of his mind," and that he had "gone mad."[104]

These cycles of depression continued well into his late twenties. With the family's reputation at sake, and as a last desperate resort, a physician was called to have Nānak treated. The physician arrived and grabbed Nānak's wrist to take his pulse. But Nānak withdrew his arm, sat up, and asked the physician what he was doing. "I am diagnosing the illness which has disturbed your state of mind," the physician replied. Nānak laughed and responded with the following words, which came to be recorded in the *Ādi Granth* under the musical register of *rāg malār*:

The physician was sent to prescribe a remedy; he takes my hand and
    feels my pulse,
But the ignorant fool knows not that the pain is my mind.

Physician, go home; take not my curse with you.
What use is this medicine when my sickness is also my state of love?
When there's pain, the physician stands ready with his store of pills.
My body weeps, the soul cries out, "Give me none of this medicine."
Go home, physician, few understand the source of my pain.
The One who gave me this pain will remove it.[105]

Soon after this episode Nānak left his family to find work at Sultanpur and took up a post as the village accountant. His life had settled into a more regulated pattern. The cycles of depression eventually gave way to nightly sessions of singing and performing *kīrtan*, bathing in the nearby river at dawn, followed by work as an accountant during the day. On one occasion, though, Nānak failed to return from his regular morning dip in the river and was feared to have drowned. However, after three days Nānak mysteriously returned but had once again become silent and withdrawn, refusing to speak and responding to all questions with the perplexing statement: "There is no Hindu, there is no Muslim."

After a short stay Nānak left Sultanpur. Accompanied by his faithful musician, Mardānā, he embarked on a series of travels that lasted twelve years. During this time his earlier silence was transformed into an outpouring of words that eventually came to be transcribed into the hymns of Sikh scripture. It is generally agreed that the event at Sultanpur (Nānak's *absence* followed by his mysterious *return*) was the pivotal experience that gave Nānak a task and project that would not only define the rest of his life but extend well beyond it. However, the nature of this experience is not generally considered beyond the idea of Nānak's meeting with God, a meeting in which God revealed to Nānak the task of spreading the Name. Such an interpretation of course sets up a sacred origin that constitutes the meaning for all future Sikh experience, repetition, and history. As we have seen, while traditionalist historians see this as legitimizing the break with the Hindu past ("the night of the Hindu womb," as I referred to it in chapter 3) and the start of "Sikh history," Western historicism posits a sacred origin for the purpose of demarcating a separation between the "religious" (whose meaning is given by transcendence of time, which translates as nonactivity in the world or detachment from the world) and the secular, or the "political," which is defined by activity or engagement in the world. The history of religions, in other words, posits a sacred origin in order to sanction the division between the religious and the political, and in order to reserve the task of secular politics to itself by demarcating the meaning of the other as religious.

But is it possible to interpret the Sultanpur event in a manner that avoids reference to sacred origin and its attendant problems? I want to argue that there is a way of thinking differently about such events, but to do so we must avoid thinking about the event as a purely *particular* occurrence, something that could only have happened to Nānak. Rather, I'd like to suggest that, its strangeness notwithstanding, the event must be thought of as a *universal*, something that is shareable with the rest of humanity. To consider this event as universal is to bring it into the realm of ordinary human experience, something that is also closer to Nānak's own thought as outlined in his hymns. One way to do this is to consider the basic phenomenological elements of the event (Nānak's *absence* from the world followed by a *return* to the world) not as the divinizing of Nānak into a transcendent being in the world of men, but as a psychological performative. By "psychological performative" I refer to a simultaneous process in which Nānak undergoes an experience with language (Word = Guru), and subjectivity emerges as a result of this experience. The evidence of this subject's emergence is the spontaneous enunciation of the Word (*bāṇī*). In other words, Nānak becomes a subject only on the condition that the Word (language as Unconscious) speaks. When the Word speaks, Nānak himself is silent. Thus Nānak does not speak, the Word speaks—a fact that inverts the normal relationship between language and subjectivity, wherein language is merely a tool at the disposal of the subject. While this follows the phenomenological psychology of ordinary experience, it nevertheless differs fundamentally from it, in that it is an inversion of ordinary experience that uses the elements of ordinary experience.

Let me try to explain this using the Lacanian/Heideggerian model of language and subjectivity introduced earlier in this book. Under normal circumstances the first stage in the development of human subjectivity is the so-called mirror-stage. This is followed at the age of three by the child's inexorable accession to the dominant symbolic order (usually the mother tongue). With this accession, which takes place through language learning, begins a steady development of the subject as ego, which more or less matures just after adolescence. This development of subjectivity through to the mature ego depends on a nonidentification with (i.e., a repression of) those elements that do not constitute the ego (drives, emotions, etc.). Such development is synonymous with the progressive formation of boundaries between ego and non-ego. To not form these boundaries would be to fuse the self and other, ego and non-ego. Any such fusion of self and other (even to keep ajar the door between self and other) is considered dangerous to the rules of the dominant symbolic order and to the normality of the subject. These boundaries manifest themselves in and through the language to which the subject has been steadily acceding. That is to say, the ego-subject enunciates its subjectivity in terms of its compliance with the linguistic and social rules of the dominant symbolic order. To become a subject/ego it has to be able to speak in an objective-universal manner, in a manner understandable by similar egos, egos that can recognize each other as similar egos (Hegelian recognition). Its speech constitutes normal behavioral speech and accords to the parameters of everyday reality, which is dependent on the self–other distinction. Central to this normalizing function is the ability of the ego-subject to reflect on itself without loss, and thus to name itself as "I," where "I" designates my self's possession of itself. In this use of language the other is silent; thus language is silent in the speech of the ego-subject. The ego-subject simply uses language as a tool for communication between similarly constituted egos.

By contrast the passage of the mystic (in this case Nānak) into subjectivity is far more traumatic. For the mystic violently refuses to definitively close the boundary between self and other and therefore resists the accession to normal ego, which of course puts the mystic at odds with society. This refusal is first of all a refusal of normative speech, the speech that issues from the ego. Perhaps the best way to explain this is to listen to Guru Nānak's own testimony on the matter, recorded in verse after verse in the Ādi Granth, but specifically in the first few lines of *Japji*, acknowledged as Nānak's most authoritative statement. In doing this I am obviously retracing the steps of numerous commentators, not least the commentary of the Sikh reformist Bhāī Vīr Singh, which we have discussed at length in chapter 3. As I mentioned earlier, however, my purpose is to enact a different kind of repetition of Nānak's words.

To remind ourselves, the *Japji* is recited daily by Sikhs and its opening formula, the *mūl mantar*, or foundational statement, serves as the Sikh credo insofar as it is repeatedly invoked in shortened form on almost every page of the Ādi Granth and symbolically expresses the experience undergone by Nānak. Of special importance is the opening phrase *ik oaṁkār* (lit.: "One, whose expression emerges as Word"), which consists of the numeral 1 standing for the Absolute—and universally recognizable across cultures and languages—followed by the sign *oaṁ* (lit. "the unfolding or emergence of the Word"), and completed by the extended sign -kār, which connects oaṁ to the next two words in the mūl mantar: sat(i) (from the Sanskrit satya, meaning "existence" or "being") followed by nām (lit. "the Name"). The verse following the mūl mantar further elaborates the nature of the Absolute One as:

> Repeat:
> True in the beginning, true before time began
> He is true, Nānak, and ever will be true.[106]

However, an important question arises here. If, as Nānak claims, the truth of this Absolute One can be experienced here and now, what is it that stops each and every person from realizing this all the time? What stops us repeating such an experience of the One or of being One? More important, how could such an experience be repeated?

The answer for Guru Nānak is relatively straightforward. From the standpoint of someone who has actualized Oneness in his or her own existence, the Absolute is One (ik) and the One is Absolute. But the standpoint from which we normally relate to this One prevents us from actualizing Oneness in our lived existence.[107] What does this mean? What Nānak seems to be suggesting is that the numeral One is not a numeral among other numerals. Rather, One is simultaneously the most unique and the most deceitful. One is most unique in the sense that there is no other like it insofar as it names the truth of existence itself (satnām); it is a "1" that cannot be owned or appropriated and thereby made part of a series of numbers $(1+n)$. On the other hand, "1" is the most deceitful.[108] This "1" is the basis of knowledge as calculation that evaluates—measures—each "1" against every other "1" and thus sets up a difference between them based on this evaluation. It is the "1" that we regard as everyday normality but which is in fact mediated through the structure of the ego, the self that asserts its being on the basis of individuation (haumai, or self-attachment, as the mechanism of a subject that returns the self to self, generating the sense of "I am my own self" or "I am self-existent"). This oneness makes ego the prior basis of all relationality. The fundamental problem with this "1" is that it projects itself as an infinite proximity between the numeral "1" as the signifier of unity and identity, and the word "I" as the signifier of the self's identity. For Nānak, the correspondence between numeral and word, "1" and "I," is deceitful in that it reproduces this self as an identity that sets itself up in opposition to anything that is different. The ego thereby maintains its existence by erecting barriers against the outside world. It sees itself as a subject fundamentally separated from everything else, which becomes an object for it. Nānak likens the subject-object mode of relating to delusion (*bharam*) created by duality (*dubidā:* seeing the "1" as two).[109]

But the problem, as Nānak sees it, goes much further than the simple assumption that the ego is the source of duality/deceit. For as he explains in the first stanza of *Japji*, from the standpoint of ego, the Absolute "1" cannot be attained either through conceptual thought or through ritual purity no matter how much one repeats such thinking or ritual.[110] Neither can the Absolute "1" be obtained by practicing silent austerities,[111] since these too fail to silence the ego's constant chatter, nor indeed by satisfying one's innermost cravings.[112] The ego works by routing our experience of the Absolute "1" through all manner of repetition: concepts, rituals, or austerities. Consequently the Absolute "1" always fails to be experienced as such; the nearest we get is to represent it as an object or an idol to constantly gratify the ego's desire for permanence. How then does one overcome egotism? How can the ego's illusory barriers be broken?[113] How does one become self-realized?[114]

Guru Nānak answers this in the first and second stanzas of *Japji*. The ego's boundary is broken by orienting the self toward an imperative that is always already inscribed with(in) the self.[115] But in order to understand and follow this imperative the ego must become silent so that one can resist saying "I am *my*-self" even as ego continues to be formed. For Nānak this silencing of the ego is not to be understood literally. Silence refers to a process of withdrawal at the very moment that the self names itself as "I" and thus becomes an origin, a starting point for any relationship to another.[116] To assert one's existence in the world through self-naming is, for Nānak, a fundamental misuse of language.

So the problem and its solution, according to Nānak, lie in understanding the nature of the ego. Stated differently, the ego may be the problem, but the solution to this problem also lies in the constitution of the ego.[117] How can this be possible? To grasp what Nānak is saying here it is helpful to look more carefully at the term *man* (pronounced "mun"), which refers to the totality of human experience prior to its being split through the function of the self-conscious ego, and for which the corresponding English terms would be "psyche," "mind," "memory," "consciousness," "heart," etc. *Man* (or mind) has two aspects for the Sikh Gurus. There is on the one hand the mind-as-ego, which causes the split or separation in the first place. As self-conscious, mind-as-ego possesses a discriminatory awareness, a sense of duality that grasps or rejects something external; fundamentally, it is that which falsely posits an other (dūjā) as the basis of external reference and projects itself as the basis of normative reality. From Nānak's perspective, this mind-as-ego is afflicted by a chronic sickness (dīragh rog). This happens to be the aspect of mind that calculates, desires, manipulates, flares up in anger, and indulges in negative emotions. It needs to constantly assert and reaffirm its existence by fragmenting, conceptualizing, and solidifying our experience of the temporal world. In fact Nānak refers to the mind-as-ego as man pardesī — "my mind that has become a foreigner to itself." By creating a defensive boundary around itself it becomes estranged from what Nānak refers to as its true home, its beloved "object," the mind-as-non-ego, or simply mind-as-other. Yet even though it is the one estranged from its beloved, the mind-as-ego disavows its own estrangement by positing that from which it is separated as stranger, as the other. In other words it projects its own activity and its guilt onto its other. Though separated by ego activity, however, the two aspects are intimately drawn to each other like lover and beloved. Together these aspects comprise a psychic whole.[118]

The split (but ultimately unified) nature of man raises questions about the "standpoint" from which Nānak enunciates, and particularly about his signature (the proper name "Nānak"), which accompanies all of his hymns. Who is it that speaks in these invocations? Precisely to whom is Nānak's utterance addressed? Who is the other of Nānak's speech? Is it God? Is it the reader? The answer to both of these must be an emphatic "no!" Rather, Nānak almost always speaks to his own mind, addressing it at times through tender love, as when he says "my beloved mind," at times by cajoling it, as in "my foolish mind," and at other times beseeching it as a lover beseeches her beloved not to leave her. However, because almost every hymn in the Ādi Granth ends with the invocation "O, Nānak," the impression may be given that through the use of his proper name, Nānak is signatory to his own words, that these words belong to the person Nānak, thereby marking them with a seal of authority. In this case Nānak's enunciation would be just another form of communication from A to B (where B might be another person, the reader, or God). Closer scrutiny, however, shows that Nānak's speech is primarily directed to himself, to his own mind. More specifically, Nānak's enunciation is invariably directed toward the ego-mind and comes from his unconscious mind (the mind that is at home) as a form of supplication beseeching his conscious ego-mind (the mind which has become a stranger to itself) to join together in union.

If the ego-mind is to respond to the supplication of the unconscious mind, it can do so only through the gesture of renunciation. By renouncing its self-naming as "I," it can unite with its (beloved) other from which it has come to be separated. This gesture of withdrawal is deeply traumatic for the ego-mind, for it requires the ego to cross the very barrier that it has erected as its own defense. Such a crossing constitutes a death (ego-loss). However, what is absolutely clear in the Gurus' teachings is that they do not advocate any kind of annihilation of the ego or its repression through excessive discipline, for as Nānak says, the ego contains its own cure (*dārū bī is mahi*)! Its cure is contained within itself as its most intimate kernel, namely its beloved other. Because the nature of ego is intrinsically time, the cure involves not a struggle against the world but a struggle to exist within the world while being connected to the unconscious mind. This struggle, however, can only be waged through the language of love ("Beloved mind, come back to me," etc.). If ego-mind is to come back it must cross its own boundary, and in so doing it must die to itself.

The real importance of this concept of *man* as Nānak elaborates it is that it at once refines and negates the monotheistic concept of self/God as a relationship between inside and outside. In Nānak's teaching this relationship is played out "in the mind" as it were, as the movement of love between lover (unconscious mind as non-ego) and beloved (mind-as-ego). Monotheism in the strict sense becomes almost redundant in the movement and crossings of love. When this love relationship is consummated (fusion), its outward manifestation is as an existence in the world that is radically interconnected to all others. This death of ego-mind, or its capitulation to the embrace of the lover (unconscious mind), is constituted as a realization that our singularity is punctuated by the presence of other existing beings, not simply humans—a fact that opens up the possibility of ethics and politics based on a state of mind that keeps its two halves fused together in a state of balance. Let us try to untangle these ideas a little more carefully.

Part of the problem of monotheism, as we have already noted, is that it remains within a standpoint from which reality is perceived dualistically in terms of either/or oppositions: One/many, existence/nonexistence, form/formlessness, good/evil, etc. Such a standpoint, however, replaces the immediate experience of the One with the dualistic representation of that experience. For Nānak the One cannot be attained by simply annihilating such oppositions or by elevating one term over another. Rather, the unity proper to the Absolute must remain a paradox, that is, as the minimal coincidence of self with other, or what Slavoj Žižek calls a "minimal noncoincidence of the self." Nānak's term for this coincidence of self and other is *birhā*. Resisting all description except through paradox, *birhā* signifies a link between self and other that exists only in erasing itself. *Birhā* is a point at which self and other touch and fuse but are ever in danger of separating.[119] In *birhā* separation is the same as union and vice versa. To speak of this state the Gurus invoke the intensely emotional imagery of the virgin bride who anticipates the embrace of her husband on her wedding night, or the wife's longing for her husband's return from a far-off land. Bride, virgin, wife are simply metaphors for a self that is individuated and that pines for union with the other. The emotion invoked here is that of intensely painful longing combined with the ecstasy of fusion. The pain signifies the minimal link to the self that cannot be broken, for otherwise fusion would mean annihilation of self and world. Hence, self and therefore separation always remain, but within ecstasy. Alternatively, the ecstasy of fusion is always there but tinged with the pain of separation. This state of fusion-separation where knowledge becomes nonknowledge is not a metaphysical ideal but a lived reality, a state of liberation, in which the liberated person *instinctively* avoids relating to everything else in terms of subject-object duality. Such a realized person no longer represents the Absolute since the conscious distinction between self and other, I and not-I, lover and beloved, *nirgun* (nonexistence or a being that cannot be predicated) and *sargun* (existence or a being that can be predicated) has disappeared, leaving an ecstatic and purely spontaneous form of existence (*sahaj*: lit. "equipoise").

In the writings of the Sikh Gurus, a person who maintains this state of *birhā*, and its attendant balance of separation-fusion, self-other, action-inaction, attachment-detachment in the course of daily life, is known as *gurmukh* (lit. "one whose speech is centered around the Guru-Word, the Unconscious Word, the *satguru*"). The *gurmukh* lives in stark contradiction to the *manmukh* (one whose existence is self-centered). The distinction between *gurmukh* and *manmukh* is more than just an ethical one since "ethic" implies some minimal binding to some norm or duty. Rather the distinction implies a freedom from the bindings of the self, which gives rise not to an annihilation of self but to a spontaneity of speech-thought-action. Whether this transition is viewed epistemologically—as a shift from duality to Oneness—or existentially—from *manmukh* to *gurmukh*—the transition itself revolves around the efficacy of the Name (*nām*), which is both the object of love and the means of loving attachment to one's beloved. The term *nām* names the impossible point of contact between self-other, separation-fusion. Attunement to *nām* constitutes a wordless communication between self and other that corresponds to the primordial love through which all existent things relate to each other before individuation takes over.

In Guru Nānak's hymns *nām* is not a particular word or mantra. It is inscribed within, yet manifests as, speech in which traces of ego are constantly erased as they arise. As the constituting link between interiority and worldly action, *nām* arises involuntarily in the *gurmukh*'s speech through the practice of constantly holding in mind the remembrance of death (*nām simaraṇ*). But *nām* cannot be obtained through self-effort alone. Its attainment depends on the grace or favorable glance (*kirpā, nadar*) of a spiritual preceptor or a guru. Nānak's own preceptor, however, was not a human guru but an impersonal principle: the Word (*śabda*), which Nānak also calls *satguru* (lit. "the only real guru"), is a term that implies a personal relation to the Word. Personal or impersonal, only the Word speaks truly about the nature of existence. The idea of *kirpā/nadar* is that the ego's effort to erase itself can be blunted if it thinks it is doing this itself. Grace as *kirpā/nadar* implies the possibility of a helping hand from the unconscious other, which deflects this possibility of a return to self and therefore slipping back into the cycle of self-production.

A variation on the terms *śabda* and *satguru* is *anhad śabda* or *anhad nād* (lit. the "unspoken Word" or "unstruck Sound"), inherited by the Sikh Gurus from their predecessors the Sants, such as Kabir, who in turn borrow the term from the Siddhās and Nāths, the expert practitioners of Haṭha Yoga. According to Nāth usage *anhad śabda* refers to the "Eternal Sound" that is heard at the climax of the Haṭha Yoga process. In the context of the Sants and the Sikh Gurus the term refers to words or language that is not tainted by traces of ego, and therefore not like ordinary communication between egos in which words are merely labels for things.

As *anhad śabda* the Word itself speaks or resounds without being spoken. This sounds like a tautology but actually indicates a mode of communication in which ego no longer controls the production of words, nor indeed the process of making words into things. Removed from the grasp of ego, words are no longer given value according to their degree of correspondence to things, but instead arise from an internalized mode of speech that occurs between conscious (ego) and unconscious (non-ego) mind. The unspoken Word arises from a mode of communication in which the mind speaks with itself, giving the impression of a departure from the standards of everyday social reality in which speech is meaningful if it makes sense to everybody. The point of this seemingly impossible communication is to rejoin the two aspects of the dualistic mind separated by ego-sense. Devoid of ego-traces, the Word that is so minted in the mind appears as an expression of wonder (*vismād*) at the nature of existence, that things exist at all rather than nothing. Just as all creation simply happens without asking why, so the unspoken Word arises without connection to intention, desire, or will.

Thus Guru Nānak's authority, what makes him Guru or *gurmukh*, is derived from the *satguru* (= *śabda*). But *satguru* as *śabda-guru* manifests only when the ego erases its own traces *without* annihilating itself. This self-erasure is another name for the love between self and other that enables them to be One even in separation. So Nānak's authority is his own experience of the One.

Liberation is for Nānak primarily a reorientation of consciousness, albeit a radical one. The reorientation that the Sikh Gurus are looking for must happen primarily at the level of language or Word (*śabda*), such that one's ordinary relationship to language, which is based on self-naming (where the "I" is attached to a primary identification to its own image and name), is transformed by its attunement to the Word as *nām* (the Name). *Nām* is the link by means of which all existing things acknowledge their nonexistent source, as well as the means by which each self acknowledges its link to its voided other.

As the Sikh Gurus articulate it, insofar as *nām* cannot simply be reduced to God's Name, or to the names of individual gods, it illustrates the paradox of the One and the Many. Throughout the Ādi Granth, *nām* serves to replace what is named in other (especially religious and philosophical) traditions as "God," whose name is no more than a tool for calling this entity to mind at will. In contradistinction, *nām* makes superfluous the need for such an entity and thereby constitutes the single most important term for deriving a posttheistic *gurmat*. For the Gurus, any "God" or "god" that is outside of the ego is to remain subject to the operation of *māyā*, the veil of illusion generated by the ego. Although "God" is referred to as the highest or ultimate, etc., these superlatives still only refer to a highest or ultimate entity that remains within a scale determined by man. Thus, whereas "God" is liable to be turned into an idol, and therefore never experienced as God, *nām* signifies that divinity can be experienced only through the meeting of eternity and time, absolute and finite. *Nām* is therefore not so much an indicator of transcendental experience as it is of the possibility of all possible experience. The term *nām* is as much theological as it is political. To see how this might be the case, it is helpful to relate our discussion of *nām* to two other terms used by Guru Nānak to refer to his experience of the One: *nirguṇ* and *sarguṇ*.

Nirguṇ, the experience of the divine as ineffable, without qualities, beyond naming, signifies the divinity's detachment or nonexistence; hence either "God" has no Name or God's Name is the signifier of emptiness. *Sarguṇ*, on the other hand, signifies that "God" has infinite names, corresponding to infinite attributes, and signifies absolute fullness, or a full involvement of the divinity in all things. Yet for Nānak these two opposing terms are also the same: *nirguṇ āp sarguṇ bī ohī* ("being absent the same One is also fully present," or "the one detached is the same as the one involved").[120] So "God" is beyond, yet "God" actualizes himself through the relation of equivalence, and therefore substitutability, between all names and things. As there is an equivalence between all things, so God's ineffability/absence and his fullness/presence are different aspects of the same formless one: *sarguṇ nirguṇ niraṁkār*.[121]

Nām therefore names this equivalential connection (*sarguṇ-nirguṇ*) as an ineffable fullness, which is to say that *nām* is a signifier of emptiness, an empty signifier. So what we regard as an entity called "God" is better termed *nām*, such that *nām* implies an entity that is involved in the world but is at the same time absent. Only *nām* can signify this impossible relation between absence/presence, nonexistence/existence, empty/full, etc. And *nām* can do this not because it has any metaphysical characteristics, but precisely because it is part of an already existing discursive network of signifiers, a symbolic order that we call language. *Nām*, in other words, is part of the fabric of ordinary and everyday experience. *Nām* therefore helps us make sense of the divine paradox (*nirguṇ-sarguṇ*) by putting the impossible, the beyond, the absent, to play in the context of finitude.[122] I can only experience the Absolute as utterly empty (*nirguṇ*) if I can project it into the contingent, everyday experience of particulars (*sarguṇ*) and therefore be involved in the world. Consequently *nām*, as experience, is to experience the detachment (*nirguṇ*) while living, speaking, and being involved in ordinary worldly experience (*sarguṇ*). If something is experienced by the mystic, then this experience, if it is not to remain abstract or detached, must actualize itself through attachment to a particular, to that which is finite, and, therefore, to contingent events. If *nām* names the mystical experience that desires ultimate fullness, then *nām* must accompany all positive experience. This is also the condition of all authority, of all sovereignty, and consequently of the political. Authority or sovereignty is such only if it is radically empty or represented through the empty signifier that is *nām*.

This is why the Gurus prefer *nām*, a term that names the intricate link or experience between self and other. In contradistinction to the "I" generated by ego's cravings, which operates an economy of narcissism precisely to gain a return-to-oneself, hence self-ownership as the beginning of ownership of the other, Name is the only capital that cannot be reduced to the status of a thing and circulated in an economy of exchange. Nānak's instruction in this regard is very pragmatic: one cannot simply escape the economic nature of one's existence in the world driven by the self's desire to make everything its own property. But it is possible to change the very nature of this economy by transforming narcissistic self-love into a love of the Name.

Moreover, the Gurus suggest a practice for transforming the ego-based economy of ordinary life in which we accumulate knowledge, exchange entities, transact commerce, follow reasonable rules, conceive of plans and projects, practice rites and rituals. This practice is *nām simaran*: the constant holding in remembrance of the Name, which goes beyond mechanical repetition to become a spontaneous form of love between self and other. The paradoxical dialectic here between appropriation of *nām* and disappropriation of ego becomes more evident from the etymology of the word *simaran*. Derived from the Indo-European root *smr-* ("to remember, hold in mind") the term has traditionally been understood to resonate with the Sanskrit terms *mr-* and *maranā*, to die or pass away, suggesting that *simaran* is a form of remembrance that automatically lets go or renounces. Stated differently, *simaran* is first of all remembrance of ones own mortality, of the ego's death, remembering which one awakens to the Name. *Nām simaran is therefore the condition of experience of finitude. Alternatively, the experience of finitude is the condition for the experience of nām.*

Because *nām simaran* is not a metaphysical concept but a concrete sacrificial practice for transforming memory, as that function of mind which weaves time into the structures that manipulate our existence and thinking, it can also be viewed as a way of transforming worldly time and existence. It provides a means for the individual to participate and make changes in the world. *Nām simaran* is as inherently political as it is spiritual. As a result such conceptual dualities as those between religion and politics, or mysticism and violence, become superfluous. This is evident in the lives of the Sikh Gurus, for whom there was no contradiction between mystical experience and the life of a soldier, householder, or political leader.

6   Decolonizing Postsecular Theory

The Cultural Bias of Theory

In the previous chapter I argued that it may be possible to break the cycles of repetition that produce identity politics centered around structures of transcendence. These structures have continued to govern the modern and postmodern (globalized) forms of Sikhism and Hinduism by limiting their engagements in the world to revivals or retrievals of an essence or an original identity. For Sikhs such a break can be effected through interpretations of texts such as the Guru Granth Sāhib, which are inherently capable of posing resistance to the *sui generis* model of religion, thereby allowing us to connect central terms in the teachings of the Sikh Gurus (*gurmat*), such as *nām* and *nām simaraṇ*, to frameworks grounded in finitude and contingency that had been repressed under the sign of the nation and the metaphysical frameworks spawned by it. The immediate outcome of this break with the nationalist schema is that it allows us to rethink *gurmat* as a teaching that engenders different ways of engaging in the world, a teaching centered on human action rather than a transcendental philosophy. This break is not a simple eradication of neocolonial representations of *gurmat* as "Sikh theology." It can be more usefully considered as a gesture that refuses the call for identity politics by reviving a prior relationship with temporality or finitude. This regrounding of *gurmat* in structures of contingency and finitude results in a secularization of *gurmat*. However, this secularization of *gurmat* does not necessarily indicate a Westernization of Sikh thought, or the implementation of a distinction between religion and secularism, but rather a form of thought that remains embedded in the specific contexts and conditions that are very different from those in which Western secularism developed. It challenges the idea that secularism is specific to the West, and suggests that alternative forms of secularization arise from within the Sikh texts. Another way to think about this is to reenvisage *gurmat* as a "political theology,"[1] which, properly speaking, corresponds more closely to the idea of *gurmat* as an self-emptying concept, a concept that places as much emphasis on the absence or loss of the divine as it does on divine presence.

In many ways the central themes of this postcolonial form of *gurmat* appear to converge with other idioms of emancipation from modernity/ nationalism/metaphysics. I refer to discourses that are prefixed with the "*post-*," namely, postmodernism and especially postsecularism, which coincides with the reemergent idiom of "political theology" or "political theologies."[2] The similarity between these "*post-*" discourses and the self-emptying idiom of *gurmat* seems to suggest the possibility of theoretical and political convergences between them. At the very least, movements such as postsecularism and political theology appear to provide a more hospitable forum not only for *gurmat* to do its critical work within the humanities, but more broadly as a staging ground for a renewed intellectual encounter between colonizer/colonized, West and non-West. Could Sikh, and more broadly South Asian, thought join the democratic spirit of dialogue with Western thought on more equal terms, that is, outside the religion/secularism binary and without needing to revive religious and ethnic identities? Could South Asian texts, literature, and subject formations enter what is called the mainstream in both a political and a theoretical sense? In a globalized world, could there now be something like an equal exchange of ideas? Can the subject of South Asia, normally regarded as a particular (i.e., belonging to a geopolitical area), be regarded as something that actively shares in the universal, in the sense that it is shareable with the rest of humanity?

Given the impact of postmodernist and postsecular thought within the humanities, both of which have in different ways helped to problematize modernity, colonialism, and the nation-state, one might be forgiven for assuming that something like this had been happening for some time. But the reality is quite different. Far from there being a mutual exchange of ideas, the reality is a more sophisticated segregation of knowledge along the lines of universal and particular within the humanities and social sciences. Despite the proliferation of knowledge about almost every aspect of non-Western cultures, scholars of religion have assumed that incorporating the appropriate methodology (in the case of disciplines such as history of religions, Asian studies, and postcolonial studies) or critical theory (in the case of theology or the philosophy of religion) would absolve them from the effects of this segregation. As theory has become increasingly central to the study of religion in recent years, the earlier divide between philosophy of religion/theology and the history of religions (which reflected the universal/particular or theory/empiricism division of knowledge in the humanities) has become increasingly blurred. Ironically, this blurring is a consequence of a split within the domain of theory itself, which has normally been considered inseparable from the broad swathe of secular humanist cultural criticism that has defined the humanities and social sciences.

What seems to have changed in recent years is the understanding of humanist cultural criticism as secular. Due to an entire range of intellectual influences whose combined effect has been to problematize the opposition between the secular and the religious, what used to be called simply "critical theory," or just "theory," has itself dissociated into two more-or-less distinct strands. One strand, derived from Marx, might be regarded as conventionally secular critical theory. This was the form of theorization adopted by Edward Said, and which runs through the work of the subaltern studies group and South Asianist scholarship more generally. The other is a form of theorization that recognizes that the normally opposed categories of "religion" and "politics," or "religion" and the "secular," implicate each other much more than was previously thought, indeed, that secularity as it has developed in the West is a religious phenomenon. At a stretch this second strand of theory could include perspectives as diverse as those of the political theorist William Connolly, the anthropologist Talal Asad,[3] or scholars of religion whose insights are derived from recent continental philosophy, which has come to call itself by various names, including, "continental philosophy of religion," "secular theology," "religious theory," or simply "postsecular theory." In other words, not only is theory itself split in a way that mirrors the religious/secular divide, but both forms of theory continue to derive their materials and impetus primarily from Western tradition and phenomena. Nowhere is this better illustrated than the way in which critical theory and cultural theory have differently impacted the study of Western versus South Asian religions within the discipline of religious studies

As far as the study of so-called Western traditions is concerned, not only has critical theory helped to dismantle well-worn dualisms such as religion/secularism, theism/atheism, and sacred/secular, but it has also helped to narrow the gap between academic practices and cultural practices (such as religion) that has preoccupied much scholarship in religious studies.[4] That is to say, critical theory has simultaneously problematized and challenged essentialist and theological tendencies (dreams of absolute principles, supernatural origins, ahistorical authorities, pure traditions, etc.) *and* scholars' claims to methodological objectivity and impartiality, since the humanities, far from being a site of neutral value-free analysis, is itself thoroughly implicated in cultural realities.[5] In what might be seen as a reversal of critical theory's atheistic roots in the "masters of suspicion" (Marx, Nietzsche, Freud), contemporary cultural theory has been adopted by scholars to successfully dispute the atheistic presuppositions of modern secular thinking in the social sciences, thereby revitalizing religious and theological reflection in the Christian and Judaic traditions. As a result theory has been used to legitimize the use of phenomena from Judeo-Christian traditions as resources not only for thinking critically about religion, but for thinking more critically about theory itself, thereby helping to push cultural and critical theory into a "postcritical" phase.[6] As I noted in chapter 2, perhaps the clearest indication of this is the conspicuous return by leading thinkers of the Left (such as Žižek, Badiou, and Vattimo, among others) to the religious sources of Western culture in order to revitalize the projects of political and cultural theory.

By contrast, the effects of theory on the study of South Asian "religions" has had precisely the opposite effect. Here the effects of critical theory seem to have reinforced the priority of the secular. To quote Dingwaney and Rajan again, "religion," "the religious," and "the theological" are concepts that encounter a notable impasse in the work of most contemporary postcolonial intellectuals, for whom critical theory is governed by the demands of historicism and the need for historical explanation.[7] Yet as I have demonstrated earlier, historicism itself is unstable. Taken to its limits, historicism is codependent and coemergent with religion or theology.

A more convincing explanation for this impasse has been given by the postcolonial theorist Dipesh Chakrabarty, who points out the very different interventions of critical theory in Western and South Asian traditions. Chakrabarty argues that in the Western intellectual traditions key thinkers who are long dead and gone are treated not only as people belonging to their own times, but also as though they were contemporaries.[8] The thinkers and traditions of South Asia, however, once unbroken and alive in their native languages, are now matters of historical research. These traditions are treated as truly dead, as history. Few if any social scientists working in the history of religions—or for that matter in the philosophy of religion, or cultural theory—would ever try to make the concepts of these traditions into resources for contemporary critical theory. And yet "past Western thinkers and their categories are never quite dead for us in the same way. South Asian(ist) social scientists would argue passionately with a Marx, or a Weber without feeling any need to historicize them in their European intellectual contexts."[9]

Such remarks are part of a broader argument put forward by scholars in different disciplines about the viability of secular humanism as an adequate model for a global understanding of the humanities.[10] In Chakrabarty's case, even though the humanities were a fundamental part of the project of European colonialism, his own task of "provincializing Europe" retains a certain ambivalence. For on the one hand Chakrabarty insists on retrieving "radically heterogeneous" forms of belief, knowledge, and social habitus that many Indian secularists, following colonial trends, tended to repress or relegate to the domain of the "religious" or, what amounts to the same thing, the "prepolitical."[11] But on the other hand he emphasizes the destructive and repressive nature of the West's humanist Enlightenment, in the sense that the idea of "political modernity" is "impossible to *think* of anywhere in the world without invoking categories and concepts, the genealogies of which go deep into the intellectual and even theological traditions of Europe."[12] Chakrabarty's search for a non-Western modernity seems to be tinged by a "politics of despair," as he acknowledges that this task is "impossible within the knowledge protocols of academic history, for the globality of academia is not independent of the globality that the European modern has created."[13]

Although Chakrabarty's questions are targeted at the discipline of history, they find equal if not greater cogency in the discipline of religious studies. Following Chakrabarty we could ask why, given that South Asian culture has been part of the comparative study of religion and philosophy for more than two centuries, the ideas and phenomena of South Asian traditions still do not find similar contemporaneity. Why has critical theory's intervention in the study of religions specifically, and more broadly in the humanities, been limited to Western religious traditions? What prevents non-Western traditions of thought and practice (*gurmat*, *bhakti*, etc.) from being used as resources for conceptual thinking/theory rather than being regarded as living relics? Why is it that despite the proliferation of postcolonial critiques, the humanities and social sciences continue to reconstitute the hegemony of theory as specifically Western and/or the division of intellectual labor between universal and particular knowledge formations? Is this due only to silence on the part of South Asianists? I am not suggesting here that South Asianists have not invested in theory. The existence of the field of postcolonial theory, which has been dominated by South Asianists in the guise of "subaltern studies," would be proof to the contrary. What I'm suggesting though is that the problem goes deeper. For as I briefly alluded to in the first two chapters, "theory" for postcolonial theorists continues to be defined by Marx's secular injunction against religion: "The criticism of religion is the premise of all criticism."[14] Accordingly, most postcolonial theorists have treated the activity of *thinking about religion* as an oxymoron, thus forgetting that the activity of thinking (theory) and the work of religion-making have been inextricably connected in the history of Western thought and, of course, within the colonial project. By overinvesting in historicism, postcolonial studies never really touched the home ground of theory, namely, religion. Having relegated the task of thinking about religion to the "prepolitical," postcolonial theory took one step forward and one step back, effectively consigning its own emancipatory project, the "*post-*" of the postcolonial project, to a kind of evolutionary historicism—the idea that whatever developed first in European modernity would inevitably follow later in the modernizing of the non-Western world. This evolution is just as evident in the development of theory (various "*post-*"s) in the humanities: postmodernism, posthumanism, postsecularism.

It would appear, then, that the stage is set for a more productive encounter between postcolonial theory and what is variously termed "continental philosophy of religion," "secular theology," "religious theory," or simply "postsecular theory," and thus for taking theory itself beyond the religion/secularism divide in such a way that it becomes more amenable to thinking about South Asian cultures. One way to achieve this is to retrieve the "semantic potentials" of the concept of secularization from within South Asian traditions, as I have indicated earlier. This is not essentially different from the procedures adopted by postsecular theory.

The only difference here is that South Asian traditions and their thinkers would be brought into contact with the sources of Western thought as if they were coeval and contemporaneous—the clear implication of this being that what we call Western thought, exemplified by the humanities and theory as such, would no longer be able to call itself "Western" as opposed to the "non-Western." It might simply be referred to as global thought, or a "global humanities."

However, it is important to understand that before this could become a reality, a major lacuna in many of the influential versions of contemporary postsecular theory must be resolved, one which prevents any meaningful encounter with postcolonial theory. Recent articulations of postsecular theory inherit a critical narrative that simply repeats a past imperialism. The main form of this past imperialism is a move that forecloses the very kind of secularization that can be claimed to be already present in South Asian traditions. This critical move denies coevalness to South Asian traditions by keeping the "*post-*," or "movement beyond," safely within the domain of Western conceptuality. What allows this to take place is the continuing assumption of historical difference between West and non-West, and the reason this assumption is still in place—even today when theory considers itself to be utterly radicalized—is that theory continues to access the other through the problematic idiom of the history of religions. This is very different from the scenario in which, let us say, South Asians or South Asian traditions access, let us say, continental philosophy. The problem, therefore, is no longer that of trying to locate and define the incommensurability or difference of non-Western traditions, but rather the more difficult one of revealing the denial of access to theory itself.

This may sound strange, but I believe that lodged within the very movement by which Western thought appears to overcome itself, the so called *post-* of postmodernity, postsecularism, etc., there is an ethnocentrism that keeps these newer stages of Western thought effectively tied to oppressive structures that were part of modernity and colonialism. The question, then, is how postsecular thought derived from recent continental philosophy can be made to recognize this implicit ethnocentrism and ultimately go through a process of decolonization, something it believes it has already achieved. At stake here is whether it is possible to conceive the "*post-*" otherwise than as a function of the West, and of the Enlightenment. Or, to put it differently: in order to make the postcolonial task viable, is it not necessary to distinguish the "*post-*" of postcoloniality from the evolutionary historicism of Western thought itself, which, in its recent (re)turn to religion, continues to maintain its self-definition as Western? Does the viability of the postcolonial task not depend on interrogating the self-referential *post-* movements that continue to keep theory on what is considered to be its home ground?

In what follows I want to look more closely at the mechanism(s) that continue to close off South Asian or non-Western thought and phenomena from the supposed ground of theory. One way of doing this is to look more closely at the narratives that write the script of emancipation, the various "*post-*"'s that aim to liberate us initially from religion, then from modernity, and finally(?) from secularism, in order to arrive at a nuanced understanding of the globalized condition of mankind. We need to look for the signs that keep these narratives of freedom revolving around its solar principle, namely, the idea of the West. It is possible to pin down this interrogation even further by focusing on the narrative that has become a conventional wisdom in the history of modern ideas, which regards the "intrinsic connection between the metaphysical-epistemological project that seeks an absolute ground for thought in reason, and the philosophical project of finding a ground in reason for the modus operandi of a moral and political subject."[15] This refers to a connection between theory and politics provided by subjectivity, which in turn finds its inspiration in the concept of religion.

One of the clearest indications of this continual self-referencing that goes on, particularly within postsecular theory, is the return of Hegel into contemporary critical and cultural theory. The figure of Hegel not only mirrors the "return of religion," or the crisis of secularism, in contemporary politics and theory, it happens to be a key link in the construction of the various narratives of overcoming and liberation. Indeed one could go so far as to say that when cultural theorists distinguish between the various theoretical movements that I shall refer to as modernism (or humanism), postmodernism[1], postmodernism[2], and postsecularism, the very differences between these movements are constituted as different ways of appropriating Hegel's thought.[16] Thus, for example, while humanism is broadly Hegelian, postcolonialism, postmodernism[1], and postmodernism[2] are anti-Hegelian, though in different ways. Postsecularism, on the other hand, begins by positing itself as truly anti-Hegelian, but then oddly mutates into a "true" Hegelianism.

But why does the figure of Hegel continue to haunt the site of theory in the humanities? Why do such different movements as the resolutely secular postcolonial theory and postsecular religious theory define their respective projects in relation to Hegel? Why is Hegel so pivotal to the form of theorizing that seeks emancipation *by turning away from religion* and embracing secularism, and to the form of theorizing that seeks emancipation *by returning to religion* through a deconstruction of the secular? What specifically interests me is whether a more critical reading of these narratives can help us rethink the task of postcoloniality. More specifically, what are the implications of Hegel's return for thinking about the postcolonial subject as the subject of politics?

To begin answering some of these questions I want first to work through the central contours of these successive theoretical movements: humanism, postmodernism[1] (which was inspired by the work of Lyotard, Foucault, Derrida, and Lacan, and which becomes synonymous with conventional secular postcolonial theory, as exemplified by Homi Bhaba, Gayatri Spivak, and Edward Said), and postmodernism[2] (which is basically globalization theory inspired by Deleuze and Guattari and taken up by leftist political theorists such Michael D. Hardt, Antonio Negri, and Susan Buck-Morss). What is striking about these theoretical movements is their neglect of the question of religion and secularism as central to the quest for liberation and therefore to the task of theorizing postcoloniality. Because of this neglect, and because of the centrality of religion and secularism to the colonial project, I argue that it is necessary for postcolonials to engage with the idiom of postsecular theory (or political theology), which radically reformulates the religion/secularism issue and develops a more nuanced reading of the relationship between subjectivity and the political. Nevertheless, I also argue that this engagement must be tempered by a realization that even the most radical versions of postsecular theory, represented by thinkers such as Slavoj Žižek and Mark C. Taylor, need to undergo a further decolonization due largely to the centrality of Hegel and the reconstitution of a new kind of Eurocentrism.

Reassessing the Narratives of Emancipation

Humanism

As we have seen in chapter 4, humanism denotes "a tradition of political thought (presupposed by contemporary liberals and conservatives alike) that understands human beings firstly as moral agents who ought to be free of, or elevate themselves above, oppressive structures and secondly as reducible to universal though interior mental processes shared by all human beings."[17] Humanism is committed to the ideology of the sovereign subject and the principle of disinterestedness — that Truth is external to and the adversary of power and politics.

Within the humanities and especially within the study of religion, the influence of humanism can be felt in the writings of phenomenologists of religion who interiorize some aspect of human experience and practice, thereby removing it from history. Consequently the ideology of humanism enters the discipline of religious studies by appealing to the abstract universality of "faith," "belief," etc., that "we" all share, thus allowing scholars to equate the *study* of religion with the *practice* of religious pluralism. As we have seen, however, there are two components to this seemingly benign pluralism: first, that identity constitutes the condition for difference; and second, that identity operates through the political psychology of recognition (i.e., ascribing "religion" or religious identity as a central category of the other) in order to reduce the subversive threat of emergent differential constituencies — e.g., bodies of marginalized texts or marginalized social groups — by accommodating them to a humanist core, namely the *anthropologos*, or the figure of Man. Despite its claim that the *anthropologos* implies the death of God (or its becoming immanent within humanity), the disinterestedness of humanistic inquiry is grounded within ontotheological structures of transcendence, which perceive temporality from the end or from an elevated position.

In practice the ideology of humanism translates itself into the accommodational politics of liberal democracy, whose coercions are concealed in the illusion of individual sovereignty and governed by metaphysical oppositions (public/private, religion/secular) where religion is an interior private affair and must cede to the rule of Law. This ideology finds its most powerful theoretical expression in the writings of Hegel, who anticipated its colonial and liberal multiculturalist forms. We can see how this works in the case of modern Sikhism. Since the Sikh subject has been determined as an essentially religious subject, then any aspiration that Sikhs have for political expression or subjectivity is necessarily a deviation from its religious nature. In order to reside in a pluralistic multicultural society, Sikh subjectivity must conform to the rule of the State. Any deviancy in the form of political action must be subject to correction. In other words, Sikhism must revert to its "original," "peaceful" state. "True" Sikhism is Sikhism without a desire for sovereignty, a Sikhism that has already renounced politics through the interiorization of Law. For liberal humanists, the only postcolonial form of Sikhism is one that has learned to limit its subjective possibilities to retrievals of identity that conform to the rules of secular democracy. A Sikh subject can be regarded as postcolonial only insofar as s/he is able to retrieve its identity but in that moment of retrieval recognizes its own limits and finds satisfaction in these limits.

Postmodernism[1]

As the prefix "post-" suggests, postmodernist theories and critiques seek to liberate us from past forms of domination and their legacies in the present. At the risk of generalizing about the sheer variety of discourses that come under the rubric of postmodernism, one could safely say that most of them begin with critiques of transcendence and the model of subjectivity upon which Enlightenment thought is based, and then go on to challenge binary oppositions that define self and other. In doing so postmodernism provides resources for those who struggle to challenge modern discourses of oppression, in particular racism, patriarchy, and colonialism. Postmodernists argue that culture's intrinsic hybridity and ambivalence challenge such binary oppositions. They insist on a politics of difference that defies universalizing discourses and structures of power. By affirming fragmented social identities as means for contesting the sovereignty of the humanist subject, postmodernist critique represents a break with the modern conception of sovereignty vested in the nation-state. Nevertheless, postmodernist theory has no desire to simply do away with the Enlightenment tradition or with modernity. Rather they distinguish between two ideologically opposed strands of the Enlightenment. One strand, associated with thinkers of immanence such as Duns Scotus and Spinoza, had a potentially liberating effect. The other strand, best represented by Hegelian dialectic, reimposed transcendental structures inherent within the concept of modern sovereignty and ended up controlling the earlier strand's liberating tendency. These transcendental structures provided new dualisms that mediated our understanding of reality and were incorporated into the intellectual project of European imperialism. Hence postmodernist theory is better seen as a challenge to the transcendentalism inherent within Hegelian dialectic, which constitutes the central logic of modern processes of domination, exclusion, and the subsuming of multiplicities to a unitary order. Accordingly, "if modern power is dialectical, . . . then the postmodern project must be non-dialectical," a politics of difference that dissolves the very power of binaries and sets differences to play across boundaries.[18]

Given that modern sovereignty was identified with the European tendency toward global domination, postmodern thought inevitably converged with an influential strand of postcolonial theory. While early versions of postcolonial theory were reliant on Marx and Sartre, the discourse soon appropriated various strands of French poststructuralism, with Said using Foucault, Fanon using Lacan, Spivak cultivating Derrida, and Bhabha using Derrida and Lacan. Of these thinkers, the work of Homi Bhabha is probably the best example of the convergence between postmodernist and postcolonial discourses. As Bhabha presents it, the postcolonial project is defined by its resistance toward the binary oppositions on which the colonialist worldview is based. This conception of the world gave rise to the essentialism and homogeneity of the identities across the boundary that separates the binary oppositions. For Bhabha, the crucial link that holds these binaries together is the Hegelian dialectic. But once this dialectic is recognized, it is possible to foster relationships between the binaries and across the boundaries that separate them. Bhabha does this by using concepts such as "mimicry," which becomes a specific form of intervention in the colonizer's discourse:

> Mimicry marks those moments of civil disobedience within the discipline of civility: signs of spectacular resistance. When the words of the master become the site of hybridity . . . then we may not only read between the lines but even seek to change the often coercive reality that they so lucidly contain.[19]

Because the colonized's mimicry of the colonizer's discourse is a form of repetition that transforms the original as it mimics, it becomes possible for the colonized to rearticulate the very notion of identity and separate it from essence. Thus, cultures are never coherent wholes but already partial and hybrid formations. For Bhabha, the concept of hybridity contains a subversive logic that can politically contest forces of social oppression by affirming the multiplicity of differences in order to subvert the power of ruling binary structures.

Postmodernity[2]

Although postmodernist critiques successfully contested liberal humanism until the early 1990s, postmodernism has, since the end of the

Cold War and the passage of the world into global capitalism, itself become the target of a countercritique from political theorists who form the vanguard of the New Left. While the passage from modernity to late modernity and globalization has been universally accepted by liberal humanists, Marxists, and postmodernists alike, there has not been a concomitant recognition of the transformation of the form of power in the new globalized society. To remedy this lack, political theorists such as Michael Hardt and Antonio Negri argue that the contemporary processes of globalization have torn down many of the boundaries of the colonial world and as a result the modern forms of power that postmodernists have taken such pains to describe and contest no longer hold sway.[20] Postmodernists, they argue, continue to combat what's left of a past form of domination to the extent that they have failed to recognize the new form of power that has constituted itself through the processes of global capitalism. A new paradigm—Empire as globalization—has come to replace the modernist paradigm, and it exerts power through the very hybridities and fragmentary subjectivities that postmodernists celebrate.

Because of this shift in the paradigm of power, globalization is much more than a phenomenon or a set of processes. It is now a central and unavoidable *concept* of contemporary cultural theory for understanding the transition of human society into a new political order. It is precisely this transition that Hardt and Negri try to explicate in their book *Empire*.[21] The term "Empire" is meant to displace the idea of territorial acquisition, which belongs to the period of European colonization. Against the spatial concept of territory or "place," the term "Empire," Hardt and Negri insist, signifies a new epoch, a "space of imperial sovereignty" that is in effect a "nonplace."[22] Ironically, it is within the "nonplace" of Empire that there emerges a supposedly mobile and innovative force that Hardt and Negri refer to as the "multitude," which can be liberated from the constraints of modernity and the nation. This passage of sovereignty is therefore a move toward immanence, consisting in the informatization of the economy that leads to the dominance of the world-market over the nation-state. By arguing that the establishment of Empire is a progressive move—"globalization . . . is really a condition of liberation of the multitude"—Hardt and Negri reject any political strategy that seeks to return power to the nation-state so that it can challenge global capital from the outside.[23] Indeed there is no outside of Empire and therefore no capacity to organize resistance from the outside. Rather, a politics of resistance, intellectual or otherwise, must come from within it.[24]

In particular Hardt and Negri target prominent postcolonial theorists such as Bhabha, Spivak, and Said, arguing that while "postcolonialist theory is a very productive tool for rereading history, it is entirely insufficient for theorizing contemporary global power."[25] By failing to recognize the contemporary object of critique, postmodernists and postcolonialists, they argue, mistake today's real enemy, which has in fact mutated from the old imperialism in such a way as to depotentialize any possible challenge. The "new enemy is not only resistant to the old weapons of critique but actually thrives on them, and thus joins its would-be antagonists in applying them to the fullest: 'Long live difference! Down with essentialist binaries!'"[26] For Hardt and Negri postcolonial and postmodern discourses are limited to being attacks on the dialectical form of modern sovereignty. In short, postcolonial and postmodern analyses continue to be haunted by the very specter that they seek to confront, namely, the Hegelian dialectic.

As Pal Ahluwalia has argued, proponents of postcolonial theory, on the other hand, have cautioned against the optimism of Hardt and Negri's thesis, suggesting that the postcolonial nation-state, instead of disappearing, has simply been restructured or that the way in which global modernity is being advanced is itself "profoundly colonial," as can be seen by the perverse persistence of identity politics in previously colonized countries.[27] "Perverse" because the form of sovereignty reproduced by ex-colonized peoples and groups is merely a mimicked form of identity based on a prior accession to Western ideals. It is therefore never sovereign, but always borrowed, and ultimately illegitimate. The greatest weakness of Empire is the desire for commodities and the patterns of consumption between and within nations, which lead to boundaries between those people and groups of people who benefit from it and those who don't.[28] It is precisely the maintenance of such boundaries between the Western and the postcolonial world and especially the deep investment in identity politics that, for postcolonialists, undermines Negri and Hardt's thesis.

The political theorist Susan Buck-Morss appears to sympathize with the concerns of postcolonial theorists and in a recent work offers an apology for the unequal and uneven nature of globalization:

> How to write for a global public that does not yet exist? We, the multitude who might become that public, cannot yet reach each other across the excluding boundaries of language, beneath the power distortions of global media, against the muffling exclusions of poverty

and the disparities of information. We are therefore to be forgiven for relying on the discourses that that we possess in common as members of partial publics—(discourses such as) religion, national belonging, Western knowledge, global business, ethnic traditions. It is understandable that we wish our particular discourses to have universal status although we're aware of the extent to which the appearance of universality is an effect of power. As there is currently no global debate, dominant ideas exist in a social context of domination that affects their truth content irrefutably.[29]

However, Buck-Morss immediately qualifies the above statement with a move that is common to theorists of globalization on the left: she invokes the notion of global immanence, the fact that in an era of global capital, global production, global labor migrations, and penetration by communications technologies, there is no spatial outside.[30] There is no other of peoples, territories against which we can define ourselves. We're all connected economically or otherwise. Because of this interconnectedness the state of immanence is inherently complex. Those who deny the truth of global immanence fuel fundamentalism. And the "mark of fundamentalism is not just religious belief but dogmatic belief" irrespective of whether this is preached by heads of state, by religious organizations, or by the IMF.[31]

Though formulated differently, the notion of immanence is also central to Hardt and Negri's notion of Empire. Through the transition to Empire the multitude can be liberated from the constraints of the nation. Hardt and Negri identify liberation with the "constituent power" of pure immanence, an uncontainable power, infinitely protean and continually creative. This power is contrasted to a "constituted power" that is always set in a constricting transcendence. The move toward immanence is also a move toward a state of complexity as opposed to the organic simplicity of the nation-state. Immanence-qua-complexity is a condition for the liberation of the multitude. And Hardt and Negri reject any political and intellectual strategy that seeks to challenge global capital from the outside. In effect, as Jacques Rancière notes, because Hardt and Negri reject any inherent negativity in political subjects, it follows that the power inherent in the multitude, and hence any politics of resistance, has to be a disruptive power, "lodged in all state of domination as its ultimate content, a content destined to destroy all barriers. 'Multitudes' have to be a content whose continent is Empire."[32]

Postsecularism

Though seemingly opposed, globalization theorists and post-colonial theorists share a common blindspot in regard to the nature of contemporary globalization. This blindspot causes them to ignore the role of religion in the shaping of global politico-economic realities and the role of Hegel in conceptualizing them. As William D. Hart and Mark C. Taylor have independently pointed out (the former with respect to postcolonial theory influenced by Said, and the latter with respect to Hardt and Negri's *Empire*), the two share a broadly Marxist perspective in which cultural perspectives can always be reduced to a material economic base[33] and critical theory to historicism.[34] Notwithstanding Hardt and Negri's claim that their theory of Empire goes beyond the critique of binaries, what in fact links their theorization of Empire to the issue of modern sovereignty is Hegel and the Hegelian dialectic. More precisely, it is the return of a certain strand of Hegelian ideology, namely, the thought of religion, once repressed by liberal and Marxist forms of secularism, which continues to haunt postcolonial critiques of imperialism and postmodern theories of Empire.

Many scholars still accept the standard Marxist narrative about Hegel, which suggests that Hegel's *Lectures on the Philosophy of History* constitutes an Ur-text that provides the matrix for colonial and neocolonial representations of non-Western cultures. Once the theological bias of Hegel's reading of history has been corrected, the narrative goes, the way is cleared for a truly secular (humanist/anthropological) framework conducive to postcolonial thinking (colonialism is equated with the unhealthy influence of theology). This narrative is based on Foucault's notion that there are fundamental epistemic ruptures in Western consciousness and that the Enlightenment turn toward secular humanism constitutes one such rupture. As I have argued earlier in this book, however, Heidegger's critique of ontotheology effectively demolishes this thesis, showing in such essays as "Age of the World-Picture" that the humanist-anthropological phase of secular Enlightenment in fact recuperates the very metaphysics/ontotheology that historicism purports to have overcome. In Heidegger's destructive genealogy of humanism the form of metaphysics that is recuperated is a historically constructed metaphor of presence, i.e., a spatial figure or schematic diagram that comes out in its practical applications. The complex interplay of theology and historicism in Hegel's schema for representing cultural and religious identities anticipates the kind of constellation that Heidegger calls the "Age of the World-Picture"—that is, the form of representation that is pertinent to the age of Empire and the globalization of cultures. Moreover, as Gianni Vattimo notes, this form of globalization is a global order based on economics. It consists in the "invasion of the political by the socio-economic."[35]

But as Mark C. Taylor has pointed out,[36] Hegel also anticipated Marx's analysis of money. In order to develop his account of money and capital, Marx tended to rely on Hegel's interpretation of the Absolute. In Marx's treatment, money becomes the middle term that mediates opposites and thus plays the role that Hegel elsewhere assigns to the Absolute: "Marx develops his critique of political economy by inverting Hegel's speculative idealism to create a dialectical material that is grounded in social practices. As Marx unfolds his analysis of money, however, he indirectly reintroduces the very idealism for which he criticizes Hegel."[37] Money thus becomes the "creative-destructive medium, a circuit of exchange in which economic value arises and passes away."[38] Just like Hegel's Absolute, which mediates the transition from particular to universal, money secures the unity in difference that transforms opposition into reciprocity. As money circulates it repeats the rhythmic cycle of the Absolute Idea.[39] The Hegelian Idea becomes incarnate in capital to form the Economic Absolute, whose manifest form today is the world market or global capital, or, to use Hardt and Negri's political term, Empire.

In short, the intrinsically connected roles of Hegel and of religion remain the "resonant unthought" in the work of globalization and postcolonial theorists. It is not surprising, therefore, that these theorists are silent about the unprecedented global "returns of religion" not only as an unwanted and irrepressible "fundamentalism"—the specter of Islam versus the West is an obvious example—but, more poignantly, as an engine of some of the world's largest and most stable democracies (U.S.A., India) and also in countries where democracy has served to repress religion (Europe). Hardt and Negri reduce the return of religion to the return of "fundamentalisms"[40] and fundamentalisms are in every way a postmodern phenomenon, while for postcolonial theorists the return of religion represents little more than simply the return of the nationalist subject as an illegitimate subject. Mis-cognizing the vehicle by which colonized cultures emerged into modernity and postmodernity, both groups therefore maintain an uneasy silence about the postnationalist *subject*, indeed, that there can even be a postnationalist subject (a subject capable of resisting and struggling) without breaking the connection to religion. While postcolonial theorists seem to have settled for a multiculturalist recognition of the Other's difference, Hardt and Negri's concept of multitude seems to have done away with the question of the subject as a locus of resistance. All resistance for them must come from the multitude.

Ernesto Laclau challenges this overly secular notion of immanence, contending that the very assertion of radical immanentism can be traced, at the very least, back to one of the key theological questions that preoccupied St. Augustine, namely, how to make compatible the existence of evil in the world with divine omnipotence. If God is responsible for evil he can't be absolutely Good. If he's not responsible for evil he can't be Absolute. With modernity, as immanence ceases to be a theological concept and becomes fully secularized, so the concept of evil becomes the kernel of what Laclau calls "social antagonism."[41] Moreover, Laclau argues, it is only in accepting this notion of social antagonism, and hence social division, that we are confronted with forms of social resistance that we call "political." The ability and will to resist can't simply be presupposed as inherent to the multitude. Rather, the ability and will to resist require "subjective transformations" that are the product of struggles themselves and that are totally contingent, i.e., they can equally fail to take place at all. Consequently what's missing from Hardt and Negri's theory of globalization is "any coherent theory of political subjectivity. Psychoanalysis, for instance, is entirely absent."[42]

It is here that Slavoj Žižek's psychoanalytically oriented interventions in cultural theory provide an important corrective to the versions of postmodernist and postcolonial theory that dominate current academic discourse.[43] Although Žižek's "engaged political interventions" are primarily intended to reformulate a leftist anticapitalist political project in an era of global capitalism and its ideological supplement, liberal-democratic multiculturalism, they also pose important questions for postcolonial theory in an age of the return of the religious and the crisis of secularism. In the following section I shall work through aspects of Žižek's theory of subjectivity that are relevant to his theoretical and his political projects. Žižek develops his theory of subjectivity through a novel rereading of the Hegel/Schelling debate, which allows him to retrieve the excluded other of Descartes "cogito." This retrieval, which allows him to develop a more nuanced position in regard to the conventional opposition between religion and secularism and the question of universals, also brings his reinterpretation of political subjectivity remarkably close to premodern

Indic formulations of subjectivity, and inadvertently opens up the issue of culturally shared logics and existence. What intrigues me, though, is why Žižek opts instead to close off this possibility—a possibility that would also open up the political to be theorized from non-Western perspectives—and develops a new "Eurocentrism of the Left" based on the return to central Christian doctrines. In what sense do Žižek and other thinkers of the postsecular remain trapped in and by a metatheoretical assumption of historical difference between West and non-West, which serves simply to exclude non-Western sources from theory, the political, and subjectivity? How can this almost intractable problem be opened up to a decolonization?

Europe's Secret Responsibility and Fundamental Fear

While academic discourses present themselves as different from each other, in Žižek's view they entail a commonality that overrides their differences. For Žižek that commonality is the legacy of the Cartesian subject, which all of the major academic discourses seem anxious to disown and have, it seems, entered into an alliance to exorcize.[44] Against this alliance Žižek endeavors to reassert the Cartesian subject "not in order to return to the cogito in the form in which this notion has dominated modern thought (the self-transparent thinking subject) but to bring to light its forgotten obverse, the excessive, unacknowledged kernel of the cogito which is far from the pacifying image of the transparent self."[45] This "extimate philosophical kernel" of modern subjectivity, as Žižek calls it, is the "constitutive madness of reason," which Lacanian psychoanalysis renders visible but which normative philosophy and, following its example, the other human sciences seek to disown and keep at a safe distance.[46] All of modern Western thought, from Descartes onward, has involved an inherent reference to madness, which is then excluded by drawing a line between the transcendental subject (the philosopher, phenomenologist, hermeneuticist, etc.) and its excessive underlying madness (the madman, fanatic, delinquent, etc.). The result of excluding the cogito's madness has been twofold: (i) the assertion of a unified transcendental Subject (God, Man, Nation, etc.) as in the case of nationalism, totalitarianism, or liberal-democratic humanism; and/or (ii) the rejection of this unified transcendental subject—that is, the death of the Cartesian subject, whose void is filled by a proliferation of decentered multiple subjectivities (gay, feminine, ethnic, religious) corresponding to the theoretical movements postmodernism, postcolonial theory, and their ideological compliment, New Age gnosticism.[47]

Žižek confronts these false alternatives by using Lacanian psychoanalysis to reappraise the standard narrative of German idealism. Far from being a triumphant march of Reason resulting in the transcendental Ego, German idealism involves a "missing link," an unnoticed "passage through madness," indeed, a relationship to madness that is in fact central to the work of Schelling *and* Hegel.[48] The usual representation of Schelling is of course as the philosopher who dared to take madness and illusion seriously (as seen in his positive readings of Indian philosophemes such as *maya* and the *yugas*), whereas Hegel throws this very madness back into the void and reasserts the dominance of Reason/*logos* (as seen in his consigning of Indian thought to prehistory). Žižek's reading, on the other hand, presents Schelling and Hegel as thinking about the same thing—the nature of the Absolute and/or the constitution of human freedom, or, how to conceive the passage from the infinite freedom of the void to contingent human freedom—*but from different perspectives*! Whereas Schelling speaks not of man but about how the Absolute *becomes* Subject—i.e., Schelling applies to the Absolute the "fundamental postulate of temporality-contingency-finitude" so that God does not create the universe ex nihilo, but out of the conditions that were found and imposed on him[49]— Hegel speaks about man, specifically how man becomes subject and asserts his freedom within a world that is imposed on him.

Central to both these perspectives is the problem of evil. For Schelling the very possibility of thinking evil-qua-freedom resides in accepting a necessarily distorted view of God: that "there is something in God that is not God," that is, a contradiction within God, on account of which God is never able to attain full identity: "God needs a foreign body in his heart since without this minimum of contractive force, he wouldn't be 'himself'—what, paradoxically, prevents God from attaining full self-identity is the very impenetrable kernel of his *selbstheit*."[50] This contradiction in God means that what we normally consider to be God's "perfection of fullness" (namely his existence) coincides intimately with what we normally consider as God's imperfection (his nonexistence or absence). Though seemingly opposed, for Schelling the two attributes have to intersect if we are to conceive true completeness as a unity of the two. For Hegel this intersection between the two attributes (perfection/imperfection, existence/void) is the core of the subject as the inherent gap, self-deferral, distance-from-itself, which prevents full self-identity from being attained. As Žižek argues:

> This basic insight of Schelling whereby, prior to its assertion as the medium of rational Word, the subject is the pure "night of the Self," "the infinite lack of being," the violent gesture of contraction that negates every being outside itself, also forms the core of Hegel's notion of madness: when Hegel determines madness as withdrawal from the actual world, the closing of the self into itself, its "contraction," the cutting-off of its links with external reality, he all too quickly conceives this withdrawal as a "regression" to the level of "animal soul" still embedded in its natural environs and determined by the rhythm of nature (night and day, etc.). Does this withdrawal on the contrary, not designate the severing of the links with the *Umwelt*, and the end of the subject's immersion in its immediate natural surroundings, and is it as such not the founding gesture of "humanization"? Was this withdrawal into self not accomplished by Descartes in his universal doubt, which, as Derrida pointed out in his "Cogito and the History of Madness," also involves a passage through the moment of radical madness? Are we not thus back at the well-known passage from *Jenaer Realphilosophie* where Hegel characterizes the experience of pure self qua "absolute negativity," the "eclipse of (constituted) reality," the contraction into self of the subject, as the "night of the world"?[51]

What these new metaphors for the subject—"night of the Self" (Schelling), "night of the world" (Hegel)—do is to invert the Enlightenment equation of the subject with the light of reason (*logos*) that prevents the regression back into madness. Rather, for Hegel and Schelling, if madness is ontologically constitutive of subjectivity, the real question is "how the subject is to climb out of madness and to reach 'normalcy.'"[52] Stated differently, the true question is how the subject is able to elevate itself from the abyss and either *create* a symbolic order *ex nihilo* (God/World) or successfully *insert itself* into an existing symbolic order (man/society). In narrative form what's involved in becoming subject for God and man is an act of passage or translation from void to world/society. However, there is no narrative continuity in going from the "night of the world" to the daylight of self-awareness, from nature to culture. Rather something intervenes between the voided subject and normal subject, a gap or inter-space that Žižek calls the "vanishing mediator."[53] This "vanishing media-tor" is in effect a primordial impulse that sets in motion the gradual self-limiting and self-determination of the initially void subject. This elevating impulse is at once a spark that ignites the subject's elevation from its own void and an obstacle that resists the subject's boundless expansion. While this movement of subjectivity appears in the form of the classic Hegelian triad universal-particular-individual (the vanishing mediator that is consti-tutive of the universality of mankind; the particular division into opposites or differences that cut into that universality; the overcoming of these op-posites through the minimal distance or noncoincidence with itself that is constitutive of the individual contracted subject), its driving mechanism is what Hegel calls "negation of negation."[54] That is, the Hegelian sub-ject consists in nothing more than the movement of the hubris of positing oneself in one's exclusive particularity, which dialectically reverses itself into its opposite and ends up in a self-negation. Hence the process of be-coming subject through negation of negation, which drives the elevation, is nothing more than the movement of unilateral self-deception. Yet this movement of self-deception is not external to the subject but in fact con-stitutes it. Negation of negation, as Žižek explains, is the logical matrix of the failure of subjectivity to absolutely coincide with itself. Subjectivity is only that which acknowledges within itself, as its own movement and at its very core, the presence of an irreducible otherness, of absolute contin-gency. The subject *becomes* only through its realization that it comprises the couple self-other/other-self, a couple that can cohere only through the love of self for other and other for the self. Or, stated in terms with which Žižek may not entirely agree, there can be "authentic" subjectivity only insofar as it includes its own self-effacement.

Such a definition or realization of subjectivity can only lead to a con-cept of reality that's rarely ever associated with Hegel: if the subject is constituted by a "minimal difference" that divides one and the same sub-ject from itself, if this difference from itself is the true identity of the subject, then subjectivity is inherently "pathological" (biased, limited, etc.).[55] Hegel combines the ontologically constitutive character of the subject's freedom/movement with its irreducible pathological bias. When these two features are brought together, the result is somewhat startling: pathological bias constitutes "reality" itself; every field of reality is al-ways already enframed, witnessed through an invisible frame.[56] These two frames never overlap though; they are separated by an invisible gap.

Once introduced, the gap between reality and appearance is thus immediately complicated as reality turns into appearance. Things only appear to appear. All of this arises from the notional contradiction or inconsistency that is the *spiritus movens* of the subject and therefore of reality.[57] Yet far from being a failure of our thought to grasp reality, this inconsistency of the conceptual apparatus means nothing more or less than that the status of reality is purely parallactic. It has no substantiality in itself. It is simply the gap between two points of view, perceptible in the shift from one to the other.[58] Yet this "parallax view" is the ultimate proof that we are able to reach "reality" itself.

Žižek's (and Hegel's) reformulation of the Cartesian subject as a paradoxical subject—one that coincides with itself only if we accept the figure One as nonidentical to itself—has clear implications for the notion of universal(ity). Once we accept that the core of the subject is its own self-contradiction or inconsistency, then it is no longer possible to posit the idea of a universal that is true for all time and for all people, like for example, the proverbial concept of man as a universal, or human subjectivity as universal. Such universals are purely abstract. Hegel's (and Žižek's) point is that just like the concept of the subject, universality is not a neutral and therefore peaceful medium that includes all particulars, the totality of everything that exists, including all concepts. Rather, universality is the site of an unbearable antagonism, of a noncoincidence or minimal difference with itself. The universal is therefore the site of a progressive battle of these particulars with each other, a constant struggle in which they try to resolve the inherent tension within it. This is why instead of the abstract universal, Hegel emphasizes the notion of "concrete universals."[59] That is, universality can only be true to its underlying principle of unicity if it asserts itself in the guise of some particular content that in turn claims to embody it directly, excluding all the content as merely particular. Thus, universality as such can only be concrete (structured through particulars) precisely because it is forever prevented from acquiring a figure that would be adequate to its notion. In other words there is universality only insofar as there is a gap or lack within its underlying principle (the One). Because of this inherent lack, universality is "forced" to take on concrete forms, as such and such a particular.[60]

Žižek's detour through Hegel (via Lacan and vice versa) thus yields definitions of the subject that are certainly more conducive to understanding the intractability of subjectivity and the political: the subject is simultaneously the ontological gap between particular and universal and the act/decision by which we pass from the one to the other; the subject is the contingency that sustains the positive ontological order of being, which includes society and politics; the subject is the "vanishing mediator," whose self-effacement transforms the preontological chaotic multitude into the objective order of reality.[61] So the subject is both the madness of radical self-withdrawal and the gesture of subjectivization, which, by means of a short circuit between universal and particular, heals the wound of the gap. This emergence of the subject is the event of the political and vice versa. The political emerges only with the event of subjectivity.

Subjectivity qua the political is therefore the name for a power of resistance that resists not external forces but an obstacle or resistance that is absolutely interior, namely, the madness of self-withdrawal or self-effacement that is the subject itself. The political therefore consists in the tension between: (i) the structured social body (positive ontological order of being) in which each part has its designated place, and (ii) the excluded part, the "part with no part," which unsettles this order by challenging its governing principle (Law) on account of the empty principle of universality. Politics is therefore a "short circuit" between universal and particular, the paradox of a singular universal, a singular that appears as a stand-in for the universal, thereby destabilizing the supposedly "natural" order of relations in the social body.[62] That is to say, subjectivity and the political are two sides of the same coin; they emerge when the excluded element in the normal social order identifies itself with the universal. Yet this happens only when a universal takes the form of a particular that is structurally displaced, out-of-joint, such that it asserts its minimal difference to itself and therefore does not coincide with itself. It is precisely this element (which prevents itself from actualizing its particular identity) that stands in for the universal. In short subjectivity/political, political/universalization, or subjectivity/universalization are not mutually exclusive but are rather intertwined.[63]

However, for Žižek and Hegel these short circuits between universal and particular, subjectivity/political, subjectivity/universality, etc., find their paradigmatic example not only in religion but specifically in Christian religion, as centered on the Event (to use Badiou's term) of Christ's arrival, death, and resurrection and first formulated in the writings of St. Paul. Contrary to appearances, though, this is not a simple assertion of Christian superiority. Rather what Žižek has in mind is Christianity as the explanation of the Hegelian notion of concrete universality insofar as its universality is based on an exception (i.e., its exclusion from a preexisting

social structure and law, namely Judaism and paganism). Insofar as Christ·
is man as such, Christianity is then the "universalized exception." Universality "appears as such" only in its exception, and therefore in its inherent
self-contradiction. But again, as Žižek is quick to point out, St. Paul's universalism is not a simple form of Christian exclusivism. Rather

> Christian universality, far from excluding some subjects, is *formulated
> from the position of those excluded*, of those for whom there is no spe-
> cific place in the existing order, although they belong to it; universality
> is strictly codependent with this lack of specific place/determination.[64]

The truly revolutionary move on St. Paul's part was to break the link between law and sin, not through the vicious cycle of prohibition/transgres-
sion itself fostered by law, but by a simultaneous enactment of radical
withdrawal from the world, as a dying to the law and an embracing of
the Other within, as universal love that connects all men beyond earthly
laws, an enactment that was first done by Christ. Hence:

> The accusation against St. Paul's exclusivism misses the true site of
> universality: the universal dimension he opened up is not the "nei-
> ther Greek nor Jew but all Christians" which implicitly excludes non-
> Christians; *it is rather the difference Christians/non-Christians itself
> which, as a difference, is universal*, that is to say, cuts across the entire
> social body, splitting, dividing from within every substantial ethnic,
> etc., identity—Greeks are divided into Christians and non-Christians,
> as well as Jews. . . . [Consequently] universal Truth is accessible only
> from a partially engaged subjective position.[65]

Postcolonial Assessments

Let me pause briefly at this stage in order to assess some possible
implications of Žižek's relocation of Cartesian subjectivity via Hegel (and
Lacan) for thinking about a postnationalist subjectivity. Prior to Žižek, the
standard Marxist-Hegelian reading held that the formation of Indian national identity through resistance to colonialist domination was preceded
by self-enclosed ethnic or mythico-religious consciousness, which lacks
the strong will to resist and assert its own identity against the colonizer.
Only as a reaction to European domination—i.e., only by becoming fully

integrated—was this consciousness transformed into an active political will, which in turn spawned two kinds of national identification: a purely secular national identity (Indian Congress, Indian Marxism) and a variety of religious or sectarian identities (Hindu, Sikh, Muslim, etc.).

Psychologically, although the weaker ego of colonized Indians has been supplemented by or mimics the strong ego of the European colonizer, this supplementation/mimicry is actually enunciated as a return to an originally pure self as a way of asserting one's cultural independence from the colonizer. In terms of the dialectic it remains at the level of negation (the negation of the colonizer's identity and the negation [repression] of its weak, i.e., pre-nationalist self) and therefore merely reactive rather than active and ever dependent on the idealogical movement of the dominant culture. It cannot ever become a true political subject because its master-signifier (the signifier to which it attaches in order to appear as universal, e.g., nation, world religion, democracy) is always already given by the hegemonic culture. As such it cannot resist the challenges of global capitalism. According to Žižek, what's needed is the negation of that first negation, which would involve rendering visible—i.e., bringing to the level of enunciation—the "ex-timate kernel" of modern subjectivity, its innermost core, the "night of the self" that nationalization had to repress on the grounds of conceptual inconsistency, contradictoriness, etc. It would mean enunciating oneself not as one's own, but as a stranger.

One might be forgiven here for experiencing a feeling of déjà vu. For is the description of the "ex-timate kernel," the voided subject, not uncannily close to the selves of Indian culture prior to nationalization? A form of self that was, moreover, rejected most emphatically by Hegel? On closer inspection, virtually all of the categories Žižek attributes to the "real" Hegel are uncomfortably close to the very categories that Hegel had attributed to Hindus and that Indologists such as Trumpp had given to Sikhs, in order to deny them passage to religion, to history, and ultimately to humanity. Take for example Žižek's descriptions of a "God who is never fully himself," or the "mad God at odds with his own nature," "God in a state of blind rotary motion prior to the externalization of the Word," "a God who can never attain full self-identity," a God who "needs a foreign body," a God who contains "evil with his own nature."[66] Is this God not to be found in abundance in the Hindu *purānas*, or in the theory of the *guṇas*?[67] Did Schelling (unlike Hegel) not already locate all of these tendencies in Hindu literatures and incorporate them in his own radical philosophy of freedom? Or take Žižek's attribution to Hegel of the consequence of the voided subject for the notion of reality: that what appears as an epistemological limitation on our capacity to grasp reality (which we perceive only from our finite perspectives) is the positive ontological condition of reality. What is this other than the notion of *māyā*, understood not as its stereotypical meaning of "illusion," but as the form of reality mediated by ego? Doesn't the concept of *māyā* imply contingent mediated reality and the negation of reality or contingency? Is *māyā* not so much the power of nature's illusion but the power of the self to deceive itself by weaving a form of self that simply returns to self?[68] Schelling himself translates *māyā* not as "illusion" but as "*Möglichkeit*" (=possibility in contingent reality).

These examples could easily be proliferated. However, my point here is not simply to present Indian categories as already acknowledging the moves that Žižek/Hegel make to reclaim the "ex-timate kernel" of subjectivity, which they clearly do, as so many scholars have pointed out. Nor is it to deny the insightfulness and relevance of Žižek's argument. Rather, my point is to draw attention to the fact that Žižek denies the full consequences of his own insights, a denial that is in part inherited from Hegel. For if colonized Indians had, as a reaction to colonization, managed to climb out of the void according to the mechanism of Hegelian dialectic (as negation of the colonizer), would it not seem that the logical move beyond the nationalist schema would be the negation of negation? This would allow them to reclaim the minimal gap, that is, the connection to the void that they already had, thereby avoiding the fake return to self that is constitutive of secular and religious (Indian) nationalism.

Surprisingly, it is this very move, the negation of negation, that Žižek (following Hegel) seems to deny to postcolonials! This move, which would allow Indian postcolonials to elevate themselves into political subjectivity that might resist global capitalism, is already closed off. The question here is why Žižek—one of the most vocal champions of the right of *all* to resist every kind of domination—would even wish to deny Indian postcolonials this possibility. To ask this question is to suggest that perhaps the problem with appropriating the political subjectivization that is intrinsic to the move beyond nationalist subjectivity is not primarily a problem of Indians (to do or not to do this) or of Indian culture. Rather, it may be that something else, perhaps even a meta-ideology, is at work here, and this meta-ideology (the ideology of all ideologies) may be responsible for a gesture of foreclosure that goes well beyond Žižek's work, and is perhaps inherent to theory, the political, and therefore the humanities itself.

Let me therefore return to Žižek's argument by recalling that the elements of the nexus subjectivity/political/universalization are thoroughly connected. Thus, political subjectivization is not simply the demand to be included as a particular identity among all other particular identities within global social space, but the demand to restructure the entire space itself. That is, it is a demand for politics to be universalized. In saying this, then, Žižek opposes globalization against universalization. Globalization is a disavowal of the political, and this disavowal is embodied by a paradoxical alliance between fundamentalism (racial and religious) and the kind of multiculturalism, espoused by postmodernists and liberal-humanists, that excludes the right to resist for all. This ideology of globalism-plus-particularization is exemplified by the economic partnerships between America and its third-world dependents. Political subjectivization would be an Event that breaks this vicious cycle of globalism-plus-particularization by reasserting the dimension of universality against global capitalism. Following Badiou and Hegel, Žižek locates the paradigmatic occurrence of this Event, or what he calls the creation of a "short circuit" in subjectivity/political/universality, in the intersection between: (i) religion, specifically Christian religion, and (ii) the political tradition of European democracy.[69]

This is not, as it might appear, a simple assertion of either old-style imperialist Eurocentrism or fundamentalist Christian exclusivism. What Žižek has in mind is a simultaneous appropriation of the leftist core of the European political tradition and the truth event that is Christianity as expounded in the writings of St. Paul. The leftist core of the European political tradition begins in ancient Greece with the struggle of the *demos*—those excluded from the social edifice—against those in power by presenting themselves as stand-ins for the whole of society and therefore for true universality.[70] Today this tradition of struggle continues to signify both the acceptance of antagonism and struggle as constitutive of society (no neutral/peaceful space) and the need to remain universalist. The leftist gesture par excellence is to identify universality with the point of exclusion, i.e., to equate assertion of universalism with a militant position of engaged struggle for the truth that motivates them. Because there is no neutral space in society, the leftist position is always recognizable by its readiness to suspend the space of law, which poses as an abstract neutral ethico-moral frame that holds all of society together.

In a similar manner, Žižek sees Christianity as the paradigm of "concrete universality" because its universality is based on an exception (i.e., its exclusion from a preexisting social structure). Insofar as Christ is man as such, Christianity is then the universalized exception. Universality appears in its exception and therefore in its inherent self-contradiction. To put this in Hegel's terms: there is a speculative identity between the political tradition of Europe and its religious tradition, an ideological convergence that in today's conditions of globalization reinvents the space of the political.[71] This ideological convergence, what Žižek calls a "progressive Eurocentrism" or a "leftist Eurocentrism,"[72] provides the best possibility of a defense against a globalism driven materially and ideologically between a mutual convergence of "American global Empire and its third-world colonies."[73] If the word "Christianity" is missing from progressive or leftist Eurocentrism it is because this reinvention of the true space of political/subjectivity/universality is the "highest example of Hegelian Aufhebung."[74] That is, progressive Eurocentrism simply retrieves the fragile core of Christianity after Christianity has sacrificed its institutional form. In other words, the form of Christianity is no longer the Church (or its shadow the nation-state) but a leftist Eurocentrism.

But is this all that postcolonials can hope for? That, yes, you have to resist if you're to attain subjectivity, but the truth of your resistance, the only hope that your resistance will not be compromised by global capitalism, lies in the central truth of Christianity's self-sacrificial resurrection as leftist Eurocentrism and only in this Truth, since all other truths do not have the power to resist, where resistance is defined in terms of the ability to negate negation, to self-sacrifice? How different is this from the self-understanding of the European mission of redeeming India through the central truth of Christ's life, death, and resurrection?

Let me be perfectly clear about my tone of dissent against Žižek's position. It is not that Žižek's insights are wrong—far from it. Žižek clearly shows the way to resist various forms of global capitalism: liberal-multiculturalism, fundamentalisms, postmodernisms/New Age movements, etc. Nor should the reason for dissent be a desire for inclusion within European Christianity's club, of which it is the only member, the universal genus of which it is its own species (although this desire is by no means unwarranted, it should not have to be asked for). A more valid reason for dissent would be that Žižek cannot follow through on his most fundamental insight, that of self-sacrifice as the ultimate source of elevation and resistance. For any self-sacrifice to be self-sacrifice, self must be given without expectancy of return (to self). This giving begins and ends with love. The question here is whether the transformation of Christian form into leftist Eurocentrism is compatible with love. Is this move motivated by love, or by something else entirely?

Historical Difference in Theory

Once again, this transformation of Christian form into leftist Eurocentrism has a precedent in Hegel's project. Let us recall from chapter 2 that in his project of organizing knowledge about India in relation to the domains of religion, history, and the question of origin, Hegel was confronted with two distasteful possibilities: *either* the origin is contaminated with difference—i.e., there is no pure origin as such, only difference in God and in the subject, the unbearable absolute proximity of the Other—hence the *Aufhebung* is not in natural difference between cultures but emerges through the human desire for cultural domination—i.e., the tension of the gap cannot simply be externalized into culture; *or*, there are two kinds of *Aufhebung*, two kinds of elevation (consistent and inconsistent).

As I have argued earlier, when it came to a real confrontation with the other, and the possibility that the other (India) might touch (i.e., contribute to) the project of universal knowledge (Hegel) or become involved with thinking subjectivity/politics/universalization (Žižek), Hegel gave in to his fundamental anxiety at the approach of the other and opted to reject the first choice. It was safer for him to reframe concepts rather than share the very ground of knowledge and conceptuality, for it was not just a question of sharing knowledge/conceptuality, but the notion that sharing conceptuality meant sharing being/existence itself. What Hegel repressed was the most radical implication of his own thought (an implication on which Schelling at least tried to follow through): not simply that the One is noncoincident with itself but that this minimal difference means being-with others, or consciousness of others as an imperative to share existence, that affects not just bodies but more intimately the nature of thought and logic itself.

It is not enough simply to glimpse the void in one's subjectivity and then to continue to dialectize this in order to prove that one has properly to climb out of the void and that others cannot. The true consequence of the madness in subjectivity is not a choice between staying in the void and climbing out. My point is that there is more than one way of climbing out. What Hegel does is to climb out but simultaneously closes the void behind him. He gives total precedence to the return of reflective consciousness to itself. Anything other than reflective consciousness cannot count as knowledge or as proper subjectivity. In his method of climbing out Hegel identifies himself with the subject who displaces onto an other (India) the fundamental passivity/madness of his experience of the void by saying, "When I'm active (look at my culture) there is another who is passive for me," or, "I'm Western/European insofar as I have successfully displaced the void/passivity onto an Other (Orient) who stands in for its passivity." In this way, Hegel's climbing out constitutes a return to self, an almost perfect self-affection, that excludes consciousness of others, being-with-others, as this would ruin his very identity (as the universal identity). As we know, the consequences of this exclusion are far reaching.

But does Žižek not make the same move in his effort to reconstitute a "progressive/leftist Eurocentrism" out of Christianity's self-sacrifice? Does his argument not follow the familiar pattern of first establishing a difference in the ability of other cultures to elevate themselves out of the void? And does this externalized difference (attachment) not *repress* the internal gap (detachment)? Is it not the case then that, like Hegel, while Žižek can sacrifice religion in order to resurrect it as a "left Eurocentrism" (political), what he cannot concede is the political itself? The political at all costs remains within a sphere that is most properly European. The only way for Žižek/Hegel to exist with others, to confront the anxiety of having to really exist with others, which means sharing thought/conceptuality in the sense of thought itself being touched by and touching foreign logics, would be to always have a firm handle on the concept of the political. But in order to repeat this condition (where the subject is able to climb out of the void and assert itself as the universally elevated), Žižek and Hegel have to remain within the charmed circle of religion and the political—charmed because of the almost invisible role of language in this process.

To illustrate the anxiety that comes from the danger of moving outside this charmed circle, let me turn to one of Žižek's favorite targets: multiculturalism. Following Lacan, Žižek notes that "multiculturalism suspends the traumatic kernel of the Other, reducing it to an aseptic folklorist entity."[75] Žižek's point is that the very purpose of multiculturalism's conferral of recognition/identity/autonomy to the other is precisely *not* to confer autonomy to the other. The paradox here revolves around the fact that the "real" other exists as a "fallout" of the very process of identification itself. It is an "indivisible remainder," an unfathomable substance X that must always be repressed in order for autonomy to be conferred. What then appears as the identical or autonomous entity is merely that part of the other that seems like the culture of multiculturalist ideology. For Žižek, the real is the "unfathomable remainder of the ethnic substance" that cannot be assimilated by multiculturalism:

> [W]hen do I encounter the Other "beyond the wall of language," in the real of his or her being? Not when I am able to describe her, not even when I learn her values, dreams, and so on, but only when I encounter the Other in the moment of her jouissance. This encounter of the real is always traumatic, there is something at least minimally obscene about it, I cannot integrate it into my existence.[76]

> The "Real" is the unfathomable X at stake in our cultural struggles; it is that on account of which, when somebody learns too much of our culture, he or she "steals" it from us; it is that on account of which, when somebody shifts allegiance to another culture, he or she "betrays" us and so on. Such experiences prove that there must be some X that is "expressed" in the cultural set of values, attitudes, rituals that materialize our way of life. What is stolen, betrayed . . . is the little piece of the Real.[77]

Ironically, however, although Žižek rightly exposes the central anxiety of multiculturalism here (why it needs to repress the "Real" of the other), in essays published after 9/11 (here the central topic under discussion is the triumphalism of American global power and the failure of Europe to pose a political and intellectual alternative to America, as exemplified by the postmodernist relativism of the traditional Left) he falls prey to these very anxieties and reverts back to the "real" of Western European modernity, namely, Christianity. Weighing heavily on Žižek's mind, it seems, is the potential access of *other* religions to the European mindset as a result of globalization. The real danger is not so much the Americanization of the planet but what lurks behind it, namely, the whole medley of "New Age spiritualisms" and "paganisms"—effectively code words for Indian and Chinese traditions—which because of American globalization are given increasingly greater access to the Western/European market:

The ultimate postmodern irony is thus the strange exchange between Europe and Asia: at the very moment when, at the level of "economic infrastructure," "European" technology and capitalism are triumphing worldwide, . . . the Judeo-Christian legacy is threatened in the European space itself by the onslaught of the New Age "Asiatic" thought, which . . . is establishing itself as the hegemonic ideology of global capitalism.[78]

In other words, "the onslaught of the New Age 'Asiatic' thought" poses a danger by exploiting the political void created by a postmodernist America allied with third-world cultures in order to export their ideologies of noninvolvement and disinterested action. Consequently for Žižek the "[t]arget on which we should focus . . . is the very ideology which is proposed as a potential solution—for example Oriental spirituality (Buddhism) with its 'gentle,' balanced, holistic, ecological approach."[79] For Žižek these ideologies serve as an example of yet another third-world, or "premodern," society that has nothing to offer in the way of intellectual or religio-cultural solutions in any present or future global problems because its contributions to human development have long since been exhausted, which is precisely why they can only ever be regarded as "premodern societies." This fear is expressed even more forcefully in his recent book on the U.S.-Iraq war, where he pleads for a "renewed leftist Eurocentrism":

> To put it bluntly: do we want to live in a world in which the only real choice is between American civilization and the emerging Chinese authoritarian-capitalist one? If the answer is no, then the true alternative is Europe. The third world cannot generate a strong enough resistance to the ideology of the Americam Dream; in the present constellation only Europe can do that.[80]

Although it is not immediately obvious, Žižek's designation of "premodern societies" can be traced to a tradition of Occidentalism based on a particular concept of religion deployed by Hegel, Marx, Husserl, and to some extent even Heidegger, in which "premodern" designates those cultures that have yet to achieve a level of elevation or transcendence that is the hallmark of history and historicism. Quoting Heidegger, Žižek reminds us that the dimension of "historicity" is totally lacking in Indian and Oriental thought. Indeed the

main task of Western thought today is to defend the Greek break-
through, the founding gesture of the "West," the overcoming of the
pre-philosophical mythical "Asiatic" universe, against the renewed
"Asiatic" threat—the greatest opposite of the West is the mythical in
general and the "Asiatic" in particular.[81]

It is no surprise then to see Žižek use terms like "pagan" and "New Age
mysticism" as metaphors for the threat of Eastern nihilisms further weakening Europe. The upshot of Žižek's argument is: (i) whereas "Christian
love is a violent passion to introduce a Difference, a gap in the order of
being, to privilege and elevate some object at the expense of others," the
"Buddhist stance is ultimately one of Indifference, of quenching all pas-
sions that strive to establish differences"[82]—consequently, insofar as the
"violent Love" of Christianity establishes the order or the act and therefore the domain of the political, it is the essential part of the European
legacy worth fighting for, a legacy that Christianity and Marxism should
fight for on the same side of the barricade against the onslaught of new
spiritualisms;[83] (ii) that other religions, especially pagan/premodern religions, their disclaimers notwithstanding, are also based on the structure
of belief. Secretly, Žižek argues, we're all believers and Asian spiritu-
alities, far from espousing an ego-less and heterological standpoint that
might be a stumbling block for global capitalism, in fact form a perfect
ideological supplement to it.

A possible objection might be raised here. It could be argued that
the "Asiatic," as Žižek uses it, does not refer to the "real" Asia or Asian
thought, but only to a Western caricature of it. However, such an objection does not hold, since Žižek's argument, like that of many other
Western theorists, is reliant on precisely this caricature. The caricature
presents an Asia that has been rendered harmless within the domain of
Western conceptuality. Hence even the "real" Asiatic sources are simply the weaker mimetes of a religion-in-general for which the conceptual
model is Christian religion. Consequently theory puts into play a belief
that there is no outside to this field of conceptuality. All cultural concepts
are fully translatable within this field. Yet this belief—that there is no
outside—is little other than an assumption of the historical conditions
of cultural domination that alone allows this field to remain unscathed
by any other source. Theory therefore continues to work within the assumption of pure translatability of concepts, of which the exemplar is the
"generalized translation" of religion.

A better way of understanding the Euro-Christo-centrism of Žižek's political theory is simply to say that it inherits from intellectual predecessors going as far back as St. Paul and St. Augustine, as well as from more recent sources such as such as Hegel, Kierkegaard, Marx, Husserl, and Max Weber, the conceptual violence that imposes itself through a belief in the "fundamental translatability" of the concept of religion (imposed as the factum of determinate religions) and stemming from this a framework for creating a stereotype of the other, which in turn enables the possibility of comparing and calculating the contemporary worth of cultures. Only through the belief in a historical difference between Asia and Europe and a logic of the stereotype proper to the comparative schema spawned by such "historical difference" at his disposal is it possible to call for a "renewed left Eurocentrism" rooted in a Christian legacy and able to withstand the ideological contamination from pagan cultures and "premodern societies" like India and China.

Far from being limited to Žižek, however, the presupposition of historical difference between Asia and the West is prevalent in the thought of many postmodernist and postsecular philosophers. It constitutes an unacknowledged presupposition that underpins the work of theory even among those who consciously try to incorporate a vision of cultural pluralism, and therefore competing universals. A good example is Mark. C. Taylor's attempt to present a new theological model for a networked global society. While Taylor's attempt is certainly genuine, it nevertheless repeats a past imperialism: that the only universals that can work in an age of globalization are Western universals. In his books *Confidence Games: Money and Markets in a World Without Redemption* and *After God*,[84] Taylor argues that the search for simplicity in an increasingly connected and complex world is one of the primary reasons for the worldwide resurgence of religious fundamentalism. Religious fundamentalists of all shades and opinions have tried to

hold out the prospect of a return to the secure world of walls in a world of increasingly volatile and risky webs. This strategy is both misguided and dangerous. If we have learned anything from the economic crises of the 1990s, it is that models matter. When the models informing policies and guiding strategies are at odds with new emerging realities, the consequences can be devastating. . . .

In an increasingly networked culture, it is necessary to cultivate an appreciation for the resources and limitations of many religious tradi-

tions. Religious visions that remain stuck in the oppositions and contradictions of the past pose a threat to the future. . . . It is necessary to
develop alternative types of religious vision that might lead to new
social, political, economic, and cultural realities.[85]

Taylor proposes a different kind of theological model by expanding
Paul Tillich's earlier model, based on two types of philosophy of religion (ontological versus cosmological), to three types of theology of
culture, best described as monistic, dualistic, and complex. In Taylor's
opinion, these three types help us to understand the kind of networked
globalized society that Hardt and Negri term "Empire." This model
does not end with the dualistic theology of modernity but is able to
make the transition to the complexities of the postmodern globalized
world:[86]

monistic → dualistic → complex

The transition from monistic through dualistic to complex clearly corresponds to the historicist movement:

premodern → modern → global

The problem with this model is that it follows the Hegelian practice
of placing all non-Western cultures under the world-historical category
of monism (in their premodern form) or at best under the category of
dualism (suggesting their transition under the influence of colonialism
to modernity/nationalism, etc.). To make the transition to the complex
stage, however, non-Western cultures must look either to Christianity or
to forms of postmodern culture. In other words, the stage of complexity
is reserved for Western forms of culture. Taylor's problem is that, like
Hegel, he assumes that precolonial cultures such as Hinduism, Sikhism,
and Buddhism needed the intervention of the West in order to bring them
into supposedly more sophisticated states—first into the form of modern nationalisms and eventually into the postnationalistic complex states.
By doing so he repeats a past imperialist gesture, which refused to see
precolonial (in this case Indic) cultures as anything other than either premodern or primitive, thereby overlooking the fact that precolonial cultures demonstrated just as much, if not more, complexity as postmodern
global culture, through their intrinsic radical heterogeneity. Even today

this radical heterogeneity can be glimpsed behind the nationalist facades of Indian culture. Their resistance to European logic was taken as a sign of an inability to make the transition to modernity. What Taylor and others seem to be unaware of is that in the last fifteen years or so, the transition of previously colonized cultures like India from beyond secular nationalism to global capitalism has precipitated a return of the radically heterogenous elements that demonstrate almost exactly the same signs of complexity that Taylor and others attribute to the processes of contemporary globalization.

A better way of contextualizing the cultural attachment of theory to the idea of historical difference, perhaps even a way by which it can be justified, is to see it not as an attachment to Christian dogma but as part of a long-running "genealogy of European responsibility, that is, of responsibility *as* Europe, Europe as the very 'idea' of responsibility, somewhat after the manner of Husserl, so that the Eurocentrism remains in place."[87] In a fascinating set of comments made on Jan Patočka's *Heretical Essays in the Philosophy of History*, Jacques Derrida observes that the interests of many Euro-Christo–centrics, like Patočka, may not be in Christian doctrine or particular articles of faith, but rather in discerning the abstract, or philosophical, structures that underpin them. In *Gift of Death* Derrida maintains that it is possible for something like a Eurocentric discourse to be developed

> without reference to religion as institutional dogma, and proposing a genealogy of thinking concerning the possibility and of the essence of the religious that doesn't amount to an article of faith. Mutatis mutandis, the same thing can be said for many discourses that seek in our day to be religious—discourses of a philosophical type if not philosophemes themselves—without putting forth theses or theologemes that would by their very structure teach something corresponding to the dogmas of a determinate religion. The difference here is subtle and unstable, and it would call for careful and vigilant analyses.[88]

Indeed this would be true of the discourses of thinkers such as Kant, Hegel, Kierkegaard, Husserl, Levinas, Heidegger, Ricoeur, Patočka, and Žižek (among many others), given that they all, to a greater or lesser extent

> belong to a tradition that consists of proposing a nondogmatic doublet of dogma, a philosophical and metaphysical doublet, in any case, a *thinking* that "repeats" the possibility of religion without religion.[89]

The very idea of a "nondogmatic doublet of dogma," a thinking that repeats religion without religion, presents an intriguing possibility. But given that Derrida himself uses themes from a particular religious tradition, is he not endorsing this Eurocentrism? If so, should his name not be added to the list of philosophers above? According to John Caputo, far from trying to defend the views of Patočka and others, Derrida is trying to tease out their subversive or heretical potential. Thus the particular nondogmatic doublet of religion that Patočka proposes is precisely the Christian Hegelian philosophy of history that Derrida resists.[90] Rather, Derrida seems to be searching for the possibility of the religious unencumbered by the baggage of determinate religions and their determinate faiths—and the practice and theory of deconstruction presents just such a possibility of a religion without religion. The important question, however, is whether the possibility of a "nondogmatic doublet of dogma" is applicable to any determinate religion. Is the thinking that repeats the possibility of religion without religion applicable beyond the confines of European philosophy?

Caputo seems to interpret Derrida's messianic tone as suggesting that these possibilities are, strictly speaking, only applicable to "religions of the Book." From this standpoint Derrida's thought would appear to slip back into a familiar Eurocentrism based on the tradition of "European responsibility" (though this would not be a Christo-centrism). On Caputo's reading, although Derrida may be trying to "offer us a work of thought that thinks the structural possibility of the religious, . . . [but] without the dangerous liaisons of the particular religions, without the dogma."[91] It remains grounded within the possibilities offered by "religions of the Book," central to which is an emphatic rejection of the orgiastic mystery, and especially the concept of fusion. That is to say, despite its emphasis on hospitality, Caputo suggests that Derrida's thought can never accept the notion of fusion—the idea that freedom and individual consciousness are immersed in "sacred" or natural forces. True freedom is the result of an effort of self-differentiation, separation, individuation, the decision to be separate. The ability to make this decision, to be able to say "I am," is the mark of responsibility. However implicit this may be in his writings, it is this rejection of the concept of fusion that marks Derrida's thought, if not as Christo-centric, then at the very least as European as opposed to, say, "Asiatic."

I would beg to differ on this point. Such a reading seems to overlook certain aspects of Derrida's thought that suggest not so much a Eurocentrism but a trend toward a dislocative globalism that is as much resistive to Eurocentrism as it is Eurocentrist. Though Derrida undeniably and self-consciously works with Judeo-Christian and European concepts, his thinking about the question of religion is more inflected by a sense of postcoloniality than many of his European and American commentators would care to admit. I wonder whether it is not possible to read within Derrida's meditations on religion a nondogmatic repetition of religious thought that repeats religion, but that, more importantly, exposes the question of religion as the very boundary or frame that encloses or imprisons European critical thought. If religion is the very secret and the boundary that Europe has a special responsibility to guard, while also guarding against concepts such as fusion (which would bring it unbearably close to Asian thought), then is this secret of "European responsibility" also not its fundamental fear of becoming radically heterogenous?

Is there a way of understanding the notion of "fusion"—a fear of which seems to animate European, and more broadly Western, self-designation as "responsible"—beyond its usual stereotype? I would argue that Derrida's interconnected interrogations of language and religion provide an entry into this problem in ways that many of his more prominent readers have not fully paid attention to. In a seemingly diverse set of writings and interviews, Derrida has explored the dislocation of classical notions of personal, political, and religious identity brought about by globalization, migration, and the fragmentation of the nation-state. The result is a potential theory of what might be called a fractured or dislocated globalization, which is pursued through a critique of two interrelated phenomena: the notion that what Hardt and Negri celebrate as Empire can be more aptly referred to as globa*latin*ization, that is to say, the globalization of Christian conceptuality; and the monolingualism of the other.

The Global Fiduciary

As I mentioned briefly at the end of chapter 1, Derrida's neologism for the process of globalization is *mondialatinization*, translated by Samuel Weber as globalatinization. Derived from the Roman imperial heritage of *religio*, with help and under the threat of what he calls teletechnoscience (or the global information system), the term "globalatinization" highlights Derrida's belief that a crucial element in what we call globalization is the unhealthy and unholy alliance of religion and teletechnoscience imperialistically exported throughout the world.[92] Thus when we think of globalization, we have to think of the spread of a certain way of thinking about religion according to the Latin and therefore Christian imprint. Referring to the strange phenomenon of "Latinity and its globalization," Derrida argues that we should not be thinking of "universality" but rather of a "process of universalization that is finite and enigmatic."[93] It is a process, moreover, that "imposes itself in a particularly palpable manner within the conceptual apparatus of international law and global political rhetoric. . . . Wherever this apparatus dominates, it articulates itself through a discourse on religion."[94] Consequently world orders or attempts to order the world depend on the credit (solidity or reliability) of the dominant power in place at any given time.[95]

The term "globalatinization" is particularly helpful for understanding the paradoxical case of Indian (de)colonization. As we saw earlier, this paradox revolves around a scenario in which postcolonials in India and the Western diaspora have repeatedly engaged the question of the political through the enunciation of an identity that *once did not exist* (an identifiable mother tongue, and the ability to respond affirmatively to the word "religion," a term that is foreign to Indic cultures) but that was *brought into existence* during the colonial period *and continues to survive* through a process that is simultaneously linguistic and religious, particular and universal, whose dominant form manifests itself as a national identity (Hindu/Hindi) and a global religion (Hinduism). The paradox consists in the fact that, on the one hand, the manifestation of a national religion invokes its freedom from the ex-colonizer, but on the other hand, and through its expression as a global religion, continues to be haunted by repeated subjection to the conceptual categories of the ex-colonizer. However, the process can work only by repressing any memory of a precolonial state of radical linguistic and "religious" heterogeneity. Postcolonials participate in this repression by suturing any perceived disorder of identity through a mechanism that simultaneously enunciates a subjectivity in the name of religion ("I am Hindu/Muslim/Sikh") and a mother tongue ("My own language, the language that properly belongs to my religion, is Hindi/Urdu/Punjabi"). Between the identity's "once did not exist" and its "coming into existence," as it were, lies the psychical process of repressing the heteronomy that governed South Asian cultures prior to colonialism, and the growth of Indian "responsibility," which is more usefully seen as the translation/conversion/confession to or of modernity.

But the paradox of Indian decolonization doesn't end there. For during the last two decades, even as India has, in the full sense of the term, entered the world market, there have been increasing signs not only of the return of precolonial (premodern and pre-nationalist) cultural formations and typologies—which were thought to have been properly exorcised during India's passage to modernity and the nation-state—but of newfound abilities to redefine traditions through radical reinterpretation, translation, etc., which in turn provide resources for appropriating and at the same time countering the influences of globalization. These cultural formations, which display tendencies toward heterolingual and hetero-"religious" states (as opposed to the cleanly demarcated nationalized entities called Sikh-ism, Hindu-ism, along with their linguistic counterparts Punjabi and Hindi, respectively, which were also manufactured during the colonial period), appear today not as the other of modernity but as cultural formations that are attuned to the logic of global capitalism yet at the same time capable of resisting it through the cultivation of a nondualistic or heterological "individualism" that can easily subvert the ego-centered logic of capitalism.

Clearly, though, such formations stand in stark contrast to the dominant expression of Hinduism as a "global religion"—which, paradoxically, is the point at which Hinduism becomes most Christian-like in nature and tendency. As a "global religion" Hinduism (not unlike Islam) makes certain claims to sovereignty, but those claims are illegitimate for the very reason, as noted above, that because of the intimate nexus of Latinity and Christianity (of language and religion) the concept of global order "refers to a notion of world that remains Christian."[96]

Ironically, although "globalatinization" evokes the unilateral order of contemporary geopolitics, it signifies at the same time the illegitimacy of the plural term "global religions," despite the obvious fact that global religions like Hinduism, Islam, etc., are political in every sense of the word. Thus when Derrida says, "I am struck by the muffled and almost desperate struggle of the non-Christian religions when they attempt at the same time to Christianize themselves and to defend themselves against Christianity. . . . They seek to be different and to resemble, to acquire the global legitimacy of Christianity,"[97] he appears to be pointing out the constitutive illegitimacy of "global religions," that is, of the illegitimacy of the pluralization of the term "religion." Or when Derrida questions "what is going on when a non-Christian says Islam, Judaism, or Buddhism [let us also add Hinduism, Sikhism to this list] is *my religion*,"[98] he is inadvertently asking what made the translation of *religio* acceptable to the native elites under conditions of colonial rule. How did they manufacture consent in good faith to the translation of *religio*? How did they convert or confess to the colonizer's demand for religious identity, when that identity clearly did not exist prior to colonialism?

And yet after this conversion to modernity/confession to one's own religion in one's own mother tongue takes place, these religions are able to "present themselves on an international stage, to lay claim to a public sphere, claim the right to practice their own religion, to inscribe themselves in a political and ideological space dominated by Christianity, and therefore engage in the obscure and equivocal struggle in which the putatively 'universal' value of the concept of religion . . . has in advance been appropriated into the space of a Christian semantics." But although all of these new initiates to the global space doubtless possess a universal vocation, Derrida is adamant that "only Christianity has a concept of universality that has been elaborated into the form which today dominates both philosophy and international law."[99] In line with current thinking on this topic, Derrida traces the concept of universalism that dominates global-politico-juridical discourse to St. Paul.

This explains somewhat more clearly how and why the conversion to modernity did not happen entirely through overt physical violence. Rather it was necessary for neocolonial elites to deny the equivocation that exists in the very concept of religion and the religious, to disavow the heteronomy that governed their cultures before the colonizer's demand for religion took effect. Only through this disavowal of one's perceived lack of religion or religious identity could the heteronomial self that is other than itself be enunciated as the self of a religious *identity*, and thereby enter into the global public space in which religions appear in their plurality. To belabor a point that I stressed earlier, the pluralization of religions as "world religions" or "religions of the world" is legitimated in the first place by a structure of belief in the "unifying horizon of paternal-fraternal sameness of religions, religious cosmopolitanism," etc.[100] Following Derrida, let us call this structure of belief at the heart of globalatinization, the *global fiduciary*.

The global fiduciary, then, is a belief in a "world order" that, in "its relative and precarious stability, depends largely on the solidity and reliability, on the *credit*" accumulated by the dominant power at any given time, which might be British power, in the late nineteenth and early twentieth centuries, or American power, today.[101] This power plays the role

of the guardian of the prevailing world order. In its role as guarantor of
the entire world, this dominant power not only assures credit in the sense
of financial transactions but *credit in general*, which must include the
credit accorded to languages, laws, and political and diplomatic transactions between nations.[102] By exerting itself at every level—"technical,
military, in the media, even on the level of discursive logic"—this power
becomes the "axiomatic that supports juridical and diplomatic rhetoric
worldwide, and thus international law." To destabilize this power is effectively to destabilize the entire world. Moreover, when such a destabi-
lization occurs, what specifically comes under threat is "the system of interpretation, the axiomatic, logic, rhetoric, concepts, and evaluations that
are supposed to allow one to *comprehend* . . . the discourse that comes to
be, in a pervasive and overwhelming, hegemonic fashion, *accredited* in
the world's public space. What is legitimated by the prevailing system
(a combination of public opinion, the media, the rhetoric of politicians
and the presumed authority of all those who . . . speak or are allowed to
speak in the public space) are thus the norms inscribed in every apparently meaningful phrase that can be constructed through the lexicon of
violence, aggression, crime, war, and terrorism."[103] Furthermore, Derrida
tells us, "wherever this apparatus dominates, it articulates itself through a
discourse on religion."[104]

In other words, the global fiduciary can be envisaged as a "hermeneutic apparatus," a conceptual matrix that must govern "strategies and
relations of force" for there to be a minimal geopolitics—which would
always be the politics of the dominant power, "the one that manages to
impose and thus to legitimate, indeed to legalize (for it is always a question of law) on a national or world stage, the terminology that best suits
it in a given situation."[105] Concurring on this point with Derrida, Gianni
Vattimo similarly argues that the global fiduciary is not just a hermeneutic apparatus but hermeneutics itself as a conceptual frame that has
achieved broad currency today to the point where it functions as a *koiné*
for the theoretical orientation that is most conducive to democracy and
thus to the free market economy.[106]

In view of what I have called the "paradox of Indian (de)colonization"
(the idea that Indian cultures assert their freedom in terms of their elevation to global status/capitalism/nuclear capability, etc., by chaining
themselves to a concept that is strictly Christian), conceptual movements
such as the "return of religion" and "postsecularism" must be passed
through another decolonization. They must be considered in relation to

the process by which colonized cultures gained entry into the global fiduciary—suggesting a more equivocal and ongoing process of assenting
based on the manufacture of belief, faith, trust, etc. This is nevertheless
a belief that could be unmade, deconstructed at any moment, if one were
to suspend belief in the translatability of term *religio*, by, for example,
asking the question, "What if *religio* remained untranslatable?," which
would thereby amount to suspending belief in the global fiduciary.

"What If *Religio* Remained Untranslatable?": Geopolitics and Theory

Toward the end of their latest book, *Multitude: War and Democracy in the Age of Empire* (the 2004 sequel to *Empire*), Hardt and Negri provide an interesting example of how the global fiduciary structures
relations of force in international politics. "Contemporary geopolitics,"
they argue, "demonstrates the same logical schema that defines the contemporary theory of sovereignty and the reality of economic order."[107]
Hardt and Negri envision the nature of contemporary geopolitical command "in the shape of a wheel with the U.S. as hub with spokes extending
to each region of the globe."[108] Each region is defined from this perspective as a group of local powers plus the United States as the dominant
element. Such a model bears a clear resemblance to Hegel's panoptical
schema—formulated initially as a model for organizing knowledge in the
newly developing humanities, but eventually adapted for the purpose of
geopolitical command. Central to the Hegelian schema was a particular
formulation of the "one versus many" in his theology and the various
histories of philosophy, religion, and culture. A result of this is the development of the logic of pluralism as we find it in the intellectual formation
of "world religions," which was simply a way of "preserving Western
conceptions of universality in the language of pluralism."[109]

For Derrida, however, the indissociability of a certain juridico-po-
litical, hermeneutic, and religious system suggests that globalatinization
provides the engine not only for contemporary geopolitics but also for
contemporary theory as conceived within the framework of the humanities. In early essays such as *Sign Structure and Play* Derrida had already
begun to connect the geopolitical and theoretical command over multiple others in terms of the visual metaphorics of a centered structure,
notably the structure of the centered circle versus periphery, a model that

has enjoyed a privileged status throughout the history of Western thought and praxis. Derrida writes that the "concept of a centered structure is in fact the concept of a play based on a fundamental ground, a play constituted on the basis of a fundamental immobility and a reassuring certitude, which itself is beyond the reach of play. And on the basis of this certitude anxiety can be mastered."[110] It is a way of representing unilateralist dominance over the multiple others linked yet subordinated to the center.

Whichever way we look at it though, the panoptical hub-and-spokes model is held together, on the one hand, by the West's (Anglo-Euro-American) power of self-accreditation (the hub) accumulated through its self-representation as the "ultimate presumed unity of force and law, of the greatest force and the discourse of law,"[111] and on the other hand, by the reciprocal accreditation-by-the-other of the West's self-representation (the spokes). Of course, this reciprocal process of self-accreditation/accreditation-by-the-other can be made to work only through some minimal address between self and other. But even before this address can begin, it is dependent on the acceptance by the other of the exchange of concepts between self and other—which is to say, a minimal belief in the function of language as a neutral, perfectly translatable, medium for carrying any universal address. This is what constitutes, within the global fiduciary, any minimal social bond in all diplomatic relations between the hub (Anglo-Euro-American) and the spokes (Anglo-Euro-American + n), that is, in all relations whose element is the spoken word.

But if Derrida's globalatinization thesis is correct, this social bond can just as easily be interrupted simply because the nature of belief itself is equivocal. This interruption could have implications for both geopolitics and theory. Space prevents me from fully exploring these implications, and so it will suffice here to attend to the earlier enigmatic statement posed by Derrida as a question, and to briefly outline some possible implications it could have. The simplicity of this particular question belies its potential for reversing the conceptual violence *imposed* by the global fiduciary, belief in belief, and underlying this, the belief in the translatability of religion, all of which was self-imposed by Indians through a certain response to religion. Derrida argues that the very point at which globalatinization appears to assert total hegemony also reveals its greatest weakness. Given that this hegemony is dependent on a belief in the unhindered translatability of religion, Derrida poses the question: "*What if* religio *remained untranslatable*?."[112] Stated otherwise, what if one were not to respond to the demand for the equivocation of religion? What if Indians (and others) were to exercise a certain undecidability in the process of translating received traditions according to a mechanism that automatically inserts them into a global circulation as proper representatives of several determinate (world) religions? Let us briefly think about the geopolitical and theoretical implications of such a move.

Geopolitical

Any minimal social bond (let us say for example in all diplomatic relations between the hub [West] and the spokes [the West + n] can easily be interrupted or unraveled simply because the nature of belief itself is equivocal. It is based on the relation to the other. If, for example, the others were to assert themselves or if the social bond were to be defined in terms of the priority of the other, the hub/spokes model of unilateral command begins to come apart. In fact Hardt and Negri acknowledge this possibility when they speak of the inherent "unpredictability of these relations of force in international politics" especially when others in the peripheral regions "play a contradictory, double-edged role in unilateralist imperial geopolitics, both as necessary parts of the unified order and as potentially autonomous forces that can break that order.[113] Consequently it is more helpful to think of the relations between center and peripheral regions as "fault lines." These fault lines designate the dualistic relationship between center and peripheral zones, particularly those peripheral zones that cannot be directly included in a unipolar world order, and that, while absorbing and *capitulating* to the mechanism through which Empire exerts control, nevertheless *resist* with global aspirations of their own. Russia, China, the conglomerate of South East Asian countries, and India, with their huge manpower resources, are obvious examples.

More important, though underestimated, symptoms may include, on the one hand, through the central characteristic of Empire as complex and immanent, a *cultural resistance* to any unilateralist command (the idea that we are interconnected at every level and that simplistic models of command will no longer suffice); and on the other hand, through the very means by which Empire seeks to extend its domain, the becoming absolute of the world market through the spread of democra*cies* (or vice versa the spread of democra*cies* through the global establishment of capital). This is inevitable if Europe, China, India, and others in the Middle and Far East continue to increase their size and stake in the world market, and, in the case of China and other nondemocracies, to stabilize their sociopolitical infrastructures.

With a balancing out such as this, which would be driven, ironically, by the spread of democracy and capital, is it not viable that the hegemony of globalatinization's hermeneutical apparatus will also need to acknowledge the presence of other apparati, each with claims to universality based on its own cultural singularities (which globalatinization simply presumes to be impossible)? The presence of different global languages and conceptual frames will be the sharpest point of resistance to the continued implementation of an international law and political rhetorics that assume the unhindered translatability of the concept of religion and hence secularism. Ironically, this kind of multipolar global order, based on a notion of pluralism very different from that espoused by secular liberal democracy, was anticipated by the legal theorist Carl Schmitt. As the political theorist Chantal Mouffe argues, only a notion of pluralism that eschews the dualism inherent in the concept of "One" can allow the coexistence of conflicting principles of legitimacy in its midst. This is a notion of pluralism that

> undermines the claim of liberal democracy to provide a universal model that all societies should adopt because of its superior rationality. Such a pluralism is the one which is at stake in the multipolar project.
>
> Contrary to what liberal universalists would want us to believe, the Western model of modernity, characterized by the development of rationality and an atomistic individualism, is not the only adequate way of relating to the world and to others. It might have gained hegemony in the West, but, as many critics have pointed out, even in the West this is far from being the only form of sociality.[114]

Mouffe goes further to argue that we need to go beyond the worn-out idea of a monolithic "Enlightenment" and explore the possibility of other enlightenments that may not be limited to "endless discussions of rival solutions" within European history and culture. Few political theorists have been as explicit as Mouffe in extolling the need to think about "non-Western enlightenments," which she believes will be crucial to the formulation of the multipolar model of global order.

> The establishment of a pluralistic world order discarding the idea that there is only one possible form of globalization, the prevalent

neo-liberal one, not merely having Europe competing for its leadership with the United States. For Europe to assert its identity, it is the
very idea of the "West" that must be questioned, so as to open a new
dynamics of pluralization which would create the basis for resisting
neo-liberal hegemony. . . .

In my view a truly *political* Europe can exist only in relation to
other political entities, as part of a multipolar world. If Europe can play
a crucial role in the creation of a new world order, it is not through
the promotion of a cosmopolitan law that all "reasonable" humanity
should obey but by contributing to the establishment of an equilibrium
among regional poles whose specific concerns and traditions will be
seen as valuable, and where *different vernacular models* of democracy
will be accepted.[115] [emphasis added]

The very idea of "*different vernacular models* of democracy" signals an
important shift, for there is a tendency among globalization theorists on
the left and the right to assume that globalization=Anglophonization and
that Anglophonization equates with the universalization of Western conceptuality. This is true only to a certain extent. If one looks more closely
at previously colonized cultures, the response to imperialism by the native elites consisted in the simultaneous processes of (i) imbibing English,
(ii) the modernization of vernacular languages into national languages
through mimicry of the English standard, and (iii) the repression of heterolingual aspects incompatible with the national/modern into the realms
of private language of the home, etc. As we know from Freud, however,
the repressed is never eradicated but always returns under suitable conditions. The conditions for this return have been fostered over the last
fifty years ironically through technology: specifically television, radio,
and more recently the Internet. Not only do large heterolingual TV/radio/
Internet audiences exist outside the West—e.g. in India, China and the
Middle East—that provide a massive barrier to the entry of English, but
similar heterolingual audiences also exist within the West, thereby helping to foster conditions of heterolingual language use that existed prior to
colonialism. The designation "multiculturalism," however, makes these
audiences invisible and inaudible to the West.

Of course, I am not suggesting that these networks are entirely immune to Western influence and therefore escape the reverberations of the
translation of *religio*. In fact they exist in fluid contact with the West.
All I am suggesting is that Western conceptuality is resisted in these

spaces because its hermeneutic apparatus cannot detect these networks, because of its assumption of the universality of the dominant language. By contrast, people within these networks can simultaneously translate and *un*-translate. And, since there is no escape from the world market, even Anglophonic hegemony will not remain immune to the influences of the peripheral regions; their resistance will consist in a contestation of the translatability of *religio*, in which previously universalized categories such as *religio* will be translated back into the West and retranslated by the West, but also *refuse* to be translated. This process of retranslation, premised on the notion that "*religio* can remain untranslatable," has been underway since the beginnings of colonialism but now takes on a different trajectory. One of its consequences may be a reprogramming of the rules of the global fiduciary and hence of its legal structures.

This is something that Chantal Mouffe seems to anticipate but not state explicitly. Structures of faith, certainty, and belief in the global fiduciary, the matrix held together by a concept of a dualistic One (the One that corresponds to modern notions of sovereignty), may come to be contested by a One that is nondual, based on a mode of disenchantment whose implications are more radical than the Cartesian kind of doubt that has given rise to the doctrine of secularism. The dualistic One is also the One that is sustained by the belief that the essence of language consists in a passage of concepts/meaning from source (other, A) to target (self, B). But here there never was a real other to begin with. True disenchantment begins with the nondual One, where the other is already in the self.

Theoretical

My reasons for linking the exclusion of India and Indian phenomena from contemporary theory to the continuing influence of Hegel should now be clearer. What alarmed Occidentalists such as Hegel in the nineteenth century was a discovery that threatened to undermine the configuration of positions that legitimized "European man's" claim to be historically different from "the Rest." This threat continues to surface today in the production of knowledge and in pedagogical strategies deployed to represent non-Western phenomena and categories in the humanities. The clearest indication of this is the basic division of knowledge in the humanities, a division that is central to the two main divisions in the study of religion. This division corresponds in turn to the classical pedagogical analogues *humanitas* and *anthropos*. As the evolution of these two analogues suggests, the former refers to those who engage in knowledge production about religion through a self-reflective knowing that tries to set the conditions of knowing in advance, thereby transforming both the constitution of the object and the subjective conditions of knowing. The latter (*anthropos*) refers to those whose participation is limited primarily to the task of supplying raw data or factual knowledge.

As Naoki Sakai argues, however, the *humanitas/anthropos* distinction actually goes further than epistemic transactions. It also implies a distinction between two types of humanity. Humanity in the sense of *humanitas* has come to designate Western/European humanity, to be distinguished from "the Rest" as long as we insist on the "historical difference" of "the West."[116] Yet as I have tried to show throughout this book, the West's sense of historical difference, far from being historical, actually represses the historical. It is a manifestation of the putative unity of the West that is not in time. While historical difference, or "secularity," to use its other name, is imposed on others, it escapes or transcends the temporal by defining the very sense of transition, elevation, or movement by way of reference ultimately to religion as the solar principle of "the West." And this in turn depends on assuming religion as the universal, as perfectly translatable. As a universal, religion cannot *not* be translated, for not to do so would entail being cast outside of humanity. The results of this have been that one cannot theorize (religion) using non-Western phenomena. South Asian subjects and phenomena, for example, can only be read as a set of particulars, and therefore remain unable to actively share in the universal.

My excavation of the history of this problem has shown that these two conclusions are simply wrong, given that South Asian and European bodies have historically shared and partaken of the universal, specifically in the encounter that led to the construction of the comparative imaginary. What forces us to separate the South Asian and the Western in terms of particular and universal is the act of disavowing the memory of this encounter, in effect a disavowal of the double-sided nature of translation. How, then, does one halt the compulsion to repeat this disavowal? In doing so does one not also bring the comparative enterprise itself to a halt? Is there a way to call attention to new ways of theorizing the comparative enterprise that would redefine the present economy of the humanities? Is there an economy of the humanities that would not be driven either by the logic of "co-figuration" (Kant) or by the logic of "historical difference" (Hegel)? Is there a form of theorizing that could "remain attentive to the trans-cultural dissemination of global traces with theoretical knowledge produced in geo-specific locations and which explores how theories are themselves transformed by their practical effects in other sites"?[117]

Given the indissociability of religion from theory (or philosophy), a starting point might be to attend to Derrida's question: "What if *religio* remained untranslatable?" To pose the untranslatability of religion is not to halt the history of colonial translation of religion as if it had never happened, or to ignore the very tangible South Asian responses. Rather, it is to circumvent the ideological relay, the programmed manner, in which translation happens automatically. "Untranslatable" does not imply a refusal to translate, but rather the need to take a step back in order to allow the work of translation to be seen as being positively dependent on an *in*ability to translate. It consists in the realization that the decision that comes to be regarded as synonymous with translation is sustained by its impossibility. To allow the "untranslatable" would be to refuse the ruse of transparency that allows religion (for example) to be translated perfectly; that is, to refuse the false belief that it is possible to pass from one language/culture to another and back again without being contaminated, a ruse/belief that constitutes the enunciation of religion as a universal. It is to recognize the work of undecidability in the relation between universal and particular. In our posing the untranslatable, translation itself is not refused or prevented. All that is refused is the belief in noncontact that constitutes the operation of transparency—for religion to translate perfectly is the same as for it to remain untranslatable. A veritable paradox, from which it can be inferred that translation achieves its perfection only in a language being contaminated, or, what amounts to the same thing, in the realization that language in general is originarily contaminated. Thus to allow *religio* to remain untranslatable, to bring the ruse to light, is to bring into relief the enunciative modality that exists prior to every decision, the nonconvergence of discourses, which allows one to locate through the "ruptures of narrativity, the founding violence of an episteme."[118]

Judith Butler argues that for any claim to "compel consensus and . . . [for it] to enact the very universality it enunciates, it must undergo a set of translations into the various rhetorical and cultural contexts in which the meaning and force of universal claims are made."[119] Through emphasis on the cultural location of the enunciation of universality, it is possible to show that there is no operative notion of universality that can avoid the risks of translation. The form and content of the universal are always contested, and refer conventional universality (of religion, for example) back to the contaminating trace of its content.[120]

If, as we have seen, the ruse of *religio*'s pure translatability (its ability to avoid contamination) has historically set up the field of political relations between colonizer and colonized, and further still, the global fiduciary as the field of politics, then to pose the "untranslatability" of religion would be to question the very organization of this political field, opening it up to a competition of universals. Thus, for Butler, "universals must now be regarded as a process by which contenders compete for universal hegemony." The aim of this competition must not be to simply include what had formerly been excluded (e.g., particulars such as nationalisms), but to change the nature of universals, to pose alternate universals.

For South Asians, the possibility of staging different universals not subservient to the politico-semantic field of the global fiduciary would *not* be to refuse religion per se, but to release so-called particular political formations of resistance that are no less universal than those of the ex-colonizer that have hitherto enjoyed hegemonic acceptance. Though fully capable of offering alternative versions of universality, these particular formations came to be repressed under the sign of the nation. To take the example alluded to earlier, it would allow South Asians to feel confident again about asserting ancient and very practical notions of freedom and action based on the nondual One (as opposed to the One of monotheism), the paradoxical One that fosters a balancing and coexistence of ego and non-ego and creatively cultivates contingency through an emptying of the ego (*nirgun*) as the ground of worldly relations (*sargun*), so that one could say in response to modernity's demand, that being is first being-with, or that ego is first ego-cum. Love for the other, another name for the primordial interconnectedness of self to everything that is not self, and therefore the constitutive vacuity of the self, has been the starting point for pervasive strands of thought and social ethics associated with the constitutive heterogeneity of South Asian society and culture that is also becoming the norm for the future global society.

The challenge for such movements will be not to demand inclusion within the semantico-political field of the global fiduciary, which would retain the conventional universal/particular relationship, but to "establish practices of translation among competing universals . . . which still belong to a set of overlapping political aims,"[121] such as the various kinds of emancipation or enlightenment. The challenge is therefore to bring (un)translation in the service of the struggle for hegemony. To do this, however, "the dominant discourse must alter by virtue of its having to admit foreign words and concepts into its own lexicon."[122] For Occidentalists this reorganization of the political field may no doubt evoke deep-rooted fears of the return of "Eastern nihilisms" bringing with them a "passage to unknowingness," perhaps even a kind of collapse leading to a new nomenclature and radical rewriting of the global fiduciary, and along with this a fundamental fear of losing control of the devices that have so far prevented the threat of all manner of fusions, paganisms, pantheisms, and mysticisms infecting the heart of Europe and the West. But if we are indeed heading toward a multipolar global society, such an "exile in heterogeneity" is irreversible. As Judith Butler so eloquently puts it:

Another universality emerges from the trace that only borders on political legibility: the subject who has not been given the prerogative to be a subject, whose *modus vivendi* is an imposed catachresis. If the spectrally human is to enter into the hegemonic reformulation of universality, a language between languages will have to be found. This will be no metalanguage, nor will it be the condition from which all languages hail. It will be the labor of transaction and translation which belongs to no single site, but is the movement between languages, and has its final destination in this movement itself. Indeed, the task will not be to assimilate the unspeakable into the domain of speakability in order to house it there, within the existing norms of dominance, but to shatter the confidence of dominance, to show how equivocal its claims to universality are, and from that equivocation, track the break-up of its regime, an opening towards alternative versions of universality that are wrought from the work of translation itself. Such an opening will not only relieve the state of its privileged status as the primary medium through which the universal is articulated, but re-establish as the conditions of articulation itself the human trace that formalism has left behind.[123]

Epilogue

Each chapter in this book has, in different ways, engaged with and provided an extended critique of the concept of religion as a cultural universal. Through a case study of Sikhism, I have tried to demonstrate how certain aspects of Sikh and Hindu traditions were reinvented in terms of the category of "religion" during the late nineteenth and early twentieth centuries. As scholars working in different disciplines have increasingly recognized, the context of India's colonial encounter with the West provides fertile ground for the emergence and crystallization of concepts and categories that inform—but at the same time test the limitations of—the contemporary intellectual and political environment. Rather than looking at the process of intellectual encounter between India and the West in isolation from Europe, I have sought to shift the focus of this encounter closer to the political history of ideas that mutually shaped European and Indian modernities. This shift in focus has been achieved by grounding the critique of religion in a series of empirical and theoretical studies of translation. The aim of this approach was twofold: on the one hand, to highlight the operations of translation that were pivotal to the reformulation of Sikh and Hindu traditions in terms of religious identity, and on the other hand, and in the very same process, to recover part of Europe's repressed colonial memory, a memory that is organized around a certain translatability between religion and secularism.

Translation therefore emerges as a "critical term" that performs several functions in this study. First, it weaves together discourses such as the history of religions, (continental) philosophy of religion, and postcolonial theory. Although they rarely appear to come into contact with each other, these discourses are in fact linked by a theoretical matrix referred to by Derrida as a "generalized translation" or a "theology of translation," which enables the convergence of the concept of religion with the concept of translation. Second, the emphasis on translation not only helps to disclose the emergence of this theoretical matrix in the colonial encounter between India and the West, but, more importantly, tracks both the repetition of this matrix in the recent resurgences of religious identity politics in the lives of South Asians, and the way that such phenomena have been analyzed and deployed by the modern state and its functionaries, the media and academia. Third, the focus on translation as a "critical term" has helped to move the discussion about religion (its concept, genealogy, and contemporary influence, etc.) beyond the usual oppositional obsessions (inside/outside, constructionist/naturalist, theology/secular, sacrament/analysis, etc.) toward a realization that the entire debate has always taken place within the semantico-referential framework of European languages.

Given that this framework continues to implement the debilitating legacy of a past imperialism, postcolonials cannot simply take theory for granted. Theoretical movements such as deconstruction, postsecularism, and political theology hold very different implications and nuances for postcolonials and need to be constantly interrogated through an aporetic logic. Such a logic enables a redefining of the postcolonial as someone for whom the concept of religion may not have existed in their language(s) prior to their accession to the dominant symbolic order imposed by the colonizer/hegemon, but for whom this now exists as if it had been an indigenous concept all along. For them, the critical force of translation, unleashed in the question "What if religio remained untranslatable?," provides a means of distancing oneself from the concept of religion, while fully acknowledging that the vestiges of "religion" continue to haunt their very existence and the possibilities of cultural formation.

To advance this point a step further, it is possible to suggest that the stakes of theorizing translation in this way—of releasing its potential from the bind of the secular interdiction—also constitute a move away from the politics of comparison in the contemporary global context toward a spectral politics of the postcolonial. Such politics can work, however, only by continually establishing practices of translation among competing claims to universality between Western and non-Western thought. But for such practices of translation to take place it has to be presumed that contact has already taken place. One fails to understand translation unless it is seen as a form of contact, of mutual contamination. A spectral politics of the postcolonial, therefore, is one that allows "something to act on or affect itself or another, or to be acted on or affected by another." It is the acknowledgment of co-contamination as the original condition of culture(s), the idea that West and non-West are inextricably entwined in a process of mutual haunting. As such, this form of politics already points toward the possibility of a truly comparative cultural theory, a form of thinking that remains attentive to the global interconnectedness of both cultures and knowledge formations.

Notes

Introduction

1. William D. Hart, *Edward Said and the Religious Effects of Culture* (Cambridge: Cambridge University Press, 2000).

2. Jacques Derrida, "Faith and Knowledge: The Two Sources of 'Religion' Within the Limits of Reason Alone," in *Religion*, ed. Jacques Derrida and Gianni Vattimo (London: Polity Press, 1998), p. 30.

3. My use of the term "ontotheology" follows Martin Heidegger's destructive hermeneutics of the Western philosophical and theological traditions. As mentioned in the preface, the term "ontotheology" refers to a continuity of different moments in the Western tradition: specifically the Greek (*onto-*), the medieval-scholastic (*theo-*), and the humanist (*logo-* or *logic-*). As such this emphasis on continuity challenges the normative story in which modernity and humanism constitute a radical break with prior traditions of thought. This normative position is in part the result of literary theory's overdetermination of Foucault's notion that modernity begins with an epistemic rupture occurring in the eighteenth century, and that the history of the West is best seen as a series of ruptures (epistemes) rather than as a continuous line of thought. In thus interpreting Foucault's apparent rejection of the continuist understanding of Western history as an affirmation of historical discontinuity, Foucault's commentators, especially in the field of literary theory, have managed to crystallize as dogma something that is actually related in Foucault's discourse, namely the separation between the discourses of classical humanism and the post-Enlightenment empirical sciences, or the separation between discourses of classical humanism and

the theological. Consequently they have missed the affinities between Foucault's genealogy of the disciplinary society and what Heidegger and others call the onto-theological tradition.

In contrast to this misreading of Foucault, Heidegger's rendering of an essential continuity between the theological and the humanist positions helps to designate a more productive idea of the formation called "the West," to which I also make constant reference in this book. It also helps to forestall a possible misreading of what I mean by the West. By the mid-1990s it had become commonplace in many discourses, including postcolonial studies and South Asian studies, to eschew the previous Marxist understanding of the West as a monolithic entity that remained unaffected by what it touched through the colonial encounter, and that simply provided an ideological blueprint for colonized elites to construct resistive nationalist enterprises. Rather (according to this post-Marxist interpretation), the West was actively engaged by non-Western discursive traditions. To speak of "the West" in this manner was to deny agency to the colonized in constructing their own societies. One result of this discourse is that by the mid-1990s, it had become almost politically incorrect to speak of "the West" without at the same time implicating the colonial nationalists in the production of "the West."

While I do not disagree with this notion—indeed I strongly affirm it throughout this work—there is a way in which this seeming desire to give agency back to the colonized silently reinscribes the very idea of the West as well as its most insidious properties, namely the power to remain ahead of "the Rest," the power to occult its tangible presence. My own argument is that the critique of the West has not been taken far enough in South Asian studies, partly because the mode of actual engagement between colonizer and colonized in the form of speech relations continues to be taken for granted, for example as a "dialogue" between two intersubjective agencies. As I will argue later, this is based on the elision of the very matter of colonial discourse, namely, the nature of speech/thought/thinking itself as something that is transformed. One consequence of this, as Gayatri Spivak and others remind us, is the continuing discourse of agency between West as theoretical (knower) and South Asians as empirical agents. These empirical agents perform the task of native informancy. I am not arguing that South Asians cannot attain the position of theorists; rather, I am suggesting that there continues to be a link between theory and ontotheology (in the form of the discourse of religion) that is unacknowledged by postcolonial studies.

4. Derrida, "Faith and Knowledge," p. 14.

5. Talal Asad, "Multiculturalism and British Identity in the Wake of the Rushdie Affair," in *Genealogies of Religion: Discipline and Reasons of Power in Christianity and Islam* (Baltimore: Johns Hopkins University Press, 1993), pp. 239–268.

6. I borrow this phrase from Kenneth Surin's article, "Rewriting the Ontological Script of Liberation: On the Question of Finding a New Kind of Political Subject," in *Theology and the Political: The New Debate*, ed. Creston Davis, John Milbank, and Slavoj Žižek (Durham: Duke University Press, 2005), p. 240.

7. For more on this distinction between politics and the political, see Slavoj Žižek's *The Ticklish Subject: The Absent Center of Political Ontology* (London: Verso, 1999), and Ernesto Laclau's *Emancipations* (London: Verso, 1996).

8. Hent de Vries, *Political Theologies: Public Religions in a Post-Secular World*, (Fordham University Press, 2007), p. 3.

9. Rey Chow, *The Age of the World Target: Self-Referentiality in War, Theory, and Comparative Work* (Durham: Duke University Press, 2006); see also Naoki Sakai, *Translation and Subjectivity* (Minneapolis: University of Minnesota Press, 1997).

10. Couze Venn, *Occidentalism* (London: Sage Publications, 1999).

11. The theory-empiricism problem is taken up more fully in chapter 6.

12. Venn, *Occidentalism*, p. 3.

13. These works include: Wilfred Cantwell Smith's *The Meaning and End of Religion* (Minneapolis: Fortress Press, 1962); J. Z. Smith's *Imagining Religion: From Babylon to Jonestown* (Chicago: University of Chicago Press, 1982); Michel Despland's *La religion en Occident: Évolution des idées et du vécu*, Héritage et projet 23 (Montreal: Fides, 1979); Talal Asad's *Genealogies of Religion*; Tomoko Masuzawa's *The Invention of World Religions; or, How European Pluralism Was Preserved in the Language of Universalism* (Chicago: University of Chicago Press, 2005); Richard King's *Orientalism and Religion: India, Postcolonial Theory, and the "Mystic East"* (London: Routledge, 1999); S. N. Balagangadhara's *"The Heathen in His Blindness": Asia, the West, and the Dynamic of Religion* (Leiden: Brill, 1994); Mark C. Taylor's *After God* (Chicago: University of Chicago Press, 2007); Daniel Dubuisson's *The Western Construction of Religion: Myths, Knowledge, and Ideology* (Baltimore: Johns Hopkins University Press, 2003); Russell McCutcheon's *Manufacturing Religion: The Discourse of Sui Generis Religion and the Politics of Nostalgia* (Oxford: Oxford University Press, 1997); David Chidester's *Savage Systems: Colonialism and Comparative Religion in Southern Africa* (Charlottesville: University of Virginia Press, 1996); and Timothy Fitzgerald's *The Ideology of Religious Studies* (Oxford: Oxford University Press, 2000).

14. Dubuisson, *Western Construction of Religion*, p. 37.

15. Dubuisson, *Western Construction of Religion*, p. 15.

16. Masuzawa, *Invention of World Religions*, p. 20.

17. Dubuisson, *Western Construction of Religion*, p. 11.

18. Earlier variants of this argument can be found in Romila Thapar's "Syndicated Moksha," *Seminar* 313 (September 1985): 14–22; Balagangadhara's *"The Heathen in His Blindness"*; and Harjot Oberoi's *The Construction of Religious Boundaries: Culture, Identity, and Diversity in the Sikh Tradition* (Chicago: University of Chicago Press, 1994).

19. BJP: Bhartiya Janata Party; VHP: Visva Hindu Parishad; RSS: Rashtriya Swayamsevak Sangh.

20. Jacques Derrida, "Force of Law: The 'Mystical Foundation of Authority,'" in *Deconstruction and the Possibility of Justice*, ed. Drucilla Cornell, Michel Rosenfeld, and David Carlson (New York: Routledge, 1992), pp. 3–68.

21. Derrida, "Force of Law," p. 18.

22. Derrida, "Force of Law," p. 17.

23. Derrida, "Faith and Knowledge," p. 36.

24. See chapter 1 for an extended discussion of this term.

25. Jacques Derrida, *Monolingualism of the Other; or, The Prosthesis of Origin*, trans. Patrick Mensah (Stanford: Stanford University Press, 1998).

26. Jacques Lacan, *Seminar II: The Ego in Freud's Theory and in the Technique of Psychoanalysis, 1954–1955*, trans. J. A. Miller, ed. S. Tomaselli (New York: Norton, 1991), p. 313: see also Lacan's *The Four Fundamental Concepts of Psycho-analysis*, trans. Alan Sheridan (London: Penguin Books, 1991), pp. 51–55. For excellent discussions of Lacan's "traumatic real" see Bruce Fink, *The Lacanian Subject: Between Language and Jouissance* (Princeton: Princeton University Press, 1995), pp. 24–26; and Žižek, *Ticklish Subject,* pp. 190–191.

27. See Jacques Derrida, "Theology of Translation," *Eyes of the University: Right to Philosophy 2*, trans. Jan Plug et al. (Stanford: Stanford University Press, 2004), p. 67.

28. See, for example, Gyan Pandey, *The Construction of Communalism in Colonial North India* (New Delhi: Oxford University Press, 1990); Peter van der Veer, *Imperial Encounters: Religion and Modernity in Britain and India* (Princeton: Princeton University Press, 2001); Vasudha Dalmia, *The Nationalization of Hindu Traditions: Bharatendu Hariśchandra and Nineteenth-Century Banaras* (New Delhi: Oxford University Press, 1996); Krishna Sharma, *Bhakti and the Bhakti Movement: A Study in the History of Ideas* (New Delhi: Munshiram Manoharlal, 1986); Brian Pennington, *Was Hinduism Invented?: Britons, Indians, and the Colonial Construction of Religion* (New York: Oxford University Press, 2005).

29. Derrida, "Faith and Knowledge," p. 26.

30. I borrow the term "meaning-value" from Lydia Liu's article "The Question of Meaning-Value in the Political Economy of the Sign," in *Tokens of Exchange: The Problem of Translation in Global Circulations*, ed. Lydia H. Liu (Durham: Duke University Press, 1999), pp. 13–41.

31. Chow, *Age of the World Target*, p. 67.

32. I am aware that there were other movements—notably among the Dalits but also among the Tamils under colonial rule—that actively used the concept of religion as a defense against traditionalist Indian elites. Under the leadership of Ambedkar, the Dalit movement conveyed dissent against the Brahmanical elite leadership that dominated the Congress Party even in its early years. Ambedkar called for Dalits to convert to Buddhism as a way of expressing a radical religious dissent against Brahmanical domination. Though these experiments were largely unsuccessful, the episode nevertheless shows a alternative way in which, for some, the category of religion helped to provide an emancipatory identity. See for example: V. Geetha, "Re-Writing History in the Brahmin's Shadow," *Journal of Arts and Ideas* 25–26 (Dec. 1993): 136–137; V. Geetha and S. V. Rajadurai, *Towards a Non-Brahmin Millenium: From Iyothee Thass to Periyar* (Calcutta: Samya, 1998), pp. 96–110; G. Aloysius, *Religion as Emancipatory Identity: A Buddhist Movement Among the Tamils During Colonialism* (New Delhi: Christian Institute for the Study of Religion and Society); *The Essential Writings of B. R. Ambedkar*, ed. Valerian Rodrigues (New Delhi: Oxford University Press, 2002).

33. Quoted in Brian Keith Axel, *The Nation's Tortured Body: Violence, Representation, and the Formation of a Sikh "Diaspora"* (Durham: Duke University Press, 2001), p. 40.

34. Axel, *Nation's Tortured Body*, p. 41.

35. Mark C. Taylor, "Introduction" to *Critical Terms for Religious Studies* (Chicago: University of Chicago Press, 1999), p. 13.

36. I borrow this term from Slavoj Žižek.

37. I want to stress that this intellectual struggle should not be conceived in terms of the difference between diasporic Sikhs and Punjabi Sikhs. While I write and think from the location of the Western Sikh diaspora, it is not enough to say that I then "belong" to this diaspora or that I have a "diasporic" identity. The very invocation of diaspora implicates one in a relation to homeland. This intellectual struggle must therefore begin with a critique of area studies, particularly within the study of religion. This connection between "area" and "religion" is intellectually and existentially problematic for me. Second, I repudiate the distinction between "outsider" and "insider." This book is a critique of the very duality between these positions, since both ultimately privilege the distinctions between West versus Rest, theory versus empiricism, and ethnic versus native that are so much a part and parcel of the humanities. My critique of this positioning and its terms depends on the work of spectralizing the West by appropriating the humanities to the fullest extent, such that both knower and known, humanities and object are contaminated to the fullest. Hence the problem of Sikh identity is transposed into the problem of the identity of the West. As such the very question of identity is best conceptualized as a dis/order. See further below.

38. Andrew Benjamin, *Translation and the Nature of Philosophy* (London: Routledge, 1989).

39. Derrida, *Monolingualism of the Other*, p. 29.

40. Arjun Appadurai, *Fear of Small Numbers: An Essay on the Geography of Anger* (Durham: Duke University Press, 2006), p, 46.

41. See Appardurai, *Fear of Small Numbers*, p. 46.

42. The phrase "conversion to modernity" was coined by Peter van der Veer.

43. Jacques Derrida, "Above All, No Journalists," in *Religion and Media*, ed. Hent de Vries and Samuel Weber (Stanford: Stanford University Press, 2001), pp. 73–74.

44. Kang Nae-Hui, "Mimicry and Difference," *Traces: A Multilingual Journal of Cultural Theory and Translation* 1 (2001): 127–128.

45. Walter Benjamin, *Gesammelte Schriften*, I, ed. Rolf Teidemann and Hermann Schweppenhäuser (Frankfurt: Suhrkamp, 1972–1989), p. 480.

46. Benjamin, *Gesammelte Schriften*, I, p. 1242.

47. Benjamin, *Gesammelte Schriften*, I, p. 1242, and V, p. 591.

48. Navdeep Mandair, "Virtual Corpus: Solicitous Mutilation and the Body of Tradition," in *Difference in the Philosophy of Religion*, ed. Philip Goodchild (Aldershot, England: Ashgate 2003), pp. 101–114

49. See, for example, Vincent P. Pecora: *Secularization and Cultural Criticism: Religion, Nation, and Modernity* (Chicago: University of Chicago Press), 2006.

50. Jacques Derrida, "The Future of the Profession or the University Without Condition (Thanks to the "Humanities," What *Could Take Place* Tomorrow," in *Jacques Derrida and the Humanities: A Critical Reader*, ed. Tom Cohen (Cambridge: Cambridge University Press, 2001), pp. 26–29.

51. Derrida, "Future of the Profession," p. 28.

52. Derrida, "Future of the Profession," p. 30.

53. "Economy of lack" refers to the positive or negative signification attached by particular translators to the contents of the *Ādi Granth*. Thus, whereas Trumpp found no evidence for a coherent concept of God, the Self, etc., and so no possibility for a monotheism or for any system of ethics, Indologist Max Arthur Macauliffe finds exactly the opposite and reverses the lack by fulfilling it. Nevertheless, the economy/lack/fulfillment remains, thereby creating the possibility for desire on behalf of a subject who enters into this dialectic.

54. The crass version of this second view simply states that Sikhism was effectively part of Hinduism until the emergence of Khalsā Sikhism (particularly the Tat Khalsā of the late nineteenth century), which was primarily responsible for asserting the distinctness of Sikh identity vis-à-vis Hinduism. As I explain in chapters 1, 3, 4, and 5, this view has neglected to incorporate into its narratives the historical fact that the modern formation "Hinduism" was itself invented in the nineteenth century.

55. W. H. McLeod, "A Sikh Theology for Modern Times," *Sikh History and Religion in the Twentieth Century*, ed. W. H. McLeod, J. T. O'Connell, M. Israel, W. Oxtoby, and J. S. Grewal (New Delhi: Manohar, 1990), p. 32.

56. Simon Critchley, *The Ethics of Deconstruction: Derrida and Levinas* (Oxford: Blackwell, 1992), p. 21.

57. Hent De Vries, *Political Theologies* (New York: Fordham University Press, 2007), p. 5.

58. Chow, *Age of the World Target*, p. 61.

59. Chow, *Age of the World Target*, p. 61.

60. Chow, *Age of the World Target*, p. 66.

1. Mono-theo-lingualism: Religion, Language, and Subjectivity in Colonial North India

1. John Micklethwait, "The New Wars of Religion" and "In God's Name: A Special Report on Religion and Public Life," *The Economist*, Nov. 3, 2007, p. 15.

2. Micklethwait, p. 15.

3. Micklethwait, p. 15.

4. The term "public religions" was coined by José Casanova. See Hent de Vries, "In Media Res," *Religion and Media*, ed. Hent de Vries and Samuel Weber (Stanford: Stanford University Press, 2001), p. 6.

5. Hent de Vries, *Political Theologies: Public Religions in a Postsecular World* (New York: Fordham University Press, 2007), p. 3.

6. de Vries, *Political Theologies*, p. 3.

7. Scott M. Thomas, *The Global Resurgence of Religion and the Transformation of International Relations: The Struggle for the Soul of the Twenty-First Century* (New York: Palgrave Macmillan, 2005), pp. 24–26.

8. Thomas, *Global Resurgence*, p. 21.

9. Anuradha Dingwaney and Rajeswari Sunder Rajan, eds., "Introduction," *The Crisis of Secularism in India* (Durham: Duke University Press, 2007), pp. 1–42.

10. Gyan Pandey, *The Construction of Communalism in Colonial North India* (New York: Oxford University Press, 1990).

11. Mukul Kesavan, *Secular Common Sense* (New Delhi: Penguin Books India, 2001), p. 3.

12. G. Balachandran, "Religion and Nationalism in Modern India," in *Unravelling the Nation*, ed. Kaushik Basu and Sanjay Subrahmanyam (New Delhi: Penguin Books India, 1996), p. 100.

13. See, for example, Gurharpal Singh, *Ethnic Conflict in India: A Case Study of Punjab* (New York: St. Martin's, 2000). Also useful is Singh's earlier article, "Understanding the 'Punjab Problem,'" *Asian Survey* 37.12:1268–1277.

14. Ram Narayan Kumar (with Amrik Singh, Ashok Agrwaal, and Jaskaran Kaur), *Reduced to Ashes: The Insurgency and Human Rights in Punjab*, vol. 1 (Nepal: Jagadamba Press, 2003).

15. Aamir Mufti, "Auerbach in Istanbul: Edward Said, Secular Criticism, and the Question of Minority Culture," *Critical Inquiry* 25 (autumn 1998): 107.

16. Dingwaney and Rajan, "Introduction," pp. 22–23.

17. Dingwaney and Rajan, "Introduction," p. 22.

18. de Vries and Weber, eds., *Religion and Media*, p. 3.

19. T. N. Madan, "Secularism in Its Place," in *Secularism and Its Critics*, ed. Rajeev Bhargava (Delhi: Oxford University Press, 1998), pp. 297–320.

20. Gyan Pandey, *The Construction of Communalism in Colonial North India*, 5th ed. (New Delhi: Oxford University Press, 1997), p. 236.

21. Peter van der Veer, *Religious Nationalism: Hindus and Muslims in India* (New Delhi: Oxford University Press, 1996).

22. van der Veer, *Religious Nationalism*, p. 20.

23. van der Veer, *Religious Nationalism*, p. 20.

24. See, for example, Peter van der Veer's *Imperial Encounters: Religion and Modernity in India and Britain* (Princeton University Press, 2001); or Brian Pennington's *Was Hinduism Invented?: Britons, Indians, and the Colonial Construction of Religion* (New York: Oxford University Press, 2005).

25. van der Veer, *Imperial Encounters*, p. 24.

26. See Eric Stokes, *The English Utilitarians and India* (1958; repr., New Delhi: Oxford University Press, 1989).

27. Pennington, *Was Hinduism Invented?*, p. 19.

28. Pennington, *Was Hinduism Invented?*, p. 19.

29. See Vasudha Dalmia, *The Nationalization of Hindu Traditions: Bhāratendu Hariśchandra and Nineteenth-Century Benaras* (New Delhi: Oxford University Press, 1997).

30. For example, different kinds of nomenclature have been used by Kenneth Jones in his *Arya Dharam: Hindu Consciousness in Nineteenth-Century Punjab* (Berkeley: University of California Press, 1976), Harjot Oberoi in his *The Construction of Religious Boundaries: Culture, Identity, and Diversity in the Sikh Tradition* (Chicago: University of Chicago Press, 1994), and Vasudha Dalmia in her *Nationalization of Hindu Traditions*.

31. Dalmia, *Nationalization of Hindu Traditions*, pp. 6–8.

32. I refer to Judith Butler's *Life of Psychic Power: Theories in Subjection* (Stanford: Stanford University Press, 1997).

33. Kelly Oliver, *The Colonization of Psychic Space: A Psychoanalytic Theory of Oppression* (Minneapolis: University of Minnesota Press, 2004).

34. Ranajit Guha, *Dominance Without Hegemony: History and Power in Colonial India* (New Delhi: Oxford University Press, 1998), pp. 22–24.

35. Guha, *Dominance Without Hegemony*, p. 22.

36. See also Dalmia, *Nationalization of Hindu Traditions*.

37. Dalmia, *Nationalization of Hindu Traditions*, pp. 430–438.

38. Richard King, *Orientalism and Religion: Postcolonial Theory, India, and the "Mystic East"* (London: Routledge, 1999), pp. 96–98.

39. Pennington, *Was Hinduism Invented?*, p. 102.

40. See Pennington, *Was Hinduism Invented?*, pp. 101–137.

41. Pennington, *Was Hinduism Invented?*, p. 59.

42. Pennington, *Was Hinduism Invented?*, p. 77.

43. William Ward, *History, Literature, and Mythology of the Hindoos*, 4 vols. (1817; repr. New Delhi: LPP, 1990).

44. Pennington, *Was Hinduism Invented?*, p. 97.

45. Rammohan Roy, *The English Works of Raja Rammohun Roy*, ed. Jogendra Chunder Ghose, 4 vols. (Allahabad, India: Bahadurganj, 1906; repr., New Delhi: Cosmo, 1982).

46. Kenneth Jones, *Arya Dharam: Hindu Consciousness in Nineteenth-Century Punjab* (1976; repr., New Delhi: Manohar, 1989), pp. 27–29 and 40–43.

47. Jones, *Arya Dharam*, pp. 38 and 177–178.

48. Jones, *Arya Dharam*, pp. 67–93.

49. Jones, *Arya Dharam*, p. 67.

50. Bhai Kahn Singh Nabha, *Ham Hindu Nahin* (repr., Amritsar: Singh Brothers, 1995).

51. One of these was by Narain Singh, *Sikh Hindu Hain* (Amritsar, 1898).

52. Romila Thapar, "Imagined Religious Communities? Ancient History and the Modern Search for a Hindu Identity," *Modern Asian Studies* 23.2 (1989): 224. See also Narendra Wagle, "Hindu-Muslim Interactions in Medieval Maharastra," in *Hinduism Reconsidered*, ed. Gunther Sontheimer and Herman Kulke (New Delhi: Manohar, 1997), pp. 51–56.

53. See Dalmia, *Nationalization of Hindu Traditions*, "Introduction."

54. Pennington, *Was Hinduism Invented?*, p. 143.

55. See Nancy Cassels, *Religion and Pilgrim Tax Under the Company Raj*, South Asian Studies 17 (New Delhi: Manohar, 1988), pp. 1–7 and 147–158.

56. Dalmia, *Nationalization of Hindu Traditions*, pp. 223–334.

57. For a succinct summary of this see Vasudha Dalmia, "The Only Real Religion of the Hindus: Vaishnava Self-Representation in the Nineteenth Century," in *Representing Hinduism: The Construction of Religious Traditions and National Identity*, ed. Vasudha Dalmia and H. von Steitencron (New Delhi: Sage Publications, 1995), pp. 176–210.

58. Dalmia, "Only Real Religion," pp. 176–210.

59. Dalmia, "Only Real Religion," p. 195.

60. Krishna Sharma, *Bhakti and the Bhakti Movement: A Study in the History of Ideas* (New Delhi: Munshiram Manoharlal, 1987).

61. Monier-Williams, *Indian Wisdom or Examples of the Religious, Philosophical and Ethical Doctrines of the Hindus*, 2nd ed. (London, 1875), p. 135.

62. See Monier Monier-Williams, "The Vaishnava Religion," *Journal of the Royal Asiatic Society of Great Britain and Ireland* (1882): 296–297.

63. Monier-Williams, *Brahmanism and Hinduism; or, Religious Thought and Life in India as Based on the* Veda *and Other Sacred Books of the Hindus* (London: John Murray, 1891), p. 96.

64. Sharma, *Bhakti and the Bhakti Movement*, pp. 92–108.

65. Sharma, *Bhakti and the Bhakti Movement*, pp. 73–91.

66. Pennington takes the term "constructivist" from David Lorenzen's article "Who Invented Hinduism?," *Comparative Studies in Society and History* 41.4 (Oct. 1999): 630–659. Included within the constructivist position would be scholars such as Robert Frykenberg, Fritz Staal, Will Sweetman, and Timothy Fitzgerald, among many others.

67. Pennington, *Was Hinduism Invented?*, p. 168.

68. Pennington, *Was Hinduism Invented?*, p. 175.

69. Pennington, *Was Hinduism Invented?*, p. 172.

70. Pennington does try to show that religion is otherwise (*Was Hinduism Invented?*, pp. 175–179), but he still has to assume the concept of religion as universal to begin with.

71. Pennington, *Was Hinduism Invented?*, p. 172.

72. Oberoi, *Construction of Religious Boundaries*, p. 93.

73. Oberoi, *Construction of Religious Boundaries*, pp. 12–13.

74. Naoki Sakai, *Translation and Subjectivity: On "Japan" and Cultural Nationalism* (Minneapolis: University of Minnesota Press, 1997), p. 8.

75. Sakai, *Translation and Subjectivity*, pp. 3–6.

76. Sakai, *Translation and Subjectivity*, p. 12.

77. Sakai, *Translation and Subjectivity*, p. 15.

78. Bernard Cohn, "The Command of Language and the Language of Command," in *Colonialism and Its Forms of Knowledge* (New Delhi: Oxford University Press, 1997).

79. Cohn, "Command of Language," p. 24.

80. Cohn, "Command of Language," p. 25.

81. William Jones, "Charge to the Grand Jury, June 10, 1787," in *Works*, vol. 7 (1799; repr., Delhi: Agam Prakashan, 1979), p. 286.

82. Cohn, "Command of Language," p. 35.

83. John B. Gilchrist, "Preface" to *A Dictionary English and Hindostanee* (Calcutta: part I, 1786; part II, 1790), appendix to part II>

84. Gilchrist, *Dictionary*, pp. vii, xiv.

85. Gilchrist, *Dictionary*, p. vii.

86. See Martin Heidegger, "Knowing as Schematizing a Chaos in Accordance with Practical Need," in *Nietzsche* 2.3: *The Will to Power as Knowledge and as Metaphysics*, ed. David Farrell Krell (New York: Harper Collins, 1987), pp. 68–84.

87. Thomas Babington Macaulay, "Indian Education" (Minute of the 2nd of February, 1835), in *Prose and Poetry*, ed. G. M. Young (Cambridge: Harvard University Press, 1967), p. 719.

88. Cohn, "Command of Language," p. 50.

89. See, for example, George Nicholls, *Sketch of the Rise and Progress of the Benares Patshalla, or Sanskrit College, Now Forming the Sanskrit Department of the Sanskrit College* (written in 1848) (Allahabad: Government Press, U.P., 1907); and Christopher King, *One Language, Two Scripts: The Hindi Movement in Nineteenth-Century North India* (New Delhi: Oxford University Press, 1994), pp. 90–91.

90. NWP Educ Rpt: "Report on the State of Popular Education in the North Western Provinces," Orders of the Government, 1873–74, p. 32.

91. Nicholls, *Sketch of the Rise and Progress*, p. 99.

92. See Jacques Derrida, *Monolingualism of the Other; or, The Prosthesis of Origin*, trans. Patrick Mensah (Stanford: Stanford University Press, 1998).

93. George Grierson, "The Modern Vernacular Literature of Hindustan," *Journal of the Asiatic Society of Bengal*, part I for 1888, special number: 107.

94. Derrida, *Monolingualism of the Other*, p. 37.

95. Charles Trevelyan, *On the Education of the People of India* (London: Longman, Orme, Browne, Green, and Longmans, 1838), p. 181.

96. Trevelyan, *On the Education of the People of India*, pp. 189–192.

97. Thomas Macaulay, "Minute on Indian Education" (1835), from *Speeches of Lord Macaulay with His Minute on Indian Education*, ed. G. M. Young (Oxford: Oxford University Press, 1935), reprinted in *The Post-Colonial Studies Reader*, ed. Bill Ashcroft, Gareth Griffiths, and Helen Tiffin (London: Routledge, 1995), p. 428.

98. Sivanath Sastri, *Ramtanu Lahiri O Tatkalin Bangasamaj* (Calcutta: New Age Publishers, Bengali Year 1362), p. 72.

99. Immanuel Kant, *Critique of Pure Reason*, trans. Norman Kemp Smith (London: Palgrave Macmillan, 1992), pp. 549–550.

100. Kant, *Critique of Pure Reason*, p. 550.

101. Kant, *Critique of Pure Reason*, p. 550.

102. Sakai, *Translation and Subjectivity*, p. 34.

103. Sakai, *Translation and Subjectivity*, p. 33.

104. Jacques Derrida, "Theology of Translation," *Eyes of the University: Right to Philosophy 2*, trans. Jan Plug et al. (Stanford: Stanford University Press, 2004), p. 65.

105. Derrida, "Theology of Translation," p. 65.

106. Derrida, "Theology of Translation," pp. 78–79.

107. Derrida, "Theology of Translation," p. 80

108. Jacques Derrida, "Faith and Knowledge: The Two Sources of 'Religion' at the Limits of Reason Alone," in *Religion*, ed. Jacques Derrida and Gianni Vattimo (London: Polity Press, 1998), pp. 26–30.

109. Derrida, *Monolingualism of the Other*, pp. 30–33.

110. Willie Appollon, "Theory and Practice in the Psychoanalytic Treatment of Psychosis," in *Lacan and the Subject of Language*, ed. Ellie Ragland-Sullivan and Mark Bracher (London: Routledge, 1991), pp. 117–119.

111. Derrida, "Faith and Knowledge," p. 26.

112. Jacques Derrida, "How to Avoid Speaking: Denials," *Languages of the Unsayable: The Play of Negativity in Literature and Literary Theory*, ed. Sanford Budick and Wolfgang Iser (New York: Columbia University Press, 1989), p. 14.

113. Derrida, "How to Avoid Speaking," pp. 29–30.

114. Derrida, "Faith and Knowledge," pp. 26–27.

115. Derrida, "Faith and Knowledge," p. 27.

116. Derrida, "Faith and Knowledge," p. 27.

117. Derrida, "Above All, No Journalists," in *Religion and Media*, ed. Hent de Vries and Samuel Weber (Stanford: Stanford University Press, 2001), p. 65.

118. Derrida, "Theology of Translation," p. 78.

119. Derrida, "Faith and Knowledge."

120. Daniel Dubuisson, *The Western Construction of Religion: Myths, Knowledge, and Ideology* (Baltimore: Johns Hopkins University Press, 2003), p. 30.

121. Dubuisson, *Western Construction of Religion*, p. 31.

122. Derrida, "Theology of Translation," p. 69.

2. Hegel and the Comparative Imaginary of the West

1. See Sheldon Pollock, "Indology, Power, and the Case of Germany," in *Orientalism: A Reader*, ed. A. L. McFie (Edinburgh: Edinburgh University Press, 2000), pp. 302–323.

2. Thomas R. Trautmann, *Aryans and British India* (New Delhi: Yoda Press, 2004), p. 23.

3. See Hent de Vries and Samuel Weber's explication of the term "mediatic" in their *Religion and Media* (Stanford: Stanford University Press, 2001).

4. Pollock, "Indology, Power, and the Case of Germany," pp. 304.

5. Pollock, "Indology, Power, and the Case of Germany," p. 304.

6. See, e.g., Ronald Inden, "Orientalist Constructions of India," *Modern Asian Studies* 20.3 (July 1986): 401–446; G. C. Spivak, *A Critique of Postcolonial Reason: Towards a History of the Vanishing Present* (Cambridge, MA: Harvard University Press, 1999), pp. 40–41; Wilhelm Halbfass, *India and Europe: An Essay in Philosophical Understanding* (New Delhi: Motilal Banarsidas, 1990), pp. 36–40; Tejaswini Niranjana, *Siting Translation: History, Post-Structuralism and the Colonial Context* (Berkeley: University of California University Press, 1992); Johannes Fabian, *Time and the Other: How Anthropology Makes Its Object* (New York: Columbia University Press, 1983); Pheng Cheah, "Universal Areas: Asian Studies in a World in Motion," *Traces* 1: *Specters of the West and the Politics of Translation*, ed. Naoki Sakai and Yukiko Hanawa (Ithaca: Cornell University Press, 2001), pp. 37–70.

7. Dipesh Chakrabarty, *Provincializing Europe: Postcolonial Thought and Historical Difference* (Princeton: Princeton University Press, 2000), p. 6.

8. Such claims are made by Slavoj Žižek in his *Iraq: The Borrowed Kettle* (London : Verso, 2004). See also the discussion in chapter 6 of this book.

9. W. D. Hart, *Edward Said and the Religious Effects of Culture* (Cambridge: Cambridge University Press, 2000), p. 151.

10. Chakrabarty, *Provincializing Europe*, p. 46.

11. Notable exceptions to this are Sheldon Pollock and Wilhelm Halbfass (see further).

12. Anne Perkins, *Nation and Word: Religious and Metaphysical Language in European National Consciousness* (Aldershot: Ashgate Publishing, 1999).

13. See Perkins, *Nation and Word,* and Martin Bernal, *Black Athena: The Afroasiatic Roots of Classical Civilization* (London: Vintage Books, 1991).

14. See Bernard Reardon, *Religion in the Age of Romanticism* (Cambridge: Cambridge University Press, 1985).

15. Cited in Mark C. Taylor, *Disfiguring: Art, Architecture, Religion* (Chicago: University of Chicago Press, 1992), p. 18.

16. Oliver Goldsmith, *History of the Earth, and Animated Nature* (London, 1774), vol. 2, pp. 230–231.

17. Plato, *Epinomis* 987D; in *Plato: The Collected Dialogues*, ed. Edith Hamilton and Huntington Cairns (Princeton: Princeton University Press, 1961).

18. Aristotle, *Politics* 7.7, trans. T. A. Sinclair (London: Penguin, 1962).

19. Robert Bernasconi, "Who Invented the Concept of Race? Kant's Role in the Enlightenment Construction of Race," in *Race*, ed. Robert Bernasconi (Oxford: Blackwell, 2001), p. 11.

20. As Wilhelm Halbfass has clearly demonstrated in his important study *India and Europe*, the influence of German philosophical thought on India and Indology far outweighs the influence of British ideology. Most of his references in the nineteenth century are to German thinkers.

21. A useful account is given by Wilhelm Halbfass in his monumental study *India and Europe*, pp. 36–54.

22. Bartholomaus Ziegenbalg, *Genealogie der malabarischen Götter*, ed. W. Germann (Madras, 1867), p. 15.

23. D. S. Hawley, "L'Inde de Voltaire," *Studies on Voltaire and the Eighteenth Century* 120 (1974): 139.

24. *Ziegenbalg's Malabarisches Heidenthum,* ed. W. Caland (Amsterdam, 1926), p. 43.

25. Bernasconi, "Who Invented the Concept of Race?," pp. 11–35.

26. Sir William Jones, *The works of Sir William Jones. With a Life of the Author by Lord Teignmouth* (London: John Shore, 1807), vol. III, p. 187.

27. The term was coined by Raymond Schwab. See *The Oriental Renaissance: Europe's Rediscovery of India and the East, 1680–1880*, trans. G. Patterson-Black and V. Reinking (New York: Columbia University Press, 1984).

28. G. W. F. Hegel, *Lectures on the Philosophy of Religion*, vols. 1 and 2, ed. P. C. Hodgson (Berkeley: University of California Press, 1995) (hereafter *LPR*). Page references will be given according to the original manuscript.

29. I have in mind the section entitled "History in Its Development," which is largely concerned with the origin of History in relation to the origin of Spirit.

30. "All the people of Europe, where are they from? From Asia" (Halbfass, *India and Europe*, p. 70).

31. The term "expressivism" is developed in Charles Taylor's *Sources of the Self: The Making of the Modern Identity* (Cambridge: Cambridge University Press, 1989), and in his *Hegel* (Cambridge: Cambridge University Press, 1981).

32. F. Schlegel, *Europa* 1 (1803): 35.

33. F. Schlegel, *Athenaum* 3 (1800): 103f.

34. F. Schlegel, *Über die Sprache und Weisheit der Indier*, in *Kritische Friedrich-Schlegel-Ausgabe*, vol. 8, ed. E. Behler and U. Struc-Oppenberg (Munich: Schöningh, 1975), p. 253.

35. Andrew Bowie, *Aesthetics and Subjectivity: From Kant to Nietzsche* (Manchester: Manchester University Press, 1990), p. 8.

36. See Taylor, *Disfiguring,* and Bowie, *Aesthetics and Subjectivity*, contradicting Taylor.

37. Bowie, *Aesthetics and Subjectivity,* pp. 12–13.

38. The complex presentation of these lectures is better understood in light of two earlier phases: Tübingen to Frankfurt (1788–1801), the period of early theological writings, and the Jena period (1801–1806), corresponding to the writing of *The Phenomenology of Spirit*. During the Tübingen to Frankfurt period, Hegel was mainly preoccupied with theological issues concerned with the renewal of religion in a modern enlightened society. Religion had to become a "*Volks-religion*" a religion of and for the "common man." God, in other words, had to be made relevant to the world and to the affairs of men. This earlier preoccupation with *Volks*-religion was incorporated into the basic structure of what eventually became Hegel's mature dialectic, which first emerges in 1799 as a series of interpretations of the very different natures of the Greek, Jewish, and Christian religions. The threefold dialectic consists of three different states: (i) *Primal Unity*, corresponding to man's initial connectedness to mother nature. In Hegel's interpretation only the Greek religion still represents dim traces of this primal state. (ii) *Cleavage/separation* between the wholly transcendent being of God and the exiled being of Man. This is characterized by the figure of the Jew and Judaism. (iii) *Reconciliation*, represented by Christianity, where former opposites—Greek and Jew—are finally reconciled.

Hegel improved and extended this earlier dialectic into the better-known version published in the *Phenomenology of Spirit* (1807). Here the three steps of the dialectic trace the progressive evolution of mankind's religious consciousness in terms of a phenomenology of religions, i.e., as determinate or historical forms. Passage through the different forms of religious experience results in the increasingly adequate self-representation of spirit and correspondingly the incremental reconciliation of the human (subject) and the divine (object). The three stages in this dialectic are: *natural, artistic*, and *revealed* types of religion corresponding to the Oriental, Greek/Roman, and the Christian. In the penultimate chapter of the *Phenomenology of Spirit* there are only vague references to named religions of the Orient. The discussion focuses more on the dialectical framework for the progression of religious forms. By contrast, the *Lectures on the Philosophy of Religion* (1824–1827) contain a more detailed articulation of Hegel's analysis of the dialectic as well as extensive discussions on the Oriental religions and Hinduism in particular.

39. The kind of Orientalist material upon which Hegel mainly relied for the formulation of the Berlin lectures became available only in the 1820s. The material available to Hegel in the early period up to publication of the *Phenomenology* tended to romanticize India and took for granted the idea of an Indian Golden Age, which, at a time when neo-Hellenism was competing for precedence with Romanticism, was a serious handicap to the core principle of the *Altertumswissenschaft*, namely the image of the divine Greek, both artistic and philosophical. Not surprisingly, the *Phenomenology* is sparse on details, unlike the Berlin lectures.

40. I shall begin with the 1824 lectures (which contain the more extensive discussion connecting the "concept of religion" in general to its determinate forms) before moving on to the 1827 lectures.

41. Hegel, *LPR* (1824), vol. 2, p. 233.

42. Hegel, *LPR* (1824), vol. 2, p. 143.

43. Hegel, *LPR* (1824), vol. 2, p. 144.

44. Hegel, *LPR* (1824), vol. 2, p. 144.

45. Hegel, *LPR* (1824), vol. 2, pp. 149–154.

46. Hegel, *LPR* (1824), vol. 2, editor's footnote, p. 241.

47. Hegel, *LPR* (1824), vol. 2, editor's footnote, p. 241.

48. Hegel, *LPR* (1824), vol. 2, pp. 147–148.

49. I refer of course to works such as James Mill's *History of India*; William Ward's *Religion and Mythology of the Hindoos*, and related works by Carey and Marshman.

50. Hegel, *LPR* (1824), vol. 2, pp. 149–152.

51. Hegel, *LPR* (1824), vol. 2, p. 149.

52. Hegel, *LPR* (1827), vol. 2, pp. 415–417.

53. Hegel, *LPR* (1827), vol. 2, p. 416. Clearly, Hegel believes, and wrongly as we shall see, his concept of religious experience based on spirit to be very different from the "merely metaphysical" abstract notion attributable to both deism and Oriental versions of pantheism.

54. Hegel, *LPR* (1827), vol. 2, p. 415.

55. Hegel, *LPR* (1824), vol. 2, p. 152.

56. Hegel, *LPR* (1824), vol. 2, p. 154.

57. Hegel, *LPR* (1824), vol. 2, p. 156. The phrase occurs in the following sentence: "[T]he elaboration of what spirit is forms the entire content of the philosophy of religion," clearly illustrating the centrality of the "concept" of spirit (religious experience) to the lecture course as also to the possibility of there being a future academic subject going by the *name* "philosophy of religion."

58. Hegel, LPR (1824), vol. 2, p. 156.

59. See Jacques Derrida, *Of Spirit: Heidegger and the Question*, trans. Geoffrey Bennington and Rachel Bowlby (Chicago: University of Chicago Press, 1989).

60. Hegel, *LPR* (1824), vol. 1, p. 115.

61. Hegel, *LPR* (1824), vol. 1, p. 221.

62. Hegel, *LPR* (1824), vol. 2, p. 155.

63. Hegel, *LPR* (1824), vol. 2, p. 157.

64. Hegel, *LPR* (1824), vol. 1, pp. 115–117.

65. Hegel, *LPR* (1824), vol. 2, pp. 159–162.

66. See Derrida's *Glas,* trans. John P. Leavey Jr. (Lincoln: University of Nebraska Press, 1986), pp. 8–20.

67. Hegel, *LPR* (1824), vol. 1, pp. 115–117.

68. Hegel, *LPR* (1824), vol. 2, pp. 159–160.

69. See Jacques Derrida's reading of this in *Glas.*

70. Derrida, *Glas*, pp. 26–29.

71. Hegel, *LPR,* vol. 1, p. 280 (1827); see also p. 353 (1831).

72. Hegel, *LPR* (1827), vol. 1, p. 280 footnote 47.

73. Hegel, *LPR* (1827), vol. 1, p. 280 footnote 47.

74. Hegel, *LPR* (1827), vol. 1, p. 271.

75. Hegel, *LPR* (1827), vol. 1, p. 270.

76. Hegel, *LPR* (1827), vol. 1, part I: "The Concept of Religion," p. 280.

77. Hegel, *LPR* (1827), vol. 2, part II: "Determinate Religions," pp. 412–413.

78. Hegel, *LPR* (1827), vol. 2, p. 414 footnote 5.

79. Hegel, *LPR* (1827), vol. 2, p. 414 footnote 5.

80. Hegel, *LPR* (1827), vol. 2, p. 414 footnote 5.

81. Hegel, *LPR* (1827), vol. 2, pp. 418–419.

82. Hegel, *LPR* (1827), vol. 2, p. 414 footnote 5 and vol. 2, pp. 532–533. The separate section dealing with the Jewish/Greek/Roman religions is entitled "The Elevation of the Spiritual Above the Natural." The word "above" is prominent in Hegel's text, being used to emphasize the consistency of the elevation, its freedom (albeit partial) from the natural so that the simple blending of the natural and the spiritual, as in Oriental religion, ceases. The characteristic of this second stage is a "free subjectivity" that has "attained lordship over the finite generally."

83. Martin Heidegger, *Nietzsche* 2.3*: The Will to Power as Knowledge and as Metaphysics*, ed. David Farrell Krell (New York: Harper Collins, 1987), pp. 68–84; *The Principle of Reason*, trans. Reginald Lily (Bloomington: Indiana University Press, 1991).

84. Anselm's version of the ontological argument is to be found in chaps. 2–4 of his *Proslogion*. Among the best translations is that by M. J. Charlesworth, in *St. Anselm's Proslogion* (Oxford: Clarendon Press, 1965), pp. 5–8. For René Descartes' restatement of Anselm's ontological argument, see article 41, "Ontological Arguments," in R. Descartes, *Oeuvres des Descartes*, ed. C. Addam and P. Tannery, rev. ed. (Paris: CNRS, 1964–1976).

85. Mark C. Taylor, *Nots* (Chicago: University of Chicago Press, 1993), pp. 19–21.

86. Heidegger, *Principle of Reason*, lecture 4, pp. 26–27.

87. Things exist only where there is perception of them; contrarily, perception exists only where there are things. What sustains the cohesion or correspondence between being and perceiving is truth, which the Western metaphysical tradition has attributed to mind (*nous*) or reason *(Vernunft)*. Reason is the form of thinking that determines — i.e., takes hold of existing things as this or that quality and quantity — and

expresses itself in the assertion (*logos*) of such correspondence. Furthermore, this kind of thinking, which Heidegger refers to as the customary thinking that defines the history of Western metaphysics from Plato to Hegel, rests on a fundamental "trust" in reason, that is, a trust in reason's ability to render the truth of the relation between knower and known, the knowing subject and object of knowledge. In the Western philosophical tradition knowing is therefore the peculiar disposition where the principle of reason is already held-to-be-true or presupposed by a subject for whom it is a presupposition. According to a more precise definition of the principle of reason: reason as such demands to be resolved in the direction of a representing subject, i.e., represented by the subject and for the subject. Thus in the representing mode of behaviour toward what exists, man always already relates himself to himself as well. As indicated above, such is also the definition of truth as *veritas* or correctness bequeathed by Plato and instituted most fully by Hegel. "Correctness" means lack of contradiction between what is encountered and its representation. "Lack of contradiction" implies that only what presents itself to a subject's cognition as fixed and stable can be counted as truly existing: "It is."

88. Heidegger, *Will to Power*, p. 70.

89. Heidegger, *Will to Power*, p. 77.

90. Gayatri C. Spivak, *A Critique of Postcolonial Reason: Toward a History of the Vanishing Present* (Cambridge, MA: Harvard University Press, 1999), p. 39.

91. Spivak, *Critique of Postcolonial Reason,* pp. 39–40.

92. Hegel is referring to the "One sSubstance" (Brahman) with its three personae: Brahma (creator), Viṣṇu (preserver), and Śiva (annihilator).

93. Hegel, *LPR* (1824), vol. 2, p. 229.

94. Hegel, *LPR* (1827), vol. 2, p. 478.

95. Hegel, *LPR* (1827), vol. 2, p. 480.

96. Hegel, *LPR* (1824), vol. 2, p. 240.

97. Hegel, *LPR* (1827), vol. 2, p. 495.

98. Hegel, *LPR* (1824), vol. 2, p. 240.

99. Hegel, *LPR* (1827), vol. 2, p. 491.

100. Hegel, *LPR* (1827), vol. 2, p. 491.

101. Hegel, *LPR* (1827), vol. 2, p. 491.

102. Hegel, *LPR* (1827), vol. 2, p. 496.

103. Although he uses it in a different sense that Max Müller, Hegel nevertheless mentions "science of religion" or "scientific conception of the religious standpoint" several times in the 1827 lectures. See *LPR* (1827), vol. 1, pp. 149, 154, and 199.

104. M. Hardt and A. Negri, *Empire* (Cambridge, MA: Harvard University Press, 2000), pp. 82–84.

105. Hardt and Negri, *Empire*, pp. 74–77.

106. Hardt and Negri, *Empire*, p. 82.

107. See, for example, Mark C. Taylor, *Erring: A Postmodern A/theology* (Chicago: University of Chicago Press, 1984); John Caputo, *The Prayers and Tears of Jacques Derrida: Religion Without Religion* (Bloomington: Indiana University Press, 1998); John Milbank, *Theology and Social Theory: Beyond Secular Reason* (Oxford:

Blackwell, 1990); and Hent de Vries, *Philosophy and the Turn to Religion* (Baltimore: Johns Hopkins University Press, 1994).

108. By colonial and neocolonial formations of power, I refer to the disciplinary formations philosophy of religion and history of religions (or "world religions") in the curriculum of the modern university.

109. See, e.g., E. J. Sharpe, *Comparative Religion: A History* (London: Open Court, 1986).

110. Tomoko Masuzawa, *The Invention of World Religions; or, How European Universalism Was Preserved in the Language of Pluralism* (Chicago: University of Chicago Press, 2005), p. 19.

111. Masuzawa, *Invention of World Religions*, p. 20.

112. Masuzawa, *Invention of World Religions* (note book subtitle).

113. Martin Heidegger, "The Age of the World Picture," in *The Question Concerning Technology, and Other Essays*, trans. William Lovitt (San Francisco: Harper Torchbooks, 1977), pp. 115–154.

114. Heidegger, "Age of the World Picture," p.123.

115. Heidegger, "Age of the World Picture," p. 124.

116. Heidegger, "Age of the World Picture," p. 126.

117. Heidegger, "Age of the World Picture," p. 128.

118. Heidegger, "Age of the World Picture," p. 133.

119. Heidegger, "Age of the World Picture," p. 134.

120. Heidegger, "Age of the World Picture," p. 135.

121. Talal Asad, *Formations of the Secular: Christianity, Islam, Modernity* (Stanford: Stanford University Press, 2003), pp. 191–192.

122. Asad, *Formations*, p. 192.

123. Richard King, *Orientalism and Religion: Postcolonial Theory, India, and the "Mystic East"* (London: Routledge, 1999).

124. Vasudha Dalmia, *The Nationalization of Hindu Traditions* (New Delhi: Oxford University Press, 1997), pp. 176–210.

125. Dalmia, *Nationalization of Hindu Traditions*, p. 396.

126. Dalmia, *Nationalization of Hindu Traditions*, p. 179.

127. See, for example, Peter Harrison's argument in his *Religion and "the Religions" in the English Enlightenment*, 2nd ed. (Cambridge: Cambridge University Press, 2002).

128. Eric Alliez, *Capital Times: Tales From the Conquest of Time* (Minneapolis: University of Minnesota Press, 1996): 134.

129. E. J. Sharpe, "The Study of Religion in Historical Perspective" in *The Routledge Companion to the Study of Religion*, ed. John Hinnells (London: Routledge, 2005), p. 21.

130. Harrison, *Religion*, p. 2.

131. For a useful overview of the intellectual scope of Max Müller's work, see Lourens Peter van den Bosch's article "Theosophy or Pantheism: Friedrich Max Müller's Gifford Lectures on Natural Religion" (http://www.here-now4u.de/eng/theosophy_or_pantheism__friedr.htm).

132. F. Max Müller, *Introduction to the Science of Religion* (London: Longmans, Green, 1873), p. 226.

133. Müller, *Science of Religion*, p. 219.

134. F. Max Müller, *Natural Religion: The Gifford Lectures Delivered Before the University of Glasgow in 1888* (London: Longmans, Green, 1889), p. 11.

135. Müller, *Natural Religion*, p.12f.

136. F. Max Müller, *Theosophy; or, Psychological Religion* (London: Longmans, Green, 1893), p. 94.

137. Müller, *Theosophy*, p. 92.

138. See for example: Hans Kippenberg's *Discovering Religious History in the Modern Age* (Princeton: Princeton University Press, 2002); or Thomas Trautman's *Aryans and British India*.

139. Halbfass, *India and Europe*, p. 420.

140. Taylor, *Disfiguring*, pp. 49–96.

141. Taylor, *Disfiguring*, p. 57.

142. Halbfass, *India and Europe*, p. 345.

143. See Halbfass, *India and Europe*, pp. 344–345.

3. Sikhism and the Politics of Religion-Making

1. The word *misl* (lit. "equal") refers to Sikh military groupings of the eighteenth century. Each *misl* had its own leader as well as its own principality. All twelve *misls* were united toward the end of the eighteenth century by Maharajah Ranjit Singh, who assumed leadership of the Sikhs until his death in 1839. After annexation the *misls*, which for some time had existed as a more-or-less unified Khalsā Army during Ranjit Singh's rule, were largely incorporated into the British Indian army.

2. Polier's book was written as early as 1780 but was submitted as a paper in 1787 to the Asiatic Society of Bengal.

3. Forster's account was written in 1783 as part of his *Travelogue* but was not published until 1798. Browne's work was published in 1785 in a volume entitled *India Tracts*. For details of these accounts see Ganda Singh's *Early European Accounts of the Sikhs* (Calcutta: Maitra, 1962), Darshan Singh's *Western Perspective on the Sikh Religion* (New Delhi: Singh Brothers, 1991).

4. Cited in Ganda Singh, *Early European Accounts*.

5. Charles Wilkins, "Seeks and their College," *Asiatick Researches* 2 (1788): 288.

6. See Brian Pennington, *Was Hinduism Invented?: Britons, Indians, and the Colonial Construction of Religion* (New York: Oxford University Press, 2005), pp. 112–113.

7. John Malcolm, *Sketch of the Sikhs; A Singular Nation, Who Inhabit the Provinces of the Penjab*, 1st ed. (London: Murray, 1812), p. 144.

8. Jeffrey Cox, *Imperial Fault Lines: Christianity and Colonial Power in India, 1818–1940* (StanfordStanford University Press, 2002).

9. Malcolm, *Sketch*, p. 144.

10. Malcolm, *Sketch*, p. 148.

11. Others include Princep, Murray, Steinbach, McGreggor, and after Cunningham we have Robert Needham Cust. But these are shorter and less important than Cunningham's.

12. J. D. Cunningham, *A History of the Sikhs* (London: John Murray, 1849), p. 19.

13. Cunningham, *A History*, p. 12.

14. Cunningham, *A History*, pp. 1–2.

15. William Ward, "Account of the Shikhs," *A View of the History, Religion, and Literature of the Hindus* (London: Kingsbury, Parbury, and Allen, 1821), pp. 270–282.

16. Quoted in Martin Latham, *The Sikh State: British Evaluations (1788–1849)*, Punjab Research Group, Discussion Papers 2, pp. 13–16.

17. H. H. Wilson, "Civil and Religious Institutions of the Sikhs," reprinted in *Western Image of the Sikh Religion: A Source Book*, ed. Darshan Singh (New Delhi: National Book Organization, 1999), p. 89.

18. Wilson, "Civil and Religious Institutions," p. 89.

19. Wilson, "Civil and Religious Institutions," p. 104.

20. Wilson, "Civil and Religious Institutions," p. 99.

21. This is not to suggest that there are not close equivalents available in the Persian and Indian languages. Indeed, this is what conventional translation theory relies upon. My point of contention, however, concerns the philosophical basis of the *principle of equivalency* itself, which takes the *perceived* similarity between words in different languages as an indication of the truth or propriety of the thing/meaning/signified to which they refer. This is a theme to which I shall return constantly, particularly in relation to the problem of mimesis.

22. Again, I am not denying that the native informant reflects his or her own cultural background. For example, Brahmin native informants put their own spin on the information they provided to the European. But the interpretive grid necessary for the process of translation into European languages did not come from the native culture. This was provided by the model of communication that assumed that meaning was being transmitted from a source to a target language. See chapter 1, and also the discussion that occurs further on in this chapter.

23. Ernest Trumpp, *The Ādi Granth* (London, 1877), p. xcvii.

24. From what we know of Trumpp's background (b. 1828), it would appear that he came from a strongly Lutheran background and had been, initially at least, marked out as a future Lutheran minister. As with many of his more famous predecessors, Trumpp joined the famous Tübingen Stift, where in additions to pursuing a core curriculum consisting of theological studies, he concentrated on languages, which included, in addition to Hebrew, Sanskrit and Arabic. See Annemarie Schimmel, *German Contributions to the Study of Indo-Pakistan Linguistics* (Hamburg: German-Pakistan Forum, 1981); see also Darshan Singh, *Western Perspectives*, chap. 1.

25. Trumpp, *Ādi Granth*, p. xcvii.

26. Trumpp, *Ādi Granth*, p. xcvii.

27. Trumpp, *Ādi Granth*, pp. xcviii, xcix–c.

28. Trumpp, *Ādi Granth*, p. c.

29. Trumpp, *Ādi Granth*, pp. c, ci.

30. Trumpp, *Ādi Granth*, p. ci.

31. G. W. F. Hegel, *Lectures on the Philosophy of Religion* (1827), ed. P. C. Hodgson (Berkeley: University of California Pres, 1995), vol. 2, p. 315.

32. Trumpp makes frequent references to the lack of "teleology" or "teleological principles" in Hindu thinking.

33. Trumpp, *Ādi Granth*, p. ci.

34. The word *nirbān* is the Punjabi version of the Sanskrit term *nirvana* or the Pali term *nibbana:* lit. "the blowing out or annihilation of consciousness/desire/appearance."

35. Trumpp, *Ādi Granth*, p. cvi.

36. Trumpp, *Ādi Granth*, pp. cix, cx.

37. See Harjot Oberoi, *The Construction of Religious Boundaries: Culture, Identity, and Diversity in the Sikh Tradition* (Chicago: University of Chicago Press, 1994), p. 247.

38. Lit. "way to live"; *rahits* were documents that codified an "authentic" Sikh conduct.

39. Cunningham, *A History*, p. 34.

40. Frederic Pincott, "Sikhism," and "The Arrangement of Hymns of the Ādi Granth," *Journal of the Royal Asiatic Society* 23 (July 1886), reprinted in Darshan Singh, ed., *Western Image of the Sikh Religion* (citations and page numbers are from this volume), pp. 185–211.

41. Pincott, "Sikhism," p. 177.

42. Pincott, "Arrangement of Hymns," p. 186.

43. Pincott, "Arrangement of Hymns," p. 186.

44. See Andrew Bowie, *Aesthetics and Subjectivity* (Manchester: Manchester University Press, 1994), pp. 176–205.

45. I designate the movement as one from "prenarrative to narrative" rather than from Indic narrative to Western narrative to emphasize a particular point—the exclusion in Occidentalist discourse of Indians from history (see below).

46. See Ronald Inden, "Orientalist Constructions of India," *Modern Asian Studies*, 20.3 (1986): 401–405.

47. This second view was propounded by a succession of British historiographers of the Sikhs that included John Malcolm, J. D. Cunningham, and M. A. Macauliffe.

48. W. H. McLeod, *Textual Sources for the Study of Sikhism* (Manchester: University of Manchester Press, 1984), pp. 11–13.

49. See Darshan Singh, *Western Perspective*.

50. Krishna Sharma, *Bhakti and the Bhakti Movement* (New Delhi: Munshiram Manohar, 1987), pp. 74–91.

51. See N. G. Barrier, *The Sikhs and Their Literature: A Guide to Tracts, Books, and Periodicals, 1849–1919* (Delhi: Manohar Book Service 1970); "Trumpp and Macauliffe," in *Historians and Historiography of the Sikhs*, ed. Fauja Singh (New Delhi: Oriental, 1978); W. H. McLeod, *Sikhism* (London: Penguin, 2000).

52. Nripinder Singh, *The Sikh Moral Tradition* (New Delhi: Manohar Publishers, 1990), p. 255.

53. Donald Dawe, "Max Arthur Macauliffe (1841–1913)," in *Encyclopedia of Sikhism* (Patiala: Punjabi University, 1997), pp. 3:1–4.

54. W. H. McLeod, "A Sikh Theology for Modern Times," in *Sikh History and Religion in the Twentieth Century*, ed. J. T. O'Connell et al. (New Delhi: Manohar Publishers, 1990), pp. 32–43.

55. M. A. Macauliffe, *The Sikh Religion: Its Gurus, Sacred Writings, and Authors*, (Oxford: Clarendon Press, 1909; repr. Chand and Company, 1983), p. vi.

56. Macauliffe, *Sikh Religion*, p. vi.

57. M. A. Macauliffe, "The Holy Writings of the Sikhs," *Asiatic Quarterly Review* (1898); repr. in Darshan Singh, *Western Image*, p. 320.

58. Macauliffe, "Holy Writings," p. 320.

59. Macauliffe, "Holy Writings," p. 326.

60. Talal Asad, "The Concept of Cultural Translation in British Social Anthropology," in *Genealogies of Religion: Discipline and Reasons of Power in Christianity and Islam* (Baltimore: Johns Hopkins University Press, 1993), pp. 171–199.

61. Asad, "Concept of Cultural Translation," p. 196.

62. Naoki Sakai, *Translation and Subjectivity: On "Japan" and Cultural Nationalism* (Minneapolis: University of Minnesota Press, 1997), pp. 15–17.

63. Macauliffe, *Sikh Religion*, p. xxxix.

64. Macauliffe, *Sikh Religion*, p. lviii.

65. Macauliffe, *Sikh Religion*, p. lviii.

66. Macauliffe, *Sikh Religion*, p. lxi.

67. Macauliffe, *Sikh Religion*, p. lxi.

68. Macauliffe, *Sikh Religion*, p. lxii.

69. Macauliffe, *Sikh Religion*, p. xxxix.

70. Macauliffe, *Sikh Religion*, p. lxiii.

71. Though problematical, this distinction is best articulated by W. H. McLeod in his article "Cries of Outrage: History Versus Tradition in the Study of the Sikh Community," *South Asia Research* 14.2 (1994): 121–134.

72. McLeod, "A Sikh Theology," p. 33.

73. The difference between these two models of transcendence is discussed at length by Martin Heidegger in his important study *The Metaphysical Foundations of Logic*, trans. Michael Heim (Bloomington: Indiana University Press, 1992), pp. 159–170.

74. Nick Land, *The Thirst for Annihilation: Georges Batailles and Virulent Nihilism* (London: Routledge, 1992), p. 5.

75. The term "ontotheology" was first used by Kant and then, following him, by Hegel. Here in my text the term is meant to depict two related things: (i) following Heidegger's essay in the volume *Identity and Difference*, it refers to the entry of the Deity into any discourse based on reason, i.e., the circular dependence of the principle of reason on God; (ii) the essential continuity of the Greek (*onto*), mediaeval (*theo*), and modern humanist (*logic*) traditions as components of the broader Western religio-cultural-philosophical traditions. In this sense it is essentially continuous with the term "metaphysics." For a detailed discussion of this see Martin Heidegger, "The Onto-Theo-Logical Constitution of Metaphysics," *Identity and Difference*, trans. Joan Stambaugh (New York: Harper Torchbooks, 1969), pp. 42–74.

76. Eric Alliez, *Capital Times: Tales from the Conquest of Time* (Minneapolis: University of Minnesota Press), pp. 238–239.

77. If originality is to be accorded to anyone it has to go to Bhāī Vīr Singh, whose historical novels (such as *Sundri*, *Satwant Kaur*, *Bijai Singh*, *Baba Naud Singh*) were pivotal to the Sikh reformist effort to relocate Sikh tradition within an historical context. BVS's novels are best seen as contributions to the genre of historical fiction. That is to say, the novels were crafted in a form that used footnotes and annotations and included detailed prefaces explaining the sources of data in the novels. This particular form did much to persuade his readers that the novels were in fact historical rather than fictional. In a very real sense, therefore, BVS's novels contain the seeds of the conceptual transition from the indigenous multiplicity of narratives told in vernacular languages (N_1) to the modern nationalized narratives that are more attuned to the narrative time of empire (N_2), which carries the self-designation of "history". This shift from N_1 to N_2 is similar to but by no means the same as Dipesh Chakrabarty's transition from history 1 to history 2 (see Chakrabarty's *Provincializing Europe*, chap. 2). Despite the novelty of BVS's historical fictions, I have chosen to overlook his narrative constructions as this would take up far more space than is available here. I have therefore chosen to focus on Teja Singh's narrative, which is much shorter and more politically nuanced than BVS's narrative. Moreover, Teja's Singh's narrative is set in the crucial decade of the 1920s—the same time that the theological commentaries on scripture were being written

78. Teja Singh, *The Growth of Responsibility in Sikhism* (herafter *GRS*), 4th ed. (Amritsar, 1928), pp. iii–iv.

79. Teja Singh, *GRS*, p. 13.

80. Teja Singh, *GRS*, p. 1.

81. Homi Bhabha, *The Location of Culture* (London: Routledge, 1993), p. 143.

82. Teja Singh, *GRS*, p. 13.

83. Teja Singh, *GRS*, p. 9.

84. Teja Singh, *GRS*, pp. ii–iii.

85. Teja Singh, *GRS*, p. 13.

86. Teja Singh, *GRS*, p. 6.

87. Bhabha, *Location of Culture*, p. 144.

88. The foregoing analysis of the Singh Sabhā's narrative construction of "Sikh history" allows us to reflect briefly on the notion of "hermeneutics" itself, and particularly on the need to be more cautious about such terms, especially in a postcolonial context. My main concern, which was developed in chapter 1, is that there are increasing numbers of interpretations of South Asian religion and philosophy that simply assume that the interaction between Orientalists and native elite scholars was "dialogical"—a dialogue between tradition and texts and with the Orientalists resulting in a concordance with the narrative of Western modernity. The danger in assuming notions such as "dialogue" (and the corresponding notions of agency) in the colonial context is that: (i) they are oblivious of power relations between the parties supposed to be in dialogical communication; (ii) there is a tendency to assume a common humanistic context of communication, and thus the universal basis for cross-cultural thinking. Such interpretations rely on a facile adoption of hermeneutic theory as a paradigmatic model for communication, particularly the dialogical theory of hermeneutics expounded by Paul Ricoeur, and to an extent H.-G. Gadamer

and Charles Taylor (see Charles Taylor, *Sources of the Self* [Cambridge: Cambridge University Press, 1989]; Hans Georg Gadamer, *Truth and Method* [London: Sheed and Ward, 1989]). Ricoeur and Taylor are both leading exponents of views that seek to defend the humanistic and therefore universal basis of Western civilization. For Ricoeur, narration is the imaginative act that configures a more primordial experience into something with meaning and structure. Primordial experience has an inchoate prenarrative quality that "constitutes a genuine demand for narrative." This "demand" is, as we have seen, an imperative, a moral obligation. Ricoeur defends this moral imperative by saying that "[T]ime becomes human . . . to the extent that it is organized after the manner of a narrative." In effect, Ricoeur is stressing that narrative is based on the notion of a universal human moral order, what he calls a "transcultural necessity."

But insofar as it is *historical*, is this "transcultural *necessity*" not the same as the necessity that underpins Hegel's passage from the speculative to the historical, which, as we have seen, is not a real transition at all but a circular, i.e., metaphorical, return to self, in effect a having-never-left-the-self (having always-already-crossed-over) as the center of the speculative standpoint? Does this "necessity" not condone without question the kind of dialogue as symmetrical communicative exchange that is historically continuous with colonialism?

What Ricoeur underplays is the significance of the artifices of the literary within the purportedly "natural" origins of narrative. The move whereby literary norms were imposed through colonial education and subsequently passed off as the "naturalization" of the native mind has its roots in what has alternatively been termed the natives' acceptance of the "natural light" or "Western metaphysics," their *willing* submission to a symbolic economy of exchange, or the capitulation of native resistance through the exchange of promises. Of course, Ricoeur is not saying that prenarrative experience lacks a narrative structure. But neither does he admit that it has a fully developed (i.e., human) structure. Hence the complications of Ricoeur's theories of threefold mimesis (where emplotment takes a *pre*-figured world of action or events and proposes a *con*-figuration that organizes worldly activity into a meaningful sequence with purpose) arise from the dialectical distinction between the binary opposites—prenarrative/narrative, implicit/explicit; chaos/order, etc.—that are fundamental to the master narrative of colonialist ethnography and native informancy, and also to the Hegelian master/slave dialectic, which is based on a similar scenario. Here experience (the given) *naturally* goes over into narration, rather than certain narrative structures being imposed upon experience. The activity of going-over into narrative (which is passed off as natural or transparent) is morally justified by the practical need for the untold story to be told. However, the activity of "going-over" is, as Ricoeur states, an imaginative act, a metaphoric act, an act of ordering. It is a going-over as *meta*-pherein, one whose movement is from the sensuous realm of experience to the nonsensuous realm of the narrative's plot. The "going-over" is a moral act of crossing from a perceived or projected lack, exemplified by metonymy, to the activity of creating, exemplified by metaphor. This movement from the world of action (mimesis[1]) to the stage of creative configuration (mimesis[2]) is essentially mimetic. But the mimetic process is claimed as "natural" by native elite and colonial ethnographer alike. For them, and Ricoeur, there is no disparity, no alienation in passing from one to the other. It is an act of total exchange, typical of hermeneutic retrieval.

Ricoeur's model of threefold mimesis does not allow us to see that the activity of "going-over" is in fact a cultural translation, but imposed as a "trans-cultural (i.e., historical) *necessity*," a move that, as with Hegel, effectively negates the temporality of circumstance. While the theory is grounded on the fact that narrative involves a "search for concordance that is part of the unavoidable assumptions of discourse and communication," it fails to note that between colonizer and colonized there could not have been any communication or dialogue, except within the ambit of the colonizer's own understanding. The disparity of power relations ensured the occurrence of a form of mimesis, though it would be disguised as the "natural" humanization of native culture under the literary norm (narrative) of the dominant symbolic order.

89. Ernest Trumpp, *The Ādi Granth; or, The Holy Scriptures of the Sikhs* (1877; repr. New Delhi: Munshiram Manoharlal, 1989).

90. *Ādi Granth*, p. 940. Translation my own.

91. This is what I would call a typical Singh Sabhā translation (especially "One God exists"). Though now it is now often replaced by "One Being," etc., still the intended meaning circulates within the same metaphysical form.

92. Despite the connotations of the word "deconstruction"—associated in particular with the work of Martin Heidegger and Jacques Derrida—this mode of regressive analysis is not intended to undermine tradition but rather to recall what it was about. "Deconstruction" here means finding the rule according to which the concepts were formed out of an experience of being, and then tracing backward the motion of their genesis. Deconstruction thus involves a "double reading," which on the one hand pays close attention to the texts of a particular tradition, but on the other hand, *in that very attention*, discloses a rupture in these texts that requires a radically different reading of the tradition, thus destabilizing it and, in the undecidability thereby created, opening the possiblity of thinking differently.

93. I shall refer mainly to noted scholars such as Bhāī Vīr Singh, Kahn Singh Nabha, Teja Singh, Jodh Singh, and Sāhib Singh.

94. Teja Singh, *Śabdarth Sri Guru Granth Sāhib*, 8th ed. (Amritsar: Shiromani Gurdwara Parbandhak Committee, June 1996), p. 1.

95. *Om* was also a focal point with the Indian philosophical traditions, especially in the two main forms of Vedānta (Advaita and Visist-Advaita) and Saṁkhyā-Yoga. In the Vedāntic systems *oṁ* is the *śabdabrahman*, the word or symbol that stands for the supreme being (Brahman), which has two forms, *Nirguṇa* and *Saguṇa*. According to the standard accounts, the non-ualistic Advaita-Vedānta associated with the ninth-century Śaivite ascetic Śankara emphasized the Nirguṇa over Saguṇa aspect, with the result that sects and philosophies based on this system tended toward an abstract monism, metaphysical contemplation, or extreme asceticism. In contrast, the qualified nondualism of Visist-Advaita Vedānta associated with the twelfth-century Vaiṣṇavite thinker Ramanuja emphasized the Saguṇa aspect, either resulting in a defense of polytheism or serving as a definitive factor in the rise of the *bhakti* movement as rejuvenation of true Hindu religion.

96. Pashaura Singh, *The Guru Granth Sāhib: Canon, Meaning, and Authority* (New Delhi: Oxford University Press, 2000), pp. 249–250.

97. Taran Singh, *Gurbanī Dīān Viākhiā Pranālīān* (Patiala: Punjabi University, 1980), pp. 119–187.

98. Kahn Singh Nabha, *Gurshabad Ratnakar Mahan Kośh* (Patiala: Bhāshā Vibhāg, 1931; repr. 1981), p. 21.

99. Jodh Singh, *Gurmat Nirnai*, 9th ed. (Ludhiana: Academy Press, 1932), p. 1.

100. Bhāī Vīr Singh, *Santhyā Sri Guru Granth Sāhib* (New Delhi: Bhai Vir Singh Sahit Sadan, 1958; repr. 1997), vol. 1, p. 2.

101. BVS, *Santhyā*, p. 2.

102. BVS, *Santhyā*, p. 1.

103. J. Laplanche and J.-B. Pontalis, *The Language of Psychoanalysis* (London: Karnac Books, 1974), pp. 166–169.

104. BVS, *Santhyā*, p. 2.

105. BVS, *Santhyā*, p. 2.

106. BVS, *Santhyā*, p. 3.

107. See footnotes to BVS, *Santhyā*, p. 3.

108. BVS, *Panj Granthī Satīk* (New Delhi: Bhāī Vīr Singh Sahīt Fadan, 1962), pp. 1–2. See also *Santhyā*, p. 10.

109. Kahn Singh Nabha, *Gurshabad Ratnakar Mahan Kośh*, pp. 148–149.

110. Teja Singh, *Śabdarth Sri Guru Granth Sāhib*, p. 1.

111. Sāhib Singh, *Sri Guru Granth Sāhib Darpan* (Jullundar: Raj Publishers, 1964), vol. 1, p. 46.

112. Jodh Singh, *Gurmat Nirnai*, p. 1.

113. BVS, *Santhyā*, p. 1.

114. BVS, *Santhyā*, pp. 10–11.

115. See "Cratylus," trans. Benjamin Jowett, in *Plato: The Collected Dialogues*, ed. Edith Hamilton and Huntington Cairns (Princeton: Princeton University Press, 1961), pp. 421–474.

116. BVS, *Santhyā*, p. 7.

117. BVS, *Santhyā*, p. 10.

118. BVS, *Santhyā*, p. 11.

119. BVS, *Santhyā*, p. 11.

120. BVS, *Santhyā*, p. 11.

121. BVS, *Santhyā*, p. 11.

122. BVS, *Santhyā*, p. 11.

123. BVS, *Santhyā*, p. 12.

124. BVS, *Santhyā*, p. 16.

125. Kahn Singh Nabha, *Gurshabad Ratnakar Mahan Kośh*, p. 36.

126. Jodh Singh, *Gurmat Nirnai*, p. 1.

127. Sāhib Singh, 1964, pp. 46–47.

128. BVS, *Santhyā*, pp. 1, 27.

129. BVS, *Santhyā*, p. 27.

130. BVS, *Santhyā*, pp. 27–28.

131. The word *partīt* means "belief, faith, or trust." See BVS, *Santhyā*, pp. 27–28.

132. BVS, *Santhyā*, pp. 27–28.

133. BVS, *Santhyā*, p. 28.

134. Paulo Gonçalves, "Vital Necrographies: Deconstruction, God, and Arche-Idolatry," *Scottish Journal of Religious Studies* 19.1 (1998): 90.

135. According to this scholastic doctrine, *scientia dei*, or God's knowledge as absolute cognition, is the measure of all knowing, possible and actual (*omnitudo realitatis*). God's knowledge is the naturally necessary knowledge (*scientia necessaria naturalis*) since it belongs to the nature of God as absolute self-consciousness or absolute self-presence. God knows what is thought in this absolute thinking through his *scientia visionis*—where *visio* is a grasping in the manner of *praesens intuitus* (present intuition). In Aquinas' *Summa Theologica* the word *praesens* is understood from the perspective of eternity: *aeternitas, quae sine successione existens totum tempus comprehendit*—eternity, which, existing without succession, comprises the totality of time. Thus in contrast to *successione*, *praesens* means that God's intuition is not a temporal series of intuitive acts but realizes itself in the eternal now, or *nunc stans*. Furthermore, God's knowledge also includes all that can be stated in propositions. But the question is whether God knows possible statements through composing and dividing, as would be the case for finite human knowing, which happens successively in time: "Our intellect," states Aquinas, "proceeds from one thing to another." In God, however, there is no succession. Whereas man, because of successivity, must render what is known separately into a unity by way of composing and dividing, God knows as an original unity, all at once, in a moment that is not a *nunc fluens* but remains the same for eternity. The knowledge of God therefore flows from the eternity of God, which in turn is inferred from immutability. The order of inference in scholastic theology [*simplicitas immutabilitas aeternitas*] indicates that while God's attributes (unity, immutability, eternity) are interchangeable to the point of being indistinguishable, they all flow from absolute self-presence: the *intuitus praesens*.

136. For example, nothing like the ontological proof for God's existence can be detected in Taran Singh's analysis of the various streams of Sikh interpretive tradition (*Gurbanī Dīān Viākhiā Pranālīān*).

137. Martin Heidegger, *The Principle of Reason*, trans. Reginald Lily (Bloomington: Indian University Press, 1991), pp. 26–28.

138. Heidegger, *Metaphysical Foundations of Logic*, pp. 161–162.

139. Although space prevents me from pursuing this point in any detail, Indic notions of transcendence have been, as the Hegelian stereotype (not incorrectly) suggests, "mired" in the sensuous, in time and the body, and therefore less concerned with universals of the kind seen in Western philosophy. While the Hegelian stereotype is clearly racist, chauvinist, and imperialist, its fault lies not so much in the fact that it demarcates a difference between Oriental and Occidental forms of thinking, but rather that it enables the reproduction of this difference as evidence of an Oriental lack. Its narrative therefore exhibits a transition-to-capitalism.

140. Jacques Derrida, *Rogues: Two Essays on Reason*, trans. Pascale-Anne Brault and Michael Naas (Stanford: Stanford University Press, 2005), p. 11.

141. Derrida, *Rogues*, p. 15.

142. Derrida, *Rogues*, p. 16.

143. Derrida, *Rogues*, p. 15.

144. J. S. Grewal, "Sikh Identity, the Akalis, and Khalistan," in *Punjab in Prosperity and Violence*, ed. J. S. Grewal and Indu Bhanga (New Delhi: K. K. Publishers, 1997), p. 92.

145. *The Sikh Rahit Maryāda* (Amritsar: Shiromani Gurdwara Prabhandak Committee, 1950).

146. http://www.sgpc.net/rehat_maryada/section_one.html.

147. Probably the best example of scholarship that espouses such an approach, and the only substantial academic work on Sikh ethics, is Avtar Singh's *Ethics of the Sikhs* (Patiala: Punjabi University, 1983).

148. This is an issue that is outside the scope of this present work and will be take up elsewhere.

149. See Grace Jantzen's discussion of necrophilia in her *Becoming Divine: Towards a Feminist Philosophy of Religion* (Manchester: Manchester University Press, 1998).

150. See for example Louis Fenech, *Martyrdom in the Sikh Tradition*, Oxford, New Delhi, 2001.

151. Brian Axel, *The Nation's Tortured Body: Violence, Representation, and the Formation of a Sikh "Diaspora"* (Durham: Duke University Press, 2001).

152. Brayton Polka, "The Ontological Argument For Existence," in *Difference in Philosophy of Religion*, ed. Phillip Goodchild (Aldershot: Ashgate), pp. 15–32.

153. See Jodh Singh, *Gurmat Nirnai*.

154. See Sher Singh, *The Philosophy of Sikhism* (Amritsar: Shiromani Gurdwara Parbhandhak Committee, 1944); G. S. Talib, *Guru Nanak: His Personality and Vision* (New Delhi: Gur Das Kapur, 1969), *Impact of Guru Gobind Singh on Indian Society* (Chandigarh, 1966); Gopal Singh, *A History of the Sikh People* (New Delhi: 1969); Daljeet Singh, *Sikhism: A Comparative Study of Its Theology and Mysticism* (New Delhi: Sterling, 1979); Jasbir Singh Ahluwalia, *Sovereignty of the Sikh Doctrine* (New Delhi: Bahri, 1983); Khushwant Singh, *A History of the Sikhs* (Princeton: Princeton University Press, 1966).

4. Violence, Mysticism, and the Capture of Subjectivity

1. The Shiromani Gurdwara Parbhandhak Committee.

2. Verne Dusenbury, "'Nation' or 'World Religion'? Master Narratives of Sikh Identity," in *Sikh Identity: Continuity and Change*, ed. Pashaura Singh and N. G. Barrier (New Delhi: Manohar, 1999), p. 133.

3. Dusenbury, "Master Narratives," p. 134.

4. Dusenbury, "Master Narratives," p. 134.

5. N. G. Barrier, foreword to *Discovering the Sikhs: Autobiography of a Historian*, by Hew McLeod (New Delhi: Permanent Black, 2004), p. ix.

6. Even the most cursory account of these events would have to recall the bitter and almost suicidal conflict between Sikhs and the Indian state that became part of

the overall political drama in South Asia during the 1980s. This political drama would have to include the following events: the role of Pakistan and the CIA in manufacturing Mujahadeen and Taliban Islamic guerilla movements to oust Soviet occupancy in early 1980s; the end of the Cold War with strategic rethinking of the roles of India and Pakistan in the South Asia region; the rise of religious nationalism in the form of the Hindutva movement and a resurgent BJP's challenge to secular Congress I control of Indian politics; internal Sikh politics in Punjab (Akalis versus Congress); Operation Bluestar (June 1984), the assassination of Indira Gandhi (Oct. 1984), the anti-Sikh pogroms in Delhi (Nov. 1984); the emergence of Sikh separatism and militant insurgency in Punjab. Linked to all of this was the mediatization of the Sikh image, that is, the creation of a "bad Sikh"/"good Sikh" media stereotype in which the "bad Sikh" is a turbaned and militant Sikh of the Khalsā, whereas the "good Sikh" is a the pacifist follower of Guru Nānak. Notwithstanding the global circulation of this media stereotype and the resultant political commentaries—which projected an image of the Sikhs as potentially unreliable, religious fundamentalists, an anti-state, separatist community, and which earned Sikhs considerable notoriety during the 1980s and 1990s—it is important to remember that the Sikhs were mostly *re*active rather than *pro*active players in the wider set of events in South Asia and beyond. Without political autonomy even in their so-called homeland of Punjab, they were effectively at the mercy of the Indian state and its machinations regarding regional and global powers. A good example of this is what Barrier terms the "wars over scholarship and Sikhism" and consequently the relationship between Sikhs and the institution of the Western university. Faced with the very negative stereotypes of Sikhs and Sikhism circulating in the mid-80s, a number of Sikh intellectuals took inspiration from the ability of the stateless Palestinians to manipulate their own image in the global media and turned to the university in the hope of using it as a venue to generate a more favorable form of knowledge about Sikhs and Sikhism and thereby stem the prevailing media representation of Sikhs as turbaned terrorists and religious fanatics.

7. McLeod, *Discovering the Sikhs.*

8. For details of this issue see, for example, Cynthia Mahmoud, *Fighting for Faith and Nation: Dialogues with Sikh Militants* (Philadelphia: University of Pennyslvania Press, 1996); J. S. Grewal, *Contesting Interpretations of the Sikh Tradition* (New Delhi: Manohar, 1998); Brian Axel, *The Nation's Tortured Body: Violence, Representation, and the Formation of a Sikh "Diaspora"* (Durham: Duke University Press, 2000).

9. I. J. Singh, *Sikhs and Sikhism: A View with a Bias* (New York, 1994), p. 78.

10. G. S. Dhillon, review of Harjot Oberoi's *The Construction of Religious Boundaries* (Chicago: University of Chicago Press, 1994), in *Sikh Review* 42.7 (July 1994): 59.

11. W. H. McLeod, "Cries of Outrage: History Versus Tradition in the Study of the Sikh Community," *South Asia Research* 14 (1994): 121–135.

12. I am aware that McLeod makes a distinction between Guru Nānak's theology and later Sikh theology (see his *Guru Nānak and the Sikh Religion* [New Delhi: Oxford University Press, 1968], p. 163). But as I shall explain, in light of his future writings on the subject, this is is largely a subterfuge.

13. W. H. McLeod, *Sikhism* (London: Penguin, 1998), pp. xxiv–xxv.

14. Readers will note that I have used two possible spellings for *nirguṇa/saguṇa* and *nirguṇ/sarguṇ*. The former terms refer to the Sanskritic tradition, and the latter refer to the Punjabi (non-Sanskritic) tradition. Strictly speaking, their meanings are pretty much the same.

15. Karine Schomer and W. H. McLeod, *The Sants: Studies in a Devotional Tradition of India* (New Delhi: Motilal Banarsidas, 1987).

16. Frits Staal, "The Ineffable Nirguṇa Brahman," in *The Sants: Studies in a Devotional Tradition of India*, ed. Karine Schomer and W. H. McLeod (New Delhi: Motilal Banarsidas, 1987), pp. 41–47.

17. See Grace Jantzen's *Becoming Divine: Towards a Feminist Philosophy of Religion* (Manchester: Manchester University Press, 1998).

18. See Richard King, *Orientalism and Religion: Postcolonial Theory, India, and the "Mystic East"* (London: Routledge, 1999), pp. 161–186.

19. McLeod, *Sikhism*, p. 14.

20. McLeod, *Sikhism*, p. 13.

21. See for example Hent de Vries' *Minimal Theologies: Critiques of Secular Reason in Adorno and Levinas* (Baltimore: Johns Hopkins University Press, 2005) and Walter Benjamin's "Theses on the Philosophy of History," in *Illumination*, trans H. Zohn (London: Fontana Press, 1992).

22. McLeod, *Sikhism*, p. 25.

23. See Tomoko Masuzawa, *In Search of Dream Time: The Quest for the Origin of Religion* (Chicago: University of Chicago Press, 1994).

24. McLeod, *GNSR*, p. 148.

25. W. H. McLeod, "A Sikh Theology for Modern Times" in *Sikh Religion and History in the Twentieth Century*, ed. W. T. Oxtoby, J. S. Grewal, Milton Israel, and W. H. McLeod (New Delhi: Manohar, 1990), p. 33.

26. McLeod, "A Sikh Theology," p. 33.

27. McLeod, "A Sikh Theology," pp. 32–33.

28. McLeod, *GNSR*, p. 168.

29. McLeod, *GNSR*, p. 175.

30. McLeod, *GNSR*, p. 190.

31. McLeod, *GNSR*, p. 191.

32. Strictly speaking, of course, the first anamneut and scribe of the *Ādi Granth* text did repeatedly raise the question concerning definitions of the Guru/Sikh, or master/pupil, relationship. But Bhāī Gurdās was largely concerned with the question "Who is the *true* Guru?," which arose in response to dissidence within the early Sikh community. However, the question referred to above, "What is a guru?," is a strictly metaphysical question that only really comes into focus after the *death* of the living (*dehdhārī*) guru and the *birth* of the *Ādi Granth* text *as a text*.

33. *Dehdhārī* is a Punjabi word composed of the words *deh* (body) and *dhārī* (manifested). Hence: "bodily manifestation."

34. See Harbans Singh, *Heritage of the Sikhs* (Delhi: Manohar, 1983), pp. 107–111.

35. There is no natural bond of signification that binds the terms "Khalsā" and "Panth." Both were used throughout North India (indeed "Khalsā" has its origins in the Persian *khalisa*="crown lands") during and before the time of the Sikh Gurus.

The Punjabi word "Panth" has its origins in the Sanskrit *pantha*, which denotes a way/path to be lived or followed. "Panth" is therefore temporal in signification, which contrasts sharply with the kind of spatialized signification it has received at the hands of the Singh Sabhā and other colonial interpreters, especially in relation to the Persian word *qaum*, meaning "tribe" or "people."

36. J. S. Grewal, "Ideas Operative in Early Sikh History," in *The Khalsā Over Three Hundred Years*, ed. J. S. Grewal and Indu Banga (New Delhi: Tulika), p. 23.

37. Grewal, "Early Sikh History," p. 24.

38. See J. S. Grewal, *Sikh Ideology, Polity, and Social Order* (New Delhi: Manohar, 1996), pp. 87–121.

39. See chapter 6.

40. *Time in Indian Philosophy*, J. N. Mohanty and Balslev (Leiden: Brill, 1996).

41. This rather quick summary does not do justice to a topic that is of real importance in the history of interpretation of the Sikh scriptures, namely the historical evolution of the notion of Guru and the relationship between this notion and the written text. To my knowledge there is no substantial published work in this area apart from Taran Singh's *Gurbānī dīān Viākhiā Prnālīān* (Patiala, 1980) and Darshan Singh's *Bhāī Gurdās: Sikhī de Pahle Viākhiakār* (Patiala, 1986). A shortage of space prevents me from taking up this task in the present thesis. The main reason why such a study could not have been undertaken in the last half-century or so is the stranglehold exerted by of one of the central paradigms in the study of South Asian culture generally, namely the dominance and privileging of *orality* over *writing* as this emerges from within the ancient Vedic or Brahmanic metaphysics, as well as the complicity of colonial constructions of Indo-Aryan linguistics with this ancient metaphysics. Exposing this constraining paradigm has two effects: (i) it inverts the view that metaphysics and therefore "philosophy-as-metaphysics" solely belongs to the religious and intellectual history of the West, and (ii) it questions the entire opposition between Nānak Panth and Khalsā Panth as based on the equation between Nānak's "mystical" teaching and the Sanātan tradition. These issues will be taken up more fully in chapter 6.

42. H. S. Oberoi, *The Construction of Religious Boundaries: Culture, Identity, and Diversity in the Sikh Tradition* (Oxford (1994), pp. 258–376.

43. The word *sat(i)* is translated as "true." *Sat(i)* is derived from the Sanskrit *satya* (root *asi*), which corresponds to the English verb "to be." The question, though, is what the translated word "true/truth" signifies within the Western domain, given that it is implicated within certain historical moves of translation from Greek to Latin and from Latin to the modern European languages.

44. As opposed to the question: "*What is* a guru?," implying that for the Singh Sabhā scholars also, the *Ādi Granth* was treated as an icon that *represented* the personality or living presence of the Guru rather than a text. See further on.

45. Jodh Singh, *Gurmat Nirnai*, 9th ed. (Ludhiana: Academy Press, 1932), p. 113.

46. Jodh Singh, *Gurmat Nirnai*, p. 114.

47. Jodh Singh, *Gurmat Nirnai*, pp. 113–115 (my translation).

48. While this tendency is more marked in Jodh Singh's case, it is certainly not absent in the work of other prominent Sabhā scholars. For example, Kahn Singh makes a second entry under the title *nam* in his *Gurshabad Ratnakar (Mahan Kosh)* as fol-

lows: *gurbānī vic "nām" kartā ate us dā hukam bowdak śabda bhī hain**, with the following footnote: *baibal (Bible) *vic issai nū* "Word" *likhiā hain.*

49. *Gurmat Nirnai*, pp. 211–249.

50. Lit. "unbeaten or unstruck," i.e., where the source of the sound effaces itself in the moment of being sounded. In the *Ādi Granth* the words *anhad/anāhad* are variants of the Sanskrit *anahata*. The term *śabda* often occurs within the *Ādi Granth* in combination with the term *anhad* (or its variant *anāhad*). *Anhad* has a very long tradition within Hindu—particularly Nāth and Yogic—"theories" of language. This fact was frequently used by followers of the Sanātan tradition to argue for the inclusion of Sikh scripture under the authority of Hindu tradition. The term *anhad* thus becomes a point of controversy, and as part of this controversy Jodh Singh tries to show that within Sikh usage *anhad* is significantly removed from Hinduism.

51. For details see Alain Daniélou's *Yoga: Mastering the Secrets of Matter and the Universe* (Vermont: Inner Traditions, 1991); Mircea Eliade's *Yoga: Immortality and Freedom* (Princeton: Princeton University Press, 1990); or Fernando Tola and Carmen Dragonetti's *The Yogasutras of Patañjali* (New Delhi: Motilal Banarsidas, 1987).

52. Jodh Singh, *Gurmat Nirnai*, p. 130.

53. Jodh Singh, *Gurmat Nirnai*, p. 134.

54. Jodh Singh, *Gurmat Nirnai*, p. 243.

55. Jodh Singh, *Gurmat Nirnai*, p. 220.

56. Jodh Singh, "Theological Concepts in Sikhism," paper presented at a Christian-Sikh Dialogue Conference, Baring College, Batala, 1963.

57. *rāg* = musical measure in the Indian musical system; *dhun* = "note or tune of singular quality"; *nād* = "sound."

58. Jodh Singh, *Gurmat Nirnai*, pp. 211–249.

59. Jodh Singh, "Theological Concepts in Sikhism."

60. Further and more detailed reference will be made to time in chapter 5.

61. McLeod, *GNSR*, p. 190.

62. McLeod, *GNSR*, p. 189.

63. McLeod, *GNSR*, p. 175.

64. McLeod, *GNSR*, p. 195.

65. McLeod, *GNSR*, p. 197.

66. McLeod, *GNSR*, p. 197.

67. Ernest Trumpp, *The Ādi Granth; or, The Holy Scriptures of the Sikhs* (1877; repr. New Delhi: Munshiram Manoharlal, 1989), p. 942.

68. McLeod, *GNSR*, p. 199.

69. McLeod, *GNSR*, p. 190.

70. McLeod, *GNSR*, p. 199.

71. See for example Martin Heidegger, "Words," trans. J. Stambuagh, in *On the Way to Language* (San Francisco: Harper Collins, 1971), pp. 139–158.

72. Martin Heidegger, "Lecture VI," in *What Is Called Thinking?*, trans. Fred D. Weick and John Glenn Gray (New York: Harper and Row, 1982), pp. 57–62.

73. See for example Martin Heidegger's discussion of the being of language in his essay "The Nature of Language," in *On the Way to Language*, trans. Peter Hertz (San Franscisco: Harper Collins, 1982), p. 94.

74. See Jacques Derrida, *Speech and Phenomena, and Other Essays on Husserl's Theory of Signs*, trans. David B. Allison (Evanston: Northwestern University Press, 1973); and *Edmund Husserl's "Origin of Geometry": An Introduction*, trans. John P. Leavey Jr. (Lincoln: University of Nebraska Press, 1989).

75. Edmund Husserl, *Logical Investigations, Vol. 1 (1900–1901)* (London: Routledge and Kegan, 1970), p. 274.

76. Derrida, *Speech and Phenomena*, pp. 32–45.

77. Jacques Derrida, *Positions*, trans. Alan Bass (Chicago: University of Chicago Press, 1972), p. 23.

78. Derrida, *Speech and Phenomena*, pp. 75–82.

79. Derrida, *Speech and Phenomena*, p. 77.

80. In this model of the mind, to which I shall return briefly in chapter 6, this absence is best understood as an absence of ego. This does not mean the annihilation of ego but the annulment of ego's self-attachment that normally goes on in the very moment of its speaking. When it is able to cultivate such a mode of speaking-thinking, the mind is able to remove all traces of self-relationality.

81. Jacques Derrida, *Of Grammatology*, trans. Gayatri Chakravorty Spivak (Baltimore: Johns Hopkins University Press, 1976), pp. 20–26.

82. Derrida, *Of Grammatology*, p. 11.

83. Derrida, *Of Grammatology*, p. 11.

84. Aristotle, *On Interpretation* 1.16a.3.

85. McLeod, *GNSR*, pp. vii–viii.

86. McLeod, *GNSR*, p. 148.

87. McLeod, *GNSR*, pp. 148–150.

88. John Hick, *An Interpretation of Religion: Human Responses to the Transcendent* (Basingstoke: Macmillan Academic, 1989).

89. William James, *The Varieties of Religious Experience: A Study in Human Nature* (London: Longmans, Green and Co., 1928).

90. Hick, *An Interpretation of Religion*, p. 156.

91. Hick, *An Interpretation of Religion*, p. 157.

92. Hick, *An Interpretation of Religion*, p. 158.

93. Russell McCutcheon, *Manufacturing Religion: Sui Generis Religion and the Politics of Nostalgia* (New York: Oxford University Press, 2000).

94. McCutcheon, *Manufacturing Religion*, p. 105.

95. McCutcheon, *Manufacturing Religion*, p. 118.

96. McCutcheon, *Manufacturing Religion*, p. 70.

97. McCutcheon, *Manufacturing Religion*, p. 70.

98. McCutcheon, *Manufacturing Religion*, p. 192.

99. McCutcheon, *Manufacturing Religion*, p. 31.

100. Derrida, *Husserl's "Origin of Geometry,"* p. 76.

101. Derrida, *Husserl's "Origin of Geometry,"* pp. 66–71.

102. Derrida, *Husserl's "Origin of Geometry,"* p. 77.

103. Derrida, *Husserl's "Origin of Geometry,"* p. 86.

104. Derrida, *Husserl's "Origin of Geometry,"* pp. 114–115.

105. Derrida, *Husserl's "Origin of Geometry,"* p. 111.

106. Derrida, "Theology of Translation," *Eyes of the University: Right to Philosophy 2*, trans. Jan Plug et al. (Stanford: Stanford University Press, 2004), p. 75.

107. Derrida, "Theology of Translation," p. 73.

108. There is an obvious connection here between Derrida's notion of "generalized translation" and Heidegger's explication of humanism as inaugurating "the age of the world picture."

109. Michel Foucault, *Discipline and Punish: The Birth of a Prison* (New York: Pantheon, 1977), p. 201.

110. McLeod, "Cries of Outrage," p. 126.

111. McLeod, "Cries of Outrage," pp. 132–133.

112. Tomoko Masuzawa, *In Search of Dreamtime: The Quest for the Origin of Religion* (Chicago: University of Chicago Press, 1994), p. 15.

113. Masuzawa, *In Search of Dreamtime*, p. 168.

114. See for example Russell McCutcheon's discussion of liberalism in the study of religion in his *The Discipline of Religion: Structure, Meaning, Rhetoric* (New York: Routledge, 2003), p. 32.

115. Michael D. Hardt and Antonio Negri, *Multitude: War and Democracy in an Age of Empire* (New York: Penguin, 2004), p. 25.

116. Hardt and Negri, *Multitude*, p. 29.

117. See Derrida, "Faith and Knowledge," pp. 33 and 58.

118. "Lost in the Terrorist Theater," *Harper's*, October 1984, 43.

119. Melanie McAlister, "Iran, Islam, and the Terrorist Threat, 1979–1989," in *Terrorism, Media, Liberation*, ed. J. David Slocum (New Brunswick: Rutgers University Press, 2005), pp. 151–157.

120. See Brian Axel's *The Nation's Tortured Body: Violence, Representation, and the Formation of a Sikh "Diaspora"* (Durham: Duke University Press, 2001), pp. 110–112. Axel provides a very useful discussion of the strategies used by the Indian state to produce national integration and unity (*rashtriya ekta*). Particularly after the 1950s there were concerted attempts by the ruling Congress party to bring about national unity. As Axel argues: "The repeated address of *ekta*, or integration/oneness, has been organized and mediated, historically, by the procedures of the National Integration Committee (NIC). . . . The NIC was initially convened by the Congress Working Committee in 1958, after the 1957 'Jabalpur riot,' to address the emerging problem of 'fissiparious tendencies in the body-politic of our country.' . . . In the 1970s the NIC turned its efforts to the problems of 'internal dangers': casteism, communalism, and separatism. Between 1983 and 1992, the activities of the NIC were almost exclusively concerned with the threat of Sikh 'terrorists.'" Indira Gandhi often presided over the NIC between 1960 and 1984.

121. Christophe Jaffrelot, *The Hindu Nationalist Movement and Indian Politics: 1925–1990s* (London: Hurst, 1996), pp. 346–353.

122. Richard Davis, "The Iconography of Ram's Chariot," in *Making India Hindu: Religion, Community, and the Politics of Democracy in India*, ed. David Ludden (New Delhi: Oxford University Press, 1996), p. 40.

123. For details see, for example: Gurharpal Singh, *Ethnic Conflict in India: A Case Study of Punjab* (London: Macmillan, 2000); Giorgio Shani, *Sikh Nationalism and Identity in a Global Age* (London: Routledge, 2008).

124. See, for example: J. S Grewal, "Sikhs, Akalis, and Khalistan," in *Punjab in Violence and Prosperity*, ed. J. S. Grewal and Indu Bhanga (New Delhi, 1997); Giorgio Shani, *Sikh Nationalism and Identity in a Global Age* (London: Routledge, 2008); Gurharpal Singh, *Ethnic Conflict in India: A Case Study of Punjab* (New London: Macmillan, 2000).

125. Agitations against the Nirāṅkarī sect in 1978 and the assassination of their guru, Baba Gurbachan Singh in 1980, are thought to have been organized by the Dal Khalsā, which it seems was supported by the local committee in charge, the Delhi *gurdwaras,* and Congress party officials connected to these *gurdwaras.* Another prominent event was the assassination in 1981 of Lala Jagat Narayan, the editor of a Haryana-based Hindu nationalist paper. Jarnail Singh Bhindranwale was implicated in this assassination, but the likely perpetrator was Dal Khalsā.

126. In regard to the question of "religious" violence, there is now a recognized connection between academic writing, media reporting, and policies of the secular state. See for example the recent article by Richard King, "The Association of 'Religion' with Violence: Reflections on a Modern Trope," in *Religion and Violence in South Asia: Theory and Practice*, ed. John Hinnells and Richard King (London: Routledge, 2006). King's article exposes the fundamental *doxa* about religion in the work of Mark Jurgensmeyer, one of the leading experts in religious terrorism, and someone who has also written about Sikh "terrorism." There is a close connection between the concept of religion (and especially Sikh "religion") deployed by Jurgensmeyer and many of the leading scholars in Sikh studies. Indeed that connection can be traced to the early work of W. H. McLeod, whose explication of "Sikh theology" captures Sikh subjectivity and installs it into a definition that will almost never be challenged again in academic Sikh studies. Consequently, in relation to Sikhism and the Punjab problem, there have been relatively few studies that treat the relationship between religion and violence in a critical manner. Notable examples are Birinder Pal Singh's article "The Logic of Sikh Militancy," in *Punjab in Violence and Prosperity* (1997), and Cynthia Mahmoud's *Fighting for Faith and Nation: Dialogues with Sikh Militants* (Philadelphia: University of Pennsylvania Press, 1996). Even these publications, however, do not subject the category of "religion" to any searching analysis.

Within the present chapter, an obvious avenue to explore would have been the state of academic writing on Sikh "terrorism." In the 1980s and 1990s numerous articles were written by so-called academics who became "experts" in Sikh "terrorism" literally overnight. Many of their articles appeared in national newspapers, particularly within the Indian and the British press. What needs to be analyzed in light of the more nuanced understanding about "religion" that exists today is how a certain a conceptualization of Sikh "religiosity" (i.e., a complacent certainty) was translated from the work of historians of religions, into the work of academics who specialize in the study of "religious" violence, and from there to the wider sphere of media journalism. My analysis in this chapter has been very limited due to considerations of space. This is an area that needs thorough and careful exploration and one that I intend to follow up in greater detail in a future publication.

127. Puar, "'The Turban is not a Hat': Queer Diaspora and Practices of Profiling," *Sikh Formations: Religion, Culture, and Theory* 4.1 (2008): 47–91.

128. Puar, "'Turban,'" p. 57.

129. Puar, "'Turban,'" p. 54.

130. Puar, "'Turban,'" p. 56.

131. *India Abroad*, May 14, 2004.

132. King, "Association of 'Religion' with Violence," p. 251.

133. See King, "Association of 'Religion' with Violence," pp. 251–252.

5. Ideologies of Sacred Sound

1. Russell T. McCutcheon, *The Discipline of Religion: Structure, Meaning, Rhetoric* (New York: Routledge, 2003), p. 54.

2. McCutcheon, *Discipline of Religion*, p. 66.

3. Michael D. Hardt and Antonio Negri, *Empire* (Cambridge, MA: Harvard University Press, 2000), p. 83.

4. Jacques Derrida, "Sign, Structure, and Play in the Discourse of the Human Sciences," in *Writing and Difference* (London: Routledge, 1978), pp. 278–294.

5. William Spanos, *The End of Education: Toward Posthumanism* (Minneapolis: University of Minnesota Press, 1995), p. 7.

6. Derrida, "Sign, Structure, and Play," p. 280.

7. Gianni Vattimo, "Hermeneutics and Anthropology," in *The End of Modernity: Nihilism and Hermeneutics in Postmodern Culture* (Cambridge: Polity Press, 1988), pp. 145–163. The way I situate hermeneutics and anthropology follows Vattimo's superb reading of the final chapter of Richard Rorty's *Philosophy and the Mirror of Nature*. In this text Rorty argues that it is better to envisage hermeneutics and anthropology as essentially related rather than opposed disciplines. There is, as Vattimo reads Rorty, a "sort of hermeneutical vocation for entering into an extremely close relationship with cultural anthropology, or rather, for dissolving itself into the latter" (p. 146). In other words, hermeneutics determines cultural anthropology because of its basic philosophical presupposition, namely the distinction "self versus other." For Vattimo, because of this horizon, which fundamentally connects the two disciplines, anthropology and hermeneutics should not be considered either as an encounter with radical alterity or as the systematic description of the human in terms of structure (p. 161). The connection between the two is particularly evident in the way that these two disciplines have approached the study of South Asian cultures, through a convergence best demonstrated by the history of religions. See below.

8. See Gianni Vattimo's *The End of Modernity* (Cambridge: Polity Press, 1988) and his *Nihilism and Emancipation: Ethics, Politics, and Law* (New York: Columbia University Press, 2004).

9. Wilfred Cantwell-Smith, "Comparative Religion: Whither? And Why?," in *The History of Religions: Essays in Methodology*, ed. Mircea Eliade and Joseph Kitigawa (Chicago: University of Chicago Press, 1958), pp. 32–33. These sentiments were echoed in kind by Mircea Eliade, who argued that the "dialogue" between East and West will have its basis in "the coming together of previously separated worlds, the

'planetization' of culture. . . . A true dialogue must deal with the central values in the culture of the participants. Now to understand these values correctly it is necessary to know their religious sources."

10. McCutcheon, *Discipline of Religion*, p. 69.

11. McCutcheon, *Discipline of Religion*, p. 73.

12. Such a project would involve looking closely at the notion of translation that is silently elided in almost all writings on hermeneutics, even in its more radical versions. This will become part of the sequel to this volume, tentatively entitled "Sikhism and Postsecular Thought."

13. McKim Marriott, "Hindu Transactions: Diversity Without Dualism," in *Transaction and Meaning: Directions in the Anthropology of Exchange and Symbolic Behavior*, ed. Bruce Kapferer (Philadelphia: Institute for the Study of Human Issues, 1976), pp. 109–142.

14. See also McKim Marriott, *India Through Hindu Categories* (Delhi: Sage, 1990), pp. 1–39.

15. McKim Marriott and Ronald Inden, "Toward an Ethnosociology of South Asian Caste Systems," in *The New Wind: Changing Identities in South Asia*, ed. David Kenneth (Paris: Mouton, 1977), p. 229.

16. Marriott and Inden, "Ethnosociology," p. 231.

17. I refer principally to the work of Franz Boaz, Edward Sapir, Benjamin Lee Whorf and Leonard Bloomfield in North America, and the work of Ferdinand de Saussure and Claude Lévi-Strauss in Europe.

18. Terence Hawkes, *Structuralism and Semiotics* (London: Routledge, 1977). Also useful is Winfried Nöth's more recent *Handbook of Semiotics* (Indiana University Press, 1994).

19. Walter J. Ong, *Orality and Literacy: The Technologizing of the Word* (London: Routledge, 1982); Jack Goody, *The Interface Between the Written and the Oral* (Cambridge: Cambridge University Press, 1987) and *Literacy in Traditional Societies* (Cambridge: Cambridge University Press, 1968); Marshall McLuhan, *The Gutenberg Galaxy: The Making of Typographic Man* (London: Routledge and Kegan Paul, 1962); Johannes Fabian, *Time and the Other: How Anthropology Makes Its Object* (New York: Columbia University Press, 1983).

20. Goody, *Literacy in Traditional Societies*, p. 2.

21. Ong, *Orality and Literacy*, p. 105.

22. Guy L. Beck, *Sonic Theology: Hinduism and Sacred Sound* (Delhi: Motilal Banarsidass, 1995).

23. See Marriott and Inden, "Ethnosociology."

24. Beck, *Sonic Theology*, pp. 2–3.

25. Fabian, *Time and the Other*, p. 106.

26. Beck, *Sonic Theology*, pp. 2–4.

27. Peter van der Veer, *Imperial Encounters: Religion and Modernity in India and Britain* (Princeton: Princeton University Press, 2001), p. 129.

28. Van der Veer, *Imperial Encounters*, pp. 121–122.

29. Verne Dusenbury, "The Word as Guru: Sikh Scripture and the Translation Controversy," *History of Religions* 34.4 (1992): 385–402.

30. Owen W. Cole, "The Settlement of Sikhs in the United Kingdom: Some Possible Consequences," in *Punjab Past and Present* 16–17 (1982): 417–424. See also Cole's *The Guru in Sikhism* (London: Longman and Todd, 1982).

31. The *akhaṇḍ pāṭh* signifies complete and unbroken recitation of the 1,430 pages of the *Guru Granth Sāhib*. Particularly in the last three decades it has become central to worship and the performance of life-cycle rituals. Prevalent opinion among Sikhs suggests that the practice of *akhaṇḍ pāṭh* originated from the turbulent period of the mid- to late eighteenth century when Khalsā Sikhs were in constant conflict with the Mughal authorities and were forced to move from place to place, carrying with them precious manuscript copies of the *Guru Granth Sāhib*. According to this narrative, whenever they found a chance for respite, they developed the practice of orally reciting the Granth without a break.

32. A useful introduction is Kristina Myrvold's *Inside The Guru's Gate: Ritual Uses of Texts Among the Sikhs in Varanasi*, Lund Studies in African and Asian Religions 17 (Lund: Media-Tryck, 2007).

33. Dusenbury, "The Word as Guru."

34. Dusenbury, "The Word as Guru," pp. 388–389.

35. Dusenbury, "The Word as Guru," p. 393.

36. Myrvold, *Inside The Guru's Gate*, p. 235.

37. Myrvold, *Inside The Guru's Gate*, p. 457.

38. Myrvold, *Inside The Guru's Gate*, p. 460.

39. Myrvold, *Inside The Guru's Gate*, p. 468.

40. Harjot Oberoi, *The Construction of Religious Boundaries: Culture, Identity, and Diversity in the Sikh Tradition* (New Delhi: Oxford University Press, 1994), p. 93.

41. Oberoi, *Construction of Religious Boundaries*, p. 107.

42. The term "Vedic" as I use it here refers to the Veda rather than the historical period called "Vedic civilization."

43. This line of thinking takes us toward a notion of "infancy" as central to what it means to be human. I hope to treat this notion of infancy in greater detail in the sequel to this book.

44. See, for example, *Śatapatha Brāhmana* 14.7.3.15, or *Rig Veda* 1.164.43 and 50; *Rig Veda* 10.90.16.

45. The etymology of *dharma* in the Rig Veda can be traced to the Sanskrit root *dhṛ*, which means "to support," or "to uphold."

46. Although there is even in the earliest Vedic documents a clearly recognizable, though mythical, awareness of a distinction between conquering *Āryas* and the indigenous inhabitants *dāsyu* or *dāsa*, the term *dharma* becomes prominent only in the Brāhmanas period, ca. 800 B.C.

47. See for example: A. A. Macdonell's *A History of Sanskrit Literature* (New Delhi: Motilal Banarsidass, 1971); or Madhav Deshpande's *Sanskrit and Prakrit: Sociolinguistic Issues* (New Delhi: Motilal Banarsidass, 1993).

For a comprehensive discussion of Sanskrit, culture, and power see Sheldon Pollock's monumental *The Language of the Gods in the World of Men: Sanskrit, Culture, and Power* (Berkeley: University of California Press, 2006). Pollock traces the rise and fall of Sanskrit as a "vehicle of poetry and polity" and discusses its reinvention as a code for literary and political expression. What Pollock does not draw attention to, however, is the ideological effect of Sanskrit and Veda on the conceptions of Indian religion developed under the framework of history of religions and Indology.

48. Especially important in this regard is Deshpande's *Sanskrit and Prakrit*, pp. 53–74. Although Deshpande argues that Sanskrit itself is the basis of this ideological paradigm—what he calls "The Theology of Eternal Sanskrit"—I think it is also helpful to consider the *circularity* of the Veda-Sanskrit-dharma triad, with circularity itself being a metaphor for eternality.

49. The term for this sound, word, or language that cannot be heard by physical ears is *anhad*, which means unstruck, i.e., a sound that is not caused by any physical impression and hence is outside the sensory experience of the physical ear.

50. See Fritz J. Staal, *A Reader on the Sanskrit Grammarians* (New Delhi: Motilal Banarsidass, 1985).

51. Good examples of this approach are Harold Coward's *The Sphoṭa Theory of Language: A Philosphical Analysis* (New Delhi: Motilal Banarsidass, 1997), *Sacred Word and Sacred Text: Scripture in World Religions* (Orbis, 1988), or *The Philosophy of Bhartṛhari*.

52. Jack Goody, *Interface Between the Written and the Oral*, pp. 110–111. As Goody rightly points out: "Thus *oral* tradition was vested in a class of *literate* specialists. The question immediately arises, why did literates insist on the oral transmission of these sacred works and claim that the 'texts' themselves were composed orally? . . . [Yet] the claim runs against conclusions that have emerged from studies of the transmission of even narrative works, much less those of a more 'philosophical' bent, that have been carried out in cultures of a purely oral kind."

53. Deshpande, *Sanskrit and Prakrit*, p. 65.

54. Deshpande, *Sanskrit and Prakrit*, p. 73.

55. See also the very rich discussion in Pollock's *Language of the Gods*, pp. 39–48.

56. *Aitareya Āraṇyaka* 5.5.3.

57. The traditional Indian bias against writing can be traced to an ancient Indo-European hostility toward the written form that, in the case of the Vedic Aryans, had developed into an unspoken law, an economic principle, as it were, structured around speech/sound. However, the form of this economic principle as we know it today was probably exacerbated by the introduction from *outside* India [ca. 600 B.C.] of an alphabetic form of writing derived from a Middle Eastern (probably Aramaic) source. Written images of an alphabet were regarded as defilements of the sacred economy of sound, as well as a threat to communal boundaries. It is interesting to note that Paṇīni's monumental efforts to restructure the Vedic economy came during this period (500 B.C.).

58. See Fritz J. Staal, ed., *A Reader on the Sanskrit Grammarians* (New Delhi: Motilal Banarsidass, 1992). If this use of the *signifier/signified* terminology seems uncomfortably close to Ferdinand de Saussure's terminology in his *Course in General Linguistics*, Staal offers an interesting explanation. It is very likely that many of Saussure's key insights in phonetic linguistics emerged out of his tenure as professor of Sanskrit and Indo-European in Geneva during the 1880s. As with other Sanskrit professors in Europe and America, Saussure was the recipient of a considerable body

of literature on Sanskrit language and its grammatical traditions. Names such as William Jones, H. T. Colebrooke, Friedrich and August Schlegel, Wilhelm von Humboldt, Franz Kielhorn, William Dwight Whitney, Bruno Liebich, and Georg Bühler were responsible for this literature, much of which was on Paṇini's linguistics. Also relevant here is Leonard Bloomfield, the founder of American structural linguistics; Bloomfield studied Sanskrit with the noted Orientalist Hermann Oldenberg and later lectured and published on the topic of Paṇini's *"rules."*

59. Prabhatchandra Chakravarti, *The Linguistic Speculations of the Hindus* (Calcutta: University of Calcutta Press, 1933), p. 86.

60. Madhav Deshpande, "On the *Ṛk-Pratiśākhya* 13.5–6," *Indian Linguistics* 37.3 (1976): 171–181.

61. Deshpande, "*Ṛk-Pratiśākhya* 13.5–6," pp. 176–177.

62. Beck, *Sonic Theology*, pp. 38–39.

63. The following philosophical axioms were adduced to support this belief: (i) that sound is eternal like space since both are imperceptible to touch, that is, beyond the bounds of sense experience; (ii) that sound is eternal and not liable to perish immediately after its utterance insofar as it is capable of being communicated; (iii) that sound is eternal as there is no cognition of the cause that might destroy it.

64. Plato, *Cratylus,* p. 425, in the *Collected Dialogues of Plato,* ed. Edith Hamilton and Huntington Cairns (Princeton: Princeton University Press, 1961).

65. Plato, *Cratylus*, p. 428e.

66. Plato, *Cratylus*, p. 416.

67. Plato, *Cratylus*, p. 416.

68. This does not necessarily lend support for a common philosophical origin to the Platonic and later Vedic philosophies, or to any borrowing of one from the other, as is argued by neo-Hindu philosophers, such as Sarvepalli Radhakrishnan in his *Eastern Religions and Western Thought* (London: Oxford University Press, 1940).

69. If one were merely trying to demonstrate a universal basis for Indian and Western cultures, it would be possible to cite as evidence the work of an entire host of famous names, such as Das Gupta, Hiriyana, Radhakrishnan, etc. What marks out Ananda Coomaraswamy from these names—although it is also a reason for his relative obscurity within the field of comparative philosophy and religion—is the inseparability of art from the philosophy of language and religion: in other words, the centrality of aesthetics (*rūpana*) and hermenia (*nirukta*) to any interpretation of the Vedic texts; this is exemplified by Coomaraswamy's constant references to the *nāma-rūpa* thematic. Of great importance—and again, Coomaraswamy probably excels in this among modern Indian thinkers—is the use he makes of Plato, the neo-Platonics, and the scholastic tradition, particularly the theme of mimesis. As I shall try to show, the notion of mimesis is not restricted to art, but is applied to the interpretation of Vedic religion, to language, and, perhaps most important, to Coomaraswamy's political theory. It is often forgotten that Coomaraswamy was also committed to the cause of Indian nationalism, serving after 1938 as president of the National Committee for Indian Freedom.

70. Ananda Coomaraswamy, "Vedic Exemplarism," in *Metaphysics*, ed. Roger Lipsey (Princeton: Princeton University Press, 1987), p. 181.

71. This particular interpretation sets Coomaraswamy apart from the mainstream neo-Hindu philosophers, who generally translate *ātman/paramātman* from the standpoint of epistemological certainty as "transcendental Self," and places him firmly within the grammarian tradition of Paṇīni and Bhartṛhari. As Coomaraswamy himself states: "[in conventional translations] 'being' or 'essence" corresponds to *ātman* as the suppositum of accidents and sine qua non of all modality (*-māyā*). We have experimented elsewhere with a rendering of atman by 'essence,' but propose in future to adhere to a more strictly etymological equivalent, more especially inasmuch as the *ātman* doctrine in the *ṚgVeda* must be considered in connection with X.129.2, *anid āvatam*, equivalent to 'at the same time *ātmya* and anātmya,' or 'equally spirated, despirated.'" ("Vedic Exemplarism," p. 188).

Support for this view appears in the Chandogya Upaniṣad, where speech is said to result from internal air or "diffused breath," which is the same as *vāk*: "When one breathes in—that is the in-breath (*prāna*). When one breathes out—that is the out-breath (*āpana*). The intersection of the in-breath and out-breath is the diffused breath. Speech is the diffused breath (*vyāna*). Therefore one utters speech without in-breathing, without out-breathing" (Robert E. Hume, *The Thirteen Principal Upanishads* [Oxford: Oxford University Press, 1958], p. 180).

72. "The parallel is all the closer because in the first case the universal form is that of the eternal sound, in the other, that of eternal light; for light and sound are coincident in divinis" (*Metaphysics*, p. 263).

Elsewhere Coomaraswamy states: "The equivalence of life, light, and sound must be taken into account when we consider the causal relationship of Vedic nṇma (name or noumenon) to rūpa (phenomenon or figure) which is that of exemplary cause to exemplatum; for while nāma involves the concept primarily of thought or sound, rūpa involves the concept primarily of vision" (*Metaphysics*, p. 192).

73. *Metaphysics*, p. 193.

74. See the essay "Nirukta=Hermenia," in *Metaphysics*, pp. 260–263.

75. The Mīmīṁsā (varṇavāda) school also propounds the theory of a universal language, but the locus of this universality is the physical body of the Veda. The individual words/letters/phonemes (*varṇa*) comprise the prime substance of *vāk*. Clearly, however, *varṇāvāda* cannot be regarded as universal in the true sense of the word, and is better described as exclusivist.

76. These paradigms were vigorously contested by the later Singh Sabhā writers such as Jodh Singh. But as I explained in an earlier chapter, although the Singh Sabhā scholars intended to uphold the written text, they ended up interpreting the notion *śabda-guru* via Christian theology, thereby unwittingly participating in the Vedic economy.

77. See Bimal K. Matilal, "Translation: Bhartṛhari on Śabda," in *The Word and the World: India's Contribution to the Study of Language* (New Delhi: Oxford University Press, 1992), p. 120.

78. Bhartṛhari, *Vākyapadīya*, ed. K. V. Abhyankar and V. P. Limaye (Poona, 1965), verse 1.51.

79. Bhartṛhari, *Vākyapadīya*, verse 1.52.

80. Coomaraswamy, *Metaphysics*, p. 185.

81. Coomaraswamy, *Metaphysics*, pp. 192–193.

82. Coomaraswamy, *Metaphysics*, pp. 261–262.

83. See Phillipe Lacoue-Labarthe's "Typography," in *Typography: Mimesis, Politics, Philosophy*, ed. Christopher Fynsk (Cambridge, MA: Harvard University Press, 1989), pp. 43–138.

84. Jacques Derrida, *Speech and Phenomena*, trans. David B. Allison (Evanston: Northwestern University Press), pp. 71–87.

85. Kahan Singh Nabha, *Gur Shabad Ratnakar: Mahankosh* (Patiala: Bhāshā Vibhāg, 1931; repr. 1981), p. 213.

86. In the *Comparative Dictionary of the Indo-Aryan Languages*, ed. R. L. Turner (London: Oxford University Press, 1989), as also in Sanskrit dictionaries, there are two basic meanings given to the term *varṇa*: [11338]: "model, specimen, class, color, appearance"; and [11339]: "sound, phoneme, letter, syllable, musical note, timbre of voice."

87. Wilhelm Halbfass, *India and Europe: An Essay in Understanding* (Albany: State University of New York, 1988), p. 187.

88. I have cited Coomaraswamy here but could have cited many others who are even more well known, such as Aurobindo Ghosh.

89. Harjot Oberoi, *The Construction of Religious Boundaries: Culture, Identity and Diversity in the Sikh Tradition* (New Delhi: Oxford University Press, 1994). The first chapter, in which the historical demarcation is made, is entitled "Boundaries and Transgression: The Khalsā Normative Tradition."

90. In Oberoi's chapter "Early Sikh Tradition."

91. In Oberoi's chapter "Boundaries and Transgression."

92. Oberoi, *Construction of Religious Boundaries*, p. 49.

93. We may recall that this intersects neatly with W. H. McLeod's interpretation of Nānak's original mystical experience: his distinction between the reality of experience as situated in sacred (eternal) time, and its subsequent translation into the corruption and violence of writing, text, and secular time. Hence the basic thesis: that boundaries—the opposition between inside and outside—can only come about as the result of the approach and presence of what is foreign. The native elites constructed religious boundaries during the colonial era by incorporating a trait or characteristic that was fundamentally foreign to the proper Indian principle. During British domination the foreign manifests through the effect of print culture as the emergence of the native elite literati, the Tat Khalsā. But the Tat Khalsā are merely a revitalized form of the earlier Khalsā of the Guru period. The seed of the foreign, therefore, was already present before the arrival of the British, in the form of Islam, the book, and Semitic writing.

94. Cynthia Mahmoud, *Fighting for Faith and Nation: Dialogues with Sikh Militants* (Philadelphia: University of Pennsylvania Press, 1996), p. 244.

95. Laclau, *Emancipations* (London: Verso, 1996), p. 31.

96. I refer among others to the oral exegeses of Sant Singh Maskīn, Darshan Singh Rāgi (ex-jathedār of Akāl Takht, etc.), etc.

97. Laclau, *Emancipations*, pp. 20–46.

98. See Rex Butler, *Live Theory: Slavoj Žižek* (New York: Continuum, 2005), pp. 16–22.

99. Butler, *Live Theory*, p. 21.

100. I refer to the now well-documented fact that in the wake of globalization and the formation of transnational diasporas, there has been a steady implosion of nationalist identification such that, as Sikhs assert their identity in new contexts, these contexts transform that identity.

101. See, for example: Pandit Tara Singh, *Granth Guru Girarath Kos* (Lahore, 1895); Charan Singh, *Sri Guru Granth Bānī Beurā* (Amritsar, 1860); Gian Singh, *Gurbānī Sangīt* (Amritsar, 1961); Bhāī Avtār Singh and Bhāī Gurcharan Singh, *Gurbānī Sangīt Prāchīn Rīt Ratnāvalī* (Patiala, 1979); Simriti Granth, *Adutī Gurmat Sangīt Sammelan* (Ludhiana, 1991); Jasbir Kaur, "Gurmat Sangīt dā Itihāsik Vikās" (diss., Chandigarh: Punjab University, 1993); Tara Singh, *Sri Guru Granth Sāhib Rāg Ratanāvalī* (Patiala: Punjabi University, 1997).

102. Christopher Shackle and Arvind-pal S. Mandair, *Teachings of the Sikh Gurus: Selections from the Sikh Scriptures* (London: Routledge, 2005).

103. The aim of what follows is not to present an overview of the teachings of the Sikh Gurus, but to outline the contours of what a posttheistic sketch of *gurmat* might look like. The central idea here is not only to break with the ontotheological frame, originally traced out by Trumpp and Bhāī Vīr Singh, but to reveal the inherently spectral nature of Sikhism's postcoloniality: that it is never free of the vestiges of colonialism. This is part of a larger and forthcoming project, entitled "Sikhism and Postsecular Thought."

104. *Purātan Janamsākhī Sri Guru Nānak Devji*, ed. Bhāī Vīr Singh (New Delhi: Bhāī Vīr Singh Sahit Sadan, 1996), pp. 24–37.

105. *Guru Granth Sāhib*, p. 1256 (translation mine).

106. "*Ād sach, jugādh sach, hai bhī sach, Nānak hosī bhī sach*" (*Ādi Granth*, p. 1).

107. See for example the following verses in the *Ādi Granth*: "*Oaṁ gurmukhi kio akārā / Ekahi sūti parovanhārā, / Bhiṅ bhiṅ traigun bisathāraṁ, / Nirgun te sargun dristāraṁ*" (*Ādi Granth*, p. 250); "*Eka surati jete hai jīa, / Surati vihūnā koi na kīa, / Jehtī surati tehā tin rāhu*" (*Ādi Granth*, pp. 24–25).

108. See the following verses: "*Eko eku raviā sabh ṭhāī, tisu binu dūjā koi nāhi, / Ādi madhi anti pabhu raviā trisan bujhi bharamaṁgna*" (*Ādi Granth*, p. 1080; "*Traigun sabha dhātu hai dūjā bhāu vikāru*" (*Ādi Granth*, p. 33); "*Niraṅkāru akāru hai āpe, bharami bhulāe, / Kari kari karatā āpe vekhai, jitu bhāvai titu lae*" (*Ādi Granth*, p. 1257).

109. The following verses in the *Ādi Granth* describe the notion of delusion in relation to duality and the One: "*Hau hau kart nahī sacu pāīai, / Haumai jāi param pad pāīai (rahau-1)*" (*Ādi Granth*, p. 226); "*Hau hau mai vicahu khovai, / Dūjā metai eko hovai*" (*Ādi Granth*, p. 943); "*Haumai merā dūjā bhāiā*" (*Ādi Granth*, p. 1051).

110. "*sochai soch na hovī je sochī lakh vār*" (*Ādi Granth*, p. 1).

111. "*chupai chup nā hovī je lai rahā liv tār*" (*Ādi Granth*, p. 1).

112. "*bhukhiān bhuk nā uttarī je banīāā purīān pār*" (*Ādi Granth*, p. 1).

113. "*kiv kūrai tuṭai pāl*" (*Ādi Granth*, p. 1).

114. "*kiv sachiārā hoaia*" (*Ādi Granth*, p. 1).

115. "*hukam rajāī chalaṇā, Nānak likhiā nāl*" (*Ādi Granth*, p. 1).

116. "*haumai kahai nā koī*" (*Ādi Granth*, p. 1).

117. "*Haumai dīrag rog hai, dārū bī is māhe*" (*Ādi Granth*, p. 466).

118. "*Mere man pardesī ve piare, āo milo, jī āo milo*" (*Ādi Granth*).

119. "*Baīar bollai mīṭulī bhāī sac kahai pir bhāe, / Birhai bedī sac vasī bhaī ad-hik rahī har nai*" (*Ādi Granth*, p. 637); "*Birhā birhā ākhīai birhā tū sultān, / Farīdā jit tan birhu na ūpjai so tan jaṇu masānu*" (*Ādi Granth*, p. 1378); "*Birhā lajāiā da-ras pāiā amio drisṭi sachiṁtī, / Binvant Nānak merī ich punī mile jis khojantī*" (*Ādi Granth*, p. 460); "*Hor birhā datu hai lagu sāhib preet na hoi, / Is man māyā mohiā ve-khan sunaṇ nā hoi*" (*Ādi Granth*, p. 83); "*Āvau milau sahelīo sacṛa nām lāiā, / Rove birhā tan kā apṇā sāhib samālihā*" (*Ādi Granth*, p. 579).

120. "*nirguṇ āp sarguṇ bī ohī, / kalā tār jin saglī mohī*" (*Ādi Granth*, p. 287).

121. "*sarguṇ nirguṇ niraṁkār ṣun samādhī āp, / āpan kiā Nānakā āpe hī phir jāp*" (*Ādi Granth*, p. 280).

122. "*sarguṇ nirguṇ thāpe nāo, / doh mil ekai kīnau tāo*" (*Ādi Granth*, p. 387).

6. Decolonizing Postsecular Theory

1. I am keenly aware of the problems involved with using terms such as "political theology" or "secularism," both of which signal a connection to religion and espe-cially to Christianity. But short of inventing new words I think this policy has more pros than cons.

2. See Hent de Vries, "Introduction," *Political Theologies: Public Religions in a Postsecular World*, ed. Hent de Vries and Lawrence E. Sullivan (New York: Fordham University Press, 2006), pp. 1–90.

3. I am well aware that Asad's work in particular can bridge the overtly secular disciplines of postcolonial theory (especially the South Asian or subaltern studies ver-sion) and the more recent phase of postsecular theory. My reasons for including him (and Connolly) broadly within the postsecular school are primarily heuristic and will become clearer as this chapter progresses. In the end, though, I am not totally con-vinced that Asad can help me think through the argument for the untranslatability of religion that I present later in this chapter.

4. Sheila Greeve Davaney, "Rethinking Theology and Religious Studies," in *Re-ligious Studies, Theology, and the University: Conflicting Maps, Changing Terrains*, ed. Linell Cady and Delwin Brown (Albany: State University of New York Press, 2002), p. 140.

5. Davaney, "Rethinking Theology," p. 140. See also Mark C. Taylor's introduc-tion to *Critical Terms for the Study of Religion* (Chicago: University of Chicago Press, 1998).

6. John Caputo, *On Religion* (London: Routledge, 2001), p. 38.

7. Anuradha Dingwaney Needham and Rajeswari Sundar Rajan, eds., *The Crisis of Secularism in India* (Durham: Duke University Press, 2007), p. 23.

8. Dipesh Chakrabarty, *Provincializing Europe: Postcolonial Thought and His-torical Difference* (Princeton: Princeton University Press, 2000), p. 5.

9. Chakrabarty, *Provincializing Europe*, p. 6.

10. Vincent P. Pecora, *Secularization and Cultural Criticism: Religion, Nation, and Modernity* (Chicago: University of Chicago Press, 2006), pp. 195–208.

11. Pecora, *Secularization*, p. 201.

12. Chakrabarty, *Provincializing Europe*, p. 4.

13. Chakrabarty, *Provincializing Europe*, p. 46.

14. Robert C. Tucker, ed., *The Marx-Engels Reader* (New York: Norton), pp. 48, 50.

15. Kenneth Surin, "Rewriting the Ontological Script of Liberation: On the Question of Finding a New Kind of Political Subject," in *Theology and the Political: The New Debate*, ed. Creston Davis, John Milbank, and Slavoj Žižek (Durham: Duke University Press, 2005), p. 240.

16. My use of the distinction between postmodernism1 and postmodernism2 follow to some extent that of Michael D. Hardt and Antonio Negri in their *Empire* (Cambridge, MA: Harvard University Press), pp. 137–143.

17. Russell McCutcheon, *The Discipline of Religion: Structure, Meaning, Rhetoric* (London: Routledge, 2003), p. 32.

18. Hardt and Negri, *Empire*, p. 140.

19. Homi K. Bhabha, "Signs Taken for Wonders: Questions of Ambivalence and Authority under a Tree Outside Delhi, May 1817," in *Europe and Its Others*, 2 Vols, ed. Francis Barker et al. (Colchester: University of Essex, 1985).

20. Hardt and Negri, *Empire*, pp. 138–139.

21. For a helpful gloss on this subject see Pal Ahluwalia's article: "Empire or Imperialism," *Social Identities: Journal of Race Nation and Culture* 10.5 (2004): 205–218.

22. Hardt and Negri, *Empire*, p. 190.

23. Hardt and Negri, *Empire*, p. 52.

24. Ahluwalia, "Empire or Imperialism," p. 208.

25. Hardt and Negri, *Empire*, p. 146.

26. Hardt and Negri, *Empire*, p. 138.

27. Ahluwalia, "Empire or Imperialism," pp. 208–210.

28. Ahluwalia, "Empire or Imperialism," p. 209.

29. Susan Buck-Morss, *Thinking Past Terror: Islamism and Critical Theory on the Left* (London: Verso, 2003), p. 92.

30. Buck-Morss, *Thinking Past Terror*, p. 93.

31. Buck-Morss, *Thinking Past Terror*, p. 93.

32. Quoted in Paul A. Passavant and Jodi Dean, eds., *Empire's New Clothes: Reading Hardt and Negri* (New York: Routledge, 2004), p. 30.

33. See, for example, Mark C. Taylor, *Confidence Games: Money and Markets in a World Without Redemption* (Chicago: University of Chicago Press, 2004).

34. William D. Hart, *Edward Said and the Religious Effects of Culture* (Cambridge: Cambridge University Press, 2000).

35. Gianni Vattimo, *Nihilism and Emancipation: Ethics, Politics, and Law* (New York: Columbia University Press, 2003), p. 120.

36. See, for example, Taylor's *Disfiguring: Art, Architecture, Religion* (Chicago: University of Chicago Press, 1992), and *Confidence Games*.

37. Taylor, *Disfiguring*, p. 148.

38. Taylor, *Confidence Games*, p. 106.

39. Taylor, *Confidence Games*, p. 105.

40. See Hardt and Negri, *Empire*, pp. 146–148.

41. Ernesto Laclau, "Can Immanence Explain Social Struggles?," in *Empire's New Clothes: Reading Hardt and Negri*, ed. Paul A. Passavant and Jodi Dean (New York: Routledge, 2004), p. 23.

42. Laclau, "Immanence," p. 28.

43. Slavoj Žižek, *The Ticklish Subject: The Absent Centre of Political Ontology* (London: Verso, 1999); *The Abyss of Freedom/Ages of the World* (Ann Arbor: University of Michigan Press, 1997); *Cogito and the Unconscious*, ed. Slavoj Žižek (Durham: Duke University Press, 1998); *The Parallax View* (Cambridge, MA: MIT Press, 2006).

44. Žižek, *Ticklish Subject*, p. 1.

45. Žižek, *Ticklish Subject*, p. 2.

46. Slavoj Žižek, "The Cogito as Shibboleth," in *Cogito and the Unconscious*, ed. Slavoj Žižek (Durham: Duke University Press, 1998), p. 2.

47. Žižek, "Cogito as Shibboleth," pp. 3–7.

48. Žižek, *Ticklish Subject*, pp. 34–41.

49. Žižek, *Ticklish Subject*, p. 88.

50. Žižek, *Abyss of Freedom*, p. 6.

51. Žižek, *Abyss of Freedom*, p. 8.

52. Žižek, *Abyss of Freedom*, p. 9.

53. Žižek, *Abyss of Freedom*, p. 9 and Žižek, *Parallax View*.

54. Žižek, *Ticklish Subject*, pp. 70–75.

55. Žižek, *Ticklish Subject*, p. 78.

56. Žižek, *Parallax View*, p. 29.

57. Žižek, *Parallax View*, pp. 29–30.

58. Žižek, *Parallax View*, p. 26.

59. Žižek, *Ticklish Subject*, pp. 98–103; *Parallax View*, pp. 30–31.

60. Žižek, *Ticklish Subject*, p. 103.

61. Žižek, *Abyss of Freedom*, p. 28; *Ticklish Subject*, p. 158.

62. Žižek, *Ticklish Subject*, p. 188.

63. Žižek, *Ticklish Subject*, p. 227.

64. Žižek, *Parallax View*, p. 35.

65. Žižek, *Parallax View*, p. 35.

66. Žižek, *Abyss of Freedom*, pp. 4–21. See also Žižek's *The Indivisible Remainder: On Schelling and Related Matters* (London: Verso, 2007), pp. 13–39.

67. See for example Jason Wirth's chapter "Purusottama," in *The Conspiracy of Life: Meditations on Schelling and His Time* (New York: State University of New York Press, 2003), pp. 219–233.

68. See Wendy Doniger, *Dreams, Illusions, and Other Realities* (Chicago: University of Chicago Press, 1984).

69. Žižek, *Ticklish Subject*, pp. 205–215.

70. Žižek, *Parallax View*, p. 35.

71. Žižek, *Ticklish Subject*, p. 231.

72. Žižek, *Ticklish Subject*, pp. 205–210.

73. Slavoj Žižek, *Iraq: The Borrowed Kettle* (London: Verso, 2004), p. 33.

74. Slavoj Žižek, *The Puppet and the Dwarf: The Perverse Core of Christianity* (Cambridge: MIT Press, 2003), p. 171.

75. Žižek, *Abyss of Freedom*, p. 26.

76. Žižek, *Abyss of Freedom*, p. 25.

77. Žižek, *Abyss of Freedom*, p. 27.

78. Slavoj Žižek, *On Belief* (London: Routledge, 2001), p. 12.

79. Žižek, *The Puppet and the Dwarf*, p. 26.

80. Žižek, *Iraq*, pp. 32–33.

81. Žižek, *On Belief*, pp. 10–11.

82. Žižek, *The Puppet and the Dwarf*, p. 33.

83. Slavoj Žižek, *The Fragile Absolute; or, Why the Christian Legacy is Worth Fighting For* (London: Verso, 2000), p. 2.

84. Mark C. Taylor, *Confidence Games: Money and Markets in a World Without Redemption* (Chicago: University of Chicago Press, 2004); *After God* (Chicago: University of Chicago Press, 2007).

85. Taylor, *Confidence Games*, pp. 312–313.

86. Adapted from Taylor, *Confidence Games*, p. 317.

87. John Caputo, *The Prayers and Tears of Jacques Derrida* (Bloomington: Indiana Univertsity Press, 1997), p. 194.

88. Jacques Derrida, *The Gift of Death* (Chicago: University of Chicago Press, 1995) p. 49.

89. Derrida, *Gift of Death*, p. 49.

90. Caputo, *Prayers and Tears*, p. 195.

91. Caputo, *Prayers and Tears*, p. 195.

92. Jacques Derrida, "Faith and Knowledge: The Two Sources of 'Religion' at the Limits of Reason Alone," in *Religion*, ed. Jacques Derrida and Gianni Vattimo (London: Polity Press, 1998), p. 29.

93. Derrida, "Faith and Knowledge," p. 30.

94. Derrida, "Faith and Knowledge," p. 29.

95. Derrida, "Autoimmunity: Real and Symbolic Suicides," in *Philosophy in a Time of Terror: Dialogues with Jürgen Habermas and Jacques Derrida*, ed. Giovanna Borradori (Chicago: University of Chicago Press, 2004), pp. 93 and 105.

96. Jacques Derrida, "Above All, No Journalists!," in *Religion and Media*, ed. Hent de Vries and Samuel Weber (Stanford: Stanford University Press, 2001), p. 66.

97. Derrida, "Above All, No Journalists," p. 73.

98. Derrida, "Above All, No Journalists," p. 74.

99. Derrida, "Above All, No Journalists," p. 74.

100. Derrida, "Above All, No Journalists," p. 89.

101. Derrida, "Autoimmunity," p. 93.

102. Derrida, "Autoimmunity," p. 94.

103. Derrida, "Autoimmunity," p. 93.

104. Derrida, "Faith and Knowledge," p. 29.

105. Derrida, "Autoimmunity," p. 105.

106. Gianni Vattimo, *The End of Modernity* (London: Polity Press, 1988).

107. Michael Hardt and Antonio Negri, *Multitude: War and Democracy in the Age of Empire* (New York: Penguin, 2004), p. 314.

108. Hardt and Negri, *Multitude*, p. 317.

109. Tomoko Masuzawa, *The Invention of World Religions; or, How European Pluralism Was Preserved in the Language of Universalism* (Chicago: University of Chicago Press, 2005).

110. Jacques Derrida, "Sign, Structure, and Play in the Discourse of the Human Sciences," in *Writing and Difference,* trans. Alan Bass (London: Routledge, 1978), p. 279.

111. Derrida, "Autoimmunity," p. 95.

112. Derrida, "Faith and Knowledge," p. 30.

113. Hardt and Negri, *Multitude*, p. 318.

114. Chantal Mouffe, *On the Political* (London: Routledge, 2005), p. 123.

115. Mouffe, *On the Political*, pp. 127–129.

116. Naoki Sakai, "The Dislocation of the West," *Traces: A Multilingual Journal of Cultural Theory and Translation* 1 (2001): 71–94.

117. Naoki Sakai, *Translation and Subjectivity* (Minneapolis: University of f Press, 1997), p. 91.

118. Judith Butler, "Restaging the Universal," in *Contingency, Hegemony, Universality: Contemporary Dialogues on the Left*, ed. Judith Butler, Ernesto Laclau, and Slavoj Žižek (London: Verso, 2000), p. 37.

119. Butler, "Restaging the Universal," p. 35.

120. Butler, "Restaging the Universal," pp. 37–39.

121. Judith Butler, "Competing Universalities," in *Contingency, Hegemony, Universality: Contemporary Dialogues on the Left*, ed. Judith Butler, Ernesto Laclau, and Slavoj Žižek (London: Verso, 2000), p. 167.

122. Butler, "Competing Universalities," p. 168.

123. Butler, "Competing Universalities," pp. 178–179.

Glossary of Indic Terms

Ādi Granth. Lit. "the first or original text," i.e., the sacred scripture of the Sikhs; also known as the *Guru Granth Sāhib.*

Akālī. Member of the Akālī Dal, a Sikh political party.

Akālī Dal. Political party represented Sikh and Punjabi interests in Punjab.

Akāl Purakh. "The Timeless Being"; God.

Akāl Takht. The principal center of Sikh temporal authority, this institution is located immediately adjacent to the Harimandir Sahib, or Golden Temple.

amrit. Lit. "nectar of immortality"; sweetened water used in Sikh initiation ceremony.

amritdhārī. A Sikh who has undergone initiation and become a member of the Khalsā.

anhad (anāhat) śabda. "Unstruck" sound or word; poetic language in which ego-traces are erased.

artha. The meaning of a word or sentence.

Āryā Samāj. A Hindu reformist movement founded by Dayananda Saraswati in the late nineteenth century.

avatār. A "descent" or incarnation of deity, usually Viṣṇu.

bhagat (bhaktā). Exponent of *bhakti.*

bhakti. Form of loving devotion directed toward a personal or impersonal divine.

bhāī. "Brother"; honorific applied to Sikhs of learning or piety.

brahman. The absolute as described in the Upaniṣads; self-appointed highest caste in Hindu caste hierarchy.

Chief Khalsā Diwan (CKD). A Sikh institution formed in 1902 to conduct the affairs of the Lahore and Amritsar Singh Sabhās.

darśan. The act of seeing or having an audience with the divine.

Dasam Granth. A Sikh scripture, parts of which are attributed to the authorship of the tenth Sikh Guru, Gobind Singh.

dharam (Skt. dharma). Duty, righteousness, law, sacred duty.

fakir (faqir). A Muslim ascetic; term loosely used to designate Sufis.

gian (Skt. jñāna). Wisdom or knowledge.

Granth. Lit. "text," referring to the *Guru Granth Sāhib*, or central Sikh scripture.

guṇa. Attribute or quality.

gurbānī. "Utterance of the Guru"; compositions of the Sikh Gurus.

Gurbilās. "Praise of the Guru"; hagiographical literature about the lives of the sixth and tenth Gurus.

gurdwara. A Sikh temple.

gurmat. Teachings of the Sikh Gurus.

gurmat sangīt. Sikh musicology; sacred music of the Sikhs.

gurmukh. One who lives according to the guru's teaching; one who has overcome ego.

gurmukhī. Lit. "from the Guru's mouth"; the Punjabi script.

guru. A spiritual master; either a person or a mystical inner principle that aids emancipation of the disciple.

Guru Granth Sāhib. The *Ādi Granth* in its role as Guru.

Guru Granth. The Granth, or text, in its role as Guru.

Guru Panth. The community, or Panth, in its role as Guru.

gurumatā. "Intention of the Guru"; a resolution passed by the Sarbat Khalsā (wider community of Khalsā Sikhs) in the presence of the *Guru Granth Sāhib*.

Harimandir Sahib. The Golden Temple.

haṭha-yoga. Yoga of physical exercises practiced by adherents of the Nath tradition.

haumai. "I am myself"; self-centeredness.

hukam. Order.

ik oaṁkār. The one being manifest as Word; the opening words of Sikh scripture.

janamsakhī. Hagiographical narratives based on the life of Guru Nānak.

jap. The act of repeating the divine name, mantras, or sacred texts.

jñāna. (Punjabi: gian). Knowledge, wisdom.

jñāna mārg. "Path of wisdom"; Vedānta.

kāl. Time or death.

kathā. Homily.

Khalistan. "Land of the Pure"; a name adopted by supporters of an independent Sikh state.

Khalsā. A spiritual-cum-military order of Sikhs established by Guru Gobind Singh in 1699.

kīrtan. Singing of hymns (see *gurmat sangī*).

Krishna. Hindu god; narrator of the *Bhagvada Gita*.

man. (pronounced "mun"). Mind; a common Indian term for the complex of heart, mind, and soul.

manmukh. One who acts according to egotistical desires; trapped within the structure of the ego.

mantar. (Skt. mantra). A verse, phrase, or syllable invested with spiritual efficacy that is repeated by sounding.

mat(i). Intellect.

māyā. The illusory status of reality.

mīrī-pīrī. Doctrine of combined temporal (*mīrī*) and spiritual (*pīrī*) authority attributed initially to the living Sikh Guru but later adopted by the Khalsā.

muktī (moksha). Ultimate freedom; liberation from the cycle of transmigration.

mūrtī. Form or image of a deity in Hinduism.

nām. The Name; a term expressing the central attribute of a paradoxical divine that is existent and nonexistent at the same time.

nāda. Sound.

nadar. Sight; divine grace.

Nāmdhārī. Member of the Sikh sect called Namdharis (also known as Kuka Sikhs).

nām japanā. Repetition of the divine Name.

nām simaraṇ. Devotional practice of meditating on the Name initially through vocalized repetition and eventually through interiorized repetition.

Nath tradition. Practitioners of hatha yoga; yogic sect influential in Punjab prior to and during the time of the Sikh Gurus.

nirbāṇ (nirvana). Extinction of suffering; without form.

nirguṇ (Skt. nirguṇa). Without qualities or attributes, not incarnated.

Nirmalā. A sect of celibate Sikhs influential in the nineteenth century.

nit-nem. Daily rituals; Sikh liturgy.

oṁ (aum). The primal syllable, said to contain the entire Sanskrit alphabet in seed form.

Panth. Lit. "the way"; the Sikh community.

pāṭh. Recitations or readings from Sikh scriptures.

prāna. Life-force, breath.

pūjā. Hindu worship.

Puraṇā. Early Hindu literatures containing mythologies and detailing sectarian rites.

Puratan janamsakhi. One of the oldest extant collections of biographies of Guru Nānak.

rāg (Skt. rāga). A traditional melodic type in Hindustani music, consisting of a theme that expresses an aspect of spiritual feeling and sets forth a tonal system on which variations are improvised within a prescribed framework of typical progressions, melodic formulas, and rhythmic patterns.

ṛṣis. Seers who apparently revealed the Veda to mankind.

śabda (or shabad). Word, language; verse or hymn of the *Guru Granth Sāhib.*

śabda-guru. The word-as-guru; guru-as-word.

sabha. Society or association.

sādhan. Method or technique of spiritual achievement.

sadhu. A renunciate, mendicant, or ascetic.

sarguṇ(Skt. saguṇa). Lit. "with qualities"; possessing form or attributes.

Śaivā (Saivism/Śaivite). Worshiper of the god Śiva.

sahaj. Naturally achieved condition of equipoise or bliss resulting especially from the practice of *nām simaraṇ.*

Sahajdhari. A non-Khalsā Sikh.

samādhi. State of deep absorption and concentration, especially in yoga.

Sāṁkhya. Pertaining to numerology; analytical system of Hindu philosophy.

sampradaya. Sect holding certain beliefs; traditional doctrine; a school of thought.

saṁsāra. The material world; cycle of rebirth.

saṁskāra. Trace; sacrament.

sanātan. Without origins; eternal; that which does not cease to be.

sanātan dharma. Eternal tradition referring also to Vedic dharma and tradition.

Sanātan Sikhs. Those who (mistakenly) considered Guru Nānak to be an incarnation or avatar of the Hindu deity Viṣṇu and thereby aligned Sikh traditions with the Hindu traditionalist (i.e., Brahmanical) social structure based on *varṇāśrama dharma*, or caste ideology.

Sant. Person who has discovered the truth of existence and nonexistence; teacher of *gurmat*.

Sant tradition. A spiritual tradition of North India that stressed the need for interiorized devotion.

sat(i) (Skt. satya). Truth, existence.

sati. Practice of burning widows or concubines on the husband's funeral pyre.

satinām (also satnām). Lit. "truth is (your) Name."

satsang. Gathering of seekers after truth; Sikh congregation.

seva. Service.

SGPC. Shiromani Gurdwara Prabandhak Committee—a committee that controls the Sikh places of worship.

Śiva. One of the great gods of Hinduism.

siddha. Men highly adept in yogic practice and believed to have attained immortality through it.

Siddh Goṣṭ. Composition in *Guru Granth Sāhib* representing a dialogue between Guru Nānak and adepts of yoga named Siddhas.

Singh Sabhā. Sikh reform movement initiated in 1873 that split into two factions in response to stigmatization from Hindu reformist and traditionalist groups.

smṛti. Post-Vedic Hindu scripture.

sphoṭa. The bursting forth of meaning from a sentence in the grammarian tradition.

Sphoṭavada. Sentence-meaning comprehension in the grammarian tradition.

śruti. Lit. "that which is heard"; the Vedas and Upaniṣads.

Sūfī. Member of a Muslim mystical order.

Sūtra. Concise text expounding a teaching.

Udāsī. Member of Udāsīs, an order of ascetics claiming Sri Chand (elder son of Guru Nānak) as their progenitor.

Upaniṣads. Fourth division of Hindu literatures; wisdom texts.

Vaiṣṇava. Follower of the god Viṣṇu.

vāk. Lit. "saying"; randomly chosen passage from the *Guru Granth Sāhib*; in Hinduism early Vedic term for the divine Word and the goddess of speech.

varṇa. Lit. "color"; caste hierarchy comprising Brahman, Kshatriya, Vaishya, and Sudra; individual letter in the Sanskrit language.

Varṇavāda. The Mīmāmsa tradition of comprehending sentence-meaning by means of individual letters.

Veda. Lit. "knowledge"; earliest texts of the Hindus.

Vedānta. The last part of the Veda; Upaniṣads.

viraha/biraha. Pining or longing for the beloved from whom one is separated.

vismād. Wonder; awe.

yoga. Lit. "yoke"; system of Indian philosophy and practice in which the mind is brought under control.

Index

Ādi Granth, 27, 211, 261, 266, 281–285, 353, 359, 436; extracts from, 213–215, 216, 365–366, 369, 476nn107–117, 477nn118–122; *gurmat* and, 204, 213, 217, 363; hymns in, 361, 371; *Japji* in, 368; McLeod and, 273–274; mysticism and, 363; *nām* in, 369, 374; translation of, 29, 175, 176, 212; orality and, 325–327, 465n50; *rāg* and, 269, 365; readers of, 219; as Sikh scripture, 29, 254, 255, 263, 271–272, 435; themes in, 364–365; Trumpp and, 186–194, 212, 232, 440n53; Wilson on, 182–183. *See also Guru Granth Sahib*

Advaita Vedānta, 68, 74, 76, 81, 170, 458n95

agency, 53, 78, 83, 96, 109, 229, 329; of colonized, 195, 313, 321, 356, 436n3; of Guru, 328, 329, 330; nature of, 78–79, 357; repetition and, 329, 355, 356. *See also* colonial agency

Akali Dal: 304, 305; nonviolence of, 48, 302; as Sikh political party, 8, 22, 241, 302, 303

Akāl Takht, 23, 435, 475n96

Akhand pānṭh, 325–328, 348, 471n31

Alliez, Eric, 163, 206

America, Americans, 21, 45, 114, 305–308, 319, 406, 411; academy, 239, 316; European-, 3–4, 50, 108, 423; global power of, 110, 407, 410, 420; new world order and, 314–315; as West, 3, 423. *See also* United States

Amir Khusrau, 249, 254

Amman, Mir, 92, 99

Amritsar, 8, 48, 67, 69, 241, 326

amritdhari, 23, 435

anhad śabda, 267, 268, 374

Anglicists, 57, 63, 72, 92; on Hinduism, 71, 91; Orientalists vs., 57, 62, 64, 65, 91

Anglo-Sikh wars (1848), 18, 176

Anglo-vernacular (A/V) schools, 14, 93–97, 101, 104–105, 199; of missionaries, 29, 67, 68, 17, 235

Anselm, Saint, 148, 238, 449n84

anthropology, anthropologists, 38, 109, 201, 205, 242, 281, 315, 316, 381, 388; anthropological religion and, 166; classic, 319, cultural, 317,

Indian democracy, 35, 49–50, 54, 299, 355, 395
Indian languages, 80, 84–91, 119, 124, 241, 321, 453n21. *See also under names of specific languages*
Indian Marxists, 8, 37, 49, 60, 404
Indian National Congress. *See* Congress Party
Indian nationalism, 3, 17–18, 38–39, 48, 54–56, 301, 304, 323, 352, 405, 473n69
Indian religions, 8, 9, 118, 131, 143, 152, 171, 187, 194, 423–424; antiquity of, 138–139, 354; classification of, 138; conceptions of, 472n47; Hegel and, 110–111, 138–141; identification and, 7; monotheism and, 112; public image of, 72; spirituality and, 39; Western thought and, 12–17. *See also* Oriental religions; pantheism; *and under names of specific religions*
Indians, 330, 347, 454n45; encounter of, with European colonialism, 53, 57, 61–62, 76, 87, 404–405; identification of, 7, 47, 95; Indian nationalism and, 39, 55; mono-theo-lingualism and, 15; orality and, 338; public sphere and, 83; self-perception of, 47. *See also* colonized; Hindus; native elites; Sikhs; *and Indian headings*
Indian secularism, secularists, 8, 49, 383. *See also* secularism
Indian state, 22, 55, 467n120; Sikhs and, 22–23, 26, 35, 245, 300–306, 461–462n6. *See also* State, the
Indic culture, 16, 32, 139, 164, 313, 354, 414, 418
Indologists, 16, 18, 65, 94, 134, 160, 162, 186, 193, 197, 360, 404, 440n53; *bhakti* and, 75–77, 196; British, 74, 182, 239; concept of religion of, 14, 77; emergence of Sikh theology and, 31; Germans as, 29, 38, 161, 175–176, 185, 239; native elites and, 75, 112; as translators, 16, 29, 165, 176, 183. *See also* Indology; *and under names of individual Indologists*
Indology, 2, 14–16, 31–32, 58, 62, 65, 74, 106, 177, 188, 472n47; Brahmanism and, 323–324; British,

116–117; as discipline, 31, 65, 74, 112, 116, 177; discourse of, 14, 111, 117; German, 38, 106, 116–117, 121, 446n20; Hegel and, 111, 121, 131, 164, 168; literature of, 61, 352; pantheism and, 122–128, 202; phases of, 112, 153, 162, 164, 196; reconstitution of, 152, 153, 161–165, 171; reform, theosophy, and, 165–171, 352. *See also* Indologists; Orientalism
Indomania, 62, 107, 126
Indo-Pakistan War (1971), 20, 21–22
Indophobia, 62, 161
interdict, 10, 95, 101, 199, 200
Islam, 5, 26, 29, 35, 46, 83, 93, 114, 156, 192, 320, 395, 462n6; corruption of, 87, 88, 93; Hinduism and, 301, 419; in India, 74, 75, 354, 475n93; monotheism of, 74, 192, 196; terrorism and, 300, 305. *See also* Muslims

Jacobi, Hermann Georg, 123, 151
jats, 250, 256
Jena Romantics, 15, 127, 131, 169
jñāna (*gian*; knowledge/philosophy), 74, 76, 436; *jñāna mārg*, 75
Jodh Singh, 30, 69, 208, 219, 224, 229, 239, 333, 458n93, 465n48, 465n50, 475n76; Bhāī Vīr Singh and, 238, 260–261; *Gurmat Nirnai*, 31, 35–36, 238–239, 259–271; as indigenous scholar, 31, 262
Jones, Kenneth, 53, 441n30
Jones, Sir William, 117–120, 162, 178, 473n58; linguistic work by, 87–88, 99, 122, 124, 131, 322; as Orientalist, 62, 107, 167, 196, 322; philosophy of, 63, 139, 179
Judaism, Jews, 157, 180, 307, 320, 322, 382, 403, 419, 447n38, 453

Kahn Singh Nabha, Bhai, 30, 31, 69; "*Ham Hindu Nahin*," 70, 199, 208, 236
Kant, Immanuel, 119, 125, 234, 288, 429, 455n75; co-figuration of, 99, 150, 157, 429; *Critique of Pure Reason*, 98; as Enlightenment thinker,